ICC Arbitration in Practice

ICC Arbitration in Practice

Second Revised Edition

Herman Verbist
Erik Schäfer
Christophe Imhoos

Stämpfli Verlag

Wolters Kluwer

Published by:
Kluwer Law International
PO Box 316
2400 AH Alphen aan den Rijn
The Netherlands
Website: www.wklawbusiness.com

Sold and distributed in North, Central and South America by:
Aspen Publishers, Inc.
7201 McKinney Circle
Frederick, MD 21704
United States of America
Email: customer.service@aspenpublishers.com

Sold and distributed in all other countries by:
Turpin Distribution Services Ltd
Stratton Business Park
Pegasus Drive, Biggleswade
Bedfordshire SG18 8TQ
United Kingdom
Email: kluwerlaw@turpin-distribution.com

Sold and distributed in all countries by:
ICC Services S.A.S., Affiliate of the International Chamber of Commerce (ICC)
33-43 avenue du Président Wilson
75116 Paris, France
Website: www.storeiccwbo.org
Email: publications@iccwbo.org

Library of Congress Cataloging-in-Publication Data is available.

Printed on acid-free paper.

ISBN 978-90-411-3171-3 (Kluwer Law International)
ISBN 978-3-7272-7757-3 (Staempfli)
ISBN 978-92-842-0378-9 (ICC Services)

Printed and Bound by CPI Group (UK) Ltd, Croydon, CR0 4YY.

NOTICE

The explanations given in this book should not be taken as the official position of the ICC International Court of Arbitration or its Secretariat.

ICC arbitration, like international arbitration in general, is constantly evolving under the influence of changing practices, legislative reform and developments in case law. The practice of the ICC International Court of Arbitration and its Secretariat based on the ICC Rules of Arbitration likewise evolves. It is therefore advisable, in any given case, to check up on current practice with the Secretariat of the Court, whose address is as follows:

International Court of Arbitration

International Chamber of Commerce

Headquarters

33-43 Avenue du Président Wilson
75116 Paris
France

Telephone: +33 1 49 53 29 05
Fax: +33 1 49 53 29 33
E-mail: arb@iccwbo.org
Web site: <www.iccarbitration.org>

Asia

Secretariat of the International Court of Arbitration of the International Chamber of Commerce
Asia Office

Ms Cheng-Yee Khong
Director and Counsel
Suite 2, 12/F, Fairmont House
8 Cotton Tree Drive
Central
Hong Kong

Tel.: +852 3607 5600
Fax: +852 2523 1619
Email: ica8@iccwbo.org

North America

International Chamber of Commerce (ICC)
International Court of Arbitration®
SICANA Inc.
Ms Rocío Digón
Counsel
1212 Avenue of the Americas
9th floor
New York, NY 10036
USA

Tel.: +1 646 699 5704
Fax: + 1 212 221 12 95
Email: ica9@iccwbo.org

General inquiries on ADR and Requests for ADR:

International Centre for ADR
33-43 avenue du Président Wilson
75116 Paris
France

Tel: +33 1 49 53 30 52
Fax: +33 1 49 53 30 49
Email: adr@iccwbo.org

CONTENTS

NOTICE **v**
FOREWORD **xv**
PREFACE **xvii**
THE AUTHORS **xix**
ABBREVIATIONS **xxi**

CHAPTER 1
INTRODUCTION **1**

A. ARBITRATION AS A PRIVATE METHOD OF SETTLING DISPUTES 1
1. Arbitration as an Alternative to Court Proceedings 1
2. Arbitration as an Alternative to Court Proceedings in International Legal Relations 2
3. Relation between Arbitration and Other Methods of Settling Private Disputes Out of Court 2

B. LINKS BETWEEN ARBITRATION AND STATE COURTS 3

C. '*AD HOC*' ARBITRATION PROCEDURE 6
1. Initiation of the Arbitration and Constitution of the Arbitral Tribunal 6
2. Conduct of Arbitration Proceedings 7

D. INSTITUTIONAL ARBITRATION 10

E. ICC ARBITRATION 10

CHAPTER 2
THE INTERNATIONAL CHAMBER OF COMMERCE AND ITS COURT OF ARBITRATION **13**

A. THE INTERNATIONAL CHAMBER OF COMMERCE AS AN INSTITUTION 13

B. THE ICC DISPUTE RESOLUTION SERVICES 13

C. THE HISTORICAL BACKGROUND OF THE RULES OF ARBITRATION 14

D. THE ICC INTERNATIONAL COURT OF ARBITRATION AND ITS SECRETARIAT 15
1. The Structure of the ICC International Court of Arbitration 15
2. The Role of the ICC International Court of Arbitration 15

3. How the ICC International Court of Arbitration Works 16
4. Avoiding Conflicts of Interest 18
5. The Composition of the Secretariat 18
6. The Tasks of the Secretariat 19
7. How the Secretariat Works 20

CHAPTER 3
ARBITRAL PROCEEDINGS UNDER THE ICC RULES OF ARBITRATION OF 2012 **23**

A. INTRODUCTORY PROVISIONS **23**
1. Definitions (Art. 2) 23
2. Written Notifications or Communications; Time Limits (Art. 3) 24

B. COMMENCING THE ARBITRATION **26**
1. The Request for Arbitration (Art. 4) 26
2. The Answer to the Request and Counterclaims (Art. 5) 38
3. The Effect of the Arbitration Agreement (Art. 6) 45

C. MULTIPLE PARTIES, MULTIPLE CONTRACTS AND CONSOLIDATION **52**
1. The Joinder of Additional Parties (Art. 7) 53
2. Claims between Multiple Parties (Art. 8) 56
3. Multiple Contracts (Art. 9) 59
4. Consolidation of Arbitrations (Art. 10) 60

D. THE ARBITRAL TRIBUNAL **63**
1. General Provisions (Art. 11) 63
2. The Constitution of the Arbitral Tribunal (Art. 12) 72
3. Appointment and Confirmation of Arbitrators (Art. 13) 78
4. Challenge of Arbitrators (Art. 14) 88
5. Replacement of Arbitrators (Art. 15) 92

E. THE ARBITRAL PROCEEDINGS **97**
1. Transmission of the File to the Arbitral Tribunal (Art. 16) 97
2. Proof of Authority (Art. 17) 100
3. Place of the Arbitration (Art. 18) 101
4. Rules Governing the Proceedings (Art. 19) 105
5. Language of the Arbitration (Art. 20) 109
6. Applicable Rules of Law (Art. 21) 113
7. Conduct of the Arbitration (Art. 22) 120
8. Terms of Reference (Art. 23) 126
9. Case Management Conference and Procedural Timetable (Art. 24) 135
10. Establishing the Facts of the Case (Art. 25) 139
11. Hearings (Art. 26) 148
12. Closing of the Proceedings and Date for Submission of Draft Awards (Art. 27) 153
13. Conservatory and Interim Measures (Art. 28) 155

F. EMERGENCY ARBITRATOR PROCEEDINGS 158
1. General Remarks 162
2. Commencement of the Emergency Arbitrator Proceedings 164
3. Appointment of the Emergency Arbitrator (App. V – Art. 2) 167
4. Challenge of the Emergency Arbitrator (App. V – Art. 3) 168
5. Proceedings before the Emergency Arbitrator (Art. 29(1); App. V – Art. 4 and 5) 168
6. Order of the Emergency Arbitrator – Effect on the Arbitration Proceedings 169
7. Costs of the Emergency Arbitrator Proceedings (App. V – Art. 7) 171
8. General Rule (App. V – Art. 8) 172
9. An Application to a Judicial Authority does not Infringe the Emergency Arbitrator Provisions (Art. 29(7)) 172
10. Limitation of Liability (Art. 40) 173

G. ARBITRAL AWARDS 173
1. Time Limit for the Final Award (Art. 30) 173
2. Awards (Art. 31) 175
3. Award by Consent (Art. 32) 180
4. Scrutiny of Award by the Court (Art. 33) 182
5. Notification, Deposit, Enforceability of Awards (Art. 34) 187
6. Correction and Interpretation of Awards; Remission of Awards (Art. 35) 191

H. COSTS AND ADVANCES 195
1. Advance to Cover the Costs of the Arbitration (Art. 36) 195
2. Decision as to the Costs of the Arbitration (Art. 37) 212
3. Costs and Fees (Appendix III, Art. 2) 213

I. MISCELLANEOUS PROVISIONS 226
1. Modified Time Limits (Art. 38) 226
2. Waiver (Art. 39) 227
3. Limitation of Liability (Art. 40) 228
4. General Rule Aimed at Filling Gaps (Art. 41) 229

CHAPTER 4
THE STANDARD ICC ARBITRATION CLAUSE 231

A. ARBITRATION CLAUSES IN GENERAL 231

B. RULES OF LAW APPLICABLE TO THE ARBITRATION AGREEMENT 233

C. QUESTIONS CONCERNING SPECIFIC SUPPLEMENTARY PROVISIONS IN THE ARBITRATION AGREEMENT 234
1. The Requirement to Attempt Mediation First and Other Prior Conditions 234
2. Arbitral Tribunals Composed of Two or an Even Number of Members 235
3. Nomination of Arbitrators by Third Parties 236
4. Possibility of Derogating from Certain Provisions of the ICC Rules 236
5. Items Worth Including in an Arbitration Agreement 237

CHAPTER 5
OVERVIEW OF THE TIME LIMITS LAID DOWN IN THE ICC RULES OF ARBITRATION **239**
1. Article 3(4) of the Rules: How Time Limits are Calculated 239
2. Article 4(2) of the Rules: Start of the Arbitral Proceedings 239
3. Article 4(4) of the Rules: Prerequisites for Filing a Valid Request for Arbitration 239
4. Article 5(1) and (2) of the Rules: Filing of an Answer to the Request for Arbitration 239
5. Article 5(6) of the Rules: Claimant's Reply to a Counterclaim 240
6. Article 11(2) of the Rules: Qualified Statement of Independence from an Arbitrator 240
7. Article 12(2) of the Rules: Nomination of Co-Arbitrators after the Court has Decided in Favour of a Three-Member Tribunal 240
8. Article 12(4) of the Rules: Nomination of Co-Arbitrators where the Parties Agree on a Three-Member Tribunal 240
9. Article 12(5) of the Rules: Nomination of the Person who will act as President of a Three-Member Tribunal 240
10. Article 12(3) of the Rules: Nomination of a Sole Arbitrator 240
11. Article 13(3) of the Rules: Appointment of a Co-Arbitrator upon the Proposal of a National Committee or Group when a Party Fails to make the Necessary Nomination 241
12. Article 14(2) of the Rules: Challenges of Arbitrators by Parties 241
13. Article 15(3) of the Rules: Replacement of Arbitrators by the Court 241
14. Article 23(2) of the Rules: Terms of Reference 241
15. Article 24(1) of the Rules: Case Management Conference 241
16. Article 24(2) of the Rules: Procedural Timetable 241
17. Article 27 of the Rules: Closing of the Proceedings 242
18. Article 27 of the Rules: Announcement of the Submission of the Draft Award to the Court 242
19. Article 30 of the Rules: The Award 242
20. Article 35 of the Rules: Correction of an Award 242
21. Article 35 of the Rules: Interpretation of an Award 242
22. Article 35(4) of the Rules: Remission of an Award 243
23. Article 36(1) of the Rules: Payment of the Provisional Advance on Costs 243
24. Article 36(6) of the Rules: Payment of the Advance on Costs 243
25. Article 38 of the Rules: Modification of Time Limits by the Parties 243
26. Article 39 of the Rules: Waiver 243
27. Article 1(8) of Appendix II to the Rules: Return of Documents at the End of the Arbitration 243

CHAPTER 6
OTHER METHODS OF DISPUTE RESOLUTION UNDER ICC RULES **245**

A. GENERAL REMARKS 245

B. ICC RULES FOR A PRE-ARBITRAL REFEREE PROCEDURE 246
1. Suggested ICC Pre-Arbitral Referee Clause 246
2. Characteristics 247
3. Powers of the Referee 247

4. Costs 248

C. ICC MEDIATION RULES **248**
1. Mediation / Amicable Dispute Resolution 248
2. Suggested ICC Mediation Clauses 251
3. Commencement of Mediation Proceedings 252
4. Mediator 253
5. Conduct of Mediation Proceedings 254
6. Termination of Mediation Proceedings 255
7. Confidentiality 255
8. Limitation of Liability 256
9. Costs 256
10. Prior ICC Arbitration 257
11. Value Added Tax (VAT) 258
12. ICC as Appointing Authority 259

D. ICC EXPERT RULES **259**
1. Proposal of Experts 261
2. Appointment of Experts 262
3. Administration of Expert Proceedings 263
4. Suggested Clauses for ICC Administered Expert Proceedings 266

E. ICC DOCDEX RULES **267**
1. Conduct of DOCDEX Proceedings 269
2. DOCDEX Decision 270

F. ICC RULES FOR DISPUTE BOARDS **271**
1. Dispute Board Proceedings 271
2. Suggested Clauses for ICC Dispute Board Proceedings 273

CHAPTER 7
STATISTICAL INFORMATION ON ICC ARBITRATION **277**

CHAPTER 8
BIBLIOGRAPHY ON ICC ARBITRATION **289**

A. ICC ARBITRAL AWARDS 289

B. BOOKS ON ICC ARBITRATION 290

C. DOSSIERS OF THE ICC INSTITUTE OF WORLD BUSINESS LAW 291

D. WEB SITES CONTAINING Materials AND INFORMATION ON INTERNATIONAL ARBITRATION 292
1. Materials Referred to in this Book 292
2. Other Internet Resources 292

APPENDIX 1
ICC RULES OF ARBITRATION (1 JANUARY 2012) 295

APPENDIX 2
ICC ARBITRATOR STATEMENT OF ACCEPTANCE, AVAILABILITY, IMPARTIALITY AND INDEPENDENCE (2012 RULES) 327

APPENDIX 3
MODEL CURRICULUM VITAE FOR ICC ARBITRATORS 329

APPENDIX 4
SECRETARIAT'S NOTE TO PARTIES IN PROCEEDINGS UNDER THE 2012 ICC RULES OF ARBITRATION 333

APPENDIX 5
SECRETARIAT'S NOTE ON ARTICLE 36(4) OF THE 2012 ICC RULES OF ARBITRATION 337

APPENDIX 6
SECRETARIAT'S NOTE ON ICC EMERGENCY ARBITRATOR PROCEEDINGS (2012 RULES) 339

APPENDIX 7
EMERGENCY ARBITRATOR'S STATEMENT OF ACCEPTANCE, AVAILABILITY, IMPARTIALITY AND INDEPENDENCE (2012 RULES) 341

APPENDIX 8
SECRETARIAT'S ICC EMERGENCY ARBITRATOR ORDER CHECKLIST (2012 RULES) 343

APPENDIX 9
SECRETARIAT'S NOTE TO THE ARBITRAL TRIBUNAL ON THE CONDUCT OF THE ARBITRATION (2012 RULES) 345

APPENDIX 10
SECRETARIAT'S NOTE ON ADMINISTRATIVE ISSUES IN PROCEEDINGS UNDER THE 2012 ICC RULES OF ARBITRATION 355

APPENDIX 11
SECRETARIAT'S ICC AWARD CHECKLIST (1998 AND 2012 RULES) 357

APPENDIX 12
SECRETARIAT'S NOTE ON CORRECTION AND INTERPRETATION OF ARBITRAL AWARDS (1998 AND 2012 RULES) 361

APPENDIX 13
SECRETARIAT'S CHECKLIST ON CORRECTION AND INTERPRETATION OF AWARDS (1998 AND 2012 RULES) 365

APPENDIX 14
EFFECTIVE MANAGEMENT OF ARBITRATION: A GUIDE FOR IN-HOUSE COUNSEL AND OTHER PARTY REPRESENTATIVES (2014) 369

APPENDIX 15
COMMISSION REPORT/SECOND EDITION – TECHNIQUES FOR CONTROLLING TIME AND COSTS IN ARBITRATION (2012) 401

APPENDIX 16
COMMISSION REPORT – ARBITRATION INVOLVING STATES AND STATE ENTITIES UNDER THE ICC RULES OF ARBITRATION (2012) 421

APPENDIX 17
COMMISSION REPORT – TECHNIQUES FOR MANAGING ELECTRONIC DOCUMENT PRODUCTION WHEN IT IS PERMITTED OR REQUIRED IN INTERNATIONAL ARBITRATION (2012) 433

APPENDIX 18
COMMISSION REPORT – ISSUES FOR ARBITRATORS TO CONSIDER REGARDING EXPERTISE (2010) 471

APPENDIX 19
ISSUES FOR EXPERTS ACTING UNDER THE ICC RULES FOR EXPERTISE OR THE ICC RULES OF ARBITRATION (2009) 493

APPENDIX 20
RULES OF ICC AS APPOINTING AUTHORITY IN UNCITRAL OR OTHER AD HOC ARBITRATION PROCEEDINGS (1 JANUARY 2004) 515

APPENDIX 21
ICC RULES FOR A PRE-ARBITRAL REFEREE PROCEDURE (1 JANUARY 1990) 519

APPENDIX 22
PRE-ARBITRAL REFEREE'S STATEMENT OF ACCEPTANCE, AVAILABILITY AND INDEPENDENCE 525

APPENDIX 23
ICC MEDIATION RULES (1 JANUARY 2014) 527

APPENDIX 24
ICC MEDIATION CLAUSES (2014) 535

APPENDIX 25
ICC EXPERT RULES (1 FEBRUARY 2015) 539

APPENDIX 26
ICC EXPERT CLAUSES (2015) 559

APPENDIX 27
ICC DOCDEX RULES (1 MAY 2015) **563**

APPENDIX 28
ICC DISPUTE BOARD RULES (1 OCTOBER 2015) **571**

APPENDIX 29
ICC DISPUTE BOARD CLAUSES (2015) **587**

INDEX AND TABLE OF FIGURES 591
A. Alphabetical Index 591
B. Table of Figures 606

FOREWORD

Almost a century after its creation in 1923, the ICC International Court of Arbitration remains the pre-eminent international arbitral institution. It has administered more than 20,000 cases involving parties from some 200 different countries. The ICC International Court of Arbitration administers cases in Paris – where it is headquartered – as well as in Hong-Kong and New York. The Court's Secretariat works in more than 25 different languages and the Court avails itself, when selecting arbitrators, of a unique network of more than 90 ICC National Committees and Groups throughout the world in addition to its own considerable 'institutional memory'. One of the principal strengths of ICC arbitration is that it does not reflect the influence of any one particular national law or culture. ICC arbitration reflects the wide diversity of the parties involved in international trade worldwide and the ICC International Court of Arbitration is the only truly global arbitration institution.

Decisions made by ICC tribunals have considerable scientific and persuasive authority. Awards, which are of particular importance in themselves or which inform legal thinking in a manner susceptible to general application are made available (in redacted form to protect the identities of the parties) through various publications by both the ICC itself and by specialist arbitration journals and press reports. These awards contribute significantly to the development of international trade law and the definition of trade usages.

The 2012 rules revision was conducted on the basis of a uniquely broad based and transparent consultative process. A drafting sub-committee was created, comprising 12 members drawn from senior members of the ICC Commission on Arbitration (as it was then known), the Court and the Secretariat, together with prominent corporate counsel, international arbitration practitioners and academics. The sub-committee prepared a draft based upon feedback received from members of the Commission and its Rules Revision Task Force and members of the arbitral community as well as from the public at large, who had responded to a call for comment. The draft was then submitted to ICC national committees in more than 90 countries and discussed by the more than 100 members of the ICC Commission on Arbitration and ADR and the 90 members of the Court. The resulting text is the fruit of these in-depth exchanges of views between practitioners from different cultures and legal traditions. It reflects the experience of the ICC International Court of Arbitration in applying the 1998 rules, but it also contains a number of important improvements, which are considered by the authors of this book in a meticulous and clear manner. The new provisions of the rules concerning multiparty and multicontracts arbitrations, as well as consolidation, set out in the clearest terms the practice that the Court will follow when it is called upon to consider a case involving multiple parties. These revisions leave the ICC rules better adapted to the growing complexity of arbitration – indispensable in circumstances in which some 30% of the Court's caseload comprises multiparty cases. The 2012 rules also place great emphasis on the need for arbitration proceedings to be conducted in an expeditious and cost-effective manner. Parties, their counsel and tribunals will often apply some, if not all, of the provisions of the Appendix on case management techniques, which was quickly acknowledged to provide a readily adaptable framework for the conduct of international arbitration proceedings. The 2012 rules also contain new provisions for the appointment of an Emergency Arbitrator and changes intended to meet the concerns of States and state entities, which arise in the context of arbitrations to which they are parties.

The authors are both experienced arbitration practitioners, who have in addition held positions as counsel within the Secretariat of the ICC Court. They come from countries with traditionally strong links with ICC arbitration. I am sure that their achievement in bringing this new edition of their work to fruition will contribute to a broadening of the reach of ICC arbitration and to popularize arbitration in general.

Mr. Alexis Mourre
President of the ICC International Court of Arbitration
Paris, France

PREFACE

The Rules of Arbitration of the International Chamber of Commerce, whose headquarters are in Paris, date from 1922. Their application is overseen by the ICC International Court of Arbitration, whose members come from various sectors of society. During their 90-year history, the rules have had a strong and lasting influence on the development of international arbitration. Many of the world's most reputed international arbitrators have acted in proceedings conducted under the auspices of ICC, thereby contributing significantly to the recognition of ICC arbitration in industrial and commercial circles. The ICC arbitration clause is today used in countless contracts of all kinds. Over 21 000 cases have been filed with the ICC since the inception of ICC arbitration.

The ICC International Court of Arbitration has always been attentive to changing needs and has periodically adapted its rules. The most recent revision – the tenth since the institution's creation – came into force on 1 January 2012. This new version of the Rules, still in force today, is the subject of this book.

Arbitration as conceived by and intended for the business community has developed into a specialized procedure dominated by lawyers specially initiated into its particularities. Although there is no reason to decry this situation, it does mean that many parties, whatever their background, find it difficult to understand how international arbitration proceedings – including those of the ICC – are conducted. There is certainly no lack of literature on ICC arbitration, but most of it is intended for practitioners already conversant with the subject.

ICC Arbitration in Practice is intended above all for readers who are unfamiliar with international arbitration and the ICC rules of 2012 and wish to be able to assess the pros and cons of entering into an arbitration clause referring to the ICC rules and to know how to proceed in a given situation. For this reason, the authors have deliberately avoided the use of footnotes and a detailed bibliography.

The first edition of this book dealt with the ICC Rules of arbitration of 1998. This second edition follows the structure of the first edition, but examines in addition the new provisions introduced with the 2012 Rules and the amendments made to the 1998 Rules. The most recent statistics have been included where available. Other dispute resolution services of the ICC such as mediation, expertise and dispute boards, including the 2014 revision of the ICC Mediation Rules, the 2015 revision of the ICC Expert Rules and the 2015 revision of the ICC Dispute Board Rules are examined in separate chapters. The book contains references to a selected number of national laws.

For ease of reading and the convenience of readers from different backgrounds, the authors have limited their use of capital letters to proper nouns and terms that have a particular meaning in the context of ICC arbitration (e.g. Terms of Reference). This explains the typographical differences that will sometimes be observed between the authors' commentary and the quotations from the rules.

Given the practical purpose of this book, the authors welcome comments and suggestions. These may be sent by e-mail to the following address: mail@arbitris.com (web site: < www.arbitris.com >).

The Authors
Ghent/Brussels, Düsseldorf, Geneva
September 2015

THE AUTHORS

HERMAN VERBIST

Herman Verbist, a Belgian lawyer, was born in 1959 and studied at the Universities of Brussels and Leuven in Belgium, as well as at the University of Tübingen in Germany and King's College, London, in England. He obtained his doctorate in law at the University of Ghent, Belgium, in 2008 with a doctoral thesis on '*De rechtsbescherming van partijen in privaatrechtelijke handelsarbitrage*' (The Legal protection of the parties in commercial arbitration under private law). He was admitted to the Brussels Bar in 1983 and to the Ghent Bar in 2007. From 1988 to 1996, he held the position of counsel at the Secretariat of the ICC International Court of Arbitration. He then returned to practice as a lawyer, currently with the firm Everest attorneys. He specializes mainly in domestic and international arbitration and has acted both as counsel and arbitrator in arbitration proceedings under the ICC Rules of Arbitration and under the rules of other arbitration institutions and also in '*ad hoc*' arbitrations. From 1996 until 2013, he has been visiting professor for the course on international arbitration at the University of Ghent, in Belgium, and since 1998 he has been a consultant with the International Trade Centre UNCTAD/WTO in Geneva. He is a member of the Belgian Centre for Arbitration and Mediation (CEPANI) and of the Board of CEPANI, and also a member of the German Arbitration Institute (DIS), the French Arbitration Committee, the Swiss Arbitration Association (ASA), the London Court of International Arbitration, the American Arbitration Association, the Belgian-German Association of Lawyers, the European Lawyers Association, the International Bar Association, of the International Council for Commercial Arbitration and of its Publications Advisory Board. He is on the lists of arbitrators of a number of arbitration institutions in different countries (Madrid Court of Arbitration, International Arbitral Centre of the Austrian Federal Economic Chamber, Court of Arbitration attached to the Polish Chamber of Commerce, Court of Arbitration attached to the Hungarian Chamber of Commerce and Industry, Arbitration Court attached to the Economic Chamber of the Czech Republic and Agricultural Chamber of the Czech Republic, Permanent Arbitration Court of the Croatian Chamber of Commerce, International Roster of Arbitrators and Mediators of the International Centre for Dispute Resolution of the American Arbitration Association, Jerusalem Arbitration Center in association with the International Chamber of Commerce, Kuala Lumpur Regional Centre for Arbitration, Hong Kong International Arbitration Centre, Singapore International Arbitration Centre). As a representative of CEPANI, he participates in the working group of UNCITRAL on arbitration and conciliation. He is contributor for Belgium to the online UNCITRAL Guide on the Convention on the Recognition and Enforcement of Foreign Arbitral Awards (New York, 1958).

Herman Verbist continues to have links with the ICC as a member of the ICC Commission on Arbitration and ADR, where he participated in several task forces, and as a member of the ICC Institute of World Business Law. He is also registered as a mediator with the Belgian Federal Mediation Commission. He is a member of the editorial board of several legal periodicals in the field of arbitration and alternative dispute resolution in Belgium and in the Netherlands (*'b-Arbitra'*, *'Tijdschrift voor Arbtrage'*, *'Nederlands-Vlaams Tijdschrift voor Mediation en Conflictmanagement'*). He published as author or as co-author several books and articles on arbitration and alternative dispute resolution and is a frequent speaker at conferences on these topics.

ERIK SCHÄFER

Erik Schäfer, a German lawyer who qualified for the Bar in 1987, was born in 1957 and studied at the Universities of Freiburg (Germany), Dijon (France) and London (England). He is admitted to practise in all local and district courts in Germany and in all of Germany's higher regional courts. He began his career in 1988 as counsel at the Secretariat of the ICC International Court of Arbitration in Paris. In 1992, he took up a position as an in-house lawyer in the intellectual property department of a company and in 1993 moved to the Dresden office of a law firm specializing in competition law, intellectual property law and commercial law. In 1997, he joined Cohausz & Florack, a Düsseldorf inter-professional law firm, which handles all aspects of intellectual property and advises on the protection and exploitation of technology and scientific know-how, and of which he is now a partner. Erik Schäfer also represents parties in arbitral proceedings and acts as arbitrator. In addition, Erik Schäfer is a trained mediator. He was recently appointed member of the board of trustees of the DIAC. He is on the list of arbitrators of the VIAC, the SIAC, the KLRCA, and the Danish Institute of Arbitration. He is a member of several professional organizations, including the German Arbitration Institute (DIS), the Swiss Arbitration Association (ASA), the Club Español del Arbitraje, the German intellectual property rights association GRUR, the German branch of the Licensing Executives Society (LES), and the International Bar Association. As German delegate to the ICC Commission on Arbitration and ADR, he has participated in various task forces and co-chairs the task force on information technology in arbitration and expertise proceedings.

CHRISTOPHE IMHOOS

Christophe Imhoos, a Swiss lawyer, was born in 1959 and studied at the Universities of Geneva (Switzerland) and New York (USA). After his admission to the Geneva Bar in 1985, he held the position of counsel at the Secretariat of the ICC International Court of Arbitration from 1987 to 1991. Since 1992, he has been a partner of the law firm Jean-Pierre and Christophe Imhoos in Geneva and acts as counsel and arbitrator in international trade disputes. He is a member of the Swiss Arbitration Association and of the ICC Commission on Arbitration and ADR. He is also on the WIPO panel of experts on domain names, in which capacity he has rendered a number of decisions. Some years ago, he worked as consultant with the United Nations Development Programme for the start of the OHADA Common Court of Justice and Arbitration in Côte d'Ivoire. Since 2007, he has considerably extended his practice to domestic and international mediation in all fields. He is an accredited mediator with CEDR (London), CMAP (Paris) and SCCM (Switzerland). He very often represents and assists clients in mediations. He is adjunct professor in conflict management (negotiation, mediation) at the Geneva *Ecole d'Advocature* (ECAV) attached to the Geneva University School of Law.

ABBREVIATIONS

The following legal instruments are referred to throughout this book using the abbreviations indicated below:

JC:	Belgian Judicial Code (*Code Judiciaire/Gerechtelijk Wetboek*)
NCPC:	French New Code of Civil Procedure (*Nouveau Code de procédure civile*)
New York Convention:	United Nations Convention on the Recognition and Enforcement of Foreign Arbitral Awards, opened for signature in New York on 10 June 1958
PILA:	Swiss Private International Law Act (*Bundesgesetz über das internationale Privatrecht/Legge federale sul diritto internazionale privato/Loi fédérale sur le droit international privé*)
Rome Convention:	European Community Convention on the Law Applicable to Contractual Obligations, opened for signature in Rome on 19 June 1980 replaced by Regulation (EC) N° 593/2008 of the European Parliament and of the Council of 17 June 2008 on the law applicable to contractual obligations ('Rome I')
UNCITRAL Model Law:	Model Law on International Commercial Arbitration of the United Nations Commission on International Trade Law
ZPO:	German Code of Civil Procedure (*Zivilprozessordnung*)

CHAPTER 1

INTRODUCTION

An introduction to the Rules of Arbitration of the International Chamber of Commerce, as in force from 1 January 2012, calls firstly for a general presentation of private arbitration and how it fits into the legal system as a whole. This will be followed by a description of institutional arbitration, in which the ICC Rules of Arbitration have a special place.

A. ARBITRATION AS A PRIVATE METHOD OF SETTLING DISPUTES

1. Arbitration as an Alternative to Court Proceedings

Throughout history people have settled their differences by seeking advice or a ruling from a chosen third person or body. In contemporary society, decisions putting an end to legal conflicts are commonly sought from courts, whose rulings may be forcibly executed by the state. The courts rendering such decisions are authorized to hear the dispute, irrespective of the parties' wishes, by the fact that the applicable procedural law gives them jurisdiction territorially and on account of the nature of the dispute. The parties have no say in the applicable rules of procedure regarding the court, the language or the duration of the proceedings.

Like litigation, the purpose of arbitration is to obtain a final and binding ruling on a dispute. The difference with arbitration is that before the dispute arises or after it has arisen the parties make a valid agreement with each other to use arbitration. By doing so, they exclude recourse to state courts and decide that disputes will be settled by an arbitral tribunal. As we shall see from the example of the ICC Rules of Arbitration, the arbitral tribunal and the parties may together extensively influence the organization of the arbitral proceedings, so long as they respect certain minimum standards. Arbitration is also distinguished by the fact that in most cases no more than one action is required to obtain a final decision.

When an arbitral award is accepted and carried out by the parties, no state intervention is necessary. This is not to say that arbitration is conducted outside any legal framework. In most national legal systems, arbitration is considered to have the same value as court proceedings. For instance, Article 1055 of the German Code of Civil Procedure (hereinafter 'ZPO') and Article 1713(9) of the Belgian Judicial Code (hereinafter 'JC') clearly state that an arbitral award shall have the same effects as a binding and final judgment. According to Article 8(1) of the Model Law on International Commercial Arbitration adopted by the United Nations Commission on International Trade Law on 21 June 1985 and amended on 7 July 2006 (hereinafter 'UNCITRAL Model Law'), when a matter which is the subject of an arbitration agreement is brought before a court, the court shall refer the parties to arbitration if one of them requests it to do so at the start of the proceedings, unless it finds that the agreement is null and void, inoperative or incapable of being performed. Similar provisions are also found in the arbitration laws of other countries, such as Belgium (Article 1682(1) JC) and France (Article 1448 of the New Code of Civil Procedure (hereinafter 'NCPC')). There is no equivalent provision, on the other hand, in Swiss international arbitration law.

2. Arbitration as an Alternative to Court Proceedings in International Legal Relations

There is no international court of justice for private international disputes. In such cases, litigants are therefore obliged to turn to national courts. The jurisdiction of the national courts, which is determined by the procedural law to which they are subject and depends on territorial and substantive criteria, will usually contain special provisions for cases with foreign connections. The procedure in the relevant national court, however, will be governed by rules specific to that court.

The situation is somewhat different when it comes to international arbitration. There is no legal requirement for arbitration proceedings to be conducted at the place where one of the parties is legally established. On the contrary, a neutral place is usually chosen. Another typical feature of arbitration is the a-national character of the arbitral tribunal: the nationality and place of residence of the arbitrators are normally independent of the place of the arbitration, unless the parties have expressly decided otherwise.

International arbitration proceedings are not, however, completely removed from national legal systems. The most important link is the seat of the arbitral proceedings, since the law applicable at such place often contains provisions allowing state courts there to review the procedure and the arbitral award if so requested by one of the parties. Some national laws contain specific rules for international arbitration proceedings distinct from those governing purely domestic arbitration. This should be checked in each case. The seat of the arbitral proceedings is also relevant as national arbitration laws often treat the recognition and enforcement of arbitral awards differently depending on whether they are domestic or foreign. A foreign award is any award that is not rendered within the state where it is to be enforced.

3. Relation between Arbitration and Other Methods of Settling Private Disputes Out of Court

Arbitration is often compared with conciliation or mediation. The comparison is not entirely inappropriate, as experience shows that a considerable number of arbitration cases end with a mutually agreed settlement. Arbitration, however, is distinguished by the fact that it leads to a final decision on the dispute with the same value as a court ruling. Although based on the parties' agreement to submit any disputes to arbitration, the decision does not in itself require their consent. When deciding the substantive issues, the arbitral tribunal must apply the rules of law agreed by the parties or which it has itself determined on the basis of the applicable legal provisions. It may sidestep the rules of applicable law to render a decision based on equity only if the parties have expressly authorized it to do so, as is possible in Switzerland under Article 187 of Chapter XII of the Federal Act on Private International Law (hereinafter 'PILA') and under the laws of Belgium (Article 1710(3) JC), France (Article 1478 NCPC), Germany (Article 1051(3) ZPO) and the UNCITRAL Model Law (Article 28(3)).

The purpose of conciliation or mediation, on the other hand, is for the parties to reach an agreement putting an end to their dispute. This is true not only of traditional conciliation, in which the third party suggests to the parties his or her own solutions for settling their dispute, but also of methods strongly orientated towards negotiation, such as mediation, where the third party guides the parties but is not required to suggest solutions. There are also hybrid procedures in which the third party has certain decision-making powers with respect to the dispute, especially when it concerns a contract (e.g. the expert adjudicator ('Schiedsgutachter') in Germany or dispute review boards in the construction field). Decisions of this kind are not normally equivalent to judgments handed down by state courts.

B. LINKS BETWEEN ARBITRATION AND STATE COURTS

In the previous section the particularities of arbitration as compared with litigation were identified. Consideration will now be given to the relationship between arbitration proceedings and state courts. These are of practical significance when a party does not fulfil its obligations under the arbitration agreement, notably by preventing the arbitration from being conducted correctly or by refusing to comply with the terms of the arbitral award. In the first case, the tribunal may not have been constituted. In the second, a decision by the arbitral tribunal dismissing the claims of one of the parties is unacceptable to that party. Since, in the latter case, the arbitral tribunal is no longer seized of the matter, the dissatisfied party cannot request it to reverse or alter its decision on the merits. In such situations, the dissatisfied party has no choice but to take its case to the courts, unless another procedure allowed by law has been agreed.

National arbitration laws contain specific provisions giving courts prerogatives with respect to:

- measures related to the constitution of the arbitral tribunal;
- decisions on challenges and the replacement of arbitrators;
- decisions on applications for an arbitral award to be set aside;
- decisions on applications for the recognition or enforcement of arbitral awards.

The first two are fall-back powers. Measures related to the constitution of the arbitral tribunal are required only if, for example, the parties have not agreed on an independent procedure for constituting the arbitral tribunal, or if disagreement between the parties raises problems with regard to the appointment of a member of the arbitral tribunal, as when a party refuses to collaborate for example. This explains why national arbitration laws contain provisions indicating how arbitral tribunals should be constituted when the question is not dealt with in the parties' agreement. Examples of such provisions may be found in Articles 1684–1685 JC, Article 179(2) PILA (which refers to cantonal law), Article 1451-1454 NCPC, Articles 1034-1039 ZPO, and Article 11(3) of the UNCITRAL Model Law. The prerogatives listed above usually lie with the court designated by the procedural law at the place agreed upon as the seat of the arbitration. With respect to challenges of arbitrators, see for instance Article 1687 JC, Article 180(3) PILA, Article 1456 and 1459 NCPC and Article 13(3) of the UNCITRAL Model Law.

Serious jurisdictional problems and conflicts may arise when, in international arbitration proceedings, the parties have not agreed on the seat of the arbitration or have agreed that it will be determined by a third party. If one party is resident or, in the case of a legal entity, has its headquarters in Germany, German courts will have jurisdiction over that person for a certain number of measures set out in Article 1025(3) the ZPO. The Belgian arbitration law (Article 1676(6) and 1676(8) JC) provides that Belgian Courts have jurisdiction territorially to take certain measures, even if the place of the arbitration is not situated in Belgium

Unless otherwise agreed by the parties, decisions relating to challenges and replacements of arbitrators are generally made by the courts at the seat of the arbitration that have jurisdiction territorially and on account of the nature of the dispute according to the procedural law applicable to them (cf. Articles 1687 (2) JC and Article 180 (3) PILA). The question of whether a decision by a third party to which the parties have agreed to refer matters relating to the challenge or replacement of an arbitrator may be reviewed by the appropriate court will depend above all on the applicable arbitration law or even the procedural law governing such court. If the parties have not agreed on the seat of the arbitration, and unless they have arranged for it to be fixed by a third party, the seat of the arbitration will in such cases normally be fixed by the arbitral tribunal. Similar provisions are found in the arbitration legislation of other states (for Germany see Article 1043(1) ZPO; for Belgium see Article 1701(1) JC and for Switzerland Article 176 (3) PILA, see also Article 20 (1) of the UNCITRAL Model Law).

The competent court at the place of the arbitration also normally decides on applications for arbitral awards to be set aside. It will do so on the basis of the arbitration law in force at the place of the arbitration (see, for example, Article 1059 ZPO; Article 1717 JC; Articles 191 and 190(2) PILA; see Articles 1491-1493 and 1518-1520 NCPC; for other countries).

The competent court at the place of the arbitration does not have exclusive jurisdiction, however, when it comes to decisions on applications for the recognition and enforcement of arbitral awards in international matters. This is understandable, since the compulsory enforcement of arbitral awards, which have the same value as court decisions, lies within the sole jurisdiction of the legal authorities of the state where the award is to be enforced. The arbitral tribunal itself has no means of compelling compliance with the award. In practice, international arbitration awards usually have more weight than foreign judgments, which, like arbitral awards, must also be registered for execution in the country of enforcement. The conditions under which such enforcement of an arbitral award is granted are those provided by the law applicable to the relevant authority in the country of enforcement (see, for example, Articles 1060-1061 (arbitral awards) and 722–723 (foreign judgments) ZPO, Articles 1719–1721 (arbitral awards) and 570 (foreign judgments) JC; Articles 25–32, 190(2) and 194 PILA; Articles 1487-1488 and 1514-1517 NCPC).

In international relations, problems of some importance are often encountered when it comes to enforcing decisions of foreign courts, unless there is a bilateral or multilateral international treaty between the state in which the decision has been rendered and that in which it is to be enforced. An example of such an agreement in Europe is the European Regulation of 12 December 2012 on jurisdiction and the recognition and enforcement of judgments in civil and commercial matters N° 1215/2012 (Recast). However, there is no guarantee that a similar regulation or convention will exist in the wider geographical context. This explains why arbitration is in a much more advantageous position, on account of the Convention on the Recognition and Enforcement of Foreign Arbitral Awards concluded in New York on 10 June 1958 (hereinafter the 'New York Convention'). There are currently over 154 parties to this convention, including all the Member States of the European Union, Switzerland, the USA, the Russian Federation, the People's Republic of China and all other major or salient emerging industrial countries. The convention provides for the recognition and enforcement of foreign arbitral awards which may be refused only on the basis of one or more grounds stated in a limited list of grounds concerning important procedural defects. It does not allow for the merits of the decision to be reviewed, unless the subject matter of the dispute is not arbitrable according to the applicable law in the country of enforcement, or if public policy provisions applicable to international arbitration proceedings in the country of enforcement would be infringed by the enforcement of the arbitral award. This standardization of the requirements for the enforcement of foreign arbitral awards is one of the major advantages of international arbitration. It may be assumed that the mere fact of knowing that it is easier to have arbitral awards recognized and enforced in foreign countries encourages parties to perform international arbitral awards spontaneously.

Another aspect of the relationship between state courts and arbitration is that arbitration laws sometimes allow parties, and sometimes also the arbitral tribunal, to apply to the relevant court at the place of the arbitration for assistance in the enforcement of certain measures that are necessary during the arbitration proceedings. Given that arbitral tribunals cannot, for example, compel themselves a witness to appear, the law may allow courts to summon witnesses within their jurisdiction to arbitration proceedings as they would to judicial proceedings. This of course presupposes that the witness is in the country where the court is located, which is likely to be rare in international arbitration proceedings (see Articles 184(2), 185 and 176(1) PILA). In Germany, for instance, foreign arbitral tribunals and parties in proceedings outside Germany, may seek assistance from German courts (Article 1025(2) and 1050 ZPO). In Belgium, parties involved in a foreign arbitration may, with the approval of the arbitral tribunal, apply to a Belgian Court to seek such assistance (Article 1676(8) JC). In Switzerland, assistance is available only when the place of the arbitration is in Switzerland (Article 184(2) combined with Article 176(1) PILA). Model Law. See also Article 27 of the UNCITRAL Model Law.

Furthermore, state courts have jurisdiction to order conservatory and interim measures, even when parties have agreed to give an arbitral tribunal sole jurisdiction over their disputes (see Article 1041 ZPO, Articles 1691 JC and Article 193 PILA in conjunction with cantonal law; see also Article 9 of the UNCITRAL Model Law). As to the question of whether or not an arbitral tribunal has jurisdiction to order such measures, answers vary from one country to another. Often a country's law contains no provision for the enforcement of such decisions when made by an arbitral tribunal. This is especially so when the decision takes the form of an order, but also – depending on the law applicable to the proceedings – when the interim or conservatory measure takes the form of an arbitral award. In addition, it will sometimes be necessary to initiate proceedings for the recognition or enforcement of the award that is duly rendered, which will lead to extra time and expense.

Another practical problem is that an interim protective measure might be required before the arbitral tribunal has been constituted. As a general rule, the time required for constituting the arbitral tribunal and setting the proceedings in motion is hardly consistent with the need for rapid assistance. This is why many national arbitration laws that allow arbitrators to order interim measures nonetheless provide for the possibility of recourse to state courts notwithstanding the existence of an arbitration agreement and without affecting the arbitral tribunal's exclusive jurisdiction to decide on the merits. Under the 2012 ICC Rules of Arbitration, however, the parties can call upon an emergency arbitrator for such interim protective measures, unless they have opted out of this mechanism or unless they have agreed upon another pre-arbitral procedure for the granting of such measures.

C. '*AD HOC*' ARBITRATION PROCEDURE

All commercial arbitration proceedings break down into two stages. The first stage is devoted to the constitution of the arbitral tribunal and the second to the actual conduct of proceedings before that tribunal. Arbitration laws typically provide for proceedings that do not involve arbitration institutions or 'permanent' arbitral tribunals. In such cases, if the parties have not made any arrangements beyond the basic provisions which the arbitration agreement is legally required to contain, the applicable arbitration law will fill the gaps. Arbitrations of this kind are referred to as '*ad hoc*'.

1. Initiation of the Arbitration and Constitution of the Arbitral Tribunal

An '*ad hoc*' arbitration is initiated by the claimant when it informs the respondent of its intention to resort to arbitration and takes the steps laid down in the arbitration agreement and applicable arbitration law. When, for example, the arbitration agreement provides for the constitution of a three-member tribunal and does not depart from the traditional arrangement whereby each party appoints a co-arbitrator, the claimant names an arbitrator when informing the other party of the initiation of proceedings and invites that party in turn to appoint an arbitrator within a given time limit. Once they have been appointed, these arbitrators then usually appoint a third arbitrator to chair the tribunal. If the parties have decided that a sole arbitrator will be appointed, the claimant will usually suggest one or more names when informing the other party of its intention to resort to arbitration, unless the parties have agreed otherwise. The purpose of making suggestions at this stage is to enable the parties then to agree on one of the names put forward. A sole arbitrator may also be appointed by a third party or an institution such as ICC.

If the constitution of the arbitral tribunal poses problems, for example when the parties cannot agree on the required appointment, the proceedings will take place in accordance with the provisions of the arbitration agreement or, failing this, those of the applicable arbitration law. If, for example, the parties have not fixed the number of arbitrators in their arbitration agreement and are unable to decide upon it, German law and Belgian law provide that the tribunal will in that case comprise three arbitrators (Article 1034(1) ZPO; Article 1684(3) JC). French and Swiss law require the dispute to be settled by an odd number of arbitrators, usually one or three (see Article 1451 NCPC; Article 179(2) PILA, which refers to cantonal law, namely Articles 10 and 11 of the Intercantonal Arbitration Concordat). Mention should also be made of Article 10 of the UNCITRAL Model Law, which provides that in the event that the parties have not come to an agreement on the number of arbitrators, they shall be three in number.

In '*ad hoc*' proceedings, once the arbitrators have been appointed, the parties usually enter into an agreement with them, confirming their appointment and settling the questions of their remuneration and the reimbursement of their expenses. This agreement may also contain provisions essential to the ensuing proceedings. It is not, however, a prerequisite for the arbitral proceedings to take place, should a party refuse to take part or to collaborate. If this happens, the relevant provisions of the applicable arbitration law will apply.

On the basis of the arbitration agreement and the applicable arbitration law, the arbitral tribunal will then ask the parties to pay an advance intended to cover the arbitrators' fees and expenses. They will normally be asked to pay the advance in equal shares. The arbitral tribunal may, and generally does, make its acceptance of its assignment conditional upon prior payment of the advance.

2. Conduct of Arbitration Proceedings

It should be noted that, as far as international arbitration is concerned, the initiation of the proceedings and the form and content of written communications may vary depending upon the legal background of the parties' representatives and the origins of the arbitrators. Flexibility is therefore a necessary part of arbitration proceedings and the way they are conducted.

Such flexibility also distinguishes arbitration from civil proceedings in a state court, even though, as described above, arbitral awards rank equally with court judgments. Despite this flexibility, certain minimum legal requirements must be met, failing which the arbitrators could be challenged or replaced or the award set aside. Consideration should also be given to the grounds upon which recognition and enforcement of awards may be refused, to the extent that the likely place of enforcement is already known. Usually, however, it will not have been determined with certainty and in this case reference should be made to the conditions laid down in the New York Convention. The arbitration law applicable at the place of the arbitration, also known as '*lex arbitri*', will be decisive. The '*lex arbitri*' consists of rules that may vary from one country to another and, even if they are identical, the related case law may nonetheless vary. For this reason, the observations made here must be of a general nature.

The procedural flexibility and the diverging legal cultures to which international arbitration practitioners pertain are sometimes also perceived as the curse of arbitration since they reduce the foreseeability of the proceedings and make it more difficult to develop procedural strategies and tactics. This has led to the general trend that professional associations such as the International Bar Association (IBA) and institutions have commenced to issue 'rules' on certain procedural issues (e.g. conflicts, ethics, taking of evidence, etc.) or guidelines. Unless agreed by the parties or ordered to be applicable by the arbitral tribunal, these rules or guidelines are not binding in the strict sense of the word, but they often have a strong persuasive character that impacts the way proceedings are conducted. Especially the rules or guidelines issued by IBA have a strong factual impact on the way international arbitrations are conducted worldwide. However, the field of actual procedural practice is very dynamic and ever changing.

To give an example: In the first edition of this book we stated that when fixing the initial period of time for the payment of the advance to cover the costs of the arbitration, the arbitral tribunal will usually instruct the parties to exchange written communications. It will set a date by which the request for arbitration must be filed if the request was not formulated when notification of the arbitration procedure was served upon the other party. Otherwise, a deadline will be set for the respondent's answer. Today, one would rather expect the parties having initially filed rather succinct initial briefs. While the arbitral tribunal would still commence with securing its costs and fees at the outset, it would now be more likely that it would quickly schedule in consultation with the parties a case management conference to discuss and – to the extent possible – agree on the way written proceedings leading up the oral hearing are to be organized and a comprehensive calendar with periods of time. The result of this initial meeting would be recorded in the first procedural order. This provides counsel with the desired foreseeability before the substantive submissions are made.

The arbitration laws known to the authors require arbitral tribunals to guarantee that the parties are given the right to present their cases. This means that they must be allowed to describe the facts that have given rise to the dispute and the legal issues resulting therefrom, insofar as these are essential to the award. The tribunal has a duty to assess these facts and issues when making its award. It is therefore necessary to give the parties the opportunity to present their respective case. They must be treated equally. The parties have the right to be assisted and represented in arbitration proceedings by counsel, both technical and legal counsel. As the rules and norms developed for party representation in domestic judicial litigation may not be well adapted to deal with legal and cultural differences among participants in international arbitration proceedings, the International Bar Association has developed in 2013 Guidelines on Party Representation in International Arbitration. The parties may adopt these Guidelines or a portion thereof by agreement. Arbitral tribunals may also apply the Guidelines in their discretion, subject to any applicable mandatory rules, if they determine that they have the authority to do so (The Guidelines can be consulted on the website of the International Bar Association: < www.ibanet.org >).

It frequently happens that parties are late in presenting their arguments. Whether or not such arguments can be rejected is a question that laws and arbitration rules frequently fail to address adequately. An arbitral tribunal may normally reject them if it has previously given the parties sufficient opportunity to express themselves and if the proceedings have been declared closed. It is debatable whether or not it may do so at earlier stages of the proceedings. However, there need be no hesitation if the parties have been set a clear time limit within which to express themselves and told that no further arguments will be allowed thereafter. The arbitral tribunal also normally has the power not to accept evidence that it considers to be irrelevant. In this regard, arbitrators usually show restraint for fear of being accused of a denial of justice or unequal treatment.

In all other respects, the arbitral proceedings must be conducted in accordance with the arrangements agreed by the parties, provided these are not contrary to any mandatory provisions of the '*lex arbitri*', such as the right to present one's case. For instance, the parties may in their arbitration agreement rule out certain methods of disclosing evidence, such as pre-trial discovery, a feature of US procedural law requiring parties to produce large quantities of documents. However, few arbitration agreements go into such detail. The parties are free to agree on the application of the IBA Rules on the Taking of Evidence in International Commercial Arbitration which were adopted in 1999 and revised in 2010 or they may find guidance in these rules for the taking of evidence proceedings in the arbitration.

The arbitral tribunal is responsible for the conduct of proceedings. In international arbitration, in particular, it would be well advised to organize the conduct of the proceedings in coordination with the parties, if there is a risk of misunderstandings or complications due to the differing conceptions of arbitration that parties from different legal backgrounds may have. This may concern such important questions as evidence offered by witnesses or the nature of the questioning. In many countries, for instance, it is customary for parties to call their own experts, whereas in other countries experts are appointed by the arbitral tribunal. Views often diverge as to who can or cannot be a witness. Added to which, arbitral tribunals, unlike some state courts, are not under an obligation to provide comments or clarification. Nor are they limited to considering only the evidence offered by the parties. This means that arbitral tribunals may in theory order the disclosure of essential evidence and introduce into the proceedings factual material of which they themselves are aware. However, international arbitrators generally show restraint in this regard.

As a general rule, discussions take place orally in arbitration. It is current practice in international arbitration for them to be mostly prepared in writing. They cannot be dispensed with, even at a party's request. Like the proceedings as a whole, the conduct of oral proceedings will be largely influenced by the participants' experience of their own national procedural law. Thus, although the overall conduct of discussions will remain in the hands of the arbitral tribunal, parties – through their counsel – will have a more prominent role in proceedings marked by a common law approach than would be the case, for instance, in proceedings involving German, Spanish or Latin American parties. These differences also affect the duration of the oral proceedings.

It is possible for a decision to be made without a hearing, on the basis of the documents submitted, provided no party has requested otherwise and none of the parties objects. The principle according to which facts that have not been challenged are deemed to have been accepted does not apply in arbitral proceedings. The arbitral tribunal must verify the essential facts by assessing the evidence, which in certain circumstances it may have asked to be submitted of its own accord.

When the arbitral tribunal considers that the parties have had sufficient opportunity to present their arguments and that the facts of the case have been established, it declares the proceedings closed and begins deliberating prior to making its award. An arbitral tribunal may choose to make more than one award, if it considers this to be necessary. It may, for instance, make separate awards on jurisdiction, the merits and the sums claimed. In this case, the terms partial, interim and final awards will be used. Where an arbitral tribunal comprises more than one member, the award is rendered unanimously or, failing this, by a majority of its members. If the arbitration agreement or the '*lex arbitri*' so provides, the decision may be made by the chair of the tribunal alone if the members of the tribunal are unable to agree with each other or to find a majority decision. However, this is rarely the case.

In order to be enforceable and not risk being set aside, arbitral awards must be limited to the issues on which a decision has been requested pursuant to the arbitration agreement. These will in other words generally be the claims. Conversely, the tribunal must settle all such issues and all claims brought before it. In so doing, it will apply the substantive law agreed by the parties. If, however, the parties have failed to agree on the applicable substantive law, this will be determined by the arbitral tribunal on the basis of the provisions contained in the arbitration rules chosen by the parties or the '*lex arbitri*'. These provisions may call for the applicable law to be determined directly rather than by using choice of law rules (this is the approach taken in Article 21(1) of the current ICC Rules of Arbitration), or in accordance with choice-of-law rules (as was the case in the ICC Rules of Arbitration prior to 1998), or in accordance with an independent choice-of-law rule. When this procedure is respected, leading to the determination of a particular law, mistakes in the application of that law cannot be reviewed by a court to which application is made for the award to be set aside or for its recognition and enforcement, unless the mistakes make the award contrary to international public policy in the state where the court is situated. Arbitral tribunals may not rule in equity ('*ex aequo et bono*'), as is commonly thought, unless they have been expressly authorized to do so by the parties.

In addition to deciding on the merits, the final award also decides on the costs of the proceedings, including any reimbursement of expenses, and how the arbitral tribunal's costs are to be borne by the parties. The arbitral tribunal cannot in fact order a payment to be made to itself, but this is in any case unnecessary on account of the advance already paid.

Arbitral proceedings do not necessarily end with a final award. It is not uncommon for a settlement to be reached during the proceedings, with or without the tribunal's help. In this case, the proceedings may be brought to an end through the withdrawal of the request for arbitration. The arbitral tribunal may also be requested to render an award, the wording of which has been agreed by the parties. The rights and obligations resulting from the parties' settlement are thereby enshrined in a binding decision that is enforceable just like any other arbitral award.

D. INSTITUTIONAL ARBITRATION

Institutional arbitration differs from '*ad hoc*' arbitration in that the parties include in their arbitration agreement a reference to an institution's arbitration rules.

Arbitration institutions may take the form of independent legal entities, such as non-profit organizations, whose statutes and rules establish the infrastructure necessary for them to carry out their tasks. They may also be set up as part of a larger organization, such as a chamber of commerce. The ICC International Court of Arbitration is an example of the second kind of institution.

The arbitration rules of such institutions are characterized by the fact that they contain rules that complement the minimum contents of an arbitration agreement. A further characteristic is that if difficulties are encountered in setting up the arbitral tribunal, the arbitration institution will have the powers to take the necessary steps. This is the case when a party fails to comply with its duty to collaborate or when the parties are unable to come to an indispensable agreement. Given that the parties may themselves decide on the composition of the arbitral tribunal, they may also empower a third party to make the relevant decisions when there is no agreement. In '*ad hoc*' arbitration proceedings, the parties must make contractual arrangements or follow the applicable procedural law. They should also make sure that the third party they have chosen has the will and the means to take the necessary decisions if required. This calls for considerable effort, which explains why parties generally avoid such arrangements.

Few arbitration institutions confine themselves to offering assistance in connection with the appointment and replacement of arbitrators. More often than not, their arbitration rules also contain procedural rules intended for the arbitral tribunal. The reason for this is that the provisions in national laws relating to arbitration are for the most part intended for the courts. The few provisions that relate to procedure before arbitral tribunals will have a fall-back role, unless they express basic principles of procedure. Moreover, given that the place of the arbitration in international cases will very often be in a third country foreign to the parties and the arbitrators, it is desirable to keep the procedure before the arbitral tribunal distinct from national procedural law. Specific rules will therefore be necessary. Understandably, parties often opt for a set of neutral rules made available by an arbitration institution, as they usually have no wish to spend time negotiating special rules of their own when drawing up their contract. Many institutions also include in their rules schedules of costs and fees to cover the financial relations between the parties and the arbitral tribunal.

E. ICC ARBITRATION

The Rules of Arbitration of the International Chamber of Commerce, which give supervisory and decision-making powers to the ICC International Court of Arbitration and its Secretariat to enable them to administer the entire proceedings, establish prerogatives that go beyond those usually assigned to arbitration institutions in their rules. These prerogatives include in particular:

- fixing all the financial rights and duties relating to the proceedings, including the arbitrators' fees;
- the logistical support offered to arbitral tribunals by the Secretariat of the ICC International Court of Arbitration, including help in seeking experts through the ICC International Centre for ADR;
- monitoring the time limit within which arbitral awards must be rendered;
- scrutiny of draft awards by the ICC International Court of Arbitration.

These powers and their practical application in accordance with the ICC Rules of Arbitration are discussed in the following pages. First, however, after a brief look at the past, attention will be given to the current composition of the ICC International Court of Arbitration and its Secretariat and the tasks assigned to them by the parties as a result of opting for the ICC Rules of Arbitration.

CHAPTER 2

THE INTERNATIONAL CHAMBER OF COMMERCE AND ITS COURT OF ARBITRATION

A. THE INTERNATIONAL CHAMBER OF COMMERCE AS AN INSTITUTION

The International Chamber of Commerce was set up in Paris in 1919, shortly after the First World War, on the initiative of a group of businessmen. It is a non profit-making organization under French law and heads a network of national committees and groups whose members are economic and industrial players. It is not an interstate organization, as it is run by private enterprise. Nor is it an interstate chamber of commerce and industry. In fact, it is much more than this, being a body that represents the interests of the international business community.

B. THE ICC DISPUTE RESOLUTION SERVICES

The ICC Dispute Resolution Services consist of: 1) the International Court of Arbitration; and 2) the ICC International Centre for ADR.

The ICC International Court of Arbitration was established in 1923 pursuant to the ICC Rules of Arbitration adopted in 1922. According to its Statutes, the ICC International Court of Arbitration has certain organizational powers, which are conferred upon it by the parties' agreeing to submit to ICC arbitration. These powers are described below.

Although part of the institution known as ICC, the ICC International Court of Arbitration and its Secretariat are in practice run as an independent body, which ensures confidentiality. This is clearly stated in the ICC International Court of Arbitration's Statutes: 'As an autonomous body, it carries out these functions in complete independence from the ICC and its organs. Its members are independent from the ICC National Committees and Groups.' (Article 1, paragraphs 2 and 3, of Appendix I to the ICC Rules of Arbitration). The headquarter of the Secretariat of the ICC Court is in Paris, but the Secretariat has opened in 2008 an office in Hong Kong and in 2013 in New York. The New York office operates under SICANA Inc., an entity incorporated under US law.

The ICC International Centre for ADR is the administrative body that oversees the application of the ICC Mediation, Expert, Dispute Board and DOCDEX Rules. The Centre encompasses the ICC International Centre for Expertise and the ICC International Dispute Board Centre but is a separate entity from the ICC International Court of Arbitration and its Secretariat, which exclusively manages ICC Arbitration proceedings.

In addition, the Centre is the organizer of the annual ICC Mediation Week which takes place every year in February in Paris, France. ICC's Mediation Week encompasses

ICC's biggest educational event, the ICC International Commercial Mediation Competition as well as the in-house counsel-focused International Mediation Conference.

The Centre may also from time to time consult national committees on possible candidates for appointment in the context of other ICC dispute resolution services, notably ICC Expertise or ICC Mediation.

Since the establishment of the DOCDEX system, the ICC International Centre for Expertise (now called ICC International Centre for ADR) has been appointing documentary credits and demand guarantee experts from a list established and maintained by the Banking Commission. Nominations for inclusion on this list are the responsibility of national committees through the Banking Commission (<www.iccwbo.org/about-icc/organization/dispute-resolution-services/icc-international-centre-for-adr/>).The International Centre for ADR consists of one team, led by a counsel and a manager.

ICC Dispute Resolution Services has regional directors for the promotion of arbitration, ADR and other activities by the directors in their respective region. They organize and participate in a wide range of conferences and seminars so as to help increase the awareness and understanding of the ICC's dispute resolution services throughout the region. The executive director for North America with two deputy directors is based with SICANA Inc. in New York. The regional director for Latin America with a deputy director is based in Panama City in Panama. The regional director for Asia is based in Singapore. The regional director for Eastern Mediterranean, Middle East & Africa is based in Tunis, in Tunisia, and also in Dubai, in the United Arab Emirates. The Young Arbitrators Forum (YAF) of the International Chamber of Commerce (ICC) is a forum for young professionals (40 years and under) to learn from experienced practitioners about career development and issues of interest in arbitration (<www.iccwbo.org/training-and-events/young-arbitrator-forum/>).

C. THE HISTORICAL BACKGROUND OF THE RULES OF ARBITRATION

There have been ten revisions of the ICC Rules of Arbitration since the original version of 1922. The current version, in force since 1 January 2012, contains significant changes, but leaves the structure of ICC arbitration proceedings unchanged. The purpose of this latest revision was to take into account recent developments in arbitral practice and offer a number of new possibilities to conduct arbitrations more rapidly and with greater cost efficiency, and also to provide additional transparency with respect to practices of the Court and the Secretariat, given the increasing number of cases referred to ICC and the complexity of the disputes, especially from a procedural point of view. Important novelties are the provisions dealing with various aspects of multiparty disputes, the requirement for arbitrators to organize a case management conference with the parties when drawing up the Terms of Reference or shortly thereafter, the possibility for parties to have urgent provisional or conservatory measures taken by an emergency arbitrator before an arbitral tribunal is constituted.

The initiative for the new ICC Rules of Arbitration was taken in 2008 by the Commission on Arbitration (now called Commission on Arbitration and ADR) of the ICC, ten years after the 1998 Rules had become operative. During more than three years a Task Force with more than 200 members from different countries and legal cultures and a Drafting Sub-Committee of about 20 members examined and discussed what amendments to the Rules of Arbitration were desirable or necessary. The national committees and groups of the ICC have also been able to submit their comments during the discussions. The new Rules were approved by the ICC World Council in June 2011 and published on 12 September 2011.

As required by the Statutes of the International Court of Arbitration (Appendix I, Article 7), the revision of the ICC Rules of Arbitration was laid before the ICC Commission on Arbitration and ADR before submission to the Executive Board of the ICC for approval.

Prior to the revision of the ICC Rules of Arbitration, the ICC Commission on Arbitration and ADR had published in 2009 a report 'Techniques for Controlling Time and Costs in Arbitration'. Based on this report, an Appendix IV has been added to the Rules listing some case management techniques that can be used by arbitrators and parties for controlling time and costs. The full text of the second edition of this report of 2012 may be found in Appendix 15 below.

The terms 'Rules' and 'Rules of Arbitration' should be understood in the present context to mean the 2012 version of the ICC Rules of Arbitration.

D. THE ICC INTERNATIONAL COURT OF ARBITRATION AND ITS SECRETARIAT

The composition and powers of the ICC International Court of Arbitration and its Secretariat are defined in Article 1 of the ICC Rules of Arbitration and Appendices I and II to these Rules. Appendix I contains the Statutes of the International Court of Arbitration and Appendix II its Internal Rules.

1. The Structure of the ICC International Court of Arbitration

The ICC International Court of Arbitration consists of a President, Vice-Presidents and members. For reasons of gender neutrality, the new Rules use the term 'President', whereas the 1998 version of the Rules still used the term 'chairman'. Likewise, the new Rules describe the 'chairman of the arbitral tribunal' henceforth as 'president of the arbitral tribunal'.

The members, whose term of office lasts three years, are appointed by the ICC World Council upon proposals by national committees and groups. Each national committee and group proposes one member and may also propose an alternate member. The ICC Court currently has 142 members, including alternate members, from 89 countries and territories. The President of the Court is elected by the ICC World Council upon the recommendation of the Executive Board of the ICC. The Vice-Presidents are appointed by the ICC World Council and may be chosen from amongst the members of the ICC International Court of Arbitration or elsewhere. There are currently 17 Vice-Presidents of the ICC Court..

The work of the ICC International Court of Arbitration is generally done on a voluntary basis, although there are certain exceptions. The President, for instance, receives an allowance to take account of his duties and responsibilities. The Court members are for the most part lawyers with a business background or from law firms who have experience in the field of international commercial arbitration and/or investment arbitration.

2. The Role of the ICC International Court of Arbitration

The ICC International Court of Arbitration is not a judicial body. Its decisions are not equivalent to those of arbitral tribunals or state courts. It does not itself settle disputes; the arbitral tribunals alone do this (Article 1(2) of the Rules). Whereas the 1998 version of the Rules stipulated that the function of the Court was 'to provide for the settlement by arbitration of business disputes of an international character', the new Rules have not maintained this phrasing. Although the majority of the disputes submitted to ICC arbitration are disputes of an international character, the Court can also be seized of other types of disputes, even if they are not international. The new wording of Article 1(2) makes it clear that the ICC Court can administer a wide range of 'disputes', including disputes involving states and disputes involving trusts, if the parties have agreed on the application of the ICC Rules of Arbitration.

According to the Rules, the ICC International Court of Arbitration's function is to ensure the application of those Rules (Article 1(2) of the Rules). When the parties agree upon an arbitration clause referring to the ICC Rules of Arbitration, they thereby entrust the ICC International Court of Arbitration with certain decision-making powers assigned to it under the Rules. For instance, the Court is empowered to make decisions regarding arbitrators. This is made possible by the fact that, when agreeing to serve, arbitrators implicitly promise the parties and ICC that they will abide by the Rules of Arbitration (Article 11(5) of the Rules). In practice, the relations between the different players involved do not cause problems. It may simply be noted at the present juncture that the Court's decision-making powers have a contractual basis. This however raises the question of whether the parties, or the arbitrators with the parties' agreement, are entitled to modify the provisions of the Rules of Arbitration. Although the parties are free to agree, to some extent, to modifications to the Rules, the Court has no obligation to administer cases where the modifications agreed between the parties do no respect the spirit of the Rules (Article 1(2), second sentence, of the Rules). The Court will refuse any substantial alteration of its powers and of core features of ICC arbitration, such as the obligation to establish Terms of Reference, the scrutiny of arbitral awards and the Court's power to fix the costs of the arbitration.

The 2012 Rules explicitly indicate that the ICC Court is the only body authorized to administer arbitrations under the ICC Rules of Arbitration. It is therefore not possible for another body or another institution to administer an arbitration under the ICC Rules. Should this nevertheless be done, then this would seriously put at risk the enforceability of the arbitral award rendered in such arbitration proceedings.

The ICC Court's decision-making powers will be examined in the following pages in connection with the individual provisions of the Rules, notably those concerning the appointment of arbitrators on behalf of parties who fail to nominate one, challenges of arbitrators, approval of arbitral awards as to their form and the fixing of arbitrators' fees.

3. How the ICC International Court of Arbitration Works

Given the rise in the number of requests for arbitration filed with the ICC International Court of Arbitration each year (from 250 in 1980 to 580 in 2003 and 767 in 2013)(see the first edition of this book published in 2005, and '2013 Statistical Report' published in *ICC International Court of Arbitration Bulletin*, Paris, Vol. 25/Nr. 1 - 2014, p. 5), a system in which members from a large number of countries with national committees or groups (some eighty-seven at the present time) meet once a month to make delicate and often difficult decisions is clearly not the most efficient way of working. Hence it was decided in the nineteen eighties that, in addition to the monthly plenary sessions (Article 4 of Appendix I to the Rules), a committee with the power to make routine decisions such as the confirmation and appointment of arbitrators would be established (Article 1(4) of the Rules, Article 5 of Appendix I to the Rules, Article 4 of Appendix II to the Rules). The committee consists of two rotating members of the ICC International Court of Arbitration and the President or one of the Vice-Presidents. Their decisions are made unanimously. However, cases that raise unexpected difficulties or in which no unanimous decision can be reached are referred to the next plenary session of the Court (Article 4(5) of Appendix II to the Rules). The committee initially met twice a month, but now meets once or twice a week, at different times to allow the participation of staff in New York, Hong Kong and Paris. Decisions made by the committee are brought to the attention of the Court at its next plenary session (Article 4(5) of Appendix II to the Rules).

When a decision is too urgent to wait for an ordinary Court session, it is made by the President or, with the President's authorization, by one of the Vice-Presidents. The Court is notified of the decision at its next session (Article 1(3) of the Rules).

Only members of the ICC International Court of Arbitration and of its Secretariat may attend sessions of the Court, whether plenary or meeting as a committee (Article 1 of Appendix II to the Rules). Parties, their representatives and arbitrators are therefore excluded. The members due to attend receive beforehand a file of documents prepared by the Secretariat. For each case to be considered, there is a summary of the facts of the case, an explanatory note intended for the committee meeting and a recommendation as to the decision to be made. They may be accompanied by important documents from the case file. For the appointment of an arbitrator, the arbitrator's declaration of independence vis-à-vis the parties and curriculum vitae are provided. Usually, therefore, only a part of the file is presented to the meeting, unless special circumstances require that the Secretariat present the entire file so as to throw light on aspects of the case relevant to the decision to be made. At plenary sessions, in addition to the Secretariat report, a written report is also drawn up by a member of the Court with a recommendation as to the decisions to be made. All decisions and the related reports are discussed orally, which may take several hours in difficult cases. Decisions are preferably made unanimously, or otherwise by a majority of members. The Court sessions take place at the ICC headquarters in Paris, but Court members may participate by video or telephone conference.

According to the standard practice, no reasons are given for the decisions made by the ICC International Court of Arbitration, as they are of an administrative, not of a judicial, nature. In October 2015, however, the ICC Court announced a policy change in this respect. In response to growing users' demand, the ICC Court announced that it will communicate reasons for many of the administrative decisions it is called to take under the ICC Rules of Arbitration. Where all the parties to a case so agree, the ICC Court may communicate henceforth the reasons for its decisions made on the challenge of an arbitrator and on a decision to initiate replacement proceedings and subsequently to replace an arbitrator on the Court's own motion. The Court may also communicate the reasons for its decisions regarding the consolidation of arbitration proceedings and '*prima facie*' decisions on jurisdiction, if all the parties to a case agree so. A request for the communication of reasons must be made in advance of the relevant decision in respect of which reasons are sought. The Court may subject the communication of reasons to an increase of the administrative expenses, normally not to exceed US$ 5 000. By changing its practice, the ICC Court tries to respond to arbitration users' frequent request that the decisions of the Court be more predictable on the basis of past practice. If the Court communicates reasons for its decisions, this does not alter the administrative nature of its decisions. More information on this new policy will be available at the ICC website at <www.iccwbo.org> and in the ICC Dispute Resolution Library at <www.iccdrl.com>.

The Court's decisions are recorded by the Secretariat and notified in writing to the parties and the arbitrators. They are in theory final, and the Rules of Arbitration do not allow for a file to be reconsidered unless there are special reasons for doing so, as when circumstances or information likely to influence the initial decision subsequently come to light. In this case, one of the parties involved in the proceedings must submit a request to the Secretariat asking for the decision to be reviewed.

English and French are the working languages of the ICC International Court of Arbitration, so all internal documents are drafted in one of these languages. Occasionally, committee sessions of the Court are held in other languages, such as Spanish, German or Portuguese, for the scrutiny of draft awards in those languages with a view to avoiding delays and costs with the translation of the draft awards in one of the working languages of the Court. ICC arbitral proceedings can, of course, be conducted in any other language. Where necessary, the Court is presented with translations of important documents such as requests for arbitration and draft awards. In actual fact, to the extent allowed by the linguistic skills both within the Secretariat and of the Court member chosen as 'rapporteur', every attempt will be made for these documents to be read in their original language.

4. Avoiding Conflicts of Interest

The duty of the members of the ICC International Court of Arbitration and the staff of the Secretariat to respect confidentiality is not the only principle legally established by the Rules of Arbitration and the Statutes and Internal Rules of the ICC International Court of Arbitration (Article 6 of Appendix I to the Rules, Articles 1 and 3(2) of Appendix II to the Rules). There are also rules for avoiding conflicts of interest so as to ensure that cases are properly handled. Firstly, the President of the ICC International Court of Arbitration and the staff of the Secretariat are forbidden to act as arbitrators or to represent parties in cases submitted to ICC arbitration (Article 2(1) of Appendix II to the Rules). The Vice-Presidents and other members of the Court may act as arbitrators in cases submitted to ICC arbitration only if proposed by one or more parties or pursuant to a procedure agreed by the parties (Article 2(2) of Appendix II to the Rules). They cannot therefore be appointed by an ICC body. In addition, the members of the Court and the Secretariat must immediately inform the Secretary General of the Court as soon as they are aware that they might in any way be involved in a case pending before the Court (Article 2 (3) of Appendix II to the Rules). This rule, which is interpreted broadly in the event of doubt, is particularly aimed at situations where there are commercial or family links with a party, the party's representative, or an arbitrator. Such situations will mainly, although not exclusively, be those in which the member in question, or another lawyer in the firm to which he or she belongs, is counsel to a party in a particular case, or customarily acts as the party's counsel. In such cases, the person involved is excluded from all discussions within the Court as well as within the Secretariat (Article 2(4) of Appendix II to the Rules) and will not receive any internal documents or other information pertaining to the file (Article 2(5) of Appendix II to the Rules).

5. The Composition of the Secretariat

The Secretary General of the ICC International Court of Arbitration is responsible for the day-to-day running of the Secretariat of the Court. Whereas the Rules in 1998 stated that the Secretariat of the Court shall have it seat at the headquarters of the ICC, this wording was not maintained in the new version of the Rules of 2012 (Article 1(5) of the Rules). This wording had to be deleted, as the Secretariat had opened an office in Hong Kong in 2008. After the new Rules entered into force, the Secretariat also opened an office in New York in 2013, which operates under SICANA Inc.

The Secretary General is assisted by a Deputy Secretary General. Together, with the support of other specialist staff, they plan and oversee operations. The General Counsel provides legal advice to the Court and its Secretariat and coordinates any litigation in which the Court may be involved. The Managing Counsel assists the Secretary General and the Deputy Secretary General in managing the caseload. The counsel are responsible for relations with the arbitrators and parties in the cases assigned to them. They are assisted by a team comprising two or more deputy counsel and two or more secretaries. There are presently nine teams within the Secretariat of the Court (seven of which are in Paris, one in Hong Kong and one in New York). The Secretariat's staff counts almost 100 persons encompassing 30 different nationalities.

Attention is paid to ensuring that different nationalities are represented when making appointments to the position of counsel. All counsel and most of the deputy counsel have full legal training and some of them have also obtained additional qualifications outside their native countries. All members of the Secretariat are fluent in at least English and French and sometimes in a third or even more languages.

6. The Tasks of the Secretariat

As far as the work of the Secretariat is concerned, a distinction needs to be made between (a) the powers that derive from the Rules of Arbitration and their Appendices I and II, and (b) tasks which are not regulated in detail but which the Secretariat is required to perform in the course of its relations with the arbitral tribunal, the arbitrators and the parties.

a) The Secretariat's Decision-Making Powers

The Secretariat and more particularly the Secretary General has certain administrative decision-making powers. Routine decisions may be made quickly by the Secretary General, whereas major decisions are required to be submitted to the ICC Court. The Secretary General may thus confirm the appointment of arbitrators nominated by the parties. This also applies to the appointment of sole arbitrators or presidents of the arbitral tribunals based on a joint proposal by the parties or a procedure mutually agreed by the parties, if the arbitrators have provided an unqualified statement of impartiality and independence (Article 13(2) of the Rules). The Secretary General may also confirm an arbitrator who has filed a qualified statement, provided that the parties have not objected to the confirmation of the arbitrator within the time limit fixed by the Secretariat for comments (Article 13(2) of the Rules). Failing this, the ICC International Court of Arbitration will decide on the confirmation of arbitrators after receiving the parties' comments (Article 13(1) and (2) of the Rules). The Secretary General may also fix a provisional advance to cover the costs of the arbitration until the Terms of Reference have been drawn up (Article 36(1) of the Rules). The definitive amount of the advance to cover the costs of the arbitration is set by the ICC Court (Article 36(2) of the Rules). If the advance is not paid, the Secretary General may direct the arbitral tribunal to suspend its work and may set a time limit for payment, after which the request will be considered as withdrawn if payment is still outstanding (Article 36(6) of the Rules).

The Secretary General is empowered to issue parties with copies of their award, certified as true (Article 34(2) of the Rules).

In the absence of the Secretary General or otherwise at the Secretary General's request, the Deputy Secretary General and/or the General Counsel shall have the authority to refer matters to the Court, confirm arbitrators, certify true copies of awards and request the payment of a provisional advance, respectively provided for in Articles 6(3), 13(2), 34(2) and 36(1) of the Rules (See Article 5(1) of Appendix II to the Rules).

It is up to the Secretariat, in the person of the counsel responsible for the file or one of the deputy counsel, to set time limits and to make sure they are respected by the parties, save those which solely the ICC Court or the arbitrators may set. The Secretariat is expressly empowered to extend time limits for filing an answer to the request for arbitration and a reply to any counterclaim(s) (Article 5(2) and (6) of the Rules).

b) The Secretariat's Focal Role in the Arbitration Proceedings

The ICC International Court of Arbitration's relations with the parties and the arbitrators are conducted through the Secretariat, specifically through the counsel responsible for the file and his or her deputy counsel, who sign correspondence and have telephone contact with the parties and the arbitrators. Each team within the Secretariat is thus the focal point or relay station for the cases it handles.

The Secretariat may, with the approval of the Court, issue notes and other documents for the information of the parties and arbitrators, or as necessary for the proper conduct of the arbitral proceedings (Article 5(2) of Appendix II to the Rules).

The notes and documents issued by the Secretariat for information of the parties and the arbitrators are enclosed below as appendices. They include:

- Note to Parties in Proceedings under the 2012 ICC Rules of Arbitration (Appendix 4 below);
- Note on Article 36(4) of the 2012 ICC Rules of Arbitration (Appendix 5 below);
- Note on ICC Emergency Arbitrator Proceedings (Appendix 6 below);
- Note to the Arbitral Tribunal on the Conduct of the Arbitration (Appendix 9 below);
- Note on Administrative Issues in Proceedings under the 2012 ICC Rules of Arbitration (Appendix 10 below)
- ICC Award Checklist (1998 & 2012 Rules) (Appendix 11 below);
- Note on Correction and Interpretation of Arbitral Awards (Appendix 12 below);
- Checklist on Correction and Interpretation of Awards (1998 and 2012 ICC Rules of Arbitration)(Appendix 13 below).

7. How the Secretariat Works

The Secretary General gives each new request for arbitration a number in a chronological sequence that began when the institution was first created. The request is then handed to a team, which is identified by the initials of the counsel in charge of the file, mentioned after the case number. The team is chosen in light of its experience, workload and any linguistic skills the case may call for.

The team cursorily examines the request for arbitration, which is immediately notified to the respondent(s) named therein. It is therefore up to the claimant alone to ensure that the respondent's full contact details are correctly provided. If problems are encountered preventing notification of the request for arbitration, the claimant must provide the Secretariat with the necessary instructions so as to allow proper and valid notification to be given. The Secretariat sends the respondent an accompanying letter informing it of the steps it is required to take within a period of thirty days.

Until such time as the file is transmitted to the arbitral tribunal, all pleadings and other correspondence are notified through the Secretariat. At this stage of the proceedings, the team's job is to obtain all information and explanations required by the Rules or any special agreements between the parties, so as to allow the arbitral tribunal to be constituted without delay. Difficulties frequently arise in cases where one of the parties wishes additional parties to be involved, or where the procedure is instituted on the basis of a pathological arbitration clause, i.e. one that is confusing or incomplete.

When the Secretariat considers it necessary that a decision is taken with respect to the case management pursuant to the Rules, it draws up a report following a predefined structure, which is put through the Court's decision-making process in compliance with a strict timetable. The report contains basic information relating to the proceedings, a summary of the salient points of the case and characteristics of the dispute, together with explanations and a recommendation for the decision to be made by the Court. These reports are then distributed to the Secretary General, the Deputy Secretary General, counsel and deputy counsel for discussion at a weekly staff meeting. Although discussions are led by the Secretary General, all participants may contribute. Once the report has been approved at a staff meeting, it is submitted to the next meeting of the Court. Shortly before the meeting – be it a committee or a plenary session – the members of the Court who are to attend are provided with the files containing the reports and accompanying documents such as Terms of Reference and draft awards.

At the Court meetings the reports are discussed in the presence of Secretariat staff, who are able to provide additional explanations and comments. The Secretariat, through its teams, then informs the parties concerned and/or the arbitrators of the decisions that the Court has made.

The Secretariat is also available to answer in writing or by telephone any questions the parties, their counsel and the arbitrators may have concerning the Rules and their application. In so doing, the Secretariat acts with the discretion that neutrality requires. The Secretary General is also available to provide the ICC Court, in particular the President and the 'rapporteurs', with any information required for the understanding of the file.

The teams also handle payments. They make sure that the advances fixed by the Court are timely paid. They also deal with the arbitrators' requests for the reimbursement of expenses and arrange for the payment of the arbitrators' fees. In addition, the teams will also handle advances on fees and expenses of experts if arbitral tribunals request them to do so (Article 1(12) of Appendix III to the Rules). Lastly, if asked to do so by the arbitrators, the Secretariat will assist in the organization of meetings (rental of premises for hearings, hiring of stenographers and interpreters, and such like).

Recently, the Secretariat has adopted the practice of asking parties and arbitrators, when the case comes to a close, to provide it with their comments on the way it has handled the proceedings, thereby remaining receptive to the reactions of ICC arbitration users. It also tries to obtain information on the parties' compliance with awards made in ICC arbitrations.

CHAPTER 3

ARBITRAL PROCEEDINGS UNDER THE ICC RULES OF ARBITRATION OF 2012

A. INTRODUCTORY PROVISIONS

1. Definitions (Art. 2)

Article 2 of the Rules of Arbitration reads:

> 'Definitions
>
> In these Rules:
>
> (i) "arbitral tribunal" includes one or more arbitrators.
>
> (ii) "claimant" includes one or more claimants, "respondent" includes one or more respondents, and "additional party" includes one or more additional parties;
>
> (iii) "party" or "parties" include claimants, respondents or additional parties;
>
> (iv) "claim" or "claims" include any claim by any party against any other party;
>
> (v) "Award" includes, inter alia, an interim, partial or final Award.'

This provision serves merely to aid understanding and calls for no further explanation. Unless otherwise stated, these definitions will also apply to the terms as used in this book.

The definitions of the terms 'party', 'additional party' and 'claim' have been added to those already included in the 1998 Rules. The definition of 'additional party' is added as a consequence of the new provision allowing the joinder of a party to an arbitration. The definition of the term 'claim' is added so to make it clear that claims not only can be filed by a claimant against a respondent and by a respondent against a claimant, but also by a claimant and/or a respondent against an additional party and also by an additional party against a claimant and/or a respondent. The term 'cross-claim' has not been used as this is not a term that is universally understood.

Whereas the 1998 version of the Rules used capital letters for the terms 'arbitral tribunal', 'claimant', 'respondent', 'arbitral tribunal', 'award', the use of the capital letters for these terms has been abandoned in the 2012 version of the Rules. The use of the capital letters in the new rules has been reserved to a limited number of words, such as 'Article', 'Rules', 'Court', 'President', 'Secretariat', 'Secretary General', 'National Committee', 'Group', 'Request for Arbitration', 'Answer', 'Terms of Reference', 'Emergency Arbitrator', 'Order'. The words written with capital letters in the Rules are defined terms in the Rules.

2. Written Notifications or Communications; Time Limits (Art. 3)

Article 3 of the Rules of Arbitration reads:

> 'Written Notifications or Communications; Time Limits
>
> 1. All pleadings and other written communications submitted by any party, as well as all documents annexed thereto, shall be supplied in a number of copies sufficient to provide one copy for each party, plus one for each arbitrator, and one for the Secretariat. A copy of any communication from the arbitral tribunal to the parties shall be sent to the Secretariat.
>
> 2. All notifications or communications from the Secretariat and the arbitral tribunal shall be made to the last address of the party or its representative for whom the same are intended, as notified either by the party in question or by the other party. Such notification or communication may be made by delivery against receipt, registered post, courier, email, or any other means of telecommunication that provides a record of the sending thereof.
>
> 3. A notification or communication shall be deemed to have been made on the day it was received by the party itself or by its representative, or would have been received if made in accordance with Article 3(2).
>
> 4. Periods of time specified in or fixed under the Rules shall start to run on the day following the date a notification or communication is deemed to have been made in accordance with Article 3(3). When the day next following such date is an official holiday, or a non-business day in the country where the notification or communication is deemed to have been made, the period of time shall commence on the first following business day. Official holidays and non-business days are included in the calculation of the period of time. If the last day of the relevant period of time granted is an official holiday or a non-business day in the country where the notification or communication is deemed to have been made, the period of time shall expire at the end of the first following business day.'

a) General Remarks

Article 3 contains essential rules relating to exchanges of correspondence and the setting of time limits in ICC arbitration proceedings. These details are necessary in order to establish a uniform framework of provisions that are as far as possible independent of any national arbitration law or legal system that may be applicable. They set clear legal parameters for the parties from the outset of the proceedings, which would otherwise be lacking if the place of the arbitration has at that stage not been agreed or fixed. Parties and arbitral tribunal are, however, free to agree on specific methods for notifications and communications in the course of an arbitration. This is often done when the arbitral tribunal and the parties establish the Terms of Reference.

b) The Number of Copies to be Filed (Art. 3(1))

It goes without saying that all pleadings and correspondence concerning the arbitral proceedings must be supplied, at least in the form of photocopies, to all the members of the arbitral tribunal and all the parties concerned. If an additional party is joined in the course of the arbitration, this additional party will also need to receive a copy of all pleadings and correspondence submitted by the other parties in the arbitration. If a party is represented by more than one law firm, the Secretariat will usually request that a copy of the pleadings and correspondence be provided for each law firm.

It is obvious that the Secretariat must also receive a copy of these documents until such time as the file is transmitted to the arbitral tribunal. Thereafter, the need to send documents to the Secretariat is explained by the ICC International Court of Arbitration's role in overseeing the time limits set for rendering the award, ruling on challenges of arbitrators and approving awards. The files held by the Secretariat may also serve as a repository of evidence, although the restrictions resulting from the need to maintain confidentiality must be fully respected.

This obligation does not of course cover correspondence between the parties in connection with amicable negotiations conducted at the same time as the proceedings or as part of their discussions on the appointment of arbitrators. Also, it does not apply to internal correspondence between the members of the arbitral tribunal. It is an obligation which applies only to documents that are part of the adversarial proceedings as such.

c) The Delivery of Documents (Art. 3(2))

It is important for documents to be delivered to the address of a party as last indicated by that party itself or the other party, especially when a party does not take part in the proceedings. If a party ceases to participate in the proceedings after the Terms of Reference have been signed, the address to be used will be the one mentioned in the Terms of Reference. It is the responsibility of the party that has initiated the proceedings, not ICC or the arbitral tribunal, to provide the last known address for the delivery of documents. Parties should be particularly attentive to this point, as many national arbitration laws, as well as Article V(1)(b) of the New York Convention, allow an award to be set aside or not to be recognized if the party concerned has not been properly informed of the appointment of an arbitrator and of the arbitration proceedings.

The Rules contain an important provision indicating how to deliver documents effectively. No difficulties arise with those methods of delivery where an acknowledgment of receipt is issued or returned, as there is proof of delivery in these cases. However, caution is today still required when it comes to delivery by electronic means, whereby only a journal is created and this is thought to suffice. No objections can in theory be made on legal grounds to the use of such procedures, which the parties have accepted and agreed upon by the very fact of referring to the Rules of Arbitration. However, the electronic transmission of procedural documents electronically currently still may occasionally give rise to problems in some countries on account of the case law on this subject, which continues to be restrictive. Besides, from a purely technical viewpoint, it can be said that a journal does not automatically imply that the document sent has in fact been received. The appropriate level of care therefore needs to be taken when choosing such means of communication, given the difficulty of predicting what an arbitral tribunal's attitude will be as to whether or not delivery has actually been accomplished, especially in the light of the aforementioned Article V(1)(b) of the New York Convention.

Sooner or later, all participants in proceedings will be forced by the distance separating them to use the electronic means available. In practice, this happens frequently and uneventfully in ICC arbitral proceedings. The liberal stance taken by the Rules of Arbitration in this regard corresponds to practical experience. However, it is recommended that this provision be expanded in the Terms of Reference so as to neutralize as far as possible any objections that may be made later. If delivery gives rise to problems, if there is doubt as to whether procedural documents and other communications have reached their destination, or if a party does not take part in the proceedings, it is worthwhile taking the precaution of delivering by traditional means as hard copies anything procedurally relevant that has been transmitted electronically, so as to be able to provide evidence that delivery has been accomplished.

Whereas the 1998 Rules still provided that notifications or communications could be made by 'facsimile transmission, telex, telegram', the mention of these communication methods has not been maintained, although 'facsimile transmission' can still be used. The new Rules wish to reflect the evolution in the communication and information technology, and therefore inserts 'email' as possible method for notifications and communications. The Rules do not refer to other electronic devices or methods, such as the use of USB-sticks or electronic platforms where various participants can log-in and file or consult documents, but it is not excluded to use such techniques in an arbitration. The use of such techniques will, however, need to be discussed between the parties and the arbitral tribunal and may need to be accompanied by certain security measures to restrict access and to avoid computer viruses.

d) The Date of Delivery and Time Limits (Art. 3(3)-(4))

The date of delivery is the day on which the document was actually received or the date on which delivery should have taken place if carried out in accordance with Article 3(2) of the Rules. The notification date can be important if a discussion arises as to the starting date or expiry date of a time limit provided in the Rules or set by the arbitral tribunal. For example, Article 5(1) provides that the respondent shall submit an answer to the request for arbitration within 30 days from the receipt of the request from the Secretariat.

The hypothetical situation contemplated in the second part of Article 3(3) does not cover cases in which, as far as the other participants are aware, the items sent have gone astray before reaching their destination or have been destroyed. It refers to situations in which no proof of delivery can be obtained or in which delivery has been made to the last known address of a party no longer participating in the proceedings. Given the risks involved and despite this fiction to which the parties have agreed, the reader is referred back to the explanations given above in connection with Article 3(2) of the Rules.

Time limits should be expressed in a simple and consistent way. When stating the length of the time limits, consideration should always be given to public holidays and non-business days in the country where documents are to be delivered, although this may be difficult to determine in individual cases.

B. COMMENCING THE ARBITRATION

1. The Request for Arbitration (Art. 4)

Article 4 of the Rules reads:

> 'Request for Arbitration
>
> 1. A party wishing to have recourse to arbitration under the Rules shall submit its Request for Arbitration (the "Request") to the Secretariat at any of the offices specified in the Internal Rules. The Secretariat shall notify the claimant and respondent of the receipt of the Request and the date of such receipt.

2. The date on which the Request is received by the Secretariat shall, for all purposes, be deemed to be the date of the commencement of the arbitration.

3. The Request shall contain the following information:

a) the name in full, description and address and other contact details of each of the parties;
b) the name in full, description and address and other contact details of any person(s) representing the claimant in the arbitration;
c) a description of the nature and circumstances of the dispute giving rise to the claims and of the basis upon which the claims are made;
d) a statement of the relief sought, together with the amounts of any quantified claims and, to the extent possible, an estimate of the monetary value of any other claims;
e) any relevant agreements and, in particular, the arbitration agreement(s);
f) where claims are made under more than one arbitration agreement, an indication of the arbitration agreement under which each claim is made;
g) all relevant particulars and any observations or proposals concerning the number of arbitrators and their choice in accordance with the provisions of Articles 12 and 13, and any nomination of an arbitrator required thereby; and
h) all relevant particulars and any observations or proposals as to the place of the arbitration, the applicable rules of law and the language of the arbitration.

The claimant may submit such other documents or information with the Request as it considers appropriate or as may contribute to the efficient resolution of the dispute.

4. Together with the Request, the Claimant shall:

a) submit the number of copies thereof required by Article 3 (1); and
b) make payment of the filing fee required by Appendix III ("Arbitration Costs and Fees") in force on the date the Request is submitted.

In the event that the claimant fails to comply with either of these requirements, the Secretariat may fix a time limit within which the claimant must comply, failing which the file shall be closed without prejudice to the claimant's right to submit the same claims at a later date in another Request.

5. The Secretariat shall transmit a copy of the Request and the documents annexed thereto to the respondent for its Answer to the Request once the Secretariat has sufficient copies of the Request and the required filing fees.'

a) General Remarks

ICC arbitration proceedings begin with the filing of a request for arbitration. The ICC Rules of Arbitration, on the one hand, require more than a mere notification of the commencement of proceedings, as is sometimes provided for in '*ad hoc*' proceedings and under the rules of other institutions, where the claimant informs the other party of its intention to resort to arbitration and asks it to nominate an arbitrator, but submits its actual request for arbitration at a later stage.

The ICC Rules, on the other hand, require the initial submission to contain only a summary of the main facts of the dispute as well as a statement of the relief sought, so

Figure 1. Communications between the parties, the Secretariat of the ICC Court and the arbitral tribunal

(a) Before the file is transmitted to the arbitral tribunal

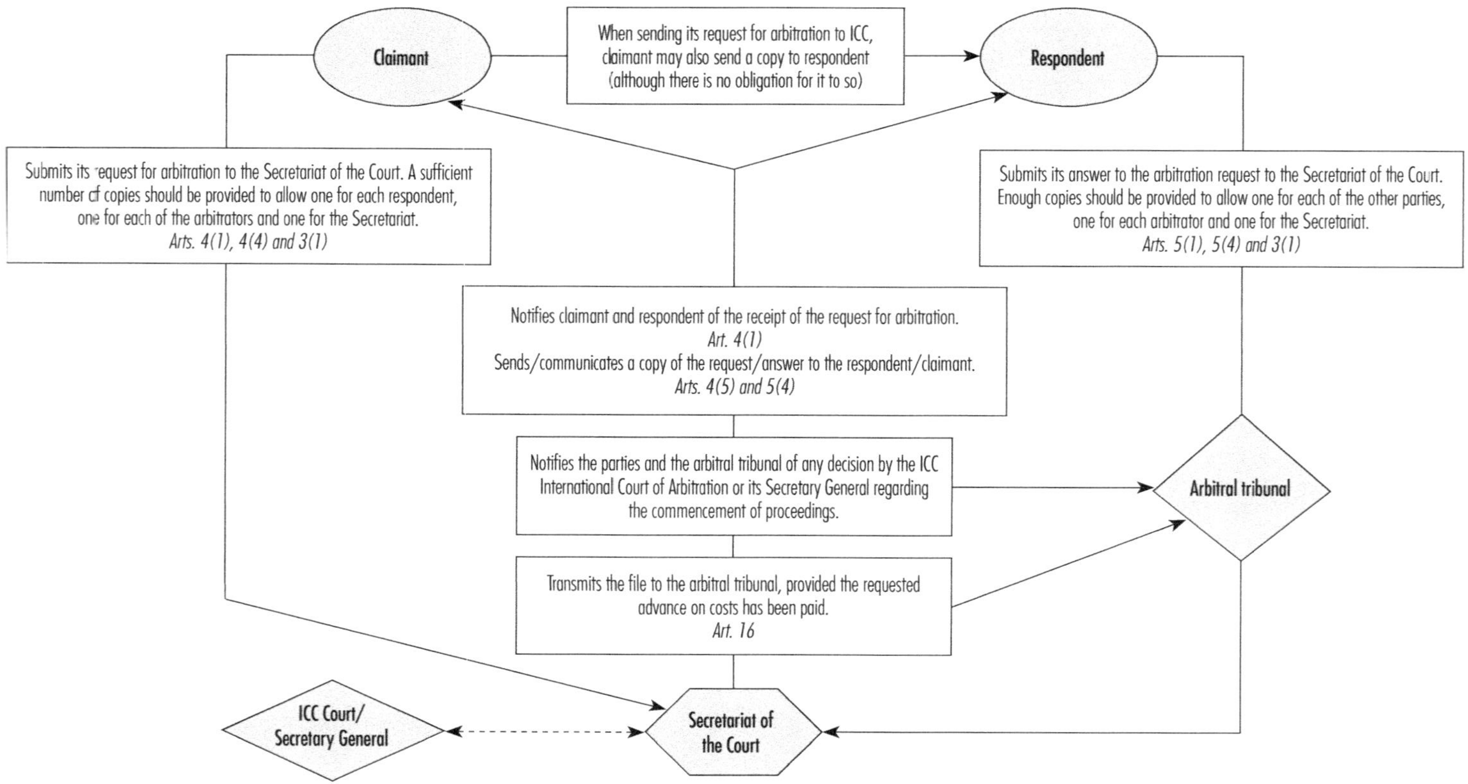

(b) After the file has been transmitted to the arbitral tribunal

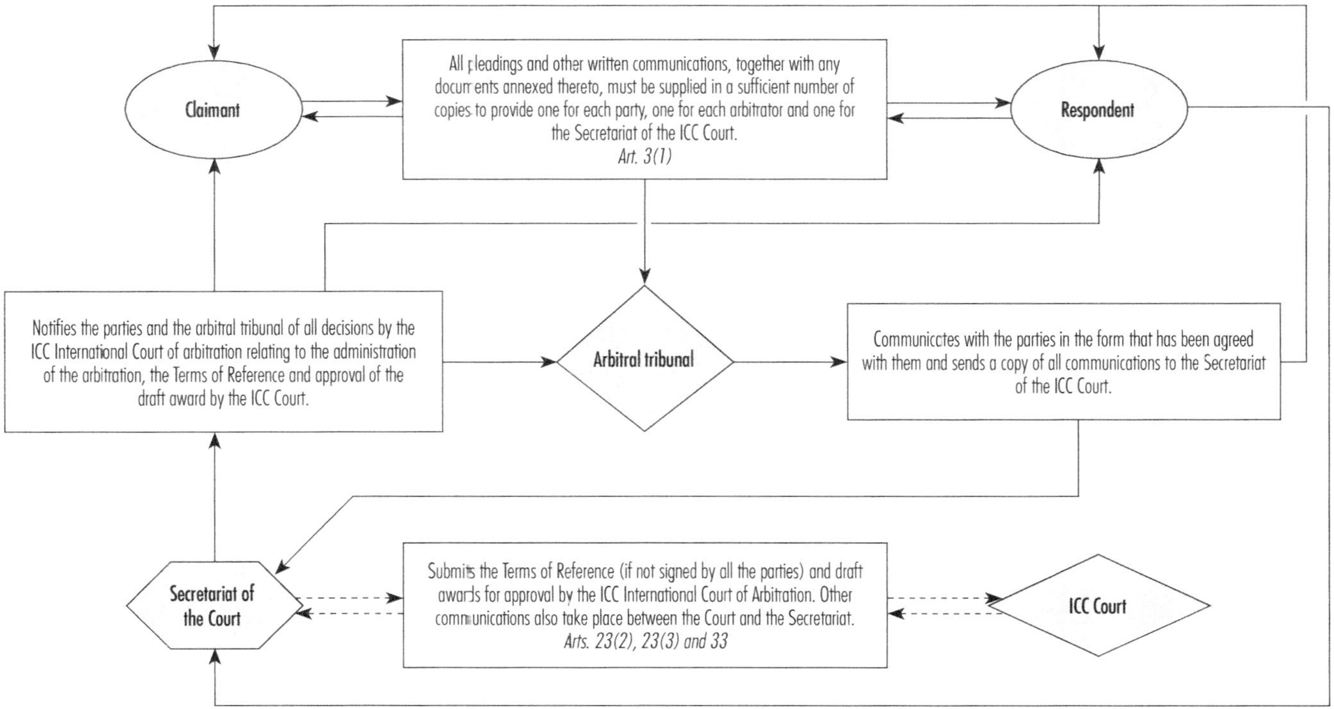

as to speed up the proceedings. The claimant may of course choose to submit a more detailed request, describing the position both in fact and at law and including supporting documents as well as evidence from witnesses and expert opinions. However, this is not compulsory and it is indeed unusual outside German-speaking jurisdictions. In international arbitration evidence is generally presented later in the proceedings. It may be noted that there are no special rules determining the style and structure of a request for arbitration, which, like all other pleadings presented during the proceedings, will in practice depend on the requirements of the courts to which the parties' counsel are accustomed. It is not unusual in ICC proceedings for pleadings to be very long and richly documented, and they may sometimes contain a summary or a list of contents at the beginning or the end to facilitate the arbitral tribunal's task when reading them.

Information on the main aspects of the dispute, as detailed below, is required for the request for arbitration, as it is useful when drawing up the Terms of Reference and helps the proceedings to be conducted more quickly. This information also enables the ICC International Court of Arbitration and its Secretariat to set the proceedings in motion without delay, and gives the respondent a clear idea of the action that has been brought against it.

Moreover, as the filing of a request for arbitration will stop the prescription period for certain claims, the facts asserted in the request for arbitration may be relevant when determining whether or not this is the case.

b) The Request for Arbitration

(1) Submission of the Request for Arbitration (Art. 4(1)).

The claimant does not send its request for arbitration directly to the respondent but to the Secretariat of the ICC International Court of Arbitration, as it is the Secretariat's responsibility under the Rules to notify the request for arbitration to the respondent(s) (Article 4(1)). Of course, there is nothing to stop the claimant at the same time informing the respondent of its action by sending it a copy of the request for arbitration.

The request for arbitration must be sent to the Secretariat of the ICC Court and can no longer be sent to an ICC national committee, as was possible prior to 1 January 1998. The request for arbitration can be filed with the Secretariat's headquarters in Paris or with its office in Hong Kong or in New York. As the Secretariat opened offices in Hong Kong and New York and as there are fully constituted teams of the Secretariat working in these offices, the teams in these offices are in a position to receive the request for arbitration and take the necessary administrative steps pursuant to the Rules.

The addresses of the Secretariat are:

International Court of Arbitration

International Chamber of Commerce

Headquarters

33-43 Avenue du Président Wilson
75116 Paris
France

Telephone: +33 1 49 53 29 05
Fax: +33 1 49 53 29 33
E-mail: arb@iccwbo.org
Web site: <www.iccarbitration.org>

Asia

Secretariat of the International Court of Arbitration of the International Chamber of Commerce
Asia Office
Suite 2, 12/F, Fairmont House
8 Cotton Tree Drive
Central
Hong Kong

Tel.: +852 3607 5600
Fax: +852 2523 1619
Email: ica8@iccwbo.org

North America

International Chamber of Commerce (ICC)
International Court of Arbitration®
SICANA Inc.
1212 Avenue of the Americas
9th floor
New York, NY 10036
USA

Tel.: +1 646 699 5704
Fax: + 1 212 221 12 95
Email: ica9@iccwbo.org

In light of Article 4(1) it is advisable to file the request for arbitration in such a way that proof of receipt by the ICC is obtained. It is possible to submit a request for arbitration by email or by fax, always provided that the originals are sent to the Secretariat immediately afterwards. The request for arbitration may be submitted by the claimant's lawyer or any other authorized person. Proof of authorization is not required at this stage under the Rules. If need be, the question may be taken up later by the arbitral tribunal, once it has been formed and entrusted with the case.

When confirming receipt of the request for arbitration, the Secretary General of the ICC Court informs the claimant and the respondent of the date on which the request was submitted (Article 4(1)).

It is not excluded for claimant and respondent parties to file a request for arbitration jointly. In practice, this is however very rarely done.

A party submitting a request for arbitration must pay the required filing fee before the request will be notified by the Secretariat to the respondent(s) (Article 4(4)(b) of the Rules and Article 1(1) of Appendix III to the Rules).

(2) Commencement of Proceedings (Art. 4(2)).

The date on which the request for arbitration is filed with the Secretariat of the ICC International Court of Arbitration marks the point at which the case becomes pending (Article 4(2)). This date is crucial: for instance, it determines the starting point of any interruption or suspension under statutes of limitation and is also a means of checking that certain other time limits are respected.

(3) Information to be Included in the Request for Arbitration (Art. 4(3)).

As already mentioned, the request for arbitration is more than a mere summons to arbitration proceedings. Article 4 (3) of the Rules sets forth the minimum information it must contain. This provision gives the claimant considerable scope to determine how it will present its case, leaving it free to decide for instance which facts and legal issues it will raise in its request.

The request for arbitration must include at least the following information:

(a) *Full details of the parties* (Art. 4(3)(a)).

The claimant is required to state the exact details of the parties, especially of the respondent(s). The address provided for respondent(s) in the request for arbitration will be used by the ICC Court Secretariat for the purpose of notifying the request for arbitration. Multiple claimants may file a request for arbitration jointly.

Not all the parties named in the request for arbitration will finally be the parties involved in the arbitration. If a respondent contests to be bound by an arbitration agreement and raises a plea for lack of jurisdiction, the ICC Court may have to decide pursuant to Article 6(4) whether or not the arbitration shall proceed or whether the arbitration shall proceed against all the respondents. A respondent may, pursuant to Article 7, decide to join an additional party, so that, subject to the provisions of Article 6(3)-6(7) and 9, more parties may become involved than solely those named by the claimant in the request for arbitration.

(b) *Full details of the person(s) representing the claimant(s)* (Art. 4(3)(b))

The claimant must also provide the name and address of its lawyer or other representative, if any, for the purpose of correspondence. This is explicitly stated as a new requirement in the 2012 Rules, although parties already in the past generally gave such information from the outset. It is not required for a party to be represented by a lawyer in an arbitration, but mostly parties do have a lawyer to represent them in arbitration. Parties may also be represented by several lawyers or law firms.

Pursuant to Article 17 the Secretariat or the arbitral tribunal, once constituted, may request at any time proof of authority of the person(s) representing the claimant(s).

(c) *A description of the nature and circumstances of the dispute giving rise to the claim(s) and of the basis upon which the claims are based* (Art. 4(3)(c)).

The claimant must present at least a summary of all the facts and legal arguments necessary for a decision to be made in its favor. A new requirement of the 2012 Rules is that the claimant also has to give a description of the basis upon which the claims are based. This should enable the respondent(s) to have a clearer idea as to whether the claims are based on a contract, on which contractual stipulations, in tort, or on a trust instrument or an international treaty. This is particularly important in the event that the respondent declines to participate in the proceedings.

However, the Rules of Arbitration do not require the claimant at this stage to submit a fully detailed statement of claim. For instance, it is not necessary to take into consideration the arguments that are likely to be raised in defense or to provide full evidence. Nevertheless, as is generally the case, it is recommended that all documents essential to the dispute be annexed to the request for arbitration. This helps the ICC Court and its Secretariat to understand the dispute and to identify those aspects that will be relevant to the constitution of the arbitral tribunal. A sufficiently accurate presentation of the dispute and in particular of claimant's case with supporting documentation is also very useful to the arbitral tribunal, which must draw up the Terms of

Reference once it has received the file. This information is also relevant for dealing with certain issues such as requests for document production or other procedural issues such as timing which need to be addressed early on. It is also advisable to mention in the request for arbitration any other arbitral proceedings related to those pending or any proceedings in state courts.

(d) *The relief sought, together with the amounts of any quantified claims and, to the extent possible, an estimate of the monetary value of any other claims* (Art. 4 (3) (d)).

The ICC Rules of Arbitration require the purposes of a request for arbitration to be specified, as the Terms of Reference are drawn up on the basis of the request and the respondent's answer. Once the Terms of Reference have been signed, no new claims may be allowed unless they lie within the limits of the Terms of Reference or, failing this, have been authorized by the arbitral tribunal in accordance with Article 23(4) of the Rules.

Parties filing claims are required under the 2012 Rules of Arbitration to provide the amount of any quantified claim and to estimate the monetary value of any other claims. As the scales of arbitrators' fees and ICC administrative expenses are based on the amounts in dispute, it is appropriate that parties themselves can specify or estimate the values of their claims from the start of an arbitration. This will allow the Secretary General or the Court to fix an appropriate advance to cover the costs from the outset and avoid the need for readjustment later on (see Article 36). It is the Court's practice not to include claims for interest and for costs in the calculation of the amount in dispute. If the parties have not specified the amount in dispute, in spite of the requirement to do so, the Court shall fix the arbitrators' fees and the administrative expenses at its own discretion (Article 2(1) of Appendix III to the Rules).

(e) *Any relevant agreements and, in particular, the arbitration agreement(s)* (Art. 4(3) (e)).

The claimant must provide all relevant provisions of the contract or, if the claim is made under a treaty, of the treaty in the request for arbitration. These necessarily include the arbitration agreement, as well as all other provisions relating to the arbitration proceedings covering such matters as the language and the place of the arbitration and any other relevant documents containing information on these matters. It does not suffice for claimant to cite the arbitration agreement(s), it should also attach a copy of the documents containing the arbitration agreement.

Information on the arbitration agreement is also essential to enable the ICC International Court of Arbitration to declare whether or not it is '*prima facie*' satisfied that an arbitration agreement under the Rules may exist, in the event that the respondent denies the existence of such an agreement or refuses to take part in the arbitration. If the Court's answer is positive, the Secretariat may then transmit the file to the arbitral tribunal for it to decide on the matter (Article 6(3)).

(f) *Indication of the arbitration agreement under which each claim is made, if claims are made under more than one arbitration agreement* (Art. 4(3)(f))

The 2012 ICC Rules of Arbitration explicitly provide in Article 9 that claims arising out of or in connection with more than one contract may be made in a single arbitration. The Rules accept that this can be done not only if claims are made under one arbitration agreement, but also if claims are submitted under more than arbitration agreement under the ICC Rules of Arbitration. If a claimant files claims under different arbitration agreements, it has to indicate in its request for arbitration for each of the claims under which arbitration agreement they are filed. These indications will be relevant, if the Court will have to take a decision regarding the setting in motion of the arbitration pursuant to article 6(4)(ii).

(g) *Relevant particulars regarding the number and choice of arbitrators* (Art. 4(3)(g)).

(i) The number of arbitrators.

The claimant's request for arbitration must state whether the dispute is to be decided by a sole arbitrator or by three arbitrators, according to what has been specified in the arbitration agreement. If nothing has been agreed on this matter, the claimant should indicate whether it prefers one or three arbitrators.

(ii) The nomination of arbitrators.

If the arbitration agreement provides for the dispute to be settled by a sole arbitrator, the claimant should include in its request for arbitration any information that may be useful when, in accordance with Article 12(3) of the Rules, the parties seek to jointly nominate an arbitrator, within 30 days from the date on which the respondent is notified of the request. The claimant may therefore suggest one or several prospective arbitrator(s) already at this early stage of proceedings.

If the number of arbitrators is not indicated in the arbitration agreement and the claimant's wish is for a sole arbitrator, this should also be specified in the request for arbitration in view of Article 12(2) of the Rules. The claimant should make known to the other party the kind of person it has in mind for joint nomination by both parties, thereby enabling the respondent to react quickly to its suggestion.

A claimant wishing to have three arbitrators when nothing is specified in the arbitration agreement may speed up proceedings not only by specifying in the request for arbitration its wish for a three-member tribunal but also by nominating already one co-arbitrator. This is not compulsory, however, as Article 12(2) of the Rules merely requires the claimant to nominate an arbitrator within 15 days of being informed of the Court's decision to submit the dispute to three arbitrators. In this case, it is in the claimant's interest to nominate an arbitrator without delay, so that the arbitral tribunal may be constituted as quickly as possible.

Only if the arbitration agreement provides for a three-member arbitral tribunal is it necessary for the claimant to nominate an arbitrator in the request for arbitration in accordance with Article 12(4).

Parties are free to modify an earlier agreement on the number of arbitrators. If the claimant wishes to have a sole arbitrator, whereas the arbitration agreement provided for three arbitrators, it may indicate this in the request for arbitration. In such case, nevertheless, it will be obliged to nominate an arbitrator in the request for arbitration in accordance with Article 12(4) as long as it is not certain that respondent accepts claimant's request to alter the number of arbitrators.

If a three member arbitral tribunal must be constituted, the claimant should not only nominate an arbitrator in the request for arbitration, it may also provide already its comments and make proposals regarding the selection of the president of the arbitral tribunal, or the qualifications which in its view the president should have. The respondent will then be able to provide its comments thereto in the answer to the request for arbitration and this may accelerate the constitution of the arbitral tribunal.

(h) *Comments as to the place of the arbitration, the applicable rules of law and the language of the arbitration* (Art. 4(3)(h)).

If these points have been settled in the arbitration agreement or explicitly in a subsequent agreement, the claimant need simply refer to and briefly describe the provisions of such agreements. The situation is more complex when the parties have not reached an agreement on these questions prior to the arbitral proceedings. Although under no obligation, the claimant would be well advised to state its position with respect to these matters, insofar as it considers them to have an important bearing on the conduct of the proceedings. The following points may be noted in this connection:

(i) The place of the arbitration.

According to Article 18(1) of the Rules, the place of the arbitration is fixed by the Court if not agreed by the parties. The Court will generally decide on a neutral place which, in the light of its knowledge of the dispute, will be acceptable to all the parties (see comments on Article 18). Therefore, if a claimant refrains from indicating the place of the arbitration that would suit it, there is a risk that, when making its decision, the Court will overlook information that is essential for the claimant but of which it has not been made aware. On the other hand, it is also true that information of this kind might cause the respondent to challenge the claimant's preference as to the place of the arbitration for tactical reasons. This might then make it more difficult for the Court to select the same place, even if it considers it to be the most appropriate place of the arbitration in the absence of any information from the claimant.

(ii) The applicable rules of law.

Under Article 21(1) of the Rules, if the parties have not themselves agreed upon the applicable rules of law, the arbitral tribunal shall apply those it considers to be appropriate (see comments on Article 21(1)). Although according to Article 4(3) of the Rules there is no requirement to give details regarding the applicable rules of law at this stage of the proceedings, such information will nevertheless be important to the Court as a criterion for selecting a sole arbitrator or president of an arbitral tribunal, as well as to the arbitral tribunal, which has the task of drawing up the Terms of Reference as soon as the file has been transmitted to it (see comments on Articles 21 and 23).

(iii) The language of the arbitration.

If the parties have not already agreed on the language of the arbitration, it is up to the arbitral tribunal to determine the language(s) to be used (see comments on Article 20). However, in the absence of a prior agreement, it is useful for the claimant to state its position on this question, even at this early stage of proceedings. This too may serve as a criterion when the Court selects a sole arbitrator or president of an arbitral tribunal. It should be borne in mind that although it is not unusual for parties to have differing opinions on the appropriate language for the arbitration at the start of the proceedings, the question is usually settled by the arbitral tribunal as soon as it receives the file (i.e. when nothing more than the request for arbitration, the answer and an exchange of correspondence have been submitted) and often even before the Terms of Reference have been drawn up. Consequently, if the claimant states its position at the outset, this will help to speed up the proceedings and clarify the issue to be determined. The factors to be taken into consideration when deciding on the language of the arbitration are discussed below in the section on Article 20.

The question remains as to what language should be used for the request for arbitration itself. When a language has been agreed, this alone should be used. Otherwise, the claimant will draft the request for arbitration in accordance with the position it has taken with respect to Article 4(3)(h) of the Rules.

(i) *Other documents or information* (Art. 4(3) last sentence)

In addition to the information claimant is required to provide in its request for arbitration, it may submit with the request for arbitration also other documents or information which it considers appropriate or which may contribute to the efficient resolution of the dispute. Such documents or information may become relevant, if the Court will have to take a decision regarding the setting in motion of the arbitration pursuant to Article 6(4).

(4) Number of Copies of the Request for Arbitration and the Advance Payment on Administrative Expenses (Art. 4(4)).

The interpretation of this provision does not raise any particular problems. The Secretariat will notify a request for arbitration only after the advance on administrative expenses was paid. According to Article 1(1) of Appendix III to the Rules, this advance is currently set at US$ 3 000. Also, the number of copies of the request for arbitration and its attachments that are supplied must be sufficient to allow one copy for each party, one for each arbitrator and one for the Secretariat (Article 3(1)). It may be, however, that the parties have not decided on the number of arbitrators. In this case, it is usually appropriate for the number of copies supplied for the arbitrators to be equivalent to the number of arbitrators specified in the request. Admittedly, this may cause some delay later if a claimant has expressed a wish for a sole arbitrator and supplied only one copy but a three-member tribunal is formed, requiring two additional copies to be supplied and possibly delaying the transmission of the file to the arbitral tribunal.

Should an insufficient number of copies of the request for arbitration have been submitted or the advance to cover administrative expenses not have been paid within the time allowed, this has no effect on the moment at which the proceedings commence under Article 4(2) of the Rules. According to the second sentence of Article 4(4), when acknowledging receipt of the request for arbitration, the Secretariat may set the claimant an appropriate time limit within which to regularize the request, failing which the file will be closed. However, the same provision clearly states that the claimant retains the right to introduce a new request with the same object at a later stage. The question of whether the statutory limitation period was suspended between the moment when the request for arbitration was filed and the moment when the file was closed will be addressed in any subsequent arbitral proceedings that may be commenced. The arbitral tribunal will make its decision in the light of the particular circumstances of the case and the applicable rules of law. However, it may rightly be argued that a limitation period is neither interrupted nor suspended in the event of an incomplete request for arbitration. This is because the respondent is not informed of such a request, which should therefore be considered as non-existent.

(5) Notification of the Request for Arbitration (Art. 4(5)).

If enough copies of the request for arbitration have been filed and the advance payment on the administrative expenses has been made, the Secretariat sends a copy of the request and its attachments to the respondent(s) for an answer, in accordance with the instructions and guidelines for notifications given in Article 3(2) of the Rules. It should be noted that the claimant is answerable for any difficulties linked to inaccuracies in the addresses and details of parties. It should therefore undertake the necessary research so as to provide the Secretariat with all information required for the notification to be effective.

In the cover letter that the Secretariat sends to the respondent when notifying the request for arbitration, the respondent is expressly requested to answer the request for arbitration within thirty days of receiving it. A copy of the Rules of Arbitration is normally sent with the notification. The respondent is also requested to state its position on all points relevant to the setting in motion of the proceedings, beginning with the constitution of the arbitral tribunal. This means that it should nominate a co-arbitrator when the parties have agreed to submit their dispute to three arbitrators. It should be noted that the Secretariat does not scrutinize the request for arbitration when notifying the respondent or later on, to check that it satisfies the requirements laid down in Article 4(3) of the Rules, mainly because there is no provision for such scrutiny in Article 4(5). In practice, the Secretariat asks the claimant to provide all information relevant to the constitution of the arbitral tribunal. However, it does not have a duty to do so, as the Rules allow the Court to constitute the arbitral tribunal when such information is lacking.

With the letter notifying the request for arbitration and the documents annexed thereto to the respondent(s) the Secretariat shall enclose some additional documents on ICC arbitration, including the Secretariat's 'Note to the Parties in Proceedings under the 2012 Rules' (see Appendix 4 below), the Secretariat's 'Note on Administrative Issues' (See Appendix 10 below) and the ICC Rules of Arbitration. At the same time, the Secretariat sends a letter to the claimant(s) with which it informs the claimant(s) that the request for arbitration is notified to the respondent(s) and invites the claimant(s) to pay the provisional advance fixed by the Secretary General pursuant to Article 36(1) of the Rules, while adding thereby a table on the financial aspect of the arbitration. Both in its letter to the claimant(s) and to the respondent(s), the Secretariat points out that the parties are free to settle their dispute amicably at any time during an arbitration and that the parties may wish to consider conducting an amicable dispute resolution procedure pursuant to the ICC Mediation Rules.

Lastly, it should be mentioned that the amount of US$ 3 000 paid as an advance on administrative costs can under no circumstances be refunded to the claimant (Article 1(1) of Appendix III to the Rules). Therefore, if the advance on costs has been paid but there is still an insufficient number of copies of the request for arbitration at the end of the period set for making up the number, or if the parties have in the meantime settled their dispute amicably, the case will be considered to have been withdrawn and the Secretariat will not refund the advance payment.

When the Secretariat informs the Claimant that the request for arbitration has been notified to the respondent(s), it requests the Claimant to pay the provisional advance pursuant to Article 36(1). This provisional advance is fixed by the Secretary General in an amount intended to cover the costs of the arbitration until the Terms of Reference are established.

(6) Amendments to the Request for Arbitration.

Although the Rules do not explicitly state that the claimant may amend its request for arbitration, it follows from Article 23(4) that a claimant, as well as any other party in the arbitration, may file new claims until the Terms of Reference have been established, without any leave from the Court or the arbitral tribunal being required. Likewise, the claimant may modify the amount of its claims. The claimant should be aware, however, that an increase of the amount in dispute may lead to an increase of the advance on costs fixed by the Secretariat. Also, it should be aware that a decrease of the amount in dispute will not necessarily lead to a reduction of the advance on costs. If the arbitrators have accepted to act as arbitrators on the basis of information provided at the time of their appointment including the advance on costs and the expected fees, they might be unwilling to further proceed if they would not have the same fee expectations in case the advance on costs were to be decreased.

Filing claims against an additional party after the request for arbitration is submitted will only be accepted under the condition set forth in Article 7. No additional party may be joined after the confirmation or appointment of any arbitrator, unless all parties, including the additional party, otherwise agree.

2. The Answer to the Request and Counterclaims (Art. 5)

Article 5 of the Rules reads:

> 'Answer to the Request; Counterclaims
>
> 1. Within 30 days from the receipt of the Request from the Secretariat, the Respondent shall submit an Answer (the "Answer") which shall, inter alia, contain the following information:
>   a) its name in full, description, address and other contact details;
>   b) the name in full, address and other contact details of any person(s) representing the respondent in the arbitration;
>   c) its comments as to the nature and circumstances of the dispute giving rise to the claim(s) and the basis upon which the claims are made;
>   d) its response to the relief sought;
>   e) any observations or proposals concerning the number of arbitrators and their choice in light of the claimant's proposals and in accordance with the provisions of Articles 12 and 13, and any nomination of an arbitrator required thereby; and
>   f) any observations or proposals as to the place of the arbitration, the applicable rules of law and the language of the arbitration.
>
> The respondent may submit such other documents or information with the Answer as it considers appropriate or as may contribute to the efficient resolution of the dispute.
>
> 2. The Secretariat may grant the respondent an extension of the time for submitting the Answer, provided the application for such an extension contains the respondent's observations or proposals concerning the number of arbitrators and their choice and, where required by Articles 12 and 13, the nomination of an arbitrator. If the respondent fails to do so, the Court shall proceed in accordance with these Rules.
>
> 3. The Answer shall be submitted to the Secretariat in the number of copies specified by Article 3(1).
>
> 4. The Secretariat shall communicate the Answer and the documents annexed thereto to all other parties.
>
> 5. Any counterclaims made by the respondent shall be submitted with the Answer and shall provide:
>   a) a description of the nature and circumstances of the dispute giving rise to the counterclaims and of the basis upon which the counterclaims are made;

b) a statement of the relief sought together with the amounts of any quantified counterclaims and, to the extent possible, an estimate of the monetary value of any other counterclaims;
c) any relevant agreements and, in particular, the arbitration agreements; and
d) where counterclaims are made under more than one arbitration agreement, an indication of the arbitration agreement under which each counterclaim is made.

The respondent may submit such other documents or information with the counterclaims as it considers appropriate or as may contribute to the efficient resolution of the dispute.

6. The claimant shall submit a reply to any counterclaim within 30 days from the date of receipt of the counterclaims communicated by the Secretariat. Prior to the transmission of the file to the arbitral tribunal, the Secretariat may grant the claimant an extension of time for submitting the reply.'

a) General Remarks on the Answer to the Request

The answer to the request is the first significant communication from the respondent. In it the respondent confronts the request and decides whether to reject to all or merely some of the claims submitted by the claimant, and whether to make other pleas in its defense. Like the request, the answer is important for constituting the arbitral tribunal, fixing the place of the arbitration and for all the other issues mentioned above in connection with the request for arbitration and the arbitral tribunal's task of drawing up the Terms of Reference. The answer to the request may be accompanied by a counterclaim. It is also possible for respondent to set off counterclaims against claims of the claimant at this early stage of proceedings.

In case the request for arbitration is filed against several respondents, the respondents may submit an answer to the request for arbitration jointly or each respondent may choose to submit an answer separately. Likewise, the respondents may submit a counterclaim jointly, or they may choose to submit counterclaims individually. If there are several claimants, the respondents may choose to submit a counterclaim against all the claimants or only against one or some of them.

Whereas under the 1998 Rules of Arbitration the respondent could only file an answer against the parties who initiated the arbitration, the 2012 Rules allow respondents to file claims also against parties other than those who initiated the arbitration through a request for joinder (see Article 7 below). A respondent may also file a cross-claim against another respondent (see Article 8 below).

b) The Contents of the Answer to the Request (Art. 5(1))

As in the case of the request for arbitration, the Rules do not require any particular form or structure for the answer. Article 5(1) merely contains a non-exhaustive list of basic points to be covered in the answer. Like the claimant, the respondent is free to decide to what extent and how it will comment on claimant's assertions regarding the subject of the dispute and how it will organize its defense. Full evidence is usually not produced at this stage of the proceedings, as the parties may submit more detailed pleadings after the file has been transmitted to the arbitral tribunal.

The remarks made in relation to the contents and language of the request for arbitration apply *mutatis mutandis* to the contents of the answer, to the extent described below.

(1) Full Details of the Parties (Art. 5(1)(a)).

The requirement to give full details of the parties implicitly allows the respondent to fill any gaps or correct any inaccuracies in the request for arbitration. This is generally done in the Terms of Reference.

(2) Full Details of the Person(s) representing the Respondent(s) (Art. 5(1)(b)).

The respondent should give the name and address of any representative it may have engaged to represent it. This is explicitly stated as a new requirement in the 2012 Rules, although parties already in the past generally gave such information from the outset. As already indicated, it is not required for a party to be represented by a lawyer in an arbitration, but mostly parties do have a lawyer to represent them in arbitration. Parties may also be represented by several lawyers or law firms.

It is advisable to mention whether subsequent communications should be sent directly to the party representative named.

Pursuant to Article 17, the Secretariat or the arbitral tribunal, once constituted, may request at any time proof of authority of the person(s) representing the respondent(s).

(3) Respondent's Position as to the Nature and Circumstances of the Dispute and the basis upon which the Claims are made (Art. 5(1)(c)).

The respondent should provide its comments on the nature and circumstances of the dispute as set out in the request for arbitration. A new requirement of the Rules is that the respondent also has to give comments as to the basis upon which the claims are based. Pursuant to the new requirement in Article 4(3)(c), claimant must set out in the request for arbitration whether its claims are based on a contract, on which contractual stipulations, in tort, or on a trust instrument or an international treaty. Respondent must provide its comments thereto in its answer to the request for arbitration.

(4) Response to the Relief Sought (Art. 5(1)(d)).

Respondent is under no obligation to give full details of its defense in the answer to the request for arbitration or to attach essential documents. This ensures that the parties are treated equally, as Article 4 of the Rules does not require the claimant either to produce full evidence in support of its claim. The extent of detail the respondent will provide in its answer may be a tactical matter and may also depend on the extent of details provided by claimant in the request for arbitration. The content and coverage of the answer to the request match those of the request itself. In any event, the respondent should give sufficient reasons to justify the prayers for relief formulated in its answer, which more often than not will be aimed at the rejection of the request.

It may be advisable for the respondent to indicate that it reserves the right to add to its pleadings with regard to both facts and law.

Article 5(1) does not expressly require the respondent to include in its response any objections it may have to the jurisdiction of the ICC International Court of Arbitration or the arbitral tribunal, or the arbitrability of the subject matter of the dispute. However, it is advisable for it to do so. Otherwise, there is little chance that the Court would refuse to set the proceedings in motion on the basis of Article 6(4) or that these defense pleas would be included in the initial draft of the Terms of Reference. Furthermore, if a respondent omits to challenge or raise objections over the arbitral tribunal's jurisdiction in general or with respect to certain issues or claims, it risks being barred from doing so if it tries to do so later in the proceedings (see, for example, Articles 1690(2) and 1717(5) JC, Article 1466 NCPC, Article 1040(2) ZPO, Article 186(2) PILA, and Article 16(2) of the UNCITRAL Model Law), although it is only in the context of Article 19 that this question is dealt with explicitly in the Rules.

In the event of unquantified claims, for the reasons explained in connection with the request for arbitration, it is advisable for the respondent also to state its position with respect to any information on the amount in dispute provided by claimant. There is no provision in the Rules or any other text allowing or prohibiting the arbitral tribunal to fix the amount in disputes. Nevertheless, in practice and if appropriate, arbitral tribunals will often raise this issue during the case management conference or at any other appropriate moments with the parties, and seek their agreement on the monetary value of unquantified claims. When submitting prayers for relief, the respondent should not omit to request that the claimant be ordered to reimburse its costs and expenses incurred in relation to the arbitration. Despite Article 37 of the Rules and given that different countries adopt different solutions on the question of the reimbursement of costs, it cannot be assumed that an arbitral tribunal will decide and assess a party's costs if the party concerned has not requested a decision in this respect.

(5) Comments Concerning the Number and Choice of Arbitrators (Art. 5(1)(e)).

The influence the parties may have on the composition of the arbitral tribunal at the very beginning of the proceedings is an expression of one of their fundamental rights. To the extent allowed by the arbitration agreement, it is in the respondent's interest to consider carefully the proposals made by the claimant in the request for arbitration concerning the constitution of the arbitral tribunal, so as to decide whether or not they are acceptable, and, if not, to put forward other suggestions.

If the parties have not provided otherwise with respect to the number of arbitrators, an arbitral tribunal comprising one or three arbitrators will be set up by the ICC International Court of Arbitration (Article 12(1)). In this case, the respondent must consider whether or not it is desirable to have a three-member tribunal. To this end, like the claimant, it will also give consideration to the difficulty of the case, the amount in dispute, as well as the consequences on the costs of the proceedings and the advance that will be fixed. When stating its position on the number of arbitrators, the respondent will also take account of the fact that the Court generally tends not to appoint a sole arbitrator when the amount in dispute is above US$ 30 000 000, and that the Court tends not to decide for the constitution of an arbitral tribunal with three arbitrators when the amount in dispute is below US$ 5 000 000 (see J. Fry, S. Greenberg and F. Mazza, *The Secretariat's Guide to ICC Arbitration*, ICC Publication No. 729 E, Paris, 2012, p. 140. This book is on sale in the ICC store at <www.storeiccwbo.org>). This means that if the amount in dispute is less than US$ 5 000 000, the respondent must provide persuasive reasons for constituting a three-member tribunal. The same applies to cases in which the amount in dispute is more than US$ 30 000 000 and the respondent desires a sole arbitrator.

When the arbitration agreement provides that the case will be decided by a sole arbitrator, or when the respondent agrees with such a suggestion made by the claimant, the parties may, within 30 days of the respondent being notified of the request for arbitration, jointly agree upon the nomination of a sole arbitrator for confirmation by the Secretary General or the Court, as the case may be. The 30-day time limit may be extended by the Secretariat (Article 12(3)) or by agreement between the parties. It is of course possible in such cases for the parties to agree directly on the nomination of an arbitrator without waiting for the answer to the request for arbitration.

When the arbitration agreement provides for the constitution of a three-member arbitral tribunal, or when the respondent accepts the claimant's request for such a tribunal, the respondent must nominate an arbitrator in its answer to the request for Arbitration (see Article 12(4)). Where there are multiple respondents, they should jointly nominate an arbitrator for confirmation by the Court (Article 12(6)). Where an additional party has been joined, the additional party may, jointly with the claimant(s) or with the respondent(s), nominate an arbitrator for confirmation by the Court (Article 12(7)). In the absence of a joint nomination and where all parties are unable to agree to a method for the constitution of the arbitral tribunal, the Court may appoint each member of the arbitral tribunal and shall designate one of them to act as president. In such case, the Court shall be at liberty to choose any person it regards as suitable to act as arbitrator (Article 12(8)). The respondent should also consider making comments or proposals on the selection process for the president of the arbitral tribunal or on qualifications expected from the president of the arbitral tribunal.

What, it may be asked, should be done if, when the arbitration agreement does not fix the number of arbitrators, the claimant asks for a three-member tribunal to be constituted but fails to nominate an arbitrator. The answer may be found in Article 12(2), where it is stated that the claimant shall first nominate a co-arbitrator. If the claimant fails to nominate a co-arbitrator, the respondent may initially refuse to name an arbitrator in its answer to the request for arbitration and ask the Secretariat to give the claimant a deadline for nominating 'its' co-arbitrator and only after this will the respondent in its turn nominate an arbitrator in the time limit set for it to do so.

(6) Comments Concerning the Place of the Arbitration, the Applicable Rules of Law and the Language of the Arbitration (Art. 5(1)(f)).

The place of the arbitration, the applicable substantive rules of law and the language of the arbitration may have an important part to play in the choice of the arbitrators. The respondent must state its position on all these points when they are not settled clearly in the arbitration agreement and when it finds the claimant's position fully or partly unacceptable. As far as the respondent's position with respect to the place of the arbitration, the applicable rules of law and the language(s) of the proceedings is concerned, the reader is referred to the discussion of these points in connection with the request for arbitration (compare Articles 4(3)(h), 18(1), 20 and 21).

(7) Other documents or Information (Art. 5(1) last sentence).

In addition to the information respondent is required to provide in its answer to the request for arbitration, it may submit with the answer also other documents or information which it considers appropriate or which may contribute to the efficient resolution of the dispute. Such documents or information may become relevant, if the Court has to take a decision regarding the setting in motion of the arbitration pursuant to Article 6(4).

c) The Time Limit for Filing the Answer to the Request for Arbitration (Art. 5(1)-(2))

The respondent must send its answer to the request for arbitration to the Secretariat within thirty days of receiving from the Secretariat the request for arbitration (Article 5(1)). Even if the respondent has already received a copy of the request for arbitration directly from the claimant, this time limit still remains the same. It begins at the time specified in Article 3(3) of the Rules, that is to say when the respondent receives the request for arbitration or should have done so if notification was made in accordance with Article 3(2). The end of the time limit is calculated in accordance with Article 3(4) of the Rules.

According to Article 5(2), the Secretariat may extend the time allowed for answering the request for arbitration subject to the following conditions:

- in its request for an extension, the respondent must give all the necessary information mentioned in Article 5(1)(e) of the Rules;
- the request for an extension and the necessary accompanying information must be sent to the Secretariat within the initial thirty-day period allowed for filing an answer to the request for arbitration.

This therefore means that if the respondent wishes the period for filing its answer to be extended, within thirty days it must provide all the information required for the constitution of the arbitral tribunal according to the Rules of Arbitration. If the arbitration clause provides for a three-member tribunal and the claimant has already nominated an arbitrator in the request for arbitration, the respondent is likewise required to nominate an arbitrator within thirty days. This allows the Court to proceed with the constitution of the arbitral tribunal, regardless of whether or not the respondent has filed a full answer to the request for arbitration.

If the respondent wishes to challenge the jurisdiction of the ICC or of the arbitral tribunal constituted in accordance with the Rules of Arbitration, it is advisable for it to raise this objection when applying for the time limit to be extended, especially if the extension of the time limit is conditional upon an arbitrator having been nominated. It is worth noting that in some legal systems a party's unreserved cooperation in constituting the arbitral tribunal, especially by designating an arbitrator, may bar it from raising any objections later relating to this matter.

Although Article 5(2) does not specify the length of the extension for filing an answer to the request for arbitration, the Secretariat normally allows an additional thirty days. A longer extension could be granted only if the respondent were able to put forward special reasons or the claimant were in agreement. In the past, the Secretariat has routinely granted a 30-day extension when requested to do so and provided the conditions laid down in Article 5(2) related to Article 5(1)(e) had been met. The Secretariat does not, however, have the power to decide of its own accord to extend the period of time for submitting comments concerning the constitution of the arbitral tribunal or, as the case may be, the nomination of an arbitrator. The parties may extend this kind of time limit themselves whenever they wish.

If the respondent fails to file its answer to the request for arbitration in time or omits to seek in time an extension of the time limit, there is a risk that the Court will decide on the constitution of the arbitral tribunal, the place of the arbitration and the advance to cover the costs of the arbitration without considering the respondent's position (Article 6(8)). It should be pointed out that the Rules do not 'penalize' a respondent for failing to file its pleadings in time. Respondent is therefore not prevented from presenting its defense arguments and producing evidence later in the proceedings. However, in such cases, consideration should be given to Article 23(4), any special agreements between the parties and the rules of procedure that may have been determined by the arbitral tribunal in accordance with Article 19, as these may bar the respondent from doing so.

d) Counterclaims (Art. 5(5))

As far as the description of any counterclaims and related facts are concerned, the reader is referred to our explanations given in connection with the request for arbitration.

If a respondent wishes to file a counterclaim, the moment to do so is when answering the request for arbitration or, at the very latest, when the Terms of Reference are drawn up. Although not compulsory, this is recommendable, since any counterclaim raised after the Terms of Reference have been drawn up and lying outside their ambit must be expressly authorized by the arbitral tribunal under Article 23(4). Thus, if a respondent does not adhere to Article 5(5), any counterclaim it presents too late is susceptible of rejection by the arbitral tribunal. In this case, it may be necessary for the respondent to file a separate request for arbitration. Under Article 10, this request could be joined to the pending case, but if in that pending case the Terms of Reference have already been drawn up, the explicit authorization of the arbitral tribunal will be required. The same applies if the parties' respective claims are set off against each other, although in civil law systems set-off is considered to have the effect of extinguishing the claim by operation of the law. There is no certainty that an international arbitral tribunal would treat a claim for set-off in this way under the applicable rules of law, given the fact that the question is dealt with differently in different legal systems.

Respondent should be aware that, if it files a counterclaim, the Court may fix separate advances on costs for the claims and the counterclaims (Article 36(3)). A decision to fix separate advances on costs is not taken systematically, when a counterclaim is filed. Normally, the Court shall fix a global advance on costs calculated on the basis of the aggregate of the principal claims and the counterclaims. However, if a party refuses to pay its share of the advance on costs because it is calculated also on the basis of the other party's claims, there could be an impasse in the arbitration proceedings. A decision to fix separate advances on costs could then provide a way out of the impasse. If separate advances are fixed by the Court, each party shall pay in full the advance on costs corresponding to its claims (Article 36(3)).

A respondent may not only submit counterclaims against the claimant, it may also file with its answer a claim against parties other than those who initiated the arbitration. If it wishes to join an additional party, respondent should file a request for joinder and comply with the requirements laid down in Article 7 (see the comments on Article 7 below).

If there are several respondents, a respondent may file a cross-claim against another respondent in accordance with the requirements of Article 8 (see the comments on Article 8 below).

e) Replies to Counterclaims (Art. 5(6))

The claimant may respond to any counterclaim made by the respondent within thirty days of being notified of the counterclaim by the Secretariat (Article 5(6)). This period may be extended by the Secretariat at the claimant's request. The Rules do not specify any special conditions to be met for this purpose.

It should be pointed out that the claimant is not compelled to file its reply within this time limit. A comparison of the English and French versions of the Rules shows this to be the case, as does the absence of any reference to the fact that replies are barred thereafter. However, as already mentioned, this does not mean that it is impossible to set a compulsory time bar. This will for instance be the case if the arbitral tribunal sets a time limit for replying to a counterclaim at a later stage of the proceedings.

f) The Number of Copies to be Filed (Art. 5(3))

As far as the required number of copies of the answer to the request for arbitration and accompanying documents and any reply is concerned, Article 5(3) of the Rules contains a similar provision to that of Article 4(5), for which the details are found in Article 3(1). The reader is therefore referred to our previous comments in this connection.

g) Notification (Art. 5(4))

The answer to the request for arbitration and any counterclaim(s), and the claimant's reply prior to transmission of the file to the arbitral tribunal, must be sent to the Secretariat, which is responsible for forwarding them to the other parties, as is the case with the request for arbitration (Article 3(2)). The Secretariat may wait with the notification of the answer to the other party or the other parties until the respondent has provided the necessary number of copies pursuant to Article 5(3).

If the respondent fails to provide its comments on important elements regarding the setting in motion of the arbitration, such as the number of arbitrators and their choice and the place of the arbitration, the Secretariat shall seek the comments of the respondent while sending a copy of the answer to the other party or the other parties.

h) Amendments to the answer or counterclaims

Although the Rules do not explicitly state that the respondent may amend its answer to the request for arbitration, it follows from Article 23(4) that a respondent, as well as any other party in the arbitration, can file new counterclaims until the Terms of Reference have been established. Likewise, a respondent can amend the amount of its counterclaims. As already indicated with respect to the principal claims being amended, the respondent should be aware that an increase of the amount in dispute may lead to an increase of the advance on costs fixed by the Secretariat. Also, it should be aware that a decrease of the amount in dispute will not necessarily lead to a reduction of the advance on costs. If the arbitrators have accepted to act as arbitrators on the basis of information provided at the time of their appointment including the advance on costs and the expected fees, they might be unwilling to further proceed if they would not have the same fee expectations in case the advance on costs were to be decreased.

Filing claims against an additional party after the answer to the request for arbitration is submitted will only be accepted under the condition set forth in Article 7. No additional party may be joined after the confirmation or appointment of any arbitrator, unless all parties, including the additional party, otherwise agree.

3. The Effect of the Arbitration Agreement (Art. 6)

Article 6 of the Rules reads:

'Effect of the Arbitration Agreement

1. Where the parties have agreed to submit to arbitration under the Rules, they shall be deemed to have submitted ipso facto to the Rules in effect on the date of commencement of the arbitration proceedings, unless they have agreed to submit to the Rules in effect on the date of their arbitration agreement.

2. By agreeing to arbitration under the Rules, the parties have accepted that the arbitration shall be administered by the Court.

3. If any party against which a claim has been made does not submit an Answer, or raises one or more pleas concerning the existence, validity or scope of the arbitration agreement or concerning whether all of the claims made in the arbitration may be determined together in a single arbitration, the arbitration shall proceed and any question of jurisdiction or of whether the claims may be determined together in that arbitration shall be decided directly by the arbitral tribunal, unless the Secretary General refers the matter to the Court for its decision pursuant to Article 6(4).

4. In all cases referred to the Court under Article 6(3), the Court shall decide whether and to what extent the arbitration shall proceed. The arbitration shall proceed if and to the extent that the Court is prima facie satisfied that an arbitration agreement under the Rules may exist. In particular:

(i) where there are more than two parties to the arbitration, the arbitration shall proceed between those of the parties, including any additional parties joined pursuant to Article 7, with respect to which the Court is prima facie satisfied that an arbitration agreement under the Rules that binds them all may exist; and

(ii) where claims pursuant to Article 9 are made under more than one arbitration agreement, the arbitration shall proceed as to those claims with respect to which the Court is prima facie satisfied (a) that the arbitration agreements under which those claims are made may be compatible, and (b) that all parties to the arbitration may have agreed that those claims can be determined together in a single arbitration.

The Court's decision pursuant to Article 6(4) is without prejudice to the admissibility or merits of any party's plea or pleas.

5. In all matters decided by the Court under Article 6(4), any decision as to the jurisdiction of the arbitral tribunal, except as to parties or claims with respect to which the Court decides that the arbitration cannot proceed, shall then be taken by the arbitral tribunal itself.

6. Where the parties are notified of the Court's decision pursuant to Article 6(4) that the arbitration cannot proceed in respect of some or all of them, any party retains the right to ask any court having jurisdiction whether or not, and in respect of which of them, there is a binding arbitration agreement.

7. Where the Court has decided pursuant to Article 6(4) that the arbitration cannot proceed in respect of any of the claims, such decision shall not prevent a party from reintroducing the same claim at a later date in other proceedings.

8. If any of the parties refuses or fails to take part in the arbitration or any stage thereof, the arbitration shall proceed notwithstanding such refusal or failure.

> 9. Unless otherwise agreed, the arbitral tribunal shall not cease to have jurisdiction by reason of any allegation that the contract is non-existent or null and void, provided that the arbitral tribunal upholds the validity of the arbitration agreement. The arbitral tribunal shall continue to have jurisdiction to determine the parties' respective rights and to decide their claims and pleas even though the contract itself may be non-existent or null and void.'

a) Referral to ICC Arbitration (Art. 6(1))

The first paragraph of Article 6 of the Rules clearly states that when parties refer to the ICC Rules of Arbitration in their arbitration agreement, they are assumed to have agreed to the version of the Rules in force at the time the request for arbitration is filed, unless the parties have agreed to the application of the Rules as in force at the date they signed their arbitration agreement.

It is not unusual for the arbitration agreement to have been made long before a dispute arises. The Rules of Arbitration may have been modified between the moment at which the agreement was made and the moment at which the request for arbitration is filed. Indeed, the International Chamber of Commerce has in the past modified its Rules of Arbitration on a number of occasions, such as in 1955, 1975, 1988, 1998 and 2012.

Even before the current version of the Rules was introduced, the ICC International Court of Arbitration adopted the practice of applying the version of the Rules in force when the request for arbitration was filed, unless the parties had agreed otherwise. Thus, in cases where the parties made an ICC arbitration agreement before 1 January 2012 but the request for arbitration based on this agreement was filed after that date, the arbitration proceedings were subject to the new Rules.

It is only when an arbitration agreement made prior to 1 January 2012 states that disputes will be subject to the Rules of Arbitration 'in effect' when the agreement or the contract was made that the latest version of the Rules will not apply. If need be, the Secretariat may draw the parties' attention to this choice with a view to enquiring whether they would nevertheless like the most recent version of the ICC Rules to be used. If the parties are unable to agree, the earlier version of the Rules will be applied in such circumstances.

b) Administration of the arbitration by the ICC Court (Art. 6 (2))

The second paragraph of Article 6 of the Rules confirms that if the parties agree to ICC arbitration, they accept that it shall be administered by the ICC Court. As already set out in Article 1(2), the ICC International Court of Arbitration is the only body authorized to administer arbitrations under the ICC Rules of Arbitration. It is therefore not possible for another body or another institution to administer an arbitration under the ICC Rules. Should this nevertheless be done, then this would probably seriously put at risk the enforceability of the arbitral award rendered in such arbitration proceedings.

The ICC Rules of Arbitration give supervisory and decision-making powers to the ICC Court and its Secretariat to enable them to administer the entire proceedings and establish prerogatives that go beyond those usually assigned to arbitration institutions in their rules (See Chapter 1.E above).

c) Decision Regarding the Continuation of the Proceedings in the Event of an Objection to ICC Arbitration (Art. 6 (3)-6(6))

May a party against which a request for arbitration under the ICC Rules is directed object to the commencement of proceedings if it believes there are no grounds for jurisdiction? What happens if a party to which a request for arbitration is notified does not answer the request for arbitration notwithstanding the invitation by the Secretariat to do so?

Normally, a party that has signed an arbitration agreement providing for ICC arbitration cannot prevent proceedings from taking place.

However, a respondent occasionally tries to prevent the arbitration from taking place by objecting to the existence, validity or scope of the arbitration agreement. Sometimes a respondent even brings proceedings in a state court while seeking to resist arbitration. Under national laws and, in the field of international arbitration, applicable international treaties relating to the recognition and enforcement of foreign arbitral awards, the state court will usually refuse to accept jurisdiction when informed by the other party that an arbitration agreement has been made between the two parties, unless it considers this agreement to be ineffective.

What kinds of objections may a party raise with respect to an arbitration agreement? What kinds of situations are encountered in practice? The following examples may shed light on these questions: A party may allege that an arbitration agreement in the general terms and conditions issued by the party with which it contracted is null and void. It may also claim that it is not bound by those general terms and conditions and that the parties are instead bound by its own general terms and conditions. This kind of situation is referred to as a battle of forms. Sometimes, a party may allege that the arbitration agreement has no effect because the contract has been terminated, or that it is inapplicable because the parties have not made a prior attempt to resolve their dispute amicably. A party may also claim that the arbitration agreement was signed by a person who was not empowered to do so.

There are occasionally differences of opinion concerning the arbitration agreement, especially its scope, as parties do not always include in their contracts the standard clause recommended by ICC (see Chapter 4 below). Parties sometimes contend that under the terms of the arbitration agreement, the arbitral tribunal is not authorized to decide all the claims and issues in dispute. For instance, if the arbitration agreement refers to 'all disputes arising from the performance of the contract', it is conceivable that a party might object to the jurisdiction of the arbitral tribunal to decide on a dispute concerning the interpretation of the agreement or problems of liability. In other situations a respondent may argue that the agreement to arbitrate is inoperative because the subject matter of the dispute is exclusively to be determined by the state courts of a given country. If the arbitration institution is incorrectly named in the arbitration agreement, this can also be a basis for challenging its jurisdiction. If a party raises a jurisdictional objection of any kind at the start of the arbitration proceedings, the ICC International Court of Arbitration decides whether or not to set the proceedings in motion (first sentence of Article 6(2)). Before making such a decision, it usually gives the parties – especially the claimant – a chance to submit its comments.

An objection concerning the existence, validity or scope of an arbitration agreement does not normally prevent the arbitral proceedings from continuing; for the arbitral tribunal will then be required to decide, as it is entitled to do, whether and to what extent it has jurisdiction to hear the dispute (Article 6(9)). The purpose of Article 6(4) is to allow flagrant instances of abuse to be excluded at the very outset.

(1) The Initial Screening by the Secretary General (Article 6(3)).

The 2012 Rules have altered the review mechanism that existed under the 1998 Rules in Article 6(2), given the increasing number of cases where a decision under Article 6(2) needed to be taken by the Court. In 2011 this was the case in more than 40% of the arbitrations initiated, although the Court refused the arbitration from proceeding only in very few cases (in only 4% of those cases; see J. Fry, S. Greenberg and F. Mazza, *The Secretariat's Guide to ICC Arbitration*, ICC Publication No. 729 E, Paris, 2012, p. 68 and p. 74). As the screening process by the ICC Court under the 1998 Rules generally delayed the setting in motion of the arbitration with one month or sometimes more, it has been decided to give an initial screening function to the Secretary General under the 2012 Rules.

The gatekeeping function of the Secretary General under Article 6(3) gives him or her the power to decide that an arbitration may proceed in the situations described in Article 6(3) or to refer the matter to the Court for a decision to be taken by the Court pursuant to Article 6(4).

In the event of an objection to jurisdiction, or if a party fails to answer the request for arbitration, the Secretary General will allow the arbitration to proceed if he or she 'is *prima facie* satisfied that an arbitration agreement under the Rules may exist'. This is also the criterion used by the ICC Court when it has to decide pursuant to Article 6(4) whether or not an arbitration can proceed, and which already was the criterion applied under Article 6(2) of the 1998 Rules. Article 6(3) provides a third type of situation where the Secretary General has the power to decide whether an arbitration shall proceed. In case an arbitration is initiated on the basis of multiple arbitration agreements, as Article 9 of the 2012 Rules allows, the Secretary General shall decide whether all the claims may be determined in a single arbitration or whether they should be filed in separate arbitrations.

If the Secretary General decides pursuant to Article 6(3) that, notwithstanding an objection from a respondent, the arbitration shall proceed or that the claims may be determined in a single arbitration, it shall be for the arbitral tribunal to decide upon its own jurisdiction once it is constituted. This is an application of the well known principle 'Kompetenz-Kompetenz' or 'competence competence', which gives the power to the arbitral tribunal to decide on its own jurisdiction.

In case the Secretary General decides to refer the matter to the Court for a decision to be taken pursuant to Article 6(4), he or she shall inform the parties thereof and will invite them to comment before a decision is taken by the Court.

The purpose of granting the Secretary General the gatekeeping function is to identify at an early stage cases in which there is no significant chance that the Court will take a negative decision that the arbitration shall not proceed. Any case that might reasonably result in a negative decision will always be presented to the Court for its decision. The administrative '*prima facie*' decision that a case may not proceed, or at least not between all named parties, may only be taken by the Court, and not by the Secretary General. The Secretary General's role is limited to the screening process and to possibly taking an administrative '*prima facie*' decision that the arbitration may proceed and that the matter shall be submitted to the arbitral tribunal.

(2) The Screening by the ICC Court (Article 6(4)-(6)).

When a matter is referred by the Secretary General pursuant to Article 6(3) of the 2012 Rules for a decision to be taken by the Court, the latter shall apply the same test as already applicable under the 1998 Rules, namely whether it is '*prima facie* satisfied that an arbitration agreement under the Rules may exist'.

Article 6(4) provides, however, an additional power of the Court in this respect. The Court may also decide 'to what extent' the arbitration shall proceed. This additional power has been added so to be able to deal with requests for arbitration filed under the new multiparty and multicontract provisions of the Rules. Article 6(4) gives guidance as to how the Court should take a decision in different kinds of situations in this connection.

The first situation is the multiparty situation where the request for arbitration is based on one arbitration agreement. If more than two parties are named in the request for arbitration, meaning more than one claimant and/or more than one respondent, and an objection is raised by a respondent against the setting in motion of the arbitration with all the parties named in the request, the Court shall decide that the arbitration may proceed if it is '*prima facie* satisfied that an arbitration agreement under the Rules that binds them all may exist'. The Court will examine with respect to all these parties whether '*prima facie*' they are bound or may be considered to be bound by one arbitration agreement among them (Article 6(4) second sentence (i)).

The second situation is the multiparty situation where the request for arbitration is based on more than one arbitration agreement. If more than two parties are named in the request for arbitration, meaning more than one claimant and/or more than one respondent, and an objection is raised by a respondent against the setting in motion of the arbitration with all the parties named in the request, the Court shall decide that the arbitration may proceed if it is '*prima facie* satisfied (a) that the arbitration agreements under which those claims are made may be compatible, and (b) that all parties to the arbitration may have agreed that those claims can be determined together in a single arbitration'. The Court will examine with respect to all these parties whether they have '*prima facie*' agreed that all the claims be handled in one arbitration. Furthermore, it will also examine whether the arbitration agreements are compatible with each other. Incompatibilities can arise from different constitutions of the arbitral tribunal, from different places of the arbitration, from different languages, from different time limits or from other procedural aspects, preventing the claims under the different agreements from being handled in a single arbitration. If the parties cannot subsequently reach agreement so as to remedy the incompatibility, the Court may decide that the arbitration cannot be set in motion with all the parties in a single arbitration. It may then decide towards which parties the arbitration may be set in motion, and towards which parties the arbitration shall not proceed (Article 6(4) second sentence (ii)).

The third situation is the multicontract situation where the request for arbitration is based on more than one arbitration agreement between the claimant and the respondent. If an objection is raised by the respondent against the setting in motion of the arbitration on the basis of the different contracts invoked by the claimant, the Court shall decide that the arbitration may proceed if it is '*prima facie* satisfied (a) that the arbitration agreements under which those claims are made may be compatible, and (b) that all parties to the arbitration may have agreed that those claims can be determined together in a single arbitration'. The Court will examine with respect to the parties whether they have '*prima facie*' agreed that all the claims be handled in one arbitration, but it also will examine whether the arbitration agreements are compatible with each other. As already set out, incompatibilities can arise from different constitutions of the arbitral tribunal, from different places of the arbitration, from different languages, from different time limits or from other procedural aspects, preventing the claims under the different agreements from being handled in a single arbitration. If the parties cannot subsequently reach agreement so as to remedy the incompatibility, the Court may decide that the arbitration cannot be set in motion with respect to all the claims in a single arbitration. It may then decide towards which claims the arbitration may be set in motion, and towards which claims the arbitration shall not proceed (Article 6(4) second sentence (ii)). The criteria applied in this third situation are similar to those which the Court will apply when it must decide about a consolidation of two or more arbitrations between the same parties, where claims are made under more than one arbitration agreement (See Article 10(c) below).

The fourth situation is where a respondent wishes to join an additional party to the arbitration pursuant to Article 7. If one of the other parties, the claimant or the additional party, objects against the additional party being involved in the arbitration, the Court shall decide that the arbitration may proceed if it is '*prima facie* satisfied that an arbitration agreement under the Rules that binds them all may exist'. The Court will examine with respect to all these parties whether they are bound or may be considered to be bound by one arbitration agreement among them (Article 6(4) second sentence (i)).

If a party named as such in one of these situations is not a signatory to the contract containing the arbitration agreement, the Court will be cautious before deciding whether or not to allow the arbitration to proceed with that party. The parties will be invited to submit further evidence, and it will be on the basis of all the evidence submitted that the Court will assess whether there is '*prima facie*' evidence that might be sufficient to support the request to involve this party in the arbitration.

The Court's '*prima facie*' decision allowing an arbitration to proceed as described above is not a formal ruling on jurisdiction with the binding force of a judicial decision. Pursuant to the Rules (Article 6(5)), it is then up to the arbitral tribunal to rule on the objection to jurisdiction raised by the respondent. If, on the other hand, the ICC Court is not satisfied that '*prima facie*' an arbitration agreement under the ICC Rules of Arbitration may exist, it informs the parties that the arbitration cannot take place (Article 6(6)) as requested.

According to the standard practice, no reasons are given for the decisions made by the ICC International Court of Arbitration, as they are of an administrative, not of a judicial, nature. In October 2015, however, the ICC Court announced that it adopted a new policy in response to growing users' demand (see Chapter 2 above; see also the ICC website at < www.iccwbo.org > and the ICC Dispute Resolution Library at < www.iccdrl.com >). Where all the parties to a case so agree, the ICC Court may communicate henceforth reasons for its '*prima facie*' decisions on jurisdiction. A request for the communication of reasons must be made in advance of the relevant decision in respect of which reasons are sought. The Court may subject the communication of reasons to an increase of the administrative expenses, normally not to exceed US$ 5 000.

Each party retains the right to refer the case, if so desired, to a state court for a decision on whether or not there is a binding arbitration agreement between the parties in dispute. A handful of cases have in the past been referred to the Paris Court of Appeal (within whose jurisdiction the Paris-based International Chamber of Commerce lies) after the ICC International Court of Arbitration had decided that the arbitration could not take place or, where there was more than one respondent, could not take place against one or more of the respondents. It is conceivable that a state court could decide in such event that the arbitration should go ahead.

The number of cases in which the ICC Court has considered that '*prima facie*' there was no agreement referring to ICC arbitration is very small. These are usually cases in which there is every reason to believe that if the case were to go before an arbitral tribunal, it could not decide otherwise, even after hearing all parties and receiving full evidence.

(3) Decision on Jurisdiction Taken by the Arbitral Tribunal (Article 6(5)).

If the ICC Court decides that the arbitration can proceed pursuant to Article 6(4), any decision on jurisdiction of the arbitral tribunal shall be taken by the arbitral tribunal. This is an application of the principle 'competence competence' (see also Article 6(3) above). Accordingly, the arbitral tribunal shall have the power to decide whether it has jurisdiction, after the ICC Court has decided pursuant to Article 6(4) to join an additional party (Article 7) or to set in motion an arbitration with claims between multiple parties (Article 8) or to set in motion an arbitration with claims arising out of more than one contract (Article 9).

When the ICC Court has decided to consolidate one or more arbitrations (Article 10), the arbitral tribunal may still have to examine its jurisdiction in case a plea for lack of jurisdiction is raised. However, the arbitral tribunal will not be able anymore to decide in such case as to whether or not the consolidation decided by the arbitral tribunal was appropriate.

d) Reintroduction of claims at a later date in other proceedings (Art. 6(7))

In case the Court decides pursuant to article 6(4) that the arbitration cannot proceed in respect to some of the claims, this does not prevent the party having filed these claims from submitting them again in other proceedings at a later date. The term 'proceedings' is generic and, consequently, may refer to a new arbitration or to proceedings in a state court. The Rules do not say anything as to whether there may be a time bar issue, since the issue of time bar of claims depends on the applicable law that varies from case to case.

e) The Autonomy or Separability of the Arbitration Agreement (Art. 6(9))

It should be noted that, unless otherwise agreed, any claim that the contract containing the arbitration agreement is null and void or non-existent does not deprive the arbitral tribunal of its jurisdiction to hear the case provided that it upholds the validity of the arbitration agreement (Article 6(9)).

If the arbitral tribunal considers the arbitration agreement to be valid, it normally has jurisdiction to decide on the parties' respective rights and their claims, even if it decides that the contract is non-existent or null and void. This is due to the principle of the autonomy or separability of the arbitration agreement. Pursuant to these legal concepts the invalidity of the main contract does not automatically also cause the arbitration agreement to be invalid or inoperative as the arbitration clause is considered to be legally distinct from the contract containing it.

C. MULTIPLE PARTIES, MULTIPLE CONTRACTS AND CONSOLIDATION

The 1998 rules contained only one provision on multiparty arbitration, more particularly on the joinder or consolidation of requests for arbitration, in Article 4(6). However, the Court and the Secretariat had to deal with a number of requests for joinder of parties, consolidation of arbitrations and claims filed under more than one arbitration agreement, to which this provision did not explicitly apply. Given the evolution of international arbitration and also of ICC arbitration since 1998, where around 30% of the arbitrations initiated involve more than 2 parties (29% in 2008, see '2008 Statistical Report' published in *ICC International Court of Arbitration Bulletin*, Paris, Vol. 20/Nr. 1 – 2009, p. 9; 31% in 2011, see '2011 Statistical Report' published in *ICC International Court of Arbitration Bulletin*, Paris, Vol. 22/Nr. 1 – 2012, p. 7; 33% in 2013, see '2013 Statistical Report' published in *ICC International Court of Arbitration Bulletin*, Paris, Vol. 25/Nr. 1 – 2014, p. 7), it was therefore considered appropriate to include in the new Rules separate provisions on multiparty arbitration which reflect the practice of the Court and the Secretariat that had emerged since the revision of the Rules in 1998. The present Rules do not contain just one provision on multiparty arbitration. They contain 4 provisions, dealing with various aspects of multiparty arbitration.

1. The Joinder of Additional Parties (Art. 7)

Article 7 of the Rules reads:

> 'Joinder of Additional Parties
>
> 1 A party wishing to join an additional party to the arbitration shall submit its request for arbitration against the additional party (the "Request for Joinder") to the Secretariat. The date on which the Request for Joinder is received by the Secretariat shall, for all purposes, be deemed to be the date of the commencement of arbitration against the additional party. Any such joinder shall be subject to the provisions of Articles 6(3)–6(7) and 9. No additional party may be joined after the confirmation or appointment of any arbitrator, unless all parties, including the additional party, otherwise agree. The Secretariat may fix a time limit for the submission of a Request for Joinder.
>
> 2 The Request for Joinder shall contain the following information:
> a) the case reference of the existing arbitration;
> b) the name in full, description, address and other contact details of each of the parties, including the additional party; and
> c) the information specified in Article 4(3) subparagraphs c), d), e) and f).
>
> The party filing the Request for Joinder may submit therewith such other documents or information as it considers appropriate or as may contribute to the efficient resolution of the dispute.
>
> 3 The provisions of Articles 4(4) and 4(5) shall apply, mutatis mutandis, to the Request for Joinder.
>
> 4 The additional party shall submit an Answer in accordance, mutatis mutandis, with the provisions of Articles 5(1)-5(4). The additional party may make claims against any other party in accordance with the provisions of Article 8.'

a) General Remarks on the Request for Joinder

Article 7 provides that any party to an arbitration may join an additional party to that arbitration by submitting to the Secretariat a request for joinder against the additional party. This means that not only a respondent but also a claimant can file a request for joinder against an additional party. Moreover, an additional party against whom a request for joinder is filed can itself also file a request for joinder against another party. This provision allows to bring together in one arbitration all parties involved in or concerned by a complex legal relationships, such as construction projects where several contractors and sub-contracts may be involved in addition to the owner of the works, even if the claimant has not included all these parties in its initial request for arbitration. The request for joinder must be filed in writing with the Secretariat and must comply with certain requirements. If these requirements are fulfilled, the Secretariat shall proceed with the notification of the request for joinder to the other parties and invite them to file a response thereto before any further decision is taken in this regard.

b) Time limit for the Filing of a Request for Joinder (Art. 7(1))

Article 7(1) stipulates that a request for joinder can only be filed before any arbitrator has been confirmed or appointed, unless all parties, including the additional party, agree otherwise. With this provision the Rules seek to avoid any potential problem that could arise by the joining of a party who has not been able to participate in the constitution of the arbitral tribunal. Nevertheless, the Rules do not exclude that an arbitral tribunal can still accept the joinder of an additional party, after it has been constituted. This will be possible if all parties, including the additional party, agree on the joinder and on the constitution of the arbitral tribunal as already made.

The Secretariat has the power to set a time limit for parties to file a possible request for joinder. The Secretariat may do so in particular when it has been informed of a party's intent to file request for joinder and if this party waits to do so. In fixing a time limit, the Secretariat assures that the setting in motion of the arbitration and the process of constituting the arbitral tribunal are not unnecessarily delayed. The Secretariat may thereby bring to the attention of the parties that the joinder of an additional party will not be possible upon simple request after any arbitrator has been confirmed or appointed.

In regard to the additional party the arbitration commences on the date on which the request for joinder is received by the Secretariat (Article 7 (1)). From that moment onwards, the additional party is considered to be a party in the same way as any of the other entities already named as a party in the arbitration. However, the fact that an entity is named as a party in the arbitration, does not necessarily mean that it shall remain a party to the arbitration. As the Rules indicate, any request for joinder is subject to the provisions of Article 6(3)-6(7) (See the comments on Article 6(3)-6(7) and see also hereafter).

c) Formal Requirements for a Request for Joinder (Art. 7(2)-(3))

The request for joinder must include a claim against the additional party and must contain the information referred to in Article 7(2). The request must specify the case number of the arbitration already filed with the ICC and to which the additional party is requested to be joined. The request should also state the names in full, description, addresses and other contact details of all the other parties to the arbitration including the additional party.

Moreover, the request for joinder should contain the information required by Article 4(3)(c) to (f), namely: (i) a description of the nature and circumstances of the dispute giving rise to the claims against the additional party and the basis upon which the claims are made (Article 4(3)(c)); (ii) a statement of the relief sought against the additional party together with the amounts of any quantified claims and, to the extent possible, an estimation of the monetary value of any other claims (Article 4(3)(d)); (iii) any relevant agreement(s) and, in particular, arbitration agreement(s) (Article 4(3)(e)); and (iv) where claims are made under more than one arbitration agreement, an indication of the arbitration agreement under which each claim is made (Article 4(3)(f)). As a consequence, a party wishing to file a request for joinder against an additional party may not just reserve its right to do so. It should explicitly do so in accordance with the requirements of Article 7(2), failing which no request for joinder shall be accepted, and certainly not after an arbitrator has been appointed or confirmed.

A party wishing to join an additional party is free to submit other documents or other information which it considers appropriate with respect to its request. In addition to the information this party is required to provide under the Rules in its request for joinder, it may submit with the request for joinder also other documents or information which it considers appropriate or which may contribute to the efficient resolution of the dispute. Such documents or information may become particularly relevant, if the Court has to take a decision pursuant to Article 6(4) regarding the setting in motion of the arbitration in general or regarding the request for joinder in particular.

The party filing a request for joinder must supply its request in hard copy for each other party and for each arbitrator as well as one copy for the Secretariat (Article 7(3) and 4(4)). Moreover, the party seeking to join another party must file with its request a filing fee of US$ 3 000, which is not refundable (Article 7(3) and Article 4(4)). The Secretariat shall delay the notification to the other parties until these requirements are fulfilled (Article 7(3) and Article 4(5)).

d) Answer to the Request for Joinder (Art. 7(1) and (4))

The additional party to whom the Secretariat notifies the request for joinder if the requirements of Article 7(2) and 7(3) are fulfilled will be invited to comment on the request for joinder within a time limit set by the Secretariat (Article 7(4)). Although the Rules do not explicitly state so, the Secretariat shall also notify the request for joinder to the other parties to the arbitration and also give them the opportunity to comment within the time limit set by the Secretariat. For this reason, Article 7(3) stipulates that the provisions of Article 4(4) apply *mutatis mutandis* and that the party filing a request for joinder must submit its request in the number of copies required by Article 4(4) and by Article 3(1) (to which Article 4(4) refers).

Article 7 (4) requires the additional party to submit an answer to the request for joinder in accordance with Article 5(1)-5(4). The additional party may, in accordance with Article 8, make claims against any other party.

The additional party becomes a party to the arbitration as soon as the request for joinder is filed, just like the respondent becomes a party to the arbitration as soon as the request for arbitration is filed against it. This is an important change compared to the practice under the 1998 Rules, where a third party could become a party to the arbitration only after the Court had decided to join such party to the arbitration proceedings.

However, the additional party against whom a request for joinder is filed, will not necessarily remain a party to the arbitration. The situation is the same like with a respondent against whom a request for arbitration is filed. Just like any other party, including a respondent, the additional party can file a plea regarding the existence, validity or scope of the arbitration agreement or concerning whether all the claims filed in the arbitration may be determined together in single arbitration (Article 6(3)). The screening process set out in Article 6(3) will then be applied by the Secretary General with regard to the 'jurisdictional' pleas raised by the additional party or also if the additional party does not submit an answer. If the Secretary General is '*prima facie*' satisfied that an arbitration agreement may exist among all of the parties including the additional party, he or she will decide to refer the matter to the arbitral tribunal. Referring to what was already set out with respect to Article 6(3), the Secretary General cannot take the negative decision that the matter shall not proceed in regard to the additional party. Any case that might reasonably result in such a negative decision will always be submitted to the Court for its decision. Pursuant to Article 6(4), the Court will allow the matter to proceed against the additional party only if it is satisfied that '*prima facie*' the additional party may be bound by the invoked arbitration agreement. In case the request for joinder is based on another arbitration agreement than the one arbitration agreement between the other parties (e.g., claimant(s) and respondent(s)), the Court will in its decision as to whether the arbitration may proceed against the additional party also have to consider whether the arbitration agreements are compatible and whether the parties may '*prima facie*' have agreed that those claims can be determined in a single arbitration. The Court may decide that the arbitration cannot be set in motion with all the parties in a single arbitration. It may also decide that the arbitration may proceed with respect to some claims and that the arbitration may not be set in motion with respect to other claims.

If the Secretary General refers the matter to the arbitral tribunal pursuant to Article 6(3), the arbitral tribunal will have the jurisdiction to decide on the pleas raised by the additional party and, therefore, to decide also whether or not the additional party shall remain in the arbitration.

e) Advance on costs (Art. 36(4))

When a request for joinder is made and the Secretary General or the Court decides that the matter shall proceed, the Court shall fix one or more advances on costs that shall be payable by the parties as decided by the Court. In most cases the Court is likely to fix one advance on costs, as is set out in a Secretariat's 'Note on Article 36(4) of the 2012 ICC Rules of Arbitration' (see Appendix 5 below). Where the Court apportions the advance on costs, it determines the amount that each party must pay towards the advance on costs. When doing so, the Court will ensure that a party shall only contribute towards the claim or claims in which it is involved. The amount payable by each party shall be proportionate to the value of those claims in relation to the total amount in dispute in the arbitration. Should a party fail to pay one or more of the amounts payable that forms its share of the advance on costs, the Secretariat will invite the other parties involved in that set of claims to pay the outstanding amounts payable.

If an advance on costs was already fixed, it will be adjusted after the additional party has been joined to the arbitration and the amounts already paid by the parties will be credited to their portion of the advance on costs as fixed after the joinder. In case separate advances on costs were fixed, such advances shall be replaced by the advance fixed pursuant to Article 36(4) and the amount of any advance already paid by any party will be credited as a partial payment by such party of its share of the advance(s) on costs fixed by the Court pursuant to Article 36(4).

2. Claims between Multiple Parties (Art. 8)

Article 8 of the Rules reads:

> 'Claims Between Multiple Parties
>
> 1 In an arbitration with multiple parties, claims may be made by any party against any other party, subject to the provisions of Articles 6(3)–6(7) and 9

and provided that no new claims may be made after the Terms of Reference are signed or approved by the Court without the authorization of the arbitral tribunal pursuant to Article 23(4).

2 Any party making a claim pursuant to Article 8(1) shall provide the information specified in Article 4(3) subparagraphs c), d), e) and f).

3 Before the Secretariat transmits the file to the arbitral tribunal in accordance with Article 16, the following provisions shall apply, mutatis mutandis, to any claim made: Article 4(4) subparagraph a); Article 4(5); Article 5(1) except for subparagraphs a), b), e) and f); Article 5(2); Article 5(3) and Article 5(4). Thereafter, the arbitral tribunal shall determine the procedure for making a claim.'

a) General Remarks on the Submission of Claims against a Party

Article 8 formulates an important new principle with respect to multiparty arbitration, which confirms a practice that had developed in the past, even if this principle was not yet explicitly contained in the 1998 Rules.

The provision of Article 8(1) confirms the definition of the term 'claim' given in Article 2(iv). This includes that in an arbitration with more than two parties, any party may make a claim against any other party as long as the Terms of Reference have not been signed or approved by the Court. Once the Terms of Reference have been signed or approved by the Court, any new claims by a party against any other party may only be filed with the authorization of the arbitral tribunal pursuant to Article 23(4).

The following situations are henceforth permitted under the Rules:

(i) If there are multiple respondents, a respondent can file a claim against another respondent. This type of claim is sometimes referred as 'cross-claim'. However, the Rules do not use the term 'cross-claim' as this term is not a term that is universally understood.

(ii) If there are multiple claimants, a claimant can also file a claim against another claimant.

(iii) If an additional party is joined pursuant to Article 7, the additional party may file a claim against one or – if there are multiple claimants – more claimants and against one or – if there are multiple respondents – more respondents.

(iv) Also, if an additional party is joined to the arbitration following a request for joinder pursuant to Article 7, the other party or parties who did not file the request for joinder may make a claim against the additional party.

(v) If multiple additional parties are joined to the arbitration, an additional party may make a claim against any other additional party. However, if an additional party wishes to file a claim against a party not yet named in the request for joinder, it should file itself a request for joinder pursuant to Article 7.

b) Limits of Article 6(3)-(7)) and Article 9

Article 8(1) stipulates that a claim by a party against any other party may only be made subject to Articles 6(3)-(7) and 9.

As already set out above, the reference to Article 6(3)-(7) means that in case a party fails to answer to a claim made against it or in case a party raises a plea concerning the existence, validity or scope of the arbitration agreement or whether all the claims made in the arbitration may be determined in a single arbitration, the screening process set out in Article 6(3) will take place. The Secretary General may decide that the matter shall proceed if he is satisfied that '*prima facie*' an arbitration agreement under the Rules may exist or, in case of doubt, he shall submit the matter to the Court for its decision pursuant to Article 6(4). In case it is decided that the arbitration may proceed with the claims pursuant to Article 6(3) or Article 6(4), the jurisdictional decision on the claims or the decision whether all the claims may be handled in a single arbitration shall be taken by the arbitral tribunal. If the Court decides that the arbitration may not proceed with respect to some or all of the claims, the parties are not prevented pursuant to Article 6(7) from reintroducing the claim at a later date in other proceedings.

The reference to Article 9 means that under the Rules claims can be made under more than one contract, irrespective of whether or not the claims are made under one arbitration agreement or under more than one arbitration agreement. However, if claims are made under more than arbitration agreement, the '*prima facie*' assessment test of Article 6(3) and 6(4) will be applied, as already explained.

c) Procedural Requirements (Art. 8(2)-(3))

The Rules do not specify requirements as to the form in which a claim must be filed, except that there is a need to do it in writing. Therefore, parties are free to choose the form in which they make a claim. They can do so with a brief or memorandum, with a letter or e-mail or any other communication which makes it clear that the claim is made. However, as required by Article 8(2), any claim should contain the information required by Article 4(3)(c) to (f), i.e.: (i) a description of the nature and circumstances of the dispute giving rise to the claims against the additional party and the basis upon which the claims are made (Article 4(3)(c)); (ii) a statement of the relief sought against the additional party together with the amounts of any quantified claims and, to the extent possible, an estimation of the monetary value of any other claims (Article 4(3)(d)); (iii) any relevant agreement(s) and, in particular, arbitration agreement(s) (Article 4(3)(e)); and (iv) where claims are made under more than one arbitration agreement, an indication of the arbitration agreement under which each claim is made (Article 4(3)(f)).

Article 8(3) sets out a number of procedural requirements for making and notifying claims by referring to various provisions of the Rules which are applicable. In accordance with Article 4(4)(a) the claim must be submitted in the number of copies required by Article 3(1). This means that the claim must be provided in a number of copies sufficient to provide one copy for each other party, for each arbitrator and one copy for the Secretariat. In accordance with Article 4(5) the Secretariat shall transmit the claim to the other parties, as soon as it has the sufficient number of copies. In accordance with Article 5(1) the Secretariat shall ask the party against which the claim is made to provide its comments as to the nature and circumstances of the dispute giving rise to the claim and the basis upon which the claims are made (Article 5(1)(c) and any observations or proposals concerning the number of arbitrators and their choice in the light of the claimant's proposals and in accordance with the provisions of Articles 12 and 13, and make any nomination of an arbitrator required thereby (Article 5(1)(e). The Secretariat may grant an extension of the time limit to respond in accordance with Article 5(2). In accordance with Article 5(3) the answer to the claim should be submitted to the Secretariat in the number of copies specified by Article 3(1). There is no requirement for a party making a claim under Article 8 to pay a filing fee, as the provision of Article 4(4)(b) only applies to the filing of a Request for Arbitration.

If new claims are filed after the arbitral tribunal has been constituted, it will be for the arbitral tribunal to determine the procedure for the filing of claims under Article 8.

d) Advance on costs (Art. 36(4))

Parties should realise that if they file cross-claims or other claims from one party against another party in the arbitration, they will all be added all together so as to constitute the amount in dispute on which basis the advance on costs will be calculated pursuant to Article 36. In most cases the Court is likely to fix one advance on costs, as is set out in a Secretariat's 'Note on Article 36(4) of the 2012 ICC Rules of Arbitration' (see Appendix 5 below). Where the Court apportions the advance on costs, it determines the amount that each party must pay towards the advance on costs. When doing so, the Court will ensure that a party shall only contribute towards the claim or claims in which it is involved. The amount payable by each party shall be proportionate to the value of those claims in relation to the total amount in dispute in the arbitration. Should a party fail to pay one or more of the amounts payable that forms its share of the advance on costs, the Secretariat will invite the other parties involved in that set of claims to pay the outstanding amounts payable. In case separate advances on costs were fixed, such advances shall be replaced by the advance fixed pursuant to Article 36(4) and the amount of any advance already paid by any party will be credited as a partial payment by such party of its share of the advance(s) on costs fixed by the Court pursuant to Article 36(4).

If an advance on costs was already fixed, it will be adjusted after all the claims have been filed and have been taken into account. In case separate advances on costs are fixed, the amounts already paid by the parties will be credited to the advance on costs fixed for their claim(s).

3. Multiple Contracts (Art. 9)

Article 9 of the Rules reads:

> 'Multiple Contracts
>
> Subject to the provisions of Articles 6(3)-6(7) and 23(4), claims arising out of or in connection with more than one contract may be made in a single arbitration, irrespective of whether such claims are made under one or more than one arbitration agreement under the Rules.'

a) General Remarks on Claims under Multiple Contracts

Article 9 formulates another important new principle with respect to multiparty arbitration, which confirms a practice that had developed in the past, even if this principle was not yet explicitly contained in the 1998 Rules.

This provision confirms that claims arising out of or in connection with different contracts may be submitted in one arbitration. Article 9 is applicable to different types of situations:

(i) where a claimant makes claims against a respondent under different contracts between the same parties.

(ii) where a claimant makes claims against more than one respondent under different contracts made by the same parties.

(iii) where a claimant makes a claim against a respondent under one contract and the respondent submits a counterclaim against claimant under another contract.

(iv) where a claimant files a claim against a respondent under one contract and respondent files a request for rejoinder making a claim against an additional party under another contract.

b) Limits of Article 6(3)-(7) and Article 23(4)

Article 9 stipulates that claims arising out of or in connection with more than one contract may be made in a single arbitration, subject to Articles 6(3)-(7) and 23(4).

The reference to Article 6(3)-(7) means, as already set out above, that in case a party fails to answer to a claim made against it or in case a party raises a plea concerning the existence, validity or scope of the arbitration agreement or whether all the claims made in the arbitration may be determined in a single arbitration or in arbitration at all, the screening process set out in Article 6(3) will apply. The Secretary General may decide that the matter shall proceed if he or she is '*prima facie*' satisfied that an arbitration agreement under the Rules may exist or, in case of doubt, he or she shall submit the matter to the Court for its decision pursuant to Article 6(4).

In accordance with Article 6(4) the Court may decide, in case claims pursuant to Article 9 are made under more than one arbitration agreement, that the arbitration shall proceed for those claims with respect to which the Court is '*prima facie*' satisfied that two conditions are fulfilled: (i) that the arbitration agreements are compatible; and (ii) that all parties to the arbitration may have agreed that those claims can be determined together in a single arbitration. Incompatibilities can arise from different constitutions of the arbitral tribunal, from different places of the arbitration, from different languages, from different time limits or from other procedural aspects, preventing the claims under the different agreements from being handled in a single arbitration. If the parties cannot subsequently reach agreement so as to remedy the incompatibility, the Court may decide that the arbitration cannot be set in motion with all the parties in a single arbitration. It may then decide with which parties the arbitration may be set in motion, and with which parties the arbitration shall not proceed (Article 6(4) second sentence (ii)).

In case it is decided that the arbitration may proceed with the claims pursuant to Article 6(3) or Article 6(4), the jurisdictional decision on the claims or the decision whether all the claims may be handled in a single arbitration will be taken by the arbitral tribunal. If the Court decides that the arbitration may not proceed with respect to some or all of the claims, the parties are not prevented from reintroducing the claim at a later date in other proceedings pursuant to Article 6(7).

The reference to Article 23(4) means that no party shall make new claims which fall outside the limits of the Terms of Reference after the Terms of Reference have been signed or approved by the Court, unless it has been authorized to do so by the arbitral tribunal.

4. Consolidation of Arbitrations (Art. 10)

Article 10 of the Rules reads:

> 'Consolidation of Arbitrations
>
> The Court may, at the request of a party, consolidate two or more arbitrations pending under the Rules into a single arbitration, where:
>
> a) the parties have agreed to consolidation; or

b) all of the claims in the arbitrations are made under the same arbitration agreement; or
c) where the claims in the arbitrations are made under more than one arbitration agreement, the arbitrations are between the same parties, the disputes in the arbitrations arise in connection with the same legal relationship, and the Court finds the arbitration agreements to be compatible.

In deciding whether to consolidate, the Court may take into account any circumstances it considers to be relevant, including whether one or more arbitrators have been confirmed or appointed in more than one of the arbitrations and, if so, whether the same or different persons have been confirmed or appointed.

When arbitrations are consolidated, they shall be consolidated into the arbitration that commenced first, unless otherwise agreed by all parties.'

a) General Remarks on Consolidation of Arbitrations

Article 10 sets out the conditions under which the Court may consolidate two or more arbitration proceedings under the Rules. It replaces Article 4(6) of the 1998 Rules, which took a narrower view on consolidation of arbitrations. Whereas Article 4(6) of the 1998 Rules allowed the Court only to consolidate arbitration proceedings in case the parties in these different proceedings were the same, unless the parties had agreed to consolidate the proceedings, the 2012 Rules allow the Court also to consolidate even if the parties in the different proceedings are not the same and even if there is no agreement between the parties to consolidate. Under the 1998 Rules a consolidation of arbitration proceedings, could be decided before the Terms of Reference had been signed or approved. Article 10 of the 2012 Rules does not limit the possibility to consolidate arbitrations until the time the Terms of Reference are signed or approved. The Court may decide to consolidate after having taken into account any circumstances it considers relevant, including whether one or more arbitrators have been confirmed or appointed in one or more arbitration and, if so, whether the same or different persons have been confirmed or appointed.

Whereas the provisions of Articles 7, 8 and 9 are indicated to be subject to Article 6(3)-(7), Article 10 is not subject to the provisions of Article 6. A decision taken by the Court under Article 10 is a final administrative decision, not a '*prima facie*' decision. Therefore, the arbitral tribunal will not be able to decide anymore as to whether or not the consolidation decided by the Court was appropriate. The arbitral tribunal will not be able to review or to alter the Court's decision to consolidate. However, the arbitral tribunal will still be able to decide on a plea for lack of jurisdiction in accordance with the principle 'competence competence'.

According to the standard practice, no reasons are given for the decisions made by the ICC International Court of Arbitration, as they are of an administrative, not of a judicial, nature. In October 2015, however, the ICC Court announced that it adopted a new policy in response to growing users' demand (see Chapter 2 above; see also the ICC website at <www.iccwbo.org> and the ICC Dispute Resolution Library at <www.iccdrl.com>). Where all the parties to a case so agree, the ICC Court may communicate henceforth reasons for its decision regarding consolidation of arbitration proceedings. A request for the communication of reasons must be made in advance of the relevant decision in respect of which reasons are sought. The Court may subject the communication of reasons to an increase of the administrative expenses, normally not to exceed US$ 5 000.

b) Conditions for a Decision by the Court to Consolidate

The Court cannot decide at its own initiative to consolidate arbitration. It may only do so, if a party has requested it to take such decision.

The Court is not obliged to consolidate. The Court 'may' do so if the conditions of Article 10 are fulfilled. A decision to consolidate can be taken in one of the three situations described in Article 10:

(1) Where the parties have agreed to consolidate the proceedings.

It goes without saying that the parties may agree that two or more arbitration cases are joined. In so doing, however, they must agree to give jurisdiction to a single arbitral tribunal that meets the requirements of the Rules. All the arbitrations should be pending under the Rules, meaning that the parties can not join an arbitration pending under other rules with an arbitration pending before the ICC Court. Moreover, parties should address in their agreement the constitution of the arbitral tribunal in the single arbitration, more particularly if arbitrators were already confirmed or appointed in one or more of the arbitrations. Also, the parties should deal in their agreement with the place of the arbitration and other possibly relevant procedural aspects, which may be different in the arbitration clauses in the different proceedings. The Rules do not exclude the possibility for the parties to agree on a consolidation after the Terms of Reference have been established in one of the arbitrations. However, the parties will have to examine whether the agreements made in the Terms of Reference are consistent with their agreement to consolidate. The parties will therefore need to agree in such case on new/revised Terms of Reference acceptable for the consolidated arbitration and for the 'consolidated' arbitral tribunal.

(2) Where all the clams in the arbitration are made under the same arbitration agreement.

If all the claims are made under the same arbitration agreement, the Court may decide to consolidate, even if the parties are not the same in the different arbitrations and even if they do not all agree on the consolidation. Article 10(b) thus gives more powers to the Court than did Article 4(6) of the 1998 Rules, as Article 4(6) required that the parties were the same in the different proceedings. It is considered appropriate and useful to give this power to the Court, if all the parties in the different proceedings are party to the same arbitration agreement and if they were not all named together in the different proceedings. A decision to consolidate will result, in all likelihood, in more effective proceedings and avoid the risk of two arbitral tribunals reaching divergent decisions on closely related or even identical sets of facts.

(3) Where the claims in the arbitration are made under more than one arbitration agreement, if the claims are between the same parties, if the disputes in the arbitrations arise in connection with the same legal relationship, and if the Court finds the agreements to be compatible.

The more complex situation is where separate proceedings are pending before the ICC Court and where claims are made under more than one arbitration agreement. In such case, Article 10(c) allows the Court to consolidate the arbitrations if three conditions are fulfilled: (i) if the arbitrations are between the same parties; (ii) if the disputes in the arbitration arise in connection with the same legal relationship; and (iii) if the Court finds the arbitration agreements to be compatible. The first two conditions were already contained in Article 4(6) of the 1998 Rules. The second condition, namely that the disputes in the different arbitration must arise in connection with the same legal relationship is understood by the Court in the sense that all the contracts must relate to the *same economic operation*. The latter term is not defined in the Rules. The third condition is a new condition in the Rules, reflecting however a practice already adopted by the Court in multicontract situations prior to the present Rules, which is now also contained in Article 6(4)(ii) of the 2012 Rules. This third condition may be the final hurdle preventing the Court from consolidating the different arbitrations. If the Court is faced with incompatibilities in the arbitration agreements relating to procedural matters, including the constitution of the arbitral tribunal, the place of the arbitration, and possibly other procedural aspects, and if the parties fail to reach agreement on these procedural aspects, the Court will not be able to consolidate, as it will not be able to disregard the provisions of the arbitration agreements on those procedural aspects.

c) Administrative Handling of a Consolidation

When the Court decides to consolidate arbitrations or the parties agree on a consolidation of arbitration proceedings, the arbitrations shall be consolidated into the arbitration that commenced first, unless otherwise agreed by all the parties (Article 10, third subparagraph). The case reference of the arbitration that was commenced first will be the reference of the arbitration after the consolidation. The filing fee paid in the arbitration that is consolidated with the first arbitration will not be reimbursed, as there is a general principle that the filing fee (of currently US$ 3 000) is non-refundable (Article 1(1) of Appendix III to the Rules). The balance of the sums paid in the arbitration that is consolidated with the first arbitration, and of which the case reference shall no longer be used, will be credited to the portions of the parties in the consolidated arbitration.

After the consolidation, the advance on costs will be fixed, or as the case may be adjusted, on the basis of the amount in dispute of all the claims in the consolidated arbitration in accordance with Article 36 (5).

D. THE ARBITRAL TRIBUNAL

1. General Provisions (Art. 11)

Article 11 of the Rules reads:

> 'General Provisions
>
> 1. Every arbitrator must be and remain impartial and independent of the parties involved in the arbitration.
>
> 2. Before appointment or confirmation, a prospective arbitrator shall sign a statement of acceptance, availability, impartiality and independence. The prospective arbitrator shall disclose in writing to the Secretariat any facts or circumstances which might be of such a nature as to call into question the arbitrator's independence in the eyes of the parties, as well as any circumstances

that could give rise to reasonable doubts as to the arbitrator's impartiality. The Secretariat shall provide such information to the parties in writing and fix a time limit for any comments from them.

3. An arbitrator shall immediately disclose in writing to the Secretariat and to the parties any facts or circumstances of a similar nature to those referred to in Article 11(2) concerning the arbitrator's impartiality or independence which may arise during the arbitration.

4. The decisions of the Court as to the appointment, confirmation, challenge or replacement of an arbitrator shall be final and the reasons for such decisions shall not be communicated.

5. By accepting to serve, arbitrators undertake to carry out their responsibilities in accordance with these Rules.

6. Insofar as the parties have not provided otherwise, the arbitral tribunal shall be constituted in accordance with the provisions of Articles 12 and 13.'

a) The Arbitrator's Impartiality and Independence (Art. 11(1))

It is a general principle of international commercial arbitration that arbitrators should be independent and impartial when carrying out their duties, regardless of whether they have been appointed by a party or an arbitration institution.

When the arbitrators have been nominated by the parties, doubt may be casted on the adherence to these requirements in certain cases. It may occasionally happen in purely domestic arbitrations that arbitrators support or favor to some extent the party that has nominated them, and in very rare cases this may even be regarded as somehow legally acceptable. This is clearly not so in Germany (see Article 1036 ZPO), Belgium (see Article 1686 JC), France (see Article 1456 NCPC) and Switzerland (see Article 180(1)(c)) PILA). See also Article 12 of the UNCITRAL Model Law.

In order to deal appropriately with this kind of issue in a foreseeable way that is detached from any eventually surprising local custom, Article 11(1) of the Rules provides that every arbitrator must be and remain impartial and independent of the parties to the arbitration. No arbitrator may have a direct or even remote or potential personal interest in a specific outcome of the dispute. The 1998 Rules stipulated in the general provision of (then) Article 7 only that the arbitrator had to be and remain independent of the parties, but Article 15(2) also specified that the arbitrator in the conduct of the proceedings should act fairly and impartially. In the 2012 Rules the term impartiality has been included in a number of provisions, more particularly in Articles 11(1), 11(2), 11(3) and 14(1), so as to stress that the requirement of the arbitrator's impartiality is as important as his or her independence. These requirements apply to all arbitrators, whether they are appointed or confirmed, and whether they serve as sole arbitrator, president of an arbitral tribunal or as co-arbitrator. The Rules do not define the notions of 'impartiality' and 'independence'. The international nature of ICC arbitration makes it impossible to provide a universal definition of impartiality and independence.

The concept of independence must be construed in each individual case in light of the geographical and cultural background of the arbitrators and the parties and having regard to the relevant legal systems. Generally, it can be said that the independence of the arbitrator means that the arbitrator may not have any ties with any of the parties, their related entities or their lawyers, whether personal, professional, financial or of any other kind. Should there be any such ties, the arbitrator should not accept to act as arbitrator or, in case of doubt, the arbitrator should make as full a disclosure as possible pursuant to Article 11(2) on facts or circumstances which might be of such a nature as to call into question the arbitrator's independence in the eyes of the parties. A lot of attention is given to the independence of arbitrators who are working as lawyers in large law firms. Lawyers working in a large international law firm with offices in different parts of the world and with clients all over the world will have to check and ensure that the law firm they are working for has no ties with any of the parties, their related entities or their lawyers. This will have to be checked not only at the moment they are asked to serve as arbitrator, but also during the course of the arbitration (pursuant to Article 11(3)). This may turn out to be cumbersome, as the arbitrator may have difficulties in checking whether lawyers in offices of the firm in other jurisdictions are working or have been working for parties to the arbitration or related entities (e.g. holding company or subsidiary).

The concept of 'impartiality' is interpreted as the arbitrator's requirement to be neutral and to act in neutral way towards the parties. Whereas the 1998 Rules focused in Article 15(2) solely on the arbitrators' impartiality in the conduct of the arbitration, the 2012 Rules make the impartiality a condition to be fulfilled so as to be appointed or confirmed as arbitrator. This brings forward the question, which is sometimes raised in treaty-based investor state arbitrations, whether an arbitrator can still be considered as impartial if they have served beforehand in another arbitration as arbitrator or as party counsel where they were known to have adopted a particular position on a specific issue which is also at the heart of the dispute in a new arbitration where they are also asked to serve ('*issue conflict*'). As arbitral awards in commercial arbitration, unlike awards rendered in investor-state arbitrations, generally are not published there will be less discussion about this type of issue conflict. In any event, it will be in the prospective arbitrator's interest to make as full a disclosure as possible pursuant to Article 11(2) on circumstances that could give rise to reasonable doubts as to the arbitrator's impartiality.

The Rules also require that the arbitrator must be available and able to conduct the arbitration in accordance with the Rules (Article 13(1)). These requirements were already contained in Article 9(1) of the 1998 Rules, but the 2012 Rules (Article 9(2)) stress in particular the requirement of availability with much more strength, as they require the arbitrator to confirm personally and expressly before he or she can be appointed or confirmed as arbitrator that he or she is available to conduct the arbitration.

No other requirements are laid down by the Rules for the selection of an arbitrator. The parties therefore have complete freedom in their choice of an impartial and independent arbitrator who is available and able to act as arbitrator. They are not limited by such criteria as the nationality or professional qualifications of the person they choose. It may be noted that the arbitrators appointed or confirmed by the ICC in 2013 came from 86 different countries (see '2013 Statistical Report' published in *ICC International Court of Arbitration Bulletin*, Paris, Vol. 25/Nr. 1 – 2014, p. 11; see also Chapter 7 below). Mention should also be made here of the fact that the ICC International Court of Arbitration does not maintain a list of arbitrators.

b) The Statement of Acceptance, Availability, Impartiality and Independence (Art. 11(2))

To ensure that arbitrators are impartial and independent, the ICC International Court of Arbitration requires them to submit a written 'Statement of Acceptance, Availability,

Impartiality and Independence', which it will examine before appointing or confirming them. Prospective arbitrators are thus required to state in writing all the relevant facts and circumstances which might be of such a nature as to call into question their independence in the eyes of the parties as well as any circumstances that could give rise to reasonable doubts as to the arbitrator's impartiality (Article 11(2) and (3)).

Since 2009 the Statement has been adapted so as to include also a declaration that the prospective arbitrator is available and shall devote the time necessary to conduct the arbitration diligently, efficiently and in accordance with the time limits in the Rules, subject to any extensions granted by the Court. In that respect, the prospective arbitrator must indicate in how many pending arbitration cases he or she is involved as arbitrator and/or as counsel and also in how many court litigations he or she is involved as counsel. Furthermore, the prospective arbitrator has to provide information on commitments in the forthcoming months which might preclude him or her from devoting time to the arbitration. With this detailed statement the Court seeks to have a better view on the arbitrator's real possibility of conducting the arbitration within the time limits set by the Rules or agreed by the parties The Court thus seeks to avoid that arbitrations suffer from delays due by busy arbitrators who accept to act in too many cases.

When accepting a nomination or appointment, prospective arbitrators are also required to sign a declaration confirming that they agree to act as arbitrator in accordance with the ICC Rules of Arbitration (Article 11(5)) and that they accept that their fees and expenses will be fixed exclusively by the Court.

Before completing the 'Statement of Acceptance, Availability, Impartiality and Independence', an arbitrator must consider whether he or she has, or has had, any direct or indirect relations of a financial, professional or other kind with the parties or their lawyers. If he or she lacks the required independence, the appointment must be refused. This may be considered to be the case whenever a prospective arbitrator would not be entitled to act as judge in a similar situation. If the arbitrator comes to the conclusion that he or she is independent but may have relations of the kind mentioned, the arbitrator must state his or her intention to be and remain independent of each of the parties and disclose the facts and circumstances that may be of such a nature as to call into question his or her independence in the eyes of the parties. The ICC Court advises arbitrators to reveal such facts and circumstances in the event of doubt. The test to be applied for disclosure concerning the independence of the arbitrator is 'facts or circumstances which might be of such a nature as to call into question the arbitrator's independence in the eyes of the parties'. The standard of 'in the eyes of the parties' is considered to be a subjective standard as it is to be examined by the prospective arbitrator on a case-by-case basis. However, the test to be applied for disclosure concerning the impartiality of the arbitrator is 'circumstances that could give rise to reasonable doubts'. This standard of 'reasonable doubts' is considered to be an objective standard reflecting what a 'reasonable person' standing in the shoes of a party would consider in the given circumstances, even if the prospective arbitrator must examine the matter of disclosure on a case-by-case basis.

The International Bar Association (IBA) has developed Guidelines on Conflicts on Interest in International Arbitration (2004, revised in 2014) which may give some assistance to prospective arbitrators as to whether any disclosure of information should be made by the prospective arbitrator and as to whether or not he or she may accept to serve as arbitrator. However, these Guidelines and the different lists of situations published in these Guidelines may turn out to be incompatible with the approach of the ICC Court. Whereas the purpose of the IBA Guidelines is to list situations where it is considered appropriate to make a disclosure (waivable red list and orange list) and situations where it is considered not necessary to make a disclosure (green list) as well as situations where it is held that there is a conflict of interest preventing a prospective arbitrator from being appointed or confirmed as arbitrator (non-waivable red list), the ICC Court takes a more subjective approach. A prospective arbitrator who makes an incomplete disclosure must be aware that, in case the non-disclosed information becomes known after his or her appointment or confirmation as arbitrator, may run the risk of a challenge being raised against him or her on the basis of such information. Depending on the jurisdiction and the applicable procedural law, the arbitrator's deliberate failure to disclose information relating to his or her independence or impartiality might jeopardize the award and his or her personal reputation may suffer from such attitude.

When the ICC Court has to decide whether to appoint or confirm an arbitrator, it may take into account a number of circumstances, including the possibly different regions and legal traditions of the parties involved in the arbitration. Because of the subjective standard '*in the eyes of the parties*', it is not possible in ICC arbitration to establish a list of situations that could be considered 'objectively' as situations where never a disclosure should be make like the 'green list' of the IBA Guidelines. The 'orange list' of the IBA Guidelines is also of no practical use in ICC arbitration for a prospective arbitrator to determine whether or no he or she should make a disclosure. In ICC arbitration, as the ICC statement form indicates it, any doubt should be resolved in favor of disclosure.

The ICC will not appoint or confirm a prospective arbitrator until it has in its possession a duly completed and signed Statement of Acceptance, Availability, Impartiality and Independence. In the case of party-nominated arbitrators, their forms are sent to the Secretariat and then forwarded to the parties together with a copy of the curriculum vitae which the Secretariat will have previously requested them to complete (see Appendix 2 and 3 below). If the statement is 'unqualified', in the sense that the arbitrator has not disclosed any facts or circumstances that could call into question his or her independence in the eyes of the parties or that could give rise to reasonable doubts as to his or her impartiality, the parties are not invited to comment, although they are nevertheless free to do so if they wish. If an arbitrator accepts his or her appointment but mentions circumstances of the kind described above relating to impartiality and independence, this 'qualified' statement of impartiality and independence is forwarded to the parties for their reactions. The Secretariat sets them a time limit (usually seven to ten days) for submitting any comments they may have (Article 11(2)).

If the arbitrator's statement is unqualified or, if qualified, does not give rise to any objection from any party, the Secretary General has the power pursuant to Article 13(2) to confirm arbitrators nominated by the parties or in accordance with their agreement. This allows the constitution of the arbitral tribunal to be accomplished more quickly.

If, a party objects to an arbitrator within the time limit set upon the communication of his or her statement, the Court has to decide whether or not to confirm or appoint the arbitrator pursuant to Article 13(1). For this purpose, it will consider the circumstances that have been disclosed and any additional facts that may have been submitted by the parties, and will examine these in the light of the Rules – especially Articles 11 and 41 – and the applicable law, before making its decision.

If the Court decides not to confirm an arbitrator, it asks the party having nominated the arbitrator to choose another arbitrator within a certain time limit (usually 15 days), failing which the appointment will be made by the Court itself (Article 12(2)).

ARBITRATION CASE No. ______________

2012 RULES

ICC ARBITRATOR STATEMENT OF

ACCEPTANCE, AVAILABILITY, IMPARTIALITY AND INDEPENDENCE

Family Name(s): ____________________ Given Name(s): ________________________

Please tick all relevant boxes.

1. ACCEPTANCE

Acceptance

☐ **I agree** to serve as arbitrator under and in accordance with the 2012 ICC Rules of Arbitration ("**Rules**"). I confirm that I am familiar with the Rules. I accept that my fees and expenses will be fixed exclusively by the ICC Court (Article 2(4) of Appendix III to the Rules).

Non-acceptance

☐ **I decline** to serve as arbitrator in this case. *(If you tick here, simply date and sign the form without completing any other sections.)*

2. AVAILABILITY

I confirm, on the basis of the information presently available to me, that I can devote the time necessary to conduct this arbitration diligently, efficiently and in accordance with the time limits in the Rules, subject to any extensions granted by the Court pursuant to Articles 23(2) and 30 of the Rules. I understand that it is important to complete the arbitration as promptly as reasonably practicable and that the ICC Court will consider the duration and conduct of the proceedings when fixing my fees (Article 2(2) of Appendix III to the Rules). My current professional engagements are as below for the information of the ICC Court and the parties.

Principal professional activity *(e.g. lawyer, arbitrator, academic)*:

____

Number of currently pending cases in which I am involved *(i.e. arbitrations and activities pending now, not previous experience; additional details you wish to make known to the ICC Court and to the parties in relation to these matters can be provided on a separate sheet):*

	As tribunal chair/ sole arbitrator	As co-arbitrator	As counsel
Arbitrations			
Court litigation	*Not applicable*	*Not applicable*	

Furthermore, I am aware of commitments which might preclude me from devoting time to this arbitration during the following periods:

3. INDEPENDENCE AND IMPARTIALITY *(Tick one box and please provide details below and/or, if necessary, on a separate sheet.)*

In deciding which box to tick, you should take into account, having regard to Article 11(2) of the Rules, whether there exists any past or present relationship, direct or indirect, between you and any of the parties, their related entities or their lawyers or other representatives, whether financial, professional or of any other kind. <u>Any doubt must be resolved in favour of disclosure.</u> Any disclosure should be complete and specific, identifying *inter alia* relevant dates (both start and end dates), financial arrangements, details of companies and individuals, and all other relevant information.

☐ **Nothing to disclose:** I am impartial and independent and intend to remain so. To the best of my knowledge, and having made due enquiry, there are no facts or circumstances, past or present, that I should disclose because they might be of such a nature as to call into question my independence in the eyes of any of the parties and no circumstances that could give rise to reasonable doubts as to my impartiality.

☐ **Acceptance with disclosure:** I am impartial and independent and intend to remain so. However, mindful of my obligation to disclose any facts or circumstances which might be of such a nature as to call into question my independence in the eyes of any of the parties or that could give rise to reasonable doubts as to my impartiality, I draw attention to the matters below and/or on the attached sheet.

Date: ______________________ Signature: ______________________________

The information requested in this form will be considered by the ICC Court and its Secretariat solely for the purpose of your appointment or confirmation as arbitrator in ICC proceedings. The information will remain confidential and will be stored in a case management database system. However, it may be disclosed solely to the parties and their counsel in the arbitration proceeding referenced above for the purposes of that proceeding. According to Article 32 and, in particular, Article 40 of the French law "Informatique et Libertés" of 6 January 1978, you may access this information and ask for rectification by writing to the Secretariat of the Court.

Whenever the ICC International Court of Arbitration, acting on the proposal of an ICC national committee or group, appoints a co-arbitrator on behalf of a party that has failed to nominate one, a sole arbitrator, or the president of an arbitral tribunal, it likewise examines the circumstances likely to affect the prospective arbitrator's impartiality and independence. The Court does not inform the parties of any reservations it may have, particularly if it decides not to appoint the person put forward as arbitrator by a national committee or group. It thus tries to avoid the risk of prospective appointees making a qualified statement of independence. Should this happen, the Court will generally ask the national committee or group to make another proposal. However, in exceptional circumstances, if the Secretariat considers the disclosure made by the prospective arbitrator to be of minor importance, it may decide to communicate the statement and CV of the person proposed by the ICC national committee or group for comments to the parties. If a party then objects to the person proposed, the Court will decide whether or not to appoint the person as arbitrator pursuant to Article 13(3). It may be noted that generally the Secretariat does not inform the parties of the person proposed by a national committee or group until that person has been appointed as arbitrator by the Court.

The ICC International Court of Arbitration's decision to confirm or appoint an arbitrator is final and the parties are not informed of the reasons for its decision (Article 11(4)).

c) Ongoing Duty to Disclose Information concerning the Arbitrator's Impartiality or Independence (Art. 11(3))

It should be pointed out that the requirement for the arbitrator to be and remain independent does not end with the signing of the Statement of Acceptance, Availability, Impartiality and Independence. The arbitrator should immediately inform the Secretariat and the parties in writing of any similar facts and circumstances that arise in the course of the ensuing arbitration (Article 11(3)).

Arbitrators who are members of a large international law firm with offices in different parts of the world and with clients all over the world may find it difficult to check and ensure on an ongoing basis that the law firm they are working for has no ties with any of the parties, their related entities or their lawyers. It will not be sufficient to make a statement that they cannot rule out that the law firm might be involved in matters for or against one of the parties to the arbitration during the course of the arbitration. Such statement does not exclude that an arbitrator may be challenged for a conflict of interest, should a situation arise where the arbitrator's firm has accepted to work on a matter for or against one of the parties to the arbitration or for a related entity thereof. In such case, the Court shall have to decide on the challenge pursuant to Article 14(3).

d) Finality and (Facultative) Communication of Reasons for Decisions of the Court (Art. 11(4))

Decisions taken by the Court as to the appointment, confirmation, challenge or replacement of an arbitrator (pursuant to Articles 13, 14 and 15) are final. Whereas the Court is able to reconsider other decisions taken under the ICC Rules of Arbitration, this is not so with respect to decisions taken regarding the constitution of the arbitral tribunal and the challenge or replacement of arbitrators. This provision should prevent parties from raising objections against such decisions taken by the

Court. Accordingly, this provision should allow the arbitration to proceed, as soon as the Court has taken its decision. In case the Court rejects a challenge against an arbitrator, a party is not able to ask the Court to reconsider its decision. However, this does not prevent a party from possibly raising another challenge at a later stage if is based on new facts or other circumstances than those that constituted the basis for the rejected challenge.

The reasons for decisions taken by the Court as to the appointment, confirmation, challenge or replacement of an arbitrator (pursuant to Articles 13, 14 and 15) are not communicated, unless – according to the new ICC Court policy – the parties agree otherwise and ask so in advance. When the 2012 Rules were drafted, it was discussed whether the Court‘s practice of not-communicating reasons for decisions taken by the Court as to the appointment, confirmation, challenge or replacement of an arbitrator should be maintained. It was decided at that time to leave the Rules and the Court's practice in this respect unchanged. Not only, it was felt that it would be delicate and time consuming to draft reasons for decisions on non-confirmations of arbitrators or on decisions accepting a challenge or replacing an arbitrator. Moreover, it was considered that providing reasons might lead to more discussions on these decisions and might provoke more challenges and in the end complicate and delay the arbitration proceedings. The fact that the Court does not communicate reasons for its decisions on appointments or confirmations, challenges or replacements of arbitrators does not mean that there are no reasons underlying the decision. Every decision taken by the Court is taken after careful consideration of all the facts and circumstances and is generally taken after the Secretariat has prepared a report. If a challenge is submitted to the plenary session of the Court, there will be a full debate with all the members attending the session being able to express their views and after one Court member will have made a report on the matter.

In October 2015, however, the ICC Court announced a policy change in this respect. In response to growing users' demand, the ICC Court announced that it will communicate reasons for many of the administrative decisions it is called to take under the ICC Rules of Arbitration, where all the parties to a case so agree. The ICC Court may communicate henceforth the reasons for its decisions made on the challenge of an arbitrator and on a decision to initiate replacement proceedings and subsequently to replace an arbitrator on the Court's own motion. The Court may also communicate the reasons for its decisions regarding the consolidation of arbitration proceedings and '*prima facie*' decisions on jurisdiction. A request for the communication of reasons must be made in advance of the relevant decision in respect of which reasons are sought. The Court may subject the communication of reasons to an increase of the administrative expenses, normally not to exceed US$ 5 000. By changing its practice, the ICC Court tries to respond to arbitration users' frequent request that the decisions of the Court be more predictable on the basis of past practice. If the Court communicates reasons for its decisions, this does not alter the legal nature of its decisions; the decisions are of an administrative, not of a judicial nature. More information on this new policy will be available at the ICC website (<www.iccwbo.org>) and in the ICC Dispute Resolution Library at <www.iccdrl.com>.

e) The Arbitrator's Duty to Respect the Rules (Art. 11(5))

The general provision that arbitrators, by accepting to serve, undertake to carry out their responsibilities in accordance with the Rules, entail a number of obligations. Not only the arbitrators undertake to accept the requirements of impartiality and independence in conducting the arbitration. Moreover, they may not resign without cause (in this regard, see Article 15). Article 22 also obliges the arbitrators to make every effort to conduct the arbitration in an expeditious and cost-effective manner. Pursuant to Article 24 the arbitrators shall organize a case management conference and establish a procedural timetable that they intend to follow for the conduct of the arbitration, after having consulted the parties. The arbitrators also accept to respect the time limits set by the Rules or as amended by the Court (Article 23 and 30).

f) Party Autonomy in Relation to the Constitution of the Arbitral Tribunal (Art. 11(6))

The ICC International Court of Arbitration will take account of any special agreements between the parties relating to the constitution of the arbitral tribunal that may depart from the Rules of Arbitration (see Chapter 4). If nothing has been agreed between the parties, or if a party fails to exercise its rights in this regard, the Court takes all appropriate steps in accordance with the Rules

Article 11(6) states that the arbitral tribunal is constituted in accordance with Articles 12 and 13 of the Rules, 'insofar as the parties have not provided otherwise'. It thereby recognizes the parties' freedom to choose the arbitrators and their number (again, see Chapter 4).

For instance, the parties are free to agree that they will appoint the arbitrator(s) themselves, or that the arbitrator(s) will be appointed directly by the ICC Court, or its President (or Secretary General), without the involvement of a national committee or group.

2. The Constitution of the Arbitral Tribunal (Art. 12)

Article 12 of the Rules reads:

> 'Constitution of the Arbitral Tribunal
>
> *Number of Arbitrators*
>
> 1. The disputes shall be decided by a sole arbitrator or by three arbitrators.
>
> 2. Where the parties have not agreed upon the number of arbitrators, the Court shall appoint a sole arbitrator, save where it appears to the Court that the dispute is such as to warrant the appointment of three arbitrators. In such case, the claimant shall nominate an arbitrator within a period of 15 days from the receipt of the notification of the decision of the Court, and the respondent shall nominate an arbitrator within a period of 15 days from the receipt of the notification of the nomination made by the Claimant. If a party fails to nominate an arbitrator, the appointment shall be made by the Court.
>
> *Sole Arbitrator*
>
> 3. Where the parties have agreed that the dispute shall be resolved by a sole arbitrator, they may, by agreement, nominate the sole arbitrator for confirmation. If the parties fail to nominate a sole arbitrator within 30 days from the date when the claimant's Request for Arbitration has been received by the other party, or within such additional time as may be allowed by the Secretariat, the sole arbitrator shall be appointed by the Court.

Three Arbitrators

4. Where the parties have agreed that the dispute shall be resolved by three arbitrators, each party shall nominate in the Request and the Answer, respectively, one arbitrator for confirmation. If a party fails to nominate an arbitrator, the appointment shall be made by the Court.

5. Where the dispute is to be referred to three arbitrators, the third arbitrator, who will act as president of the arbitral tribunal, shall be appointed by the Court, unless the parties have agreed upon another procedure for such appointment, in which case the nomination will be subject to confirmation pursuant to Article 13. Should such procedure not result in a nomination within 30 days from the confirmation or appointment of the co-arbitrators or any other time limit agreed by the parties or fixed by the Court, the third arbitrator shall be appointed by the Court.

6. Where there are multiple claimants or multiple respondents, and where the dispute is to be referred to three arbitrators, the multiple claimants, jointly, and the multiple respondents, jointly, shall nominate an arbitrator for confirmation pursuant to Article 13.

7. Where an additional party has been joined, and where the dispute is to be referred to three arbitrators, the additional party may, jointly with the claimant(s) or with the respondent(s), nominate an arbitrator for confirmation pursuant to Article 13.

8. In the absence of a joint nomination pursuant to Articles 12(6) or 12(7) and where all parties are unable to agree to a method for the constitution of the arbitral tribunal, the Court may appoint each member of the arbitral tribunal and shall designate one of them to act as president. In such case, the Court shall be at liberty to choose any person it regards as suitable to act as arbitrator, applying Article 13 when it considers this appropriate.'

a) General Remarks

The Rules provide that disputes are decided by a sole arbitrator or an arbitral tribunal comprising three arbitrators (Article 12(1)). In the latter case, the arbitral tribunal consists of two arbitrators designated by the parties ('co-arbitrators') and a third arbitrator who chairs the tribunal.

There are three possible scenarios at the outset of the proceedings:

(i) the parties have made no agreement on the number of arbitrators;
(ii) the parties have agreed that the case will be referred to a sole arbitrator;
(iii) the parties have agreed on the constitution of a three-member arbitral tribunal.

The particular scenario may result from the arbitration agreement or an exchange of correspondence between the parties at the start of the proceedings.

The Rules deal with each of these three situations as described below.

Article 12 of the 2012 Rules brings together Articles 8 and 10 of the 1998 Rules and divides the matter of the constitution of the arbitral tribunal in three sections: the number of arbitrators (which was contained in Article 8 of the 1998 Rules), sole arbitrator and three arbitrators. The provisions of Article 10 of the 1998 Rules dealing with multiple parties have been inserted as Article 12(6) and 12(8). A new Article

12(7) deals with the constitution of the arbitral tribunal following a Request for Joinder pursuant to Article 7.

b) No Agreement between the Parties on the Number of Arbitrators (Art. 12(2))

If there is no agreement between the parties on the number of arbitrators, the decision lies with the ICC International Court of Arbitration. This is also the case when the provisions relating to the number of arbitrators contained in the parties' agreement are not clear enough and the matter cannot be clarified, as, for instance, when the arbitration agreement provides that the dispute will be decided by one or more arbitrators and one party wants a sole arbitrator and the other party a three-member tribunal.

Article 12(2) of the Rules provides in such cases that the Court will appoint a sole arbitrator unless it considers that the case warrants the appointment of three arbitrators. The Court's decision is generally made on the basis of the following criteria: the legal and factual complexity of the case; any features peculiar to the parties, be they natural persons or legal entities; any counterclaim that may have been made; and the amount in dispute. The Court will normally not appoint a sole arbitrator when the amount in dispute is above US$ 30 000 000. It will also consider whether the case involves natural persons, legal entities or a state. If a state or state entity is involved, the Court will usually decide to submit the dispute to a three-member arbitral tribunal, unless the state or state entity specifically requests that the dispute be submitted to a sole arbitrator (J. Fry, S. Greenberg and F. Mazza, *The Secretariat's Guide to ICC Arbitration,* ICC Publication No. 729 E, Paris, 2012, p. 140).

It should be noted that when parties wish their case to be decided by a three-member tribunal and the amount in dispute is much less than US$ 5 000 000, before the arbitral tribunal is constituted the Secretariat of the Court will systematically draw the parties' attention to the financial implications of their choice.

During recent years, parties have agreed on the number of arbitrators in approximately 85% of ICC cases. In two thirds of these cases they did so in their arbitration agreement. In more than 80% of the cases where the parties had agreed on the number of arbitrators, they had opted for a three-member arbitral tribunal. In less than 20% of the cases they agreed that the dispute had to be submitted to a sole arbitrator. If the number of arbitrators was agreed subsequently by the parties, they opted in more than 60% of the cases for a sole arbitrator and in less than 40% of the cases for a three-member arbitral tribunal. Where the parties had not agreed on the number of arbitrators the Court decided in recent years in 80% of the cases that the matter had to be submitted to a sole arbitrator (see J. Fry, S. Greenberg and F. Mazza, *The Secretariat's Guide to ICC Arbitration,* ICC Publication No. 729 E, Paris, 2012, p. 139).

c) The Parties Agree on a Sole Arbitrator (Art. 12(3))

Here, there is an agreement between the parties to the effect that the dispute will be decided by a sole arbitrator. More often than not the parties will decide so after the dispute has arisen, either spontaneously or after being informed of the financial implications of their choice by the Secretariat of the Court.

The Rules provide that in such situations it is possible for the parties jointly to agree upon a person to act as sole arbitrator (Article 12(3)). This rarely happens in practice, however, so the appointment is more often than not made by the Court.

d) The Parties Agree on a Three-Member Tribunal (12(4)-(5))

Here, the parties have decided in their arbitration agreement that any disputes will be referred to three arbitrators. The agreement may sometimes be made after the dispute has arisen. Article 12(4) provides that each party – the claimant in its request for arbitration and the respondent in its answer to the request – nominates a co-arbitrator for confirmation by the ICC International Court of Arbitration. Should either party fail to do so, the appointment is made by the Court. When the parties nominate a co-arbitrator, he or she will not be confirmed by the Secretary General or by the Court until he or she has signed and submitted a statement of acceptance, availability, impartiality and independence pursuant to Article 11(2). Co-arbitrators nominated by the parties must meet the same requirements as presidents of arbitral tribunals and as co-arbitrators.

The third arbitrator, who chairs the arbitral tribunal, is appointed by the Court, unless the parties have agreed upon an alternative method of appointment (Article 12(5)). The parties have considerable freedom in this respect. The choice of the arbitrator to chair the tribunal may for instance be made directly by the parties, or by another body or a third person. Sometimes, the parties provide that the third arbitrator will be appointed directly by the President or the Secretary General of the Court (as opposed to the Court as a whole). It is more common however for the parties to give the co-arbitrators the power to choose the third arbitrator. This happens in approximately half of ICC cases involving a three-member tribunal.

If the president of the arbitral tribunal has been chosen by the parties or on the basis of a special method of appointment, the Court confirms the person appointed (first sentence of Article 12(5)), once the person concerned has submitted a statement of acceptance, availability, impartiality and independence without qualification or a qualified statement that has not given rise to any objections (Article 11(2)).

If the parties are unable to agree on the method by which the third arbitrator is to be appointed, the Court makes the appointment (second sentence of Article 12(5)). In cases where the parties or the co-arbitrators have not agreed on the person to act as president of the arbitral tribunal, but where they have reached agreement on qualifications of the president of the arbitral tribunal (e.g. nationality, language skills, legal education, technical expertise), the Court shall take these agreed qualifications into account, to the extent possible, when selecting the president of the arbitral tribunal.

e) Three-Member Arbitral Tribunals in Multiparty Arbitration (Art. 12(6)-(8))

Article 12(6)-(8) contains provisions to regulate the constitution of the arbitral tribunal in multiparty cases, i.e. those in which there is more than one claimant and/or more than one respondent.

Article 12(6) replaces Article 10(1) of the 1998 Rules and Article 12(8) replaces Article 10(1) of the 1998 Rules. These provisions came in the 1998 Rules in the wake of the decision of the French Court of Cassation in the *Dutco* case (*Sociétés BKMI et Siemens* v. *Société Dutco Construction*, Court of Cassation, 7 January 1992). The claimant, a company named Dutco, began arbitration proceedings against two respondents, Siemens and BKMI. The ICC International Court of Arbitration requested the claimant to nominate a co-arbitrator. In accordance with its practice in such situations, the ICC Court asked the two respondents jointly to nominate a co-arbitrator, as the arbitration agreement in question provided for the constitution of a three-member arbitral tribunal. The respondents questioned this decision and, not having been able to agree on a co-arbitrator, asserted that each of them had been deprived of the right to nominate 'its' co-arbitrator, as had the claimant. In support of their claim, they argued that they had conflicting interests. They ended up jointly nominating a co-arbitrator, notwithstanding all their reservations, but later applied to the French courts for the arbitral tribunal's interim award on this issue to be set aside on the ground that the arbitral tribunal had not been correctly constituted for the aforementioned reason. In its judgment on the decision reached by the Paris Court of Appeal, the French Court of Cassation held (i) that each party had a right to equal treatment when it came to constituting the arbitral tribunal and (ii) that it was not possible to waive this right in an arbitration agreement made before the dispute arose.

(1) Joint Nomination of a Co-arbitrator by Multiple Claimants or by Multiple Respondents (Art. 12(6) and (8)).

Article 12(6) confirms the rule according to which, in cases involving more than one claimant and/or respondent and a three-member tribunal, the claimants must jointly nominate an arbitrator and the respondents must jointly do so likewise. This reflects the practice adopted by the ICC International Court of Arbitration prior to the *Dutco* case.

The provision of Article 12(8), which reflects the previous Article 10(2) introduced in 1998 in the wake of the *Dutco* decision of the French Court of Cassation, specifies that (i) when the claimants or, as is more likely, the respondents have not jointly appointed an arbitrator and (ii) it proves impossible for all parties to reach a general agreement on a special method for constituting the arbitral tribunal in such situations, the ICC Court may appoint all the members of the arbitral tribunal, i.e. the two co-arbitrators and the president of the arbitral tribunal. In this case, the Secretariat of the Court will make sure that, beforehand, the claimant waives its right to nominate an arbitrator, so as to avoid any objection at a later stage. Any nomination of an arbitrator already made by the claimant will therefore be canceled. In such circumstances, the Court may select and appoint any impartial and independent person it considers suitable to act as arbitrator (Article 18(2)) and it may thereby apply Article 13 when it considers this appropriate. There is no need for the Court to seek a proposal from a national committee or group of the ICC, nor does it need to take into account the nationalities of the parties and the prospective arbitrator. Article 13(4) confirms the possibility for the Court to proceed to a direct appointment of arbitrators.

The provisions of Article 12(6) and (8) apply only when a three-member tribunal is to be constituted, as the problems it covers do not arise when a sole arbitrator is appointed.

As Article 12(8) leaves the Court free to decide how to proceed ('may appoint'), it may, where appropriate, choose to follow the practice exclusively applied prior to *Dutco* and ask the respondents jointly to nominate a co-arbitrator. The Court will, however, only rarely decide not to apply Article 12(8).

(2) Constitution of Arbitral Tribunal in case of Joinder of Additional Party (Art. 12(7)).

Since the Rules provide in Article 7 the possibility of joining additional parties, they also needed to provide how the arbitral tribunal shall be constituted if an additional party is joined to the arbitration. Given the above mentioned decision of the French

Court of Cassation, which held that each party has a right to equal treatment when it comes to constituting the arbitral tribunal, the Rules provide an equal right for the additional party to participate in the constitution of the arbitral tribunal. For that reason, an additional party may not be joined to an ICC arbitration after any arbitrator has been confirmed or appointed, unless all parties, including the additional party, agree otherwise (Article 7(1)).

Article 12(7) provides that the additional party has the choice, when a three-member arbitral tribunal must be constituted, to jointly select and nominate a co-arbitrator with the claimant(s) or to jointly select and nominate a co-arbitrator with the respondents. Should the additional party not be able to make such a joint nomination of a co-arbitrator either with the claimant(s) or with the respondent(s), Article 12(8) applies. Should the parties not be able to agree on a method for the constitution of the arbitral tribunal, the Court then appoint each member of the arbitral tribunal and designate one of them as president of the arbitral tribunal.

e) The Time Limits for Appointing Arbitrators

(1) Sole Arbitrators.

Once the Secretariat has notified the respondent of the request for arbitration in accordance with Article 3(2) of the Rules, the parties have 30 days during which to agree upon a sole arbitrator. This time limit may be extended by the Secretariat if need be (Article 12(3)). An extension will normally be granted if requested by all parties. If no nomination is made at the end of this period, the sole arbitrator will be appointed by the Court (Article 12(3)).

(2) Three-Member Arbitral Tribunal.

The claimant nominates an arbitrator in the request for arbitration, and the respondent does likewise in the answer to the request or at any rate within 30 days of receiving the request for arbitration from the Secretariat (Article 12(4)). If the respondent is granted an extension of the time limit allowed for filing an answer to the request for arbitration, this does not affect the said time limit for nominating an arbitrator (see Article 5(2)), unless the parties expressly agree otherwise.

If the parties have not agreed on the number of arbitrators and the ICC Court decides that the case should be referred to a three-member arbitral tribunal, the claimant must nominate one arbitrator within 15 days of receiving notification of the Court's decision concerning the number of arbitrators. The respondent must then nominate a co-arbitrator within 15 days of receiving notification of the claimant's nomination (Article 12(2)). The respondent is therefore obliged to nominate a co-arbitrator once the claimant has nominated one.

The ICC Court usually appoints the third arbitrator to chair the arbitral tribunal, unless the parties have agreed otherwise in writing. Should the parties have made such an agreement, the person must be nominated within 30 days from the confirmation or appointment of the co-arbitrators or any other time limit they have set or within the time limit fixed by the Court (Article 12(5)).

It should be mentioned that Article 11(6) allows parties to modify any time limits relating to the nomination of arbitrators. In doing so, however, consideration should be given to Article 38 of the Rules.

3. Appointment and Confirmation of Arbitrators (Art. 13)

Article 13 of the Rules reads:

> 'Appointment and Confirmation of the Arbitrators
>
> 1. In confirming or appointing arbitrators, the Court shall consider the prospective arbitrator's nationality, residence and other relationships with the countries of which the parties or the other arbitrators are nationals and the prospective arbitrator's availability and ability to conduct the arbitration in accordance with the Rules. The same shall apply where the Secretary General confirms arbitrators pursuant to Article 13(2).
>
> 2. The Secretary General may confirm as co-arbitrators, sole arbitrators and presidents of arbitral tribunals persons nominated by the parties or pursuant to their particular agreements, provided that the statement they have submitted contains no qualification regarding impartiality or independence or that a qualified statement regarding impartiality or independence has not given rise to objections. Such confirmation shall be reported to the Court at its next session. If the Secretary General considers that a co-arbitrator, sole arbitrator or president of an arbitral tribunal should not be confirmed, the matter shall be submitted to the Court.
>
> 3. Where the Court is to appoint an arbitrator, it shall make the appointment upon a proposal of a National Committee or Group of the ICC that it considers to be appropriate. If the Court does not accept the proposal made, or if the National Committee or Group fails to make the proposal requested within the time limit fixed by the Court, the Court may repeat its request, request a proposal from another National Committee or Group that it considers to be appropriate, or appoint directly any person whom it regards as suitable.
>
> 4. The Court may also appoint directly to act as arbitrator any person whom it regards as suitable where:
> a) one or more of the parties is a state or claims to be a state entity; or
> b) the Court considers that it would be appropriate to appoint an arbitrator from a country or territory where there is no National Committee or Group; or
> c) the President certifies to the Court that circumstances exist which, in the President's opinion, make a direct appointment necessary and appropriate.
>
> 5. The sole arbitrator or the president of the arbitral tribunal shall be of a nationality other than those of the parties. However, in suitable circumstances and provided that none of the parties objects within the time limit fixed by the Court, the sole arbitrator or the president of the arbitral tribunal may be chosen from a country of which any of the parties is a national.'

a) General Remarks

Appointing and confirming arbitrators are amongst the ICC International Court of Arbitration's key tasks. The confirmation of arbitrators, as opposed to their appointment, is peculiar to ICC arbitration. The Court will 'confirm' an arbitrator who has been nominated by a party or a third person, whereas it will 'appoint' an arbitrator who has been proposed by a national committee or group which it has chosen.

Whereas the 1998 Rules provided (Article 9(4) and (6)) a limited possibility for the Court to appoint an arbitrator without a proposal by a national committee, the 2012 Rules have expanded the power of the Court to appoint directly arbitrators without a proposal by a national committee. Moreover, the 2012 Rules also provide the possibility to call upon a group to propose an arbitrator.

b) Circumstances to be Considered when Choosing Arbitrators (Art. 13(1))

Article 13(1) of the Rules lists several criteria, in addition to the impartiality and independence required by Article 11(1), which the Secretary General or the Court, as the case may be, should take into consideration when confirming or appointing arbitrators:

(i) the person's nationality, place of residence and any other connections with the countries of which the parties or the other arbitrators are nationals, and

(ii) the person's availability and ability to conduct the arbitration in accordance with the Rules of Arbitration. Although the Rules do not specify that an arbitrator should have had legal training or experience, in most ICC arbitrations the persons appointed as arbitrators are lawyers.

These criteria are particularly important for the ICC Court when appointing a sole arbitrator or the president of an arbitral tribunal (see Article 13(5)). The reference in the Rules to the arbitrator's availability and ability to conduct the arbitration allows the Court not to confirm or appoint an arbitrator who clearly has not enough time or is unable to conduct the arbitration in accordance with the Rules (for example, due to inadequate language or other special skills, poor health, or being barred from entering the state where the place of the arbitration is situated).

The criteria listed in Article 13(1) also apply, in theory, to arbitrators nominated by the parties. However, given the importance of the parties' right to take part in the constitution of the arbitral tribunal, the Court will exercise restraint if the arbitrator's impartiality and independence are not in doubt and use the discretion it has under this provision only when faced with serious infringements.

c) Confirmation of Arbitrators (Art. 13(2))

The provision contained in Article 13(2) allows the Secretary General of the ICC International Court of Arbitration to confirm arbitrators under certain conditions. This power covers arbitrators nominated by the parties, sole arbitrators and presidents of arbitral tribunals. The purpose of the provision is to allow the arbitral tribunal to be constituted quickly in straightforward cases.

If the prospective arbitrator has (i) submitted a statement of independence without qualification regarding impartiality or independence, called an 'unqualified' statement of impartiality and independence (Article 13(2)), or (ii) a 'qualified' statement of independence regarding impartiality or independence that has not given rise to any objections from the parties, the Secretary General will confirm the arbitrator and such confirmation will be reported to the Court when it next meets (Article 13(2)). In recent years two thirds of the confirmations of arbitrators where made by the Secretary General and only one third of the confirmations of arbitrators was made by the Court.

It is not within the Secretary General's powers to refuse to confirm an arbitrator. If the Secretary General doubts that an arbitrator should be confirmed, the matter is referred to the Court. This will be the case, for example, if an arbitrator has submitted a

Figure 2. Formation of a three-member arbitral tribunal

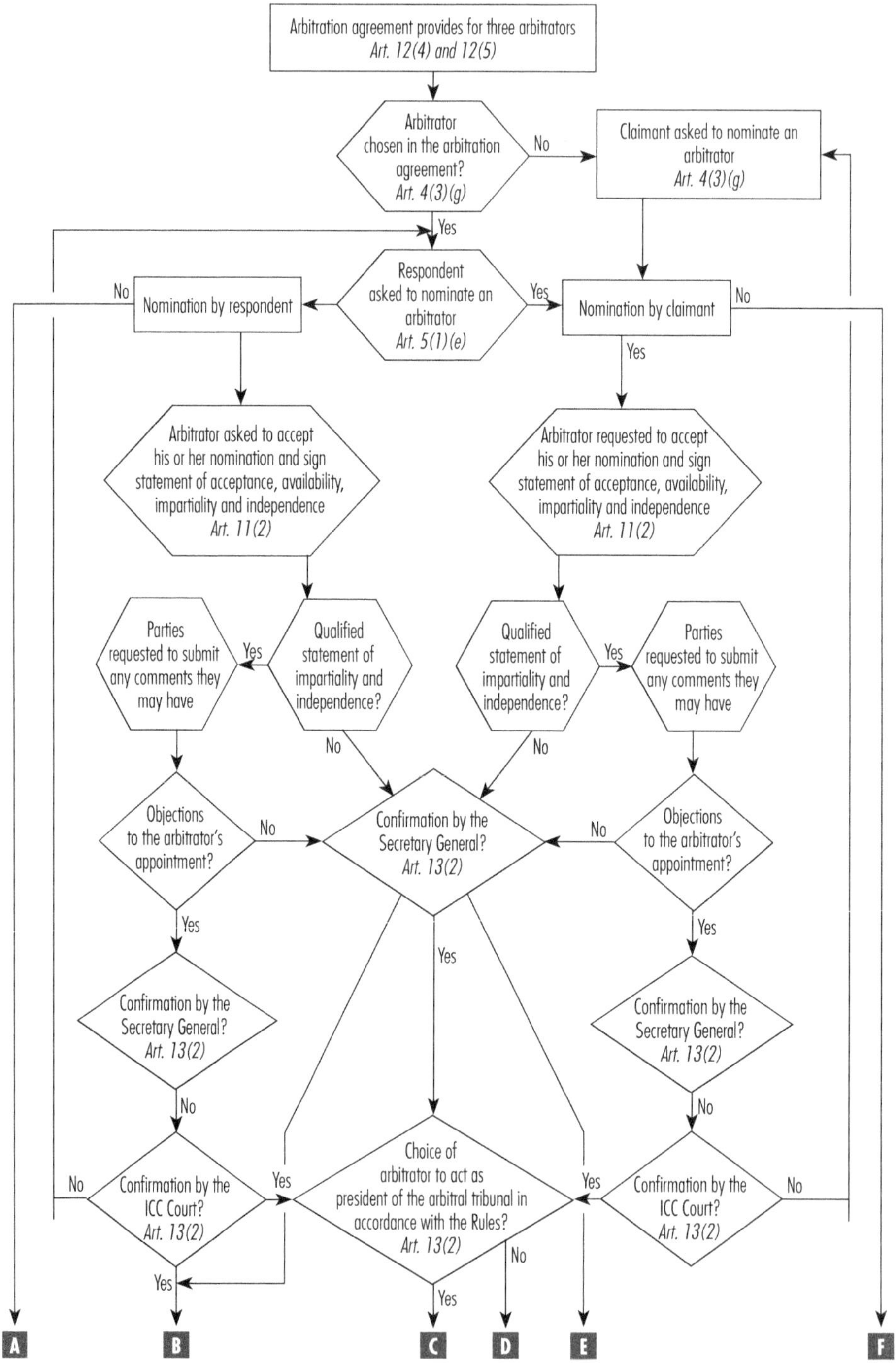

… continued on facing page

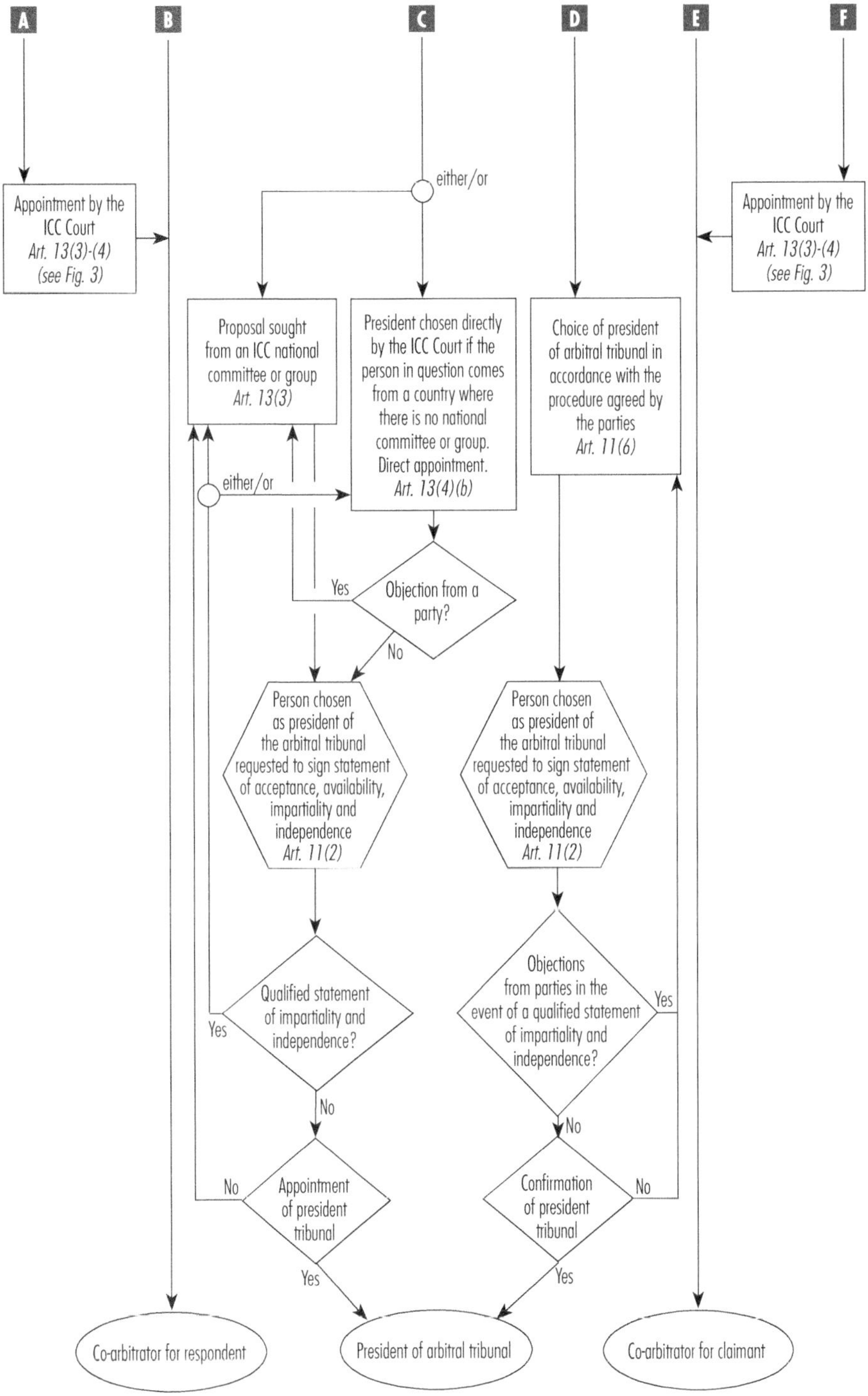
A
B
C
D
E
F
either/or
Appointment by the ICC Court Art. 13(3)-(4) (see Fig. 3)
Appointment by the ICC Court Art. 13(3)-(4) (see Fig. 3)
Proposal sought from an ICC national committee or group Art. 13(3)
President chosen directly by the ICC Court if the person in question comes from a country where there is no national committee or group. Direct appointment. Art. 13(4)(b)
Choice of president of arbitral tribunal in accordance with the procedure agreed by the parties Art. 11(6)
either/or
Yes
Objection from a party?
No
Person chosen as president of the arbitral tribunal requested to sign statement of acceptance, availability, impartiality and independence Art. 11(2)
Person chosen as president of the arbitral tribunal requested to sign statement of acceptance, availability, impartiality and independence Art. 11(2)
Qualified statement of impartiality and independence?
Yes
No
Objections from parties in the event of a qualified statement of impartiality and independence?
Yes
No
Appointment of president tribunal
No
Yes
Confirmation of president tribunal
No
Yes
Co-arbitrator for respondent
President of arbitral tribunal
Co-arbitrator for claimant

Figure 3. Appointment of an arbitrator on behalf of a party

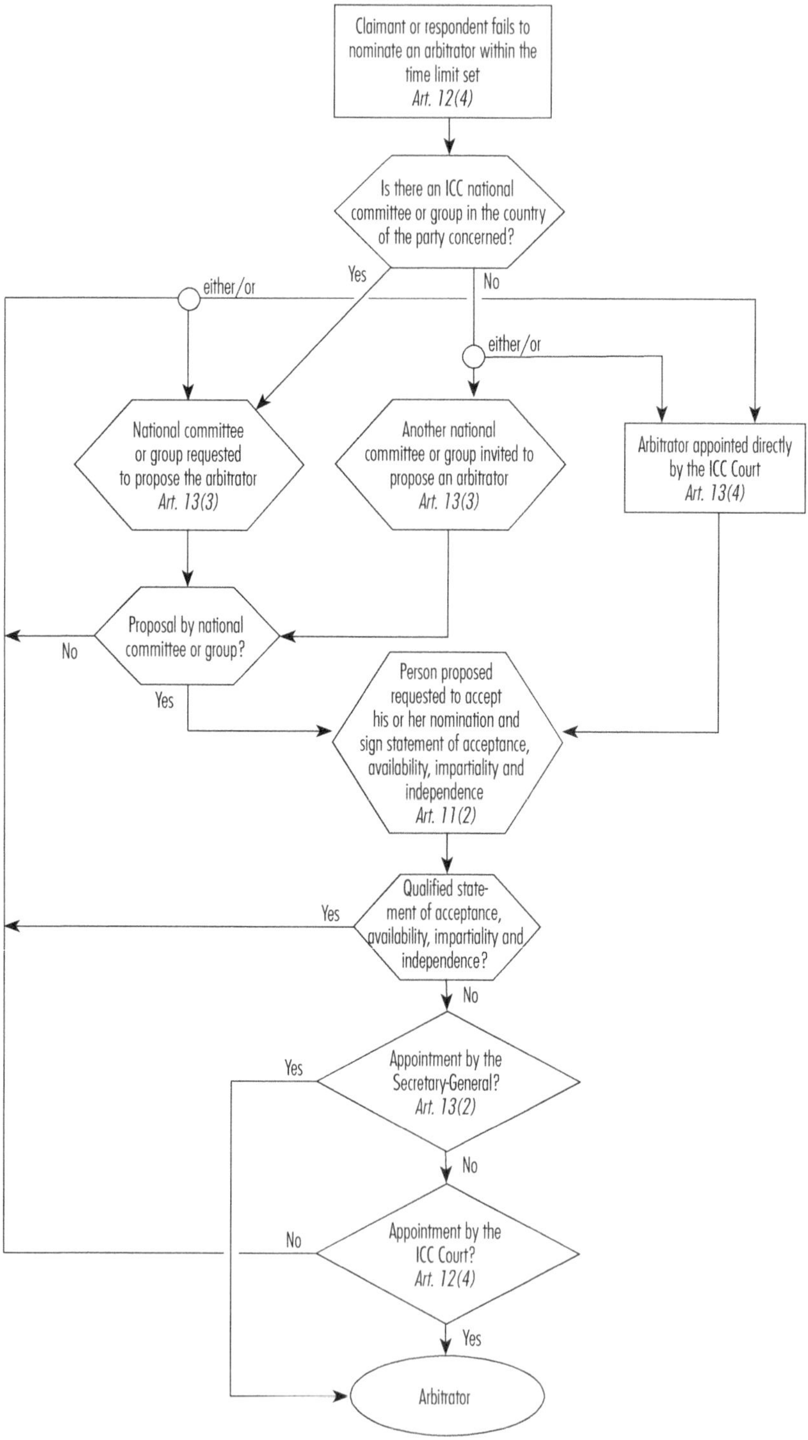

Figure 4. Arbitration agreement providing for a sole arbitrator

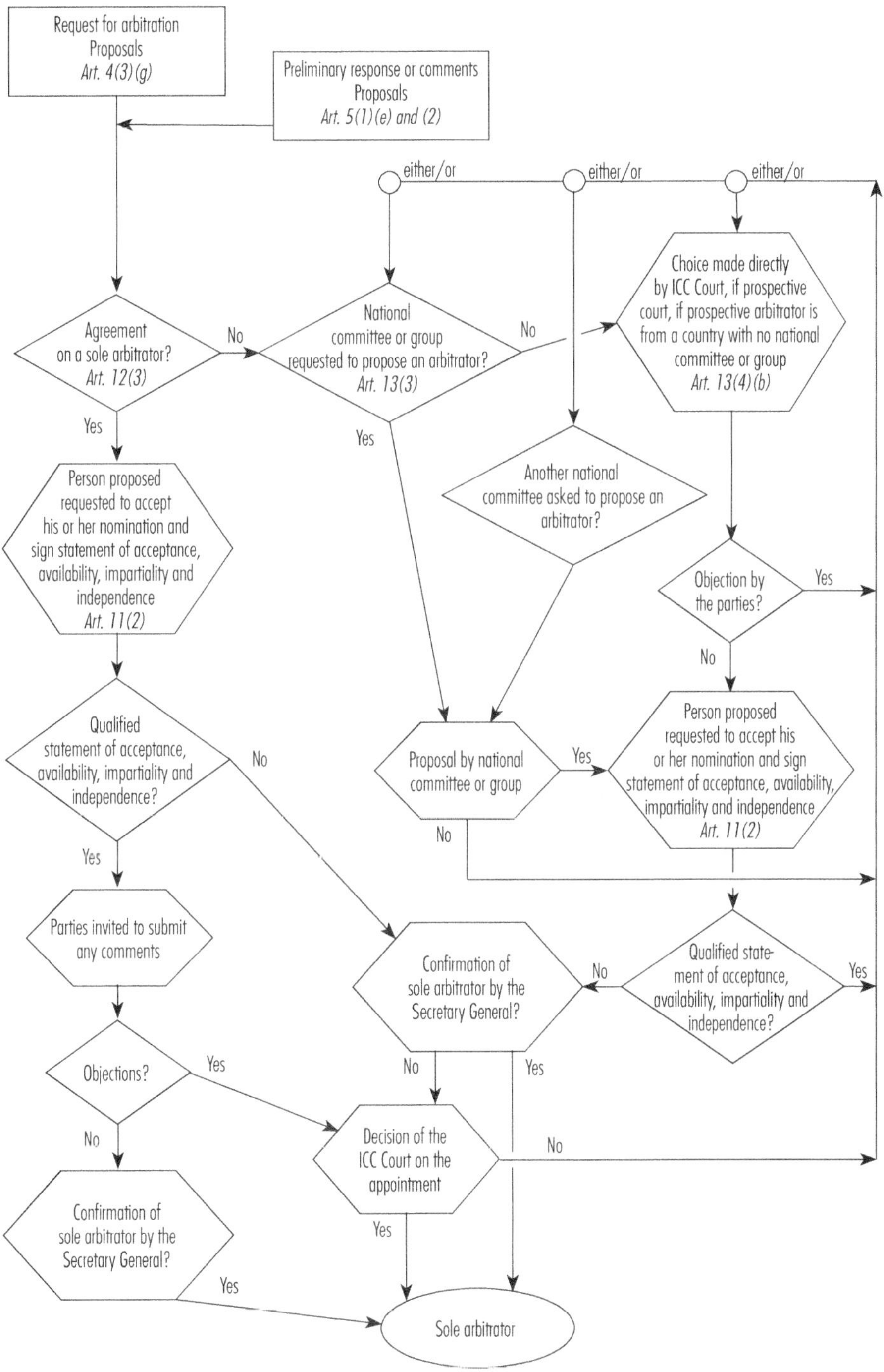

Figure 5. Unspecified number of arbitrators

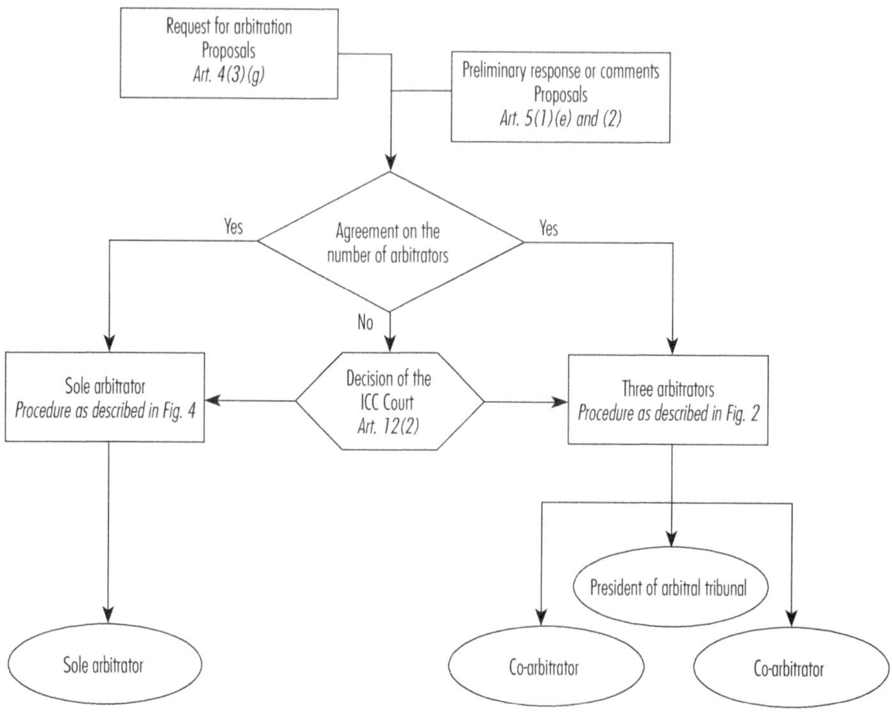

qualified statement of independence to which objections have been made by one of the parties. Should the person concerned not be confirmed as arbitrator, the nominating party will be asked to nominate another arbitrator within a given time limit (usually between 15 and 30 days).

d) Proposals by National Committees or Groups (Art. 13(3))

Appointments of sole arbitrators and presidents of arbitral tribunals are made by the Court, if the parties have not provided for an alternative method of appointment and are unable to agree upon the choice of an individual. This is also the case when parties fail to nominate an arbitrator.

Before appointing a sole arbitrator or the president of an arbitral tribunal, the Court invites one of the ICC's national committees (currently 87 in number) or groups (currently 3 in number) to make a proposal. In this connection, the Rules were changed to allow the Court to seek proposals from groups, and not only from national committees. This should allow the Court to appoint arbitrators from such territories, where there is not a national committee but where there is a community of business people that can liaise with the ICC. The ICC has meanwhile three groups in territories without a national committee, namely Hong Kong, Macao and Chinese Taipei.

The parties are never informed of the choice of the national committee or group, so as to avoid any interference in or pressure on the choice of candidate. They are simply informed that the necessary steps for appointing an arbitrator have been taken. Once the Court has selected a national committee or group, the Secretariat gives the chosen national committee or group a time limit within which to propose an arbitrator for appointment by the Court at one of its future sessions.

In most cases, the choice of the national committee or group will determine the nationality of the arbitrator, as national committees or groups generally propose citizens of their own country. When selecting a national committee or group, the Court takes into account the nationalities of the parties or the countries in which their head offices are situated and the countries from which any other persons involved in the procedure originate or where they are established, including any co-arbitrators. Where appropriate, general regional or geopolitical considerations may have a bearing on the Court's decision. The Court will also take account of any information provided by the parties, such as the applicable substantive law and the place and the language of the arbitration. Article 41 of the Rules, which obliges the Court to make every effort to ensure that the arbitral award is enforceable at law, may also affect the Court's choice, especially if it emerges that the nationality of the person proposed may be of importance, factually or at law, when it comes to enforcing the arbitral award.

e) The Procedure for Selecting Arbitrators through National Committees or Groups

The national committee or group chosen by the ICC Court proposes an arbitrator in the light of the information given to it by the Secretariat. This will include, in particular, the details of the parties, their counsel and any co-arbitrators nominated by the parties, the nature of the case, the amount in dispute, the applicable law and the place and the language of the arbitration. The proposal must be made within a given time limit – usually 15 days.

If the national committee or group does not make a proposal within the time limit it has been given – which rarely occurs in practice – the Court may renew its request or ask for a proposal from another national committee that it considers appropriate (Article 13(3)).

As soon as the national committee or group has proposed an arbitrator to the Secretariat, the proposal is immediately submitted to the Court at its next session. In most cases, the proposal will be accepted and the appointment made, whether it be a sole arbitrator or the president of an arbitral tribunal.

If the Court does not accept the proposal made by the national committee or group, for example on account of reservations made in the prospective arbitrator's statement of impartiality and independence, or because the person concerned does not possess the required qualifications for conducting the procedure (for instance, is not fluent in the language of the arbitration), the Court, through its Secretariat, will ask the national committee or group to make another proposal, or it will choose another national committee or group for this purpose.

When the Court has to appoint an arbitrator on behalf of a party that has failed to nominate one, it usually proceeds in the same way as when appointing a sole arbitrator or the chair of an arbitral tribunal. It requests a proposal from the national committee or group in the country from which the party concerned originates.

If there is no national committee or group in the country from which a party originates, or if the national committee or group fails to make a proposal within the time limit it has been given, or if its proposal is not accepted by the Court, the appointment may be made directly by the Court without going through a national committee or group (Article 13(3)). The new Rules also provide for other circumstances where the Court may directly appoint arbitrators without a proposal from a national committee, as set out in Article 13(4).

f) Direct Appointment of Arbitrators by the Court (Art. 13(4))

Whereas generally appointments of sole arbitrators and presidents of arbitral tribunals are made by the Court upon a proposal of a national committee, the Court had under the 1998 Rules (Article 9(4)) the possibility to choose the sole arbitrator or the president of the arbitral tribunal from a country where there is no national committee, if neither of the parties objected within the time limit fixed by the Court. This provision avoided the situation in which the Court was prevented from appointing a well-qualified person as arbitrator because he or she comes from a country which does not have a national committee. It also made the selection process even more international. Article 9(4) of the 1998 Rules, however, required the Court to announce in advance that it intended to select an arbitrator from a country without a national committee. As a consequence, if one of the parties made an objection, the Court was not able to choose such person from a country without a national committee and it had to follow the normal method of selecting a national committee and asking the national committee to propose an arbitrator.

The 1998 Rules also provided in Article 9(6) that, in case the Court did not accept the proposal of an arbitrator made by a national committee, or in case the national committee failed to make the proposal requested within the time limit fixed by the Court, or in case a party who failed to nominate a co-arbitrator and the country of which that party was a national had no national committee, the Court could choose any person whom it regarded as suitable. The Court had thereupon to inform the national committee, if one existed, of the country of which such person was a national.

In the past some concerns had been expressed about the standard procedure of seeking a proposal of an arbitrator from a national committee in the first instance. There was a concern that some national committees do not function properly. Some national committees refuse to propose nationals who are living abroad. Also, there was a concern that in some situations – such as investor-state disputes – an appointment of an arbitrator upon proposal of a national committee would not appear to be appropriate, because the membership of national committees is often constituted of businesses and arbitrators proposed by national committees may therefore be perceived to favor business interests. Furthermore, there was a concern that more flexibility was needed to make appointments of arbitrators within very short time limits if so required by the agreement of the parties or during periods of time in which a national committee may not be in a position to guarantee continuity of service.

The new Article 13(4) introduced in the 2012 Rules provides for three further special situations in which the Court may also directly appoint an arbitrator, in addition to the possibility of making a direct appointment pursuant to Article 13(3). These situations are: (a) when a state is a party or a party claims to be a state entity; (b) when the Court considers it appropriate to choose an arbitrator from a country or territory where there is no national committee or group; or (c) when the President of the Court certifies to the Court that circumstances exist which, in the President's opinion, make a direct appointment necessary and appropriate. However, the Rules maintain the principle that the normal method of appointment should be upon the proposal of a national committee or a group.

ICC arbitration is often used by states and state entities. Approximately 10% of ICC arbitrations involve a state or a state entity (9.5% in 2009, see '2009 Statistical Report' published in *ICC International Court of Arbitration Bulletin*, Paris, Vol. 21/Nr. 1 - 2010, p. 8; 10% in 2010, see '2010 Statistical Report' published in *ICC International Court of Arbitration Bulletin*, Paris, Vol. 22/Nr. 1 - 2011, p. 10; 10.2% in 2011, see '2011 Statistical Report' published in *ICC International Court of Arbitration Bulletin*, Paris, Vol. 23/Nr. 1 - 2012, p. 10; 9.9% in 2012, see '2012 Statistical Report' published in *ICC International Court of Arbitration Bulletin*, Paris, Vol. 24/Nr. 1 - 2013, p. 10; see also Report of the ICC Commission on Arbitration and ADR on 'Arbitration Involving States or State Entities', 2012, par. 7, Appendix 16 below). These arbitrations cover both commercial and investment disputes. Approximately 18% of bilateral investment treaties allow for the possibility of using ICC arbitration (Report of the ICC Commission on Arbitration and ADR on 'Arbitration Involving States or State Entities', 2012, par. 10). It is the Court's practice, if it has to determine the number of arbitrators in disputes involving states and state entities, to decide to constitute a three member arbitral tribunal, unless the state or state entity specifically requests that the dispute be submitted to a sole arbitrator. According to ICC statistics, states and state entities often prefer a three-member arbitral tribunal. It has been the Court's practice, when it has to appoint a co-arbitrator on behalf of a state or state entity that has failed to make a nomination, to appoint an arbitrator either from that state or from a state with which that state has cultural affinities.

The Court is increasingly using the new provision of Article 13(4) since its introduction in the 2012 Rules. Where the Court was required to make an appointment of an arbitrator in 2012, it did so in 85% of the cases upon the proposal of a national committee or group, and in the remaining 15% of the cases directly (being 53 direct appointments out of a total of 764 confirmations and appointments made in 2012, see '2012 Statistical Report' published in *ICC International Court of Arbitration Bulletin*, Paris, Vol. 24/Nr. 1 - 2013, p. 11). More than half of these direct appointments concerned co-arbitrators, more than a quarter concerned presidents of three-member arbitral tribunals and less than a quarter of the direct appointments concerned sole arbitrators. From the cases were the Court made direct appointments in 2013 (114 out of a total of 740 confirmations and appointments made in 2013; see '2013 Statistical Report' published in *ICC International Court of Arbitration Bulletin*, Paris, Vol. 25/ Nr. 1 - 2014, p. 10), more than one third of these direct appointments concerned co-arbitrators, far more than one third concerned presidents of three-member arbitral tribunals and a quarter of the direct appointment concerned sole arbitrators.

g) Nationality of the Sole Arbitrator and of the President of the Arbitral Tribunal (Art. 13(5))

For reasons of neutrality, the Rules provide that a sole arbitrator or the president of an arbitral tribunal should not have the same nationality as any of the parties. Whereas there was some discussion in the revision process as to whether or not the nationality provision should be maintained in the Rules, the general sentiment was that having a sole arbitrator or a president of an arbitral tribunal from another nationality than the nationalities of the parties is perceived to be a sign of neutrality and therefore contributes to greater confidence of the parties in the arbitral process. Nonetheless, if justified by the circumstances and none of the parties objects within the time limit set by the Court, or at the express wish of the parties, the sole arbitrator or the chair of an arbitral tribunal may be chosen from a country of which any of the parties is a national

(Article 13(5)). This happens, for instance, when the two co-arbitrators nominated by the parties are of the same nationality and the parties inform the Secretariat that they wish the tribunal to be chaired by an arbitrator of the same nationality.

4. Challenge of Arbitrators (Art. 14)

Article 14 of the Rules reads:

> 'Challenge of Arbitrators
>
> 1. A challenge of an arbitrator, whether for an alleged lack of impartiality or independence, or otherwise, shall be made by the submission to the Secretariat of a written statement specifying the facts and circumstances on which the challenge is based.
>
> 2. For a challenge to be admissible, it must be submitted by a party either within 30 days from receipt by that party of the notification of the appointment or confirmation of the arbitrator, or within 30 days from the date when the party making the challenge was informed of the facts and circumstances on which the challenge is based if such date is subsequent to the receipt of such notification.
>
> 3. The Court shall decide on the admissibility and, at the same time, if necessary, on the merits of a challenge after the Secretariat has afforded an opportunity for the arbitrator concerned, the other party or parties and any other members of the arbitral tribunal to comment in writing within a suitable period of time. Such comments shall be communicated to the parties and to the arbitrators.'

a) The Powers of the ICC International Court of Arbitration

Under the Rules, the power to decide on challenges of arbitrators lies with the ICC International Court of Arbitration. This is a purely administrative procedure concerning the organization and administration of the arbitral proceedings.

Notwithstanding the decision of the Court, the mandatory rules of law applicable to the procedure ('*lex arbitri*') often give the parties the right to apply to the relevant court for an arbitrator to be removed from office or for the arbitral award to be set aside if, for instance, the arbitral tribunal has not been correctly formed. In several countries, including France and Switzerland, state courts have decided that parties may validly decide that a private entity will have the power to hear and settle challenges on the basis of certain rules, without review by state courts. These countries also allow the parties the freedom to decide on the procedure relating to challenges. However, in some countries, including Switzerland, for example, if the Court wrongly rejects a challenge, this may be raised as an argument in support of a plea that the arbitral tribunal was incorrectly constituted when its final award comes before a state court.

Figure 6. Challenge of arbitrators

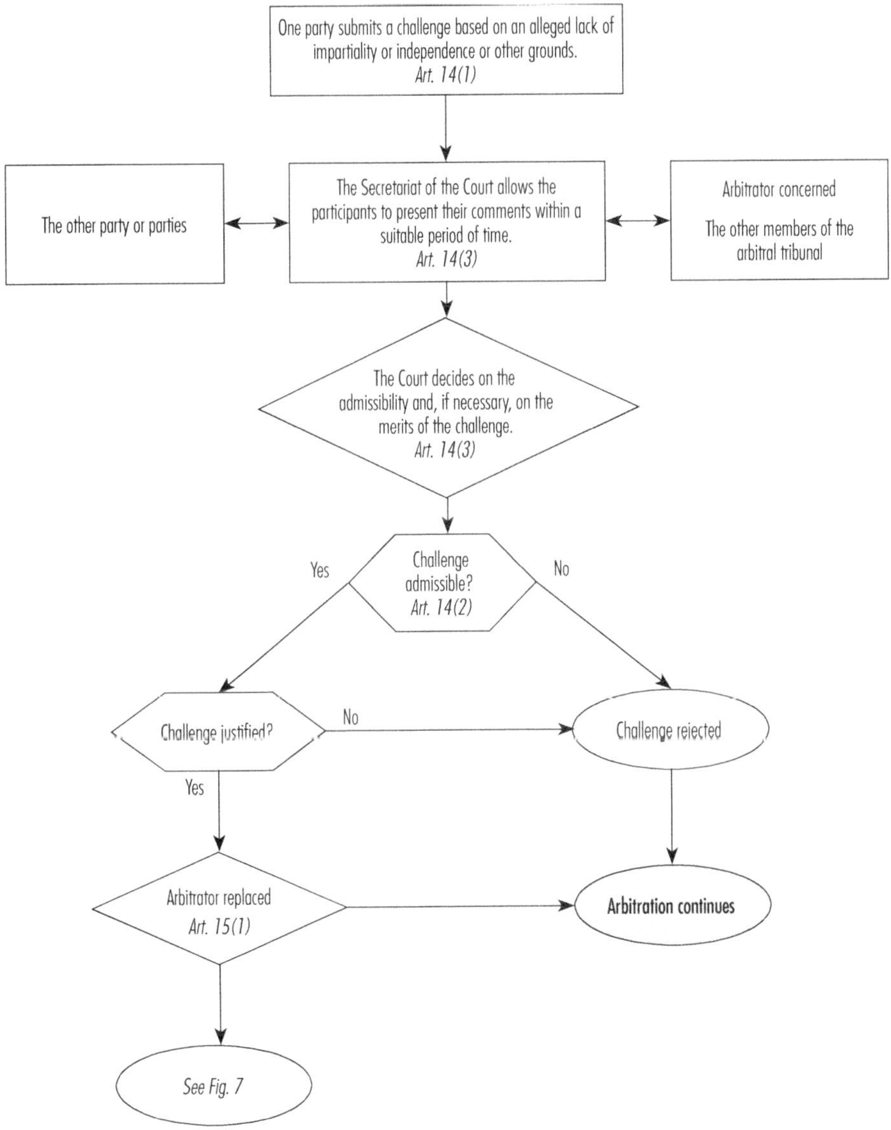

b) The Possible Grounds for a Challenge

Challenges of arbitrators in ICC arbitral proceedings may be based on an alleged lack of impartiality or independence, or any other grounds (Article 14(1)). As the 2012 Rules introduced in Article 11 explicitly the requirement that an arbitrator must not only be and remain independent, but also be and remain impartial, consequently the lack of impartiality has been added in Article 14(1) also as ground to challenge an arbitrator. The Rules leave it open which circumstances may constitute 'any other grounds'. In practice, lack of independence is the most common ground, together with the alleged violation of the obligation to disclose important circumstances relating to the arbitrator's impartiality and independence. A failure to fulfill the duties of an arbitrator, including sloth, may also be taken into account. A challenge based on lack of impartiality is less likely to succeed. These challenges are sometimes based on the conduct of an arbitrator or on comments made by an arbitrator at a hearing or during a meeting. Sometimes also challenges for lack of impartiality are based on prior writings of the arbitrator in an article or in a book on a topic which is discussed in the arbitration and which a party may perceive as going against its case in the arbitration. An important rule of good conduct is that arbitrators shall in the course of the arbitration proceedings show the utmost impartiality and shall refrain from any deeds or words that might be perceived by a party as a sign of bias, especially when asking questions at the hearing.

As far as the violation of the duty of disclosure is concerned, a party may discover during the proceedings that an arbitrator did not include in his or her statement of independence facts or circumstances likely to call into question the arbitrator's independence in the eyes of the parties (Article 11(2) and (3)). This is for instance the case when an arbitrator has relations with a party or its counsel. A person who has failed to disclose something which should reasonably have been disclosed (see the explanations relating to Article 11(3)) is deemed '*prima facie*' to have done so knowingly, and this may be considered as evidence of a lack of independence. An arbitrator may also be challenged when he or she has not given the parties or one of them a sufficient opportunity to present its case during the proceedings.

c) The Challenge Procedure

A party wishing to challenge an arbitrator must present in writing the facts and circumstances on which its challenge is based (Article 14(1)). Its presentation should be credible, reasoned and well documented, as there will usually be no further opportunity to elaborate on it. It should be borne in mind that the challenge procedure is conducted in writing only and neither the parties nor the arbitrator are given the opportunity to express themselves orally before the Court.

As soon as the Secretariat receives the challenge, it forwards it to the other party, to the arbitrator concerned and to all the members of the tribunal in compliance with Article 3(1). The Secretariat gives them an appropriate period of time (usually 15 days) in which to submit their comments in writing (Article 14(3)).

These comments are forwarded to the other parties and arbitrators for information, so as to ensure that the procedure is transparent and in compliance with Article 3(1). However, there is no provision giving the parties an opportunity to submit their reactions to these comments. It is up to the Secretariat to decide whether the parties or the arbitrators may be allowed to submit additional comments.

Once comments have been received and the period of time allowed for this purpose has expired, the Court will decide at a plenary session or, in case of a straightforward challenge, at one of the weekly committee sessions on the admissibility and, if necessary, the merits of the challenge (Article 14(3)). A member of the Court will present a report on the challenge and make a recommendation on the challenge. The Court will discuss and decide the matter on the basis of this report. If the committee session cannot reach a unanimous decision, the matter shall be submitted to the plenary session of the Court, as required by Article 4(5) of Appendix II to the Rules.

If parties wish to raise a challenge against an arbitrator for a particular fact or circumstance of which they are aware at the time of the appointment of the arbitrator or of which they become aware in the course of the arbitration proceedings, they should not postpone the challenge procedure until the arbitral award is rendered. A party which proceeds with the arbitration without raising its objection against the constitution of the arbitral tribunal or the conduct of the proceedings shall be deemed to have waived its right to object pursuant to Article 39 of the ICC Rules. Moreover, national arbitration laws will not necessarily consider an alleged lack of impartiality or independence as a ground for annulment of the arbitral award, after the arbitral award is rendered (see Article 1059 ZPO; Article 190(2) PILA; Article 1492 and 1520 NCPC; Article 1717 JC).

d) The Court's Decision on the Challenge

As already mentioned, the Court will first decide on the admissibility of the challenge. It will be admissible only if filed (i) within 30 days of receipt of the notification of the appointment or confirmation of the arbitrator who is being challenged, or (ii) within 30 days of the date on which the party making the challenge was informed of the facts and circumstances on which the challenge is based, if such date is later than that on which the aforementioned notification was received (Article 14(2)). Two different situations may therefore arise: either (i) a challenge is made just after the appointment or confirmation of an arbitrator, or (ii) the challenge is made during the arbitral proceedings. Once the time limit allowed for making a challenge has expired, a party may no longer challenge an arbitrator on the basis of facts known to it. The purpose of this strict time limit is to prevent parties from trying to delaying proceedings by filing a challenge just before they are closed, when the arbitrators are about to render their final award.

Only if a challenge has been declared admissible will the Court proceed to examine its merits. As previously mentioned, the Court is free to take whatever decision it considers appropriate. According to the standard practice, the parties and the arbitrators are not informed of the reasons for its decision (Article 11(4)); the Secretariat merely informs them whether or not the Court has accepted the challenge. In October 2015, however, the ICC Court announced that it adopted a new policy in response to growing users' demand (see Chapter 2 above; see also the ICC website at <www.iccwbo.org> and the ICC Dispute Resolution Library at <www.iccdrl.com>). Where all the parties to a case so agree, the ICC Court may communicate henceforth reasons for its decision regarding the challenge of an arbitrator. A request for the communication of reasons must be made in advance of the relevant decision in respect of which reasons are sought. The Court may subject the communication of reasons to an increase of the administrative expenses, normally not to exceed US$ 5 000.

If the Court accepts the challenge, the procedure for appointing another arbitrator is implemented (Article 15).

In practice, challenges are something of a rarity and only few of them succeed by being declared both admissible and justified. Most of them are rejected as unjustified. In 2013, 66 challenges were introduced and all but four of them were rejected (see '2013 Statistical Report' published in *ICC International Court of Arbitration Bulletin*, Paris, Vol. 25/Nr. 1 - 2014, p. 11); in 2012, 13 of the 61 challenges made were accepted (see '2012 Statistical Report' published in *ICC International Court of Arbitration Bulletin*, Paris, Vol. 24/Nr. 1 - 2013, p. 11); in 2011, 39 challenges were made and only three accepted (see '2011 Statistical Report' published in *ICC International Court of Arbitration Bulletin*, Paris, Vol. 23/Nr. 1 - 2012, p. 11); in 2010, six of the 46 challenges filed were accepted (see '2010 Statistical Report' published in *ICC International Court of Arbitration Bulletin*, Paris, Vol. 22/Nr. 1 - 2011, p. 11); in 2009, 57 challenges were made, of which five were accepted (see '2009 Statistical Report' published in *ICC International Court of Arbitration Bulletin*, Paris, Vol. 21/Nr. 1 - 2010, p. 10); and in 2008, of the 44 challenges made only one was accepted by the Court (see '2008 Statistical Report' published in *ICC International Court of Arbitration Bulletin*, Paris, Vol. 20/Nr. 1 - 2009, p. 10).

e) The Resignation of an Arbitrator Following a Challenge

According to Article 11(5), by agreeing to serve, an arbitrator undertakes to act in accordance with the Rules of Arbitration. This means that he or she can and must continue the proceedings even if challenged. The arbitrator remains in office pending the ICC Court's decision on the challenge and until such time as the Court decides to remove him or her from office.

However, the Rules do not prevent an arbitrator from deciding to resign on account of a challenge and the circumstances of the case. In all events, the arbitrator's resignation must first be accepted by the Court in order to become effective (Article 15(1)).

5. Replacement of Arbitrators (Art. 15)

Article 15 of the Rules reads:

> 'Replacement of Arbitrators
>
> 1. An arbitrator shall be replaced upon death, upon acceptance by the Court of the arbitrator's resignation, upon acceptance by the Court of a challenge, or upon acceptance by the Court of a request of all the parties.
>
> 2. An arbitrator shall also be replaced on the Court's own initiative when it decides that the arbitrator is prevented de jure or de facto from fulfilling the arbitrator's functions, or that the arbitrator is not fulfilling those functions in accordance with the Rules or within the prescribed time limits.
>
> 3. When, on the basis of information that has come to its attention, the Court considers applying Article 15(2), it shall decide on the matter after the arbitrator concerned, the parties and any other members of the arbitral tribunal have had an opportunity to comment in writing within a suitable period of time. Such comments shall be communicated to the parties and to the arbitrators.
>
> 4. When an arbitrator is to be replaced, the Court has discretion to decide whether or not to follow the original nominating process. Once reconstituted, and after having invited the parties to comment, the arbitral tribunal shall

determine if and to what extent prior proceedings shall be repeated before the reconstituted arbitral tribunal.

5. Subsequent to the closing of the proceedings, instead of replacing an arbitrator who has died or been removed by the Court pursuant to Articles 15(1) and 15(2), the Court may decide, when it considers it appropriate, that the remaining arbitrators shall continue the arbitration. In making such determination, the Court shall take into account the views of the remaining arbitrators and of the parties and such other matters that it considers appropriate in the circumstances.'

a) The Reasons for Replacement

Article 15 of the Rules specifies the situations in which arbitrators need to be replaced:

(1) Replacement Following a Challenge.

Article 15(1) follows logically from Article 14, when the challenge has been accepted.

(2) Death of an Arbitrator.

An arbitrator who dies during proceedings must be replaced.

(3) Resignation of an Arbitrator.

As already mentioned in connection with Article 11(5) and Article 14, once an arbitrator has agreed to serve, he or she must fulfill this commitment in accordance with the Rules and cannot unilaterally decide to resign. Therefore, an arbitrator cannot withdraw if, for any reason, he or she no longer wishes to continue the proceedings, or finds that his or her opinion does not prevail when the arbitral tribunal deliberates upon the award. To be effective, a resignation must first be accepted by the ICC International Court of Arbitration (Article 15(1)). Given that an arbitrator's resignation may seriously compromise the conduct of the proceedings, especially if they have reached an advanced stage, it may be refused by the Court.

The Rules do not state under what circumstances an arbitrator may resign. As a general rule, the Court accepts resignations in the event of serious illness or if arbitrators are no longer able to act in accordance with the Rules due to a change in their professional circumstances.

The Court may also accept the resignation of an arbitrator who has been challenged, if it considers that the arbitrator no longer commands the necessary authority to conduct the proceedings.

In the years 2008-2010, when the 1998 Rules were still applicable, the Court accepted 75 resignations of arbitrators, whereas in the same period only 10 challenges of arbitrators were accepted by the Court (see J. Fry, S. Greenberg and F. Mazza, *The Secretariat's Guide to ICC Arbitration*, ICC Publication No. 729 E, Paris, 2012, p. 183).

(4) Removal from Office by the Parties.

It is not possible for one party alone to remove an arbitrator from office, even if the arbitrator was nominated by that party. The Rules, however, allow parties jointly to remove an arbitrator from office (Article 15 (1)). This reflects party autonomy and is carried out in collaboration with the Court, which confirms the arbitrator's removal from office at one of its sessions.

In the years 2008-2010 the Court removed 10 arbitrators following an agreement of the parties (see J. Fry, S. Greenberg and F. Mazza, *The Secretariat's Guide to ICC Arbitration,* ICC Publication No. 729 E, Paris, 2012, p. 183).

(5) Replacement on the Court's Own Initiative.

It is possible for the Court itself to replace an arbitrator who is prevented from carrying out his or her responsibilities for legal or factual reasons, or who does not act in accordance with the Rules or within the prescribed time limits (Article 15(2)). In practice, arbitrators are rarely replaced for these reasons. The Court decided to replace an arbitrator on nine occasions in 2013 (see '2013 Statistical Report' published in *ICC International Court of Arbitration Bulletin,* Paris, Vol. 25/Nr. 1 – 2014, p. 11), on two occasions in 2011 (see '2011 Statistical Report' published in *ICC International Court of Arbitration Bulletin,* Paris, Vol. 23/Nr. 1 – 2012, p. 11), and on three occasions in 2010 (see '2010 Statistical Report' published in *ICC International Court of Arbitration Bulletin,* Paris, Vol. 22/Nr. 1 – 2011, p. 11), whereas no decisions to replace an arbitrator were taken in 2008 and 2009 (see J. Fry, S. Greenberg and F. Mazza, *The Secretariat's Guide to ICC Arbitration,* ICC Publication No. 729 E, Paris, 2012, p. 184).

b) The Replacement Procedure

In the situations mentioned in Article 15(1), the ICC International Court of Arbitration is contacted by one or all of the parties and decides whether or not the arbitrator should be replaced.

In the situations mentioned in Article 15(2), the procedure is basically the same as in the case of challenges (Article 14(3)). The only difference lies in the fact that the procedure is initiated by the Court rather than by one of the parties.

When, on the basis of circumstances brought to its knowledge, the Court contemplates to proceed in accordance with Article 15(2), it first decides at one of its committee sessions whether the arbitrator should be replaced. If it so decides, the arbitrator concerned, the parties and any other members of the arbitral tribunal are given an opportunity to submit written comments within a given time limit (normally 15 days). The Court then announces the grounds on which it contemplates replacing the arbitrator (Article 15(3)).

The comments of the arbitrator concerned, of the parties and of any other members of the arbitral tribunal are sent to all the parties and the arbitrator(s) involved in the proceedings for the sake of transparency and in compliance with Article 3(1). As with challenges, there is no provision for parties to comment again or proceed to further written exchanges. It is up to the Secretariat to decide whether the parties or arbitrators should be allowed to submit additional observations.

The Court then decides, at a plenary session, whether or not the arbitrator shall be replaced (Article 15(3)). A member of the Court prepares a report and makes a recommendation to the Court, which serve as a basis for the Court's discussions and decision.

Like the Court's decisions relating to challenges, those concerning the replacement of arbitrators are of an administrative, not a judicial, nature. They are final, unless mandatory rules provide otherwise. According to the standard practice, the reasons for these decisions are not disclosed (Article 11(4)). In October 2015, however,

Figure 7. Replacement of arbitrators

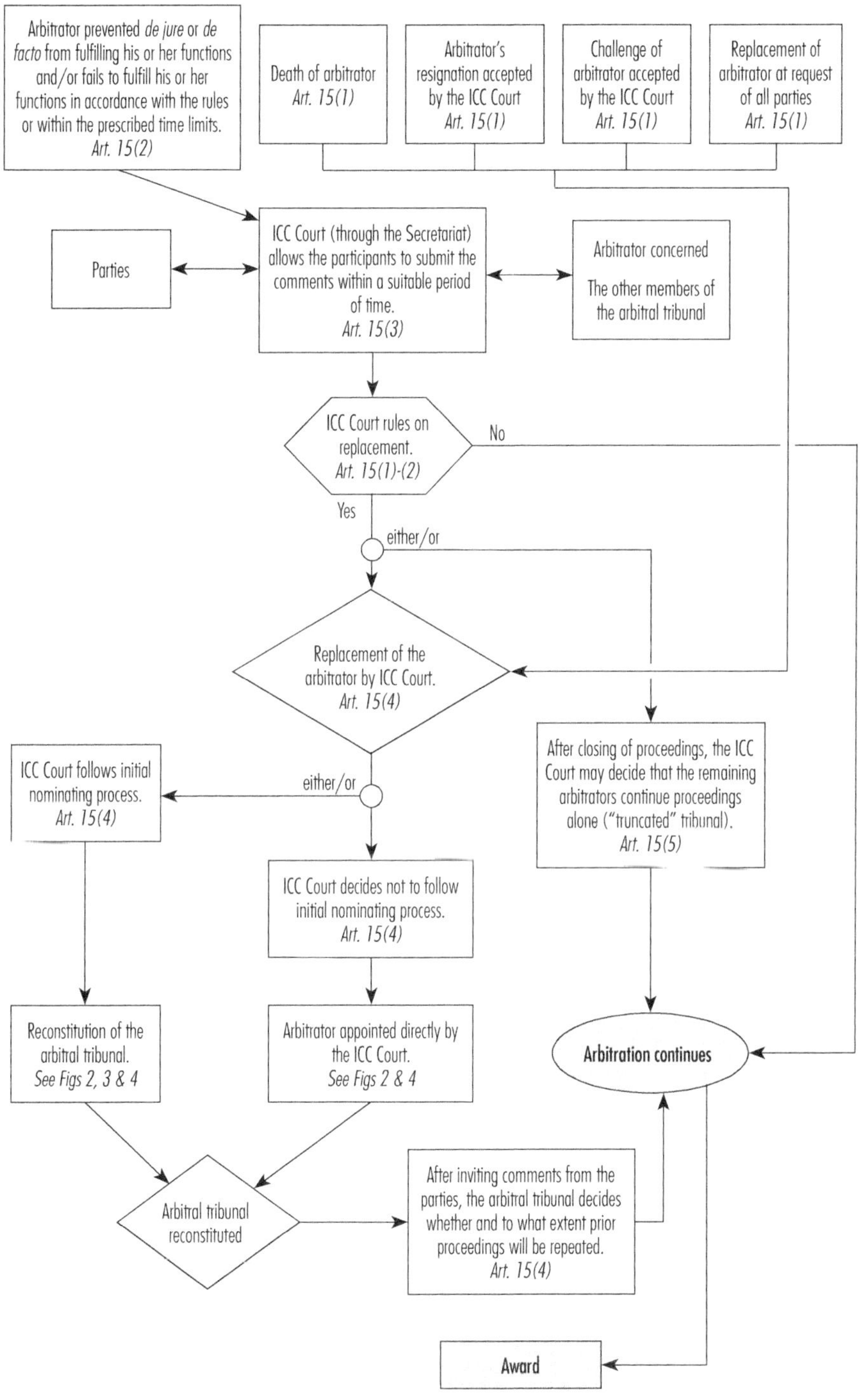

the ICC Court announced that it adopted a new policy in response to growing users' demand (see Chapter 2 above; see also the ICC website at <www.iccwbo.org> and the ICC Dispute Resolution Library at <www.iccdrl.com>). Where all the parties to a case so agree, the ICC Court may communicate henceforth reasons for its decision to initiate replacement proceedings and subsequently to replace an arbitrator on the Court's own motion. A request for the communication of reasons must be made in advance of the relevant decision in respect of which reasons are sought. The Court may subject the communication of reasons to an increase of the administrative expenses, normally not to exceed US$ 5 000.

In 2013, on 46 occasions an arbitrator was replaced: 37 of these replacements were made pursuant to Article 15(1) due to an arbitrator's death, resignation, a successful challenge or at the request of all parties; the remaining nine replacements were made by the Court on its own initiative pursuant to Article 15(2) due to the arbitrator's being prevented *de jure* or *de facto* from fulfilling his or her functions in accordance with the Rules (see '2013 Statistical Report' published in *ICC International Court of Arbitration Bulletin*, Paris, Vol. 25/Nr. 1 - 2014, p. 11). In 2012, a total of 47 replacements were made (see '2012 Statistical Report' published in *ICC International Court of Arbitration Bulletin*, Paris, Vol. 24/Nr. 1 - 2013, p. 11). In 2011, a total of 30 resignations were accepted by the Court. In addition to replacements made following a challenge or a resignation, 4 arbitrators were replaced at the request of all parties, 4 replacements were made following an arbitrator's death, and a further 2 replacements were made at the Court's initiative due to the arbitrators' failure to fulfill their functions (see '2011 Statistical Report' published in *ICC International Court of Arbitration Bulletin*, Paris, Vol. 23/Nr. 1 - 2012, p. 11).

c) The Consequences of a Decision to Replace an Arbitrator

When the decision has been made to replace an arbitrator, the necessary steps also are taken to appoint another arbitrator. The ICC Court is free to decide whether or not the initial nominating process should be followed (Article 15(4)). The Court therefore has the possibility to appoint an arbitrator directly, where appropriate, instead of letting the party that nominated the arbitrator who is being replaced name another arbitrator. It may be assumed that the Court will avail itself of this possibility only on rare occasions, as, for instance, when an arbitrator chosen by a party is replaced on grounds of partiality or complicity with the party that chose him or her, or when the Court considers that the party who nominated the arbitrator may exercise its right to nominate a new arbitrator with the negative intention of seeking to derail or frustrate the arbitration proceedings. In the Court's view, this presupposes that the party concerned has also acted reprehensibly. Before making such a decision, the Court will consider the consequences of a possible infringement of a party's rights regarding the choice of an arbitrator.

(1) Continuation of the Proceedings Before the Arbitral Tribunal whose Composition was Changed.

After an arbitrator has been replaced, the newly composed tribunal must decide whether and to what extent to repeat the prior proceedings. The reconstituted arbitral tribunal will first hear what the parties have to say (Article 15(4)), for instance on whether or not the Terms of Reference should be modified or completely rewritten, or whether witnesses should be heard again or new hearings held. In practice, it is rare for reconstituted arbitral tribunals to draw up new Terms of Reference when they already exist. This is understandable, especially if the Terms of Reference have been signed by all of the parties. Other procedural acts are very rarely repeated if the proceedings are already far advanced.

(2) The Special Case of an Incomplete or 'Truncated Arbitral Tribunal' (Art. 15(5)).

The provisions of Article 15(5), which were introduced in the 1998 version of the Rules, allow the ICC International Court of Arbitration, in special circumstances and if appropriate, to decide not to replace an arbitrator who has been removed from a three-member tribunal, but to let the two remaining arbitrators continue the proceedings. Such a decision is possible only after the proceedings have been declared closed (Article 27) and the tribunal has begun its deliberations. In addition, before deciding to let an 'incomplete' tribunal continue the proceedings, the Court must invite comments from the remaining arbitrators and the parties and take into account all relevant circumstances of the case in question. This possibility, for which similar provisions may also be found in Article 1052(2) ZPO and Article 1711(4) JC, serves above all to avoid difficulties at the stage of deliberating the arbitral award, if a member of the arbitral tribunal is no longer able or no longer wishes to take part in the deliberations and the rendering of the award (see also Articles 1480 and 1513 NCPC, Article 189(2) PILA, Articles 29 and 31(1) of the UNCITRAL Model Law).

Article 15(5) of the Rules thus allows incomplete or 'truncated' arbitral tribunals to render an award at the close of proceedings in exceptional circumstances when a member of the tribunal has died, refuses to take part in deliberations, has resigned, or when the arbitrator has been removed by the Court pursuant to Article 15(1) and 15(2) after the proceedings have been closed. Although rarely applied, this possibility may prove to be particularly useful where a member of the arbitral tribunal attempts to block the proceedings for whatever reason and to delay the rendering of the award. It also covers cases in which an arbitrator who has taken part in deliberations and approved the draft award dies before being able to sign the award once it has been approved by the Court.

It should be noted that such decisions must be taken by the ICC Court. The arbitral tribunal itself may not decide to render an award with two of the three members.

The Court has applied the provision on the 'truncated arbitral tribunal' between 2007 and 2011, pursuant to Article 12(5) of the 1998 Rules, in only four cases. This concerned situations where there was a vacancy in the arbitral tribunal because of death, resignation, a successful challenge or a removal pursuant to Article 12(2) of the 1998 Rules (now Article 15(2)) (see J. Fry, S. Greenberg and F. Mazza, *The Secretariat's Guide to ICC Arbitration*, ICC Publication No. 729 E, Paris, 2012, p. 193).

E. THE ARBITRAL PROCEEDINGS

1. Transmission of the File to the Arbitral Tribunal (Art. 16)

Article 16 of the Rules reads:

> 'Transmission of the File to the Arbitral Tribunal
>
> The Secretariat shall transmit the file to the arbitral tribunal as soon as it has been constituted, provided the advance on costs requested by the Secretariat at this stage has been paid.'

Article 16 is the first provision in the Rules relating to proceedings before the arbitral tribunal. Under this provision, the file will be transmitted to the arbitral tribunal as soon as two conditions have been fulfilled, namely that the arbitral tribunal has been constituted, i.e. all the arbitrators have been confirmed or appointed by the Court, and the advance requested by the Secretariat has been paid.

a) First Condition: Formation of the Arbitral Tribunal

In the event of a three-member arbitral tribunal, it is only once the three arbitrators have been confirmed or appointed that the file is transmitted to the arbitral tribunal, which may then begin its work. Its first task will be to draw up the Terms of Reference.

In those cases where the arbitrators named by the parties are given the power jointly to nominate a third arbitrator as president, the Secretariat will normally transmit the request for arbitration and the answer to the request to these two arbitrators for information, so that they may make an appropriate choice in light of the parties' statements. However, this does not constitute the transmission of the file as referred to in Article 16. At this stage, the two arbitrators can do no more than choose the person to preside the tribunal: they cannot undertake any procedural acts.

b) Second Condition: Payment of the Advance Requested at this Stage of the Proceedings

Even if the arbitral tribunal is complete, it will not be given the file until the advance requested has been paid. The advance due at this stage is the provisional amount fixed by the Secretary General pursuant to Article 36(1) of the Rules and Article 1(2) of Appendix III to the Rules.

The Secretary General fixes this provisional advance immediately after the request for arbitration has been filed, on the basis of the information it contains. The provisional advance is intended in all cases to cover the costs of the proceedings up to the point at which the Terms of Reference are drawn up in compliance with Article 23. Normally, it is to be paid by the claimant alone. Prompt payment will help to ensure that the file is transmitted to the arbitrators quickly.

It should be mentioned here that the provisional advance to cover the costs of the proceedings prior to the drawing up of the Terms of Reference should be rapidly adapted. It is essential that the amount required to cover the entire proceedings be requested as soon as possible, so as to prevent the proceedings from being hampered by subsequent delays in payment. In this way, the parties immediately have a clear idea of the costs they will have to bear and can accordingly decide what attitude to adopt in the proceedings.

According to Article 36(2) of the Rules and Article 1(4) of Appendix III to the Rules, the full advance on costs is fixed by the Court on the basis of the claims and counterclaims presented by the parties and may be readjusted later. The readjustment generally occurs as soon as the respondent has submitted its answer and any counterclaim.

It is the arbitral tribunal's duty to also ensure that the amount in dispute is quantified as far as possible. If the claimant has not calculated the amount of its claims or the respondent has not evaluated its counterclaim, the arbitral tribunal will ask the parties to quantify their claims when drawing up the Terms of Reference. This will allow the Court to readjust the advance on costs at the latest when the Terms of Reference are submitted to it.

The parties are informed by the Secretariat that the file has been transmitted to the arbitral tribunal. Under Article 23(2) of the Rules, it is at this moment that the two-month time limit for drawing up the Terms of Reference begins to run. The Court may extend this time limit in response to a reasoned request from the arbitral tribunal or of its own accord if it considers this to be necessary. To avoid the risk of an eventual time bar, the necessity will in theory exist so long as the Terms of Reference have not been signed or submitted to the Court.

c) Documents transmitted to the Arbitral Tribunal

The Secretariat will transmit to each member of the arbitral tribunal all the submissions filed by the parties including the exhibits. As the parties are required pursuant to Article 3(1) to submit the request for arbitration, the answer thereto and all other communications in a number of copies sufficient to provide one copy for each arbitrator, the Secretariat will dispose of the necessary number of copies of all the parties' submissions so as to provide one set for each member of the arbitral tribunal.

With its letter to the arbitrators, the Secretariat encloses a number of sheets with information on the particular case and notes on various aspects on ICC arbitration proceedings:

(1) a 'Case Information' sheet containing the contact details of the parties, of the arbitrators and of the team of the Secretariat in charge of the administrative monitoring of the case as well as a summary of information collected by the Secretariat from the documents provided by the parties and meant to give the arbitral tribunal an overall picture of the matter;

(2) a 'Financial Table' reflecting the financial situation of the arbitration;

(3) a 'Note to the Arbitral Tribunal on the Conduct of the Arbitration' (see Appendix 9 below). This note of the Secretariat provides the arbitral tribunal with information concerning the conduct of arbitrations under the 2012 ICC Rules of Arbitration. It incorporates notes previously published by the Secretariat separately on (i) personal and arbitral tribunal expenses, (ii) VAT, taxes, charges and imposts applicable to arbitrators' fees, and (iii) appointment, duties and remuneration of administrative secretaries. The note draws the attention of the arbitrators to the time limits to be respected for the establishment of the Terms of Reference and to render the award, and emphasizes the importance of conducting the arbitration proceedings as rapidly as possible. In this regard, it refers the arbitrators to the 'Techniques for Controlling Time and Costs in Arbitration' in appendix IV to the Rules and the report of the ICC Commission on Arbitration and ADR entitled 'Techniques for Controlling Time and Costs in Arbitration', available on the ICC website (see Appendix 15 below). The Secretariat's note stresses that the arbitral tribunal must declare the proceedings closed as to the issues to be decided and that it must indicate to the Secretariat an approximate date by which the draft award will be submitted for scrutiny by the ICC Court. It points out that an original of the Terms of Reference signed by the parties and the arbitral tribunal must be provided to each party, each member of the arbitral tribunal and the Secretariat and that, similarly, each party, each arbitrator and the Secretariat must receive an original of the awards signed by the arbitrators after approval of the drafts by the Court. The note reminds the arbitrators that their fees are exclusively fixed by the Court and that separate fee arrangements between the arbitrators and the parties are not permitted. The note brings to the attention of the parties

that in fixing the arbitrators' fees at the end of the arbitration, the Court takes into account the diligence and efficiency of the arbitrator, the time spent, the rapidity of the proceedings, the complexity of the dispute and the timeliness of the submission of the draft award. It stresses that the Court does not take into account the arbitrator's usual hourly rates or remuneration. It points out that when there is a three-member arbitral tribunal and, unless the Secretariat is informed in writing that the arbitral tribunal has agreed to a different allocation, the Court normally fixes the arbitrators' fees so that the president receives 40% of the total fees and each co-arbitrator receives 30%. The note invites the arbitrators to inform the Secretariat during the course of the proceedings of any developments in the value and complexity of the arbitration or any other issues they consider relevant. The Secretariat's note gives information on personal and arbitral tribunal's expenses for which reimbursement may be requested. It also draws the attention of the arbitrators to the fact that amounts paid to them do not include taxes or other charges applicable to the fees and it offers arbitrators subject to VAT and other taxes, if they request so in writing, a service allowing them to have the funds corresponding to their estimate of the VAT due on their fees and expenses administered by ICC. The Secretariat's note also sets out the policy and practice of the ICC Court and its Secretariat regarding the engagement of administrative secretaries by arbitral tribunals. Finally, the Secretariat's note indicates in its letter that the parties are free to settle their dispute amicably at any time during the arbitration and that, where appropriate, the arbitral tribunal may remind the parties of the ICC Mediation Rules (the ICC ADR Rules were replaced by the ICC Mediation Rules as of 1 January 2014, see Chapter 6 below).

(4) a 'Note on Administrative Issues' (see Appendix 10 below). With this note the Secretariat draws the attention of the arbitral tribunal to the provisions of the Rules on communications, on how to dispatch documents to ICC and brings to the attention of the arbitrators that for ICC arbitrations in Paris the hearing may take place at the ICC Hearing Centre in Paris, a wholly-owned affiliate of the ICC.

(5) an 'ICC Award Checklist (1998 & 2012 Rules') (see Appendix 11 below). This note is a checklist for arbitrators regarding the drafting of the award

If the arbitral tribunal is composed of three arbitrators, it will enclose for each arbitrator the curriculum vitae of the fellow arbitrators. A copy of the letter to the arbitral tribunal is sent by the Secretariat to the parties for their information. In its letter to the parties, the Secretariat asks the parties henceforth to correspond directly with the arbitral tribunal and to send copies of their correspondence always directly to the other party(parties) and to the Secretariat.

2. Proof of Authority (Art. 17)

Article 17 of the Rules reads:

> 'Proof of Authority
>
> At any time after the commencement of the arbitration, the arbitral tribunal or the Secretariat may require proof of the authority of any party representatives.'

Article 17 is a new provision that was not yet contained in the 1998 Rules. It explicitly gives the power to the arbitral tribunal and to the Secretariat to request any representative of a party to submit a proof that he or she is authorized to represent the party in the arbitration.

Pursuant to Article 4(3)(b), the claimant is required to provide with its request for arbitration the name in full, a description, contact details of any person representing the claimant in the arbitration and, pursuant to Article 5(1)(b), the respondent must with its answer to the request for arbitration provide the name of in full, the address and other contact details of any person(s) representing the respondent in the arbitration. The parties are not required pursuant to these provisions to submit a power of attorney for their representatives.

Article 26(4) provides that parties may appear at a hearing in person or through duly authorized representatives. In addition, they may be assisted by advisers.

Whilst in some jurisdictions there is a principle contained in the law (in Belgium this is contained in Article 440 JC), that a lawyer may represent his or her client in court proceedings without the need to provide a power of attorney (referred as a 'mandate *ad litem*'), such principle is not known in all legal systems. Therefore, an arbitral tribunal or the Secretariat must have the possibility to ask for a proof of the representation of a party. This may be of importance, in particular, if a party is represented by a person who is not a lawyer. Also, if parties are represented by lawyers, it is appropriate to ask the parties that a power or attorney be provided for the persons who will sign the Terms of Reference on their behalf, given the contractual nature of the Terms of Reference.

Given that parties and their counsel in international arbitration proceedings often have a different legal background or are based in different jurisdictions, it is fairly usual that an arbitral tribunal requests the parties to provide a written power of attorney for their representative.

In case the authority of a person representing a party is contested, the arbitral tribunal will have to take a decision whether the party is duly represented and what proof is required to provide appropriate evidence of the party representation.

3. Place of the Arbitration (Art. 18)

Article 18 of the Rules reads:

> '*Place of the Arbitration*
>
> 1. The place of the arbitration shall be fixed by the Court unless agreed upon by the parties.
>
> 2. The arbitral tribunal may, after consultation with the parties, conduct hearings and meetings at any location it considers appropriate, unless otherwise agreed by the parties.
>
> 3. The arbitral tribunal may deliberate at any location it considers appropriate.'

a) Choice of the Place of the Arbitration

(1) The Will of the Parties.

The Rules give the parties the freedom to choose the place of the arbitration, i.e. the legal seat of the arbitral tribunal. This they may do in their arbitration agreement or later (Article 18(1)). The ICC International Court of Arbitration does not intervene in any way and respects the parties' choice.

The parties had agreed on the place of the arbitration in 88.5% of the cases referred to the Court in 2013 (see '2013 Statistical Report' published in *ICC International Court of Arbitration Bulletin*, Paris, Vol. 25/Nr. 1 – 2014, p. 12). The corresponding figure was 90% in 2012 (see '2012 Statistical Report' published in *ICC International Court of Arbitration Bulletin*, Paris, Vol. 24/Nr. 1 – 2013, p. 14), 87% in 2011 (see '2011 Statistical Report' published in *ICC International Court of Arbitration Bulletin*, Paris, Vol. 23/Nr. 1 – 2012, p. 13), 89% in 2010 (see '2010 Statistical Report' published in *ICC International Court of Arbitration Bulletin*, Paris, Vol. 22/Nr. 1 – 2011, p. 13), 88.4% in 2009 (see '2009 Statistical Report' published in *ICC International Court of Arbitration Bulletin*, Paris, Vol. 21/Nr. 1 – 2010, p. 12) and 90% in 2008 (see '2009 Statistical Report' published in *ICC International Court of Arbitration Bulletin*, Paris, Vol. 20/Nr. 1 – 2012, p. 11). This is not surprising, as the ICC brochure on arbitration mentions in relation to the standard ICC arbitration clause that it may be desirable for the parties to agree on the place of the arbitration. If they have done so, the place they have chosen will be taken into account by the Court from the very beginning of the proceedings. Parties can not only agree on the place of the arbitration in the arbitration agreement in their contract prior to the arbitration, but they can still do so after the dispute has arisen. If parties wish, they may also agree to change the place of the arbitration initially agreed.

The place of the arbitration should be a city, not a country. If parties have agreed on a country, and not on a city as place of the arbitration, the Court will give them the opportunity to agree on a city at the outset of the arbitration. Should the parties not agree on a city in such case, the Court shall fix the city where the arbitration shall be conducted. The reason why it matters to fix a city is that in some countries there are different arbitration laws applicable in different parts of the country, with possibly different controlling mechanisms by national courts. In such situation, the designation of a country instead of a city as place of the arbitration could leave uncertainty regarding the applicable arbitration law and the possible controlling mechanism or assistance by local courts. Any doubt or uncertainty in regard to the applicable arbitration law or competent state courts is to be avoided by anchoring the arbitration in a specific city.

It should be noted that parties often refer in their arbitration clause to 'the Rules of Arbitration of the International Chamber of Commerce (ICC) in Paris' or 'ICC in Paris', without clearly specifying the place of the arbitration. In such cases, it is not clear whether the parties wished the arbitration to be conducted in Paris or whether the reference to Paris simply relates to the International Chamber of Commerce, whose headquarters are in Paris. If this happens, the Secretariat draws the parties' attention to this point when notifying the request for arbitration. The parties will be asked whether, by referring to Paris in the arbitration clause, they meant Paris to be the place of the arbitration. The Secretariat will point out that it is the Court's practice to fix Paris as the place of the arbitration if at least one of the parties confirms that this was its intention or if none of the parties reacts. The parties must send their reactions to the Secretariat within the 30-day period allowed for answering the request for arbitration or when the respondent asks for such period to be extended. The aim is to avoid delaying a decision by the ICC Court on this matter. No decision by the Court will of course be necessary if the parties inform the Secretariat that Paris is indeed the place of the arbitration, as they will have thereby made their intention clear. Since the 1998 Rules came into force, the Court no longer 'confirms' the place of the arbitration.

The parties should not underestimate the importance of the choice of the place of the arbitration in avoiding later complications. From a legal point of view, they should ask themselves whether the applicable law at the place of the arbitration allows arbitral awards to be set aside and on what grounds; whether it contains mandatory rules of procedure, which, if not complied with, could cause the award to be set aside; or whether it places restrictions on the arbitrability of the subject matter of the dispute. It is also important to determine whether and in what cases state courts may intervene in arbitration proceedings or provide assistance. A further matter of importance is whether or not the state in which the place of the arbitration is situated has ratified the New York Convention. Lastly, political factors, such as the independence of the judiciary, free access to the country and the risk of political disturbances should also be taken into consideration.

The ICC arbitrations commenced in 2013 were seated in 104 different cities in 63 countries. The top ten cities selected in 2013 were: Paris (118 cases), London (70), Geneva (56), Zurich (34), Singapore (33), New York (24), Hong Kong (14), Stockholm (14), Sao Paulo (12), Vienna (11), Frankfurt/Main (11) (see '2013 Statistical Report' published in *ICC International Court of Arbitration Bulletin*, Paris, Vol. 25/Nr. 1 – 2014, p. 12). ICC arbitrations initiated in 2012 took place in 92 cities in 59 countries, whereby the top 10 cities selected in 2012 were: Paris (100 cases), London (71), Geneva (62), Zurich (48), Singapore (36), New York (22), Vienna (13), Mexico (12), Frankfurt/Main (10), Hong Kong (10) (see '2012 Statistical Report' published in *ICC International Court of Arbitration Bulletin*, Paris, Vol. 24/Nr. 1 – 2013, p. 14). The place of the arbitration for the arbitrations commenced in 2011 were situated in 113 cities in 63 different countries, whereby the top 10 cities selected were: Paris (111 cases), London (62), Geneva (53), Zurich (40), Singapore (24), New York (20), Frankfurt/Main (14), Brussels (13), Madrid (13), Sao Paulo (12) (see '2011 Statistical Report' published in *ICC International Court of Arbitration Bulletin*, Paris, Vol. 23/Nr. 1 – 2012, p. 13).

(2) Fixed by the ICC International Court of Arbitration.

If the parties have not agreed on the place of the arbitration, it will be fixed by the ICC Court (Article 18(1)). In so doing, the Court will take into account any observations from the parties and the recommendations of the Secretariat and give consideration, amongst other things, to whether or not the country in which the place of the arbitration is to be situated has ratified the New York Convention or other multilateral or bilateral treaties relating to the recognition and enforcement of arbitral awards; whether or not the national law on arbitration procedure applicable to international arbitrations gives the courts at the place of the arbitration the power to intervene in arbitration proceedings; whether or not this law places any restrictions on the arbitrability of disputes; whether arbitration agreements, arbitral awards and the freedom of the parties to choose the applicable law and procedural rules are respected at the place of the arbitration.

The Court also ensures that the place it intends to choose for the arbitration will be regarded as neutral by the parties and that it is acceptable to all the participants in the proceedings, not only from a geographical point of view but also for practical reasons (such as how distant the place is, whether or not there are adequate means of communication, the quality of the infrastructure and logistics, possible problems of access and safety concerns). The Court also considers the particularities of the case in question, namely the origins of the parties and their lawyers and, if known, that of the co-arbitrators and the president of the arbitral tribunal or the sole arbitrator. The Court may also take the applicable law and the language of the arbitration into account, so that the place of the arbitration to be fixed corresponds as much as possible to the expectations of the parties.

In exceptional cases, if there is controversy between the parties regarding the interpretation of the contractual stipulation of the place of the arbitration, the Court may provisionally fix the place of the arbitration and leave it to the arbitral tribunal to finally determine the place of the arbitration. Such unusual situation could arise, for instance, if the contract between the parties stipulates two different places of the arbitration and where they cannot agree on one place. A similar situation could arise if the parties have amended their original contract and stipulated in the amended contract a different place of the arbitration, but have not been able at the start of the arbitration to reach agreement on the place where the arbitration should be conducted.

b) The Place of the Hearings

Article 18(2) expressly allows the arbitral tribunal, after first consulting the parties, to hold hearings and meetings at any location other than at the place of the arbitration, which will nonetheless remain the legal seat of the arbitral tribunal. It is not uncommon for this to happen. In practice, it may well be an advantage, or even a necessity, to hear witnesses at their place of residence or work, if this is not the same as the place of the arbitration. With regard to factual matters, it is sometimes necessary to inspect the material and equipment in dispute on site (e.g. goods delivered, a machine, a factory or other physical evidence), when they are not located at the place of the arbitration.

Before deciding to hold hearings and meetings in a place other than that of the arbitration, the arbitral tribunal must hear the parties on this matter and seek their agreement. If all the parties cannot agree, it is preferable for the arbitrators to hear them at the place of the arbitration to avoid any problems later.

Hearings can also be organized by telephone or videoconference as a means to control time and costs in an arbitration (Article 24(4) of the Rules and Appendix IV to the Rules). This can be appropriate for procedural hearings where it is not necessary to meet the parties personally or not necessary to examine witnesses. In such case, and also if none of the parties requested a hearing and the arbitral tribunal decides that it can decide the matter solely on the basis of the written submissions of the parties (Article 25(6)), the mandatory provisions of the arbitration law of the place of the arbitration confirmed or fixed by the Court must be respected. The arbitral tribunal is well advised to check whether the arbitration law applicable at the place of the arbitration does not formulate certain requirements about holding a hearing at the place of the arbitration.

The arbitrators are free to organize the hearing within the city confirmed or fixed as place of the arbitration at a location they deem appropriate. This can be in the office of one of the arbitrators or, if the parties agree, in the office of one the parties' counsel. Sometimes arbitration hearings are organized in hotels. In a number of cities there are hearing centers which are well equipped for holding hearings. The ICC has since October 2008 its own hearing center in Paris (at 112 Avenue Kléber, 75016 Paris, France).

c) The Place of the Deliberations

Article 18(3) was likewise introduced in the 1998 Rules. It provides that the arbitral tribunal may deliberate in any place it considers appropriate, which therefore need not necessarily be that of the arbitration. When deciding where to deliberate, the arbitral tribunal does not have to consult the parties or obtain their agreement.

If the members of the arbitral tribunal do not reside in the same place or at the place of the arbitration, it may well be more efficient and less costly for them not to meet at the place of the arbitration to deliberate. In this regard, the Rules fictitiously assume that the arbitral award is rendered at the seat of the arbitration (Article 31(3)).

As a matter of fact, in many instances, the arbitrators deliberate by telephone conference or by exchange of e-mails or by other means of information technology.

4. Rules Governing the Proceedings (Art. 19)

Article 19 of the Rules reads:

> 'Rules Governing the Proceedings
>
> The proceedings before the arbitral tribunal shall be governed by these Rules and, where the Rules are silent, by any rules which the parties or, failing them, the arbitral tribunal may settle on, whether or not reference is thereby made to the rules of procedure of a national law to be applied to the arbitration.'

a) Hierarchy of the Applicable Procedural Rules

Article 19 contains the highly important general provisions relating to the rules of procedure applicable to the arbitral proceedings and fixes the order in which the potentially applicable rules apply.

According to Article 19, the rules of procedure contained in the ICC Rules of Arbitration themselves should apply in the first place. However, these rules are limited in number and do not cater for all the different procedural situations that may arise. This is because they must be capable of being applied in as many jurisdictions as possible and must be acceptable to parties from different legal backgrounds. If the ICC Rules of Arbitration contained more provisions, they would be less flexible and include provisions that it would be difficult to apply in all legal systems.

b) The Parties' Freedom to Determine the Applicable Rules of Procedure

Article 19 provides that the parties may decide on any specific provisions that are not covered by the Rules themselves, thereby upholding party autonomy, which is a basic principle in arbitration. However, party autonomy is not without limits. The parties should always check that any agreement reached with regard to procedural provisions does not violate any rules that are mandatory or considered part of public policy under an applicable law on arbitration procedure. This will usually be the arbitration law applicable at the place of the arbitration.

There is no obligation upon parties to refer to a national procedural law to complement the procedural provisions in the Rules. Indeed, it is not particularly recommendable to do so, as national procedural laws are designed to meet the domestic requirements of civil trials. It is therefore stated at the end of Article 19 that there is no necessity to refer to a national law when determining the rules of procedure. This principle ensures the flexibility of arbitrations and confirms that ICC arbitration proceedings should not be conducted in the same way as court proceedings.

According to Article 23(1)(g) of the Rules, the parties' agreements on procedure should be included in the Terms of Reference. If an agreement is made between the parties fixing the rules of procedure, this is a further reflection of party autonomy and must be respected by the arbitral tribunal. Were it not to do so, Article 15(1) would entitle the parties to ask for the arbitral tribunal to be replaced. If all the parties were jointly to submit to the ICC International Court of Arbitration a request for the arbitral tribunal to be removed from office, the Court would have to accede to this joint request and replace the arbitral tribunal.

The new provision of Article 24 requires the arbitral tribunal to organize a case management conference with the parties when drawing up the Terms of Reference or shortly thereafter to discuss procedural measures that may be adopted pursuant to Article 22(2). If applicable rules of procedure are agreed between the parties during a case management conference after the Terms of Reference were established, the arbitral tribunal shall typically record the agreed rules of procedure in a procedural order.

The parties are free to agree on the application of available Rules such as the IBA Rules on the Taking of Evidence in International Commercial Arbitration which were adopted in 1999 and revised in 2010 or they may find guidance in these rules for the taking of evidence proceedings in the arbitration. The topic of the applicable rules of evidence is usually discussed within the context of the case management conference.

c) Determination of the Rules of Procedure by the Arbitral Tribunal

If the parties have not agreed on any additional rules of procedure, the arbitral tribunal will determine these to the extent necessary. It usually does so through procedural orders, which are not arbitral awards and therefore do not have to be scrutinized and approved beforehand by the ICC Court (Article 33). It is also possible for the arbitral tribunal to formulate such rules in the Terms of Reference. The signing of the Terms of Reference makes such rules part of the parties' agreement (in this regard see Article 23 of the Rules). If the arbitral tribunal is not able to decide unanimously on a procedural measure to be taken, it shall decide by majority. Should, exceptionally, the arbitral tribunal not be able to take a decision by majority, the president of the arbitral tribunal alone is able to decide on such procedural measure, by analogy to Article 31(1). This provision specifies for the arbitral award that, if no majority can be reached, the award shall be made by the president alone.

Despite the hierarchy described above, it is the arbitral tribunal's duty to check that any agreements the parties have made relating to procedural rules are not contrary to those provisions of the ICC Rules of Arbitration from which they may not derogate, or any mandatory rules of law, since this could undermine the recognition and enforcement of the arbitral award. It should not be forgotten that the arbitral tribunal, like the Court, has an obligation under Article 41 of the Rules to make every effort to ensure that the arbitral award is enforceable at law.

Rare though such agreements may be, arbitral tribunals cannot afford to disregard them and will encourage the parties to abandon them.

d) Provisions of the Rules from which the Parties may not Derogate

Not all the provisions of the ICC Rules of Arbitration are mandatory. The autonomy enjoyed by the parties allows them to make agreements that depart from the Rules. Great care should be taken however when the powers of the Court are affected.

Although it is not specified in the Rules which provisions may or may not be modified by the parties, some articles clearly give them this possibility. For instance, Article 11(6) provides that the parties may depart from Articles 12 and 13 relating to the constitution of the arbitral tribunal, and Articles 18, 20 and 21 refer explicitly to the parties' freedom to agree on the place of the arbitration, the language of the arbitration, and the rules of law applicable to the dispute.

In principle, there can be no doubt that the parties are not free to alter certain provisions containing essential features of the ICC arbitration procedure. Thus, the parties may not agree to exempt the arbitral tribunal from drawing up the Terms of Reference (Article 23) or submitting its award in draft form to the Court for scrutiny (Article 33). Also, as the Secretariat sets out in the cover letter with which it transmits the file to the arbitral tribunal, the arbitrators must convene the parties to a case management conference (Article 24) and close the proceedings as soon as possible after the last hearing day concerning matters to be decided in an award or after the filing of the last authorized substantive submissions concerning such matters (Article 27).

According to Article 1 of Appendix I to the Rules, it is the ICC International Court of Arbitration that has the final word as to whether or not provisions departing from the Rules are acceptable. If the provisions that depart from the Rules are contained in the parties' arbitration agreement, i.e. before the start of the proceedings, the Court may, if it considers the changes unacceptable, decide that the proceedings are not in fact ICC arbitration proceedings. In this case, it will refuse to administer the arbitration. These kinds of questions are sometimes unclear and, happily, they rarely arise in practice (in this regard, see our comments in relation to the arbitration agreement).

e) Procedural Agreements Against the Arbitral Tribunal's Will

Article 19 does not answer the question whether, after the arbitral tribunal has been constituted, the parties may agree upon rules of procedure without its authorization or even against its will. This rarely happens, as such behavior would be discourteous and it is in practice unlikely that parties agree on basic rules of procedure that the arbitrators would consider unacceptable. Nonetheless, it should be noted that practitioners have differing opinions on the question. Some believe that, although bound by the rules agreed by the parties, arbitrators are entitled to resign if the rules originally agreed are modified after they have taken up office. Others consider that once the arbitral tribunal has been constituted, the parties cannot make procedural agreements contrary to the will of the arbitral tribunal, as the legal relationship is no longer just between the parties alone. However, the arbitrators cannot disregard the will of the parties without good cause.

In practice, there have been cases in which the parties agreed on long extensions of time limits or the cancellation or postponement of a hearing, without taking into account the expectations of the arbitral tribunal. Given that arbitrators must plan ahead, postponements may have considerable financial consequences and make it difficult for arbitrators to render the award within the prescribed time limits. There is therefore no balanced, all-purpose solution applicable whenever this kind of situation arises.

f) The Arbitral Tribunal's Conduct

In addition to procedural provisions, the Rules establish certain principles which the arbitrators must respect when conducting an arbitration.

Throughout the proceedings, an arbitral tribunal must make sure that it acts 'fairly' and 'impartially' and gives each party 'a reasonable opportunity to present its case' (Article 22(4)). This corresponds to the principle of due process, which is well known in common law jurisdictions and which corresponds in civil law jurisdictions generally to the rights of the parties to be heard and to be treated equally (see Article 1699 JC, Article 1464 NCPC, Article 1042(1) ZPO, Article 182(3) PILA, Article 18 of the UNCITRAL Model Law). All arbitrators must respect these general principles in all proceedings, regardless of the place where they are conducted and regardless of the other procedural rules applicable to them.

What do these principles actually mean in practice?

An arbitral tribunal's duty to act 'fairly' means that it must behave in a just and well-balanced way. When conducting the proceedings, it may not do anything that favors one of the parties. The arbitral tribunal's additional obligation to act 'impartially' means that it must show no bias. It must treat the parties in the same way and always avoid being partial or appearing to be so.

The arbitral tribunal must also ensure that each party has a reasonable opportunity to present its case in fact and at law. This corresponds to the general principle guaranteeing the right to a hearing. What is actually meant by 'reasonable' can be determined by the arbitral tribunal only in the light of the circumstances of the case. A party should have the possibility to give a reasonable presentation of the factual and legal situation and to react to the presentation made by the other party, provided this is done within the prescribed time limits.

'A reasonable opportunity to present its case' implies that the arbitral tribunal will see to it that the parties have the same or an equivalent opportunity to make written submissions, to present evidence or to speak during hearings, unless there is a particular reason for doing otherwise. The arbitral tribunal should also ensure that a party does not misuse its right to have a reasonable opportunity to present its case by introducing 'last minute' pleas that could have been dealt with earlier, in an attempt to prolong and delay the proceedings or to 'ambush' the other party. If the arbitral tribunal believes that a party is unnecessarily trying to drag out the proceedings, it may refuse to allow such requests without thereby denying the party its right to a hearing.

Basically, each party has the right to demand that the arbitral tribunal respects the principles laid down in Article 22(4) of the Rules. If, after objecting, a party continues to consider that it has not been treated 'fairly', or that the arbitral tribunal or one of the arbitrators has behaved 'partially', or that it has not had 'a reasonable opportunity to present its case', it may challenge the arbitrator or arbitrators pursuant to Article 14(1) of the Rules by submitting an application to the Court (for more on this question, see our comments on Articles 14 and 15, paragraphs 2 and 3).

Lastly, it should be noted that if a party considers the arbitral tribunal to be acting unfairly or partially or not to have given it a reasonable opportunity to present its case, this should be mentioned as soon as possible. According to Article 39 of the Rules and also the '*lex arbitri*', a party loses the right to object if it 'proceeds with the arbitration without raising its objection to a failure to comply with any provision of the Rules, or of any other rules applicable to the proceedings, any direction given by the arbitral tribunal'. Therefore, a party that wishes to raise an objection due to the arbitral tribunal's partiality or the fact that it has not had a reasonable opportunity to present its case cannot wait and act against the award once it has been rendered. It is reasonable to think that the party should make its objection based on Article 14(2) before the proceedings are closed pursuant to Article 27. Indeed, it would seem implausible and improper for a party to wait until the proceedings have been closed, the arbitral tribunal has deliberated and the award rendered before objecting that it did not have a reasonable opportunity to present its case or was treated unfairly by the arbitral tribunal.

In this connection, it is worth bearing in mind Article V(1)(b) of the New York Convention and the provisions of several national arbitration laws, which provide that a party may object to the enforcement of a foreign arbitral award or apply for a domestic arbitration award to be set aside if it has been unable to assert its rights or argue its case (see also Article 1717(3)(a)(ii) JC, Articles 1492(4) and 1520(4) NCPC, Article 1059(2)(1)(b) ZPO, Article 190(2)(d) and (3) PILA, Articles 34(2)(a)(ii) and 36(1)(a)(ii) of the UNCITRAL Model Law). However, it is hardly likely that an ICC award would be challenged on the basis of such provisions, as Article 22(4) of the Rules, combined with Article 39 of the Rules, guarantees that the party was able to state its claims and defend itself. Consequently, the party forfeits its right to raise an objection if it fails to allege an infringement of its rights in a timely fashion during the course of the proceedings.

5. Language of the Arbitration (Art. 20)

Article 20 of the Rules reads:

> 'Language of the Arbitration
>
> In the absence of an agreement by the parties, the arbitral tribunal shall determine the language or languages of the arbitration, due regard being given to all relevant circumstances, including the language of the contract.'

a) The Parties' Freedom to Choose the Language of the Arbitrations

In arbitration proceedings, like in all litigation, the language is very important. It is both the means by which each party tries to prove its case to the arbitrators and the instrument with which the arbitrators conduct the proceedings and make their decisions. In international arbitrations, the parties often speak different languages, unless they come from the same linguistic region. The same may be said of the arbitrators. This may give rise to considerable problems. It should not be forgotten that, unlike state courts, arbitral tribunals are not an offshoot of the state in which the arbitration takes place and they therefore do not necessarily have to conduct the proceedings in the official language of that country.

The ICC Rules of Arbitration are neutral as far as language is concerned and allow the proceedings to be conducted in any language.

There is no particular problem if the parties have chosen a language in their arbitration agreement or subsequently. The fact that they use the same language may be construed as an implicit agreement. It should be borne in mind, however, that arbitrations conducted in more than one language present considerable difficulties as they usually necessitate simultaneous or consecutive translation at hearings, which is both time-consuming and costly. For this reason, it is preferable for the participants to agree on the use of only one language.

ICC always takes any agreement on language into account when appointing an arbitrator.

In most cases the parties have agreed or reach agreement on the language of the proceedings. A claimant filing a request for arbitration is required pursuant to Article 4(3)(h) to provide all relevant particulars and any observations or proposals on the language of the arbitration. A respondent is required to do likewise in its answer to the request for arbitration pursuant to Article 5(1)(f). During the years 2006-2010, the parties had agreed in 96% of the cases filed on the language of the arbitration. In only

4% the language of the arbitration was determined by the arbitral tribunal or agreed between the parties after the filing of the request for arbitration. Where the parties had agreed on the language of the arbitration in their arbitration agreement, they had chosen English in 76% of the cases. In the other cases they had agreed on the following languages: French (7%), Spanish (4%), German (4%), Portuguese (2%), Italian (1%), Polish (less than 1%), Czech (less than 1%), Greek (less than 1%), Turkish (less than 1%), Arabic (less than 1%), other (less than 1%), and in 2% of the cases they had chosen for a bilingual arbitration (see J. Fry, S. Greenberg and F. Mazza, *The Secretariat's Guide to ICC Arbitration*, ICC Publication No. 729 E, Paris, 2012, p. 213).

b) Determination of the Language of the Arbitration by the Arbitral Tribunal

If the parties have not agreed on the language of the arbitration and the parties use different languages in their pleadings, the language or languages of the arbitration must be determined by the arbitral tribunal, unless it manages to elicit an agreement from the parties. The arbitral tribunal is well advised to give the parties an opportunity to file further comments on the issue of the language of the arbitration before taking a decision on the language of the arbitration, as it may well be that the parties still reach agreement on the language after having given their first indications on the language of the arbitration in the request for arbitration and in the answer thereto. Although this does not have to happen at any particular time, for practical purposes the arbitral tribunal should determine the language of the arbitration at the latest when the Terms of Reference are drawn up. The Terms of Reference will then be established in the language chosen by the parties or determined by the arbitral tribunal. Moreover, the arbitral tribunal will be able to include special provisions on the language of the arbitration in the Terms of Reference.

The Rules do not provide a particular form in which the arbitral tribunal must determine the language of the arbitration. As this decision needs at best to be taken before the Terms of Reference are established, it is not appropriate to lay this decision down in an arbitral award. Such decision is generally taken through a procedural order or in a letter by the arbitral tribunal.

Besides the language of the contract, other factors to be considered, although not specified in Article 20, may include the linguistic skills of the parties and their lawyers and those of the arbitrators, as well as the language or languages used by the parties in their business relations. It is up to the parties to describe the relevant circumstances. Unless the rules of law applicable at the place of the arbitration would contain mandatory provisions on language to be taken into account, which is rarely the case, the arbitral tribunal is free to choose whatever language or languages it considers appropriate, subject to fair and equal treatment requirements. Given the importance of the language to the parties when presenting their cases, the arbitrators occasionally decide that each party may use its own language if this is justified by the parties' circumstances prior to the dispute and is within the limits of the arbitrators' own linguistic skills. In accordance with arbitral practice, the Rules expressly allow the use of more than one language. In most cases, the arbitral tribunal will decide to use only one of these languages itself, however. Only very occasionally will the parties' pleadings and the arbitral tribunal's decisions be drafted in two languages. If the parties are happy to allow this, the arbitral tribunal may suggest to confirm such an agreement in the Terms of Reference. In that case, it is important to indicate in which language the award will be rendered. In the exceptional case where the arbitral award would be rendered in two languages, the parties and the arbitral tribunal are well advised either to agree or otherwise to determine which of the two languages will be the prevailing language, so to avoid any discussion in case of possible conflicts in wording between the two language versions of the arbitral award.

In the ICC arbitrations administered in 2013, arbitral awards were rendered in 13 languages. More than 80% of the arbitral awards were rendered in English. The other awards were rendered in French (7%), Spanish (5%), German (3%), Portuguese (2%), and occasionally awards were rendered in Arabic, Bulgarian, Italian, Norwegian, Romanian, Russian and Serbian. In two cases the arbitral tribunal rendered bilingual awards: in one case the award was rendered in English and Portuguese, and in another case in English and Chinese (see '2013 Statistical Report' published in *ICC International Court of Arbitration Bulletin*, Paris, Vol. 25/Nr. 1 – 2014, p. 14). In 2012, the great majority of awards was also rendered in English (76.4%) and arbitral awards were rendered in 13 other languages: French (8.4%), Spanish (6.3%), German (3.3%), Portuguese (2.4%), Italian (0.8%), Chinese (0.6%), Norwegian (0.4%), Polish (0.4%), Czech, Dutch, Japanese, Swedish and Turkish (0.2% each) (see '2012 Statistical Report' published in *ICC International Court of Arbitration Bulletin*, Paris, Vol. 24/Nr. 1 – 2013, p. 15).

In addition to the general considerations discussed above, a certain number of specific problems should be mentioned which are sometimes given insufficient attention in practice.

c) The Nomination of Arbitrators

The ICC Court always takes any agreement on language into account when appointing an arbitrator. When parties do not agree on the language of the arbitration and a three-member arbitral tribunal must be constituted, one of the parties may try to influence the decision to be taken by the arbitral tribunal on the language of the arbitration by nominating an arbitrator who does not speak the other language to be taken into consideration. Given that the nomination of an arbitrator to serve on a three-member tribunal is one of the basic rights of the parties, a precarious situation may result. In such circumstances, especially if requested by the other party, the ICC Court may decide not to confirm the person concerned, on the basis of Article 13(1), because that person lacks a requisite skill. However, the Court is free to decide as it thinks fit, although it exercises its discretion with restraint.

d) The Language of Correspondence with the Secretariat and the Language of the Initial Pleadings

Under the Rules, the Secretariat of the Court does not have any power to decide in which language correspondence and pleadings should be sent to it. The Secretariat is able to correspond with the parties in a great number of languages, given that staff members of the Secretariat originate from around 30 different countries and speak many different languages. If nobody in the Secretariat has the requisite linguistic skills, however, it will be necessary to have the documents translated whenever they concern matters to be dealt with by the Secretariat or the Court. This may result in delays, so it is advisable to draft all important letters and submissions prior to the transmission of the file to the arbitral tribunal in one of the official languages of the Court, namely English or French. It sometimes happens that when a party files a request for arbitration in a language which is neither that of the opposite party nor the agreed language, the opposite party may claim that the request is irregular and that the period allowed for answering the request has not started to run. If the Secretariat is unable to get the parties to agree on a pragmatic solution, it will be for the arbitral tribunal to settle the matter in accordance with the Rules. Given that neither Article 4 nor 5 of the Rules lays down any requirements as to language, it could be argued that such an occurrence is of no consequence. However, it is not out of the question that an arbitral tribunal would think differently in a given case.

e) Translation of Submissions and Documents Produced as Evidence

In multilingual arbitrations, the question arises as to who should bear the costs of the necessary translations. As no two cases are alike, it is impossible to ascertain a strict rule. However, to avoid discussions over the quality and accuracy of the translations, it is preferable for each party to have its own translations of the other party's documents. In addition, it may be agreed, or the arbitral tribunal may order, that an advance be paid to cover the resulting costs and that they be claimed at the end of the proceedings along with all other procedural expenses.

The same approach may be adopted for documents produced as evidence that are in another language. However, it is not unusual for a party submitting such documents in a language other than that which has been decided upon for the procedure to provide a translation and advance the associated costs.

It is generally not required to submit certified translations of documents submitted in another language than the language of the arbitration. However, in case of controversy about the translation of a document, a party may be well advised to have the translation made by a certified translator or an arbitral tribunal may require this.

f) The Hearing of Witnesses

The witnesses are not always able to express themselves in the language of the arbitration. Their statements may need to be translated simultaneously or consecutively. It should be borne in mind that simultaneous translation is much more expensive. To ensure that the hearing runs smoothly, the arbitral tribunal should make all necessary arrangements with the interpreters and technical staff. For this purpose, it may ask the Secretariat of the Court to help setting up the necessary local contacts through the many cooperation agreements the ICC has with other arbitration bodies such as the American Arbitration Association or the German Arbitration Institute (DIS) and the ICC national committees. Sometimes, especially in England and North America, when the parties' lawyers are experienced in arbitration and have offices at the place of the arbitration, the arbitral tribunal will let them make the necessary arrangements under its instructions and supervision.

g) The Language of the Applicable Rules of Law

Often, in international arbitrations, the language of the arbitration is not the same as the language in which the applicable rules of law have been drafted and commented upon. This does not necessarily matter, however, as the difficulty at issue may be of a factual nature, calling above all for an interpretation of the contract. If this is not the case, the parties and their lawyers should ensure that the arbitrator they choose has at least some knowledge of the applicable law and the linguistic understanding to avoid having to use translations. In cases involving legal difficulties, parties should carefully describe the legal bases on which they rely, with references to case law, scholarly articles, and even expert legal opinions. These may need to be accompanied by translations. It is worth recalling that the general rule according to which the parties describe the facts and the tribunal knows and ascertains the law (*'Iura novit curia'*) does not automatically apply in international arbitration.

h) The Linguistic Skills of the Parties' Lawyers

Lastly, the parties' lawyers should also be chosen according to the languages likely to be used in the arbitration. Not only will this help to ensure that the clients' interests are effectively defended, but also avoids translating costs and the risk of delays when preparing submissions. When deadlines have been set for submitting observations, the need to obtain a translation may lead to the loss of valuable time. If the parties' lawyers have inadequate linguistic skills, this may be detrimental to the proceedings.

6. Applicable Rules of Law (Art. 21)

Article 21 of the Rules reads:

> 'Applicable Rules of Law
>
> 1. The parties shall be free to agree upon the rules of law to be applied by the arbitral tribunal to the merits of the dispute. In the absence of any such agreement, the arbitral tribunal shall apply the rules of law which it determines to be appropriate.
>
> 2. The arbitral tribunal shall take account of the provisions of the contract, if any, between the parties and of any relevant trade usages.
>
> 3. The arbitral tribunal shall assume the powers of an amiable compositeur or decide ex aequo et bono only if the parties have agreed to give it such powers.'

The first and second paragraphs of this article appear at first sight to be clear and unambiguous. The arbitral tribunal must settle the dispute on the basis of the provisions of the contract, if any, and, where these are insufficient, on the basis of the rules of law chosen by the parties, having regard to any relevant trade usages. In the 2012 Rules the words 'if any' have been inserted in Article 21(2) so to make it clear that ICC arbitration is also possible in case the arbitration agreement is not contained in a contract but in another instrument including an international investment treaty. In Article 21(3) the word 'any' was inserted before 'trade usages', because the concern had been raised that, in investment arbitration, no trade usages should normally apply (Report of the ICC Commission on Arbitration and ADR on 'Arbitration Involving States or State Entities', 2012, par. 46 and 48, Appendix 16 below).

a) Choice of the Applicable Rules of Law by the Parties

(1) Choice of the 'Rules of Law' by the Parties.

In most of the cases referred to ICC arbitration the parties have already chosen the law to be applied by the arbitral tribunal to the merits of the dispute. The parties had chosen the applicable rules of law in 90% of the contracts underlying disputes referred to the ICC Court in 2013. In 97% of contracts they chose a national law. The choices made by the parties concerned the rules of law of 93 different nations and independent territories. The rules of law most frequently chosen by the parties were: English law (15.64%), Swiss law (10.09%), US laws (8.70%), French law (7.69%), German law (7.31%), Brazilian law (4.67%), Spanish law (3.28%), Austrian law

(2.77 %), Greek law (2.14 %), Mexican law (1.89 %), Romanian law (1.89 %), Algerian law (1.77 %), Singaporean law (1.77 %), Italian law (1.64 %), Indian law (1.39 %). In 3 % of contracts, the parties chose rules or principles other than national laws for the determination of their dispute, including the United Nations Convention on Contracts for the International Sale of Goods (14 contracts), international law (6 contracts), the UNIDROIT Principles on International Commercial Contracts (2 contracts), European Union Law (1 contract), '*amiable composition*' (1 contract) and the ICC Incoterms rules (1 contract). In a few cases, the parties made negative choices, whereby they excluded the application of certain rules of law (see '2013 Statistical Report' published in *ICC International Court of Arbitration Bulletin*, Paris, Vol. 25/Nr. 1 – 2014, p. 13-14).

It should be noted that since 1998 the ICC Rules of Arbitration aimed to give parties greater freedom by allowing them to choose the 'rules of law' to be applied by the arbitral tribunal to the merits of the dispute, rather than simply the 'law' as laid down in the previous version of the Rules (Article 13(3) of the 1988 Rules of Arbitration). In so doing, they acknowledged the growing trend over recent years for parties to choose as the governing law of their contract not a national law but 'general principles of law', '*lex mercatoria*' or the UNIDROIT Principles of International Commercial Contracts (see b)(5) below).

(2) Trade Usages.

Like some international conventions, the UNCITRAL Model Law and the arbitration rules of certain other institutions, Article 21(2) requires the arbitral tribunal to take account of any trade usages even if it applies a national law.

It may often be helpful to refer to trade usages as a way of filling gaps in the applicable law. This is because usages are inclined to develop more quickly than law in the field of international trade. However, the need to take account of trade usages should not lead the arbitral tribunal to disregard the provisions of the law chosen by the parties.

Sometimes, when the parties have not specified the applicable law, arbitrators decide the case on the basis of trade usages only. They justify this approach by referring to those international conventions and institutional rules which, as mentioned above, require arbitrators in all cases to take account of trade usages.

b) Determination of the Applicable Rules of Law by the Arbitral Tribunal

The fact that since 1995 around 80 % of the contracts in the cases referred each year to ICC have contained a choice-of-law clause may lead one to think that the provision contained in the second sentence of Article 21(1) is of little practical importance. It nonetheless calls for comment, as the number of cases in which there is no choice of law is not insignificant and there are legal differences between the way an arbitral tribunal and a state court determine the applicable law.

It should be mentioned that the fact that there is no explicit choice of law in a contract does not necessarily mean that the parties have not made such a choice, as this may be implicit or result from their behavior. The arbitrators should decide whether or not this is the case on the basis of the parties' statements. In this respect, the legal background of the arbitrators may have an impact.

It should be further noted that when the applicable law has not been expressly stated in the contract, arbitrators sometimes interpret the parties' positions as implying that they have made a 'negative' choice of law, meaning that they have excluded a national law in favor of international trade usages or '*lex mercatoria*'.

Prior to 1998, the arbitral tribunal was required to apply the law designated as the proper law by the rule of conflict which it considered appropriate and was free to decide which rule of conflict this should be. The presence of this provision was due to the fact that there is not always a system of conflict rules for arbitral tribunals, as there is for courts in some countries (e.g. Germany (see Introductory Act to the Civil Code) and Switzerland (see PILA itself)). In an ICC arbitration, the seat of the arbitral tribunal will often be in a country other than the countries from which the parties come. However, it is independent of the state authorities in that country and not bound by the substantive or procedural law in force there unless such law has been chosen. Nor is it under any obligation to apply the particular rules of conflict in force at the place of the arbitration. Only the mandatory provisions of the arbitration law at the place of the arbitration are binding upon it. This law sometimes contains fall-back provisions indicating how the applicable law should be determined ('rules of conflict of laws'). Given the desirability of a minimum of predictability, it was agreed to include such a provision in the former ICC Rules of Arbitration, especially as the application of the rules of conflict of only one of the countries from which the parties originate did not seem to be a satisfactory alternative.

Those arbitral awards that have been published show the great variety of methods used by international arbitrators to determine the applicable law. More often than not, and depending on the parties' respective arguments, arbitrators determine the rules of law applicable to the merits of the dispute according to one of the following methods:

(1) Use of a Given System of Conflict-of-Law Rules.

According to this method, the arbitrator determines the applicable law using the rule of conflict he or she deems to be appropriate to the particular case. This is the principle contained in Article 13(3) of the 1988 ICC Rules of Arbitration. It may still be applied by arbitrators, even after the introduction of the 1998 and the 2012 Rules, which do not contain a similar provision.

Upon what basis should the rule of conflict to be used by an international arbitrator be determined? Should it be the rule of conflict of the country from which the arbitrator comes or is a national, or that of the country in which the arbitral tribunal has its seat or from which one or other of the parties comes? An arbitrator is not bound to follow the rules of conflict of one country rather than of another, but may choose any of the various possibilities, according to his or her preference. International arbitrators appear generally not to limit themselves to a single national system of conflict-of-laws rules.

(2) Application of the Rules of Conflict of More than One Country Connected with the Dispute Subject to Arbitration.

Pursuant to this method, the arbitral tribunal examines in turn the conflict-of-laws rules of the different legal systems connected with the dispute (e.g. those of the country from which the parties originate or those of the country in which the contract was signed or performed). If these rules point towards the same law, this is the law the arbitrator will declare to be applicable. This method has the advantage of predictability. On the other hand, it would serve little purpose if the rules of conflict were to point towards different laws.

(3) Use of the General Principles of Private International Law.

This method involves identifying common or generally accepted principles amongst the main conflict-of-laws rules. On this basis, arbitrators sometimes look for the 'center of gravity' or the 'most closely connected country'.

Although plausible, the reference to different systems of conflict-of-laws rules contains a risk of simplification, as the above-mentioned principles vary somewhat from one system to another. This perhaps explains why some arbitral tribunals prefer to refer to international conventions such as the European Union Convention on the Law Applicable to Contractual Obligations, opened for signature in Rome on 19 June 1980 (this Convention was replaced by Regulation (EC) No. 593/2008 of the European Parliament and of the Council of 17 June 2008 on the law applicable to contractual obligations (hereinafter 'Rome I')), or the Hague Convention of 22 December 1986 on the Law Applicable to International Sales of Goods.

(4) The 'Voie Directe' or Direct Method.

Under the so-called '*voie directe*', the applicable law is determined without referring to any conflict-of-laws system. Usually the arbitrator will endeavor to establish a determining or meaningful connection between the contract and the law that he or she decides to apply. This may, for instance, be the place of the performance which is characteristic of the contract, the center of gravity of the contract, the place where the contract is performed, or the seller's place of residence, etc. However, this approach may prove dangerous and questionable if the dispute is essentially about the validity of the contract or about whether or not claims are time-barred.

(5) Application of Rules other than Those of a National Law to the Merits of the Dispute.

On several occasions arbitrators have based their awards not on a given national law but on trade usages or general principles of law. Such awards have been rendered both in cases where arbitrators were vested with the powers of an '*amiable compositeur*' and those where they were not.

(a) Trade usages.

Sometimes, in cases where the parties have not specified the applicable law (see a)(2) above), the arbitral tribunal will base its decision on trade usages alone, referring for this purpose to international conventions and the rules of other arbitration institutions that require arbitrators to take account of trade usages in all cases, as mentioned above.

(b) '*Lex mercatoria*' and 'general principles of law'.

Unlike 'trade usages', these two expressions, which are often thought to be synonymous, are not used in international conventions or the rules of arbitration institutions. There has been much scholarly discussion about '*lex mercatoria*' since the seminal writings of Berthold Goldman and Clive Schmitthoff in the nineteen sixties. However, no definition that clearly describes the concept and encompasses all views expressed on the subject has so far been found. Some legal writers submit that arbitrators often do not distinguish between 'trade usages' and '*lex mercatoria*'. There have so far been very few awards based exclusively on '*lex mercatoria*', without at the same time applying a national law. Some of these awards have been challenged in state courts. Dismissing such actions, English and French courts have held that arbitrators may base their decisions on internationally recognized legal principles regulating contractual relations, or even on '*lex mercatoria*'. These decisions of both state courts and arbitral tribunals show that parties consider it acceptable to have their disputes resolved in accordance with '*lex mercatoria*' rather than a given national law.

When it comes to identifying the rules of '*lex mercatoria*' or the 'general principles of law' regarding international sales, arbitrators regularly rely on the United Nations Convention on Contracts for the International Sale of Goods, concluded at Vienna on 10 April 1980.

In May 1994, UNIDROIT (International Institute for the Unification of Private Law) published the 'Principles of International Commercial Contracts', comprising 119 general rules for international contracts. In 2004, a new, expanded edition with 185 articles was published. In 2010 a newly expanded version containing 210 articles was published. As stated in the Preamble to these Principles, '[t]hey shall be applied when the parties have agreed that their contract be governed by them. They may be applied when the parties have agreed that their contract be governed by general principles of law, the '*lex mercatoria*' or the like. They may be applied when the parties have not chosen any law to govern their contract. They may be used to interpret or supplement international uniform law instruments. They may be used to interpret or supplement domestic law. They may serve as a model for national and international legislators.' The UNIDROIT Principles will certainly help to give substance to '*lex mercatoria*' and for this reason are very useful and deserve to be used in international commercial arbitration.

(6) Practical Conclusions.

Legal counsel should give consideration to the points discussed above when the arbitral tribunal is being constituted, bearing in mind their clients' interests. They should first try to find out whether the arbitral tribunal or the sole arbitrator is likely to have allegiances towards a particular 'school'. Well-known arbitrators will often have expressed their thoughts on the matter in articles or awards.

When preparing one's defense, it may be helpful to refer to the practice of international arbitral tribunals, as reflected in the *Collection of ICC Arbitral Awards* or the *Yearbook Commercial Arbitration* which is published each year by the International Council for Commercial Arbitration (see Bibliography). The decisions of international arbitral tribunals are increasingly influenced by such practice, although it does not constitute a binding precedent.

Finally, it should be mentioned that, as a general rule, there is no obligation to apply a single law or set of rules to all aspects of the dispute. In theory, it is possible to apply to certain questions a different law from that which is applicable to the rest of the dispute, according to the method of *dépeçage* (splitting of the contract). Thus there will be different laws governing different questions: for example, the capacity to contract and powers of representation will be subject to the law of the country from which the parties originate.

c) Mandatory Rules

It goes without saying that neither the parties nor the arbitral tribunal may elude mandatory law. This having been said, it is difficult to identify mandatory law in a given arbitration. Also, opinions differ on the subject.

One of the problems that may arise in this connection and directly affects the implementation of the arbitration agreement is the arbitrability of the dispute. Most countries have laws giving state courts sole jurisdiction over certain disputes, which are consequently excluded from arbitration. They involve situations where the outcome of the dispute has an effect upon third parties (e.g. – although not the case everywhere – certain disputes concerning companies, family maintenance, or claims for the annulment or cancellation of patents and trademarks) or situations that have an important public interest aspect.

State courts will refer simply to their rules of conflict, if need be. Article 9 of the Rome I Regulation provides that the mandatory rules of a country other than that of which the law is applicable, should be respected, whenever they are regarded as crucial by a country for safeguarding its public interests, such as political, social or economic organization, to such an extent that they are applicable to any situation falling within their scope, irrespective of the law otherwise applicable to the contract. Article 19 PILA likewise provides that the mandatory law of a third country shall apply if this is appropriate from the perspective of Swiss law and provided there is a close connection with this law. However, as already mentioned, these provisions do not automatically apply to arbitral tribunals.

If the law applicable to a party's personal status limits its freedom to contract, that law must be applied whenever it is mandatory for the party concerned, even if the legal consequences of doing so are not entirely satisfying, as may be the case when a state claims immunity or when a restrictive provision seems quite unjustified in the circumstances.

When such situations arise in international arbitrations, arbitrators will try to find another criterion for characterizing them in a given case. There is a widespread tendency to subject such mandatory national provisions to the rule of reason, i.e. the mandatory provision will usually be taken into consideration only if it reflects 'international public policy'. Although not unknown in German law, this tendency has become prominent, especially in French and Swiss law, where the principles generally accepted by the international community are used as criteria. In order to determine in a European context the 'close connection', reference may be made to the second sentence of Article 9(3) of the Rome I Regulation.

There may be other mandatory rules affecting not the arbitrability of the dispute but its very subject matter. These may, for example, render certain contractual clauses null and void. Competition law may play an important but sometimes problematic role in international commercial disputes (cf. Articles 101 and 102 (formerly 81 and 82) of the Treaty on the Functioning of the European Union, and US antitrust law), especially when its application in other territories – intended by the legislator – is at issue. Arbitrators should examine whether mandatory competition rules are applicable extra-territorially.

It may be argued that mandatory law should be applied directly in situations where all the parties are clearly subject to it, if they have not submitted their dispute to an arbitral tribunal with its seat in a 'neutral' country. For instance, if a German party and a Belgian party are opposed over the performance of a exclusive sales agreement relating to Spain, European competition law must be applied even if the arbitral tribunal has its seat in Switzerland. However, it should be added that a different view is sometimes taken when, for example, the parties have agreed on the application of Swiss law to their business relations.

Embargoes constitute a special case. In international arbitration, they are sometimes characterized not as legal but factual issues preventing the performance of the contract. There is a general tendency to consider embargoes prescribed by international organizations such as the United Nations as mandatory law, whereas discriminatory embargoes (e.g. Arab states against Israel) are not taken into account as they are considered to be contrary to higher international legal principles. This is a controversial subject which cannot be developed at any greater length in the present context.

According to national arbitration laws and Article V of the New York Convention, failure to respect mandatory law, insofar as it constitutes a violation of public policy, may cause state courts to refuse the recognition of arbitral awards in exequatur proceedings. The same also applies in applications for awards to be set aside. Parties should therefore take this into account when drafting their claims. Article 41 of the ICC Rules of Arbitration calls for arbitrators to do likewise, and it is in any case unlikely that they would overlook the matter.

d) Decisions Based on Amiable Composition and Ex Aequo et Bono

There is some discussion as to what is exactly meant with the concept of '*amiable composition*' and deciding '*ex aequo et bono*'. In some legal systems this concept is well known, but it is a concept recognized in international arbitration and also in international legal instruments (see Article 28(3) of the UNCITRAL Model Law on International Commercial Arbitration).

If the parties have empowered the arbitral tribunal to act as an *amiable compositeur*, it may depart from a strict application of the law if this would lead to an unjust or inequitable result. In such situations, the arbitral tribunal has the power to settle the dispute '*ex aequo et bono*' or in equity. There is some discussion, however, as to whether or not the arbitral tribunal should apply rules of law to the dispute before determining whether these rules lead to a just or equitable result, or whether the arbitral tribunal may decide the matter purely on principles of fairness without taking into account any rules of law. It should be noted, however, that an '*amiable compositeur*' is required to respect (international) public policy to the extent described above, both when conducting the proceedings and when making a decision on the merits.

Arbitrators may act as '*amiables compositeurs*' only if they have been expressly empowered to do so by the parties. In case the power of '*amiable compositeur*' have been conferred upon the arbitral tribunal, this should be mentioned in the Terms of Reference pursuant to Article 23(1)(g). It is rare in practice for parties to authorize the arbitral tribunal to decide in equity, as provided in Article 21(3). If they do so, the arbitral tribunal's decision will be binding on them, given that it takes the form of a reasoned arbitral award.

e) Form of the Arbitral Tribunal's Decision

The Rules do not provide a particular form in which the arbitral tribunal must determine the law applicable to the substance of the dispute, if such decision needs to be taken. As it is an important decision with respect to the substance of the matter, it is necessary to formulate it in writing and to provide reasons for it. The arbitral tribunal may decide to take its decision through a procedural order or through an interim award, in case the parties expect to be informed of the arbitral tribunal's decision before they make further submissions on the substance of the matter.

If the arbitral tribunal decides to take the decision through a procedural order, the arbitral tribunal will nevertheless have to include its decision also in the arbitral award which it shall render at the end of the arbitration so that its decision can be legally enforced, if needed.

If the arbitral tribunal decides to determine the applicable law by an interim award, it has to submit the draft award first for scrutiny to the ICC Court pursuant to Article 33 of the Rules.

7. Conduct of the Arbitration (Art. 22)

Article 22 of the Rules reads:

> 'Conduct of the Arbitration
>
> 1. The arbitral tribunal and the parties shall make every effort to conduct the arbitration in an expeditious and cost-effective manner, having regard to the complexity and value of the dispute.
>
> 2. In order to ensure effective case management, the arbitral tribunal, after consulting the parties, may adopt such procedural measures as it considers appropriate, provided that they are not contrary to any agreement of the parties.
>
> 3. Upon the request of any party, the arbitral tribunal may make orders concerning the confidentiality of the arbitration proceedings or of any other matters in connection with the arbitration and may take measures for protecting trade secrets and confidential information.
>
> 4. In all cases, the arbitral tribunal shall act fairly and impartially and ensure that each party has a reasonable opportunity to present its case.
>
> 5. The parties undertake to comply with any order made by the arbitral tribunal.'

a) General Remarks

Article 22 is a new provision that reflects one of the main goals envisaged by the revision of the ICC Rules of Arbitration in 2012. The 2012 Rules are intended to offer new possibilities to conduct arbitrations more rapidly and with greater cost efficiency. Article 22 confirms the principle that arbitration proceedings can be tailor-made in accordance with the procedural expectations of the parties (Article 22(2)). But the arbitral tribunal and the parties have the duty to conduct the arbitration in an expeditious and cost-effective manner, having regard to the complexity of the dispute. Other obligations regarding the conduct of an arbitration are contained in Article 24 that requires the arbitral tribunal to convene a case management conference so as to consult the parties on appropriate procedural measures to be adopted pursuant to Article 22(2). Appendix IV to the Rules proposes several measures for controlling time and cost in arbitration. These provisions and the proposed measures result from the report of the ICC Commission on Arbitration and ADR on 'Techniques for Controlling Time and Costs in International Arbitration'. A first edition of this report was published in 2009, and a second edition in 2012 (see Appendix 15 below).

Article 22(4) confirms another important duty of the arbitral tribunal, namely that it shall always act fairly and impartially. This duty was contained in the 1998 Rules in Article 15(2).

Article 22(3) further elaborates on the provision of Article 20(7) of the 1998 Rules.

b) Controlling Time and Costs in Arbitration (Art. 22(1))

The ICC Rules of Arbitration provide a general framework for the conduct of arbitration proceedings with typical requirements such as the duty of the arbitral tribunal to establish Terms of Reference before examining the substance of the claims and to submit the arbitral award in draft form to the ICC Court before it can be rendered. The ICC Rules also provide time limits for the arbitrators to accomplish their duties. However, as arbitration is based on an agreement between parties, the parties have the liberty to choose a tailor made arbitration in accordance with their wishes and expectations. The parties are free to agree on the timetable for their submissions, on the number of submissions, on the type of taking of evidence for their arbitration, on the hearing of witnesses, on the appointment of experts, on site visits, and on other aspects relating to the procedure. When the parties do not agree on these procedural aspects, the arbitral tribunal is authorized and even required to determine them. The question whether the parties may agree on procedural aspects relating to the procedure against the will of the arbitral tribunal is a debated topic.

As parties in international arbitration often originate from different legal and cultural backgrounds, they may have different expectations and they may each wish to see procedural steps taken to which they are used in their own legal environment. This may lead to duplication of procedural steps and unnecessary delays and high costs of international arbitrations.

A study of the ICC Commission on Arbitration in 2007 on cases where an arbitral award was rendered in 2003 and 2004 had shown that in ICC arbitrations the largest part of the costs of the arbitration proceedings is related to the party costs, including lawyers' fees and expenses, expenses related to witness and expert evidence and other costs incurred by the parties for the arbitration, making up on average for 82% of the costs of an ICC arbitration. It also resulted from this study that on average 16% of the costs of an ICC arbitration covered arbitrators' fees and expenses, and that only 2% of the costs covered ICC administrative expenses (see Report of the ICC Commission on Arbitration and ADR on 'Techniques for Controlling Time and Costs in Arbitration', ICC Publication No. 843, Paris, 2009, p. 11; Report of the ICC Commission on Arbitration and ADR on 'Effective Management of Arbitration: A Guide for In-House Counsel and other Party Representatives', ICC Publication No. 866-0 E, Paris, 2014, p. 3; see Appendix 14 below).

The growing complaints about the long durations and about the high costs in international arbitrations, in particular the party costs, instigated the ICC Commission on Arbitration and ADR to establish a report on 'Techniques for Controlling Time and Costs in International Arbitration' (See Appendix 15 below). This report provides guidance to the parties not only on the drafting of their arbitration agreements but above all on the procedure during the arbitration. It provides comments and proposals on various aspects which the parties may not always think about or which they may not be familiar with and which may help to reduce time and costs in the arbitration. But many of the comments and proposals also provide practical guidance for arbitrators. These more than 80 comments and proposals deal with aspects such as the selection of counsel and of arbitrators, the preparation of the request for arbitration and of the answer thereto, multiparty and multicontract arbitrations, consolidation, emergency arbitrator proceedings, the language of the arbitration, the drafting of the Terms of Reference, the organization of the case management conference, the procedural timetable, the written submissions by the parties, the documentary evidence, the witness statements, the expert evidence, the organization of hearings, the deliberation of the arbitral award and the allocation of costs.

When the arbitral tribunal has to decide about the allocation of the costs of the arbitration, it may pursuant to Article 37(5) take into account such circumstances as it considers relevant, including the extent to which each party has conducted the arbitration in an expeditious and cost-effective manner. The arbitral tribunal is well advised to draw the attention of the parties to this provision shortly after the file was transmitted to it, so that the parties realize what the consequences may be of a procedure that is not conducted in an expeditious and cost-effective manner. Depending on the complexity of the matter, the arbitral tribunal may decide that a party should support the costs of the arbitration entirely or to a larger extent, if it has behaved in a manner which was not in accordance with the requirement of Article 22(1). Such behavior could includes: excessive document requests, excessive legal argument, excessive cross-examination, dilatory tactics, exaggerated claims, failure to comply with procedural orders, unjustified applications for interim relief, and unjustified failure to comply with the procedural calendar (Commission report on 'Techniques for Controlling Time and Costs in International Arbitration', second edition, 2012, par. 82, see Appendix 15 below). Appendix IV to the Rules 'Case Management Techniques' also stresses the particular importance to ensure that time and costs are proportionate to what is at stake in the dispute.

To stress the importance of the cost-effective conduct of an arbitration, the ICC Commission on Arbitration and ADR published in 2014 a Guide specifically for in-house counsel and party representatives (Report of the ICC Commission on Arbitration and ADR on 'Effective Management of Arbitration: A Guide for In-House Counsel and other Party Representatives', 2014, see Appendix 14 below).

Other reports were made by the ICC Commission on Arbitration and ADR with the concern to have arbitrations conducted in an expeditious and cost-effective manner, more particularly:

(i) Report on 'Techniques for Managing Electronic Document Production When it is Permitted or Required in International Arbitration' issued in 2012 (see Appendix 17 below);

(ii) Report on 'Issues for Arbitrators to Consider Regarding Expertise' issued in 2010 under the 2003 ICC Rules for Expertise and under the 1998 ICC Rules of Arbitration (see Appendix 18 below);

(iii) Report on 'Issues for Experts acting under the ICC Rules of Expertise or the ICC Rules of Arbitration' issued in 2009 under the 2003 ICC Rules for Expertise and under the 1998 ICC Rules of Arbitration (see Appendix 19 below).

c) Measures Adopted by the Arbitral Tribunal (Art. 22(2))

Article 22(2) allows the arbitral tribunal to adopt procedural measures in order to ensure an effective case management, to the extent that they are not contrary to an agreement of the parties. This provision confirms the principle of party autonomy in tailoring the proceedings. If parties reach an agreement on procedural measures during a case management conference, the arbitral tribunal is well advised to confirm these measures in writing. This is typically done in a procedural order. If a three-member arbitral tribunal is constituted, it shall generally be agreed that, for reasons of efficiency, the procedural orders may be signed by the president of the arbitral tribunal alone and that they need not be co-signed by the co-arbitrators.

In case the parties do not reach agreement on procedural measures, after they were consulted by the arbitral tribunal, the measures will have to be decided by the arbitral tribunal. Such decisions are typically in the form of a procedural order and need not to be submitted for scrutiny to the ICC Court before being rendered. An arbitral tribunal may render as many procedural orders as are necessary or appropriate in view of the developments in the arbitration proceedings.

d) The Arbitral Tribunal's Conduct (Art. 22(4))

In addition to its duty to conduct the arbitration in an expeditious and cost-effective manner, throughout the arbitration proceedings the arbitral tribunal must make sure it acts 'fairly' and 'impartially' and that it gives each party 'a reasonable opportunity to present its case'. This provision of Article 22(4) was already contained in Article 15(2) of the 1998 Rules. It corresponds to the principle of due process, which is well known in common law jurisdictions and which corresponds in civil law jurisdictions generally to the rights of the parties to be heard and to be treated equally (see Article 1699 JC, Article 1464 NCPC, Article 1042(1) ZPO, Article 182(3) PILA, Article 18 of the UNCITRAL Model Law). All arbitrators must respect these general principles in all proceedings, regardless of the place where they are conducted and the other procedural rules applicable to them.

What do these principles actually mean in practice?

An arbitral tribunal's duty to act 'fairly' means that it must behave in a just and well-balanced way. When conducting the proceedings, it may not do anything that favors one of the parties. The arbitral tribunal's additional obligation to act 'impartially' means that it must show no bias. It must treat the parties in the same way and always avoid being partial or appearing to be so.

The arbitral tribunal must also ensure that each party has a reasonable opportunity to present its case in fact and at law. This corresponds to the general principle guaranteeing the right to a hearing. What is actually meant by 'reasonable' can be determined by the arbitral tribunal only in the light of the circumstances of the case. A party should have the possibility to give a reasonable presentation of the factual and legal situation and to react to the presentation made by the other party, provided this is done within the prescribed time limits.

'A reasonable opportunity to present its case' implies that the arbitral tribunal will see to it that the parties have the same amount of time to file their documents or to speak during hearings, unless there is a particular reason for doing otherwise. The arbitral tribunal should also ensure that a party does not misuse its right to have a reasonable opportunity to present its case by introducing 'last minute' pleas that could have been dealt with earlier, in an attempt to prolong and delay the proceedings. If the arbitral tribunal believes that a party is unnecessarily trying to drag out the proceedings, it may refuse to allow such requests without thereby denying the party its right to a hearing.

In theory, each party has the right to demand that the arbitral tribunal respects the principles laid down in Article 22(4) of the Rules. If, after complaining to the arbitral tribunal, a party continues to consider that it has not been treated 'fairly', or that the arbitral tribunal or one of the arbitrators has behaved 'partially', or that it has not had 'a reasonable opportunity to present its case', it may challenge the arbitrator or arbitrators pursuant to Article 14(1) of the Rules by submitting an application to the Court (for more on this question, see our comments on Articles 14 and 15).

Lastly, it should be noted that if a party considers the arbitral tribunal to be acting unfairly or partially or not to have given it a reasonable opportunity to present its case, this should be mentioned as soon as possible. According to Article 39 of the Rules, a party loses the right to object if it 'proceeds with the arbitration without raising its objection to a failure to comply with any provision of the Rules, or of any other rules applicable to the proceedings, any direction given by the Arbitral Tribunal'. Therefore, a party that wishes to raise an objection due to the arbitral tribunal's partiality or due to the fact that it has not had a reasonable opportunity to present its case should not wait and act against the award once it has been rendered. It is reasonable to expect that the party should make its objection based on Article 22(4) before the proceedings are closed pursuant to Article 27. Indeed, it would seem implausible and improper for a party to wait until the proceedings have been closed, the arbitral tribunal has deliberated and the award rendered before objecting that it did not have a reasonable opportunity to present its case or was treated unfairly by the arbitral tribunal.

In this connection, it is worth bearing in mind Article V(1)(b) of the New York Convention and the provisions of several national arbitration laws, which provide that a party may object to the enforcement of a foreign arbitral award or apply for a domestic arbitration award to be set aside if it has been unable to assert its rights or argue its case (see also Article 1717(3)(a)(ii) and 1721(1)(a)(ii) JC, Articles 1492(4) and 1520(4) and 1522 NCPC, Article 1059(2)(1)(b) ZPO, Article 190(2) and (3) PILA, Articles 34(2)(a)(ii) and 36(1)(a)(ii) of the UNCITRAL Model Law). However, it is hardly likely that an ICC award would be challenged on the basis of such provisions, as Article 22(4) of the Rules, combined with Article 39 of the Rules, guarantees that the party was able to state its claims and defend itself. Consequently, the party forfeits its right to raise an objection if it fails to allege an infringement of its rights in the course of the proceedings.

e) Orders on Confidentiality and Protection of Trade Secrets and Confidential Information (Art. 22(3))

One of the features of arbitration that is often highlighted is the confidentiality of the proceedings. The Rules expressly state that the Secretariat staff and the members of the ICC International Court of Arbitration are required to respect the confidentiality of the proceedings (Article 6 of Appendix I and Article 1 of Appendix II to the Rules). It is not said in so many words that arbitrators are also bound by confidentiality, although this is traditionally considered to be the case. Many arbitrators, especially those who are practising lawyers, have a duty to assure discretion laid upon them by their professional code of ethics. The oral discussions before the arbitral tribunal are also confidential insofar as they are not open to the public and no person other than the parties, the experts and the witnesses may attend without the prior consent of all the parties.

The ICC Rules of Arbitration do not stipulate, however, that the arbitration proceedings are confidential. Whereas it is widely believed that parties to an arbitration are also bound by confidentiality, the Rules do not explicitly say so. Some parties, especially those listed on stock exchanges, are obliged to make disclosures and public announcements at the place where they are established. If only for this reason, secrecy cannot be absolute. In certain cases, the parties may have strong reasons, be they justifiable or not, for disclosing information about the proceedings. For instance, a party may be forced to apply to a court for conservatory and interim measures if these are not granted by the arbitral tribunal (see Article 28 on this subject). Also, the setting aside and recognition of arbitral awards necessarily brings them before the public eye, as court proceedings are usually public. This includes hearings and means that the judgments handed down by the courts are not confidential either.

In addition, as ICC administers sometimes treaty based investor-state arbitration proceedings and as these proceedings generally are publicly known, it might prevent the ICC Rules from being referred to in future investment treaties if these Rules would stipulate that ICC arbitration proceedings are confidential. At the time the revision process of the ICC Rules of Arbitration was taking place, the UNCITRAL Rules on Transparency in Treaty based Investor-State Arbitration were being elaborated. As a matter of fact, these Transparency Rules that promote the principle of transparency in investment arbitration were adopted by UNCITRAL in 2013. Moreover, in 2014 a Convention was adopted by UNCITRAL which should allow countries, upon ratification, to apply the 2013 UNCITRAL Transparency Rules also to bilateral investment treaties concluded by them in the past. The United Nations Convention on Transparency in Treaty-based Investor-State Arbitration was opened for signature in Mauritius on 17 March 2015 (see: <www.uncitral.org>).

Whereas the ICC Rules do not provide that ICC arbitration is confidential, the parties are free to make an agreement on confidentiality and ask the arbitral tribunal to confirm this agreement in a procedural order pursuant to Article 22(3). If the Terms of Reference have not yet been established, it is appropriate to record the agreement on the confidential nature of the arbitration in the Terms of Reference.

In case the parties do not reach agreement on the confidentiality of the arbitration, a party may request the arbitral tribunal to render a procedural order so as to protect information which it considers confidential. A party may have legitimate and understandable reasons for keeping the information it discloses during an arbitration from third parties, especially if such information concerns trade secrets. Usually, this is not a problem. Article 22(3) gives the arbitral tribunal the freedom to order measures to protect trade secrets and other confidential information. Although not explicitly mentioned in the Rules, the parties should be given the opportunity to make comments before any decision is made, on account of the possible conflicts of interest mentioned above. The arbitral tribunal should try as far as possible to obtain a unanimous agreement.

A more difficult situation is that in which a party demands that information it considers essential to the proceedings (whether in the form of documents, testimonies or inspections) be withheld from the other party. Its concern is to avoid the risk of wrongful use of such information by the other party. An example would be technical know-how in proceedings between direct competitors. In such cases, the arbitral tribunal must weigh the importance of protecting confidential information against the principle of due process, which includes the possibility of commenting at the appropriate moment on all the facts connected with the proceedings.

As decisions on how to protect confidential information without unduly undermining a party's rights can only be taken on a case-by-case basis, the Rules do not contain any provisions on the method to be adopted. One approach would be for the arbitral tribunal to make a prohibitory order with the possibility of a fine if it is not complied with. However, it would need to be checked that this is not forbidden by any applicable mandatory rules of law, for instance in the '*lex arbitri*'. With regard to the handling of such information, it would be possible to take steps to prevent the other party from revealing any trade secrets of which it may have become aware and which are required to remain confidential. Many questions remain unanswered as it is only in recent years that they have acquired importance. This is a further reason for trying to reach an agreement in each individual case, in consultation with the arbitral tribunal.

The 1998 Rules did not specify in Article 20(7) in what form measures for the protection of trade secrets should be taken. Article 22(3) of the 2012 Rules bring the clarification that such measures may be taken through a procedural order.

f) Obligation to Comply with Orders made by the Arbitral Tribunal (Art. 22(5))

Article 22(5) stipulates the general principle that parties undertake to comply with any order made by the arbitral tribunal. This principle applies to all sorts of orders, including orders regarding the submission of written pleadings or documentary evidence, procedural orders on confidentiality rendered pursuant to Article 22(3) and orders concerning conservatory and interim measures rendered pursuant to Article 28.

Given the hierarchy of rules governing the proceedings laid down in Article 19, an order rendered by an arbitral tribunal can not infringe upon an agreement reached between the parties.

8. Terms of Reference (Art. 23)

Article 23 of the Rules reads:

> 'Terms of Reference
>
> 1. As soon as it has received the file from the Secretariat, the arbitral tribunal shall draw up, on the basis of documents or in the presence of the parties and in the light of their most recent submissions, a document defining its Terms of Reference. This document shall include the following particulars:
>   a) the names in full, description, address and other contact details of each of the parties and of any person(s) representing a party in the arbitration;
>   b) the addresses to which notifications and communications arising in the course of the arbitration may be made;
>   c) a summary of the parties' respective claims and of the relief sought by each party, together with the amounts of any quantified claims and, to the extent possible, an estimate of the monetary value of any other claims;
>   d) unless the arbitral tribunal considers it inappropriate, a list of issues to be determined;
>   e) the names in full, address and other contact details of each of the arbitrators;
>   f) the place of the arbitration; and
>   g) particulars of the applicable procedural rules and, if such is the case, reference to the power conferred upon the arbitral tribunal to act as amiable compositeur or to decide ex aequo et bono.
>
> 2. The Terms of Reference shall be signed by the parties and the arbitral tribunal. Within two months of the date on which the file has been transmitted to it, the arbitral tribunal shall transmit to the Court the Terms of Reference signed by it and by the parties. The Court may extend this time limit pursuant to a reasoned request from the arbitral tribunal or on its own initiative if it decides it is necessary to do so.
>
> 3. If any of the parties refuses to take part in the drawing up of the Terms of Reference or to sign the same, they shall be submitted to the Court for approval. When the Terms of Reference have been signed in accordance with Article 23(2) or approved by the Court, the arbitration shall proceed.
>
> 4. After the Terms of Reference have been signed or approved by the Court, no party shall make new claims which fall outside the limits of the Terms of

Reference unless it has been authorized to do so by the arbitral tribunal, which shall consider the nature of such new claims, the stage of the arbitration and other relevant circumstances.'

a) Introduction

The Terms of Reference are a compulsory component of the ICC arbitration procedure and one of its main characteristics. Before the arbitral tribunal can deal with the substance of the dispute in an ICC arbitration, it should first establish a procedural document called the Terms of Reference. Although today they no longer have the role they originally played, they are still of practical use and were therefore kept in the 2012 version of the ICC Rules of Arbitration despite having some drawbacks.

When the ICC Rules of Arbitration were first created in 1922, the enforcement of agreements giving jurisdiction over potential commercial disputes to an arbitral tribunal was impossible in many countries, especially those belonging to the civil law tradition. In this context, the purpose of the Terms of Reference, which amounted to a contract between the parties, was to give a legal basis to the arbitral tribunal's jurisdiction. This need has been surpassed as a result of the New York Convention and the modernization of national arbitration laws. Another important purpose of the Terms of Reference has been to allow the ICC International Court of Arbitration, when scrutinizing awards, to check that the arbitral tribunal has not gone beyond its mission and has covered all the claims made by the parties (see J. Fry, S. Greenberg and F. Mazza, *The Secretariat's Guide to ICC Arbitration*, ICC Publication No. 729 E, Paris, 2012, p. 240).

Nowadays, the Terms of Reference are justified primarily by the fact that they require the arbitrators and the parties to decide early in the proceedings, by mutual agreement if possible and having regard to the requirements of the case, how the substance of the dispute and procedural matters covered only in general terms in the Rules are to be handled. Our earlier comments on Article 19 (procedural rules) and Article 20 (language of the arbitration) are relevant here too. A similar purpose also underlies the requirement to establish a procedural timetable, which appeared for the first time in the 1998 Rules.

b) Content of the Terms of Reference (Art. 23(1))

(1) The Full Names and Descriptions of the Parties (Art. 23(1)(a)).

As in civil court proceedings, it is important that the parties be correctly identified, especially if the arbitral award necessitates an enforcement order. It is up to the claimant to ensure that the respondent is correctly named and to provide the address at which the respondent should be sent notifications. The Rules do not expressly require the respondent to correct any mistakes in the details given by the claimant. However, by signing the Terms of Reference, the respondent confirms the notification address and the name and description that appear therein. By requiring these details to be included in the Terms of Reference, the Rules aim to ensure that any details that are incorrect or likely to cause confusion are amended.

In most arbitrations the parties are assisted and/or represented by lawyers. Whereas the 1998 Rules did not yet stipulate this, the 2012 Rules now confirm the general practice that the names in full, the description, address and other contact details of any person representing a party in the arbitration should also be mentioned in the Terms of Reference.

(2) The Addresses for Notifications (Art. 23(1)(b)).

The remarks made in the preceding paragraph also apply to the addresses for notifications. It should also be mentioned that in arbitration proceedings the initial request for arbitration is sent directly to the parties, whereas subsequent notifications are usually sent to their representatives. The parties' choice of domicile is also clarified by the signing of the Terms of Reference. If both parties are represented by lawyers, the further correspondence shall be conducted with the parties' lawyers.

(3) The Summary of the Parties' Respective Claims and of the Relief Sought by Each Party together with the Amounts of any Quantified Claims and, to the Extent Possible, an Estimate of the Monetary Value of Any Other Claims (Art. 23(1)(c))

More often than not, the summary of the parties' claims is prepared by the arbitral tribunal on the basis of the request for arbitration, the answer to the request and any counterclaim(s) and other submissions. The Rules do not specify how detailed this summary should be. In practice, the summary of the facts and the parties' claims is in most cases similar to those made in state court proceedings.

The reference to the relief sought should not normally be a source of problems. However, it should be recalled that the relief sought is not presented uniformly in all jurisdictions. The Rules do not contain any formal indications as to the precision or admissibility of the relief sought. There may nonetheless be cases where the relief sought is presented in such a way that the arbitral tribunal does not clearly understand what is requested. Although the Rules do not indicate how the arbitral tribunal should act in such a situation, it would seem appropriate for it to request clarification.

Parties filing claims are required under the 2012 Rules of Arbitration to provide the amount of any quantified claim and to estimate the monetary value of any other claims (Article 4(3)(d) and 5(5)(b)). The requirement to indicate the amount claimed chiefly concerns declaratory claims and claims for enforcement that are not quantified. As the scales of arbitrators' fees and ICC administrative expenses are based on the amounts in dispute, it is appropriate that parties themselves can specify or estimate the values of their claims. It is the Court's practice not to include claims for interest and for costs in the calculation of the amount in dispute. If the parties have not specified the amount in dispute, in spite of the requirement to do so, the Court shall fix the arbitrators' fees and the administrative expenses at its own discretion (Article 2(1) of Appendix III to the Rules).

(4) The List of Issues (Art. 23(1)(d)).

The list of issues to be determined is to be distinguished from the claims of the parties. Issues to be determined can be questions of fact or law that are considered to be relevant for the tribunal's decision on the claims. By specifying the issues in the Terms of Reference the arbitral tribunal can provide a frame so that the parties know on what specific questions the arbitral tribunal wants to receive arguments and evidence. Arbitral tribunals will often indicate that the list of issues mentioned in the Terms of Reference is not exhaustive and that the issues need not necessarily to be determined in the same order. Notwithstanding, the list is intended to give at least some guidance to the parties before they draft their further submissions.

In the past, the list of issues was one of the most disputed aspects of the Terms of Reference. Some arbitration practitioners believed, not entirely without reason, that this compulsory ingredient of the Terms of Reference causes the parties to take different views on the issues to be determined, which may prevent the Terms of Reference from being signed or at least delay the proceedings. They also believed that the issues to be determined could not be adequately defined so early in the proceedings and argued that this could not be done until much later in the proceedings.

Experience shows that in many – and probably most – ICC arbitrations, identifying the issues to be determined on the basis of the statements of the parties' claims makes it easier to limit the subject matter of the dispute and the parties' subsequent statements to the essential facts. Moreover, the need to reach agreement indirectly gives the parties the opportunity to consider their respective positions and allows the arbitrators to delimit the subject matter of the dispute at an early stage, which can only be beneficial to the planning of the proceedings. In practice, most Terms of Reference include a detailed list of issues, even if it is since the 1998 Rules no longer compulsory to draw up a list of issues to be determined. This allows arbitral tribunals to proceed as appropriate in a particular case. For instance, an arbitral may consider a list of issues to be inappropriate if a party tries to have the issues worded to its advantage and prevents the list from being drafted in a 'balanced' way.

The possibility of not identifying the issues to be determined should, in conjunction with Article 23(4), help to overcome any problems that might arise from the wording of any such list, since Article 23(4) allows the arbitral tribunal to accept new claims later in the proceedings. Previously, this was possible only if the parties signed a 'rider' (addendum) to the Terms of Reference specifying the new claims. For this reason, before 1998, many parties feared that they could be barred from presenting a new claim later that might prove necessary.

(5) The Full Names, Descriptions and Addresses of the Arbitrators (Art. 23(1)(e)).

This was already a requirement of the very first version of the Rules in the 1920s. Its purpose is above all one of clarification and does not call for any particular comment.

(6) The Place of the Arbitration (Art. 23(1)(f)).

Reference should be made here to the place of the arbitration agreed by the parties or fixed by the ICC Court in accordance with Article 18(1) of the Rules. The localization of the proceedings essentially serves legal purposes, as this will be the basis for determining a state court's jurisdiction under the arbitration law at the place of the arbitration. If the parties have not agreed otherwise, Article 18(2), introduced into the Rules in 1998, allows the arbitral tribunal to hold hearings and meetings at any other location that it considers appropriate, provided the parties are first consulted.

(7) Particulars of the Applicable Procedural Rules (Art. 23(1)(g)).

Particulars of the procedural rules may be included in the Terms of Reference. This does not refer to the procedural calendar or directions given by the arbitral tribunal for the further conduct of the proceedings, as it is not recommended to include them in the Terms of Reference, but rather in a separate procedural order. As the Terms of Reference are held to be a form of contract, the arbitral tribunal will not be able to amend the calendar or the procedural directions should one of the parties request new directions in light of further developments. The particulars that should be mentioned in the Terms of Reference are first of all the terms of the arbitration agreement and general rules that will not unduly 'tie the hands' of the arbitral tribunal.

Moreover, if parties have agreed on specific rules for the taking of evidence, such as the IBA Rules on the Taking of Evidence in International Arbitration (the Rules were amended in 2010, and can be consulted on the website of the International Bar Association: <www.ibanet.org>), it is recommended to mention this in the Terms of Reference. Even if it is not compulsory to include such specific rules in the Terms of Reference, it is useful to include special rules on important points, as this helps transparency and predictability and acceptance of the arbitral tribunal's conduct of the proceedings. Any procedural matters that are not dealt with in the Rules, or that have not been agreed between the parties, may be determined by the arbitral tribunal by way of decisions or procedural orders made on the basis of Article 19 and in the context of Article 25(1).

Lastly, it is possible to specify in the Terms of Reference, if this has not already been agreed, that the arbitral tribunal may decide as '*amiable compositeur*' or '*ex aequo et bono*' (in this regard, see the comments relating to Article 21(3) above). It is rather unusual, however, for this to happen.

If the parties have agreed on the rules of law applicable to the substance of the matter, it is important that this be mentioned in the Terms of Reference. In case the parties have not agreed on the rules of law applicable to the merits of the dispute, the arbitral tribunal shall have to determine the applicable law and include the question of the applicable law in the list of issues to be determined.

(8) Other Possible Elements that May Be Considered Relevant.

The parties and the arbitral tribunal are free to include in the Terms of Reference other elements that may be considered relevant for the case and on which they are free to agree.

Even if the Rules do not prescribe this, it is good practice to include in the Terms of Reference the procedural history of the case. This concerns a summary of all the steps already taken in the arbitration proceedings and the decisions taken by the Secretary General and/or the Court regarding the setting in motion of the arbitration. If a decision has been taken pursuant to Article 6(3) or 6(4) this should be mentioned, because the arbitral tribunal as a consequence needs to decide on its own jurisdiction. If the arbitral tribunal has determined the language of the arbitration before the Terms of Reference were established, this should be mentioned in the Terms of Reference and the decision taken by the arbitral tribunal should be included.

If parties have an agreement on the confidentiality of the arbitration or of certain aspects of the case, this should be included in the Terms of Reference so to give binding force to this agreement with the signature of the Terms of Reference.

c) Drawing up the Terms of Reference (Art. 23(1)–(3))

(1) The Usual Procedure.

The Terms of Reference are drawn up on the basis of the parties' most recent written submissions. Some arbitral tribunals leave it to the parties to provide a summary of their claims and simply draft the part of the Terms of Reference covering the points mentioned under a), b), e), f) and g) of Article 23(1). This is not the best way to proceed, however, as the summary of the parties' claims and the list of issues to be determined need to be analyzed by the arbitral tribunal at this stage so that any misunderstandings can immediately be removed.

Article 23(1) allows the Terms of Reference to be prepared and signed by correspondence or at a meeting with the parties. However, from a practical angle, there is often little purpose in holding a meeting for this purpose, as only in very simple cases involving few issues will it be possible to obtain the parties' agreement on the Terms of Reference at a single meeting. It may be that such agreement can equally well be obtained by correspondence, which saves time and cost. In any event, it is advisable for the arbitral tribunal to send the parties a draft first, asking them to respond quickly with their comments. Any problems identified in the first draft may be dealt with in a new draft sent out to the parties for their approval or for them to comment on within a specified time limit. If it is impossible to obtain an agreement in this way, or if the size of the case makes it necessary, a meeting will have to be quickly arranged. It will be useful for the parties to indicate their availability as soon as possible so as to avoid delays due to postponements requested when dates are proposed. The arbitral tribunal should be mindful of this.

Ideally, the arbitral tribunal will prepare the meeting in such a way that discussions are confined to the essential issues and conducted in accordance with a strict plan. Any changes to the text should be prepared beforehand so that the Terms of Reference can be signed at the end of the meeting.

It is appropriate to hold a meeting for the purpose of finalizing and signing the Terms of Reference even when the summary of the parties' claims and the list of issues do not raise any particular problems. Such a meeting provides an opportunity to discuss and decide how the ensuing proceedings will be conducted, allowing the parties to present their positions and the arbitral tribunal to take these into account. Article 24(1) stipulates that the arbitral tribunal shall convene a case management conference to consult the parties on procedural measures that shall be adopted pursuant to Article 22(2). To save time and costs in the arbitration proceedings it is good practice to organize this case management conference together with the meeting for the signature of the Terms of Reference, unless the high cost of organizing such meeting would recommend that the signature process of the Terms of Reference be handled by circulating the document.

The expectations of the parties' lawyers are sometimes influenced by the national procedural law with which they are familiar and may therefore lead to differing viewpoints on such matters as their obligations relating to the production of documents, the way in which witnesses are examined, or possible expertise proceedings. When such differences arise, it may be preferable for the ensuing proceedings to include these points in the Terms of Reference in the form of detailed rules agreed on the basis of Article 23(1)(g). Also, it is often the case in international arbitrations that some or even all of the parties do not know each other. Personal impressions gained from a meeting are likely to have a significant psychological effect on the rest of the proceedings.

An original of the Terms of Reference signed by the parties and the arbitral tribunal must be provided to each party, each member of the arbitral tribunal and the Secretariat (see Note to the Arbitral Tribunal on the Conduct of the arbitration; Appendix 9 below).

(2) The Time Allowed for Signing the Terms of Reference and Submitting Them to the ICC International Court of Arbitration (Art. 23(2)).

The arbitral tribunal has two months from the moment the file is transmitted to it during which to draw up the Terms of Reference and have them signed by all parties or, failing this, to submit them to the ICC International Court of Arbitration for approval. In many cases this time limit is not respected, not only on account of the internal deliberations necessitated by a three-member tribunal, but also due to the difficulty of finding a date when all the parties are available and the fact that they usually insist on being given adequate time to present their views. The arbitral tribunal should as a rule inform the Court and, as far as possible, indicate how it intends to continue the proceedings. On this basis, the Court will decide whether to extend the time limit as provided in Article 23(2). The Court is also free to extend the time limit of its own accord.

(3) A Party Refuses to Sign the Terms of Reference (Art. 23(3)).

Occasionally, a party fails to answer the request for arbitration or to take part in the proceedings. In such cases, the arbitral tribunal needs to ensure that all submissions are sent to that party in accordance with the provisions of Article 3 of the Rules and that it is allowed time to reply. If the Terms of Reference are drawn up in agreement with the participating party alone, the other party should be sent the final text and given a suitable period of time to sign it. At the same time, the document is circulated for signature by all other persons concerned. If the non-participating party has not signed at the end of the time limit set, the Terms of Reference will be submitted to the ICC International Court of Arbitration for approval, in accordance with Article 23(3) of the Rules. As in such circumstances it is not possible to agree on procedural details as mentioned in Article 23(1)(g), provisions regarding the procedure should be included in a procedural order issued by the arbitral tribunal on the basis of Article 19. It will not be possible for the case to be decided '*ex aequo et bono*' pursuant to Article 21(3), unless the parties have already expressly agreed to this.

Cases in which a party takes part in the proceedings but refuses to sign the Terms of Reference are more difficult to handle. It is not always easy for the arbitral tribunal to discern whether this is merely a dilatory tactic or reflects legitimate reservations or misunderstandings. Experienced arbitrators will usually be able to overcome such problems in appropriate ways. It is important that the proceedings should be conducted efficiently so as to avoid any delay in submitting the Terms of Reference to the ICC Court for approval when this is necessary. A typical instance in which a party refuses to sign the Terms of Reference is when the existence of a valid arbitration agreement between the parties is disputed. Sometimes the party disputing the validity of the arbitration agreement demands that the Terms of Reference be initially limited to the question of jurisdiction. If the arbitral tribunal accepts jurisdiction, further Terms of Reference will then be drawn up relating to the substance of the dispute. This possibility is available to arbitral tribunals in exceptional cases but it is rarely used in practice as it is uneconomical and tends to drag out the proceedings. For this reason it is not expressly mentioned in the Rules. As a rule, the aim should be to draw up Terms of Reference covering all aspects of the dispute.

It should also be pointed out that the Rules do not provide for the situation in which one of the members of a three-member arbitral tribunal does not sign the Terms of Reference. Although highly unlikely, if this were to occur it would be up to the ICC Court to decide whether or not to replace the arbitrator in accordance with Article 15(2) of the Rules combined with Articles 13(1) and 23(1). The Rules do not contain any provisions allowing the president of the arbitral tribunal or a majority of its members to sign the Terms of Reference without the recalcitrant arbitrator, as is possible with an arbitral award under Article 31 of the Rules.

The time limit of six months within which the arbitral tribunal must be rendered pursuant to Article 30(1) starts to run from the date of the last signature by the arbitral tribunal or by the parties of the Terms of Reference or, in case the Terms of Reference must be approved by the Court pursuant to Article 23(3), from the date of notification to the arbitral tribunal of the Court decision regarding the approval of the Terms of Reference.

d) New Claims (Art. 23(4))

(1) The Conditions for Bringing New Claims after the Terms of Reference have been Drawn Up

The Terms of Reference outline the subject of the dispute and contain the parties' claims which the arbitral tribunal is required to decide. The question arises as to whether the parties may add to their claims or bring new claims after the Terms of Reference have been signed. By this we do not mean a mere increase in the amount of a claim based on facts that have already been presented in time. Indeed, parties are able to increase or reduce the amounts they claim at any moment prior to the closing of the proceedings (Article 27 of the Rules), provided the facts on which the increase or the reduction is based have been raised in time. If the amount at issue is increased, the ICC International Court of Arbitration will usually increase the advance on costs accordingly, as provided in Article 36(5) of the Rules and Article 1(11) of Appendix III to the Rules. If the amount at issue is reduced, the arbitral tribunal must determine, after first hearing the parties, whether this implies the partial withdrawal of a claim.

(a) Admissibility of new claims by virtue of an explicit agreement between the parties.

Parties can of course always agree between themselves to allow new claims in the course of the proceedings after the Terms of Reference have been drawn up, even if they do not satisfy the conditions laid down in Article 23(4). In this case, the arbitral tribunal will decide on the new claims out of respect for party autonomy. The parties' agreement should be recorded in the minutes of their meeting or in a document duly signed by both of them.

It is primarily up to the arbitral tribunal to check in each case whether the unqualified acceptance of new claims by the other party can be considered under Article 39 to cure a violation of Article 23(4) or whether it amounts to a tacit agreement to include the new claims. In any event, given the possibility that the award could be challenged later for non-compliance with procedural rules, it is advisable that provision be made for an explicit agreement or, if need be, a decision by the arbitral tribunal.

(b) Authorization of new claims by the arbitral tribunal.

If new claims fall within the limits of the Terms of Reference, they are automatically admissible. It is up to the arbitral tribunal to determine, after first consulting the parties, whether or not this is the case. This decision may be made by way of a procedural order, and should not take the form of an award (see commentary on Article 31 below).

If, on the other hand, new claims do not come within the limits of the Terms of Reference, they are admissible only if accepted by the arbitral tribunal. Article 23(4) lists certain considerations to which the arbitral tribunal should give attention when deciding on the admissibility of new principal claims or counterclaims. The arbitral tribunal will take into account the 'nature' of the new claims. This normally means that it will check whether there is a relationship between the new claims and the facts on which the claims contained in the Terms of Reference are based. If the new claims deal with quite different matters from those mentioned in the Terms of Reference and are unrelated to the initial request for arbitration, they will probably not be accepted by the arbitral tribunal. For instance, if the original request for arbitration concerned a contract for the sale of goods and the new claims submitted by one of the parties after the Terms of Reference have been drawn up concern another contract between the parties, the new claims should not be accepted. However, there are times when the new claims concern the same contract and the same facts. This would be the case, for instance, if a party initially requests the payment of the sales price stipulated in the contract and then, once the Terms of Reference have been signed, claims a right to damages due to a breach of the contract. In this case, the arbitral tribunal would probably regard the new claim as related to the initial request and would therefore be more likely to consider it admissible.

When deciding on the admissibility of new claims, the arbitral tribunal will also take into account the stage the proceedings have reached. It may decide differently depending on whether the claim is introduced shortly before the closing of the proceedings or soon after the Terms of Reference have been signed. The arbitral tribunal's role is to see the proceedings through to their successful conclusion and to make an award covering all the claims as quickly as possible. If it observes that a party introduces new claims with a view to slowing down the proceedings and delaying the moment at which the award is rendered, Article 23(4) entitles it not to accept such new claims. This might happen if the respondent introduces new claims just before the proceedings are closed, after all evidence relating to the original claims has been produced, because further evidence would need to be taken.

If the arbitral tribunal refuses to authorize the new claims, separate arbitral proceedings will have to be commenced by the party that wishes to assert these claims. This means that they will be decided by another arbitral tribunal, which may be differently composed. There is therefore a risk that the new arbitral tribunal will decide differently from the initial tribunal and render an award that might even contradict that of the first tribunal. This risk should be given due consideration by an arbitral tribunal presented with new claims in the proceedings and weighed up against the need for a quick decision on the claims made in the Terms of Reference.

It should be pointed out that the late introduction of new claims does not always constitute a dilatory tactic by one of the parties. Sometimes, a case evolves in the course of the proceedings and new information emerges which was unknown at the time the case was first brought or when the Terms of Reference were signed. Sometimes, too, events giving rise to new claims occur during the proceedings. In such instances, it would often be inappropriate not to also deal with such new claims in the same proceedings as the original claims.

Notwithstanding the above, the following important limits to the admissibility of new claims must be borne in mind. In case the new claim is made against a new party not yet involved in the arbitration, the provision of Article 7 will be applicable (see comments on Article 7 above). No additional party may be joined after the confirmation or appointment of any arbitrator, unless all parties, including the additional party, otherwise agree. Any such joinder shall also be subject to the provisions of Articles 6(3)-6(7) and 9.

In case the new claim is made on the basis of another contract between the same parties in accordance with Article 9, irrespective of whether such claims are made under one or more than arbitration agreement under the Rules, such claim shall be subject to the provisions of Articles 6(3)-6(7) (see comments on Article 9 above).

(2) Increased Flexibility as Compared with the Former Rules

In addition to the 'nature' of the claims and the 'stage of the arbitration', the arbitral tribunal may also give consideration to 'other relevant circumstances' when deciding on the admissibility of new claims. The Rules therefore leave much to the arbitral tribunal's discretion and allow for more flexibility than was possible under the previous versions of the Rules.

Under the Rules in force from 1988 to 1997, parties could introduce new claims only by way of a 'rider' to the Terms of Reference. The 'rider' had to be signed by all of the parties. One of the parties could therefore prevent the other from introducing new claims by refusing to sign this 'rider'.

9. Case Management Conference and Procedural Timetable (Art. 24)

Article 24 of the Rules reads:

> 'Case Management Conference and Procedural Timetable
>
> 1. When drawing up the Terms of Reference or as soon as possible thereafter, the arbitral tribunal shall convene a case management conference to consult the parties on procedural measures that may be adopted pursuant to Article 22(2). Such measures may include one or more of the case management techniques described in Appendix IV.
>
> 2. During or following such conference, the arbitral tribunal shall establish the procedural timetable that it intends to follow for the conduct of the arbitration. The procedural timetable and any modifications thereto shall be communicated to the Court and the parties.
>
> 3. To ensure continued effective case management, the arbitral tribunal, after consulting the parties by means of a further case management conference or otherwise, may adopt further procedural measures or modify the procedural timetable.
>
> 4. Case management conferences may be conducted through a meeting in person, by video conference, telephone or similar means of communication. In the absence of an agreement of the parties, the arbitral tribunal shall determine the means by which the conference will be conducted. The arbitral tribunal may request the parties to submit case management proposals in advance of a case management conference and may request the attendance at any case management conference of the parties in person or through an internal representative.'
>
> 'APPENDIX IV : CASE MANAGEMENT TECHNIQUES
>
> The following are examples of case management techniques that can be used by the arbitral tribunal and the parties for controlling time and cost. Appropriate control of time and cost is important in all cases. In cases of low complexity and low value, it is particularly important to ensure that time and costs are proportionate to what is at stake in the dispute.
>
> a) Bifurcating the proceedings or rendering one or more partial awards on key issues, when doing so may genuinely be expected to result in a more efficient resolution of the case.
> b) Identifying issues that can be resolved by agreement between the parties or their experts.

c) Identifying issues to be decided solely on the basis of documents rather than through oral evidence or legal argument at a hearing.
d) Production of documentary evidence:
   (i) requiring the parties to produce with their submissions the documents on which they rely;
   (ii) avoiding requests for document production when appropriate in order to control time and cost;
   (iii) in those cases where requests for document production are considered appropriate, limiting such requests to documents or categories of documents that are relevant and material to the outcome of the case;
   (iv) establishing reasonable time limits for the production of documents;
   (v) using a schedule of document production to facilitate the resolution of issues in relation to the production of documents.
e) Limiting the length and scope of written submissions and written and oral witness evidence (both fact witnesses and experts) so as to avoid repetition and maintain a focus on key issues.
f) Using telephone or video conferencing for procedural and other hearings where attendance in person is not essential and use of IT that enables online communication among the parties, the arbitral tribunal and the Secretariat of the Court.
g) Organizing a pre-hearing conference with the arbitral tribunal at which arrangements for a hearing can be discussed and agreed and the arbitral tribunal can indicate to the parties issues on which it would like the parties to focus at the hearing.
h) Settlement of disputes:
   (i) informing the parties that they are free to settle all or part of the dispute either by negotiation or through any form of amicable dispute resolution methods such as, for example, mediation under the ICC Mediation Rules;
   (ii) where agreed between the parties and the arbitral tribunal, the arbitral tribunal may take steps to facilitate settlement of the dispute, provided that every effort is made to ensure that any subsequent award is enforceable at law.

Additional techniques are described in the ICC publication entitled "Controlling Time and Costs in Arbitration"."

a) General Remarks

Article 24 is one of the new provisions of the Rules, although it confirms a practice which was already adopted by some arbitrators. This new provision stresses the duty of the arbitral tribunal to consult the parties specifically on case management before it will render procedural directions in that regard. This new provision was inserted in the Rules together with the new Article 22 as a direct result of the Report of the ICC Commission on Arbitration and ADR on 'Techniques for Controlling Time and Costs in International Arbitration' (See Appendix 15 below). Moreover, a new Appendix IV to the Rules is included with examples of case management techniques that can be discussed during the case management conference and that can serve to control time and costs in the arbitration. The provision of Article 24(2) was already contained in the 1998 Rules as Article 18(4).

b) The Case Management Conference (Art. 24(1); Art. 24(3) and (4))

As already explained with respect to Article 22(1), the arbitral tribunal and the parties shall conduct the arbitration in an expeditious and cost-effective manner. In order to ensure effective case management, the arbitral tribunal may pursuant to Article 22(2), after having consulted the parties, adopt such procedural measures as it considers appropriate, provided that they are not contrary to any agreement of the parties. The consultation of the parties before adopting these procedural measures, shall occur during a case management conference. This case management conference shall be convened at the time the Terms of Reference are established or as soon as possible thereafter. It is good practice to organize the case management conference, at the same time or on the same occasion of the meeting for the signature of the Terms of Reference.

The arbitral tribunal has the power to require the parties to attend the case management conference in person or through an in-house representative (Article 24(4)). It is good practice that the parties together with their lawyers attend the case management conference. This allows the parties to get to know the arbitrators and to better understand the arbitral process and the measures adopted for the conduct of the proceedings.

The Rules do not require a physical meeting of the parties in person for organizing a case management conference. Depending on the amount in dispute and the complexity of the case, it may be too expensive to have the parties and their representatives travel to one location for attending in person. Accordingly, the arbitral tribunal may decide to conduct the case management conference also through other means, such as video conference, telephone or similar means of communication, pursuant to Article 24(4).

With a view to taking into account the expectations of the parties, the arbitral tribunal may request the parties to submit case management proposals in advance of the case management meeting (Article 24(4)). As the parties in international arbitrations often originate from different legal and cultural backgrounds, they may have different expectations and they may each wish to see procedural steps taken to which they are used in their own legal environment. This may lead to duplication of procedural steps and unnecessary delays and high costs.

Depending on the developments in the arbitration, the arbitral tribunal may adopt further procedural measures or modify the procedural timetable after having consulted the parties. Such consultation can occur by means of a further case management conference or otherwise (Article 24(3)).

c) Case Management Techniques (Appendix IV to the Rules)

Appendix IV to the Rules provides a number of examples of case management techniques that can be used by the arbitral tribunal and the parties for controlling time and cost in the arbitration. Those techniques are taken from the Report of the ICC Commission on Arbitration and ADR on 'Techniques for Controlling Time and Costs in International Arbitration' (See Appendix 15 below). Appendix IV stresses the importance that time and costs are proportionate to what is at stake in the dispute. Therefore, not each of the proposed case management techniques will be the appropriate technique in any case.

The proposed techniques include: bifurcating the proceedings by rendering one or more partial awards; identifying issues that can be resolved by agreement between the parties or their experts; identifying issues that can be decided solely on the basis of documents; controlling the production of documentary evidence; limiting the length of written submissions and of written and oral witness evidence; using telephone or video conferencing for procedural and other hearings; organizing a pre-hearing conference with the arbitral tribunal so as to discuss and make arrangements for the hearing and so as to indicate issues on which the arbitral tribunal would like the parties to focus at the hearing; informing the parties that they may seek to settle the dispute by negotiation or by mediation and informing them that the arbitral tribunal may take steps to facilitate settlement of the case.

In an effort to help in-house counsel and other party representatives, such as managers and government officials, implement the new provisions and make appropriate decisions for effective case management, the ICC published in 2014 a 'Guide for In-House Counsel and Other Party Representatives'. This guide is a practical toolkit for making decisions on how to conduct an arbitration in a time- and cost-effective manner, having regard to the complexity and value of the dispute. It provides 11 topic sheets, with questions to ask, options, pros and cons, and a cost/benefit analysis. The topic sheets deal with: the request for arbitration; the answer and counterclaims; multiparty arbitration; early determination of issues; rounds of written submissions; document production; need for fact witnesses; expert witnesses (pre-hearing issues); hearing on the merits (including witness issues); post-hearing briefs ('Effective Management of Arbitration', ICC Publication No. 866-0 E, Paris, 2014, 61pp.; see Appendix 14 below).

d) The Procedural Timetable (Art. 24(2))

Since 1998, the Rules have included (in Article 18(4) of the 1998 Rules) a provision requiring the arbitral tribunal to establish a procedural timetable. This provision is contained in the 2012 Rules in Article 24(2).

The purpose of this provision is to speed up the proceedings through improved planning. The arbitrators and the parties' lawyers often have heavy schedules, making it difficult to fix dates if this is not addressed early enough. It may be necessary to wait several months for a hearing if the date is not arranged early in the proceedings. A timetable in which these dates are fixed also makes it possible to clarify how many exchanges of pleadings there should be and how evidence should be produced. It is good practice to establish the timetable at the case management conference organized at the time the Terms of Reference are signed. If for whatever reason the timetable cannot be established at the same time as the Terms of Reference, it should be attended to as quickly as possible thereafter. The provisional timetable can of course be modified to take account of unforeseen events that may arise during the proceedings.

Article 24(2) requires that the procedural timetable should be communicated in writing to the parties. It does not prescribe a particular form for doing so. It is normal practice that the arbitral tribunal incorporates the timetable in a procedural order, which shall be communicated to the parties and to the Court.

The requirement to inform the Court of the procedural timetable and any changes made to it allows the Court, if need be, to extend the six-month time limit laid down in Article 30(1) by however long it considers necessary in the particular case, as it is entitled to do under Article 30(2).

10. Establishing the Facts of the Case (Art. 25)

Article 25 of the Rules reads:

> 'Establishing the Facts of the Case
>
> 1. The arbitral tribunal shall proceed within as short a time as possible to establish the facts of the case by all appropriate means.
>
> 2. After studying the written submissions of the parties and all documents relied upon, the arbitral tribunal shall hear the parties together in person if any of them so requests or, failing such a request, it may of its own motion decide to hear them.
>
> 3. The arbitral tribunal may decide to hear witnesses, experts appointed by the parties or any other person, in the presence of the parties, or in their absence provided they have been duly summoned.
>
> 4. The arbitral tribunal, after having consulted the parties, may appoint one or more experts, define their terms of reference and receive their reports. At the request of a party, the parties shall be given the opportunity to question at a hearing any such expert.
>
> 5. At any time during the proceedings, the arbitral tribunal may summon any party to provide additional evidence.
>
> 6. The arbitral tribunal may decide the case solely on the documents submitted by the parties unless any of the parties requests a hearing.'

a) General Remarks

Article 25 of the Rules contains fundamental provisions regarding the arbitral tribunal's powers and duties when establishing the facts of the case. These are the provisions upon which the arbitral tribunal relies when ascertaining the facts prior to deciding on the parties' claims.

Like the general principles laid down in Article 22, these obligations must be respected by any arbitral tribunal irrespective of the country in which the proceedings take place or the applicable arbitration law.

As a number of other provisions of the Rules, Article 25 also stresses the importance that the arbitral tribunal proceeds with the arbitration expeditiously.

b) Establishing the Facts by All Appropriate Means (Art. 25(1))

The arbitral tribunal's first task is to 'establish the facts of the case'. Each party describes the circumstances of the case. Their respective descriptions usually reveal contradictory positions with respect to the events underlying the dispute. The arbitral tribunal may use 'all appropriate means' to clarify these contradictions, which means that it has considerable freedom to decide how to go about establishing the facts. For example, an on-site visit, the hearing of witnesses (Article 25(3)) and the commissioning of an expert (Article 25(4)) are appropriate means. The arbitral tribunal also has complete freedom when assessing evidence. If it considers that it has been unable sufficiently to establish the facts of the case, it can ask the parties at any time to provide additional evidence (Article 25(5)). The obligation to do so 'within as short a time as possible' makes it necessary for the arbitrators to conduct the proceedings swiftly.

In practice, it cannot however be assumed that arbitrators in international proceedings will establish the facts of the case *ex officio*. The general tendency amongst different legal traditions is rather to consider that the parties should provide all factual information and supporting evidence. However, the arbitral tribunal may at any point request an expert to give an opinion on technical or economic questions.

The ways in which parties present the facts and supporting evidence may vary fundamentally. Very often, testimony is not limited to the allegations in dispute that remain to be proven. During the hearing of witnesses, facts may be revealed that were merely touched on in the pleadings. It should be noted that parties have a duty to produce documents and expert opinions, if so required by the arbitral tribunal. If they are from different cultural backgrounds, they may have different expectations regarding the presentation of evidence, in which case it may be necessary for the arbitral tribunal to let the party representatives handle the furnishing of evidence. This point will be further discussed later on.

c) Preparatory Submissions (Art. 25(2))

As stated at the beginning of Article 25(2), the arbitral tribunal should first examine the written documents submitted by the parties. Although this may seem self-evident, it reflects an approach to international arbitration that is not shared by all legal traditions, that is to say it puts written and oral submissions on an equal footing and presupposes that the hearings have usually been amply prepared by the parties' written pleadings. This approach will even apply, although to a different extent, to proceedings between parties from legal systems in which oral submissions are of greater importance than is usually the case in civil law systems.

Pleadings are exchanged in accordance with the provisions contained in the Terms of Reference or as instructed by the arbitral tribunal. After the initial request and the answer have been filed and the Terms of Reference drawn up, there are on average one or two further exchanges of pleadings before the hearing, although there may sometimes be more. In some cases, parties file certain pleadings simultaneously rather than successively.

If no detailed provisions have been agreed upon in the Terms of Reference, exchanges of pleadings are governed by Article 3(1) and (2), of the Rules. It is normally decided that pleadings will not be dispatched by the Secretariat or the arbitral tribunal, but sent directly by the party concerned to the arbitrators, the other party and the Secretariat.

It is common for evidence such as contracts, technical documents, correspondence, expert opinions and written testimonies to be attached to the pleadings. They can sometimes fill several binders. More detailed provisions on this subject may occasionally be found in the Terms of Reference or in a procedural order issued by the arbitral tribunal. They may cover such points as the translation of documents drafted in a foreign language.

d) Oral Hearing

(1) Hearing of the Parties (Art. 25(2)).

In most ICC arbitrations one or more oral hearings take place after the exchange of pleadings (Article 25(2)). If this has not been agreed with the parties or settled by the arbitral tribunal when establishing the procedural timetable (Article 24(2)), the arbitral tribunal will decide on this after hearing the parties and considering the progress of the proceedings. It is, however, a general principle of due process that if any of the parties requests an oral hearing, the arbitral tribunal shall organize an oral hearing so to hear the parties in person. If none of the parties requests a hearing, the arbitral tribunal may nevertheless of its own initiative decide to organize an oral hearing.

If a hearing has already taken place and the arbitral tribunal believes that the parties have had a reasonable opportunity to present their arguments, it may reject a request from one of the parties for another hearing. This will be the case when all the evidence has been presented in good time and the facts have therefore been established.

It is good practice for an arbitral tribunal to prepare the hearing during a case management conference (Article 24(1)) or during a specific pre-hearing conference (Appendix IV to the Rules). At such pre-hearing conference the arbitral tribunal may discuss with the parties any necessary or desirable arrangements for the hearing and it can also indicate to the parties issues on which it would like the parties to focus at the hearing.

The parties and their representatives are entitled to take part in all discussions and hearings where evidence is produced and should be summoned in accordance with Article 3(1) and (2). If one of the parties were to be excluded from a hearing or proceedings where evidence is produced, this would be a violation of due process. However, it may be necessary to limit the scope of participation in order to protect trade secrets of the other party (Article 22(3)). If a party that has been duly summoned fails to appear, it normally cannot later object that it has been denied due process (Article 26(2)). This of course would not be the case if it indicated in good time that it was unable to attend for imperative reasons beyond its control.

(2) Hearing of Witnesses, Experts and Other Persons (Art. 25(3)).

Parties may ask for witnesses or party-appointed experts to be heard. Although the arbitral tribunal is under no obligation to grant such requests, it should normally give reasons if it refuses, so as to avoid assertions of lack of due process which could affect the validity and enforceability of the award (see Article V(1)(b) of the New York Convention). An arbitral tribunal may, however, consider that the subject on which witnesses or experts can testify is not relevant to the proceedings and/or would delay them needlessly or lead to excessive expenditure. In most cases, arbitral tribunals grant the parties' requests for witnesses or party-appointed experts to be examined in order to comply with the requirements of due process. In some cases, the parties and the arbitrators agree to have a separate evidentiary hearing for examining the witnesses and the experts prior to the oral arguments on the legal issues. The question of when to organize an evidentiary hearing and, if so, how it should be organized is normally discussed at the case management conference (Article 24(1)) or at pre-hearing conference.

The arbitral tribunal may also hear 'any other person' as witness or a party-appointed expert, without necessarily being asked to do so. This could for instance be the case if the arbitral tribunal believes that such 'other person' may provide more relevant testimony than the persons identified by the parties. It is very rare for the tribunal to issue such directions, however.

The arbitral tribunal may also decide to hear one or all of the parties, if requested to do so (it would rarely do so of its own accord). National procedural laws sometimes do not distinguish between the hearing of witnesses and parties. The Rules do not specify who may be a witness. Arbitral tribunals are usually prepared to hear parties, and in particular their counsel, if asked to do so, provided this is consistent with the '*lex arbitri*'. It goes without saying that the relationship between the persons heard and one or other of the parties may have a bearing on the evaluation of their testimony.

Naturally, parties are entitled to take part in discussions and the taking of evidence, as this is generally required by the universal principle of due process. However, if a party that has been duly summoned fails to appear, this does not prevent the proceedings from continuing or the hearing from taking place (Article 20 (2)). Therefore, a party may not block arbitral proceedings by refusing to appear. This principle must also be respected by experts appointed by the arbitral tribunal, even in the arbitral tribunal's absence, when on-site visits and inspections are organized.

The Rules do not indicate how witnesses, experts and other persons should be examined. If nothing has been previously agreed, for instance in the Terms of Reference, the arbitral tribunal duly decides after first inviting the parties to express their preferences. Arbitral tribunals have quite a free hand in this respect. They often tend to follow the rules applicable to the judicial proceedings with which they are familiar. However, there is no obligation or necessity for them to do so, unless the '*lex arbitri*' contains mandatory provisions regulating the question.

In international arbitrations consideration should be given to the fact that the parties come from different countries and are used to different methods of producing evidence. In some countries, for instance, it is customary for the parties' representatives to 'coach' witnesses, whereas this would be improper in other countries. When it comes to examining witnesses and experts, parties may therefore have different expectations, which should be taken into account if an agreement is to be reached. The approaches adopted vary from one case to another. In some cases, the arbitral tribunal may decide to examine witnesses and experts itself to begin with and then give the parties the opportunity to ask questions. In other cases the parties may be allowed to examine and cross-examine the witnesses and experts first, after which the arbitral tribunal may ask any questions it considers necessary. In any event, the parties should be given a reasonable opportunity to ask any questions they may have. The Rules do not forbid the use of video conferencing for hearing witnesses. In international arbitrations testimony may also be submitted in the form of affidavits and written witness statements as a way of preparing and simplifying the hearing.

The arbitral tribunal may also decide on the admissibility of written statements from witnesses and expert opinions, if nothing has been agreed on this matter in the Terms of Reference for instance. Any agreement that may have been made on the way and form in which evidence may be submitted must of course be respected. If a party makes a timely request for a witness or an expert who has submitted a written statement to be heard, the arbitral tribunal will normally agree to this request, in which case the witness or expert will usually be called to a hearing. The question arises as to whether the arbitral tribunal may assess the contents of a written statement made by a witness without necessarily examining the witness at a hearing. The Rules do not answer this question, which must be – and usually is – settled by the arbitral tribunal in agreement with the parties either in the Terms of Reference or in preparatory discussions on the admissibility of evidence. As with other important procedural matters, the arbitral tribunal and the parties should settle the question in advance and not wait for disagreements to arise.

The Rules do not deal with the question of whether, if requested, witnesses and experts may be heard under oath. Care should be taken to make sure that this is not forbidden by the '*lex arbitri*'. Even if witnesses do not take an oath, false statements may have criminal implications. The arbitral tribunal will usually inform the witnesses of this before hearing them.

There are no provisions in the Rules requiring discussions and statements made by witnesses or expert witnesses during hearings to be recorded in writing. However, this will often be inevitable where there are a great many witnesses or experts to be examined and – especially – where evidence is given over periods of several days or even weeks. It is hardly surprising therefore that parties often expressly request a written record of evidentiary hearings despite the extra costs. The written record may take the form of a verbatim transcript. Alternatively, tape recordings may be made. Although less costly, these are harder for the arbitral tribunal and the parties to exploit however. It is up to the parties to agree, in consultation with the arbitral tribunal, whether the case warrants this extra expenditure. If they cannot agree amongst themselves, the arbitral tribunal will decide.

If agreed between the parties or allowed by the arbitral tribunal when requested by one of the parties, once all the witnesses have been heard, the parties will be given the opportunity to comment on the conclusions to be drawn from the evidence presented. It may be sufficient for them to make oral comments at the end of the hearing. This is not a requirement, however, as the Rules do not contain any provisions on the subject. Often so called post-hearing briefs are agreed or ordered, albeit with the priviso that no new facts on evidence may be adduced therewith.

Unlike courts, arbitral tribunals cannot compel witnesses to appear, even at the request of one of the parties. Normally, it is the parties themselves who ensure that their witnesses appear. Sometimes, the *'lex arbitri'* allows arbitral tribunals to turn to local courts for help in ensuring that evidence such as witness testimony is produced. Such help may involve coercion, if necessary. It should be said, however, that more often than not the person required to give evidence will be located outside the jurisdiction of the local court. The person's failure to appear will mean that the party concerned will be unable to provide the evidence it may be required to produce. Some arbitration laws provide for court assistance to arbitral tribunals seated in another country if the evidence/witness is located in the jurisdiction of that court.

Travel costs incurred by witnesses or party-appointed experts called to a hearing are usually covered initially by the party that called them. However, they are normally considered as part of the costs of the arbitration and a party may therefore ask for such costs to be awarded against the other party in the final award, in accordance with Article 37(1) and (4). Where there are costs for interpretation and making a written record of the hearing, the arbitral tribunal may request the parties to pay a special advance, which will usually be split equally between them. It is more often the case, however, that the Secretariat will charge such costs to the advance on arbitration costs already paid by the parties. If the arbitral tribunal appoints an expert, it will always fix a special advance, which may be administered by ICC under the arbitral tribunal's instructions or paid into an account specially designated for this purpose by the arbitral tribunal.

e) Appointment of Experts (Art. 25(4)).

(1) Party-Appointed Experts.

The arbitral tribunal's power to appoint one or more experts under Article 25(4) reflects general practice in continental Europe. In other legal traditions such as the common law, it is customary for the parties rather than the arbitral tribunal to appoint experts and witnesses. In this case, the parties usually prepare and agree on the written and oral statements to be made by their experts before joining them in the proceedings. It may be wise to do so especially in highly technical cases in which the issues are of a technical rather than a legal nature. In such instances a party's arguments will generally benefit from being backed up by opinions from technical experts. However, such experts are not as independent as those appointed by the arbitral tribunal.

The way in which statements made by such experts will be presented and used during the proceedings, and especially the question of whether or not recourse should also be had to an expert appointed by the arbitral tribunal, must be agreed by the parties or decided by the arbitral tribunal in each instance in light of the parties' comments. Much will depend on the origins of the parties and their representatives and the make-up of the arbitral tribunal.

(2) Experts Appointed by the Arbitral Tribunal.

If the parties do not request to present a party appointed expert or if the arbitral tribunal does not wish to, or cannot, decide the case on the basis of the parties' statements alone, Article 25(4) allows experts to be appointed by the arbitral tribunal itself, unless the parties have decided not to allow this. If the parties have agreed to ask for a neutral expert to be appointed, the arbitral tribunal will normally grant this request out of respect for party autonomy.

Article 25(4) requires the arbitral tribunal to allow the parties to comment before it makes a decision on the appointment of an expert and the expert's terms of reference. It will always allow the parties to express their views on the terms of reference to be given to the expert. At this stage of the proceedings the parties are usually better informed of the technical aspects of the dispute than the arbitrators, so it makes sense to do so. Although desirable, it is not necessary for the parties to be in agreement on the expert's terms of reference, as it is the arbitral tribunal's job to define them. By being given an opportunity to comment on the terms of reference, the parties may not subsequently object that the assignment given to the expert does not adequately reflect their pleadings and requests.

It is also desirable that the parties be given the possibility to comment on the choice of an appropriate expert, as they are often better aware of the technical side of the dispute than the arbitral tribunal at this stage. Obviously, the decision lies in the last resort with the arbitral tribunal in the event of a difference of opinion. It may for this purpose turn to organizations that have access to a network of experts, such as the ICC International Centre for ADR in Paris for international cases or chambers of commerce and industry.

Tribunal-appointed experts are appointed directly by the arbitral tribunal and act upon its instructions and also are required to be independent and impartial, like arbitrators. Arbitral tribunals will usually ask for a written confirmation of independence by the expert, although this is not compulsory.

Arbitrators who are considering whether or not to appoint an expert or who are conducting a case where parties have appointed themselves experts may find useful guidance in a report on 'Issues for Arbitrators to Consider Regarding Expertise' issued in 2010, notwithstanding the fact that this report was established under the 2003 ICC Rules for Expertise and under the 1998 ICC Rules of Arbitration (see Appendix 18 below). Persons who have been retained to serve as an expert in proceedings under the ICC Expert Rules or under the ICC Rules of Arbitration or who are contemplating such an engagement may find useful guidance in a report on 'Issues for Experts acting under the ICC Rules of Expertise or the ICC Rules of Arbitration' issued in 2009 by the

ICC Commission on Arbitration and ADR, even if this report was established under the 2003 ICC Rules for Expertise and under the 1998 ICC Rules of Arbitration (see Appendix 19 below).

The ICC has issued in 1976 Expertise Rules that were revised a few times and most recently in 2015 (see Chapter 6 and Appendix 25 below). The ICC Rules for Expertise (now called 'ICC Expert Rules') offer various options in domestic and international business matters. Upon the request of a party, the ICC International Centre for Expertise (now called ICC International Centre for ADR) proposes the name of one or more experts or neutrals in a particular field of activity (pursuant to the 'ICC Rules for the Proposal of Experts and Neutrals' in a new edition in force as from 1 February 2015, see Chapter 6 and Appendix 25 below). The Centre can appoint an expert or neutral, if the parties have agreed to the appointment of an expert or neutral and have agreed to use the Centre as the appointing authority or where the Centre is satisfied that there is a sufficient basis for appointing an expert or neutral (pursuant to the 'ICC Rules for the Appointment of Experts and Neutrals' in a new edition in force as from 1 February 2015, see Chapter 6 and Appendix 25 below). Moreover, when the parties have agreed upon the administration of expertise proceedings by the Centre or when the Centre is otherwise satisfied that there is a sufficient basis for administering expertise proceedings, the Centre will administer the proceedings pursuant to the Rules (pursuant to the 'ICC Rules for the Administration of Expert Proceedings' in a new edition in force as from 1 February 2015, see Appendix 25 below).

If an arbitral tribunal acting in an ICC arbitration requests the ICC International Centre for ADR a proposal of an expert, the services of the ICC Centre shall be provided free of charge (Article 3(1) of Appendix II to the ICC Rules for the Proposal of Experts and Neutrals, see Chapter 6 and Appendix 25 below).

Before an expertise ordered by the arbitral tribunal can be commenced, the parties, or one of them, shall pay an advance on costs fixed by the arbitral tribunal sufficient to cover the expected fees and expenses of the expert as determined by the arbitral tribunal. The arbitral tribunal shall be responsible for ensuring the payment by the parties of such fees and expenses (Article 1(12) of Appendix III to the Rules).

This advance on costs is usually split equally between the parties, although it may sometimes be paid in full by the party upon which the burden of proof falls. If the advance remains unpaid, the arbitral tribunal must consider the party concerned to be in default and decide accordingly as regards the burden of proof.

Before fixing the advance, the arbitral tribunal must enter into an agreement with the expert and discuss his or her foreseeable expenses. It will be up to the arbitral tribunal to decide which of the parties will in the end bear the costs of the expert (Article 37(1) and (4)). According to Article 37(3), this decision may be taken at any moment during the arbitration. It does not need to be made in the final award, as was the case under previous versions of the Rules prior to 1998. There is nothing in the Rules saying whether this decision should take the form of a procedural order or a partial or interim award. However, in situations where it might be necessary to order that a party be reimbursed, it is advisable for the decision to be made in the form of an award. For this reason, therefore, the decision on such costs will usually be made in the final award.

The expert's report is normally submitted in writing. This allows the parties to comment on the report. Were the arbitral tribunal to base its award on an expert's report, the contents of which remained unknown to the parties or on which they had been unable to comment, this would be contrary to due process. If the parties ask for the expert's report to be presented orally, so as to give them an opportunity to question the expert, the arbitral tribunal must agree to this (Article 25(4)).

As the arbitral tribunal has a free hand when it comes to assessing evidence, it may decide whether and to what extent to follow the expert's findings. In practice, arbitral tribunals more often than not rely on the expert's report they have themselves commissioned, unless there are strong reasons for doing otherwise. Clearly, the arbitral tribunal will give the reasons for its decision when explaining the grounds for the award, especially if it diverges fully or in part from the expert's findings. Although there is nothing in the Rules to this effect, it remains to be seen whether an award containing insufficient reasons in this regard could be considered as flawed.

(3) Decision Not to Use a Tribunal-Appointed Expert.

There may be occasions when the parties do not wish to have an independent expert appointed by the arbitral tribunal. If this is the case, the principle of party autonomy requires the arbitral tribunal to take account of their wish. However, the arbitral tribunal will normally draw their attention to the implication this will have, namely that its decision is likely to be based on where the burden of proof lies. From a practical point of view, it would be difficult for an arbitral tribunal to order an expertise against the parties' wishes, even if in theory Article 25(4) entitles it to do so, as the expert's fees and expenses are part of the costs of the arbitration (Article 37(1)) for which an advance must be paid before the expert can start work (see Article 1(12) of Appendix III to the Rules).

f) Summoning Parties to Provide Additional Evidence (Art. 25(5))

There is no automatic duty to disclose documents or a right to request or obtain document production in international arbitration (Report of the ICC Commission on Arbitration and ADR on 'Techniques for Managing Electronic Document Production When it is Permitted or Required in International Arbitration', 2012, p. 1; see Appendix 17 below). International arbitrations are sometimes influenced by the common law practice of discovery, whereby each party can require the other party to disclose certain documents relating to the merits of the dispute or (narrow) categories. Should this practice be adopted, it usually occurs after the Terms of Reference have been drawn up and before the hearing is held, so as to allow the documents produced to be taken into consideration. Parties unfamiliar with discovery will often forget, when drawing up internal documents prior to the emergence of the dispute, that it may be necessary to disclose these documents, whereas the other party, better informed of this duty, may act more cautiously. Equally important is the rejection of discovery by parties from countries where the procedural law does not require litigants to disclose documents. For all these reasons, many international arbitral tribunals tend to limit this obligation by deciding that once both sides have been heard, any documents that have not been spontaneously disclosed may be submitted only if they have been adequately described for purposes of identification and they are needed to convince the arbitrators. Nevertheless, it is not unusual for arbitral tribunals to request parties to disclose more documents than would be required by a state court in a civil law country. Whether or not a party may resist a request for disclosure from the other party and the arguments it may present to support its position will depend on the circumstances of the case. Depending on the legal system involved, confidentiality obligations, the protection of trade secrets, the secrecy of communications between lawyer and client, state secrets, or the excessive expenditure caused by disclosure may be used to ward off such a request.

The IBA Rules on the Taking of Evidence in International Arbitration provide (Article 3(3); revised edition of 2010; at <www.ibanet.org>) that a request to produce documents should contain a description of each requested document sufficient to identify it, or a description in sufficient detail of a narrow and specific requested category of documents that are reasonably believed to exist; in the case of documents maintained in electronic form, the requesting party may, or the arbitral tribunal may order that it shall be required to, identify specific files, search term, individuals or other means of searching for such documents in an efficient and economical manner. The arbitral tribunal may order the party to whom such request is addressed to produce any requested document in its possession, custody or control as to which the arbitral tribunal determines that the issues that the requesting party wishes to prove are relevant to the case and material to its outcome (Article 3(7); revised edition of 2010; at <www.ibanet.org>).

The advent of digital documents should not lead to any expansion of the traditional and prevailing approach to document production. Thus, requests for the production of digital documents, like requests for the production of paper documents – to the extent they are deemed necessary and appropriate in an arbitration – should remain limited, tailored to the specific circumstances of the case and subject to the general document production principles of specificity, relevance, materiality and proportionality (Report of the ICC Commission on Arbitration and ADR on 'Techniques for Managing Electronic Document Production When it is Permitted or Required in International Arbitration', 2012, p. 1; see Appendix 17 below).

The parties undertake to comply with any order made by the arbitral tribunal (Article 22(5)). If a party refuses to comply with an order of the arbitral tribunal to disclose required documents, the arbitral tribunal can draw an adverse inference from such failure or refusal, in accordance with a practice well established in international arbitration and foreseen in the IBA Rules on the Taking of Evidence in International Arbitration (Article 9(5); revised edition of 2010; at <www.ibanet.org>; see J. Fry, S. Greenberg and F. Mazza, *The Secretariat's Guide to ICC Arbitration*, ICC Publication No. 729 E, Paris, 2012, p. 277).

g) A Decision Without an Oral Hearing (Art. 25(6))

Some arbitration cases are of a nature that allow a decision without a hearing on the basis of the documents submitted by the parties, if none of the parties requests a hearing.

(1) Document-Based Decision with the Parties' Consent

Sometimes the parties do not request a hearing and are happy for the decision to be made on the basis of the documents they have submitted. This may, for instance, happen in minor and relatively simple cases where the parties believe that the amount in dispute does not justify the expense of organizing a hearing and the related travel costs. The Rules allow the arbitral tribunal to decide on the sole basis of the documents submitted by the parties, provided none of them requests a hearing (Article 25(6)). The arbitral tribunal is of course at liberty to hold a hearing, without having been asked to do so, if it considers this to be necessary to clarify the factual or legal situation or for other reasons.

In practice, it is rare for an ICC arbitral tribunal to wish to decide a case on the basis of the parties' documents only. If the parties have not expressly waived their right to a hearing, it is advisable for the arbitral tribunal to enquire whether this is the case, before closing the proceedings in accordance with Article 27. By doing so, it will avoid later objections by a party claiming a violation of its right to be heard.

(2) Document-Based Decision where One of the Parties is Absent.

Since ICC arbitral proceedings carry on even when one of the parties decides not to take part or to cease taking part, a decision based on documents only may be contemplated here too, provided the other party does not request a hearing. The arbitral tribunal will generally inform the parties and allow a short period for any objections they may wish to make. In practice, arbitrators generally tend to avoid such situations, so as not to jeopardize their awards. If, however, an award is made under such conditions, it is not necessarily equivalent to a judgment in default and several ICC arbitration specialists believe that a party's absence does not imply its acceptance of the facts presented by the other party. This is sometimes clearly mentioned in national arbitration laws (see Article 1048 ZPO, Article 1706 JC, Article 25 of the UNCITRAL Model Law), but no similar provision is found in the ICC Rules of Arbitration. In any event, the arbitral tribunal has a free hand when assessing evidence and may also call upon witnesses. Given that circumstances may vary considerably from one case to another, parties are advised to decide as soon as possible with the arbitral tribunal on the procedure to be followed.

11. Hearings (Art. 26)

Article 26 of the Rules reads:

> '**Hearings**
>
> 1. When a hearing is to be held, the arbitral tribunal, giving reasonable notice, shall summon the parties to appear before it on the day and at the place fixed by it.
>
> 2. If any of the parties, although duly summoned, fails to appear without valid excuse, the arbitral tribunal shall have the power to proceed with the hearing.
>
> 3. The arbitral tribunal shall be in full charge of the hearings, at which all the parties shall be entitled to be present. Save with the approval of the arbitral tribunal and the parties, persons not involved in the proceedings shall not be admitted.
>
> 4. The parties may appear in person or though duly authorized representatives. In addition, they may be assisted by advisers.'

a) Due Summoning by the Arbitral Tribunal (Art. 26(1) and (2))

When the arbitral tribunal schedules a hearing, be it at the request of a party or of its own accord, it must summon the parties in good time and in due form (Article 2(1) of the Rules).

It is advisable for the arbitral tribunal to agree with the parties on available dates first, before officially fixing the date (see Article 24(2)). It is also necessary to check that the witnesses, experts and other persons to be heard at the same time are also available to appear on the chosen date.

If no agreement can be reached between the parties, the arbitral tribunal shall fix the date of the hearing. It should make sure, however, that a 'reasonable notice' is given. The Rules do no specify what a 'reasonable notice' is. This depends on the particular circumstance of the case, taking into account the locations where the parties and their representatives are residing, the time of the year when the hearing will be organized, the duration of the scheduled hearing and the matters that will be discussed at the hearing.

The form in which the summons should be notified to the parties is determined by Article 3(1) and (2) of the Rules, if the parties have not made any specific arrangements for this purpose, for instance in the Terms of Reference (see Article 23(1)). As a general rule, it is advisable to give notification by registered letter or courier service with acknowledgment of receipt, especially if one of the parties refuses to take part in the proceedings. Notification by e-mail or by fax will nonetheless be regarded as having been properly given if in accordance with Article 3(2), especially if the parties have corresponded by e-mail or by fax previously. When parties are represented by lawyers, the notification will generally be sent to the lawyers. Normally the terms of reference will specify how the communications between the arbitral tribunal and the parties may be done.

For the sake of predictability, which is very important in arbitration, the arbitral tribunal should give the parties a clear indication of how the hearing will be conducted. This should be done at the latest when giving notice of the hearing. In addition to specifying the date and venue of the hearing, such notice should provide information on how the proceedings will be conducted so that the parties can prepare themselves. For instance, the parties should be informed in advance whether the purpose of the hearing is to take evidence from witnesses or experts and, if so, which witnesses or experts will be heard, or to allow the lawyers to present their pleadings. If the arbitral tribunal plans to hear the parties' witnesses or experts, it should indicate, no later than when giving notice of the hearing, whether they will be questioned first by the parties or whether the questioning will be done by the arbitral tribunal itself. If more than one witness or expert is to be summoned, it should be indicated whether they can or should be present throughout all the discussions.

It is not necessary to organize all hearings in the form of physical meetings. As set out in the case management techniques (Appendix IV to the Rules; see also Article 24(4) for the case management conferences), the arbitral tribunal may consider using telephone or video conferencing for procedural and other hearings where attendance in person is not essential. It may also consider using IT that enables online communication with the parties.

Arbitrators can also find guidance about whether to hold hearings and how to organize them in the UNCITRAL Notes on Organizing Arbitral Proceedings (issued in 1996 and currently under revision).

b) A Party's Failure to Appear Despite Due Summoning (Art. 26(2))

If a party that has been duly summoned to the hearing with a reasonable notice fails to appear without a valid excuse, the hearing may go ahead in its absence (Article 26(2) of the Rules). The arbitral tribunal decides on a case-by-case basis what will be deemed to constitute a 'valid excuse'. If it considers the absent party's excuse to be adequate, it will adjourn the hearing. For instance, if one of the parties comes from a country stricken by war at the time of the hearing or from a country cut off from the rest of the world by an international boycott, the party will usually be considered to have a valid excuse for not attending. If the arbitral tribunal were to go ahead with the proceedings in such situations, this could cause the ICC International Court of Arbitration to withhold its approval of the arbitral tribunal's draft award, on the basis of Article 41 of the Rules, until it is assured that due process has been respected.

Should a party face problems with traveling to the country of the place of the arbitration, the arbitral tribunal may consider, after having consulted the other party or the other parties, to relocate the hearing to another country where all parties are able to attend the hearing (see also Article 18(2)).

If the absent party fails to provide a valid justification for its absence, the proceedings may go ahead without it. The Rules do not contain any provisions allowing the absent party to ask for a new hearing to be scheduled or for the scheduled hearing to be repeated. Nor may this be inferred from other applicable rules (e.g. the '*lex arbitri*'). Having had a reasonable opportunity to present its case orally but having failed to take advantage of this opportunity, the party concerned cannot be considered to have been denied due process.

A respondent's failure to appear at a hearing does not necessarily mean that the case will be automatically decided in the claimant's favor. Although in judicial proceedings a judgment in default may sometimes be requested against a party that fails to appear (see, for example, Article 805 JC, Article 473 NCPC, Articles 330 and 331 ZPO), this possibility is not provided for in the ICC Rules of Arbitration. In particular, the Rules do not recognize the fiction whereby a defendant who fails to appear automatically admits the facts or recognizes the rights claimed. Even if the respondent does not appear at the hearing and does not take part in the proceedings, the claimant must establish that its claims are justified. The arbitral tribunal must render a reasoned award. In any event, no party should think that its failure to appear at a hearing or take part in the proceedings is without consequence (see Article 25 above).

c) The Conduct of the Hearing (Art. 26(3))

(1) The Proceedings.

In the absence of an agreement of the parties, the arbitral tribunal decides alone how the proceedings will be conducted at the hearing, although it will preferably seek the parties' views first. It is good practice for an arbitral tribunal to discuss already before the hearing the manner in which the hearing will be conducted. It is recommended to know prior to the hearing whether the parties wish to present their pleadings orally, how much time they will need for this purpose and whether they intend to ask for witnesses or experts to be heard (see in this regard Article 25(3)). The necessary arrangements can be discussed during a case management conference (see Article 24(1)) or a specific pre-hearing conference.

The arbitral tribunal is in full charge of the hearing. Should particular issues arise at the hearing which were not yet discussed, it is good practice to discuss them with the parties before the arbitral tribunal issues procedural directions. If needed, the arbitral tribunal may render at the hearing a decision in the form of a procedural order, that can be communicated orally and confirmed in the transcript of the hearing or in writing shortly thereafter.

(2) The Record of the Hearing.

The same applies to the drawing up of minutes or a tape recording of the hearing. If the parties wish, the arbitral tribunal will make the necessary logistical arrangements and, if appropriate, will fix an advance to cover the related costs. The arbitral tribunal may also decide to establish a summary or full record (verbatim transcript) of the hearing itself or to engage a secretary or court reporter. Given the extra costs that may be involved with a secretary or court reporter, the arbitral tribunal should check whether the parties or any of them are willing to bear such extra costs.

(3) An Assistant to the Arbitral Tribunal ('Administrative Secretary').

Many arbitral tribunals wish to use the services of a secretary to deal with matters relating to the administration of the arbitral proceedings. The ICC International Court of Arbitration insists on the importance of consulting the parties first, especially if the appointment of an administrative secretary puts an additional cost burden on the parties. It should be noted that the Rules, which say nothing about administrative secretaries, do not contain a rule as to who should bear such costs. If the parties fail to agree on whether or not an administrative secretary may be appointed, the arbitral tribunal should carefully consider whether in the circumstances of that particular case such an appointment is appropriate, as pointed out by the Secretariat of the ICC Court in a note to the arbitrators on the conduct of the arbitration ('Note to the Arbitral Tribunal on the Conduct of the Arbitration', see Appendix 7 below). This note is communicated to the arbitral tribunal by the Secretariat when it transmits the file in accordance with Article 16. Administrative secretaries must satisfy the same independence and impartiality requirements as those which apply to arbitrators under the ICC Rules. ICC staff members are not permitted to serve as administrative secretaries in ICC arbitration proceedings. There is no formal process for the appointment of an administrative secretary. Before it decides to appoint an administrative secretary, however, the arbitral tribunal is well advised to inform the parties of its intention to do so. Thereby, it should provide the curriculum vitae of the proposed administrative secretary as well as a statement of independence and impartiality and an undertaking of the administrative secretary that he or she shall act in accordance with the Secretariat's Note. The parties should be given the opportunity to object against the appointment of the administrative secretary.

The parties' agreement is also required in order for an administrative secretary to be able to take part in a hearing. This is a result of Article 26(3) of the Rules, which states that 'persons not involved in the proceedings' cannot attend without the consent of the arbitral tribunal and the parties. The principle of the confidentiality of arbitration proceedings prevents third parties from attending proceedings without the parties' consent.

An administrative secretary shall act upon the arbitral tribunal's instructions and under its supervision only. An administrative secretary may perform organizational and administrative tasks such as transmitting documents and communications on behalf of the arbitral tribunal, organizing and maintaining the arbitral tribunal's file and locating documents, organizing hearings and meetings, attending hearings and deliberations, taking notes or minutes or keeping time, conducting legal or similar research, proof-reading and checking citations and dates and cross-references in procedural orders and awards, correcting typographical or calculation errors. Under no circumstances may an arbitral tribunal delegate decision-making functions to an administrative secretary. With the exception of the administrative secretary's reasonable personal disbursements as detailed in the Secretariat's note, the engagement of an administrative secretary should not pose any additional financial burden on the parties (Secretariat's 'Note to the Arbitral Tribunal on the Conduct of the Arbitration', see Appendix 9 below).

(4) Witnesses.

If the arbitral tribunal wishes one or more witnesses to attend a hearing, it must decide in detail how they will be questioned (see Article 25(3)). If more than one witness is called, the arbitral tribunal will decide, after consulting with the parties, whether during the examination of one witness other witnesses may be present.

(5) Due Process.

When conducting the hearing, the arbitral tribunal should keep in mind that each side should be given sufficient opportunity to present its case. This presupposes that all the parties are given the right to take part in the discussions and the production of evidence. It is inconceivable that the arbitral tribunal should decide the dispute on the basis of circumstances unknown to one or other of the parties. In accordance with the requirement to act 'fairly and impartially', as laid down in Article 22(4) of the Rules, the arbitral tribunal will make sure that the parties have the same opportunity to present their arguments.

In international arbitration, there is controversy over the question of whether and how, during a hearing, an arbitral tribunal may engage in legal discussions in the course of which it expresses its position on factual and legal questions. The national procedural traditions to which the participants belong will be influential here. On the one hand, it is thought to be premature for the arbitral tribunal to make any comments reflecting its provisional opinion, as this is deemed to be a violation of the obligation to hear a party fully before coming to a decision and could lead to the arbitrators being challenged. On the other hand, for example, German parties tend to expect the arbitral tribunal to engage in a legal discussion. Consequently, whether and to what extent an arbitral tribunal may reveal its provisional views on the factual and legal situation in the course of a hearing must be decided in the light of each individual case in consultation with the parties.

d) Party Representation (Art. 26(4))

Parties may defend themselves or may be assisted by a person of their choice. They may also be represented by a 'duly authorized' person (Article 26(4)). In international arbitration, it is customary, although not compulsory, to be represented by a lawyer or at least to seek the assistance of a lawyer. The complexity of the proceedings and their international implications generally make this appropriate. Given that international arbitration proceedings rarely take place in the countries from which the parties originate, that foreign law is often applicable to the issues involved, and that the proceedings are frequently conducted in a language other than the parties' native languages, the assistance or at least the advice of a suitably qualified lawyer is recommended.

Given that arbitrations are generally not subject to the procedural rules applicable to court proceedings at the place of the arbitration, parties are not necessarily required to be represented by local lawyers and may therefore use the services of their regular lawyers. Difficulties may sometimes arise where national rules of law allow only locally admitted lawyers to act on behalf of parties, although this is somewhat unusual. It is not uncommon in international arbitrations for none of the parties' representatives to be established in the country where the arbitration is seated. In this case, it may nonetheless be useful to consult or collaborate with a local lawyer when checking the mandatory procedural rules applicable to arbitrations at the place of the arbitration ('*lex arbitri*').

Many legal systems require parties wishing to be represented by a lawyer to draw up a written power of attorney. However, this is not generally the case in international arbitration practice. Indeed, many legal systems assume that when a person acts as a lawyer, this automatically implies that the lawyer has been duly mandated to represent his or her client. This for instance is the case in France and in other legal systems influenced by the French system. In international arbitrations involving parties and lawyers from different legal systems and backgrounds, the arbitral tribunal will often take the precaution of checking the lawyers' authority to act on behalf of their clients in order to avoid any difficulties. Article 17 of the Rules allows arbitral tribunals to require proof of the authority of any party representatives at any time of the proceedings.

Rules developed for domestic judicial litigation only are usually not well adapted to deal with legal and cultural differences among participants in international arbitration proceedings. The International Bar Association has therefore adopted in 2013 Guidelines on Party Representation in International Arbitration. The parties may adopt these Guidelines or a portion thereof by agreement. Arbitral tribunals may also apply the Guidelines in their discretion, subject to any applicable mandatory rules, if they determine that they have the authority to do so (The Guidelines can be consulted on the website of the International Bar Association: <www.ibanet.org>). These Guidelines provide for example that, in case a change in party representation in the course of the arbitration creates a conflict of interest between a newly-appointed party representative and one or more of the arbitrators which threatens the integrity of the proceedings, the arbitral tribunal may, where it has found that it has the authority to do so, consider excluding the new representative from participating in all or part of the arbitral proceedings (Guidelines 4-5; at <www.ibanet.org>).

As already mentioned, there is no obligation to be represented by a lawyer. It is quite conceivable – although relatively rare in practice – for a company to be represented by its in-house counsel. This contrasts with mediation and other ADR procedures such as mini-trials, where parties are frequently represented by in-house counsel rather than an outside lawyer.

The arbitral tribunal shall permit the parties and their representatives to attend the hearing. Other persons, who are neither a party nor a representative nor their counsel nor a witness nor an expert, shall not be admitted to the hearing without the parties' consent. If the parties have accepted that an administrative secretary is appointed by the arbitral tribunal, such administrative secretary shall also be admitted to the hearing.

12. Closing of the Proceedings and Date for Submission of Draft Awards (Art. 27)

Article 27 of the Rules reads:

> 'Closing of the Proceedings and Date for Submission of Draft Awards
>
> As soon as possible after the last hearing concerning matters to be decided in an award or the filing of the last authorized submissions concerning such matters, whichever is later, the arbitral tribunal shall:
>
> a) declare the proceedings closed with respect to the matters to be decided in the award; and
>
> b) inform the Secretariat and the parties of the date by which it expects to submit its draft award to the Court for approval pursuant to Article 33.

> After the proceedings are closed, no further submission or argument may be made, or evidence produced, with respect to the matters to be decided in the award, unless requested or authorized by the arbitral tribunal.'

a) The Significance of the Closing of the Proceedings

These provisions, which were introduced into the Rules in 1998, are aimed at accelerating the proceedings at the time when the arbitral award must be rendered by the arbitral tribunal. They oblige the arbitrators to declare the proceedings officially closed when the parties have had a reasonable opportunity to argue their case. As already mentioned in connection with Article 22(4), the arbitral tribunal decides when the proceedings have reached the stage at which the parties may be considered to have had 'a reasonable opportunity to present their case'.

The closing of the proceedings marks the end of the submission of factual and legal assertions and submission of any evidence. From then on, the parties may not present further pleadings or new evidence. Once the arbitral tribunal has closed the proceedings, it begins its deliberations leading to the final award. Normally, any arguments presented by the parties after that moment are inadmissible and cannot be taken into consideration by the arbitral tribunal. If the parties wish to present further pleas, they may do so only if requested or authorized by the arbitral tribunal.

The arbitral tribunal may itself decide to re-open the hearing or take evidence again. For instance, it may order the parties to provide further details on certain specific points. This will be the case if the arbitral tribunal realizes during its deliberations that the assertions of one or all of the parties on an essential question are insufficient and prevent it from rendering its award or from deciding on certain of the claims made. A typical example is the issue of costs. As the arbitral tribunal has to decide in its award which of the parties should bear the costs of the arbitration and the recoverable amounts, it may need to ask the parties after the closing of the proceedings to provide details of the costs they have incurred in exercising their rights.

The provisions of Article 27 not only apply to the final award, but also to any interim or partial award 'concerning matters to be decided in an award' after the last authorized submissions on such a matter have been filed.

b) The Date on which the Award is Expected to be Rendered

When closing the proceedings, the arbitral tribunal is required to indicate when it expects to submit its draft award to the ICC International Court of Arbitration for scrutiny (Article 27(b)). It must inform the Secretariat of the Court and the parties of this date. Under the 1998 Rules there was not yet a requirement to inform the parties of this date, but the 2012 Rules now oblige the arbitral tribunal to also advise the parties thereof. The Court checks that the date is within the time limit for rendering the award laid down in Article 30 of the Rules and, if necessary, will extend this time limit. The arbitral tribunal must therefore carefully plan its deliberations.

It is appropriate to let the parties know the date on which they may expect to receive the award. The arbitral tribunal and the parties should remember that the draft award must first be submitted to the ICC Court for scrutiny and approval, which may take up to a month (see Article 33 of the Rules). This period must be added to the time required for deliberating and drafting the award including the reasons on which it is based. It is therefore not uncommon, especially in complex cases, for some months to elapse between the closing of the proceedings and the date on which the award is rendered.

13. Conservatory and Interim Measures (Art. 28)

Article 28 of the Rules reads:

> 'Conservatory and Interim Measures
>
> 1. Unless the parties have otherwise agreed, as soon as the file has been transmitted to it, the arbitral tribunal may, at the request of a party, order any interim or conservatory measure it deems appropriate. The arbitral tribunal may make the granting of any such measure subject to appropriate security being furnished by the requesting party. Any such measure shall take the form of an order, giving reasons, or of an award, as the arbitral tribunal considers appropriate.
>
> 2. Before the file is transmitted to the arbitral tribunal, and in appropriate circumstances even thereafter, the parties may apply to any competent judicial authority for interim or conservatory measures. The application of a party to a judicial authority for such measures or for the implementation of any such measures ordered by an Arbitral Tribunal shall not be deemed to be an infringement or a waiver of the arbitration agreement and shall not affect the relevant powers reserved to the arbitral tribunal. Any such application and any measures taken by the judicial authority must be notified without delay to the Secretariat. The Secretariat shall inform the arbitral tribunal thereof.'

a) The Arbitral Tribunal's Jurisdiction to Order Conservatory and Interim Measures

There are times when parties need to seek conservatory and interim measures. This for instance will be the case when damage or other unexpected events have occurred and evidence must immediately be obtained so as not to be irremediably lost. Sometimes, a party may wish to ensure that its contractual partner does not destroy or alter goods which are important to the outcome of the dispute. On other occasions, a party may wish to ensure that its opponent has provided adequate guarantees to cover the reimbursement of its expenses in the event that the award is in its favor.

It is not always easy for parties to know whether they should apply to a judicial authority or an arbitral tribunal for conservatory and interim measures. Article 28(1) provides that, 'as soon as the file has been transmitted to it', an arbitral tribunal may, at the request of one of the parties, order the conservatory and interim measures which 'it deems appropriate', 'unless the parties have otherwise agreed'. The Rules therefore expressly allow the parties to deny the arbitral tribunal jurisdiction in this regard. The parties may also agree to limit the arbitral tribunal's power to ordering certain specific conservatory and interim measures. Also, they may decide that a given judicial authority has jurisdiction for interim measures when allowed by the procedural law to which it is subjected.

If the parties have made no such agreements, the arbitral tribunal may order such measures as soon as it is in possession of the file (see Article 16 of the Rules). It therefore does not have to wait until the Terms of Reference have been drawn up or until the advance to cover the costs of the arbitration has been paid in full. Consequently, it is impossible for parties to hinder the ordering of necessary urgent measures through protraction or resistance.

It is imperative that any national rules at the place of the arbitration containing mandatory provisions restricting the arbitral tribunal's jurisdiction with respect to conservatory and interim measures be respected. For instance, Article 1691 of the Belgian

Judicial Code allows arbitral tribunals seated in Belgium to order conservatory and interim measures but expressly forbids them to order the seizure of goods. Likewise, Article 1468 NCPC allows arbitral tribunals seated in France to order conservatory and interim measures but forbids them to order conservatory attachments and judicial security. However, no such restriction is found in Switzerland (see Article 183 PILA), Germany (see Article 1041 ZPO) or under the UNCITRAL Model Law (see Article 17).

Consequently, parties may find themselves obliged to apply to a judicial authority for certain measures, even after the file has been transmitted to the arbitral tribunal. Prior to the start of the arbitral proceedings, the parties may make an application for such measures pursuant to Article 29 and the Emergency Arbitrator Rules contained in Appendix V to the Rules, unless the arbitration agreement was concluded before 1 January 2012, or unless the parties have opted out of the Emergency Arbitrator Provisions, or unless the parties have agreed to another pre-arbitral procedure that provides for the granting of conservatory, interim or similar measures. The parties can agree to have recourse to ICC's pre-arbitral referee procedure, which was introduced in 1990 and which is also specially conceived for rapid action when difficulties arise during contractual relations (see the ICC Rules for a Pre-Arbitral Referee Procedure, Chapter 6 and Appendix 21 below). Both the Emergency Arbitrator Rules and the Pre-Arbitral Referee Rules entail the appointment of a third party empowered to take urgent steps such as interim measures or to establish a neutral record of facts. The parties remain contractually bound by the emergency arbitrator's order and by the pre-arbitral referee's ruling until such time as an arbitral tribunal or judicial authority decides otherwise. If the emergency arbitrator's order or the pre-arbitral referee's ruling are not respected, the aggrieved party may be entitled to damages.

Another possibility open to parties wishing to ascertain factual issues and thereby preserve evidence is to apply to the ICC International Centre for ADR for the appointment of a duly qualified independent expert. Such an appointment may even be made at the request of only one of the parties. It should be pointed out that the resulting expert's report is not binding upon an arbitral tribunal unless the parties have agreed otherwise (see the ICC Expert Rules, Chapter 6 and Appendix 25 below).

b) The Form of the Arbitral Tribunal's Interim Decision

The Rules do not specify the form of the decision ordering conservatory or interim measures. The arbitral tribunal is not necessarily required to make an award for this purpose; a procedural order may suffice. Whether it opts for an award or a procedural order will depend on the mandatory procedural rules applicable at the place of the arbitration and the desired effectiveness of the measure.

If the measure were to take the form of an award, more time would be needed than for a procedural order as the ICC International Court of Arbitration will have to scrutinize and approve the draft award before the Secretariat notifies it to the parties. In very urgent cases, approval by the President of the Court alone, under Article 1(3) of the Rules, could be contemplated. In theory, an award has the advantage of being enforceable at law, but this will depend on the legal system at the place where the measure is to be enforced. There is much debate among practitioners as to whether or not arbitral awards ordering conservatory or interim measures are enforceable and in many countries the question remains unclear. The reason for this is that the enforcement of an award is, as a general rule, conditional upon it being final. By their very nature, interim decisions lack this quality and could be vacated or modified by an arbitral tribunal when rendering its final award or even earlier.

When conservatory and interim measures take the form of a procedural order, this is quicker than an award but offers no guarantee of enforceability as there is no international convention providing for the enforcement of procedural orders. Furthermore, it is relatively rare for national arbitration laws to provide for the enforcement of procedural orders rendered by arbitral tribunals. Sometimes they allow for arbitral tribunals to seek assistance from the courts. Article 1696(1) of the Belgian JC provides that an interim or protective measure issued by an arbitral tribunal shall be recognized as binding and, unless otherwise provided by the arbitral tribunal, enforced by the court of first instance, irrespective of the country in which it was issued, unless there is a ground of refusal pursuant to Article 1697 JC. In Germany, a court may allow a conservatory or interim measure ordered by an arbitral tribunal to be enforced at a party's request, unless application has been made to another court for a similar measure. Article 1041(2) ZPO allows the court to modify the interim measure if this is necessary for its enforcement. Pursuant to Article 22(5) of the ICC Rules of Arbitration the parties undertake to comply with any order made by the arbitral tribunal. Pursuant to Article 34(6) of the Rules every award shall be binding upon the parties and the parties undertake to carry out any award without delay. If a party does not comply with a measure imposed upon it by way of a procedural order or by way of an interim award, the arbitral tribunal will usually take appropriate account of such refusal. For this reason parties are rarely recalcitrant, even though procedural orders or interim awards are unenforceable without the assistance of judicial authorities

An arbitral tribunal may make a conservatory or interim measure conditional upon the provision of a reasonable guarantee, such as a deposit of money or other form of security. This is a way of ensuring that parties do not make unwarranted claims for conservatory or interim measures and that the party against which such measure is directed will be compensated for any harm caused if it transpires during the proceedings that there was no ground for the measure in the first place.

Irrespective of the form which the conservatory or interim measure takes, the final sentence of Article 28(1) requires the arbitral tribunal to give the reasons for accepting or refusing the request for such measure.

c) An Application to a Judicial Authority does not Infringe the Arbitration Agreement

The fact that a party applies to a judicial authority (normally a state court) for an interim or conservatory measure or the enforcement of a measure ordered by an arbitral tribunal as such does not constitute a breach of the arbitration agreement. Article 28(2) expressly provides that parties may apply to 'any competent judicial authority' for interim or conservatory measures not only prior to the transmission of the file to the arbitral tribunal, but also thereafter 'in appropriate circumstances'.

This gives the parties the freedom to choose whether to apply to an arbitral tribunal or a judicial authority for an interim or conservatory measure. However, Article 28 emphasizes that parties should apply first to the arbitral tribunal, insofar as this is possible, and turn after the dispute has been referred to an arbitral tribunal to state courts only in exceptional situations ('in appropriate circumstances') . Such exceptional situations arise in certain legal contexts in which arbitral tribunals are unable to order certain measures, or if the interim or conservatory measure requested involves a third party, and the parties therefore have no choice between an arbitral tribunal and a court. For example, if a party seeks an attachment of the other party's account with a bank that is not a party to the arbitration proceedings, it must apply to a court as arbitral tribunals cannot order measures against third parties that are not bound by the arbitration agreement. Similarly, as mentioned above, many legal systems do not allow arbitral tribunals to order certain measures. These are not the only examples covered by Article 28(2), which also allows parties to have recourse to a state court rather than the arbitral tribunal in order to obtain an order that will be quicker and easier to enforce.

When a party applies to a court for conservatory or interim measures, it must inform the Secretariat of the ICC International Court of Arbitration without delay (Article 28(2)). The Secretariat in turn immediately informs the arbitral tribunal.

F. EMERGENCY ARBITRATOR PROCEEDINGS

Article 29 of the Rules reads:

> 'Emergency Arbitrator
>
> Article 29: Emergency Arbitrator
>
> 1. A party that needs urgent interim or conservatory measures that cannot await the constitution of an arbitral tribunal ("Emergency Measures") may make an application for such measures pursuant to the Emergency Arbitrator Rules in Appendix V. Any such application shall be accepted only if it is received by the Secretariat prior to the transmission of the file to the arbitral tribunal pursuant to Article 16 and irrespective of whether the party making the application has already submitted its Request for Arbitration.
>
> 2. The emergency arbitrator's decision shall take the form of an order. The parties undertake to comply with any order made by the emergency arbitrator.
>
> 3. The emergency arbitrator's order shall not bind the arbitral tribunal with respect to any question, issue or dispute determined in the order. The arbitral tribunal may modify, terminate or annul the order or any modification thereto made by the emergency arbitrator.
>
> 4. The arbitral tribunal shall decide upon any party's requests or claims related to the emergency arbitrator proceedings, including the reallocation of the costs of such proceedings and any claims arising out of or in connection with the compliance or non-compliance with the order.
>
> 5. Articles 29(1)–29(4) and the Emergency Arbitrator Rules set forth in Appendix V (collectively the "Emergency Arbitrator Provisions") shall apply only to parties that are either signatories of the arbitration agreement under the Rules that is relied upon for the application or successors to such signatories.
>
> 6. The Emergency Arbitrator Provisions shall not apply if:
>   a) the arbitration agreement under the Rules was concluded before the date on which the Rules came into force;
>   a) the parties have agreed to opt out of the Emergency Arbitrator Provisions; or
>   a) the parties have agreed to another pre-arbitral procedure that provides for the granting of conservatory, interim or similar measures.
>
> 7. The Emergency Arbitrator Provisions are not intended to prevent any party from seeking urgent interim or conservatory measures from a competent

judicial authority at any time prior to making an application for such measures, and in appropriate circumstances even thereafter, pursuant to the Rules. Any application for such measures from a competent judicial authority shall not be deemed to be an infringement or a waiver of the arbitration agreement. Any such application and any measures taken by the judicial authority must be notified without delay to the Secretariat.'

APPENDIX V: EMERGENCY ARBITRATOR RULES

Article 1: Application for Emergency Measures

1. A party wishing to have recourse to an emergency arbitrator pursuant to Article 29 of the Rules of Arbitration of the ICC (the "Rules") shall submit its Application for Emergency Measures (the "Application") to the Secretariat at any of the offices specified in the Internal Rules of the Court in Appendix II to the Rules.

2. The Application shall be supplied in a number of copies sufficient to provide one copy for each party, plus one for the emergency arbitrator, and one for the Secretariat.

3. The Application shall contain the following information:
   a) the name in full, description, address and other contact details of each of the parties;
   b) the name in full, address and other contact details of any person(s) representing the applicant;
   c) a description of the circumstances giving rise to the Application and of the underlying dispute referred or to be referred to arbitration;
   d) a statement of the Emergency Measures sought;
   e) the reasons why the applicant needs urgent interim or conservatory measures that cannot await the constitution of an arbitral tribunal;
   f) any relevant agreements and, in particular, the arbitration agreement;
   g) any agreement as to the place of the arbitration, the applicable rules of law or the language of the arbitration;
   h) proof of payment of the amount referred to in Article 7(1) of this Appendix; and
   i) any Request for Arbitration and any other submissions in connection with the underlying dispute, which have been filed with the Secretariat by any of the parties to the emergency arbitrator proceedings prior to the making of the Application.

The Application may contain such other documents or information as the applicant considers appropriate or as may contribute to the efficient examination of the Application.

4. The Application shall be drawn up in the language of the arbitration if agreed upon by the parties or, in the absence of any such agreement, in the language of the arbitration agreement.

5. If and to the extent that the President of the Court (the "President") considers, on the basis of the information contained in the Application, that the Emergency Arbitrator Provisions apply with reference to Article 29(5) and Article 29(6) of the Rules, the Secretariat shall transmit a copy of the Application and the documents annexed thereto to the responding party. If and to the

extent that the President considers otherwise, the Secretariat shall inform the parties that the emergency arbitrator proceedings shall not take place with respect to some or all of the parties and shall transmit a copy of the Application to them for information.

6. The President shall terminate the emergency arbitrator proceedings if a Request for Arbitration has not been received by the Secretariat from the applicant within 10 days of the Secretariat's receipt of the Application, unless the emergency arbitrator determines that a longer period of time is necessary.

Article 2: Appointment of the Emergency Arbitrator; Transmission of the File

1. The President shall appoint an emergency arbitrator within as short a time as possible, normally within two days from the Secretariat's receipt of the Application.

2. No emergency arbitrator shall be appointed after the file has been transmitted to the arbitral tribunal pursuant to Article 16 of the Rules. An emergency arbitrator appointed prior thereto shall retain the power to make an order within the time limit permitted by Article 6(4) of this Appendix.

3. Once the emergency arbitrator has been appointed, the Secretariat shall so notify the parties and shall transmit the file to the emergency arbitrator. Thereafter, all written communications from the parties shall be submitted directly to the emergency arbitrator with a copy to the other party and the Secretariat. A copy of any written communications from the emergency arbitrator to the parties shall be submitted to the Secretariat.

4. Every emergency arbitrator shall be and remain impartial and independent of the parties involved in the dispute.

5. Before being appointed, a prospective emergency arbitrator shall sign a statement of acceptance, availability, impartiality and independence. The Secretariat shall provide a copy of such statement to the parties.

6. An emergency arbitrator shall not act as an arbitrator in any arbitration relating to the dispute that gave rise to the Application.

Article 3: Challenge of an Emergency Arbitrator

1. A challenge against the emergency arbitrator must be made within three days from receipt by the party making the challenge of the notification of the appointment or from the date when that party was informed of the facts and circumstances on which the challenge is based if such date is subsequent to the receipt of such notification.

2. The challenge shall be decided by the Court after the Secretariat has afforded an opportunity for the emergency arbitrator and the other party or parties to provide comments in writing within a suitable period of time.

Article 4: Place of Emergency Arbitrator Proceedings

1. If the parties have agreed upon the place of the arbitration, such place shall be the place of the emergency arbitrator proceedings. In the absence of such agreement, the President shall fix the place of the emergency arbitrator proceedings, without prejudice to the determination of the place of the arbitration pursuant to Article 18(1) of the Rules.

2. Any meetings with the emergency arbitrator may be conducted through a meeting in person at any location the emergency arbitrator considers appropriate or by video conference, telephone or similar means of communication.

Article 5: Proceedings

1. The emergency arbitrator shall establish a procedural timetable for the emergency arbitrator proceedings within as short a time as possible, normally within two days from the transmission of the file to the emergency arbitrator pursuant to Article 2(3) of this Appendix.

2. The emergency arbitrator shall conduct the proceedings in the manner which the emergency arbitrator considers to be appropriate, taking into account the nature and the urgency of the Application. In all cases, the emergency arbitrator shall act fairly and impartially and ensure that each party has a reasonable opportunity to present its case.

Article 6: Order

1. Pursuant to Article 29(2) of the Rules, the emergency arbitrator's decision shall take the form of an order (the "Order").

2. In the Order, the emergency arbitrator shall determine whether the Application is admissible pursuant to Article 29(1) of the Rules and whether the emergency arbitrator has jurisdiction to order Emergency Measures.

3. The Order shall be made in writing and shall state the reasons upon which it is based. It shall be dated and signed by the emergency arbitrator.

4. The Order shall be made no later than 15 days from the date on which the file was transmitted to the emergency arbitrator pursuant to Article 2(3) of this Appendix. The President may extend the time limit pursuant to a reasoned request from the emergency arbitrator or on the President's own initiative if the President decides it is necessary to do so.

5. Within the time limit established pursuant to Article 6(4) of this Appendix, the emergency arbitrator shall send the Order to the parties, with a copy to the Secretariat, by any of the means of communication permitted by Article 3(2) of the Rules that the emergency arbitrator considers will ensure prompt receipt.

6. The Order shall cease to be binding on the parties upon:

a) the President's termination of the emergency arbitrator proceedings pursuant to Article 1(6) of this Appendix;

b) the acceptance by the Court of a challenge against the emergency arbitrator pursuant to Article 3 of this Appendix;

c) the arbitral tribunal's final award, unless the arbitral tribunal expressly decides otherwise; or

d) the withdrawal of all claims or the termination of the arbitration before the rendering of a final award.

7. The emergency arbitrator may make the Order subject to such conditions as the emergency arbitrator thinks fit, including requiring the provision of appropriate security.

8. Upon a reasoned request by a party made prior to the transmission of the file to the arbitral tribunal pursuant to Article 16 of the Rules, the emergency arbitrator may modify, terminate or annul the Order.

Article 7: Costs of the Emergency Arbitrator Proceedings

1. The applicant must pay an amount of US$ 40,000, consisting of US$ 10,000 for ICC administrative expenses and US$ 30 000 for the emergency arbitrator's fees and expenses. Notwithstanding Article 1(5) of this Appendix, the Application shall not be notified until the payment of US$ 40,000 is received by the Secretariat.

2. The President may, at any time during the emergency arbitrator proceedings, decide to increase the emergency arbitrator's fees or the ICC administrative expenses taking into account, inter alia, the nature of the case and the nature and amount of work performed by the emergency arbitrator, the Court, the President and the Secretariat. If the party which submitted the Application fails to pay the increased costs within the time limit fixed by the Secretariat, the Application shall be considered as withdrawn.

3. The emergency arbitrator's Order shall fix the costs of the emergency arbitrator proceedings and decide which of the parties shall bear them or in what proportion they shall be borne by the parties.

4. The costs of the emergency arbitrator proceedings include the ICC administrative expenses, the emergency arbitrator's fees and expenses and the reasonable legal and other costs incurred by the parties for the emergency arbitrator proceedings.

5. In the event that the emergency arbitrator proceedings do not take place pursuant to Article 1(5) of this Appendix or are otherwise terminated prior to the making of an Order, the President shall determine the amount to be reimbursed to the applicant, if any. An amount of US$ 5,000 for ICC administrative expenses is non-refundable in all cases.

Article 8: General Rule

1. The President shall have the power to decide, at the President's discretion, all matters relating to the administration of the emergency arbitrator proceedings not expressly provided for in this Appendix.

2. In the President's absence or otherwise at the President's request, any of the Vice-Presidents of the Court shall have the power to take decisions on behalf of the President.

3. In all matters concerning emergency arbitrator proceedings not expressly provided for in this Appendix, the Court, the President and the emergency arbitrator shall act in the spirit of the Rules and this Appendix.'

1. General Remarks

In 1990, the ICC published the ICC Pre-Arbitral Referee Rules and thus provided the parties with a contractual mechanism allowing them to call upon the appointment of a third person (a 'referee'), who has the power to order provisional measures as a matter of urgency, before the case is heard by a court or arbitral tribunal (See Chapter 6 and Appendix 21 below). The measures ordered by a referee are binding until the referee, or the court or arbitral tribunal to which the case is subsequently referred, decides otherwise. The Pre-Arbitral Referee Rules turned out not to be a success, because this mechanism needed to be agreed upon separately and as the parties did not frequently do so. In order to increase the use of this contractual mechanism of calling upon a third person to order provisional measures prior to the constitution of the arbitral tribunal, the ICC has included in its new 2012 Rules the Emergency Arbitrator Provisions on an *opt-out* basis.

Article 29 is a new provision and one of the prominent novelties of the 2012 Rules. Any party has, prior to the constitution of the arbitral tribunal, the right to make an application for interim or conservatory measures that cannot await the constitution of the arbitral tribunal. The procedure is set forth in a new Appendix V – The Emergency Arbitrator Rules. The provisions of Article 29 and of Appendix V are collectively referred to as the 'Emergency Arbitrator Provisions' (Article 29(5)). The Secretariat of the ICC Court established a note on ICC Emergency Arbitrator Proceedings that emphasizes some essential elements to be taken into account by the emergency arbitrator throughout the proceedings under the Emergency Arbitrator Provisions (see Appendix 6 below).

The person deciding on the emergency measures is called 'emergency arbitrator'. He or she is to be distinguished from the 'arbitrator' who will decide on the merits of the dispute later. The Rules use the term 'emergency arbitrator' as he or she has the power, like an arbitrator, to decide the requested measures. Unlike the arbitrator who will decide on the merits, however, the emergency arbitrator may not deal with the substance of the dispute and only has the power to grant or deny temporary relief.

The Emergency Arbitrator Provisions only apply to parties having signed an ICC arbitration agreement or to the successors in law of the signatories (Article 29(5)). Moreover, they only apply if the arbitration agreement was signed after the 2012 Rules entered into force (Article 29(6)(a)), if the parties have not opted out of these provisions (Article 29(6)(b)) and if the parties have not agreed to another pre-arbitral procedure that provides for the granting of conservatory, interim or similar measures (Article 29(6)(c)). If the parties have agreed to the ICC Pre-Arbitral Referee Rules or to use a Dispute Board that may issue interim measures, such as the ICC Dispute Adjudication Boards (see Appendix 28 below; Chapter 6 below) or the FIDIC Conditions of Contract for major works providing for the appointment of a Dispute Board, this has the consequence that the ICC Emergency Arbitrator Provisions are not applicable.

Pursuant to Article 29(5), the emergency arbitrator provisions do not apply to treaty-based investor-state arbitrations, because the investor and the host state are not signatories of the arbitration agreement formed by the state's offer contained in the bilateral investment treaty and by the investor's acceptance contained in its notice of claim or request for arbitration (Report of the ICC Commission on Arbitration and ADR on 'Arbitration Involving States or State Entities', 2012, par. 52, Appendix 16 below).

The President of the Court shall verify whether the Emergency Arbitrator Provisions apply pursuant to Article 29(5) and Article 29(6) before the Secretariat may transmit the request for emergency measures to the respondent (Article 1(5) of Appendix V to the Rules). The President of the Court has the power to decide, at his discretion, all matters relating to the administration of the emergency arbitrator proceedings not expressly provided for in the Emergency Arbitrator Provisions (Article 8(1) of Appendix V to the Rules).

In 2012, the Secretariat received two applications under the Emergency Arbitrator Provisions. In the first case, the emergency arbitrator issued an order rejecting the application. In the second case, the application was held inadmissible as the contract containing the parties' arbitration agreement had been made before the entry into force of the 2012 Rules and no subsequent agreement had been reached between the parties on the application of the 2012 Rules ('2012 Statistical Report' published in *ICC International Court of Arbitration Bulletin*, Paris, Vol. 24/Nr. 1 - 2013, p. 15).

In 2013, six applications for emergency measures were filed. They were all considered admissible pursuant to Article 29(5)-(6) of the Rules. Two of the applications concerned payment obligations, two sought orders to refrain from action and two requested anti-suit injunctions. Three of the applications were granted at least in part, two were denied, and the emergency arbitrator declined jurisdiction over the remaining application ('2013 Statistical Report' published in *ICC International Court of Arbitration Bulletin*, Paris, Vol. 25/Nr. 1 - 2014, p. 14-15).

2. Commencement of the Emergency Arbitrator Proceedings

a) Submission of the Application for Emergency Measures (Art. 29(1)).

The Rules provide certain formal requirements to be complied with in order to commence emergency arbitrator proceedings. An 'application for emergency measures' must be filed so as to commence the emergency arbitrator proceedings. The formal requirements of the 'application' of Article 29 of the Rules and Article 1 of Appendix V to the Rules are largely similar to the requirements for a 'request for arbitration' pursuant to Article 4 of the Rules.

In the emergency arbitrator proceedings the term 'applicant' is used for the party requesting emergency measures, whereas the term 'responding party' is used for the respondent.

The applicant does not send its application for emergency measures directly to the responding party but to the Secretariat of the ICC International Court of Arbitration, as it is the Secretariat's responsibility under the Rules to notify the request for arbitration to the respondent(s) (Article 1(5) of Appendix V). Of course, there is nothing to stop the applicant at the same time informing the responding party of its action by sending it a copy of the application for emergency measures.

The application must be submitted in a number of copies sufficient to provide one copy for each party, plus one for the emergency arbitrator, and one for the Secretariat (Article 1(2) of Appendix V to the Rules).

b) Information to be Included in the Application for Emergency Measures (App. V – Art. 1(3))

Article 1(3) of Appendix V to the Rules sets forth the minimum information the application for emergency measures must contain. This provision gives the applicant considerable scope to determine how it will present its case, leaving it free to decide for instance which facts and legal issues it will raise in its request.

The application must include at least the following information:

(1) Full Details of the Parties (App. V – Art. 1(3)(a)).

The applicant is required to state the exact details of the parties, especially the responding party.

(2) Full Details of the Person(s) Representing the Applicant (App. V – Art. 1(3)(b))

The applicant must also provide the name and address of its lawyer or other representative for the purpose of correspondence. As it is not required for a party to be represented by a lawyer in an arbitration, it is also not required for a party to be represented by a lawyer in emergency arbitrator proceedings. However, as already set out above, mostly parties do have a lawyer to represent them in arbitration. Parties may also be represented by several lawyers or law firms.

Pursuant to Article 17, the Secretariat or the emergency arbitrator, once constituted, may request at any time proof of authority of the person(s) representing the applicant(s).

(3) A Description of the Circumstances Giving Rise to the Application and of the Underlying Dispute Referred or To Be Referred to Arbitration (App. V – Art. 1(3)(c)).

The applicant must present at least a summary of all the facts and legal arguments necessary for a decision to be made in its favor. Although the Rules do not require the applicant at this stage to submit a detailed request, it will be in its interest to provide from the outset as much information as possible given that there will be little time during the emergency arbitrator proceedings to make further submissions.

The applicant should provide information on the underlying dispute in regard to which the measures are requested and which has been or shall be submitted to arbitration. If the applicant has not yet filed a request for arbitration, it should do so at the latest within 10 days of the receipt of the application for emergency measures by the Secretariat (Article 1(6) of Appendix V to the Rules). The information provided by the applicant should allow the President of the Court to determine that the emergency arbitrator provisions apply (pursuant to Article 1(5) of Appendix V to the Rules).

(4) A Statement of the Emergency Measures sought (App. V – Art. 1(3)(d)).

The applicant should set out what emergency measures are requested.

(5) The Reasons Why The Requested measures Cannot Await the Constitution of the Arbitral Tribunal (App. V – Art. 1(3)(e)).

The applicant will have to motivate why it invokes the emergency arbitrator proceedings so as to allow the emergency arbitrator pursuant to Article 6(2) of Appendix V to decide whether the application is admissible. In case the emergency arbitrator will decide that the requested measures can await the constitution of the arbitral tribunal, it will consider the application to be inadmissible.

(6) Any Relevant Agreements and, in Particular, the Arbitration Agreement (App. V – Art. 1(3)(f)).

The applicant must provide all relevant provisions of the contract, including in particular the arbitration agreement. It does not suffice for the applicant to cite the arbitration agreement(s), it should also attach a copy of the documents containing the arbitration agreement.

Information on the arbitration agreement is essential to enable the President of the Court to decide pursuant to Article 1(5) of Appendix V to the Rules and in accordance with Article 29(5) and (6) of the Rules that the Emergency Arbitrator Provisions apply.

(7) Any Agreement as to the Place of the Arbitration, the applicable Rules of Law and the Language of the Arbitration (App. V – Art. 1(3)(g)).

In case the parties reached an agreement on the place of the arbitration, the applicable rules of law and/or the language of the arbitration proceedings, and which is not contained in the arbitration agreement, it must provide information thereof and communicate copies of the documents in which such agreement may be contained. Pursuant to Article 1(4) of Appendix V to the Rules, the application shall be drawn up in the language of the arbitration if agreed upon by the parties or, in the absence of any such agreement, in the language of the arbitration agreement. If the parties have agreed upon the place of the arbitration, such place shall be the place of the emergency arbitrator proceedings. In the absence of such agreement, the President of the Court shall fix the place of the emergency arbitrator proceedings, without prejudice to the determination of the place of the arbitration pursuant to Article 18(1) of the Rules (Article 4(1) of Appendix V to the Rules).

(8) Proof of Payment of the Filing Fee (App. V – Art. 1(3)(h))

Together with the filing of the application the applicant must pay the requested filing fee of US$ 40 000, as fixed by Article 7(1) of Appendix V to the Rules. The amount of US$ 40 000 consists of US$ 10 000 for ICC administrative expenses and US$ 30 000 for the emergency arbitrator's fees and expenses. The application shall not be notified by the Secretariat to the responding party until the payment of US$ 40 000 is received.

(9) Any Request for Arbitration and Any Other Submissions in Connection with the Underlying Dispute, which have been Filed Already (App. V – Art. 1(3)(i))

In case any of the parties to the emergency arbitrator proceedings already filed submissions in connection with the dispute prior to the application for emergency measures, these submissions should be attached to the application. This information should enable the President of the Court to verify whether the conditions for the application of the emergency arbitrator provisions are fulfilled and in particular that no arbitral tribunal was constituted yet with respect to the dispute. If an arbitral tribunal has already been constituted, the application for emergency measures shall have to be submitted to the arbitral tribunal in the arbitration proceedings.

c) Review by the President and Notification of the Application for Emergency Measures (App. V – Art. 1(5))

Article 1(5) of Appendix V to the Rules provides that the emergency arbitrator proceedings will go forward only if the President of the ICC Court considers that the emergency arbitrator provisions apply, in accordance with Article 29(5) and 29(6) of the Rules. The President takes the decision on the basis of the information submitted with the application for emergency measures. The provision of Article 1(5) of Appendix V to the Rules constitutes for the emergency arbitrator proceedings what Article 6(4) of the Rules constitutes for the arbitration proceedings. The *'prima facie'* assessment whether the emergency arbitrator provisions apply is made by the President of the Court. However, if the jurisdiction of the emergency arbitrator is contested by the responding party, the final determination on jurisdiction shall not be made by the emergency arbitrator, who will only take a decision on emergency measures. The final determination on jurisdiction shall be taken by the arbitral tribunal in the proceedings on the substance of the dispute.

In multiparty proceedings, the President of the Court has pursuant to Article 1(5) of Appendix V to the Rules the power to decide that the emergency arbitrator proceedings shall take place with respect to some but not all of the parties.

If the President decides that the Emergency Arbitrator Provisions apply, the Secretariat will transmit a copy of the application and the documents annexed thereto to the responding party. With its letter, the Secretariat will enclose some additional documents on ICC arbitration, including the Secretariat's 'Note on ICC Emergency Arbitrator Proceedings' (see Appendix 6 below), the ICC Rules of Arbitration as well as the ICC Dispute Resolution Brochure (see also at <www.iccarbitration.org>).

If the President, however, considers that the emergency arbitrator provisions do not apply with respect to some or all of the parties, the President will inform the parties thereof and will transmit a copy of the application for information to them (Article 1(5) of Appendix V to the Rules).

If the President informs the parties that the emergency arbitrator proceedings shall not take place, the President will determine the amount to be reimbursed to the applicant, if any. An amount of US$ 5 000 for ICC administrative expenses is non-refundable in all cases (Article 7(5) of Appendix V to the Rules).

The President shall terminate the emergency arbitrator proceedings if a request for arbitration has not been received by the Secretariat from the applicant within 10 days after the Secretariat received the application, unless the emergency arbitrator, if he or she has meanwhile received already the file, determines that a longer period of time should be granted to the applicant for the filing of a request for arbitration (Article 1(6) of Appendix V to the Rules).

3. Appointment of the Emergency Arbitrator (App. V – Art. 2)

The ICC emergency arbitrator proceedings provide for the appointment of a sole emergency arbitrator, and not for a three member panel.

The appointment shall be made by the President of the ICC Court within a very short time period, normally within two days after the Secretariat received the application for emergency measures (Article 2(1) of Appendix V to the Rules). Before appointing the emergency arbitrator, the President will require the prospective emergency arbitrator to sign a statement of acceptance, availability, impartiality and independence (Article 2(5) of Appendix V to the Rules; see Appendix 7 below). The prospective emergency arbitrator shall not only confirm with this statement that he or she is and shall remain impartial and independent of the parties involved in the dispute (Article 2(4) of Appendix V to the Rules), he or she shall also confirm that he or she is available to deal with the application for emergency measures within the very short time frame prescribed by the emergency arbitrator provisions. The parties receive a copy of the signed statement (Article 2(5) of Appendix V to the Rules).

The President of the Court may appoint an emergency arbitrator as long as the arbitral tribunal has not been constituted, meaning as long as the file has not been submitted to the arbitral tribunal in arbitration proceedings concerning the same dispute (Article 29(1) of the Rules; Article 2(2) of Appendix V to the Rules). The transmission of the file to the emergency arbitrator is done by the Secretariat immediately upon the appointment of the emergency arbitrator by the President of the Court. The Secretariat will immediately inform the parties thereof (Article 2(3) of Appendix V to the Rules).

If an emergency arbitrator is appointed and shortly thereafter an arbitral tribunal is constituted in arbitration proceedings concerning the same dispute, the emergency arbitrator will retain the power to make an order on the application for emergency measures within the time limit permitted by Article 6(4) of Appendix V to the Rules (Article 2(2) of Appendix V to the Rules).

The emergency arbitrator may not act as an arbitrator in any arbitration proceedings relating to the dispute that gave rise to the application for emergency measures (Article 2(6) of Appendix V to the Rules).

4. Challenge of the Emergency Arbitrator (App. V – Art. 3)

In the same way as an arbitrator can be challenged by the parties in arbitration proceedings under the ICC Rules of Arbitration (Article 14), the emergency arbitrator can be challenged by the parties in the emergency arbitrator proceedings. Unlike Article 14(1) of the Rules, the emergency arbitrator provisions do not explicitly state the grounds on which a challenge against the emergency arbitrator can be based (Article 3(1)). The same grounds as in Article 14 of the Rules can be invoked, as the emergency arbitrator must comply with the same essential requirements as an arbitrator in arbitration proceedings.

As already indicated, every emergency arbitrator shall be and remain impartial and independent of the parties involved in the dispute (Article 2(4) of Appendix V to the Rules). Moreover, the emergency arbitrator shall act fairly and impartially in all cases and ensure that each party has a reasonable opportunity to present its case (Article 5(2) of Appendix V to the Rules).

Given the short time frame within which the emergency arbitrator proceedings must take place, there is also a very short time frame foreseen for a challenge against the emergency arbitrator. A challenge against the emergency arbitrator must be made within three days after the party making the challenge was informed of the appointment of the emergency arbitrator or within three days after the party making the challenge was informed of the facts and circumstances on which the challenge is based if it became aware of such facts and circumstances at a date subsequent to the notification of the President's decision to appoint the emergency arbitrator (Article 3(1) of Appendix V to the Rules). Like a challenge raised against an arbitrator in arbitration proceedings under the ICC Rules of Arbitration (Article 14(3) of the Rules), the decision on the challenge shall be taken by the ICC Court after the Secretariat has afforded an opportunity to the emergency arbitrator and to the other party or parties to comment in writing within a suitable period of time (Article 3(2) of Appendix V to the Rules).

In case the emergency arbitrator has already made an order at the time of the challenge, this order shall cease to be binding on the parties if the Court accepts the challenge against the emergency arbitrator (Article 6(6)(b) of Appendix V to the Rules).

5. Proceedings before the Emergency Arbitrator (Art. 29(1); App. V – Art. 4 and 5)

a) Place of the Emergency Arbitrator Proceedings (App. V – Art. 4))

If the parties have agreed on the place of the arbitration for the arbitration proceedings, either in the arbitration agreement or in a later agreement, this place shall also be the place of the emergency arbitrator proceedings (Article 4(1) first sentence of Appendix V to the Rules).

Should the parties not have agreed on a place for the arbitration proceedings, the President of the Court shall fix the place of the emergency arbitrator proceedings. However, such decision will not affect the subsequent determination of the place of the arbitration by the Court in the arbitration proceedings pursuant to Article 18(1) of the Rules of Arbitration (Article 4(1) second sentence of Appendix V to the Rules).

The emergency arbitrator provisions provide that any meetings with the emergency arbitrator may be conducted at any location he or she considers appropriate (Article 4(2) of Appendix V to the Rules).

b) Procedural Timetable (App. V – Art. 5(1))

The first task of the emergency arbitrator is to prepare a procedural timetable, within as short a time as possible, normally within two days after he or she received the file from the Secretariat (Article 5(1) of Appendix V to the Rules).

The emergency arbitrator is free to conduct the proceedings in the manner which he or she considers most appropriate, taking into account the nature and the urgency of the application. In all cases, the emergency arbitrator shall act fairly and impartially and ensure that each party has a reasonable opportunity to present its case (Article 5(2) of Appendix V to the Rules).

Because the Emergency Arbitrator Provisions require the emergency arbitrator to take a decision within 15 days from the date on which the file was transmitted (Article 6(4) of Appendix V to the Rules), the emergency arbitrator shall have to schedule the procedural calendar in such a way that the 15-day time limit is respected and that the decision on the application is made within the 15-day time limit.

The President of the Court may extend the 15-day time limit pursuant to a reasoned request from the emergency arbitrator or on the President's own initiative if the President decides that this is necessary (Article 6(4) of Appendix V to the Rules).

c) Hearing or meeting (App. V – Art. 4(2))

The general rule that if a party requests a hearing in arbitration proceedings (Article 25(6) of the Rules), also applies in emergency arbitrator proceedings. If a party asks for a hearing and the emergency arbitrator refuses such hearing, this would constitute a violation of due process.

Given the 15-day time limit laid down in the emergency arbitrator provisions for the emergency arbitrator to make an order on the application for emergency measures (Article 6(4) of Appendix V to the Rules), the Emergency Arbitrator Provisions explicitly indicate that any meetings with the emergency arbitrator may be conducted by video conference, telephone or similar means of communication (Article 4(2) of Appendix V to the Rules). In any event, the hearings or meetings will have to be scheduled and organized on a very short notice, so that it may not always be feasible in practice to find a date suitable for a meeting in person with all the participants.

6. Order of the Emergency Arbitrator – Effect on the Arbitration Proceedings

a) Order of the Emergency Arbitrator (Art. 29(2); App. V – Art. 6))

The decision of the emergency arbitrator shall take the form of an order (Article 29(2) of the Rules; Article 6(1) of Appendix V to the Rules). In the order, the emergency arbitrator shall first determine whether the application for emergency measures is admissible pursuant to Article 29(1) of the Rules and whether he or she has jurisdiction to order emergency measures (Article 6(2) of Appendix V to the Rules). In case the emergency arbitrator finds that the requested measures could await the constitution of the arbitral tribunal and that there was not sufficient urgency for the requested measures, the emergency arbitrator shall reject the application.

In case the emergency arbitrator grants the application for emergency measures, he or she may make the order subject to such condition as he or she deems fit, including requiring the provision of appropriate security (Article 6(7) of Appendix V to the Rules).

The order must fix the costs of the emergency arbitrator proceedings and allocate them between the parties (Article 7(3) of Appendix V to the Rules).

Pursuant to Article 1(6) of Appendix V to the Rules, the emergency arbitrator may extend the 10-day time limit within which the applicant for emergency measures should file a request for arbitration after having filed the application for emergency measures, if the emergency arbitrator determines that a longer period is necessary in order to enable the applicant to file the request for arbitration. Should this time limit expire without the applicant having filed a request for arbitration, the emergency arbitrator proceedings shall be terminated by the President of the Court.

As a decision taken by an arbitral tribunal in arbitration proceedings (Article 31(2) of the Rules), the order of the emergency arbitrator shall be made in writing and shall state the reasons upon which it is based. It shall be dated and signed by the emergency arbitrator (Article 6(3) of Appendix V to the Rules).

As already indicated above, the order must be made within 15 days after the file was transmitted by the Secretariat to the emergency arbitrator pursuant to Article 2(3) of Appendix V. This time limit may be extended by the President pursuant to a reasoned request from the emergency arbitrator or at the President's own initiative if the President decides it is necessary to do so (Article 6(4) of Appendix V to the Rules). In any event, the emergency arbitrator is required to handle the matter with urgency, given the specificity of the proceedings and the type of measures requested.

Whilst an arbitral tribunal in proceedings under the ICC Rules of Arbitration must submit its award in draft form for scrutiny to the ICC Court and whilst the award must be approved by the ICC Court before it can be rendered (Article 33 of the Rules), such scrutiny process is not foreseen for orders made by the emergency arbitrator in emergency arbitrator proceedings. When the Secretariat transmits the matter to the emergency arbitrator after his or her appointment, it will also forward an 'ICC Emergency Arbitrator Order Checklist' (see Appendix 8 below). This checklist is intended to provide the emergency arbitrator acting under the ICC Rules of Arbitration with guidance in addition to the Note on ICC Emergency Arbitrator Proceedings. It does not constitute an exhaustive, mandatory or otherwise binding document. It is simply intended to facilitate the mission of the emergency arbitrator in drafting his or her decision in an order.

Whereas an arbitral award rendered by arbitrators in proceedings under the ICC Rules of Arbitration is notified to the parties by the Secretariat of the Court (Article 34(1) of the Rules), such notification process is not foreseen for orders made by the emergency arbitrator in emergency arbitrator proceedings. To gain time, the emergency arbitrator shall send the order directly to the parties, within the 15-day time limit prescribed by Article 6(4) of Appendix V or any extension of the time limit granted pursuant to that provision. The emergency arbitrator shall send the order to the parties, with a copy to the Secretariat, by any means of communication permitted by Article 3(2) of the Rules that the emergency arbitrator considers will be appropriate (Article 6(5) of Appendix V to the Rules).

The parties undertake to comply with any order made by the emergency arbitrator (Article 29(2) second sentence of the Rules). However, if the file has not yet been transmitted to an arbitral tribunal in arbitration proceedings, the emergency arbitrator may upon a reasoned request of a party modify, terminate or annul the order (Article 6(8) of Appendix V to the Rules).

The order of the emergency arbitrator ceases to be binding in the circumstances described in Article 6(6) of Appendix to the Rules. Accordingly, the order shall cease to be binding if the President of the Court terminates the emergency arbitrator proceedings pursuant to Article 1(6) of Appendix V (Article 6(6)(a) of Appendix V to the Rules), or if the Court accepts a challenge against the emergency arbitrator pursuant to Article 3 of Appendix V (Article 6(6)(b) of Appendix V to the Rules). As set out below, the order normally also ceases to be binding if a final award is rendered in the subsequent arbitration proceedings (Article 6(6)(c) of Appendix V to the Rules) or if the arbitration is terminated before the final award is rendered (Article 6(6)(d) of Appendix V to the Rules).

b) Effect of the Emergency Arbitrator's Order on the Arbitration Proceedings (Art. 29(3)-(4); App. V – Art. 6(6)(c))

The order of the emergency arbitrator shall not bind the arbitral tribunal seized of the dispute with respect to any question, issue or dispute determined in the order. The arbitral tribunal may modify, terminate or annul the order or any modification thereto made by the emergency arbitrator (Article 29(3) of the Rules).

Moreover, the arbitral tribunal will decide upon any party's requests or claims related to the emergency arbitrator proceedings, including the reallocation of the costs of the emergency arbitrator proceedings and any claims arising out of or in connection with the compliance or non-compliance by a party with the order of the emergency arbitrator (Article 29(4) of the Rules). The Emergency Arbitrator Provisions thus recognize that the final decision relating to a dispute is taken by the arbitral tribunal in the arbitration proceedings, and not by the emergency arbitrator.

The order of the emergency arbitrator ceases to be binding on the parties once the arbitral tribunal has rendered a final award in the arbitration proceedings, unless the arbitral tribunal expressly decides otherwise (Article 6(6)(c) of Appendix V to the Rules), and also when all the claims are withdrawn or the arbitration is terminated before the final award is rendered in the arbitration proceedings (Article 6(6)(d) of Appendix V to the Rules).

7. Costs of the Emergency Arbitrator Proceedings (App. V – Art. 7)

a) Advance on Costs for the Emergency Arbitrator Proceedings (App. V – Art. 7(1)-(2))

Together with the submission of an application for emergency measures, the applicant must pay an amount of US$ 40 000 to cover the ICC administrative expenses and the emergency arbitrator's fees and expenses (Article 7(1) of Appendix V to the Rules).

The amount of the advance on costs may be increased by the President, at any time during the emergency arbitrator proceedings, in the light of, inter alia, the nature of the case and the nature and amount of work performed by the emergency arbitrator, the Court, the President and the Secretariat. This increase shall have to be paid by the applicant for emergency measures. The Emergency Arbitrator Provisions do not provide that the responding party must take part in the payment of the advance on costs for the emergency arbitrator proceedings. If the applicant fails to pay the increase of the advance on costs within the time limit fixed by the Secretariat, the application for emergency measures shall automatically be considered as withdrawn (Article 7(2) of Appendix V to the Rules).

b) Decision on the Costs of the Emergency Arbitrator Proceedings (App. V – Art. 7(3)-(5))

The decision on the costs of the emergency arbitrator proceedings shall be taken by the emergency arbitrator in the order rendered on the application. The emergency arbitrator shall fix the costs of the proceedings and decide which of the parties shall have to bear them or in what proportion they shall be borne by them (Article 7(3) of Appendix V to the Rules). These costs include the ICC administrative expenses, the emergency arbitrator's fees and expenses, and also the reasonable legal and other costs incurred by the parties for the emergency arbitrator proceedings (Article 7(4) of Appendix V to the Rules).

In the event that the emergency arbitrator proceedings do not take place pursuant to Article 1(5) of Appendix V or are otherwise terminated prior to the making of an order, the President shall determine the amount to be reimbursed to the applicant, if any. However, an amount of US$ 5 000 for ICC administrative expenses is non-refundable in all cases (Article 7(5) of Appendix V to the Rules).

8. General Rule (App. V – Art. 8)

Appendix V does not cover all matters that can arise during emergency arbitrator proceedings. With respect to some matters, the provisions of the Rules of Arbitration may apply to the emergency arbitrator proceedings, even if this is not explicitly provided. As an example, the provisions of Article 3 of the Rules apply with respect to notifications and communications (see J. Fry, S. Greenberg and F. Mazza, *The Secretariat's Guide to ICC Arbitration*, ICC Publication No. 729 E, Paris, 2012, p. 297).

On all matters not expressly provided for in Appendix V, the President shall have the power to decide, at his or her discretion (Article 8(1) of Appendix V to the Rules). If the President is absent, or otherwise at the request of the President, any of the Vice-Presidents of the Court has the power to take decisions on behalf of the President (Article 8(2) of Appendix V to the Rules).

Similar to the general rule laid down in Article 41 with respect to ICC arbitration proceedings, the Emergency Arbitrator Provisions contain the general rule that in all matters concerning emergency arbitrator proceedings not expressly provided for in Appendix V, the Court, the President and the emergency arbitrator shall act in the spirit of the Rules and Appendix V (Article 8(3) of Appendix V to the Rules).

9. An Application to a Judicial Authority does not Infringe the Emergency Arbitrator Provisions (Art. 29(7))

The fact that a party applies to a judicial authority for an interim or conservatory measure does not constitute a breach of the arbitration agreement. Article 29(7) of the Rules expressly provides that parties may apply to 'any competent judicial authority' for interim or conservatory measures not only prior to filing an application for emergency measures, but also thereafter 'in appropriate circumstances'.

This gives the parties the freedom to choose whether to apply to an emergency arbitrator or to a judicial authority for an interim or conservatory measure before initiating arbitration proceedings. However, Article 29(7) seeks to emphasize that parties should only turn to state courts in exceptional situations ('in appropriate circumstances') after an application for emergency measures has been referred to an emergency arbitrator. Such exceptional situations arise in certain legal contexts in which arbitral tribunals, and therefore also emergency arbitrators, are unable to order certain measures, or in case the interim or conservatory measure requested involved a third party, and the parties therefore have no choice between an emergency arbitrator and a court. For example, if a party seeks an attachment of the other party's account with a bank that is not a party to the arbitration proceedings, it must apply to a court as arbitral tribunals, and therefore also emergency arbitrators, cannot order measures against third parties that are not bound by the arbitration agreement. Similarly, as mentioned above, many legal systems do not allow arbitral tribunals to order certain measures (see Article 28(2) above).

When a party applies to a court for conservatory or interim measures, it must inform the Secretariat of the ICC International Court of Arbitration without delay (Article 29(7)). The Secretariat in turn immediately informs the emergency arbitrator.

10. Limitation of Liability (Art. 40)

Article 40 of the ICC Rules of Arbitration provides a limitation of liability for the emergency arbitrator, in the same manner as for the arbitrators, the ICC Court and its members, the ICC and its employees, and the ICC national committees and groups and their employees and representatives. Accordingly, the emergency arbitrator shall not be liable to any person for any act or omission in connection with the emergency arbitrator proceedings, except to the extent such limitation of liability is prohibited by applicable law.

G. ARBITRAL AWARDS

1. Time Limit for the Final Award (Art. 30)

Article 30 of the Rules reads:

> 'Time Limit for the Final Award
>
> 1. The time limit within which the arbitral tribunal must render its final award is six months. Such time limit shall start to run from the date of the last signature by the arbitral tribunal or by the parties of the Terms of Reference or, in the case of application of Article 23(3), the date of the notification to the arbitral tribunal by the Secretariat of the approval of the Terms of Reference by the Court. The Court may fix a different time limit based upon the procedural timetable established pursuant to Article 24(2).
>
> 2. The Court may extend this time limit pursuant to a reasoned request from the arbitral tribunal or on its own initiative if it decides it is necessary to do so.'

a) Six Months for Rendering the Award

Arbitration proceedings should normally take place quickly, as this is what the parties expect. Hence, the Rules set a time limit within which the award must be rendered. This time limit is six months from the date on which the last party signs the Terms of Reference or, if one of the parties refuses to sign the Terms of Reference, the date on which the arbitral tribunal is notified of the ICC International Court of Arbitration's decision to approve the Terms of Reference (Article 23(3) and Article 30(1) of the Rules).

The arbitral tribunal must conduct the proceedings and render its final award within this period of six months. It is not sufficient for it simply to submit its draft award to the ICC International Court of Arbitration within six months; the final award approved by the Court must be signed by the arbitral tribunal and notified to the parties by the Secretariat before the six months have expired. It is the notification of the final award that marks the real end of the proceedings.

b) Fixing of a Different Time Limit

The traditional purpose of specifying an extendable time limit for rendering the award, which has been a feature of ICC arbitration from the very beginning, is to prevent proceedings from becoming void if the deadline is overrun. In the past – it is less so now – many national arbitration laws provided that arbitration proceedings and sometimes the arbitration agreement itself were invalid if the arbitral tribunal did not render its award within the time limit agreed by the parties or set by law.

The 2012 Rules provide the possibility for the Court to fix a different time limit than the six-month time limit provided by the Rules for making the award. If the parties have agreed on a procedural timetable for submissions and hearings that goes beyond the six-month time limit, the Court will take this into account when fixing the time limit for the arbitral award. The procedural timetable will normally be fixed in accordance with Article 24(2) of the Rules during or following the case management conference which the arbitral tribunal must organize pursuant to Article 24(1) of the Rules.

Normally the Court expects to receive an award within about eight weeks following the last procedural step in the arbitration, if a sole arbitrator conducts the arbitration, and within about twelve weeks, if the arbitral tribunal is composed of three arbitrators (see J. Fry, S. Greenberg and F. Mazza, *The Secretariat's Guide to ICC Arbitration*, ICC Publication No. 729 E, Paris, 2012, p. 314).

c) Extension of the Time Limit

It is not always possible to respect the time limit set by the Rules or fixed by the Court, no matter how hard one tries. Although the parties could in the past extend the time limits, there was a risk of their being unable to agree on this once the proceedings were under way. The problem therefore had to be resolved by giving the ICC International Court of Arbitration the power to extend the time limit, as is also done in Article 38(2) of the Rules.

Owing to the complexity of most ICC arbitrations, proceedings are rarely accomplished within six months and the time limit therefore often needs to be extended by the Court. At the request of an arbitral tribunal or of its own accord, the Court will decide on an extension of reasonable length. If the arbitral tribunal and the parties have agreed on a timetable for the conduct of the arbitration (Article 24(2) of the Rules) spanning more than six months, the Court will take account of this and usually grant an extension longer than the three months by which it normally extends the time limit if the procedural timetable does not contain sufficient details. Before the extension elapses, the arbitral tribunal informs the Court of the progress of the case since the last extension and the time it considers it still needs to render its final award.

As previously mentioned, Article 15(2) of the Rules allows the Court to decide to replace an arbitrator on its own initiative if it finds that the arbitrator is not fulfilling his or her functions within the time limit that has been set. However, even when the arbitral tribunal has overrun the period allowed for rendering its final award, the Court will rather extend the time limit, so as to avoid the risk of the proceedings and maybe the arbitration agreement lapsing for the simple reason that a deadline has not been extended when required by the law applicable to the proceedings (*'lex arbitri'*). The Rules do not contain any provisions covering such situations.

In rare cases, such as when none of the parties has any interest in pursuing the proceedings and they do not do so, the Court may decide not to extend the time limit at the arbitrators' request. In such situations, the proceedings will lapse *ipso jure* when the current time limit provided expires. Once the time limit has expired, the arbitral tribunal no longer has the power to render an award.

2. Awards (Art. 31)

Article 31 of the Rules reads:

> 'Making of the Award
>
> 1. When the arbitral tribunal is composed of more than one arbitrator, an award is given by a majority decision. If there is no majority, the award shall be made by the president of the arbitral tribunal alone.
>
> 2. The award shall state the reasons upon which it is based.
>
> 3. The award shall be deemed to be made at the place of the arbitration and on the date stated therein.'

a) The Difference Between an Award and an Order

According to Article 2 of the Rules, the word 'Award', as used in the Rules, refers, *inter alia*, to an interim, partial or final award.

The meaning of a final award is clear. It rules conclusively on all the claims. It may also be an award in which the arbitral tribunal declines jurisdiction. A partial award rules only on part of the claims that have been made. The definition of an interim award appears more complex. In practice, decisions on the applicable law and decisions confirming the arbitral tribunal's jurisdiction are occasionally described as interim awards. Given that the Rules do not define 'interim' and 'partial' awards, it is up to the arbitrators to decide which of these words to use to refer to awards other than final awards. There is no consistency in the use of the terms in international arbitration practice and national arbitration laws do not always define them either. These variations in terminology are unimportant in themselves, but they may lead to situations in which an arbitral tribunal rules by way of a procedural order on a matter that should have been dealt with in an award. This rarely happens in practice, however.

The question of whether a decision should, or could, be rendered in the form of an award is highly important, especially in relation to conservatory and interim measures (Article 28(1) of the Rules) and the submission of new claims during the proceedings (Article 23(4) of the Rules). It is for the arbitral tribunal to decide whether a procedural order is appropriate or whether an award is required on account of its greater force. Arbitral tribunals order conservatory and interim measures in the form of awards if the decision is likely to be enforceable and faces no legal obstacles, notably under the *'lex arbitri'* and the arbitration law in the countries where enforcement might be sought (see above with regard to Article 28(1) of the Rules). In view of the widespread opinion that conservatory and interim measures do not have the finality required by the New York Convention, awards ordering conservatory and interim measures will often come up against such obstacles.

b) Rules Applicable to the Making of an ICC Award

(1) Drafting the Award

When the Secretariat transmits the matter to the arbitral tribunal after its constitution, it will also forward an 'ICC Award Checklist' (see Appendix 11 below). This checklist is intended to provide arbitrators acting under the ICC Rules of Arbitration with guidance when drafting awards. It does not constitute an exhaustive, mandatory or otherwise binding document. It is simply intended to facilitate the mission of the arbitrators in drafting their decisions in an award.

The Rules do not provide how the arbitral award should be deliberated if the arbitral tribunal comprises three members. It is good practice for a three-member arbitral tribunal to deliberate immediately after the hearing is finished and as soon as any final written submissions have been received and the proceedings have been closed (Article 27). Before the arbitral tribunal starts to write the decisive parts of an award, it should ensure that the parties have completed their submissions within the time limit fixed by the arbitral tribunal and that no procedural steps or issues are incomplete or unresolved.

Where the arbitral tribunal comprises three members, the president of the tribunal usually is responsible for drafting the award. If the case is complex, the work of drafting the award may be split among the arbitrators, although one person, (usually the president) ought to be responsible for co-ordination and consistency of reasoning and result.

Once the proceedings have been closed, Article 27 requires the arbitral tribunal to set an approximate date for the submission of the draft award and to notify the Secretariat and the parties thereof. The Secretariat and the parties ought to be informed of any known delays that could affect that date and, of course, of any postponement of it. A timetable must therefore be devised for the production of the draft award. This is one of the responsibilities referred to in Article 11(5). The timetable must allow sufficient time for the arbitral tribunal to complete its deliberations (especially where the arbitral tribunal comprises three members and if differing views are expected), for the production of a first draft of the award, for comments on the first draft, for discussion and agreement of the final draft, and for its submission to the Court for scrutiny under Article 33.

The working draft or drafts of the award must only be circulated within the arbitral tribunal and must be kept absolutely confidential. The draft award should never be sent to or seen by the parties or to any of their representatives or to any witness or expert (including an expert appointed by the arbitral tribunal). The Secretariat should only be sent the draft which the arbitral tribunal has agreed is to be submitted to the Court for its scrutiny. The prohibition on the circulation of drafts applies equally to disagreements within the tribunal and dissenting views and opinions (see H. Lloyd, M. Darmon, J.-P. Ancel, Lord Dervaird, C. Liebscher and H. Verbist, 'Drafting Awards in ICC Arbitrations', *ICC International Court of Arbitration Bulletin*, Paris, Vol. 16/ No. 2, 2005, p. 19-40).

(2) Reasons of the Award

According to Article 31(2) of the Rules, the award must 'state the reasons upon which it is based'. It is not enough for the arbitral tribunal to decide the dispute; it must also give the reasons that have led to its decision. In other words, it must set forth the grounds justifying and explaining the operative part of the award. This means that in

ICC proceedings the reasons for an award must be given even when it is rendered in a country whose arbitration law does not contain such a requirement.

Although this rarely happens and is not recommendable, the parties may depart from the Rules by expressly authorizing the arbitrators not to state the reasons. The Court has approved such awards in the past, if there is a signed agreement in writing between the parties to have an award without reasons and if the parties have ensured that the relevant jurisdictions of the place of the arbitration and of the likely places of enforcement do not require that an award be reasoned (see J. Fry, S. Greenberg and F. Mazza, *The Secretariat's Guide to ICC Arbitration*, ICC Publication No. 729 E, Paris, 2012, p. 321).

The Rules do not mention whether the reasons must be stated briefly or in detail, leaving it to the arbitral tribunal to decide how they are to be drafted. However, the grounds given should inform the parties of the reasons for the decision, as this will encourage them to accept and comply spontaneously with the award.

The arbitral tribunal must be sure that it bases its decisions only on the facts and law presented to it by the parties or which it has ascertained (where it is permissible to do so) and on which the parties have been given a proper opportunity to file comments.

Each arbitral tribunal will decide whether the award should first consider the law or the facts (or to combine the discussion of both). Whatever approach is adopted, the award, in recording the facts upon which the arbitral tribunal relies, should make it clear which facts were not contentious and which facts were disputed and have been established by the arbitral tribunal. Facts that are not relevant to the decision should not be included or discussed, unless this is necessary in order to explain why the arbitral tribunal considers that a particular fact has been proven. Where the fact was contentious, the arbitral tribunal should briefly outline the respective positions of the parties before setting out its conclusions. Where appropriate it ought to state the rules of evidence that have been applied.

Where the parties disagree about the applicable rules of law or about the interpretation of the contract, the award ought to set out the respective positions of the parties before discussing them and arriving at its reasoned conclusions. The arbitral tribunal ought to take care to see that any discussion of the law is related to the rules of law applicable to the merits. If there is discussion about the possible application of other rules of law, then the relevance of that discussion should be made clear.

The decisions of the arbitral tribunal on the merits will be the product of a reasoned application of the relevant rules of law to the facts. They will normally be expressed as answers to the issues and will show how the dispute has been resolved (see H. Lloyd, M. Darmon, J.-P. Ancel, Lord Dervaird, C. Liebscher and H. Verbist, 'Drafting Awards in ICC Arbitrations', *ICC International Court of Arbitration Bulletin*, Paris, Vol. 16/ No. 2, 2005, p. 19-40).

(3) Deliberation of the Award

When the arbitral tribunal comprises three members, it must decide whether to meet physically to complete its deliberations and the final draft or whether it can do so by some other method of communication (correspondence by e-mail or telefax, telephone conference, video conference), since a physical meeting adds to the costs of the arbitration).

If the award (or any section of it) has been drafted by one member of the arbitral tribunal, then the other members must carefully read and comment on the draft. If a member does not agree with the substance of the draft it is often helpful to provide an alternative draft on the substance, even if the disagreement is fundamental. If the award has to be made by a majority, or by the president in the absence of a majority, the award ought to take into account the grounds for the minority view(s) and, if appropriate, will provide reasons for rejecting them. In this way the minority may not have to express a dissenting opinion. A final draft may have to use wording that is acceptable to all or to the majority but the wording ought to be free from doubt or ambiguity.

Most arbitral awards rendered by three-member arbitral tribunals are taken unanimously by the three arbitrators, but it may occasionally happen that a majority award is rendered. If, as very exceptionally happens, there is no majority, the president of the arbitral tribunal will decide alone (Article 31(1)). The Rules thus ensure that an award may be rendered, even if the members of the arbitral tribunal each have a different opinion.

Of the 431 partial and final awards rendered in 2013 in ICC arbitrations (not including awards by consent), 256 were rendered by arbitral tribunals composed of three arbitrators. 214 (84%) of those awards were rendered unanimously and 42 (16%) by a majority of the arbitrators comprising the tribunal. In 2013, the minority arbitrator expressed a dissenting opinion in the award in 17 cases and in a separate document in 19 cases. In two cases, failing a majority, the president of the arbitral tribunal decided alone on some or all of the matters decided in the award (see '2013 Statistical Report' published in *ICC International Court of Arbitration Bulletin*, Paris, Vol. 25/Nr. 1 - 2014, p. 14).

Of the 460 partial and final awards rendered in 2012 in ICC arbitrations (not including awards by consent), 273 were rendered by arbitral tribunals composed of three arbitrators. 221 (81%) of those awards were rendered unanimously and 52 (19%) by a majority of the arbitrators comprising the tribunal. In 2012, the minority arbitrator expressed a dissenting opinion in the award in 14 cases and in a separate document in 28 cases. In no case in 2012 was it necessary for the president of an arbitral tribunal to make an award alone (see '2012 Statistical Report' published in *ICC International Court of Arbitration Bulletin*, Paris, Vol. 24/Nr. 1 - 2013, p. 15).

Of the 508 partial and final awards rendered in 2011 in ICC arbitrations (not including awards by consent), 285 were rendered by arbitral tribunals composed of three arbitrators. 244 (85.6%) of those awards were rendered unanimously and 41 (14.4%) by a majority of the arbitrators comprising the tribunal. In 2011, the minority arbitrator expressed a dissenting opinion in the award in 14 cases and in a separate document in 23 cases. In no case in 2011 was it necessary for the president of an arbitral tribunal to make an award alone (see '2011 Statistical Report' published in *ICC International Court of Arbitration Bulletin*, Paris, Vol. 23/Nr. 1 - 2012, p. 15).

(4) Dissenting Opinions

The Rules do not mention dissenting opinions. Nevertheless, the ICC Court allows that an arbitrator who disagrees with the majority may submit a dissenting opinion to the other members of the arbitral tribunal and to the ICC Court. A dissenting opinion can be expressed in different forms. It may be contained in a document separate from the arbitral award, or it may be included in the award with an indication that on a particular decision there was a dissent by one of the members of the arbitral tribunal. If the dissenting opinion is contained in a separate document, it will be communicated to the Court for its information together with the draft award that will be scrutinized by the Court pursuant to Article 33. The dissenting opinion itself will, however, not be scrutinized by the Court (see comments on Article 33 below). If one of the arbitrators submits a dissenting opinion in a separate document, the Court will usually communicate the dissenting opinion for information to the parties when it notifies the arbitral award, unless it considers in accordance with the general rule laid down in Article 41 of the Rules that the disclosure of the dissenting opinion could undermine the enforceability of the arbitral award. Pursuant to this general rule the arbitral tribunal and the Court shall ascertain the parties whether the communication of the dissenting opinion to the parties could be deemed to be a violation of the confidentiality of the deliberations under mandatory rules at the place of the arbitration. This is a matter to which the ICC International Court of Arbitration also gives consideration when scrutinizing draft awards (Article 6 of Appendix II to the Rules).

Although dissenting opinions are chiefly found in common law countries, many other legal systems (e.g. German and Swiss law) do not in principle prohibit their use in arbitration. In such circumstances, an arbitral tribunal may decide that, for the parties' information, the dissenting opinion should be attached to the award when notified to them.

In 2013, of the 42 awards rendered by three-member arbitral tribunals with a majority decision, the minority arbitrator expressed a dissenting opinion in the award in 17 cases and in a separate document in 19 cases (see '2013 Statistical Report' published in *ICC International Court of Arbitration Bulletin*, Paris, Vol. 25/Nr. 1 – 2014, p. 14). In 2012, of the 52 awards rendered by three-member arbitral tribunals with a majority decision, the minority arbitrator expressed a dissenting opinion in the award in 14 cases and in a separate document in 28 cases (see '2012 Statistical Report' published in *ICC International Court of Arbitration Bulletin*, Paris, Vol. 24/Nr. 1 – 2013, p. 15). In 2011, of the 41 awards rendered by three-member arbitral tribunals with a majority decision, the minority arbitrator expressed a dissenting opinion in the award in 14 cases and in a separate document in 23 cases (see '2011 Statistical Report' published in *ICC International Court of Arbitration Bulletin*, Paris, Vol. 23/Nr. 1 – 2013, p. 15).

c) When and Where is the Award Deemed to have been Made?

The date stated in the award is deemed to be that on which it was made. As the Rules require awards to be submitted to the ICC Court in draft form for scrutiny and approval before being rendered, the date that appears in the award will always be later than that on which the draft award was approved by the Court, even if the arbitral tribunal has already terminated its deliberations.

The place where the award is rendered is the place of the arbitration as fixed or recorded by the Court (under the current version of the Rules, the Court no longer makes a decision officially confirming the place of the arbitration when chosen by the parties). This prevents the arbitral tribunal from changing the 'nationality' of the award by deliberating and signing it in another place. This could easily happen, given the various means of communication (letter, telephone, electronic) used when deliberating and the fact that the arbitrators may reside in different places. The 'nationality' of an award is highly important when it comes to its recognition and enforcement. For instance, the New York Convention applies only to 'foreign' awards, not to 'domestic' awards. In this respect, it should be borne in mind that national laws concerning the recognition and enforcement of domestic awards often differ considerably from the New York Convention and therefore the recognition of a domestic award may sometimes be refused on grounds which would not lead to refusal under the New

York Convention. Many of the member countries of the New York Convention have formulated reservations, making its application conditional upon reciprocity and/or subject to the requirement that the dispute is considered as commercial under the national law in question. (An up-to-date list of the states that are parties to the New York Convention may be found on the web site of the United Nations Commission on International Trade Law (UNCITRAL) at < www.uncitral.org > .) A description of the relevant national rules of procedure for the recognition and enforcement of foreign arbitral awards pursuant to the New York Convention in 79 countries is available in a Guide established by the ICC Commission on Arbitration and ADR. A second edition of this Guide was published in 2012 as a Special Supplement to the ICC International Court of Arbitration Bulletin (The Guide is also available at the Dispute Resolution Library of the ICC at < www.iccdrl.com >).

Article 31(3) does not require the arbitrators to sign the award at the place of the arbitration, which will usually save them from having to return to the place of the arbitration simply for this purpose.

3. Award by Consent (Art. 32)

Article 32 of the Rules reads:

> 'Award by Consent
>
> If the parties reach a settlement after the file has been transmitted to the arbitral tribunal in accordance with Article 16, the settlement shall be recorded in the form of an award made by consent of the parties, if so requested by the parties and if the arbitral tribunal agrees to do so.'

Approximately half of the ICC arbitrations are withdrawn before a final award is rendered on the merits of the dispute (see J. Fry, S. Greenberg and F. Mazza, *The Secretariat's Guide to ICC Arbitration,* ICC Publication No. 729 E, Paris, 2012, p. 323). The withdrawal of the arbitration mostly occurs when the parties have reached a settlement agreement that ends their dispute. If the parties come to a compromise over their dispute after the matter has been referred to the arbitral tribunal, they may ask the tribunal to render an award making their arrangement enforceable. Such 'award by consent' may be rendered even if the Terms of Reference have not yet been signed. There is after all little point in requiring the parties and the arbitral tribunal to prepare Terms of Reference, as this would be a waste of time and money if the dispute has already been settled. The parties are in this case asked to confirm in writing that there is no need for Terms of Reference.

There is no obligation under the Rules to render an award by consent if a case is settled. The arbitral tribunal may consider issuing such an award 'if so requested by the parties'. This wording clarifies that all parties have to request that an award by consent be rendered. This request may be included in the settlement agreement or in separate submissions. If only one party requests an award by consent, and the other party does not or even objects, no such award shall be made. If the parties forego an award by consent and are content with the settlement, they will normally ask the ICC Court to take note of the withdrawal of their claims, in order to terminate the arbitration.

The arbitral tribunal must not render an award by consent, if it considers the contents thereof to be legally unacceptable or even unlawful. The words 'and if the arbitral tribunal agrees to do so' clearly establish that the arbitral tribunal has discretion to decide not to render an award by consent. However, one may assume that the arbitral tribunal will refuse to render the award by consent only in exceptional circumstances. This might, for instance, happen if the arbitral tribunal finds the settlement agreement or the immediate effects thereof to be in violation of applicable mandatory laws, illegal or even fraudulent.

Before preparing a draft award by consent terminating the arbitration (partial awards by consent are also possible), the arbitral tribunal should reassure itself that the settlement is comprehensive, i.e. that it covers all claims, counterclaims and set-off claims. Should the arbitral tribunal find that not all claims have been settled, or should it have substantial doubts in this regard, it should preferably seek clarification from the parties and only then act accordingly.

An award by consent usually reproduces the operative part of the settlement reached by the parties, thereby obliging them to fulfill the obligations upon which they have agreed. In addition, in accordance with Article 37(4) of the Rules, the award will decide which party is required to pay the costs of the arbitration or in what proportion they shall be split between the parties. Here again, the parties' arrangement will be followed if it has dealt with this question. If not, the arbitral tribunal must rule on the costs and state the reasons for its ruling. If the arbitration terminates with a settlement agreement before the final award on the merits is rendered, the Court will fix the arbitrators' fees and the ICC administrative expenses, in accordance with Article 37(6) of the Rules and Article 2(8) of Appendix III to the Rules, at its discretion, taking into account the stage attained by the arbitral proceedings and any other relevant circumstances. In most instances this means that the Court reimburses a portion of the advance on costs (see J. Fry, S. Greenberg and F. Mazza, *The Secretariat's Guide to ICC Arbitration*, ICC Publication No. 729 E, Paris, 2012, p. 327).

Awards by consent rank as arbitral awards and must therefore meet the formal requirements of any other award in an ICC arbitration. Usually, the award by consent records the settlement agreement reached between the parties and spells out the parties' obligations under the settlement agreement. Moreover, the award by consent records the agreement of the parties on the allocation of the costs of the arbitration. The requirement of Article 31(2) to state the reasons upon which the award is based shall be restricted with respect to awards by consent. The reasons upon which the award by consent is based are, essentially, the terms of the settlement agreement and their agreement to comply with its terms.

Awards by consent have the same status as final awards and benefit from the provisions of the New York Convention when it comes to their recognition and enforcement in foreign countries. The same is also true in Germany (see Articles 1053 and 1061 ZPO), Belgium (Article 1712(1)-(2) JC) and in Switzerland (PILA contains a reference to the New York Convention in Article 194, without actually laying down any specific rule itself in this regard). See also Article 30 of the UNCITRAL Model Law.

In 2013, 40 awards by consent were rendered in ICC arbitrations (see '2013 Statistical Report' published in *ICC International Court of Arbitration Bulletin*, Paris, Vol. 25/Nr. 1 – 2014, p. 14). In 2012, 31 awards by consent were rendered in ICC arbitrations (see '2012 Statistical Report' published in *ICC International Court of Arbitration Bulletin*, Paris, Vol. 24/Nr. 1 – 2013, p. 15). In 2011, 41 awards by consent were rendered in ICC arbitrations (see '2011 Statistical Report' published in *ICC International Court of Arbitration Bulletin*, Paris, Vol. 23/Nr. 1 – 2012, p. 15).

4. Scrutiny of Award by the Court (Art. 33)

Article 33 of the Rules reads:

> 'Scrutiny of the Award by the Court
>
> Before signing any award, the arbitral tribunal shall submit it in draft form to the Court. The Court may lay down modifications as to the form of the award and, without affecting the arbitral tribunal's liberty of decision, may also draw its attention to points of substance. No award shall be rendered by the arbitral tribunal until it has been approved by the Court as to its form.'

Article 6 of Appendix II to the Rules reads:

> 'Scrutiny of Arbitral Awards
>
> When the Court scrutinizes draft awards in accordance with Article 33 of the Rules, it considers, to the extent practicable, the requirements of mandatory law at the place of the arbitration.'

a) Scrutiny as to Form

The ICC International Court of Arbitration's scrutiny of the draft award is unique in the arbitration world and constitutes one of the essential features of the ICC arbitration procedure. No award – be it an interim or final award or an award by consent – may be rendered by an arbitral tribunal without first being scrutinized and approved by the Court 'as to its form'. Although this rule has been criticized (as it delays the proceedings and could be considered as an infringement of the arbitral tribunal's freedom of decision), the Court's scrutiny is appreciated by most ICC arbitration users, including most arbitrators. The Court's scrutiny function is as an internationally recognized quality label, which makes ICC awards less prone to annulment.

The purpose of this scrutiny is to avoid the risk of an ICC award containing a serious formal defect and to enhance the quality and enforceability of the arbitral award. The Court checks, amongst other things, whether the award rules on all the claims (and no more than these), includes an operative part and gives the reasons for the arbitral tribunal's decisions. The Court will also draw attention to any typographical or computational errors which the Secretariat may point out to it.

In light of Article 6 of Appendix II to the Rules, the Court also checks whether there are any mandatory legal requirements at the place of the arbitration that may have been overlooked by the arbitral tribunal. This is in keeping with the requirement laid upon the Court by Article 41 of the Rules to make every effort to ensure that the award is enforceable at law. For instance, when there is a dissenting opinion, the Court will look into the formal question of whether there are any compulsory rules at the place of the arbitration prohibiting disclosure of dissenting opinions to parties. The Court may lay down modifications of form (Article 33 of the Rules). This means that the award is approved only after the arbitral tribunal has made the required modification(s), as the points raised may cause the arbitral tribunal to modify its award – as it is free to do – which may in turn raise further questions of form. This is, of course, an unlikely occurrence. No award may be notified to the parties until the arbitral tribunal has made the formal modifications that are required by the Court.

The scrutiny process does not allow the Court to require a modification of the substance of the decision taken by the arbitral tribunal in its award. However, it may happen that as a result of the Court drawing the attention of the arbitral tribunal to some points of substance, the arbitral tribunal modifies its decision. The Court will, however, not indicate what decision the arbitral tribunal should take, because the Court does not have the power to decide the dispute.

If the Court decides not to approve the draft award, it will send comments to the arbitral tribunal and request the arbitral tribunal to submit a revised draft award for scrutiny by the Court after having considered the Court's comments on the first draft (See J. Fry, S. Greenberg and F. Mazza, *The Secretariat's Guide to ICC Arbitration*, ICC Publication No. 729 E, Paris, 2012, p. 334).

A procedural order must not be submitted for scrutiny before it can be rendered by the arbitral tribunal. Whether a decision of an arbitral tribunal can be taken in the form of a procedural order or must be taken in the form of the arbitral award will in the first place depend on the applicable law at the place of the arbitration, but may also depend on the law applicable at the place of enforcement of the award. Whereas the arbitral tribunal has for some decisions the choice whether to include them in an award or a procedural order, e.g. interim and conservatory measures (Article 28), it will not have such choice for decisions on the merits of the dispute. As regards the determination of the applicable law, in cases where the parties have not agreed on the applicable law, the situation is somewhat different. As set out above (Article 21), the Rules do not provide a particular form in which the arbitral tribunal must determine the law applicable to the substance of the dispute, if such decision needs to be taken. As it is an important decision with respect to the substance of the matter, it is necessary to formulate it in writing and to provide reasons for it. The arbitral tribunal may decide to take its decision through a procedural order or through an interim award, in case the parties expect to be informed of the arbitral tribunal's decision before they make further submissions on the substance of the matter. If the arbitral tribunal decides to take the decision through a procedural order, the arbitral tribunal will nevertheless have to include its decision also in the arbitral award which it shall render at the end of the arbitration so that its decision can be legally enforced, if needed. If the arbitral tribunal decides to determine the applicable law by an interim award, it must submit the award first in draft form for scrutiny to the ICC Court pursuant to Article 33 of the Rules.

b) The Secretariat's ICC Award Checklist

As already set out above (Article 16 and 31), when the Secretariat transmits the matter to the arbitral tribunal after its constitution, it will forward an 'ICC Award Checklist' (see Appendix 11 below). This checklist is intended to provide arbitrators acting under the ICC Rules of Arbitration with guidance when drafting awards. It does not constitute an exhaustive, mandatory or otherwise binding document. It is simply intended to facilitate the task of the arbitrators when drafting an award.

The checklist provides a number of formal points to which all arbitrators should have regard when drafting an award. It includes general requirements, such as the need to mention the ICC case reference, the identification of the parties and their representatives, the arbitrator(s) and the arbitration agreement. Also, the checklist recommends to include in the arbitral award a history of the arbitral proceedings with a summary of all the procedural steps, the decisions taken by the ICC Court regarding the arbitration proceedings, including the time limit to render the arbitral award and any extensions granted by the Court. If the jurisdiction has been contested and the Court needed to take a decision in accordance with Article 6(4), the arbitral award should contain a decision on jurisdiction or state why such decision is not necessary.

The checklist also points out that the final arbitral award should include a decision on the costs of the arbitration and their allocation between the parties. It also provides practical recommendations for drafting the dispositive section and in particular the last page for the signature of the arbitral award.

When the Secretariat receives a draft award for scrutiny, it will first check whether all items on the checklist have been addressed. If some of these items have not been addressed, the Secretariat will resend a copy of the checklist to the arbitral tribunal and identify thereby the missing points (see J. Fry, S. Greenberg and F. Mazza, *The Secretariat's Guide to ICC Arbitration*, ICC Publication No. 729 E, Paris, 2012, p. 332).

c) The Right to Raise Points of Substance without Affecting the Arbitral Tribunal's Liberty of Decision

According to Article 33 of the Rules, the Court may draw the arbitral tribunal's attention 'to points of substance'. As the Court must respect the arbitral tribunal's liberty of decision, it does not give any instructions regarding the dispositive part (tenor) of the award. It is for the arbitral tribunal alone to decide in favor of or against one or other of the parties.

The Court may nonetheless comment on the reasons for the decision. For instance, it may draw the arbitral tribunal's attention to the fact that an award contains reasons which contradict each other and could make it partly incomprehensible. The Court could also point out that the arbitral tribunal has clearly ruled '*ultra petita*' by deciding on a point that did not form part of the claims or by awarding amounts above those requested. It may draw the arbitral tribunal's attention to compulsory statutes of limitation in a given country, which may have been ignored and could hinder the enforcement of the award.

Arbitral tribunals are of course free to modify their awards, or not, in the light of such comments. They will usually take them into account. Although such situations are not always easy to handle psychologically, arbitral tribunals usually appreciate the Court's opinion on their draft awards.

d) How is the Draft Award Scrutinized?

Initially, it is up to the counsel in charge of the matter within the Secretariat of the Court to examine the draft award before submitting it to the Court. The counsel's daily experience makes him or her well placed to know what points of form are likely to be raised by the Court. He or she may immediately draw the tribunal's attention to any typographical or computational errors. After conferring with the Secretary General and/or the Deputy Secretary General, the counsel will discuss one or more points with the president of the arbitral tribunal or the sole arbitrator, if it is thought highly likely that the Court will raise these points. Such discussions, which often take place by telephone, present two advantages. Firstly, they allow the arbitral tribunal to react quickly to clarify the formal or substantive question, without necessarily making any changes. Secondly, they allow the arbitral tribunal to decide whether any changes should be made to the draft award before it is submitted to the Court.

These informal discussions help to avoid delays, for even if the Court does no more than draw the arbitral tribunal's attention to points of substance, it will wait until these points have been clarified before approving the award as to its form. This can easily delay the proceedings by several weeks.

Given the considerable number of awards that the Court must scrutinize each year, not all drafts are put before the plenary session of the Court. Awards that clearly do not raise any problems are scrutinized and approved by a committee of the Court (see Article 5 of Appendix I to the Rules and Article 4 of Appendix II to the Rules). Draft awards which, upon examination by the Secretariat, call for a more detailed examination (because, for instance, there is a dissenting opinion or the dispute is complex or involves a state party) are submitted to a plenary session of the Court, for which one of its members prepares a report. On the basis of the report, the plenary session discusses the draft and decides whether or not to approve the award.

In exceptional circumstances, if an urgent notification of the arbitral award to the parties is required, the Court and its Secretariat can adopt an accelerated scrutiny process. Pursuant to Article 1(3), the President of the ICC Court has the power to make urgent decisions alone and exceptionally the President may use this power to scrutinize and approve an award on an urgent basis. In such case, the decision taken by the President shall be reported to the Court at its next session.

The parties will not be informed of the scrutiny process and of any comment that may be made by the ICC Court or the Secretariat on the draft award. As a consequence, the parties will not know whether the draft award was approved with its first submission, or whether particular modifications were required by the Court or whether the Court has drawn the attention of the arbitral tribunal to points of substance in the award. Once the scrutiny process is terminated and the arbitral tribunal has signed the requested number of originals of the arbitral award, the Secretariat will in its notification letter to the parties mention the date of the Court session in which the draft award was approved, without providing any further details.

The scrutiny process will normally take two to three weeks from the date the arbitral tribunal submits its draft award to the Secretariat until the arbitral tribunal receives the Court's approval or comments on the draft award. In some cases this may take more time, however, in case the draft award needs to be translated or if the length and quality of the draft award take more time for the Secretariat to examine it (see J. Fry, S. Greenberg and F. Mazza, *The Secretariat's Guide to ICC Arbitration,* ICC Publication No. 729 E, Paris, 2012, p. 337).

In 2013, no less than 471 awards were approved by the Court. These comprised 327 final awards, 104 partial or interim awards, and 40 awards by consent (see '2013 Statistical Report' published in *ICC International Court of Arbitration Bulletin*, Paris, Vol. 25/Nr. 1 – 2014, p. 14). In 2012, the Court approved 491 awards, comprising 341 final awards, 119 partial or interim awards and 31 awards by consent (see '2012 Statistical Report' published in *ICC International Court of Arbitration Bulletin*, Paris, Vol. 24/ Nr. 1 – 2013, p. 15). In 2011, a total of 508 awards were approved by the Court, comprising 347 final awards, 120 partial or interim awards, and 41 awards by consent (see '2011 Statistical Report' published in *ICC International Court of Arbitration Bulletin*, Paris, Vol. 23/Nr. 1 – 2012, p. 15). In 2010, the Court approved 479 awards, comprising 305 final awards, 130 partial or interim awards, and 44 awards by consent (see '2010 Statistical Report' published in *ICC International Court of Arbitration Bulletin*, Paris, Vol. 22/Nr. 1 – 2011, p. 15). In 2009, the total number of awards approved by the Court was 415, comprising 265 final awards, 111 partial or interim awards, and 39 awards by consent (see '2009 Statistical Report' published in *ICC International Court of Arbitration Bulletin*, Paris, Vol. 21/Nr. 1 – 2010, p. 14). In 2008, 407 awards were approved, namely 261 final awards, 109 partial or interim awards, and 37 awards by consent (see

'2008 Statistical Report' published in *ICC International Court of Arbitration Bulletin*, Paris, Vol. 20/Nr. 1 – 2009, p. 14).

According to the statistics published by the Court, the latter gave an unqualified approval to only 5 draft awards in 2013. The remaining 466 awards were approved subject to modifications of form or with the attention of the arbitrators being drawn to points of substance, in order to enhance the quality and enforceability of the award. 40 draft awards were not approved, but sent back to the arbitral tribunal to be reworked and resubmitted (see '2013 Statistical Report' published in *ICC International Court of Arbitration Bulletin*, Paris, Vol. 25/Nr. 1 – 2014, p. 14). In 2012, the Court required modifications as to form and drew the attention of the arbitral tribunal to points of substance when approving 483 (98%) awards. On a further 59 occasions, the Court requested that the arbitral resubmit its award for approval (see '2012 Statistical Report' published in *ICC International Court of Arbitration Bulletin*, Paris, Vol. 24/Nr. 1 – 2013, p. 15). In 2011, the Court used its power to require modifications as to form and draw the attention of the arbitral tribunal to points of substance when scrutinizing 496 (97.6%) of the awards. On a further 37 occasions, the Court requested that the arbitral tribunal resubmit its award for approval (see '2011 Statistical Report' published in *ICC International Court of Arbitration Bulletin*, Paris, Vol. 23/Nr. 1 – 2012, p. 15). In 2010, the Court used its power to require modifications as to form and draw the attention of the arbitral tribunal to points of substance when scrutinizing 444 (92.7%) of the awards. On a further 43 occasions, the Court requested that the arbitral tribunal resubmit its award for approval (see '2010 Statistical Report' published in *ICC International Court of Arbitration Bulletin*, Paris, Vol. 22/Nr. 1 – 2011, p. 15). In 2009, the Court required modifications as to form and/or drew attention to points of substance when approving 382 awards, leaving 33 awards approved without commentary by the Court. On a further 34 occasions, the Court requested that the arbitral tribunal resubmit its award for approval (see '2009 Statistical Report' published in *ICC International Court of Arbitration Bulletin*, Paris, Vol. 21/Nr. 1 – 2010, p. 14). In 2008, the Court used its power to require modifications as to form and draw the attention of the arbitral tribunal to points of substance when scrutinizing 363 of the awards, leaving 44 awards approved without commentary by the Court. On a further 25 occasions, the Court requested that the arbitral tribunal resubmit its award for approval (see '2008 Statistical Report' published in *ICC International Court of Arbitration Bulletin*, Paris, Vol. 20/Nr. 1 – 2009, p. 14).

The above figures reflect both the quality of arbitrators in ICC proceedings and the way in which the Court pertinently and discreetly exercises its powers. It may be assumed that parties generally appreciate the strong encouragement given to arbitrators to carry out their work conscientiously so as to ensure as far as possible the enforceability of ICC awards.

e) Is a Dissenting Opinion Scrutinized?

The ICC Rules do not provide for the scrutiny of any dissenting opinions. If a member of a three-member arbitral tribunal has written a dissenting opinion, it will be submitted together with the draft award to the ICC Court. When scrutinizing the draft arbitral award, the ICC Court will read the dissenting opinion but it will not take a decision on the dissenting opinion contained in a separate document, as such dissenting opinion is not considered to be a part of the arbitral award (on dissenting opinions, see also the comments with respect to Article 31 above).

Should the ICC Court in reading the dissenting opinion find that issues raised in the dissenting opinion are not dealt with in the majority award or should the dissenting opinion question whether the arbitral tribunal's deliberations or the arbitration proceedings were conducted correctly, the ICC Court may invite the majority to deal with these issues or it may draw the majority's attention to the possibility to strengthen its reasoning in relation to issues raised by the dissenting arbitrator (see J. Fry, S. Greenberg and F. Mazza, *The Secretariat's Guide to ICC Arbitration,* ICC Publication No. 729 E, Paris, 2012, p. 319).

5. Notification, Deposit, Enforceability of Awards (Art. 34)

Article 34 of the Rules reads:

> 'Notification, Deposit and Enforceability of the Award
>
> 1. Once an award has been made, the Secretariat shall notify to the parties the text signed by the arbitral tribunal, provided always that the costs of the arbitration have been fully paid to the ICC by the parties or by one of them.
>
> 2. Additional copies certified true by the Secretary General shall be made available on request and at any time to the parties, but to no one else.
>
> 3. By virtue of the notification made in accordance with Article 34(1), the parties waive any other form of notification or deposit on the part of the arbitral tribunal.
>
> 4. An original of each award made in accordance with the Rules shall be deposited with the Secretariat.
>
> 5. The arbitral tribunal and the Secretariat shall assist the parties in complying with whatever further formalities may be necessary.
>
> 6. Every award shall be binding on the parties. By submitting the dispute to arbitration under these Rules, the parties undertake to carry out any award without delay and shall be deemed to have waived their right to any form of recourse insofar as such waiver can validly be made.'

a) Notification of the Award (Art. 34(1))

After the Court has approved the draft award, the Secretariat will check whether the arbitral tribunal has taken into account the comments made by the Court in the scrutiny process. Arbitral tribunals are therefore well advised, after they were informed of the Court decision regarding the award, to submit a corrected draft first to the Secretariat so to allow it to check whether the Court's comments were taken into account. Also, in case the Court has approved a final award and fixed the costs of the arbitration proceedings, the Secretariat will check whether the amount of the costs is included in the award.

It is understandable that the award will be notified only after all the costs of the arbitration mentioned in Article 37(1) of the Rules have been paid to the ICC in accordance with Article 36 of the Rules, given that an award may order one of the parties to reimburse the other for its costs, but does not provide the ICC or the arbitrators with an enforceable title in respect of the payment of the costs due (ICC administrative expenses and the fees and expenses of the arbitrators). The ICC and the arbitrators would be obliged to resort to ordinary legal remedies in order to claim payment of their expenses and fees from the defaulting party or parties, which is likely to waste time and cause considerable problems. Hence, the right to withhold the award is, in practice, the only effective means of recourse they have. The question arises as to whether the ICC may withhold an award if any taxes due by the parties, as mentioned in Article 2(13) of Appendix III to the Rules, remain unpaid. The answer is likely to be no in the present circumstances. For this reason, arbitrators should take whatever steps are necessary vis-à-vis the parties in this regard during the proceedings.

When all the costs have been paid, the Secretariat (not the arbitral tribunal) notifies the award to the parties in accordance with Article 3(2) of the Rules and the indications given in the Terms of Reference.

The arbitral tribunal should provide the arbitral award to the Secretariat unbound in as many signed originals as there are parties and arbitrators as well as an original for the Secretariat (see Note to the Arbitral Tribunal on the conduct of the arbitration; Appendix 9 below). The addressees for the notification of the arbitral award shall be those listed in the Terms of Reference pursuant to Article 23(1)(b) of the Rules, unless some amendments thereto will have been made afterwards.

In its letter notifying the arbitral award to the parties, the Secretariat draws the attention of the parties to the provision of Article 34(6) of the Rules and reminds the parties that every award shall be binding on the parties and that, by submitting the dispute to arbitration under the Rules, the parties undertake to carry out any award without delay and shall be deemed to have waived their right to any form of recourse insofar as such waiver can validly be made. In case the arbitral award rendered and notified is a final award, the Secretariat informs the parties of the decision taken by the Court with regard to the costs of the arbitration, and indicates thereby how this amount is composed (administrative expenses, the fees for each of the arbitrators, expenses incurred by the arbitrators). If a balance of the advance on costs remains to be reimbursed, the Secretariat shall set out which amount shall be reimbursed and how it shall be apportioned between the parties. The Secretariat also points out in the notification letter, in case the arbitral award is a final award, that it shall close the file and that it shall, pursuant to Article 1(8) of Appendix II to the Rules, destroy any documents submitted by the parties or the arbitrators unless a party or an arbitrator requests in writing within 30 days that its documents should be returned. All related costs and expenses shall be paid by the requesting party. The Secretariat thereby brings to the attention of the parties that it will retain originals of the Terms of Reference and of the arbitral award(s) rendered, as well as copies of all correspondence with the Secretariat and records of the Court's decisions. Finally, the Secretariat sends with the notification letter an evaluation form, which it invites the parties to complete and return to the General Counsel at their convenience. The Secretariat thereby clarifies that the answers given in the evaluation form will be kept strictly confidential and that they will allow the Secretariat to evaluate the quality of its services and to improve them if need be.

At the same time when notifying the originals of the arbitral award to the parties, the Secretariat informs the arbitrator(s) that the originals of the award are sent to the parties and, in case the fees were fixed by the Court, that the ICC accounting department shall pay the fees and any outstanding expenses. The Secretariat encloses for the information of the arbitrator(s) the Secretariat's Note on Correction and Interpretation of Arbitral Awards (see Appendix 12 below). In the case the arbitral award is a final award, the Secretariat also brings to the attention of the arbitrator(s) that it shall close the file and that it shall, pursuant to Article 1(8) of Appendix II to the Rules, destroy any documents submitted by the parties or the arbitrators unless a party or an arbitrator requests in writing within 30 days that its documents should be returned. As with the letter sent to the parties, the Secretariat sends to the arbitrator(s) an evaluation form, which it invites the arbitrator(s) to complete and return to the General Counsel at their convenience. The Secretariat thereby also clarifies that the answers given in the evaluation form will be kept strictly confidential and that they will allow the Secretariat to evaluate the quality of its services and to improve them if need be.

b) Issuing of Copies Certified as True (Art. 34(2))

When required in order to obtain the compulsory enforcement of awards and also for other reasons, the Secretary General of the ICC International Court of Arbitration issues copies certified as true for submission to the relevant authorities, especially in connection with applications for enforcement orders in accordance with Article IV(1)(a) of the New York Convention or in compliance with applicable national laws. Confidentiality requires such copies to be supplied to the parties alone. If need be, ICC will also provide authentication and copies with the Hague Convention 'apostille' certificate. In the absence of the Secretary General or otherwise at the Secretary General's request, the Deputy Secretary General and/or the General Counsel shall have the authority to certify true copies of the award, as set out in Article 5(1) of Appendix II to the Rules.

c) Deposit with the ICC and Waiver of any other Form of Notification or Deposit (Art. 34(3)-(4))

By having recourse to ICC arbitration, the parties accept that the notification of the arbitral awards is done in accordance with Article 34(1) by the Secretariat of the ICC Court. They thus waive any other form of notification on the part of the arbitral tribunal, to the extent that such waiver can validly be made.

Many arbitration laws require awards rendered within their jurisdiction to be deposited with a judicial authority. The basic point of such a provision is to ensure legal certainty and conserve evidence. Article 34(3)-(4) takes a different line by requiring awards to be deposited with the ICC. In the context of enforcement proceedings this does not cause any problems, because the question of whether it is permissible to waive deposit of an award in the country where it was rendered is irrelevant. More often than not, such a waiver may be made. If a party is established in the country where the award was rendered, it may nevertheless be appropriate to check that the award does not have to be filed with the relevant authority. Particular attention should be given to any deadlines that may be applicable, so as not to be barred from filing the award in the event of problems.

A description of the relevant national rules of procedure and requirements for the recognition and enforcement of foreign arbitral awards pursuant to the New York Convention in 79 countries is available in a Guide established by the ICC Commission on Arbitration and ADR. A second edition of this Guide was published in 2012 as a Special Supplement to the ICC International Court of Arbitration Bulletin (The Guide is also available at the Dispute Resolution Library of the ICC at <www.iccdrl.com>).

d) Assistance in Complying with any other Necessary Formalities (Art. 34(5))

This paragraph is somewhat vague, leaving a question mark over what formalities are involved. Basically, it refers to the formal requirements of mandatory law at the place of the arbitration applicable to the proceedings. An example would be any provisions relating to the deposit of the award that have to be complied with. Sometimes, such formalities will prove to be necessary on account of the requirements of mandatory law applicable in the country of enforcement. Information may be required to show that specific aspects of the proceedings have been conducted in the appropriate way. However, this provision does not as such imply that the ICC and the arbitral tribunal are obliged to take part, as participants, in any setting-aside or enforcement proceedings.

e) Compulsory Nature of the Award and Waiver of any Form of Recourse (Art. 34(6))

Arbitration is distinguished by the fact that the arbitral tribunal's decisions, including the award deciding the dispute, are not subject to appeal before a judicial authority in order to obtain a different decision. The parties may of course agree otherwise, but this is uncommon and not provided for in the Rules. The principle stated in the first sentence of Article 34(6) is particularly important in the context of Article V(1)(e) of the New York Convention, according to which the recognition and enforcement of an award may be refused if it has not yet become 'binding' upon the parties. The opening sentence of Article 34(6) aims to prevent such a refusal.

This does not, however, mean that an award cannot be void or that it will automatically be enforced. Indeed, national laws applicable to arbitration proceedings by virtue of the place of the arbitration provide that awards may be set aside if there are fundamental defects in the proceedings. Such defects include the absence or nullity of the arbitration agreement, the fact that the subject matter of the dispute is not capable of settlement by arbitration, and serious infringements of procedural rules. More detailed information on this matter may be found, for example, in Article V of the New York Convention, Article IX of the 1961 Geneva Convention, national arbitration laws (e.g. Articles 1059 and 1061 ZPO, Articles 190 and 194 PILA, Articles 1716-1721 JC, and Articles 34-36 of the UNCITRAL Model Law), and scholarly literature.

At an international level, a particular problem may be posed by Article V(2)(b) of the New York Convention and corresponding provisions in national laws. These provisions allow an award to be refused enforcement or to be set aside if 'public policy' has been violated. The notion of 'public policy' refers to compulsory provisions which have to be respected on account of their overriding legislative importance. It is in certain cases interpreted broadly by national courts (see previous discussion of Article 21 of the Rules).

Since in most countries only serious procedural 'defects' may be cause for setting aside an award or refusing its enforcement, it is understandable that the same principle applies to arbitration proceedings as is found, for instance, in German procedural law, namely that it is forbidden to waive forms of recourse in advance. The Rules take account of this principle insofar as the waiver concerning forms of recourse, to which the parties agree by incorporating the Rules in their arbitration agreement, concerns only those forms of recourse which they may validly waive.

The parties' duty to carry out the award without delay is notably aimed at making them mindful of their obligations. It also forms part of their arbitration agreement, which incorporates the Rules by reference. It is therefore a contractual obligation which, if disrespected, may in theory be sanctioned through compensation for harm caused.

In some countries, however, including Belgium (Article 1718 JC), Switzerland (Article 192(1) PILA), Sweden (Article 51 of the Swedish Arbitration Act) and Tunisia (Article 78-6 of the Tunisian Arbitration Act), arbitration law gives parties the possibility of excluding actions to set aside the award at the place of the arbitration, provided none of them is established or habitually resident or has a branch in the country concerned. In France, the parties to an international arbitration may waive their right to bring an action to set aside an arbitral award, even if they are established or resident in France (Article 1522 NCPC). In such cases, the parties may exclude such actions when they enter into their arbitration agreement or at any time prior to the closing of the proceedings.

6. Correction and Interpretation of Awards; Remission of Awards (Art. 35)

Article 35 reads:

> '**Correction and Interpretation of the Award: Remission of Awards**
>
> 1. On its own initiative, the arbitral tribunal may correct a clerical, computational or typographical error, or any errors of similar nature contained in an award, provided such correction is submitted for approval to the Court within 30 days of the date of such award.
>
> 2. Any application of a party for the correction of an error of the kind referred to in Article 35(1), or for the interpretation of an award, must be made to the Secretariat within 30 days of the receipt of the award by such party, in a number of copies as stated in Article 3(1). After transmittal of the application to the arbitral tribunal, the latter shall grant the other party a short time, normally not exceeding 30 days, from the receipt of the application by that party, to submit any comments thereon. The arbitral tribunal shall submit its decision on the application in draft form to the Court not later than 30 days following the expiration of the time limit for the receipt of any comments from the other party or within such other period as the Court may decide.
>
> 3. A decision to correct or to interpret the award shall take the form of an addendum and shall constitute part of the award. The provisions of Articles 31, 33 and 34 shall apply mutatis mutandis.
>
> 4. Where a court remits an award to the arbitral tribunal, the provisions of Articles 31, 33, 34 and this Article 35 shall apply mutatis mutandis to any addendum or award made pursuant to the terms of such remission. The Court may take any steps as may be necessary to enable the arbitral tribunal to comply with the terms of such remission and may fix an advance to cover any additional fees and expenses of the arbitral tribunal and any additional ICC administrative expenses.'

a) General Remarks

The task of the arbitral tribunal ceases when it renders its final award. From that moment it is usually '*functus officio*', that is to say divested of its powers, unless the parties or the '*lex arbitri*' have provided otherwise. It may happen that the parties disagree on the terms of the decision, which may contain typographical or computational errors, or because the operative part of the award or the grounds upon which it is based are not clear, or so they claim. The Court's scrutiny of the draft arbitral award (Article 33) is intended to avoid that any such typographical or computational errors or errors of similar nature are contained in the award. If such errors are nevertheless found after the award has been notified to the parties, the question therefore arises as to whether the parties may turn again to the same arbitral tribunal or whether new proceedings must be commenced.

The ICC Rules provide in Article 35 a procedure and time limits for the correction and interpretation of awards, as it would lead to unacceptable uncertainty to allow applications for correction or interpretation to be made at any time after the award has been notified.

Besides, it is essential to have rules laying down the procedure to be followed, so as to make it clear to the parties whether they should file their application with the ICC or with the arbitral tribunal. The provisions contained in the Rules correspond in principle to those found in the UNCITRAL Model Law (Article 33), the UNCITRAL Arbitration Rules (Articles 37 and 38), and ZPO (Article 1058) (see also Article 1715 JC and Article 1485 and 1506 NCPC). In Switzerland, the PILA does not contain any rules on the subject, but the Swiss Federal Court has held recently that an arbitral tribunal has jurisdiction to interpret its award and correct an oversight.

The provisions on correction and interpretation of an award apply to all sorts of arbitral awards, including interim awards, partial awards, final awards and also awards by consent, in accordance with the broad definition of 'award' in Article 2 of the Rules.

As an 'addendum' correcting or interpreting an award constitutes a part of the award (Article 35(3)), the 'addendum' may also be the subject of an application for correction or interpretation by a party or of a correction at the initiative of the arbitral tribunal. If the application for a correction or interpretation of the award submitted by a party is rejected and no order is made on costs, the arbitral tribunal's decision will be called 'decision'. Such 'decision' is not considered by the Court to constitute a part of the award. However, the provisions of Article 31 (Making of the Award), Article 33 (Scrutiny of the Award by the Court) and Article 34 (Notification, Deposit and Enforceability of the Award) apply both to the 'addendum' and to the 'decision' (see J. Fry, S. Greenberg and F. Mazza, *The Secretariat's Guide to ICC Arbitration,* ICC Publication No. 729 E, Paris, 2012, p. 354).

In 2011, 45 addenda correcting and/or interpreting an award were issued and 33 decisions rejecting applications for the correction and/or interpretation of an award (see '2011 Statistical Report' published in *ICC International Court of Arbitration Bulletin*, Paris, Vol. 23/Nr. 1 – 2012, p. 15). In 2011, 4 addenda had been rendered by arbitral tribunals on their own initiative to correct their award (see J. Fry, S. Greenberg and F. Mazza, *The Secretariat's Guide to ICC Arbitration,* ICC Publication No. 729 E, Paris, 2012, p. 348)

In 2010, 34 addenda correcting and/or interpreting an award were issued and 23 decisions rejecting applications for the correction and/or interpretation of an award (see '2010 Statistical Report' published in *ICC International Court of Arbitration Bulletin,* Paris, Vol. 22/Nr. 1 – 2011, p. 15). In 2010, 6 addenda had been rendered by arbitral tribunals on their own initiative to correct their award (see J. Fry, S. Greenberg and F. Mazza, *The Secretariat's Guide to ICC Arbitration,* ICC Publication No. 729 E, Paris, 2012, p. 348)

In 2009, 28 addenda correcting and/or interpreting an award were issued and 31 decisions rejecting applications for the correction and/or interpretation of an award (see '2009 Statistical Report' published in *ICC International Court of Arbitration Bulletin*, Paris, Vol. 21/Nr. 1 – 2010, p. 14). In 2009, 2 addenda had been rendered by arbitral tribunals on their own initiative to correct their award (see J. Fry, S. Greenberg and F. Mazza, *The Secretariat's Guide to ICC Arbitration,* ICC Publication No. 729 E, Paris, 2012, p. 348)

Applications for interpretation (as opposed to correction) of an award are rarely accepted. Many applications for interpretation amount to attempted appeals aimed at altering an award, raising an additional issue or attempting to have the arbitral tribunal reconsider its decision or the evidence (see J. Fry, S. Greenberg and F. Mazza, *The Secretariat's Guide to ICC Arbitration,* ICC Publication No. 729 E, Paris, 2012, p. 351).

b) Formal Conditions

Applications based on Article 35 of the Rules must be sent to the Secretariat by the parties within thirty days following the notification of the award, in as many copies as required under Article 3(1) of the Rules. In the event of failure to comply with the latter obligation, is there any cure? Although this would be desirable, the question remains open, as does that of whether, if a party is not responsible for overrunning the time limit (as, for instance, in a case of *force majeure*), the time limit may be reset. This would be desirable in the event of *force majeure*, but here too it is not possible to affirm with any certainty that the Court would allow this.

An application for correction or interpretation also has financial implications. According to Article 2(10) of Appendix III to the Rules, the Court may fix an advance to cover additional fees and expenses of the arbitral tribunal and additional ICC administrative expenses and make the transmission of the application to the arbitral tribunal subject to prior payment of the entire advance in cash.

A note from the Secretariat on the correction and interpretation of arbitral awards was published in the ICC International Court of Arbitration Bulletin (Vol. 10/No. 2 – Fall 1999). It describes the circumstances in which applications for the correction and interpretation of awards may be made. This note is reproduced in Appendix 12 below. Moreover, the Secretariat has established a 'Checklist on Correction and Interpretation of Awards' (See Appendix 13 below) which is intended to provide arbitrators acting under the ICC Rules of Arbitration with additional guidance.

In all cases, the arbitral tribunal must first ensure that mandatory rules of law at the place of arbitration do not exclude the correction or interpretation of an award by the arbitral tribunal.

c) Correction of the Award

Although the ICC Court's scrutiny of draft awards is in principle designed to avoid the need for correction once the award has been rendered, there are nevertheless times when an award contains typographical or computational errors or other mistakes that must be corrected before the award can be carried out.

The initiative may be taken by the parties or the arbitral tribunal. Even without being asked, the arbitral tribunal may correct any errors it may find in its award, provided it does so within 30 days following the date of the award (not 30 days following the date of notification – Article 35(1)).

The correction may also be requested by one of the parties, within 30 days from the date on which the party requesting the correction was notified of the award (Article 35(2)). This time limit is calculated in accordance with Article 3 of the Rules. The application must be sent to the Secretariat, which then forwards it to the arbitral tribunal. If the 30-day time limit has expired, the application is inadmissible.

Once it has received the application for correction and before making a decision, the arbitral tribunal begins by inviting the other party to submit its comments. The maximum time allowed for this is 30 days.

Following the expiration of the time limit for the submission of the other party's comments, the arbitral tribunal then has a further period of 30 days, which may be renewed by the Court, to rule on the application. If the arbitral tribunal decides that the award should be corrected, it issues an 'addendum' to the award. Like all awards, the 'addendum' must be scrutinized by the Court in accordance with Article 33 of the Rules. Not until the 'addendum' has been approved by the Court does it become an integral part of the award and is notified to the parties by the Secretariat.

An application for the correction of an award cannot lead to a change in the arbitral tribunal's decision. It may only concern the correction of typographical or computational errors. A correction could, for instance, be occasioned by the fact that a party was ordered to pay 100 000 dollars in the operative part of the award, whereas this figure appears as 1 000 000 dollars in the presentation of the grounds leading to the decision. Like an award, an addendum may be rendered by a majority of the members of the arbitral tribunal or by the president alone, pursuant to Article 31(1) of the Rules. A majority decision is possible even when the award concerned was rendered unanimously.

d) Interpretation of the Award

The Rules also allow for the interpretation of an award. Although the procedure is basically the same as for corrections, a distinction should be made between the interpretation and the correction of an award. The essential difference lies in the fact that the arbitral tribunal cannot interpret an award unless requested to do so by the parties (Article 35(2)).

The Rules make the interpretation of awards subject to very strict conditions, so as to prevent parties from resisting the enforcement of an award by opening a discussion on its interpretation. The arbitral tribunal may of course dismiss the application for interpretation if it considers that the award is clear and does not need interpreting. It will naturally do so if it comes to the conclusion that the application is an improper attempt to reopen discussions. The arbitral tribunal cannot change its decision once it has ruled on the dispute, which means that an application for interpretation cannot be intended to alter the decision.

Once the time limit given to the other party to submit its comments has expired, the arbitral tribunal has 30 days in which to rule on the application for interpretation. However, this time limit may be extended by the Court. If the arbitral tribunal finds that the award needs to be interpreted, it will do so in an 'addendum' to the award. As in the case of corrections, the arbitral tribunal must submit its draft 'addendum' to the Court for scrutiny and approval (Article 33 of the Rules). Only then will it become an integral part of the award.

Under Article 31(1) of the Rules, an 'addendum' interpreting an award need not necessarily be decided by all members of the arbitral tribunal, even if the award involved was rendered unanimously.

e) Dismissal of an Application under Article 35 of the Rules

If an Article 35 application has been made too late and is therefore inadmissible, if there are mandatory rules in the '*lex arbitri*' prohibiting the correction or interpretation of an award, or if the application is unjustified, the arbitral tribunal will dismiss the application by way of a 'decision', stating its reasons. The parties are notified of the decision by the Secretariat.

f) Remission of an Award (Article 35(4))

Under some arbitration laws, where setting aside proceedings were initiated against an arbitral award before a state court, the state court may give an opportunity to the arbitral tribunal to resume the arbitration proceedings or to take such other action as in the opinion of the arbitral tribunal will eliminate the grounds for the setting aside of the award. Such possibility is foreseen in the arbitration law in Belgium (Article 1717(6) JC) and in Germany (Article 1059(4) ZPO) in accordance with the UNCITRAL Model Law (Article 34(4)), but is also permitted by Courts in Switzerland.

Article 35(4) is a new provision inserted in the 2012 Rules so as to be able to handle remission procedures concerning arbitral awards rendered in ICC arbitrations. If an award is remitted by a state court to the arbitral tribunal, the provisions of Article 31 (Making of the Award), Article 33 (Scrutiny of the Award by the Court) and Article 34 (Notification, Deposit and Enforceability of the Award) as well as Article 35 (Correction and Interpretation of the Award) are applicable. The Court may take any steps as may be necessary to enable the arbitral tribunal to comply with the terms of such remission and may fix an advance to cover any additional fees and expenses of the arbitral tribunal and any additional ICC administrative expenses.

As remissions are rare and can vary in scope, the ICC Court and its Secretariat have no fixed practices in dealing with them (see J. Fry, S. Greenberg and F. Mazza, *The Secretariat's Guide to ICC Arbitration*, ICC Publication No. 729 E, Paris, 2012, p. 359).

H. COSTS AND ADVANCES

1. Advance to Cover the Costs of the Arbitration (Art. 36)

Article 36 of the Rules reads:

> 'Advance to Cover the Costs of the Arbitration
>
> 1. After receipt of the Request, the Secretary General may request the claimant to pay a provisional advance in an amount intended to cover the costs of the arbitration until the Terms of Reference have been drawn up. Any provisional advance paid will be considered as a partial payment by the claimant of any advance on costs fixed by the Court pursuant to this Article 36.
>
> 2. As soon as practicable, the Court shall fix the advance on costs in an amount likely to cover the fees and expenses of the arbitrators and the ICC administrative costs for the claims which have been referred to it by the parties, unless any claims are made under Article 7 or 8 in which case Article 36(4) shall apply. The advance on costs fixed by the Court pursuant to this Article 35(2) shall be payable in equal shares by the claimant and the respondent.
>
> 3. Where counterclaims are submitted by the respondent pursuant to Article 5 or otherwise, the Court may fix separate advances on costs for the claims and the counterclaims. When the Court has fixed separate advance on costs, each of the parties shall pay the advance on costs corresponding to its claims.
>
> 4. Where claims are made under Article 7 or 8, the Court shall fix one or more advances on costs that shall be payable by the parties as decided by the Court. Where the Court has previously fixed any advance on costs pursuant

to this Article 36, any such advance shall be replaced by the advance(s) fixed pursuant to this Article 36(4), and the amount of any advance previously paid by any party will be considered as a partial payment by such party of its share of the advance(s) on costs as fixed by the Court pursuant to Article 36(4).

5. This amount of any advance on costs fixed by the Court pursuant to Article 36 may be subject to readjustment at any time during the arbitration. In all cases, any party shall be free to pay any other party's share of any advance on costs should such other party fail to pay its share.

6. When a request for an advance on costs has not been complied with, and after consultation with the arbitral tribunal, the Secretary General may direct the arbitral tribunal to suspend its work and set a time limit, which must be not less than 15 days, on the expiry of which the relevant claims shall be considered as withdrawn. Should the party in question wish to object to this measure, it must make a request within the aforementioned period for the matter to be decided by the Court. Such party shall not be prevented, on the ground of such withdrawal, from reintroducing the same claims at a later date in another proceeding.

7. If one of the parties claims a right to set-off with regard to any claim, such set-off shall be taken into account in determining the advance to cover the costs of the arbitration in the same way as a separate claim insofar as it may require the arbitral tribunal to consider additional matters.'

Article 1 of Appendix III to the Rules reads:

'Advance on Costs

1. Each request to commence an arbitration pursuant to the Rules must be accompanied by an advance payment of US$ 3,000. Such payment is non-refundable and shall be credited to the claimant's portion of the advance on costs.

2. The provisional advance fixed by the Secretary General according to Article 36(1) of the Rules shall normally not exceed the amount obtained by adding together the ICC administrative expenses, the minimum of the fees (as set out in the scale hereinafter) based upon the amount of the claim and the expected reimbursable expenses of the arbitral tribunal incurred with respect to the drafting of the Terms of Reference. If such amount is not quantified, the provisional advance shall be fixed at the discretion of the Secretary General. Payment by the claimant shall be credited to its share of the advance on costs fixed by the Court.

3. In general, after the Terms of Reference have been signed or approved by the Court and the provisional timetable has been established, the arbitral tribunal shall, in accordance with Article 36(6) of the Rules, proceed only with respect to those claims or counterclaims in regard to which the whole of the advance on costs has been paid.

4. The advance on costs fixed by the Court according to Article 36(2) or 36(4) of the Rules comprises the fees of the arbitrator or arbitrators (hereinafter referred to as 'arbitrator'), any arbitration-related expenses of the arbitrator and the ICC administrative expenses.

5. Each party shall pay its share of the total advance on costs in cash. However, if a party's share of the advance on costs is greater than US$ 500,000 (the "Threshold Amount"), such party may post a bank guarantee for any amount above the Threshold amount. The Court may modify the Threshold Amount at any time at its discretion.

6. The Court may authorize the payment of advances on costs, or any party's share thereof, in instalments, subject to such conditions as the Court thinks fit, including the payment of additional ICC administrative expenses.

7. A party that has already paid in full its share of the advance on costs fixed by the Court may, in accordance with Article 36(5) of the Rules, pay the unpaid portion of the advance owed by the defaulting party by posting a bank guarantee.

8. When the Court has fixed separate advances on costs pursuant to Article 36(3) of the Rules, the Secretariat shall invite each party to pay the amount of the advance corresponding to its respective claim(s).

9. When, as a result of the fixing of separate advances on costs, the separate advance fixed for the claim of either party exceeds one half of such global advance as was previously fixed (in respect of the same claims and counterclaims that are the subject of separate advances), a bank guarantee may be posted to cover any such excess amount. In the event that the amount of the separate advance is subsequently increased, at least one half of the increase shall be paid in cash.

10. The Secretariat shall establish the terms governing all bank guarantees which the parties may post pursuant to the above provisions.

11. As provided in Article 36(5) of the Rules, the advance on costs may be subject to readjustment at any time during the arbitration, in particular to take into account fluctuations in the amount in dispute, changes in the amount of the estimated expenses of the arbitrator, or the evolving difficulty or complexity of arbitration proceedings.

12. Before any expertise ordered by the arbitral tribunal can be commenced, the parties, or one of them, shall pay an advance on costs fixed by the arbitral tribunal sufficient to cover the expected fees and expenses of the expert as determined by the arbitral tribunal. The arbitral tribunal shall be responsible for ensuring the payment by the parties of such fees and expenses.

13. The amounts paid as advances on costs do not yield interest for the parties or the arbitrator.'

a) General Remarks

It is a general principle in arbitration that prior payment is needed before the arbitration can proceed. This means that at the various stages of the proceedings, the parties must pay the advances on costs fixed so as to cover the costs of the arbitration until its completion. There is no reason to object to this principle, which is not limited to the ICC Rules. The arbitration institution and the arbitrators cannot be expected to wait until the award has been rendered before their expenses and fees are paid, especially in an international context where the collection of such expenses and fees is much more difficult and costly than in purely domestic matters. Besides, the losing party will see little point in paying procedural costs and the winning party will not always be prepared to cover the costs once it has managed to have the award carried out.

This principle means that when a party fails to pay its share of the advance on the costs of the arbitration, the proceedings are suspended or sometimes even terminated, unless the outstanding amount is paid by the other party, by way of substitution, in addition to its own share.

The advance on costs is intended to cover the administrative expenses of the ICC International Court of Arbitration and the fees and expenses of the arbitrators. It is calculated on the basis of the sum in dispute using the financial scales referred to in the Rules. This method of calculation allows the parties and the arbitrators to have an idea of the Court's administrative expenses and the anticipated arbitrators' fees (which, except in special cases, vary between a minimum and a maximum,) at the very outset of the proceedings. The parties should bear in mind that the calculation of the advance is directly affected by the amount in dispute: the greater this amount, the greater the advance. They should therefore as far as possible avoid making excessive or frivolous claims.

b) Provisional Advance on Costs (Article 36(1))

Article 36(1) of the Rules, which should be read in conjunction with Article 1(2) of Appendix III to the Rules, was introduced for the first time in the 1998 version of the Rules in order to accelerate proceedings by allowing the file to be transmitted to the arbitral tribunal sooner than was previously possible. Under this provision, the claimant may have its request for arbitration transmitted to the arbitral tribunal more quickly by paying a provisional advance on costs fixed by the Secretary General. The amount of this provisional advance is based on the claim and is intended to cover the costs expected to be incurred until the Terms of Reference are drawn up. As a rule, the Secretary General fixes the amount of this provisional advance when the request for arbitration is notified to the respondent.

In order not to overburden the claimant, who is responsible for paying this advance, the amount is usually kept to a minimum. Article 1(2) of Appendix III to the Rules states that this advance should normally not exceed the sum of the following amounts: (i) the ICC administrative expenses, (ii) the minimum arbitrator's fees based on the amount in dispute using the scale in Article 4 of Appendix III to the Rules, and (iii) the reimbursable expenses likely to be incurred by the arbitral tribunal in connection with drawing up the Terms of Reference. If the amount in dispute is not quantified, the provisional advance on costs will be fixed at the discretion of the Secretary General.

As a general rule, when the amount in dispute is quantified, the Secretary General adds half of the administrative expenses to half of the minimum arbitrator's fees (multiplied by three when there are three arbitrators) using the relevant scales, and adds the expected expenses of the arbitral tribunal at the commencement of the proceedings. If the amount in dispute is not quantified, the Secretary General will fix the provisional advance at his or her discretion thereby taking into account the number of arbitrators to be appointed. Only the amount in dispute stated in the request for arbitration will be used for fixing the provisional advance. No consideration can be given to possible counterclaims, given that the provisional advance is fixed immediately after the request for arbitration has been received.

The amount fixed by the Secretary General must be paid by the claimant as quickly as possible, so as to allow the file to be transmitted to the arbitral tribunal as soon as it has been constituted. Usually, the claimant is asked to pay the provisional advance on costs within 30 days. If the claimant fails to pay the provisional advance on costs, the Secretariat will not transmit the file to the arbitral tribunal in accordance with Article 16.

The provisional advance on costs is to be distinguished from the filing fee which a claimant must pay when it submits a request for arbitration (Article 4(4) of the Rules and Article 1(1) of Appendix III to the Rules) or when it files a request for joinder (Article 7(3) of the Rules). The filing fee is a fixed amount, which currently amounts to US$ 3 000 (Article 1(1) of Appendix III to the Rules). The filing fee paid by the claimant is credited to its part of the provisional advance on costs.

The provisional advance on costs fixed by the Secretary General pursuant to Article 36(1) is also to be distinguished from the 'definitive' advance on costs which is fixed by the Court pursuant to Article 36(2) or Article 36(4) to cover the costs of the arbitration until the end of the proceedings. According to Article 36(2) of the Rules, such advance, which is fixed 'as soon as practicable', is payable in equal shares by the parties. It should be noted that the fixing of the advance on costs and its payability are not dependent on payment by the claimant of the provisional advance. This will simply be deducted from the claimant's share of the 'definitive' advance.

c) Advance on Costs (Article 36(2))

(1) When is it Fixed?

Article 36(2) of the Rules states that the advance on costs should be fixed 'as soon as practicable', but does not specify exactly when. In practice, the Secretariat submits the case to the ICC International Court of Arbitration for the advance to be fixed as soon as it has the necessary information. Advances on costs are usually fixed by a committee of the Court when the Secretariat initially submits the case, referred to at that stage as a 'new case'. This generally occurs after the respondent has filed an answer to the claim, or after it has presented its comments on the constitution of the arbitral tribunal when an extension of the 30-day time limit for filing an answer is requested, or after the 30-day time limit when the respondent does not react at all. When calculating the advance, the Secretariat will take into account any counterclaim that may have been made at this point.

(2) How is it Fixed?

The advance on costs is fixed by the ICC International Court of Arbitration in accordance with Article 1(4) of Appendix III to the Rules. It comprises the fees of the arbitrator(s), the arbitral tribunal's expenses and the ICC administrative expenses and is intended to cover all of these fees and expenses until the completion of the proceedings. This advance does not cover the costs relating to any expertise proceedings. Under Article 1(12) of Appendix III to the Rules, expertise costs are covered by a separate advance, fixed and administered by the arbitral tribunal itself or by the Secretariat acting on the arbitral tribunal's instructions.

In practice, the advance on costs is calculated using the scales set forth in Appendix III to the Rules. New scales became effective as of 1 January 2012. Article 4(1) of Appendix III to the Rules states that the new scales will be applied to all arbitrations commenced on or after 1 July 2012, irrespective of which version of the ICC Rules of Arbitration applies. A set amount is added to cover the expected expenses of the arbitral tribunal (such as travel to the place of the arbitration or elsewhere to hear the parties or witnesses, room hire for the estimated number of hearings, etc.).

The ICC Court provides at its website a cost calculator allowing the parties to have in advance an estimate of the amount of the advance on costs that shall be fixed on the basis of their claims. The parties merely need to insert the amount of their claims and to indicate whether the arbitral tribunal shall be composed of one or three arbitrators, whereupon the calculator immediately states the amount of the ICC administrative expenses, the minimum, the maximum and the average fees for the arbitrators calculated on the basis of the amount in dispute and the aggregate sum of the ICC administrative expenses and of the average fees for the arbitrator(s). This aggregate sum does not include an amount for the expenses of the arbitrators, as these expenses may vary from one arbitration to another in the light of travel requirements of the arbitrators, the taking of evidence, the appointment of experts and other circumstances that may increase the expenses. In any event, the ICC costs calculator is a useful tool that allows every party prior to an arbitration to check what the expected costs of the arbitration proceedings may be.

The amount in dispute used for the application of the scales is based on the sum of the parties' quantified claims, including any counterclaims. Only the principal claims are taken into account, not the associated claims for interest (whether contractual or statutory) or claims for reimbursement of costs, except when the claim for payment of interest is itself the subject of the request for arbitration. It will be noted that the ICC cost scales use the US dollar as the reference currency. Any claims made in another currency are converted into US dollars using the official rate in force on the date when the request for arbitration is received by the Secretariat of the Court. This rate remains applicable throughout the entire proceedings, even if the amount in dispute changes during this time.

If the parties' claims are not quantified or do not concern the payment of a sum of money, the ICC International Court of Arbitration will fix the ICC administrative expenses and the arbitrators' fees at its discretion, as permitted by Article 2(1) and Article 2(5) of Appendix III to the Rules. If the amount in dispute is known, the arbitrators' fees lie between the minimum and the maximum as calculated according to the applicable scale. As it is difficult to estimate at the beginning of the proceedings the amount of the arbitrators' fees that will be fixed upon termination of the proceedings, it is the Court's practice, when fixing the advance on costs, to take a figure midway between the maximum and the minimum. However, it is under no obligation to do so and may fix the fees above or below that figure when it considers this to be appropriate.

The following example illustrates the practice described above:

Amount claimed by claimant:	US$ 500 000
Amount claimed by respondent:	US$ 500 000
Total amount in dispute:	US$ 1 000 000
Arbitral tribunal:	3 arbitrators (Swiss chair; French and Belgian co-arbitrators, like the parties, whose offices are in their respective countries of origin)
Place of the arbitration:	Geneva, Switzerland

On the basis of the tables for calculating fees and administrative expenses, the advance on costs will be as follows:

ICC administrative expenses:		US$ 21 715
Arbitrators' fees:		
minimum:	US$ 14 627	
maximum:	US$ 64 130	
average:	US$ 39 378 × 3	US$ 118 135
Arbitrators' expected expenses		US$ 10 150
Advance on costs:		US$ 150 000

(3) Reconsideration of the Advance on Costs (Art. 36(5)).

As provided in Article 36(5) of the Rules, the advance on costs may be readjusted at any moment during the proceedings, for instance so as to take into account fluctuations in the amount in dispute, changes in the amount of the arbitral tribunal's expenses, or the evolving difficulty or complexity of the arbitration (Article 1(11) of Appendix III to the Rules).

In practice, it is rare for the advance on costs to be reduced, except where the parties considerably lower the amount in dispute. The amount of the advance is quite often increased after the Terms of Reference and the procedural timetable have been drawn up and when they show the amount in dispute to have risen considerably, or when the dispute turns out to be more difficult and complex than was assumed at the outset, requiring more work from the arbitral tribunal.

On the other hand, the ICC International Court of Arbitration is disinclined to increase the amount of the advance when the arbitration has reached a very advanced stage, namely when the award is about to be rendered. The reason for this is to protect the arbitrators against parties that might attempt to block the proceedings in their final stages upon realizing that they are likely to lose the case. Therefore, arbitrators themselves should always immediately inform the ICC of any changes relating to the amount in dispute or the proceedings (greater complexity of the case, the arbitrators' progress in the proceedings, the costs already incurred), so as to make it possible for the Secretariat to ask the Court in good time to reconsider the amount of the advance, if necessary.

Before asking the Court to consider increasing the advance on costs, the Secretariat will usually inform the parties of its intention and allow them to make any comments, although it is not obliged to do so under the Rules. In any event, the Court decides at its own discretion whether an increase in the advance is appropriate in the circumstances. If so, it will be up to the Court to determine the new amount.

d) Obligation to Pay the Advance on Costs in Equal Shares (Art. 36(2))

Article 36(2) of the Rules lays down the principle according to which advances on costs fixed by the ICC International Court of Arbitration are payable in equal shares by the claimant and the respondent. The provisional advance already paid by the claimant is deducted from its share pursuant to Article 36(1). This obligation in no way predetermines the arbitral tribunal's decision as to how the costs of the arbitration will be borne in the final analysis when it renders its final award. It is possible that the winning party will ask to be reimbursed by the other party for all or part of the sums paid as an advance on costs.

According to Article 1(5) of Appendix III to the Rules, each party must pay its share of the advance in cash. ICC indicates the bank account into which it is to be paid. However, where one party's share of the advance exceeds the amount of US$ 500 00 (the 'Threshold Amount'), that party may pay the additional amount in the form of a bank guarantee, as described below (Article 1(5) of Appendix III to the Rules).

As a general rule, the Secretariat asks the parties to pay their respective shares of the advance on costs usually within 30 or, at the very most, 60 days of being notified of the Court's decision. This time limit corresponds to the period within which the Terms of Reference must be drawn up according to Article 23(2) of the Rules. A time limit of 60 days is usually allowed if the claimant has paid the provisional advance in full. If the claimant has not paid the provisional advance when the Court fixes the advance on costs, a time limit of 30 days is usually set for payment of the advance, so as not to delay transmission of the file to the arbitral tribunal. The Secretariat is authorized to extend this time limit upon request, whenever justified.

It should be noted that the parties are not entitled to any interest on the sums they pay as an advance on costs, even if some or all of this money remains unused until the end of the proceedings. This well-established practice of the Court is confirmed in the 2012 Rules in Article 1(13) of Appendix III to the Rules. In the course of the proceedings, the advance on costs paid by the parties may be used by the Secretariat to reimburse the arbitrators for their expenses or to pay advances on fees, if the arbitrators so request. It should be pointed out that without the interest earned on such sums ICC would be obliged to increase its administrative expenses by an equivalent amount to cover the actual operating costs of the Court and its Secretariat. It should also be borne in mind that the administrative expenses do not, in every case, cover the costs actually incurred by the Court and its Secretariat.

e) Separate Advances (Article 36(3))

As mentioned above, the parties have a duty to pay the advance on costs in equal shares. It is generally assumed that each party will fulfill its obligation. However, as an exception to this general rule, the ICC International Court of Arbitration may fix separate advances, notably when there is a counterclaim or a claim for set-off in addition to the principal claim. In case the Court decides to fix separate advances on costs for the principal claim and for the counterclaim, the separate advances must be paid separately in full by the parties concerned (Article 36(3) of the Rules and Article 1(8) of Appendix III to the Rules).

Separate advances are fixed by the ICC Court when (i) the claimant and the respondent have each asserted monetary claims against each other and (ii) when the global advance on costs remains unpaid by one or all of the parties, as is the case when one of them fails to pay its share of the global advance fixed by the Court and the other refuses to pay in its place.

That each party should be able to ask for separate advances to be fixed arises from the fact that a party should not be obliged to pay an advance that – albeit in part – has been fixed on the basis of claims directed against it. The aim here is above all to prevent dilatory tactics, especially by a respondent that asserts exorbitant or frivolous claims aimed at making it onerous or even impossible for the claimant to pay its share of the advance or to pay in place of the respondent in default with paying its share, thereby causing the proceedings to come to a standstill or even an end.

When fixing separate advances, the Court follows the procedure described above and applies the scales of administrative expenses and arbitrators' fees separately to the principal claims and the counterclaims or set-off claims. Given that the percentages in these scales decrease as the amount in dispute rises, it is not usually in a party's interest to ask for separate advances to be fixed, because the aggregate sum of these separate advances will always be higher than a global advance covering all the claims involved. In the example given above, the parties each made claims amounting to US$ 500 000 and the global advance was fixed at US$ 150 000, payable by the parties in equal shares, i.e. US$ 75 000 each. If separate advances were fixed, each party would have to pay an advance of US$ 105 000 using the same cost scales and dividing the expected expenses of the arbitral tribunal between the two parties (i.e. approximately US$ 5 000 each), as shown below.

On the basis of the tables for calculating fees and administrative expenses, the advance on costs when calculated separately for the parties' respective claims will be as follows:

Amount claimed by claimant:	US$ 500 000	
Amount claimed by respondent:	US$ 500 000	
ICC administrative expenses:		US$ 14 165
Arbitrators' fees:		
minimum:	US$ 9 857	
maximum:	US$ 43 990	
average:	US$ 26 923 × 3	US$ 80 770
Arbitrators' expected expenses:		US$ 10 065
Separate advance on costs for claimant:		US$ 105 000
Separate advance on costs for respondent:		US$ 105 000
Sum of the separate advances on costs:		US$ 210 000

The only situation in which it might be to a party's advantage to have separate advances on costs fixed is when there is a substantial difference between the amount of the principal claim and that of the counterclaim. In this case, the party with the smaller claims is likely to have to pay less than what would be its share of the global advance.

The Court will not fix separate advances on costs without a request from a party. Moreover, if a party requests for separate advances on costs, the Secretariat will first inform the parties of the financial consequences thereof.

If the Court fixes separate advances on costs, this does not mean that the ICC will receive a higher amount of administrative expenses and that the arbitrator's will receive a higher amount of fees than in a case with one global advance on costs, as the ICC Court will, at the end, fix the ICC administrative expenses and the arbitrators' fees on the basis of the scale for the aggregate amount of the claims handled in the arbitration (see J. Fry, S. Greenberg and F. Mazza, *The Secretariat's Guide to ICC Arbitration*, ICC Publication No. 729 E, Paris, 2012, p. 375-376).

f) Advance on Costs in Case of Joinder of a Party and in Multiparty Arbitrations (Article 36(4))

Article 36(4) is a new provision in the 2012 Rules which was not yet contained in the 1998 Rules. It is added as a consequence of the new Article 7 allowing the joinder of a party to an arbitration and of Article 8 allowing claims in a multiparty arbitration to be made by any party against any other party. The new Article 36(4) gives the Court in such cases the possibility to deviate from the general principle laid down in Article 36(2) pursuant to which the advance on costs shall be payable in equal shares by the claimant and the respondent.

In arbitrations where claims are made under Article 7 or 8 of the Rules, the Court has the discretionary power: (i) to fix one or more advances on costs, and (ii) to decide about the apportionment of the payment of such advance(s) as it deems appropriate. In most cases the Court is likely to fix one advance on costs, as is set out in a Secretariat's 'Note on Article 36(4) of the 2012 ICC Rules of Arbitration' (see Appendix 5 below).

Where the Court apportions the advance on costs, it determines the amount that each party must pay towards the advance on costs. When doing so, the Court will ensure that a party shall only contribute towards the claim or claims in which it is involved. The amount payable by each party shall be proportionate to the value of those claims in relation to the total amount in dispute in the arbitration. The calculation of the apportionment of the shares of the parties in such multiparty situation or in case of joinder of an additional party is done in different steps as follows:

- (i) The Court will first calculate the advance on costs due in case all the claims are added up and in case one 'global advance' were to be fixed.
- (ii) Thereupon it calculates the advances due for each set of claims made by identical claiming parties against identical responding parties ('partial advances').
- (ii) It then adds up these 'partial advances' so as to calculate the 'total amount'.
- (iii) On the basis of this 'total amount' it calculates the percentage that each 'partial advance' forms as part of the total amount.
- (iv) These percentages are then applied to the amount calculated first as the 'global advance on costs' so to end up with the respective amounts payable by each party in relation to each set of claims.

Accordingly, the parties will not pay a higher amount as advance on costs in case an apportionment is decided pursuant to Article 36(4) (see Secretariat's 'Note on Article 36(4) of the 2012 ICC Rules of Arbitration', Appendix 5 below; see also J. Fry, S. Greenberg and F. Mazza, *The Secretariat's Guide to ICC Arbitration*, ICC Publication No. 729 E, Paris, 2012, p. 380-382).

In case the Court had first fixed a global advance and decides subsequently to apply Article 36(4), such advance shall be replaced by the new advance(s) fixed pursuant to Article 36(4) and the amount of any advance previously paid by any party will be considered as a partial payment by such party of its share of the advance(s) on costs as fixed by the Court pursuant to Article 36(4).

Unless the parties reach a different agreement, if the Court apportions the advance on costs, it will determine the apportionment as follows:

- (i) For each set of claims, the portion shall be payable fifty percent by the parties bringing said claims and fifty percent by the parties defending said claims.
- (ii) If there are multiple parties either bringing or defending each set of Claims, the co-claimants or co-respondents respectively will bear their fifty percent share equally.

Should a party fail to pay one or more of the amounts payable that form its share of the advance on costs, the Secretariat will invite the other parties involved in that set of claims to pay the outstanding amounts payable (see Secretariat's 'Note on Article 36(4) of the 2012 ICC Rules of Arbitration'; Appendix 5 below).

g) Non-Payment by a Party of its Share of the Advance on Costs (Art. 36(5))

If a party fails to pay its share of the global advance on costs, the other party is free to pay the whole of the advance according to Article 36(5) of the Rules. In other words, it substitutes for the party that has failed to comply with its obligation to pay. In most cases, it is the respondent that defaults on payment, leaving the claimant with the option of either paying the whole of the advance or posting a bank guarantee to cover the respondent's share of the advance. When the respondent has made a counterclaim or asked for its claims to be set off against those of the claimant, the latter may ask for separate advances to be fixed, as described above (Article 36(3)).

The Secretariat will only invite a party to substitute for another party if the latter party has failed to pay its share after several reminders.

If a party encounters difficulties to pay its share but nevertheless confirms that it is prepared to do so, the Court may authorize this party to pay the advance on costs, or a part thereof, in installments, subject to such conditions as the Court thinks fit, including the payment of additional ICC administrative expenses (Article 1(6) of Appendix III to the Rules).

Where a party fails to pay its share of the advance on costs and the other party has to substitute for it, the latter party may request a decision from the arbitral tribunal ordering the defaulting party to reimburse it. There are examples of ICC awards both accepting and rejecting such requests (see J. Fry, S. Greenberg and F. Mazza, *The Secretariat's Guide to ICC Arbitration*, ICC Publication No. 729 E, Paris, 2012, p. 385-386).

h) Consequences of Non-Payment of the Advances (Art. 36(6))

The Rules do not penalize a party for not paying its share of the advance, so long as the other party pays the whole of the advance or posts a bank guarantee, as described below. In particular, the defaulting party is in no way prevented from taking part in the proceedings or asserting its rights with respect to both form and substance.

There are however two situations in which the Rules provide for adverse effects: (i) where neither of the parties pays its share of the global advance, and (ii) where at least one party fails to pay its separate advance which was set following the failure of one of the parties to pay its share in the global advance. In such situations, once the time limit for payment has expired, the Secretariat will apply the procedure described in Article 36(6). This means that the arbitral tribunal will first suspend its proceedings, and the ICC International Court of Arbitration may then decide that the claims for which the advance has not been paid should be considered as withdrawn. This does not prevent the party that brought such claims from reintroducing them again later in different proceedings.

The effects of this provision vary according to the stage of the proceedings reached when it is applied. At the beginning of the proceedings, a failure to pay the provisional advance or to pay the global advance fixed by the Court or to pay the separate advances that may have been fixed by the Court will have as a consequence that the file is not transmitted to the arbitral tribunal. Later in the proceedings, when the arbitral tribunal has been constituted and separate advances have been fixed, if one of the

Figure 8. Advance on costs (i)

a) Filing fee

b) Provisional advance on costs

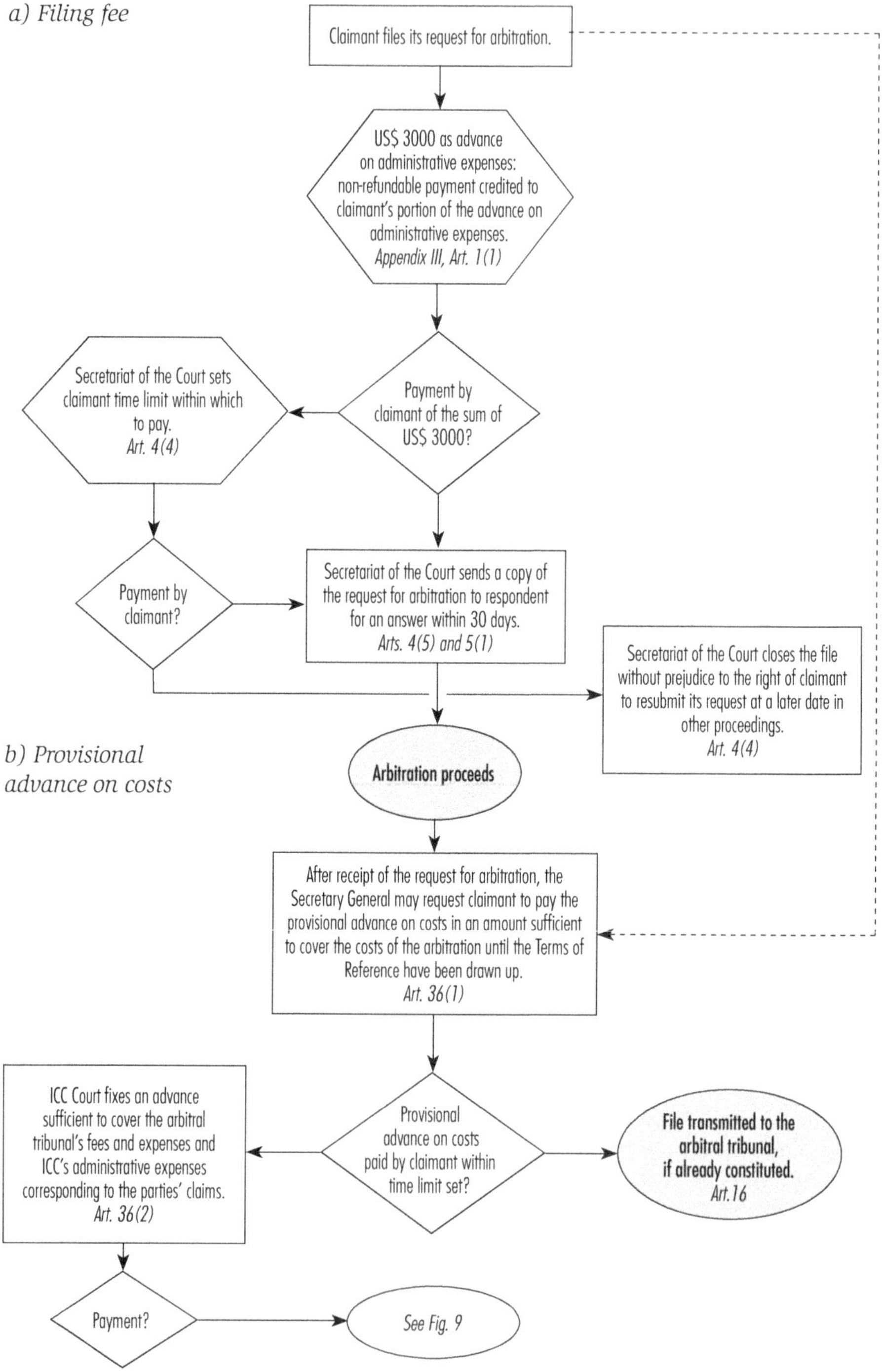

Figure 9. Advance on costs (ii)

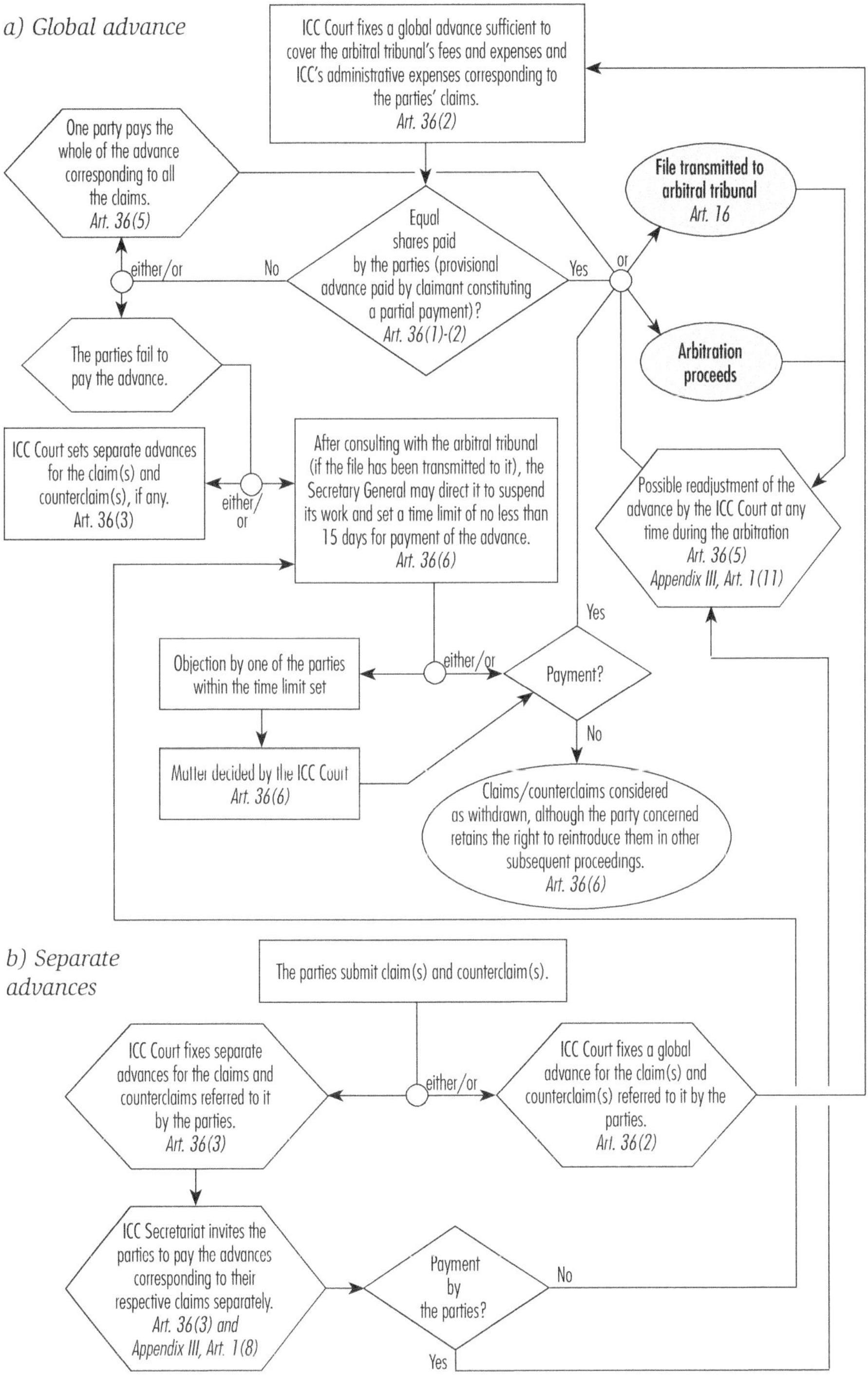

Figure 10. Advance on costs (iii)

Payment by bank guarantee

(a) In the event of a global advance

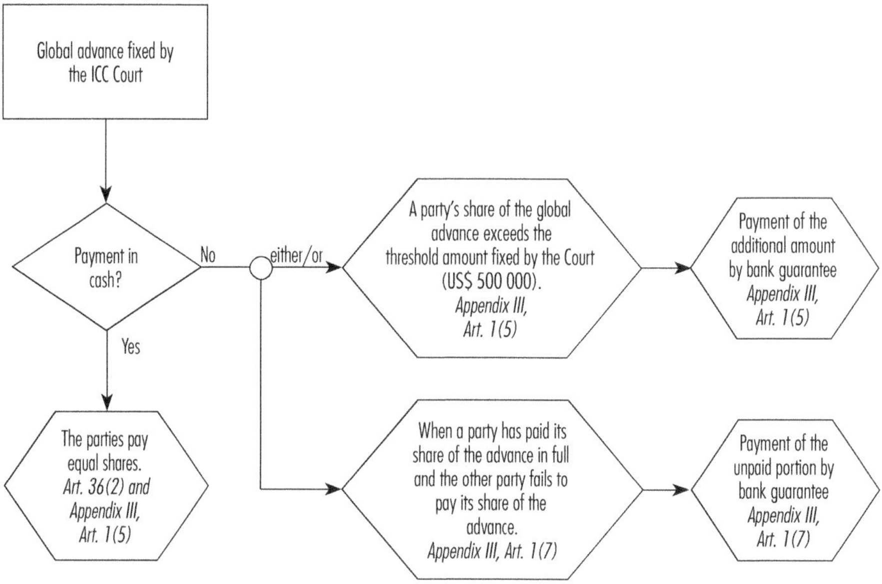

(b) In the event of separate advances

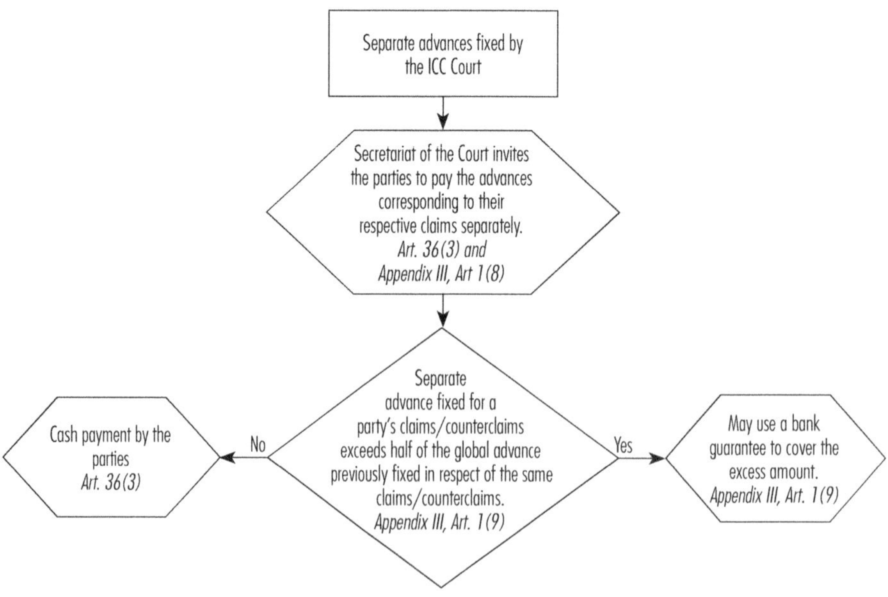

Figure 11. Advance on costs during the arbitration

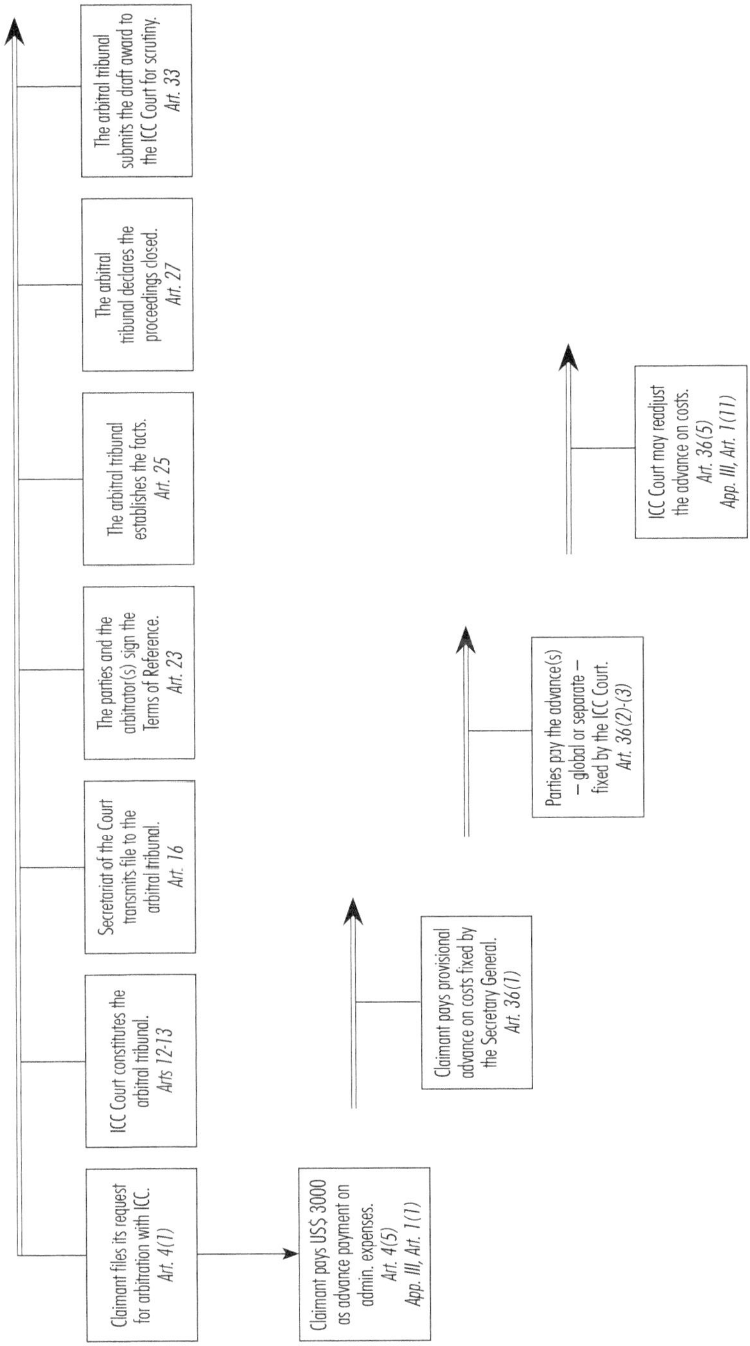

parties pays 'its' advance, the arbitral tribunal will examine that party's claims but not those submitted by the other party. In case the Court decides to readjust and increase the global advance on costs and the parties fail to pay the balance after the increase of the advance on costs, the Secretary General may direct the arbitral tribunal to suspend the entire arbitration until the advance on costs is fully paid.

In practice, until such time as the Secretary General considers that Article 36(6) should be applied and until the Court decides that the claims should be considered as withdrawn under Article 36(6) of the Rules, the arbitral tribunal will nonetheless include in the Terms of Reference the claims of the other party whose advance remains unpaid, although this would be an unusual occurrence, given that the provisional advance is fixed on the basis of the request for arbitration and is intended simply to cover the costs of the arbitration until the Terms of Reference have been forwarded to the Court. Article 1(3) of Appendix III to the Rules provides that once the Terms of Reference have been transmitted to the Court, only those claims for which the whole of the advance on costs has been paid shall be dealt with by the arbitral tribunal.

Although the Secretariat is flexible in its handling of this provision, it checks that the sums paid as an advance are sufficient to cover all the costs incurred thus far in the proceedings, including those arising at that point if the arbitration were to end. The Secretariat nevertheless allows a short period to elapse before the Secretary General consults with the arbitral tribunal (if constituted) with a view to directing it to suspend its work. If separate advances have been fixed, it is possible that the arbitral tribunal will be directed to suspend its work only with respect to the claims for which a separate advance remains unpaid.

When directing the arbitral tribunal to suspend its work, the Secretary General gives the defaulting party or parties a time limit in which to fulfill their financial obligations. The Rules state that at least 15 days should be allowed for payment. The time limit actually set by the Secretariat will take account of special circumstances such as any currency exchange rules to which the defaulting party might be subject and which make it difficult or impossible for it to comply with its obligation to pay within the time limit set. ICC must be in receipt of the payment by the date on which the time limit expires. Failing this, the principal claims or counterclaims will be automatically considered as withdrawn. The arbitration will lapse if separate advances have not been fixed.

The Rules expressly state that the party concerned still has the right to reintroduce the same claim at a later date. However, this must be done in a new arbitration (Article 36(6) of the Rules). In cases where such a time limit for payment is set, if the party concerned wishes to object, it may request that the matter be referred to the ICC Court. Its request will be admissible only if made within the payment deadline set by the Secretariat. If not, the Court will be unable to consider it.

In conclusion, it should be noted that the time limits discussed above have no direct effect on the time limit within which the arbitral award must be rendered according to Article 30(1) of the Rules. In any event, this time limit starts to run on the date on which the last signature is added to the Terms of Reference or, if a party refuses to sign, the date on which the arbitral tribunal is notified of the Court's approval of the Terms of Reference. There is no requirement that the advance on costs be paid in full before the six-month time limit for rendering the award begins to run. However, if the advance that has been paid is insufficient to cover the costs of the proceedings, including the arbitrators' fees, the Secretariat may direct the arbitral tribunal to suspend its work, as described above.

During the five-year period from 2007 until 2011 in total 166 cases were considered withdrawn following a failure to pay the advance on costs (under Article 30(4) of the 1998 Rules, now Article 36(6) of the 2012 Rules). These cases deemed withdrawn represented 10% of the total number of cases withdrawn during this five-year period (see J. Fry, S. Greenberg and F. Mazza, *The Secretariat's Guide to ICC Arbitration*, ICC Publication No. 729 E, Paris, 2012, p. 389).

i) Claim for Set-Off (Art. 36(7))

If a party claims a right to set-off with respect to a claim that has been made, Article 36(7) of the Rules provides that this set-off will be treated in the same way as a separate claim when calculating the advance on costs, if it is likely to require the arbitral tribunal to consider additional matters.

The Rules do not define the term 'a right to a set-off', because the term may have different meanings in different cases depending on the applicable rules of law. Therefore, when such a claim is made, it is necessary to know whether it requires the arbitral tribunal to consider additional matters, in order to determine whether it should be treated in the same way as a counterclaim. Such additional matters might consist of the need to consider factual issues, additional evidence or legal issues which the arbitral tribunal would not have to consider in connection with the claims filed by the claimant. This matter is dealt with by the Secretariat in consultation with the arbitral tribunal.

If 'a right to a set-off' is taken into account when fixing the advance on costs, it may be treated in the same way as a counterclaim for the purpose of fixing separate advances, since it is considered to be a 'claim'.

There is a problem as to the legal consequences of a set-off in respect of which separate advances have been set and which is considered as withdrawn under Article 36(6) of the Rules. In German and Swiss law, set-off leads *ipso jure* to the extinction of the claims in respect of which the set-off is requested. It could be argued that the fiction of withdrawal is irrelevant, because it is precisely the arbitral tribunal's task to decide on the claim in regard of which extinction by way of set-off is being asserted. However, arguably this argument is incompatible with the Rules, which the parties have agreed.

j) Bank Guarantees

The Rules refer to three situations in which parties have the possibility to provide a bank guarantee instead of paying their respective share of the advance in cash.

The first situation is that in which a party's share of the advance exceeds the 'Threshold Amount' fixed by the ICC International Court of Arbitration. In the 2012 Rules this Threshold Amount is fixed at US$ 500 000, but the Court may modify this amount at any time at its discretion, under Article 1(5) of Appendix III to the Rules. The party concerned may provide a bank guarantee for the amount of the advance in excess of US$ 500 000. Under the 1998 version of the Rules, whereby the Threshold Amount was not yet stated in the Rules, the Secretariat of the Court allowed a party to post a bank guarantee when it was required to pay an advance in excess of US$ 300 000.

The second situation is when a party has fully paid its share of the advance and is requested to pay on behalf of a defaulting party in order to allow the proceedings to continue. In doing so, it may provide a bank guarantee covering the unpaid portion of the advance owed by the defaulting party (Article 1(7) of Appendix III to the Rules). Appendix III does not set a minimum amount for posting bank guarantees. It is possible for the bank guarantee to cover the defaulting party's entire share of the advance, irrespective of its amount.

The third situation is when the ICC Court has fixed separate advances (see above). If it turns out that the advance fixed for a party's claim exceeds half of the global advance initially determined on the basis of the principal claims and counterclaims, that party is required to pay in cash only the equivalent of half of the global advance and may post a bank guarantee for the rest (Article 1(9) of Appendix III to the Rules). This provision is intended to prevent a party from having to pay as a separate advance in cash a higher amount than it would have had to pay if the global advance had been maintained. In the event that the amount of the separate advance is subsequently increased, at least one half of the increase shall be paid in cash. As a general rule and for the economic reasons mentioned above, separate advances are fixed only if a party fails to pay its share of the advance, as it is required to do.

If a party wishes to provide a bank guarantee to cover part of the amount due as an advance, it should contact the Secretariat of the Court for information on the terms required by the ICC for such bank guarantees (Article 1(10) of Appendix III to the Rules).

At the end of an arbitration, when the ICC Court fixes the arbitrators' fees and settles the accounts, the Secretariat informs parties that have provided bank guarantees that it is possible for them to pay in cash the sums covered by the guarantees which fall due for arbitration costs, expenses and fees of the arbitral tribunal. In this case, the guarantees will not be called but simply released. Many parties prefer to do so for understandable reasons.

k) Advances for Expertise Costs

As mentioned in Article 25(4) of the Rules, the arbitral tribunal may appoint one or more experts after first consulting the parties. Such experts are paid for the services they render.

Like arbitrators, experts shall not begin their work until the relevant advance intended to cover their fees and expenses has been paid. It is up to the arbitral tribunal, not the ICC International Court of Arbitration, to take the necessary steps for this purpose. After conferring with the expert(s) to assess the likely fees and expenses that are anticipated by the expertise, the arbitral tribunal will fix an appropriate advance, which it will request the parties to pay in accordance with Article 1(12) of Appendix III to the Rules. This advance is not subject to the ICC Rules concerning the costs of the proceedings. It is therefore up to the arbitral tribunal to take whatever measures may be appropriate regarding the conduct of the expertise if the advance remains unpaid.

As already indicated above (see Article 25(4)), if an arbitral tribunal acting in an ICC arbitration requests the ICC International Centre for ADR a proposal of an expert, the services of the ICC Centre shall be provided free of charge (Article 3(1) of Appendix II to the ICC Rules for the Proposal of Experts and Neutrals, see Chapter 6 and Appendix 25 below).

2. Decision as to the Costs of the Arbitration (Art. 37)

Article 37 of the Rules reads:

> 'Decision as to the Costs of the Arbitration
>
> 1. The costs of the arbitration shall include the fees and expenses of the arbitrators and the ICC administrative expenses fixed by the Court, in accordance

with the scale in force at the time of the commencement of the arbitration, as well as the fees and expenses of any experts appointed by the arbitral tribunal and the reasonable legal and other costs incurred by the parties for the arbitration.

2. The Court may fix the fees of the arbitrators at a figure higher or lower than that which would result from the application of the relevant scale should this be deemed necessary due to the exceptional circumstances of the case.

3. At any time during the arbitral proceedings, the arbitral tribunal may make decisions on costs, other than those to be fixed by the Court, and order payment.

4. The final award shall fix the costs of the arbitration and decide which of the parties shall bear them or in what proportion they shall be borne by the parties.

5. In making decisions as to costs, the arbitral tribunal may take into account such circumstances as it considers relevant, including the extent to which each party has conducted the arbitration in an expeditious and cost effective manner.

6. In the event of the withdrawal of all claims or the termination of the arbitration before the rendering of a final award, the Court shall fix the fees and expenses of the arbitrators and the ICC administrative expenses. If the parties have not agreed upon the allocation of the costs of the arbitration or other relevant issues with respect to costs, such matters shall be decided by the arbitral tribunal. If the arbitral tribunal has not been constituted at the time of such withdrawal or termination, any party may request the Court to proceed with the constitution of the arbitral tribunal in accordance with the Rules so that the arbitral tribunal may make decisions as to costs.'

3. Costs and Fees (Appendix III, Art. 2)

Article 2 of Appendix III to the Rules reads:

'Costs and Fees

1. Subject to Article 37(2) of the Rules, the Court shall fix the fees of the arbitrator in accordance with the scale hereinafter set out or, where the amount in dispute is not stated, at its discretion.

2. In setting the arbitrator's fees, the Court shall take into consideration the diligence and efficiency of the arbitrator, the time spent, the rapidity of the proceedings, the complexity of the dispute and the timeliness of the submission of the draft award, so as to arrive at a figure within the limits specified or, in exceptional circumstances (Article 37(2) of the Rules), at a figure higher or lower than those limits.

3. When a case is submitted to more than one arbitrator, the Court, at its discretion, shall have the right to increase the total fees up to a maximum which shall normally not exceed three time the fees of one arbitrator.

4. The arbitrator's fees and expenses shall be fixed exclusively by the Court as required by the Rules. Separate fee arrangements between the parties and the arbitrator are contrary to the Rules.

5. The Court shall fix the ICC administrative expenses of each arbitration in accordance with the scale hereinafter set out or, where the amount in dispute is not stated, at its discretion. In exceptional circumstances, the Court may fix the ICC administrative expenses at a lower or higher figure than that which would result from the application of such scale, provided that such expenses shall normally not exceed the maximum amount of the scale.

6. At any time during the arbitration, the Court may fix as payable a portion of the ICC administrative expenses corresponding to services that have already been performed by the Court and the Secretariat.

7. The Court may require the payment of administrative expenses in addition to those provided in the scale of administrative expenses as a condition to holding an arbitration in abeyance at the request of the parties or of one of them with the acquiescence of the other.

8. If an arbitration terminates before the rendering of a final award, the Court shall fix the fees and expenses of the arbitrators and the ICC administrative expenses at its discretion, taking into account the stage attained by the arbitral proceedings and any other relevant circumstances.

9. Any amount paid by the parties as an advance on costs exceeding the costs of the arbitration fixed by the Court shall be reimbursed to the parties having regard to the amounts paid.

10. In the case of an application under Article 35(2) of the Rules or of a remission pursuant to Article 35(4) of the Rules, the Court may fix an advance to cover additional fees and expenses of the arbitral tribunal and additional ICC administrative expenses and may make the transmission of such application to the arbitral tribunal subject to the prior cash payment in full to the ICC of such advance. The Court shall fix at its discretion the costs of the procedure following an application or a remission, which shall include any possible fees of the arbitrator and ICC administrative expenses, when approving the decision of the arbitral tribunal.

11. The Secretariat may require the payment of administrative expenses in addition to those provided in the scale of administrative expenses for any expenses arising in relation to a request pursuant to Article 34(5) of the Rules.

12. When an arbitration is preceded by proceedings under the ICC Mediation Rules, one half of the ICC administrative expenses paid for such proceedings shall be credited to the ICC administrative expenses of the arbitration.

13. Amounts paid to the arbitrator do not include any possible value added tax (VAT) or other taxes or charges and imposts applicable to the arbitrator's fees. Parties have a duty to pay any such taxes or charges; however, the recovery of any such charges or taxes is a matter solely between the arbitrator and the parties.

14. Any ICC administrative expenses may be subject to value added tax (VAT) or charges of a similar nature at the prevailing rate.'

a) Definition of the Arbitration Costs (Art. 37(1))

Article 37(1) of the Rules defines the costs of the arbitration, which are fixed in accordance with Article 37(2) and (4) of the Rules. The arbitration costs include (i) the arbitrators' fees, (ii) the arbitral tribunal's expenses, (iii) ICC's administrative expenses, (iv) the fees and expenses of any experts appointed by the arbitral tribunal, and (v) the reasonable legal and other costs incurred by the parties for the arbitration.

A study of the ICC Commission on Arbitration in 2007 on ICC cases that went to a final award in 2003 and 2004 has shown that in ICC arbitrations the largest part of the costs of the arbitration proceedings is related to the party costs, including lawyers' fees and expenses, expenses related to witness and expert evidence, and other costs incurred by the parties for the arbitration, making up on average for 82% of the costs of an ICC arbitration. It also resulted from this study that on average 16% of the costs of an ICC arbitration were arbitrators' fees and expenses, and that only 2% of the costs covered ICC administrative expenses (see Report of the ICC Commission on Arbitration and ADR on 'Techniques for Controlling Time and Costs in Arbitration', ICC Publication No. 843, Paris, 2009, p. 11; Report of the ICC Commission on Arbitration and ADR on 'Effective Management of Arbitration: A Guide for In-House Counsel and other Party Representatives', 2014, p. 1; see Appendix 14 below).

Given the concerns that are increasingly raised in relation to the costs of arbitration proceedings, the ICC Commission on Arbitration and ADR published a report in a first edition in 2009, and in a second edition in 2012, providing guidance and techniques which are aimed at reducing procedural costs connected with the parties' presentation of their cases ('Techniques for Controlling Time and Costs in Arbitration', see Appendix 15 below). Based on this report, an Appendix IV has been added to the Rules listing some case management techniques that can be used by arbitrators and parties for controlling time and costs.

(1) The Arbitrators' Fees

The arbitrators' fees are fixed in accordance with Article 37(1) of the Rules and Article 2(1) of Appendix III to the Rules using the scales set forth in Article 4 of Appendix III to the Rules, unless exceptional circumstances require to do otherwise, as allowed by Article 37(2) of the Rules. The applicable scales are those in force when the proceedings are commenced, not those that applied when the arbitration agreement was made. It should be noted that new scales became effective as of 1 January 2012. As stated in the revised Article 4(1) of Appendix III to the Rules, the new scales are applied to all arbitrations commenced on or after 1 January 2012, irrespective of which version of the ICC Rules of Arbitration applies.

The arbitrators' fees do not include any expenses the arbitrators may incur nor any taxes (including value added tax) that may apply to their fees (Article 2(13) of Appendix III to the Rules).

The arbitrators' fees are usually set at an amount between the minimum and maximum resulting from the application of the scales to the amount in dispute. In the case of an arbitral tribunal comprising three members, the ICC International Court of Arbitration normally fixes the fees of the president of the arbitral tribunal and of each of the other two arbitrators separately on a 40/30/30 percentage basis. The larger proportion is attributed to the president of the arbitral tribunal to reflect the fact that he or she usually has more work than the co-arbitrators, who each receive 30% of the total amount. However, the arbitrators are at liberty to share the total amount differently, provided they all agree (see Note to the Arbitral Tribunal on the conduct of the arbitration; Appendix 9 below).

When setting the fees of the arbitrators, the ICC Court takes into consideration (i) their diligence and efficiency in conducting the proceedings, (ii) the time spent, (iii) the rapidity, (iv) the complexity of the dispute and (v) the timeliness of the submission of the draft award, so as to arrive at a figure within the limits indicated in the scales or, in the special cases referred to in Article 37(2) of the Rules, outside those limits (Article 2(2) of Appendix III to the Rules; see also the Secretariat's 'Note to the Arbitral Tribunal on the Conduct of the Arbitration', Appendix 9 below). However, the setting of higher or lower fees than those indicated in the scales must be justified by 'exceptional circumstances'. In practice, the Court rarely fixes fees that are outside the limits of the scales. For the sake of the predictability of the arbitration costs, it prefers to set the fees at a figure which is consistent with the parties' expectations. It will proceed otherwise only if the application of the scale of arbitrators' fees would lead in a given case to fees that are obviously too low for the work done or too high. At the end of the proceedings, the Secretariat asks the arbitrators to indicate how much time they have each spent on the case and to provide any other information relevant to the fixing of their fees. On the basis of the information collected by the Secretariat, the Court assesses the case and fixes the fees appropriately.

The arbitrators' fees may be fixed only by the Court on the basis of the Rules. Parties and arbitrators may not make separate fee arrangements, because this is contrary to the Rules (Article 2(4) of Appendix III to the Rules).

The Rules do not specify at which moment during the proceedings the ICC International Court of Arbitration fixes the arbitrators' fees. In practice, the arbitrator's fees are normally fixed when the Court approves the draft final award pursuant to Article 33 of the Rules, in other words at the end of the proceedings. This means that the arbitrators are paid only when the award has been notified to the parties. However, it is possible for the arbitrators to ask the Court for an advance on fees, which will be granted only if 'concrete' stages have been reached in the proceedings. For instance, an advance on fees will never be granted before the file has been transmitted to the arbitral tribunal.

If the arbitration terminates before a final arbitral award is rendered, the Court will fix the fees at the session during which it takes note of the withdrawal of the arbitration (Article 37(6)). In case an arbitrator is replaced upon death, upon acceptance by the Court of the arbitrator's resignation, upon acceptance by the Court of a challenge, or upon acceptance by the Court of a request of all parties in accordance with Article 15(1), the arbitrator's fees are fixed by the Court at the session during which the decision to replace the arbitrator is taken. Before the Court decides on the arbitrator's fees, the Secretariat will invite the arbitrator to provide information on the time spent as arbitrator in the arbitration proceedings as well as information on the work done in the arbitration and any other elements that may be deemed relevant for the fixing of the fees of the arbitrator.

(2) The Arbitrators' Expenses

The arbitrators' expenses are not subjected to any scales. They are reimbursed on the basis of statements of expenses with supporting documents submitted by the arbitrators to the Secretariat of the Court. The reimbursement is made out of the advance on arbitration costs paid by the parties.

The Secretariat has produced in the past a note on personal and arbitral tribunal expenses, which is sent to arbitrators. With the revision of the Rules in 2012 the content of this note was included in a note to the Arbitral Tribunal on the Conduct of the Arbitration (reproduced in Appendix 9 below) that is sent to the arbitrators when the file is transmitted to them pursuant to Article 16. It covers travel expenses, as well as expenses for accommodation and meals, which may be reimbursed on a lump-sum basis (*per diem*) or on the basis of actual expenditure supported by documentary evidence. It also covers room hire for meetings and secretarial and telecommunications costs. If the arbitral tribunal retains the services of an assistant, known as an administrative secretary, he or she will usually be paid out of the fees of the arbitrator(s). Such assistants are usually young associates of one of the arbitrators. The payment of the fees and expenses of administrative secretaries hired with the parties' consent is reimbursed as an expense of the arbitral tribunal only if the parties did agree to this.

The Secretariat of the Court keeps an account of the arbitral tribunal's expenses in each case. It may be disclosed to the parties at their express request.

(3) The Administrative Expenses

Like the arbitrators' fees, the administrative expenses of the ICC International Court of Arbitration, known simply as 'administrative expenses', are fixed using the scale for administrative expenses in force at the start of the arbitration. If the amount in dispute has not been specified, the arbitration expenses are fixed at a standard amount. According to Article 2(5) of Appendix III to the Rules, the Court may fix the administrative expenses at a figure higher or lower than that which results from the applicable scale if justified by the exceptional circumstances of the case. The administrative expenses normally will not exceed the maximum amount resulting from the application of the scale and it is indeed rare for this to happen in practice.

The administrative expenses are fixed as a lump sum on the basis of the amount in dispute. They include the cost of services rendered by the ICC International Court of Arbitration and its Secretariat (e.g. case management costs and associated postal, international courier, telephone, fax and photocopying charges). The advantage of fixing the administrative expenses as a lump sum based on the amount in dispute is that they are predictable for the parties if the amount in dispute is known. Although parties sometimes consider the administrative expenses as being expensive, it should be pointed out that the ICC's activity is more extensive than that of other arbitration institutions, which usually deal only with the constitution of the arbitral tribunal.

If the arbitration has been preceded by an aborted attempt to resolve the dispute amicably using the ICC Mediation Rules, Article 2(12) of Appendix III to the Rules provides that half of the administrative expenses paid for the mediation proceedings are credited to the amount required for the ICC administrative expenses of the arbitration.

The Court normally fixes the ICC administrative expenses when it approves the final award. Pursuant to the new Article 2(6) of Appendix III to the Rules, however the Court may decide at any time during the arbitration that a portion of the administrative expenses is due and payable for services that have already been performed by the Court and the Secretariat. If the arbitration terminates before a final arbitral award is rendered, the Court shall fix the administrative expenses when it takes note of the withdrawal of the arbitration (Article 37(6)).

(4) The Fees and Expenses of Experts Appointed by the Arbitral Tribunal

As already mentioned, the arbitral tribunal has the power to appoint experts. According to Article 37(1) of the Rules, the fees and expenses of any experts appointed by the arbitral tribunal are part of the costs of the arbitration. It is the arbitral tribunal, not the ICC International Court of Arbitration, that must fix a deposit securing the later payment of these costs before the expert starts working (Article 1(12) of Appendix

III to the Rules). The fees and expenses of party-appointed experts are not concerned here, but they may be included in the costs which a party incurs for the arbitration and for which it claims reimbursement.

(5) The Costs incurred by the Parties for the Arbitration

Article 37(1) of the Rules provides that the costs of the arbitration also include 'the reasonable legal and other costs incurred by the parties for the arbitration', without actually defining them. These costs include, amongst other things, the fees and expenses of the lawyer(s) representing a party, the costs of experts commissioned by a party, the costs of consultants and witnesses, the costs of sending documents and attending hearings, translation, interpretation and transcription costs. These costs are fixed by the arbitral tribunal on the basis of information provided by the parties. Usually, at the end of the proceedings, the arbitral tribunal asks the parties to provide it with details of these costs. It has considerable freedom to fix the amount it thinks fit.

b) The Court's Decision on Costs (Article 37(1)-(2))

The ICC International Court of Arbitration fixes the amounts due to ICC and to the arbitral tribunal on the basis of the amount in dispute, using the applicable scales. The arbitral tribunal's expenses and the costs and expenses of any experts appointed by it are added to these amounts. The parties' costs and their other expenses, including those of any experts commissioned by them, are not fixed by the Court, but by the arbitral tribunal.

Together, these amounts constitute the costs of the arbitration. The resulting sum is formally determined by the arbitral tribunal in its final award, after the ICC International Court of Arbitration has approved the award and fixed the administrative expenses and the arbitrators' fees. The date on which this sum is deemed to have been fixed is normally that on which the Court approves the award. As a general rule, the costs of the arbitration are fixed in the arbitral tribunal's final award, whereby the tribunal decides which of the parties shall bear the costs of the arbitration or in what proportion the costs shall be borne by the parties (Article 37(4)).

According to the new provision of Article 2(6) of Appendix III to the 2012 Rules, the Court may at any time during the arbitration fix as payable a portion of the ICC administrative expenses corresponding to services that have already been performed by the Court and the Secretariat.

If parties wish to put an arbitration in abeyance, or if one party requests so with the acquiescence of the other, the Court may require the payment of administrative expenses in addition to those provided in the scale of administrative expenses (Article 2(7) of Appendix III to the Rules). Such additional amount for administrative expenses may fall due if an arbitration is to be kept in abeyance for a longer period and since the Court will have to ensure in the meantime that the time limit foreseen in Article 23(2) for the establishment of the Terms of Reference or, as the case may be, the time limit foreseen in Article 30(1) to render the final award is duly extended. 'Abeyance fees' are not included in the calculation of the ICC administrative expenses when fixed by the Court at the end of the arbitration (see J. Fry, S. Greenberg and F. Mazza, *The Secretariat's Guide to ICC Arbitration*, ICC Publication No. 729 E, Paris, 2012, p. 403).

Should the arbitration end before a final award is rendered – as might happen, for instance, if the case is withdrawn as a result of an amicable settlement of the dispute, or in the event of an award by consent – the Court fixes the costs of the arbitration at its discretion (Article 37(6)). In taking its decision, the Court will take into consideration the stage the proceedings have reached and any other relevant circumstances (Article 2(8) of Appendix III to the Rules). When fixing the arbitrators' fees, the criteria mentioned in Article 2(2) of Appendix III to the Rules will be taken into consideration. The Court may also take account of any other circumstances, such as the arbitral tribunal's possible involvement in the amicable settlement of the case. If the parties have not agreed upon the allocation of the costs of the arbitration or upon other relevant issues with respect to costs, the arbitral tribunal shall decide on the allocation of the costs between the parties (Article 37(6)).

If the parties have not agreed on the allocation of the costs and if the arbitration is to be withdrawn before the arbitral tribunal is constituted, a party may request the Court to proceed with the constitution of the arbitral tribunal so that the arbitral tribunal may take a decision on the sole issue of the allocation of the costs of the arbitration pursuant to the new provision of Article 37(6).

Once the costs have been settled by the payment of fees and expenses to the arbitrators and to eventual tribunal appointed experts and by the ICC administrative expenses, and if there is a balance in the parties' favor, the Secretariat will reimburse them in proportion to the share of the advance on costs they have each paid. Unless instructed by parties acting in common, the ICC International Court of Arbitration will not take account of what the award decides regarding how the costs are split between the parties, because the ICC does not involve itself in the execution of the award (Article 2(9) of Appendix III to the Rules).

For example, if the advance has been fixed at US$ 20 000 and the claimant has paid US$ 15 000, of which US$ 5 000 was paid in place of the respondent, that paid only US$ 5 000, then the balance will be refunded as follows:

If the arbitration costs are finally fixed at US$ 15 000, the US$ 5 000 balance belongs to the claimant.

If, on the other hand, the arbitration costs are fixed at US$ 4 000, the following amounts will be repaid to the parties:

To claimant:	US$ 15 000	(already paid)
less	US$ 2 000	(claimant's share of the costs as fixed)
Refund:	US$ 13 000	
To respondent:	US$ 5 000	(already paid)
less	US$ 2 000	(respondent's share of the costs as fixed)
Refund:	US$ 3 000	

If a party requests the correction of an error in the award or the interpretation of the award under Article 35(2), or if a state court remits an arbitral award to the arbitral tribunal pursuant to Article 35(4) of the Rules, the ICC International Court of Arbitration may fix an advance intended to cover additional fees and expenses of the arbitral tribunal. When approving the arbitral tribunal's decision on the application, the Court is at liberty to fix any fees it may consider appropriate to grant to the arbitral tribunal (Article 2(10) of Appendix III to the Rules).

If a party requests under Article 34(5) for assistance from the Secretariat in complying with any formalities that may be necessary after the notification of an arbitral award, the Secretariat may require the payment of administrative expenses in addition to those provided in the scale of administrative expenses (Article 2(11) of Appendix III to the Rules).

c) The Arbitral Tribunal's Decision on Costs (Art. 37(3)-(5))

The provision of Article 37(3) confirms that an arbitral tribunal may already take a decision during the arbitral proceedings on costs other than those that shall be fixed by the Court (Article 31(2) of the 1998 ICC Rules). The arbitral tribunal may not decide on the ICC administrative expenses and on the arbitrators' fees and expenses, as these shall be fixed by the ICC Court pursuant to Article 37(1). The arbitral tribunal may, however, decide on costs for any phase of the arbitration and order the payment of such costs. The reference here concerns costs of experts the arbitral tribunal has appointed and the various costs and expenses incurred by the parties for the arbitration.

In certain circumstances, the arbitral tribunal may also grant relief in relation to the payment of the advance on costs. Where a party fails to pay its share of the advance on costs and the other party has to substitute for it, the latter party may request a decision from the arbitral tribunal ordering the defaulting party to reimburse it. It is for the arbitral tribunal to decide whether a procedural order is appropriate or whether an award is required to grant such relief on account of its greater force (see above with regard to Article 28(1) and Article 31 of the Rules). There are examples of ICC awards both accepting and rejecting such requests (see J. Fry, S. Greenberg and F. Mazza, *The Secretariat's Guide to ICC Arbitration*, ICC Publication No. 729 E, Paris, 2012, p. 385-386 and p. 406).

According to Article 37(4) of the Rules, the arbitral tribunal has an obligation to decide in the final award on the proportion of the costs of the arbitration to be borne by each party. The parties have the opportunity to plead on this issue before the proceedings are closed.

The new provision of Article 37(5) confirms that, in making decisions as to costs, the arbitral tribunal may take into account such circumstances as it considers relevant, including the extent to which each party has conducted the arbitration in an expeditious and cost-effective manner. This provision allows the arbitral tribunal to take into account whether or not the conduct of a party during an arbitration has helped to control the time and costs during the arbitration proceedings. This provision may serve to sanction dilatory tactics adopted by a party in an arbitration. The arbitral tribunal should consider drawing the attention of the parties to this provision as a tool to encourage greater efficiency in their conduct in the proceedings during the case management conference organized in accordance with Article 24. Any decision taken by the arbitral tribunal on costs should state the reason(s) on which it is based as required by Article 31(2). Before taking its decision, the arbitral tribunal should allow the parties the opportunity to submit their comments and substantiate their claims with regard to the costs of the arbitration.

The decision on how the costs should be divided between the parties is often influenced by the legal background of arbitrators and parties and their practice in national courts or under national laws which may vary from one jurisdiction to another. There is no single, universal approach to costs allocation in international arbitration, as it was observed by the Task Force on Decisions as to Costs of the ICC Commission on Arbitration and ADR. Usually, one of the following solutions is adopted:

(i) the parties bear the costs of the arbitration equally;
(ii) the costs are divided between the parties on the basis of the outcome of the case (in accordance with the well-known principle 'costs follow the event', e.g. in the proportion 60/40 or 75/25);
(iii) each party bears entirely its own costs regardless of the outcome of the case.

The arbitral tribunal has considerable freedom when making its decision. However, the reasons for the decision must be stated in compliance with Article 31(2) of the Rules. The arbitral tribunal is also free to decide that some of the costs claimed should not be reimbursed, or that the sums requested (e.g. lawyers' fees) should be reduced.

d) Costs in the Event of Withdrawal of Claims (Art. 37(6))

During the five-year period from 2007 until 2011, there was a withdrawal of claims in 51% of all the cases ended during the period and in an additional 6% of the cases ended there was an award by consent rendered. In 42% of the cases ended during these five years there was a final award rendered and in 1% of the cases there was a negative decision taken by the ICC under Article 6(2) of the 1998 ICC Rules so that the arbitration could not proceed (see J. Fry, S. Greenberg and F. Mazza, *The Secretariat's Guide to ICC Arbitration*, ICC Publication No. 729 E, Paris, 2012, p. 412).

The withdrawal of the arbitration mostly occurs when the parties have reached a settlement agreement that ends their dispute. If the parties come to a compromise over their dispute after the matter has been referred to the arbitral tribunal, they may ask the tribunal to render an award by consent even if the Terms of Reference have not yet been signed. There is, however, no obligation under the Rules to render an award by consent if a case is settled (see comments on Article 32 above). The parties may also agree to withdraw their claims without requesting an award by consent. A case may also be considered as withdrawn if the parties do not pay the advance on costs fixed by the Court (Article 36(6)).

When the advance on costs has already been paid at the time the claims are withdrawn, the Court will determine the costs of arbitration when it takes note of the withdrawal of the claims and it will determine at the same time whether or not there will be a partial reimbursement of the amounts paid. When only the non-refundable filing fee has been paid (Article 1 of Appendix III to the Rules), no reimbursement will be made and the Court in such situation will fix the costs of the arbitration at the amount of US$ 3 000 paid by the Claimant as filing fee.

Sometimes a situation arises where parties agree on the withdrawal of their claims in the arbitration, without agreeing on the allocation of the costs among them. In such case, the arbitral tribunal may be asked to decide in accordance with article 37(4) which of the parties shall bear the costs of the arbitration or in what proportion they shall be borne by the parties. If the arbitral tribunal has not yet been constituted at the time of such withdrawal or termination, the new provision of Article 37(6) allows a party to request the Court to proceed with the constitution of the arbitral tribunal so that the arbitral tribunal can take a decision as to the costs of the arbitration.

e) Value Added Tax (VAT)

Since 1998, the Rules have included a provision dealing with the question of taxes that may be due on the arbitrators' fees. Article 2(13) of Appendix III to the Rules states that the amounts paid to arbitrators do not include value-added tax or any other taxes, charges and imposts that may be applicable to arbitrators' fees. It goes on to establish that the parties have a duty to pay such taxes and charges. Their recovery is a matter for the arbitrators and the parties alone and does not involve ICC. Although not specifically mentioned, it may be understood that income tax is not covered by this provision.

Given that such taxes become due once arbitrators have received their fees, i.e. after the award has been notified to the parties, arbitrators may encounter difficulties when seeking repayment from the parties. Article 2(13) of the Rules makes it clear that the parties have an obligation to pay such taxes and charges, although it does not indicate how payment should be made or how it may be guaranteed.

The question of whether VAT is applicable to arbitrators' fees and, if so, the amount of such tax depends on the applicable tax law and relevant conventions. The tax law to which arbitrators are subject is determined by their place of residence and for this reason cannot be determined by the Rules. In 1997, the European Court of Justice held that a German professor who had acted as arbitrator in proceedings based in Paris should pay VAT on his fees (case C-145/96, *B. von Hoffmann* v. *Finanzamt Trier*, 16 September 1997).

The Rules do not state how and when the parties may be asked to pay any amounts that may be due. One solution would be for the arbitrators to request an advance for this purpose early in the proceedings, although the Rules do not mention what the consequences of non-payment of such advance would be. Some arbitrators have developed the practice of mentioning in the Terms of Reference that the parties have an obligation to pay VAT on fees when it becomes due. In this case, the arbitrators would have additional grounds for requesting the parties to pay any VAT that may be due on their fees at the end of the arbitration. It is advisable to seek further information from the Secretariat of the ICC Court as and when the need arises.

Arbitrators may request that the Secretariat set up a VAT account at the outset of the arbitration. In such case, the arbitrators must inform the parties of the amount to be paid into the account and seek confirmation from the Secretariat that the payments have been made. In such case, when the Secretariat pays the arbitrator's fees, it will also pay any amounts contained in the VAT account in accordance with the arbitrator's instructions (see Secretariat's 'Note to the Arbitral Tribunal on the Conduct of the Arbitration', Appendix 9 below; see also J. Fry, S. Greenberg and F. Mazza, *The Secretariat's Guide to ICC Arbitration*, ICC Publication No. 729 E, Paris, 2012, p. 400).

f) How to Calculate the Administrative Expenses and Fees on the Basis of the Amount in Dispute

Article 4 of Appendix III to the Rules reads:

> '**Scales of Administrative Expenses and Arbitrator's Fees**
>
> 1. The Scales of Administrative Expenses and Arbitrator's Fees set forth below shall be effective as of 1 January 2012 in respect of all arbitrations commenced on or after such date, irrespective of the version of the Rules applying to such arbitrations.
>
> 2. To calculate the administrative expenses and the arbitrator's fees, the amounts calculated for each successive tranche of the amount in dispute must be added together, except that where the amount in dispute is over US$ 500

million, a flat amount of US$ 113,215 shall constitute the entirety of the ICC administrative expenses.

3. All amounts fixed by the Court or pursuant to any of the appendices to the Rules are payable in US$ except where prohibited by law, in which case the ICC may apply a different scale and fee arrangement in another currency.'

(1) Which Version of the Scales should be Used?

The costs of the arbitration are fixed by the Court in accordance with the scales of administrative expenses and arbitrators' fees in force at the time of the commencement of the arbitration (Article 37(1)). As a consequence, if the Court adopts new cost scales in the course of an arbitration, such new cost scales will not be applicable and the cost scales in force at the time of commencement of the arbitration will remain applicable. This is in accordance with the principle of predictability, as the parties do not wish to be taken by surprise by an increased cost scale of which they were not aware when the arbitration was commenced.

The scales of administrative expenses and arbitrators' fees currently applicable are those which came into force on 1 January 2012, following the revision of the scales in the 2012 Rules. These scales apply to all arbitrations commenced on or after 1 January 2012, including those conducted on the basis of an arbitration agreement that refers to an earlier version of the Rules.

(2) The Method of Calculation

(a) ICC administrative expenses

ICC's administrative expenses are calculated using a sliding scale depending on the amount in dispute. This scale ranges from a minimum of US$ 3 000 to a maximum of US$ 113 215. The percentages used to calculate the administrative expenses decrease as the amount in dispute increases. Article 2(5) of Appendix III to the Rules allows the Court to depart from the scale in exceptional circumstances and fix the administrative expenses at a figure higher or lower than that which would result from its application. However, when doing so, it should not normally go beyond the maximum amount of the scale.

The administrative expenses are the sum of the amounts obtained by multiplying each portion of the amount in dispute mentioned in the scales by the corresponding percentage. To facilitate this calculation, Appendix III contains an additional table which allows the administrative expenses to be determined by simply multiplying the portion of the amount in dispute in excess of the uppermost amount of the preceding portion by the percentage indicated. The resulting figure should then be added to the amount stated for the relevant portion.

(b) Arbitrators' fees

Arbitrators' fees are similarly calculated using a sliding scale in which decreasing percentages are applied to successive portions of the amount in dispute to give minimum and maximum figures. The ICC Court has considerable freedom when applying this scale and may fix the fees within the range resulting from the scale or beyond it if special circumstances make this necessary (Article 37(2) of the Rules). Arbitrators' fees are generally set around the middle of the range. To calculate the fees, the second and third of the tables on the following pages are applied in the same way as for the administrative expenses. When a case is submitted to more than one arbitrator, the

Court, at its discretion, shall have the right to increase the total fees up to a maximum which shall normally not exceed three times the fees of one arbitrator (Article 2(3) of Appendix III to the Rules).

The arbitrators' fees are fixed exclusively by the Court. Separate fee arrangements between the parties and the arbitrator(s) are contrary to the Rules (Article 2(4) of Appendix III to the Rules).

A. ADMINISTRATIVE EXPENSES

Amount in dispute (in US Dollars)				**Administrative expenses(*)**
up to			50,000	$3,000
from	50,001	to	100,000	4.73%
from	100,001	to	200,000	2.53%
from	200,001	to	500,000	2.09%
from	500,001	to	1,000,000	1.51%
from	1,000,001	to	2,000,000	0.95%
from	2,000,001	to	5,000,000	0.46%
from	5,000,001	to	10,000,000	0.25%
from	10,000,001	to	30,000,000	0.10%
from	30,000,001	to	50,000,000	0.09%
from	50,000,001	to	80,000,000	0.01%
from	80,000,001	to	500,000,000	0.0035%
over	500,000,000			$113,215

(*) For illustrative purposes only, the table on the following page indicates the resulting administrative expenses in US$ when the proper calculations have been made.

B. ARBITRATOR'S FEES

Amount in dispute (in US Dollars)				**Fees (**)** **minimum**	**maximum**
up to	50,000			$3,000	18.0200%
from	50,001	to	100,000	2.6500%	13.5680%
from	100,001	to	200,000	1.4310%	7.6850%
from	200,001	to	500,000	1.3670%	6.8370%
from	500,001	to	1,000,000	0.9540%	4.0280%
from	1,000,001	to	2,000,000	0.6890%	3.6040%
from	2,000,001	to	5,000,000	0.3750%	1.3910%
from	5,000,001	to	10,000,000	0.1280%	0.9100%
from	10,000,001	to	30,000,000	0.0640%	0.2410%
from	30,000,001	to	50,000,000	0.0590%	0.2280%
from	50,000,001	to	80,000,000	0.0330%	0.1570%
from	80,000,001	to	100,000,000	0.0210%	0.1150%
from	100,000,001	to	500,000,000	0.0110%	0.0580%
over	500,000,000			0.0100%	0.0400%

(**) For illustrative purposes only, the table on the following page indicates the resulting range of fees in US$ when the proper calculations have been made.

AMOUNT IN DISPUTE (in US Dollars)	A. ADMINISTRATIVE EXPENSES (*) (in US Dollars)	B. ARBITRATOR'S FEES (**) (in US Dollars)	
		Minimum	Maximum
up to 50,000	3,000	3,000	18.02% of amount in dispute
from 50,001 to 100,000	3,000 + 4.73% of amt. over 50,000	3,000 + 2.6500% of amt. over 50,000	9,010 + 13.568% of amt. over 50,000
from 100,001 to 200,000	5,365 + 2.53% of amt. over 100,000	4,325 + 1.4310% of amt. over 100,000	15,794 + 7.6850% of amt. over 100,000
from 200,001 to 500,000	7,895 + 2.09% of amt. over 200,000	5,756 + 1.3670% of amt. over 200,000	23,479 + 6.8370% of amt. over 200,000
from 500,001 to 1,000,000	14,165 + 1.51% of amt. over 500,000	9,857 + 0.9540% of amt. over 500,000	43,990 + 4.0280% of amt. over 500,000
from 1,000,001 to 2,000,000	21,715 + 0.95% of amt. over 1,000,000	14,627 + 0.6890% of amt. over 1,000,000	64,130 + 3.6040% of amt. over 1,000,000
from 2,000,001 to 5,000,000	31,215 + 0.46% of amt. over 2,000,000	21,517 + 0.3750% of amt. over 2,000,000	100,170 + 1.3910% of amt. over 2,000,000
from 5,000,001 to 10,000,000	45,015 + 0.25% of amt. over 5,000,000	32,767 + 0.1280% of amt. over 5,000,000	141,900 + 0.9100% of amt. over 5,000,000
from 10,000,001 to 30,000,000	57,515 + 0.10% of amt. over 10,000,000	39,167 + 0.0640% of amt. over 10,000,000	187,400 + 0.2410% of amt. over 10,000,000
from 30,000,001 to 50,000,000	77,515 + 0.09% of amt. over 30,000,000	51,967 + 0.0590% of amt. over 30,000,000	235,600 + 0.2280% of amt. over 30,000,000
from 50,000,001 to 80,000,000	95,515 + 0.01% of amt. over 50,000,000	63,767 + 0.0330% of amt. over 50,000,000	281,200 + 0.1570% of amt. over 50,000,000
from 80,000,001 to 100,000,000	98,515 + 0.0035% of amt. over 80,000,000	73,667 + 0.0210% of amt. over 80,000,000	328,300 + 0.1150% of amt. over 80,000,000
from 100,000,001 to 500,000,000	99,215 + 0.0035% of amt. over 100,000,000	77,867 + 0.0110% of amt. over 100,000,000	351,300 + 0.0580% of amt. over 100,000,000
over 500,000,000	113,215	121,867 + 0.0100% of amt. over 500,000,000	583,300 + 0.0400% of amt. over 500,000,000

(*)(**) See preceding page

g) Costs for the Appointment of Arbitrators in Non-ICC Arbitrations (Art. 3 of Appendix III to the Rules)

The International Chamber of Commerce is sometimes called upon to appoint arbitrators and decide on challenges of arbitrators in cases that are not subject to its Rules of Arbitration. Article 3 of Appendix III to the Rules states that in such instances a non-refundable sum of US$ 3 000 must be paid when the request is filed with the ICC and that the ICC is at liberty to charge a sum of no more than US$ 10 000 to cover administrative expenses for additional services. A request to appoint an arbitrator and to decide on the challenge of an arbitrator in a non-ICC arbitration will be treated in accordance with the Rules of the ICC as Appointing Authority in UNCITRAL or Other '*Ad Hoc*' Arbitration Proceedings, which are reproduced in Appendix 20 below.

I. MISCELLANEOUS PROVISIONS

1. Modified Time Limits (Art. 38)

Article 38 of the Rules reads:

> 'Modified Time Limits
>
> 1. The parties may agree to shorten the various time limits set out in the Rules. Any such agreement entered into subsequent to the constitution of an arbitral tribunal shall become effective only upon the approval of the arbitral tribunal.
>
> 2. The Court, on its own initiative, may extend any time limit which has been modified pursuant to Article 38(1) if it decides that it is necessary to do so in order that the arbitral tribunal and the Court may fulfil their responsibilities in accordance with the Rules.'

a) The Parties' Decision to Shorten the Time Limits: 'Fast-Track Arbitration' (Art. 38(1))

The time limits laid down in the Rules (i.e. two months for drawing up the Terms of Reference and six months for rendering the final award) are sometimes longer than the parties wish. If this is the case, parties may agree on shorter time limits, which in practice they do either in their arbitration agreement or at a later stage. Some years ago, a case was referred to ICC in which the parties had agreed that the award would be rendered within two months of the filing of the request for arbitration. The request for arbitration was filed shortly before Christmas and the proceedings were accomplished within the agreed time limit thanks to the cooperation and intensive work of all those involved.

Sometimes, parties may require a quick decision for justifiable reasons, such as the interpretation of contractual provisions relating to prices or adaptations required by a change of circumstances. Even before 1998, respect for party autonomy led the ICC International Court of Arbitration to implement time limits shortened by agreement of the parties, to the extent that these were consistent with the Rules. It was therefore logical to include in 1998 in the ICC Rules of Arbitration a provision that expressly regulated such cases. Rather than devising a special set of rules for fast-track procedures, as some other arbitration institutions have done (e.g. the World Intellectual Property Organization (WIPO), with its Expedited Arbitration Rules of 1994), the ICC simply included a provision expressly allowing for time limits to be shortened. At the same time, however, limits are set upon party autonomy, as it is expressly stated that the ICC Court may extend time limits that have been shortened by the parties. This was the real innovation, and a very necessary one, given that, no matter how hard they try, it is not always possible for the ICC and the arbitral tribunal to implement shortened time limits for reasons of a practical nature or beyond their control, as when one of the parties refuses to cooperate. The Court must therefore be able to extend the time limit for the reasons mentioned earlier in connection with Article 30 of the Rules. This is the purpose of Article 38(2) (which was introduced in the 1998 Rules as Article 32(2)). Parties risk running into difficulties if they agree on shortened time limits in their arbitration agreement. Therefore, they are advised to do so only in very special cases where there are compelling reasons for doing so.

b) The Shortening of Time Limits with Respect to the Arbitral Tribunal

If parties decide to shorten time limits after the arbitral tribunal has been constituted, the new time limits will be valid only if agreed by the arbitrators (second sentence, Article 38(1) of the Rules). It is logical that an arbitrator who has agreed to serve in the knowledge that the time limits would be those laid down in the Rules should not then be forced against his or her will to respect shorter time limits.

If the parties have at the outset agreed on shortened time limits, the arbitrator must decide whether he or she is prepared to comply with the deadlines before agreeing to serve. Once the time limits have been accepted, they must of course be respected.

2. Waiver (Art. 39)

Article 39 of the Rules reads:

> 'Waiver
>
> A party which proceeds with the arbitration without raising its objection to a failure to comply with any provision of the Rules, or of any other rules applicable to the proceedings, any direction given by the arbitral tribunal, or any requirement under the arbitration agreement relating to the constitution of the arbitral tribunal or the conduct of the proceedings, shall be deemed to have waived its right to object.'

A party is entitled to raise an objection if, for instance, it realizes that the arbitral tribunal was not constituted in accordance with the arbitration agreement or that an order issued by the arbitral tribunal violates a provision in the Rules or in other rules applicable to the proceedings. However, the objection must be raised as soon as the party becomes aware of the alleged violation. If it allows the proceedings to continue without objecting, the objection will no longer be admissible, even if entirely justified at the outset.

The aim of Article 39 of the Rules is to prevent parties from claiming late in the proceedings, or just after the award has been drafted, or even thereafter, that the arbitration has been conducted irregularly, in a deceitful attempt to delay the rendering of the award or hinder its performance.

Article 39 does not provide for a time limit for raising an objection. This will depend on the particular circumstances. If all the circumstances on which the objection is based are known to the party concerned, the objection must be made immediately and certainly within the time limit mentioned in Article 14(2) of the Rules (for a challenge of an arbitrator to be admissible), which may be applied by analogy, i.e. within 30 days of the parties becoming aware of those circumstances. The fact that the parties have decided on the application of the ICC Rules of Arbitration (see Article 6(1) of the Rules) means that this provision is a procedural rule to which they have agreed and which must be applied both by the arbitral tribunal and the ICC International Court of Arbitration, as the case may be, when a party raises an objection. As already indicated above (see comments on Article 22 of the Rules), if a party considers the arbitral tribunal to be acting unfairly or partially or not to have given it a reasonable opportunity to present its case, this should be mentioned as soon as possible. A party that wishes to raise an objection due to the arbitral tribunal's partiality or the fact that this party has not had a reasonable opportunity to present its case under Article 22(4) cannot wait and act against the award once it has been rendered. If a party does not comply with an order made by the arbitral tribunal in spite of its undertaking to do so under Article 22(5), the other party may be considered to have waived its right to object against such failure to comply. The same principle may apply if a party does not comply with any order made by the emergency arbitrator in spite of its undertaking under the Rules (Article 29(2) second sentence of the Rules). If one of the parties wishes to object to specific conduct some time after the event, it must prove that it was not aware – or could not have been aware – of the alleged violation of the Rules or the applicable procedural rules and was thus prevented from raising its objection immediately. This is no easy matter in practice, especially if the objection concerns a violation of the Rules. It should of course be borne in mind that the ICC Court (pursuant to Article 1(1) of Appendix I to the Rules) and its Secretariat (pursuant to Article 1(5) of the Rules) exercise their supervisory powers throughout the proceedings with a view to ensuring compliance with the Rules and the parties' agreements concerning the constitution of the arbitral tribunal and the conduct of the proceedings.

If a party raises its objection in a state court – whether in connection with an application for arbitrators to be removed from office or, at a later date, for an award to be set aside or not recognized – the court must decide, having regard to its own law or the applicable foreign law, whether Article 39 of the Rules deprives the parties of their right to raise an objection and whether, notwithstanding this provision, the objection should be considered late or be dismissed for other reasons (see, for example, Article 1717(5) JC, Article 1466 NCPC, Article 1027 ZPO, Article 4 of the UNCITRAL Model law).

If a party fails or ceases to take part in the proceedings, a late objection relating to procedural defects might sometimes be considered inadmissible under other applicable rules of procedure or the applicable arbitration law.

3. Limitation of Liability (Art. 40)

Article 40 of the Rules reads:

> 'Limitation of Liability
>
> The arbitrators, any person appointed by the arbitral tribunal, the emergency arbitrator, the Court and its members, the ICC and its employees, and the ICC National Committees and Groups and their employees shall not be liable to any person for any act or omission in connection with the arbitration, except to the extent such limitation of liability is prohibited by applicable law.'

This article deals with the question of liability or, rather, its exclusion. Even in arbitration, there is an increasing risk for the arbitration institutions and the arbitrator(s) of being sued for liability on grounds of alleged misconduct, although this is rarely justified. Sometimes parties use the possibility of suing the arbitrators and/or the institution as a means of exerting pressure on them. This runs counter to the independence required of them and hence undermines the supreme power of decision conferred upon them by applicable rules.

Article 40 is worded in such a way so as to exclude liability to the extent possible. Not only the arbitrators, but also any person appointed by the arbitral tribunal, the emergency arbitrator, the arbitration institution, including the ICC International Court of Arbitration, the Secretariat staff, the National Committees and Groups and their employees must be protected from any complaint. Whereas the ICC 1998 Rules when introducing a provision on liability provided for a full exclusion of liability (in Article 34), it has been added in the 2012 Rules that a full exclusion of liability will not be possible 'to the extent such limitation of liability is prohibited by applicable law'. Here, the Rules have followed the position taken by many other arbitration institutions. It is worth remembering that judicial immunity may vary from one country to another. So too may national rules concerning the exclusion or limitation of the liability of arbitrators and arbitration institutions. In many countries arbitral tribunals enjoy the same immunity as courts as far as liability is concerned. In other countries, such as the USA, arbitrators and arbitration institutions are exempt from liability when this is expressly mentioned in arbitration rules or in a contract. In some other countries, complete exclusion of liability is not foreseen or not allowed. It will therefore be up to national courts to decide whether and to what extent Article 40 of the Rules may be effective in a specific case.

4. General Rule Aimed at Filling Gaps (Art. 41)

Article 41 of the Rules reads:

> 'General Rule
>
> In all matters not expressly provided for in the Rules, the Court and the arbitral tribunal shall act in the spirit of the Rules and shall make every effort to make sure that the award is enforceable at law.'

Article 41 of the Rules is a general provision covering situations in which the other provisions of the Rules do not apply directly. It may be inferred from the first part of this provision that the ICC International Court of Arbitration and arbitral tribunals have the necessary powers for this purpose. When exercising these powers, they must act 'in the spirit of the Rules'. This general provision is particularly significant, for it means that the Court may adapt the practice of the ICC arbitration procedure to developments in international arbitration.

The second part of Article 41 allows the Court and arbitral tribunals to do all they can to ensure that the award rendered is flawless and enforceable internationally. Although they cannot always guarantee this completely, for reasons beyond their control, they should constantly endeavor to observe the general principles of sound and fair arbitration procedure in order for the award to be enforceable.

Although parties usually seems to perform awards spontaneously and rarely have to be compelled to perform them, there are occasions when the review of an award by a national court in enforcement or setting-aside proceedings reveals a procedural defect that could cause it to refuse enforcement or to set aside the award.

It is impossible for arbitral tribunals and the ICC International Court of Arbitration to make sure that awards will always successfully pass such a review. There are a number of reasons for this: the arbitral tribunal and the Court cannot always predict in which country or countries the award will in the end be enforced, nor can they anticipate how the judicial authorities there will react. The country or countries where an award is enforced will usually depend above all on the place where the losing party has assets that could be seized by the winning party.

Applications for an award to be set aside, on the other hand, can usually only be brought in the competent court at the place of the arbitration. Arbitral tribunals and the ICC Court are aware of the legal rules that need to be respected in order to limit the chances of success of a possible application for the award to be set aside at the place of the arbitration. As already mentioned, when scrutinizing draft awards under Article 33 of the Rules, the Court takes into account, to the extent practicable, the requirements of mandatory law at the place of the arbitration (Article 6 of Appendix II to the Rules).

CHAPTER 4

THE STANDARD ICC ARBITRATION CLAUSE

The standard arbitration clause recommended by ICC is worded as follows:

> 'All disputes arising out of or in connection with the present contract shall be finally settled under the Rules of Arbitration of the International Chamber of Commerce by one or more arbitrators appointed in accordance with the said Rules.'

If the parties wish to exclude any recourse to the Emergency Arbitrator Provisions, they must expressly opt out by adding the following wording to the standard arbitration clause:

> 'The Emergency Arbitrator Provisions shall not apply.'

A. ARBITRATION CLAUSES IN GENERAL

Like any other arbitration proceedings, those conducted under the ICC Rules presuppose that the parties have made a valid agreement to arbitrate. Book 10 of the German ZPO, for example, which is based on the UNCITRAL Model Law, defines what an arbitration agreement is in Article 1029(1) and the form it should take in Articles 1029(2) and 1031. Book 6 of the Belgian Judicial Code, which also is based on the UNCITRAL Model law, defines the arbitration agreement in Article 1681 and does not require a written form for the validity of the arbitration agreement, whereas a written form will only be necessary to prove the existence of the arbitration agreement (See also Articles 1442 and 1443 NCPC, Article 178(1) PILA, Article 7 of the UNCITRAL Model Law).

According to Article 7(1) of the UNCITRAL Model Law, an arbitration agreement is 'an agreement by the parties to submit to arbitration all or certain disputes which have arisen or which may arise between them in respect of a defined legal relationship, whether contractual or not'. The second sentence of this article goes on to indicate that such an agreement may be made within a contract or separately. Once made, it binds the contracting parties and occasionally other parties that are also to be regarded as contracting parties.

The arbitration agreement does not mean that any dispute arising between these parties has to be submitted to arbitration, but only those resulting from the specific legal relationship to which the agreement relates. This condition is expressed as follows in the ICC standard clause: 'All disputes arising out of or in connection with the present contract will be finally settled ... by one or more arbitrators ...'

The questions of how many arbitrators will comprise the arbitral tribunal and how these shall be appointed remain open. If the German ZPO is applicable, the number of arbitrators will be decided in accordance with Article 1034(1). In the case of the Belgian JC, it will be determined in accordance with Article 1684 and in the case of the Swiss PILA in accordance with Article 179(2), which refers to cantonal law, and if the French NCPC is applicable in accordance with Article 1451. (See also Article 10 of the UNCITRAL Model Law). As far as the appointment of arbitrators is concerned, the relevant provisions are Article 1035(3) and (5) ZPO, Article 1685 JC, Articles 1451 to 1454 NCPC and Article 179(2) PILA, which refers to cantonal law, and Article 11 of the UNCITRAL Model Law. The place of the arbitration will then be fixed by the arbitral tribunal in accordance with Article 1043 ZPO, if applicable (cf. Article 1701(1) JC, Article 176(3) PILA, Article 20 of the UNCITRAL Model Law).

In an international context, it may be difficult to determine which national court has jurisdiction since the parties reside in different countries and the place of performance or the place where the damage occurs may be in yet another country. Nor is it always easy in such situations to know which procedural law is applicable if the dispute is to be submitted to a national court.

There is no need to determine or refer to a national procedural law if a dispute is submitted to arbitration, especially that of an institution like ICC. It is sufficient to include in the arbitration agreement a reference to the institution's rules, as is found in the ICC standard clause ('shall be finally settled under the Rules of Arbitration of the International Chamber of Commerce by one or more arbitrators appointed in accordance with the said Rules').

However, the parties should always check whether there are any mandatory requirements for an arbitration agreement at the place of the arbitration and at potential place(s) of enforcement of any arbitral award. In this respect, ICC indicates that it is prudent for parties wishing to have an ICC arbitration in China to include in their arbitration clause an explicit reference to the ICC International Court of Arbitration. The following clause is suggested for this purpose (see J. Fry, S. Greenberg and F. Mazza, *The Secretariat's Guide to ICC Arbitration*, ICC Publication No. 729 E, Paris, 2012, p. 449):

> 'All disputes arising out of or in connection with the present contract shall be submitted to the International Court of Arbitration of the International Chamber of Commerce and shall be finally settled under the Rules of Arbitration of the International Chamber of Commerce by one or more arbitrators appointed in accordance with the said Rules.'

The effect of the reference to the ICC Rules of Arbitration is to make the Rules part of the parties' arbitration agreement, which thereby deals with both the constitution of the arbitral tribunal and the determination of the place of the arbitration. This is supported by Article 6(1) of the Rules:

> 'Where the parties have agreed to submit to arbitration under the Rules, they shall be deemed to have submitted *ipso facto* to the Rules in effect on the date of commencement of the arbitration, unless they have agreed to submit to the Rules in effect on the date of their arbitration agreement.'

The standard clause leaves open the questions of how many arbitrators will comprise the arbitral tribunal in a given case, where the arbitration will be seated and in what language it will be conducted. Given that the latter two questions are often a cause of disagreement between the parties when negotiating the arbitration clause, the use of the standard clause as it is usually saves time and avoids problems. However, it should not be forgotten that parties need to be able to predict such matters when signing a contract and, for this reason, arbitration agreements usually indicate the number of arbitrators and the place and language of the arbitration.

It is possible to agree on other aspects of the procedure too. However, anyone who is not fully conversant with arbitration and the ICC Rules should be very careful when including any additional wording, in order to avoid unexpected problems.

To sum up, parties who enter into an ICC arbitration agreement undertake to use arbitration to obtain a final decision relating to one or more specified, or at least clearly definable, legal relationships, and must at the same time include a reference to the ICC Rules and clearly express their agreement to the application of the rules.

B. RULES OF LAW APPLICABLE TO THE ARBITRATION AGREEMENT

The arbitration agreement is subject to the provisions governing contracts contained in the applicable rules of law. Like any contract, the arbitration agreement may be void or voidable. However, this does not result from the mere fact that the contract, or legal relationship, for which the arbitration agreement was made is void or voidable. Even if the arbitration agreement takes the form of a clause inserted in the contract rather than a separate document, it is currently considered by lawyers internationally to be legally independent of the main contract. This is clearly stated in Article 6(9) of the Rules:

> 'Unless otherwise agreed, the arbitral tribunal shall not cease to have jurisdiction by reason of any allegation that the contract is non-existent or null and void, provided that the arbitral tribunal upholds the validity of the arbitration agreement. The arbitral tribunal shall continue to have jurisdiction to determine the parties' respective rights and to decide their claims and pleas even though the contract itself may be non-existent or null and void.'

This provision enshrines the principle of jurisdiction over jurisdiction in ICC arbitration. This principle, otherwise known as 'Kompetenz-Kompetenz' or 'Competence competence', asserts the arbitral tribunal's power to decide on its own jurisdiction. It is a principle recognized in many countries.

Article V(1)(a) of the New York Convention allows the recognition and the enforcement of an award to be refused if one of the parties provides the relevant authority with proof that the parties to the arbitration agreement 'were, under the law applicable to them, under some incapacity, or the said agreement is not valid under the law to which the parties have subjected it or, failing any indication thereon, under the law of the country where the award was made'. Equivalent or similar provisions are found in the laws of countries where courts have jurisdiction over applications for an award to be set aside.

Before an arbitration agreement is made, even in the form recommended by ICC in its standard clause, it is advisable to check that the parties have the legal capacity to enter into such an agreement. If there are multiple parties, or if the parties are legal entities, powers of attorney necessary for this purpose must be checked, as must the arbitrability of the dispute according to the applicable law. Without going into the various situations that may be encountered, it is worth mentioning that in ICC arbitrations problems in this regard have generally arisen in connection with contracts in which one of the parties is a state authority or a state-owned undertaking.

C. QUESTIONS CONCERNING SPECIFIC SUPPLEMENTARY PROVISIONS IN THE ARBITRATION AGREEMENT

1. The Requirement to Attempt Mediation First and Other Prior Conditions

Arbitration clauses that contain conditions to be fulfilled before a request for arbitration may be filed are often a source of problems. The wording of a well-intentioned clause requiring the parties to attempt to settle their dispute amicably through a mediation before resorting to arbitration may at the very least be a cause of delay, if one of the parties claims that no such attempt has been made by the other party. Attempts to reach an amicable settlement, even with the involvement of a neutral third party (mediator) are, of course, usually to be welcomed, provided parties ensure that they are not used to hinder any arbitration proceedings that may prove to be necessary. Similar precautions should be taken with respect to any other condition relating to the commencement of arbitration proceedings.

ICC offers a range of standard clauses for different combinations of procedures which are available in several languages at <www.iccarbitration.org>.

If parties wish to create an obligation to refer a dispute to proceedings under the ICC Mediation Rules before starting an arbitration, but without requiring the parties to conclude the mediation process or without a requirement to wait for an agreed period of time before commencing arbitration proceedings, ICC suggests the following clause (ICC Publication No. 865-0 E, Paris, 2013, p. 89):

> '(x) In the event of any dispute arising out of or in connection with the present contract, the parties shall first refer the dispute to proceedings under the ICC Mediation Rules. The commencement of proceedings under the ICC Mediation Rules shall not prevent any party from commencing arbitration in accordance with sub-clause y below.
>
> (y) All disputes arising out of or in connection with the present contract shall be finally settled under the Rules of Arbitration of the International Chamber of Commerce by one or more arbitrators appointed in accordance with the said Rules.'

This clause allows judicial, arbitral or similar proceedings to be commenced in parallel with proceedings under the ICC Mediation Rules.

If parties wish to create an obligation to refer a dispute to proceedings under the ICC Mediation Rules before starting an arbitration, however, while requiring the parties to wait until an agreed period of time has elapsed following the filing of a request for mediation before they can commence arbitration proceedings, ICC suggests the following clause (ICC Publication No. 865-0 E, Paris, 2013, p. 90):

> 'In the event of any dispute arising out of or in connection with the present contract, the parties shall first refer the dispute to proceedings under the ICC Mediation Rules. If the dispute has not been settled pursuant to the said Rules within [45] days following the filing of a Request for Mediation or within such other period as the parties may agree in writing, such dispute shall thereafter be finally settled under the Rules of Arbitration of the International Chamber of Commerce by one or more arbitrators appointed in accordance with the said Rules of Arbitration.'

If parties wish to exclude any recourse to the Emergency Arbitration Provisions, they must expressly opt out by adding wording as indicated above.

If parties wish to exclude any recourse to the Emergency Arbitration Provisions, they must expressly opt out by adding wording as indicated above.

If parties wish to have recourse to ICC arbitration as well as to the ICC pre-arbitral referee procedure, a specific reference to both procedures should be stipulated. For that purpose, ICC recommends the following clause (ICC Publication No. 864-0 E, Paris, 2008, p. 11):

> 'Any party to this contract shall have the right to have recourse to and shall be bound by the pre-arbitral referee procedure of the International Chamber of Commerce in accordance with its Rules for a Pre-Arbitral Referee Procedure. All disputes arising out of or in connection with the present contract shall be finally settled under the Rules of Arbitration of the International Chamber of Commerce by one or more arbitrators appointed in accordance with the said Rules of Arbitration.'

As ICC indicates, the extent to which the ICC Rules for a Pre-Arbitral Referee Procedure are recognized and accepted may vary from one country to another depending on the applicable law(s). Parties wishing to have recourse to these Rules should ensure that they conform with the law(s) applicable to each case.

If parties wish to create an obligation to submit a dispute to non-binding administered expert proceedings under the ICC Rules for the Administration of Expert Proceedings before starting an arbitration, the following clause may be used (ICC Publication No. 869-1 E, Paris, 2015, p. 35):

> 'In the event of any dispute arising out of or in connection with clause [X] of the present contract, the parties agree to submit the dispute, in the first instance, to administered expert proceedings in accordance with the Rules for the Administration of Expert Proceedings of the International Chamber of Commerce. After the International Centre for ADR's notification of the termination of the administered expert proceedings, the dispute, if it has not been resolved, shall be finally settled under the Rules of Arbitration of the International Chamber of Commerce by one or more arbitrators appointed in accordance with the said Rules of Arbitration.'

Other combinations of services are also possible. For instance, arbitration may be used as a fallback to dispute boards under the ICC Dispute Board Rules.

2. Arbitral Tribunals Composed of Two or an Even Number of Members

The ICC Rules of Arbitration state that arbitral tribunals may be composed of one or three members. This avoids the risk of an impasse, as Article 31(1) makes it clear that the arbitral tribunal will always be able to make a decision. There have been cases in practice where parties agreed upon a two-member tribunal, or a tribunal comprising more than three arbitrators, as has happened in multiparty arbitrations for instance. Such situations should no longer arise, as the ICC International Court of Arbitration will consider such exceptions as unacceptable, unless the parties have provided for solutions to possible deadlocks. Such a solution could be an agreement to appoint an additional arbitrator, known as an umpire, who will have the same rights as a president of the arbitral tribunal under Article 31(1) of the Rules. Failing this, there is a strong risk that the ICC Court would refuse to set the proceedings in motion, on the grounds that it does not qualify as an ICC arbitration. In light of Article 11(6) of the Rules and the principle of party autonomy with regard to the constitution of the arbitral tribunal, the Court will of course try to give effect to the arbitration clause by allowing the proceedings to be set in motion whenever it considers this to be possible under the Rules.

It is not uncommon for national laws to require arbitral tribunals to be composed of an odd number of members (see, for example, Article 1684(1) JC and Article 1451 NCPC). If such a law is applicable, failure to comply with this requirement could render the arbitration agreement invalid.

3. Nomination of Arbitrators by Third Parties

Occasionally, an ICC arbitration agreement may provide that a sole arbitrator, the president of an arbitral tribunal or a co-arbitrator that a party has failed to appoint will be nominated by a third party rather than by the ICC International Court of Arbitration. Such third party might be the president of another chamber of commerce or the presiding judge of a national court. The Court usually accepts this, as long as the conditions relating to the impartiality and independence of the arbitrator and the process of confirmation, which necessarily apply here too, are met. This is why, in such cases, the Court's confirmation of such arbitrators is also necessary. In actual practice, such agreements are not really useful, given that they exclude the possibility of drawing on the pool of arbitrators of the ICC national committees. Problems may also arise if the third party chosen by the parties is prevented for legal or other reasons from nominating an arbitrator. Already for this reason, it is inadvisable to agree on the nomination of arbitrators by third parties.

It is useful and even recommendable to empower the co-arbitrators of a three-member tribunal to choose the president of the arbitral tribunal. (In 2013, 194 of the 355 arbitrators appointed to chair a tribunal were proposed by the co-arbitrators, 19 selected directly by the parties, 94 were appointed upon the proposal of an ICC national committee or group, 45 were appointed directly by the Court and 3 were appointed by an authority other than the ICC Court; see '2013 Statistical Report' published in *ICC International Court of Arbitration Bulletin*, Paris, Vol. 25/Nr. 1 – 2014, p. 10, In 2012, 175 of the 335 arbitrators appointed to chair a tribunal were proposed by the co-arbitrators, 26 directly by the parties, 119 were appointed upon the proposal of an ICC national committee or group and 15 were appointed directly by the Court; see '2012 Statistical Report' published in *ICC International Court of Arbitration Bulletin*, Paris, Vol. 24/Nr. 1 – 2013, p. 11) If the co-arbitrators are unable to agree on their choice of the third arbitrator, it will be up to the ICC International Court of Arbitration to make the appointment.

4. Possibility of Derogating from Certain Provisions of the ICC Rules

Except for a few provisions that explicitly allow for alternative arrangements by the parties, it is not advisable to derogate from individual provisions of the Rules, as they are interdependent. Like its predecessors, the 2012 version of the Rules does not contain any formal rule on permissible or prohibited derogations. There is, therefore, a risk that, not only in the cases mentioned previously where an even number of arbitrators has been agreed upon without any stop-gap mechanism, the ICC International Court of Arbitration may decide that it was not the parties' intention to have their dispute settled under the ICC Rules. This will also be the case when the parties choose to depart from the provisions relating to the Terms of Reference, the submission of the draft award to the Court for approval as to its form, or ICC's responsibility for managing costs and fixing fees. It is not possible to provide detailed information on this risk as the Court's decisions in this regard are not made public.

5. Items Worth Including in an Arbitration Agreement

Firstly, one of the chief points to be included in the arbitration agreement are the rules of law applicable to the contract and the performance thereof, which therefore will be the rules of law applied by the arbitral tribunal when resolving a dispute. It is generally advisable to agree on the applicable rules of law in international contracts (see the commentary on Article 21 of the Rules).

Secondly, the place of the arbitration needs to be specified. More often than not, it is located in a country other than where any of the parties is based. It should not be chosen solely for its ease of access for the parties and for the infrastructure it offers for the conduct of the proceedings, but also and above all because its legislation and courts are favorably disposed towards arbitration. A further point to check is that in the countries where the arbitral award is likely to be performed the recognition and enforcement of awards are guaranteed through international conventions such as the New York Convention or through bilateral agreements between the country where the place of the arbitration is located and the country where the arbitral award is likely to be performed.

It is worth noting that the ICC International Court of Arbitration and a number of state courts have in the past interpreted the inclusion of the words 'in Paris' after the reference to the International Chamber of Commerce in the ICC standard clause and similarly worded arbitration agreements to mean the place of the arbitration rather than the location of the ICC International Secretariat (see the commentary on Article 18 of the Rules).

Thirdly, the language of the arbitration should be mentioned (see the commentary on Article 20 of the Rules). Specifying the language of the arbitration will help when selecting arbitrators, as it will be clear what linguistic requirements they need to satisfy.

Fourthly, the parties may decide whether to submit the dispute to one or three arbitrators. Parties often prefer to specify three arbitrators in their arbitration agreement, as this gives them a feeling of greater security in the decision-making process and as the ICC Rules contain a presumption in favour of a sole arbitrator (Article 12(2) of the Rules). This will usually be appropriate if the amount in dispute is sizable, although a sole arbitrator can usually conduct the proceedings more rapidly – at least in theory – as there is no need to consult other arbitrators. If the amount in dispute is small, the choice of a three-member tribunal may make the cost of the arbitration disproportionately high.

Other aspects of the procedure – such as the production of evidence – should be mentioned in the arbitration agreement only if absolutely necessary and after first consulting arbitration specialists.

CHAPTER 5

OVERVIEW OF THE TIME LIMITS LAID DOWN IN THE ICC RULES OF ARBITRATION

1. Article 3(4) of the Rules: How Time Limits are Calculated

Periods of time begin to run on the day after that on which the notification or communication is deemed to have been made in accordance with Article 3(3). If such day is an official holiday or a non-business day in the country where notification is made, the period of time does not start to run until the first following business day.

Periods of time expire on the last day, unless this day is an official holiday or non-business day in the country where notification is made, in which case the expiry date will be the first following business day.

2. Article 4(2) of the Rules: Start of the Arbitral Proceedings

The date on which the request for arbitration is received by the Secretariat of the ICC International Court of Arbitration is regarded, for all purposes, as the date of commencement of the arbitral proceedings.

3. Article 4(4) of the Rules: Prerequisites for Filing a Valid Request for Arbitration

If the claimant does not comply with the conditions set forth in Article 3(1) (number of copies required) and Article 4(4) (advance payment on administrative expenses), the Secretariat of the Court may set the claimant a time limit for compliance with these conditions. If the claimant has still not complied upon the expiry of the time limit, the arbitration file will be closed, although the claimant retains the right to file a new request at a later date. The practice of the Secretariat is to set a time limit of **around ten days** in such situations.

4. Article 5(1) and (2) of the Rules: Filing of an Answer to the Request for Arbitration

The respondent's answer must be filed **within 30 days** of receiving the request for arbitration from the Secretariat of the Court (paragraph 1).

This time limit may be extended by the Secretariat at the respondent's request. When making such a request, the respondent must give its views on the number and choice of arbitrators and nominate an arbitrator, if necessary, in accordance with Articles 12 and 13. The Secretariat's practice is usually to extend the time limit by **approximately 30 days**.

If the respondent fails to submit an answer, the Secretary General (Article 6(3)) or the ICC International Court of Arbitration (Article 6(4)) may decide that the arbitration shall proceed in accordance with the Rules.

5. Article 5(6) of the Rules: Claimant's Reply to a Counterclaim

The claimant has **30 days** in which to respond to a counterclaim from the moment it receives the counterclaim from the Secretariat of the Court.

This time limit may be extended by the Secretariat, in which case an extension of **around 30 days** is common practice.

6. Article 11(2) of the Rules: Qualified Statement of Independence from an Arbitrator

The Secretariat of the Court will forward to the parties for their comments a qualified statement of independence submitted by an arbitrator. The Secretariat sets a time limit (**usually 15 days**) for the parties to indicate whether they are in favor of accepting the arbitrator or have objections.

7. Article 12(2) of the Rules: Nomination of Co-Arbitrators after the Court has Decided in Favor of a Three-Member Tribunal

If the parties have not agreed on the number of arbitrators and the ICC International Court of Arbitration considers a three-member arbitral tribunal to be warranted, the **claimant** nominates an arbitrator **within 15 days** of receiving notification of the Court's decision and the **respondent** nominates an arbitrator **within 15 days** of receiving notification of the person nominated by the claimant.

8. Article 12(4) of the Rules: Nomination of Co-Arbitrators where the Parties Agree on a Three-Member Tribunal

If the parties have agreed that their dispute shall be resolved by a three-member arbitral tribunal, the claimant nominates an arbitrator in the request for arbitration and the respondent nominates an arbitrator in its answer to the request for arbitration, both arbitrators being subject to confirmation (respectively Articles 4(3) and 5(1) and (2); see 3 and 4 above).

If a party fails to nominate an arbitrator, the ICC International Court of Arbitration will appoint the arbitrator instead.

9. Article 12(5) of the Rules: Nomination of the Person who will act as President of a Three-Member Tribunal

When the parties have agreed on the procedure for appointing the third arbitrator who will act as president of the arbitral tribunal, the nomination should be made within **30 days** from the confirmation or appointment of the co-arbitrators or any other time limit agreed by the parties or fixed by the ICC International Court of Arbitration.

If the nomination is not made within the 30 days-time limit or within any other time limit agreed by the parties or fixed by the Court for this purpose, the third arbitrator will be appointed by the Court.

10. Article 12(3) of the Rules: Nomination of a Sole Arbitrator

When the parties have agreed that the dispute will be resolved by a sole arbitrator, they may nominate an arbitrator for confirmation, by mutual agreement, **within 30 days** of the respondent receiving notification of the request for arbitration, or within any additional time limit allowed by the Secretariat of the Court.

11. Article 13(3) of the Rules: Appointment of a Co-Arbitrator upon the Proposal of a National Committee or Group when a Party Fails to make the Necessary Nomination

When the ICC International Court of Arbitration has to appoint an arbitrator on behalf of a party that has failed to nominate one, it makes the appointment on the basis of a proposal from the ICC national committee or group that it considers to be appropriate. The proposal is to be made within the time limit set by the Court, which is usually **around 15 days**.

If the national committee or group does not make a proposal within the given time limit, the Court may repeat its request, or request a proposal from another national committee or group that it considers to be appropriate, or appoint directly any person whom it regards as suitable.

12. Article 14(2) of the Rules: Challenges of Arbitrators by Parties

To be admissible, a challenge must be made **within 30 days** of receipt of notification of the appointment or confirmation of the arbitrator, or **within 30 days** from the date on which the party making the challenge was informed of the **facts and circumstances** on which its challenge is based, if this date is later than the receipt of the aforementioned notification.

According to Article 14(3), the Court gives all those involved in the arbitration an opportunity to express their views in writing before it makes its decision. The customary time limit for this is **around 15 days**.

13. Article 15(3) of the Rules: Replacement of Arbitrators by the Court

When, on the basis of information that has come to its attention, the ICC International Court of Arbitration considers replacing an arbitrator, it makes its decision after first giving the arbitrator concerned, the parties and any other members of the arbitral tribunal a suitable time to submit written comments. The time allowed is **usually 15 days**.

14. Article 23(2) of the Rules: Terms of Reference

The Terms of Reference, signed by the parties and the arbitral tribunal, are submitted to the ICC International Court of Arbitration **within two months** of the file being transmitted to the arbitral tribunal by the Secretariat of the Court.

This time limit may be extended, if the arbitral tribunal makes a reasoned request to this effect, or upon the Court's own initiative if it considers this to be necessary.

If one of the parties refuses to sign the Terms of Reference, the arbitration proceeds according to Article 23(3) of the Rules, once the Terms of Reference have been signed in accordance with Article 23(2) or approved by the Court.

15. Article 24(1) of the Rules: Case Management Conference

When the Terms of Reference are drawn up, or as soon as possible thereafter, the arbitral tribunal shall convene a case management conference to consult the parties on procedural measures that may be adopted pursuant to Article 22(2).

16. Article 24(2) of the Rules: Procedural Timetable

During the case management conference organized pursuant to Article 24(1), or as soon as possible thereafter, and after consulting the parties, the arbitral tribunal draws up a procedural timetable that it intends to follow for the conduct of the arbitration.

17. Article 27 of the Rules: Closing of the Proceedings

As soon as possible after the last hearing concerning matters to be decided in an award or the filing of the last authorized submissions concerning such matters, whichever is later, the arbitral tribunal declares the proceedings closed.

18. Article 27 of the Rules: Announcement of the Submission of the Draft Award to the Court

When the arbitral tribunal declares the proceedings closed, it indicates to the Secretariat of the ICC International Court of Arbitration and to the parties the date by which it expects to submit the draft award to the Court for approval in accordance with Article 33.

19. Article 30 of the Rules: The Award

The arbitral tribunal renders its award **within six months** from the date of the last signature by the arbitral tribunal or by the parties of the Terms of Reference or, if a party refuses to sign them, within six months from the date on which the Secretariat notifies the arbitral tribunal of the Court's approval of the Terms of Reference.

This time limit may be extended by the Court if the arbitral tribunal makes a reasoned request to this effect or upon the Court's own initiative, if it considers this to be necessary.

20. Article 35 of the Rules: Correction of an Award

The arbitral tribunal may, on its own initiative, correct any clerical, computational, typographical or similar error contained in the arbitral award, as long as such correction is submitted to the ICC International Court of Arbitration for approval **within 30 days from the date of the award** (Article 35(1)).

A party may apply to the Secretariat of the Court for the correction of an award **within 30 days of being notified** of such award (Article 35(2)).

The application is forwarded to the arbitral tribunal, which gives the other party a period of time, **normally not exceeding 30 days** from that party's receipt of the application, in which to submit its comments.

If the arbitral tribunal decides to correct the award, it submits its decision in draft form to the Court **no later than 30 days** after the expiry of the period of time allowed for receipt of comments from the other party or within any other time limit set by the Court.

21. Article 35 of the Rules: Interpretation of an Award

A party may apply to the Secretariat of the Court for the interpretation of an award **within 30 days of being notified** of such award (Article 35(2)).

The application is forwarded to the arbitral tribunal, which gives the other party a period of time, **normally not exceeding 30 days** from that party's receipt of the application, in which to submit its comments.

If the arbitral tribunal decides to interpret the award, it submits its decision in draft form to the Court **no later than 30 days** after the expiry of the period of time allowed for receipt of comments from the other party or within any other time limit set by the Court.

22. Article 35(4) of the Rules: Remission of an Award

Where a court remits an award to the arbitral tribunal, the provisions of Articles 31, 33, 34 and 35 shall apply. The Court may take any steps as may be necessary to enable the arbitral tribunal to comply with the terms of such remission.

23. Article 36(1) of the Rules: Payment of the Provisional Advance on Costs

The provisional advance on the costs of the arbitration fixed by the Secretary General of the ICC International Court of Arbitration must be paid by the claimant as quickly as possible so as not to delay the transmission of the file to the arbitral tribunal once it has been constituted. As a general rule, the claimant is requested to pay this provisional advance **within 30 days**.

24. Article 36(6) of the Rules: Payment of the Advance on Costs

When a request for an advance on costs has not been complied with, the Secretary General of the ICC International Court of Arbitration may direct the arbitral tribunal to suspend its work, after first consulting it on the matter. The Secretary General may set a time limit, that must be no less than **15 days**, upon the expiry of which the relevant claims will be considered as withdrawn.

Should the party concerned wish to object to this measure, it must make a request, within the time limit mentioned above, for the matter to be decided by the Court.

25. Article 38 of the Rules: Modification of Time Limits by the Parties

The parties may agree to shorten the various time limits referred to in the Rules of Arbitration. If such an agreement is made after the arbitral tribunal has been constituted, it will become effective only if approved by the arbitral tribunal (Article 38(1)).

The ICC International Court of Arbitration may, on its own initiative, decide to extend any time limit that has been modified by the parties pursuant to Article 38(1), if it considers this to be necessary in order to allow it or the arbitral tribunal to fulfill their duties in accordance with the Rules (Article 38(2)).

26. Article 39 of the Rules: Waiver

A party is deemed to have waived its right to object to a failure to comply with any provision of the Rules, any other rules applicable to the proceedings, any direction given by the arbitral tribunal, or any requirement under the arbitration agreement relating to the constitution of the arbitral tribunal or the conduct of the proceedings, if it proceeds with the arbitration without immediately raising its objection before the arbitral tribunal.

27. Article 1(8) of Appendix II to the Rules: Return of Documents at the End of the Arbitration

Any documents, communications or correspondence submitted by the parties or the arbitrators may be destroyed unless a party or an arbitrator requests in writing, within a period fixed by the Secretariat of the Court, the return of such documents. The cost of their return is borne by the party or arbitrator making the request.

CHAPTER 6

OTHER METHODS OF DISPUTE RESOLUTION UNDER ICC RULES

A. GENERAL REMARKS

In recent times, ICC has adopted or updated a number of other sets of dispute resolution rules, which can be considered as complementary to its Rules of Arbitration.

ICC's very first set of dispute resolution rules covered conciliation as well as arbitration. In the 1920s, the process of conciliation was well received by the business community as a useful technique for settling disputes and indeed gave rise to more cases at that time than arbitration. However, it was subsequently overshadowed by arbitration, whose success owed much to the fact that arbitration led to a binding decision enforceable in a growing number of countries across the world following the adoption and ratification of various international conventions. Of these, the convention that has most contributed to the success of arbitration is the Convention on the Recognition and Enforcement of Foreign Arbitral Awards, done in New York on 10 June 1958 (the 'New York Convention'), now in force in over 150 countries throughout the world.

Over the years, arbitration has evolved into a more complex and costly procedure than it was initially. This deters some parties from using arbitration to resolve their disputes and over the last twenty to twenty-five years has led to a growing need and search for other methods of dispute resolution.

ICC itself felt that its conciliation rules, which were originally adopted in 1922 and modified in 1927, 1933, 1947, 1955, 1975 and 1988, no longer met current business needs. When revising its Rules of Arbitration in the 1990s, it therefore decided to separate arbitration and conciliation and remove the reference to conciliation in the standard ICC arbitration clause. ICC was nonetheless fully aware of the need to respond to an increasing demand for alternatives to arbitration that do not normally end in an enforceable award.

As early as 1976, it made a first move to widen its dispute resolution services by creating its International Centre for Expertise. The ICC Rules for Expertise, administered by the Centre (now called the International Centre for ADR), were amended in 1993, in 2003 and in 2015. In 1990, ICC adopted Rules for a Pre-Arbitral Referee Procedure and in 1997 Rules for Documentary Credit Dispute Resolution Expertise, known as DOCDEX. The DOCDEX Rules were revised in 2002 and new DOCDEX Rules entered into force as from 1 May 2015. In 2001, ICC introduced ADR Rules to replace the former Rules of Optional Conciliation. In 2014, the ADR Rules were replaced by the Mediation Rules. In 2004, ICC adopted rules relating to Dispute Boards (Dispute Review Boards (DRB)/Dispute Adjudication Boards (DAB)) and new Dispute Board Rules entered into force as from 1 October 2015. The ICC International Centre for ADR provides the necessary services of the ICC under the Mediation Rules, the Expert Rules, the Dispute Board Rules and the DOCDEX Rules, whereas the Secretariat of the ICC International Court of Arbitration provides the necessary services of the ICC under the Pre-Arbitral Referee Rules. Together, these various sets of rules, including those relating to arbitration, provide the framework for ICC's comprehensive set of dispute resolution services.

It is worthwhile looking briefly at the rules mentioned above, which are complementary to arbitration and, in certain situations, may be used in combination with arbitration to settle disputes. The official English and French texts of the rules, together with a number of translations, can be consulted on the following web pages: <www.iccarbitration.org>, <www.iccmediation.org>, <www.iccadr.org>, <www.iccexpertise.org> and <www.iccdocdex.org>. For the sake of convenience, the current English versions of the ICC Rules for a Pre-arbitral Referee Procedure, the ICC Mediation Rules, the ICC Expert Rules, the ICC Dispute Board Rules and the ICC DOCDEX Rules are reproduced in appendices at the end of this book. Readers should consult the ICC web pages for any updates following the publication of this book.

B. ICC RULES FOR A PRE-ARBITRAL REFEREE PROCEDURE

During the performance of a contract, problems can arise that need to be attended to immediately through urgent, binding measures. If the factual situation is likely to change, it may not be possible or desirable to wait for the matter to be dealt with by an arbitral tribunal once arbitration proceedings have been set in motion. The ICC Rules for a Pre-Arbitral Referee Procedure, which came into force on 1 January 1990, are intended to respond to this specific need (see Appendix 21 below). They provide for the appointment of a third person, referred to as a 'referee', who has the power to order provisional measures as a matter of urgency, before the case is heard by an arbitral tribunal or a court (Article 1(1)). The measures ordered are binding until the referee, or the court or arbitral tribunal to which the case is subsequently referred, decides otherwise (Article 6(3)). Parties may use these rules only if they have agreed in writing to do so. It is worth noting that if the parties have agreed to the ICC pre-arbitral referee procedure, this shall have as a consequence under Article 29(6) of the 2012 ICC Rules of Arbitration that the Emergency Arbitrator Provisions (contained in Article 29 of the Rules of Arbitration and in Appendix V to the ICC Rules of Arbitration) will not be applicable.

ICC has handled only ten pre-arbitral referee cases since the Rules were adopted in 1990. The ICC Rules for a Pre-Arbitral Referee Procedure may be found in Appendix 21 below.

1. Suggested ICC Pre-Arbitral Referee Clause

ICC recommends the following pre-arbitral referee clause:

> 'Any party to this contract shall have the right to have recourse to and shall be bound by the Pre-Arbitral Referee Procedure of the International Chamber of Commerce in accordance with its Rules.'

A standard clause referring to both the pre-arbitral referee procedure and arbitration is also available for use by parties wishing to provide for both procedures in their contracts.

2. Characteristics

The essential features of these rules are speed and efficiency. After being notified directly by the claimant of the request for the appointment of a referee, the respondent has eight days in which to file an answer, which is sent directly to the claimant and to any other party, as well as to the Secretariat of the ICC International Court of Arbitration, using the quickest available method of delivery (Article 3(4)). The referee is appointed by the President of the ICC International Court of Arbitration, upon the expiry of the eight-day time limit allowed for the respondent to submit an answer to the request and after having verified the '*prima facie*' existence of the agreement of the parties. Alternatively, the parties may choose a referee by agreement, before or after the filing of the request (Article 4(1)).

As with arbitrators under the ICC Rules of Arbitration, a prospective referee will first be asked to sign a statement of acceptance, availability and independence and to reveal to the Secretariat any facts or circumstances that could call into question his or her independence in the eyes of the parties (See Appendix 22 below).

The referee has thirty days in which to make an order (Article 6(2)). The Secretariat notifies the parties of the order, provided that the full amount of the advance on costs previously fixed by it has been paid (Article 6(5)). The proceedings are conducted in an adversarial manner and the respondent is given the opportunity to submit comments and documents. Before delivering an order, the referee is entitled to make any investigations, decide on any interim measures and request any expert opinions that may be considered appropriate (Article 5(3)).

3. Powers of the Referee

According to Article 2(1) of the rules, the referee can:

- order any conservatory measures or measures of restoration urgently needed to prevent immediate damage or irreparable loss, so as to safeguard any of the rights or property of one of the parties;
- order a party to make any payment that needs to be made to any other party or any other person;
- order a party to take any step required by the contract between the parties, including the signing or delivery of any document or the procuring by a party of the signature or delivery of a document;
- order any measures necessary to preserve and establish evidence.

The referee cannot make an order other than that requested by a party (Article 2(2)).

The referee's order does not pre-judge the substance of the case, nor is it binding on any arbitral tribunal or national court that may hear any question, issue or dispute in respect of which the order has been made. The order remains in force unless and until the referee or the arbitral tribunal or national court decides otherwise (Article 6(3)).

The referee's order includes the reasons on which the decision is based. The carrying out of the order may be made subject to the fulfillment of any other conditions thought fit by the referee, such as the commencement of proceedings on the merits before the arbitral tribunal or national court within a certain time limit, or the provision of adequate security by the party for whose benefit the order is made (e.g. the production of guarantees) (Article 6(4)).

By agreeing to use these rules, the parties undertake to carry out the referee's order without delay and waive their right to appeal against or oppose the implementation of the order, insofar as such waiver can validly be made (Article 6(6)). Since the referee's order is not an award, no application can be made for it to be set aside.

If a case is referred to a court or arbitral tribunal after the referee has been appointed, the referee retains the power to make an order within thirty days of being given the file, unless the parties agree otherwise or the court or arbitral tribunal decides otherwise (Article 2(4)).

A referee is forbidden to act as arbitrator in any subsequent proceedings between the same parties or in other connected cases, unless the parties agree otherwise in writing (Article 2(3)).

4. Costs

When filing a request under the ICC Rules for a Pre-Arbitral Referee Procedure, the requesting party must pay US$ 5 000, of which US$ 2 500 constitutes a non-refundable administrative charge and US$ 2 500 an advance on the fees and expenses of the referee and any expert (Appendix – Costs and Payment for a Pre-Arbitral Referee Procedure, part B(1)). ICC will deal with the request only if it is accompanied by this payment. The Secretariat of the ICC International Court of Arbitration will then fix an advance to cover the estimated costs of the pre-arbitral referee procedure as soon as possible after the file has been sent to the referee. The advance is paid by the party or parties seeking the order (Appendix, part B(2)). No order can be notified until payment has been made in full (Article 6(5)) of the Rules; Appendix, part B(3)).

The amount of the referee's fees and expenses are fixed by the Secretary General of the ICC International Court of Arbitration at the end of the proceedings (Appendix, part A(2)). This amount is stated in the referee's order, which also indicates in what proportion these costs are to be borne by the parties (Article 7(1) of the Rules).

C. ICC MEDIATION RULES

1. Mediation / Amicable Dispute Resolution

The ICC Mediation Rules, which entered into force on 1 January 2014 and replace the 2001 ICC ADR Rules, are intended to offer business partners a means of resolving disputes amicably, in the way best suited to their needs. The ICC Mediation Rules may be found in Appendix 23 below.

Whereas the acronym 'ADR' is generally considered to stand for 'Alternative Dispute Resolution' in the sense of an alternative to litigation in the courts, for ICC, however, 'ADR' meant 'Amicable Dispute Resolution'. ICC preferred not to use the acronym ADR to mean alternative dispute resolution, which in several countries, including the USA, includes arbitration, whereas ICC has a separate set of rules for arbitration.

The ADR Rules were revised in 2014 so as to make them consistent with the 2012 ICC Rules of Arbitration, and also to update the Rules to reflect developments in ADR and mediation practice and to better reflect the current practices of the ICC International Centre for ADR under existing ADR Rules, while maintaining flexibility in the process. The first and most obvious difference between the ADR Rules and the Mediation Rules is the change of name. It reflects the fact that in the 180 cases conducted under the ADR Rules in more than 90% of these cases mediation was chosen by the parties as the settlement technique or became the settlement technique pursuant to the default mechanism foreseen in the ADR Rules (Art. 5(1) of the 2001 ADR Rules). Consistent with the change of the name of the Rules, the term 'neutral' of the ADR Rules has been abandoned and replaced by 'mediator' throughout the Rules (see 'The New ICC Mediation Rules' published in *ICC International Court of Arbitration Bulletin*, Paris, Vol. 24/Nr. 2 - 2014, p. 6-7).

The new ICC Mediation Rules will apply to all contracts signed after their entry into force on 1 January 2014. If, prior to the date of entry into force of the Rules, the parties have agreed to refer their dispute to the former ICC ADR Rules, the parties shall pursuant to Article 10(1) be deemed to have referred their dispute to the ICC Mediation Rules, unless any of the parties objects thereto, in which case the ICC ADR Rules shall apply.

Although conciliation and mediation are often considered, broadly speaking, synonymous and may refer to the same kind of process, there are significant differences between the rules that formerly governed ICC conciliation proceedings and those that govern processes under the 2001 ICC ADR Rules or under the 2014 ICC Mediation Rules. Under the ICC Rules of Optional Conciliation, proceedings could only start if one of the parties filed a request for conciliation. ICC notified the request to the other party, which could either accept or reject it. ICC ADR proceedings and ICC Mediation proceedings, on the other hand, can be commenced with a joint request from all parties. Also, the ADR Rules and the Mediation Rules allow for the use of several different techniques of dispute resolution, whereas the conciliation rules covered conciliation as the only available method.

There is also a clear difference between mediation and arbitration. Whereas the purpose of mediation is to bring parties to a dispute to an amicable settlement, arbitration is a process in which the issues are decided by an external person, the arbitrator, whose decision is binding upon the parties.

Whilst being quite distinct mechanisms for resolving disputes, mediation and arbitration may be complementary. It is possible for parties to agree that they will first attempt to resolve their differences through mediation, failing which they will resort to arbitration (see the escalation clauses recommended by ICC in Chapter 4 above). Conversely, parties who are already engaged in arbitration proceedings or litigation may, in the course of proceedings, agree to suspend the arbitration or litigation and attempt mediation. Furthermore, a mediation process can even be considered in parallel to arbitration or litigation proceedings. An important difference between mediation and arbitration or litigation is that the mediation process can help the parties to acquire a better understanding of each other's needs and interests so that they can look for a solution which accommodates these needs and interests as far as possible. If parties attempt to reach a settlement in the course of arbitration or litigation proceedings, however, they will focus on factual and legal elements put forward in these proceedings and, in doing so, their bargaining positions may be limited.

ICC mediation is designed to be a rapid, non-contentious and inexpensive dispute resolution method. It not only allows parties to avoid the expense of contentious proceedings, but is also more likely to preserve relations, allowing them to enter into new contracts or continue ongoing or long-term relationships. It allows the parties to terminate their contracts other than by litigation or arbitration. For this to be possible, all parties should, of course, have an interest in settling their dispute in another way than by adversary proceedings. Failing such common interest, or if a party's interest is not to settle in a non-contentious manner, there is little hope for a successful outcome of the mediation.

Together with the Rules, ICC also published 'Mediation Guidance Notes', in a separate publication, numbered 870. The 'Mediation Guidance Notes' give explanations on the provisions of the rules. They set out that mediation as referred to in the ICC Mediation Rules and in the Mediation Guidance Notes is a concept sufficiently broad to encompass both mediation and conciliation ('Mediation Guidance Notes', ICC Publication No. 870, Paris, 2013, p. 4). The ICC Mediation Rules do not provide a definition for mediation. The 2014 Mediation Rules contain ten articles, whereas the 2001 ADR Rules contained only seven articles; this small number is intended to leave the parties and the mediator with as much flexibility as possible in the mediation process in trying to achieve a settlement. As set out in Article 1(3) of the Rules, mediation shall be used under the Rules unless, prior to the confirmation or appointment of the mediator, or with the agreement of the mediator, the parties agree upon a different settlement procedure or a combination of settlement procedures. The Rules are not, however, appropriate for Dispute Review Boards and Dispute Adjudication Boards, which are usually established through detailed contractual provisions specifying the rules to be followed in such cases.

The breadth and flexibility of the Mediation Rules is made clear from the outset. Article 1(4) states that the provisions of the Rules may be modified by agreement of all the parties, subject to the approval of the ICC Centre. As with arbitration and other alternatives to litigation, mediation presupposes an agreement by the parties to use this method to resolve their disputes. This agreement will typically be found in a mediation clause contained in the business contract signed by the parties. However, the parties can also agree to mediation later, once a dispute has arisen, as with arbitration. In the first case, the way the parties word their clause will determine whether mediation is optional or obligatory and whether, if unsuccessful, it will be followed by arbitration. There have recently been decisions by the courts in some countries, including France and the United Kingdom, holding that such clauses placed the parties under an obligation to attempt mediation before being able to refer their disputes to the courts.

During the first ten years when the ICC ADR Rules were in force, the ICC Centre administered over 100 cases, including corporate and State parties from all continents, disputes spanning construction, M&A, insurance, intellectual property and finance with amounts ranging from US$ 30 000 to more than US$ 450 million. The results of the cases were that approximately 80% of the cases transferred to the mediator settled less than four months after transfer of the file and after an average of one to two mediation meetings (H. Tümpel and C. Sudborough, 'ICC's ADR Rules 2001-2010: Current Practices, Case Examples and Lessons Learned', in A. Ingen-Housz (Editor), 'ADR in Business, Practice and Issues across Countries and Cultures', Vol. II, Kluwer Law International, Alphen aan den Rijn, 2011, p. 257). From 2001 until 2013, the Centre administered over 180 cases under the ADR Rues ('The New ICC Mediation Rules', ICC *International Court of Arbitration Bulletin*, Paris, Vol. 24/Nr. 2 – 2013, p. 6).

In 2013, 32 requests for ADR were filed. Mediation was the settlement technique used in 17 cases, conciliation was chosen in three cases, and the remaining 12 cases were withdrawn before the parties decided on the settlement technique. Half of the cases were initiated pursuant to a dispute resolution clause providing for ICC ADR followed in most cases by ICC arbitration if no settlement was reached. The other half were initiated by a unilateral request in the absence of a prior agreement between the parties to refer their disputes to the ICC ADR Rules. In the five cases that were settled before the end of the year, the duration of the proceedings between the transfer of the file to the neutral and the reaching of a settlement averaged 70 days (see '2013

Statistical Report' published in *ICC International Court of Arbitration Bulletin*, Paris, Vol. 25/Nr. 1 – 2014, p. 15-16).

In 2012, 21 cases were filed under the ICC ADR Rules. Mediation was the settlement technique used in 16 cases, conciliation was chosen in two cases, and in one case a combination of neutral evaluation and mediation was chosen as settlement technique. The remaining two cases were withdrawn before the settlement technique had been fixed. In 16 of the cases, the proceedings were initiated pursuant to a dispute resolution clause providing for ICC ADR followed by arbitration in the event mediation was unsuccessful. In three of the cases the proceedings were initiated pursuant to an agreement after the dispute had arisen or at the request of one party accepted by the other party. Two mediations were conducted concurrently with an ICC arbitration, which was stayed for the duration of the mediation (see '2012 Statistical Report' published in *ICC International Court of Arbitration Bulletin*, Paris, Vol. 24/Nr. 1 – 2013, p. 16).

In 2011, 27 cases were filed under the ICC ADR Rules. Mediation was the settlement technique used in 15 cases, conciliation was chosen in one case, and in one case a combination of neutral evaluation and mediation was chosen as settlement technique. The remaining two cases were either resolved or withdrawn before the settlement technique had been fixed. In 21 of the cases, the proceedings were initiated pursuant to a dispute resolution clause contained in the contract giving rise to the dispute and 17 of those clauses provided for a two-tiered dispute resolution process, with arbitration as a second step if the ADR proceedings were unsuccessful (see '2011 Statistical Report' published in *ICC International Court of Arbitration Bulletin*, Paris, Vol. 23/Nr. 1 – 2012, p. 16).

In 2010, 13 cases were filed under the ICC ADR Rules. Mediation was the settlement technique used in 9 cases, adjudication in 2 cases, conciliation in 1 case and in the remaining case both mediation and neutral evaluation was used. All but one of the cases were commenced on the basis of a clause in the parties' contract specifying ICC ADR. In 8 cases, the dispute resolution clause provided for an escalation process, with arbitration as a second step if the case could not be resolved by ADR. The parties reached a settlement in 10 of the cases commenced in 2010 (see '2010 Statistical Report' published in *ICC International Court of Arbitration Bulletin*, Paris, Vol. 22/Nr. 1 – 2011, p. 15).

In 2009, 24 requests for ADR 13 cases were filed under the ICC ADR Rules. Mediation was chosen as the settlement technique in almost 90% of the cases. Other techniques chosen included conciliation and neutral evaluation. The average duration of the proceedings, from the filing of the request for ADR to the completion of the case, was 117 days, while the cost of the proceedings, including the neutral's fees and expenses and ICC's administrative costs, averaged less than US$ 20 000 (i.e. approximately 0.1% of the average amount in dispute) (see '2009 Statistical Report' published in *ICC International Court of Arbitration Bulletin*, Paris, Vol. 21/Nr. 1 – 2010, p. 15-16).

2. Suggested ICC Mediation Clauses

Parties wishing to use proceedings under the ICC Mediation Rules should consider using one of the clauses recommended by ICC, which cover different situations and needs (see Appendix 24 below; see also Chapter 4 above):

a) Option to Use the ICC Mediation Rules:

> 'The parties may at any time, without prejudice to any other proceedings, seek to settle any dispute arising out of or in connection with the present contract in accordance with the ICC Mediation Rules.'

b) Obligation to Consider the ICC Mediation Rules:

> 'In the event of any dispute arising out of or in connection with the present contract, the parties agree in the first instance to discuss and consider referring the dispute to the ICC Mediation Rules.'

c) Obligation to Refer Dispute to the ICC Mediation Rules While Permitting Parallel Arbitration Proceedings if Required:

> '[x] In the event of any dispute arising out of or in connection with the present contract, the parties shall first refer the dispute to proceedings under the ICC Mediation Rules. The commencement of proceedings under the ICC Mediation Rules shall not prevent any party from commencing arbitration in accordance with sub-clause [y] below.
>
> [y] All disputes arising out of or in connection with the present contract shall be finally settled under the Rules of Arbitration of the International Chamber of Commerce by one or more arbitrators appointed in accordance with the said Rules of Arbitration.'

d) Obligation to Refer Dispute to ICC Mediation Rules, Followed by ICC Arbitration if Required:

> 'In the event of any dispute arising out of or in connection with the present contract, the parties shall first refer the dispute to proceedings under the ICC Mediation Rules. If the dispute has not been settled pursuant to the said Rules within [45] days following the filing of a Request for Mediation or within such other period as the parties may agree in writing, such dispute shall thereafter be finally settled under the Rules of Arbitration of the International Chamber of Commerce by one or more arbitrators appointed in accordance with the said Rules of Arbitration.'

Parties are free to amend the chosen clause for their particular requirements. Parties may wish to specify the use of a settlement procedure other than mediation. Further they may wish to stipulate the place of any mediation and/or arbitration proceedings (ICC Publication No. 865-0 E, Paris, 2013, p. 88).

If the parties choosing clauses c) and d) above wish to exclude any recourse to the Emergency Arbitrator Provisions, they must expressly opt out by adding the following wording to the standard arbitration clause:

> 'The Emergency Arbitrator Provisions shall not apply.'

At all times, care must be taken to avoid any risk of ambiguity in the drafting of the clause. Unclear wording causes uncertainty and can hinder or delay the dispute resolution process.

3. Commencement of Mediation Proceedings

The Rules distinguish between those cases where the parties have agreed to have recourse to the ICC Mediation Rules (Article 2) and those where there is no such agreement (Article 3). In both instances, however, the proceedings commence with the filing of a request for mediation with the ICC International Centre for ADR (the 'Centre').

In those cases where an agreement to use ICC mediation already exists, any party or parties may file a request for mediation, in which they are required to state their own addresses and those of their representatives, provide a description of the dispute and, if possible, an assessment of its value, indicate any agreement to use a settlement procedure other than mediation or, in the absence thereof, any proposal for such other settlement procedure, mention any agreement as to the time limit, the language of the location for conducting the mediation or, in the absence thereof, any proposal thereto, and jointly nominate a mediator or indicate the qualifications a mediator should have if appointed by the ICC. The request should be accompanied by a copy of the written agreement under which it is made and a non-refundable registration fee of US$ 2 000 (Article 1 of the Appendix to the Rules).

If the request is not filed jointly by all of the parties, although there is an agreement to submit disputes to ICC mediation, the party or parties filing the request must simultaneously send the request to the other party or parties (Article 2(3)).

If the parties have not previously agreed to refer their dispute to ICC mediation, the Centre sends the request to the other party or parties, asking them to advise it within 15 days or within an additional time limit determined by the Centre whether they agree or decline to participate in the mediation proceedings. If they refuse to participate or if they fail to respond, the request will be considered to have been declined and consequently the mediation proceedings will not commence (Article 3). If they agree to take part in the mediation proceedings, they may propose one or more mediators to be designated by all the parties or make any proposal regarding the qualifications of a mediator to be appointed by ICC (Article 5).

4. Mediator

The parties are free to select between themselves the mediator who will conduct the mediation proceedings (Article 5(1)). However, if they cannot agree upon the person to act in this capacity, the Centre shall, after consulting the parties, either appoint a mediator or propose a list of mediators to the parties (article 5(2)). In practice, the second option is generally used. The parties can select from such list their preferred candidate for appointment by the Centre or, as it is done quite often, they may specify the qualifications that the Centre should take into account before making a proposal or the appointment.

Like arbitrators, every prospective mediator should complete a curriculum vitae form and a statement of acceptance, availability, impartiality and independence. If there are facts or circumstances that could call into question the prospective mediator's independence in the eyes of the parties as well as any circumstances that could give rise to reasonable doubts as to the mediator's impartiality, these should be disclosed with the statement of acceptance, availability, impartiality and independence (Article 5(3)).

If the Centre appoints the mediator, the parties have 15 days from the time they are notified of the appointment in which to file objections against the person appointed. The objections must be sent to the Centre and to the other party or parties. Thereupon, the Centre is required to appoint another mediator (Article 5(5)).

The parties can agree to have more than one mediator conduct the proceedings (Article 5(6)). The appointment of two or more mediators may be appropriate in certain circumstances, for instance when the parties wish to have mediators with different qualifications or professional backgrounds or when the complexity or the number of parties involved warrant a co-mediation.

5. Conduct of Mediation Proceedings

The Rules allow the parties and, in the event they are unable to agree, the mediator, considerable freedom to conduct the mediation proceedings as they think fit (Article 7(1)). The mediation can be adapted to the needs of the parties, including their cultural and legal backgrounds, and any elements of the dispute other than a legal component. The parties can also agree on specific modalities of the mediation proceedings, such as whether submissions are to be filed, or whether there is to be a site visit, although mediation can and should not mimic legal proceedings. After having discussed this with the parties, the mediator shall provide a written note informing the parties of the manner in which the mediation shall be conducted (Article 7(2)). Informal by nature, such a note should simply clarify which technique(s) the mediator shall use throughout mediation.

By agreeing to refer a dispute to the ICC Mediation Rules, each party takes the commitment to participate in the proceedings at least until the receipt of the written note from the mediator with which the mediator sets out how the mediation shall be conducted (Article 7(2)).This provision is inspired by the 2001 ICC ADR Rules (Article 5(1) thereof) which stipulated that the parties could not withdraw from the ADR proceedings prior to the first meeting with the neutral.

During mediation sessions, the mediator may meet with all parties together in a joint meeting or have separate meetings with each of the parties or certain party representatives. Because mediation essentially is a third party assisted negotiation process in which legal aspects are normally only part of many other relevant factors such as underlying party interests, the procedural concept of 'due process' is not directly applicable to mediation, irrespective of the fact that mediation will only properly function, if it is being perceived by all stakeholders as fair and reasonable. The Mediation Rules merely state that in all cases the mediator shall be guided by the principles of fairness and impartiality and by the wishes of the parties (Article 7(3)). If one or both of the parties wish(es) to provide the mediator with documents or other information that should not be communicated to the other party, these will be kept confidential by the mediator ('Mediation Guidance Notes', ICC Publication No. 870, Paris, 2013, p. 6). This reflects the fact that ICC mediation provides essentially for third-party-assisted negotiations, with the parties remaining in ultimate control. They should therefore not be considered as subject to the same principles as judicial proceedings. Accordingly, the ICC 'Mediation Guidance Notes' (ICC Publication No. 870, Paris, 2013, p. 6) also underscore that aspects of due process are not being applied in mediation to the same extent as in arbitration and court proceedings.

During all meetings (both joint and private) the mediator will seek to create an environment conducive to constructive negotiations; some meetings may be used by the parties and/or their lawyers to make presentation to each other; others may be used for the mediator to explore the background and unrevealed elements of the dispute, especially identify the interests and needs of each of the parties (as opposed to pure elements of facts and law) for their mutual benefit and consider any alternative options for settlement instead of focusing on adversary debates ('Mediation Guidance Notes', ICC Publication No. 870, Paris, 2013, p. 7).

The mediator determines the language or languages of the proceedings (Article 4(2)) and the place where meetings will be held, if the parties have not already agreed on them (Article 4(1)). Although it is generally useful for the parties and the mediator to meet, conversations can also take place by telephone conference, videoconference or any other suitable means.

As regards the participation of the parties in mediation proceedings, the rules require each party to cooperate in good faith with the mediator (Article 7(4)). It is important that there be at least a discussion between the parties and the mediator, regardless of whether or not it leads to a settlement, mediation being an important and useful channel of communication between parties in dispute.

6. Termination of Mediation Proceedings

The rules describe a number of situations in which the mediation proceedings end (Article 8). Clearly, the best possible situation is when both parties reach a settlement agreement that terminates their dispute (Article 8(1)(a)). The parties will normally confirm their agreement in writing. The rules do not state whether the mediator should be involved in the drafting of the settlement agreement or should sign it. This will be a matter to be discussed and decided with the parties, when the situation arises. There may be times, albeit unusual, when parties reach a settlement agreement among themselves, the full details of which are unknown to the mediator. The mere indication by the parties to the mediator that the dispute has been settled should suffice to put an end to the proceedings. In some instances, it is worth considering the possibility to incorporate the settlement agreement in an award by consent within the meaning of Article 32 of the ICC Rules of Arbitration (see comments on Article 32 of the ICC Rules of Arbitration above) in order to facilitate the international enforcement of the settlement agreement (e.g. pursuant to the 1958 New York Convention on the recognition and enforcement of foreign arbitral awards).

Mediation proceedings can also terminate without a settlement being reached. This can occur when one of the parties informs the mediator in writing that it no longer wishes to pursue the mediation proceedings, after it has received the mediator's note referred to in Article 7(2)) (Article 8(1)(b)), or when the mediator informs the parties that, in his or her opinion, the mediation will not resolve the dispute between the parties (Article 8(1)(d)). The mediation proceedings will also terminate, without a settlement, when the mediator informs the parties in writing that the mediation has been completed (Article 8(1)(c)). Similarly, when the mediator informs the parties that a time limit set for the mediation proceedings has expired and has not been extended by all the parties (Article 8(1)(e)), the mediation proceedings will come to an unsuccessful end.

There are also situations in which mediation proceedings terminate at a very early stage, even before they have really commenced. This can happen, for instance, when the Centre considers that there has been a failure to nominate a mediator or that it has not been reasonably possible to appoint a mediator (Article 8(1)(g)). Early termination will also occur when the ICC notifies the parties and the mediator that a due payment has not been made at least seven days after payment should have been made (Article 8(1)(f)).

7. Confidentiality

ICC Mediation proceedings are confidential. The Mediation Rules put in place maximum safeguards to that effect in order to ensure efficiency in the process. Article 4 of Appendix I – Statutes of the Standing Committee confirms the principle of the confidential nature of the work of the Standing Committee and of the Centre.

Article 9(1) of the Rules states that, unless agreed otherwise by the parties or unless prohibited by applicable law, the mediation proceedings, but not the fact that they are taking place, have taken place or will take place, are private and confidential (Article 9(1)(a)). If a settlement agreement is reached, this must likewise be kept confidential, unless a party is required by law to disclose its contents, or this is necessary for its implementation or enforcement (Article 9(1)(b)). As a result, parties may not produce any information in proceedings before a court or arbitral tribunal that was submitted by the other party or by the mediator in the mediation proceedings, unless such information can be obtained independently (Article 9(2)(a)). Nor may a party disclose any views expressed or suggestions put forward by any party or by the mediator (Article 9(2)(b)), or any admissions made by the other party during the mediation proceedings (Article 9(2)(c)).

If the parties have not agreed in their contract on the application of the Mediation Rules and if one party requests the commencement of Mediation proceedings and the other party rejects this request, there will have been no agreement on the application of the Mediation Rules, including its confidentiality provisions. In such a situation, there is no guarantee that the unilateral request for mediation will be kept confidential.

Unless the parties agree otherwise, the mediator may not act as a judge, arbitrator, expert or representative of a party in any judicial, arbitration or similar proceedings relating to the dispute that is the subject of the mediation proceedings (Article 10(3)). Unless required by applicable law or unless the parties agree otherwise, the mediator shall not give testimony in any judicial, arbitration or similar proceedings relating to the dispute that is the subject of the mediation proceedings (Article 10(3)).

8. Limitation of Liability

Like the Arbitration Rules, the Mediation Rules contain a provision excluding the liability of the expert or neutral, the Centre, ICC and its employees, and the ICC national committees and groups and their employees and representatives, for any act or omission in connection with the mediation proceedings, except to the extent that such limitation of liability is prohibited by law (Article 10(5)).

9. Costs

The Centre will process a request for mediation only if it is accompanied by payment of the required registration fee (Article 2(2)). As indicated in the Appendix to the Rules, this registration fee currently amounts to US$ 2 000. This is not refundable, even if the mediation proceedings are not set in motion (Appendix, Fees and Costs, Article 1).

Upon receipt of a request for mediation, in the absence of an agreement by the parties to refer their dispute to mediation under the Rules, the Centre may request the party filing the request for mediation to pay a deposit to cover the administrative expenses of the Centre (Article 6(2)). Following the commencement of the mediation proceedings, the Centre shall request the parties to pay a deposit to cover the expected administrative expenses of the ICC and fees and expenses of the mediator (Article 6(3)). The Centre may stay or terminate the mediation proceedings if this amount is not paid (Article 6(4)). The parties are required to pay the deposit in equal shares, unless they have agreed otherwise in writing. If one of the parties fails to pay its share, the other party will be invited to substitute for the defaulting party (Article 6(6)). A party's other expenditure shall remain the responsibility of that party, unless otherwise agreed by the parties (Article 6(7)).

Upon termination of the proceedings, the Centre shall fix the total costs of the mediation proceedings and shall, as the case may be, reimburse the parties for any excess payment or bill the parties for any remaining balance required pursuant to the Rules (Article 6(5)).

The ICC's administrative expenses for mediation are fixed at its discretion, depending on the tasks it carries out, and taking into account the amount in dispute. However, they may not exceed a maximum amount of US$ 30 000 (Appendix, Fees and Costs, Article 2(1)). Where the amount in dispute is not stated, the administrative expenses may be fixed by the Centre at its discretion, taking into account all the circumstances of the case, including indications regarding the value of the dispute, but they shall normally not exceed US$ 20 000 (Appendix, Fees and Costs, Article 2(2)). In exceptional circumstances, the Centre may fix the administrative expenses at a higher figure than that which would result from the scale, without however exceeding the maximum amount for administrative expenses foreseen in the scale (Appendix, Fees and Costs, Article 2(3)). If the parties or one of them with the acquiescence of the other requests to hold the mediation proceedings in abeyance, the Centre may request the payment of an abeyance fee which shall normally not exceed US$ 1 000 per party per year (Appendix, Fees and Costs, Article 2(4)).

Unlike the ICC Rules of Arbitration, the mediator's fees are not fixed on the basis of a scale. The mediator is remunerated on the basis of an hourly rate fixed by the Centre in consultation with the mediator and the parties (Appendix, Fees and Costs, Article 3(1)). It is stated in the Appendix that this hourly rate must be reasonable in amount and shall be determined in light of the complexity of the dispute, and any other relevant circumstances. In practice, the prospective mediator is invited to provide the Centre and the parties with his or her hourly rate for approval. However, if agreed by the parties and the mediator, the Centre may fix the mediator's fees on the basis of a single fixed fee for the whole proceedings rather than on the basis of an hourly rate (Appendix, Fees and Costs, Article 3(2)). It is stated in the Appendix that this single fee must be reasonable in amount and shall be determined in the light of the complexity of the dispute, the amount of work that the parties and the mediator anticipate will be required of the mediator, and any other relevant circumstances. In addition, the mediator is reimbursed for reasonable expenses fixed by the Centre (Appendix, Fees and Costs, Article 3(3)).

10. Prior ICC Arbitration

Parties are free to agree upon mediation even after a request for arbitration is filed. When the Secretariat of the ICC International Court of Arbitration notifies a request for arbitration to the respondent(s), the Secretariat also points out that the parties are free to settle their dispute amicably at any time during an arbitration and that the parties may wish to consider conducting an amicable dispute resolution procedure pursuant to the ICC Mediation Rules (see comments on Article 4(5) of the ICC Rules of Arbitration above).

When the parties in an arbitration agree to conduct a mediation pursuant to the ICC Mediation Rules, the filing fee paid for the arbitration proceedings shall be credited to the administrative expenses of the mediation, if the total administrative expenses paid with respect to the arbitration exceed US$ 7 500 (Appendix, Fees and Costs, Article 4).

The parties may agree that the arbitrator (sole arbitrator) or a member of the arbitral tribunal (usually the president) or all arbitrators assist the parties in negotiating a settlement of their dispute by acting as mediator. The parties may also agree that if the mediation does not lead to a settlement of all the issues in dispute in the arbitration, then the mediator may return to the role of arbitrator and proceed to make or participate in the making of an award in the arbitration. This practice should be handled with care, so that it may not jeopardize the arbitral process and the enforceability of the arbitral award rendered by an arbitrator who has acted before as mediator in the same dispute. The key concerns are that during mediation information is being elicited from the parties which would normally not be part of the factual assertions of any of the parties and that such information could lead to 'extra-legal' psychological influences during the decision-making process. This problem is aggravated when information is provided during a private meeting (caucus)of a party with the mediator(s). Because of the potential risks to the integrity of the arbitral proceedings in some jurisdictions, Article 10(3) allows a mediator to act as arbitrator in the same dispute only when all the parties have consented thereto in writing ('Mediation Guidance Notes', ICC Publication No. 870, Paris, 2013, p. 15). In practice it is highly recommendable that the arbitral tribunal informs the parties of what such a change of procedure and the role from arbitrator to mediator implies and seek informed acceptance thereof from all parties before engaging in the mediated settlement efforts. Such acceptance should normally be made in writing and include an explicit waiver of future challenges of the proceedings for the sole reason that the arbitrator(s) acted as mediator(s) during an aborted settlement attempt. Notwithstanding, such change between the role of mediator and the role of arbitrator may nevertheless be appropriate when the parties, once a written settlement has been reached, wish to have it incorporated in an arbitral award by consent (see comments above) so as to ensure the enforcement of the settlement agreement.

In certain jurisdictions arbitrators frequently engage during a hearing in discussions aiming at facilitating settlement. In such cases the arbitral tribunal in most instances will share its provisional view of the strengths and weaknesses of the parties' respective positions in a hearing and engage in a 'learned' discussion with the party representatives. This resembles more to what is known as claims based early neutral evaluation and less to interest driven mediation, especially, because the tribunal only works with the information the parties have already submitted and does not purposefully elicit additional information. Furthermore, caucusing is normally not part of this approach. In our view the procedural rules of due process and fair and equal treatment of the parties remain applicable during such discussions. Therefore, and because the approach remains claims based this form of settlement facilitation is not to be confounded with mediation. It is argued that during such discussions the arbitral tribunal prematurely makes up its mind and prejudges the case before hearing all arguments and evaluating all evidence. How serious this argument is being taken appears to be a cultural issue. However, the described concerns should not be bluntly dismissed as irrelevant, wherefore also in such cases it is highly recommendable in international arbitration to first seek the parties' informed consent before embarking in this kind of evaluative settlement facilitation.

11. Value Added Tax (VAT)

Article 5(2) of the Appendix, Fees and Costs, states that amounts paid to the mediator do not include value-added tax or any other taxes, charges and imposts that may be applicable to the mediator's fees. It goes on to say that the parties have a duty to pay such taxes and charges. Their recovery is a matter for the mediator and the parties alone and does not involve ICC. Although not specifically mentioned, it may be understood that income tax is not covered by this provision.

Article 5(3) of the Appendix, Fees and Costs, sets out that any ICC administrative expenses may be subject to value added tax or charges of similar nature at the prevailing rate.

12. ICC as Appointing Authority

The International Chamber of Commerce is sometimes called upon to appoint a mediator in proceedings that are not conducted under the ICC Mediation Rules. In such case, the request to appoint a mediator will be treated in accordance with the ICC Rules for the Appointment of Experts and Neutrals (see Chapter 6 and Appendix 25 below) and shall only be processed if accompanied by a filing fee of US$ 3 000 per mediator (ICC Rules for the Appointment of Experts and Neutrals, Appendix II – Costs, Article 1). This filing fee is not refundable. For additional services, the ICC may at its discretion decide to fix ICC administrative expenses, which shall be commensurate with the services provided and which shall normally not exceed the maximum amount of US$ 10 000 (ICC Rules for the Appointment of Experts and Neutrals, Appendix II – Costs, Article 5).

D. ICC EXPERT RULES

The ICC Expert Rules offer users a broad range of options. Experts may be required in a number of different settings. An expert opinion may be required to settle a technical issue, such as the compliance of natural or manufactured products with contractual specifications, trade customs or other standards, as well as legal or financial and accounting issues. The circumstances in which expert opinions are needed also vary greatly. For instance, there may be times when parties agree to have an issue determined urgently during the performance of a contract. It may happen that a party needs an expert opinion to prepare litigation but has difficulty finding an appropriately qualified person or wishes to increase the expert's credibility by having him or her selected by an independent institution. In other cases, parties may need a neutral expert opinion during post-contractual amicable settlement negotiations, when they agree on the broad framework but not on the particular issue that they decide to submit to the expert.

Independent expert proceedings normally are used without relation to arbitration at an earlier stage of the parties' relationship. In certain areas, expert determination outside of a DRB (Dispute Resolution Board; see ICC Rules for Dispute Boards hereafter) is quite often used. One example among others are post Merger & Acquisition price adjustments.

Expertise also plays an important role in international arbitration procedures. Disputes referred to arbitration often involve technical issues. Arbitrators, who are usually lawyers, may find it necessary to seek an opinion from an expert with specialized technical or other knowledge (e.g. accounting, damage assessment, etc.). The ICC Rules of Arbitration explicitly allow arbitral tribunals to have recourse to experts in the course of arbitration proceedings (Article 25(4) of the ICC Rules of Arbitration).

The functions experts fulfill may vary depending on the legal system under which the parties have chosen to have their dispute settled. In the context of arbitration and litigation, experts are generally called upon to provide neutral opinions in civil law countries, whereas in common law countries parties often expect experts to act as witnesses and use experts' opinions to assert their respective cases. A slightly different, independent and neutral, type of expert skill may be required where parties have agreed to empower the expert to determine an issue in a manner that is binding upon them.

Since 1976, the ICC has offered specific services relating to expertise through its International Centre for Expertise (now called ICC International Centre for ADR). These services are set out in the ICC Rules for Expertise, which cover the proposal of experts, the appointment of experts and the administration of expertise proceedings. In the 2003 version of the Rules the provisions for the proposal and appointment of experts and for the administration of expertise proceedings were contained in a single set of rules entitled 'ICC Expertise Rules'. In the new 'ICC Expert Rules' applicable as from 1 February 2015, the different functions of proposal, appointment and administration are set out in separate sections so that the users may find the three services offered by ICC more accessible: the 'ICC Rules for the Proposal of Experts and Neutrals' (Articles 1 to 4); the 'ICC Rules for the Appointment of Experts and Neutrals' containing (Articles 1 to 5); the 'ICC Rules for the Administration of Expert Proceedings' (Articles 1- 14). Each section is completed with an 'Appendix I – Statutes of the Standing Committee' (Articles 1 to 4) and an 'Appendix II – Costs' (Articles 1 to 6). The 2015 ICC Expert Rules may be found in Appendix 25 below.

Arbitrators who are considering whether or not to appoint an expert or who are conducting a case where parties have appointed themselves experts may find useful guidance in a report on 'Issues for Arbitrators to Consider Regarding Expertise' issued in 2010, notwithstanding the fact that this report was established under the 2003 ICC Rules for Expertise and under the 1998 ICC Rules of Arbitration (see Appendix 18 below). Persons who have been retained to serve as an expert in proceedings under the ICC Expert Rules or under the ICC Rules of Arbitration or who are contemplating such an engagement may find useful guidance in a report on 'Issues for Experts acting under the ICC Rules of Expertise or the ICC Rules of Arbitration' issued in 2009 by the ICC Commission on Arbitration and ADR, even if this report was established under the 2003 ICC Rules for Expertise and under the 1998 ICC Rules of Arbitration (see Appendix 19 below).

In 2013, 27 requests were received under the ICC Expertise Rules: 16 for the proposal of an expert, 7 for the appointment of an expert and 4 for the administration of expertise proceedings. The requests were made by ICC arbitral tribunals in 11 cases, by other arbitral tribunals in 2 cases and by the parties in the remaining 14 cases. The majority of requests were for technical experts. Financial or legal experts were needed in a smaller number of cases. 5 cases required a combination of technical, financial and/or legal experts (see '2013 Statistical Report' published in *ICC International Court of Arbitration Bulletin*, Paris, Vol. 25/Nr. 1 – 2014, p. 16-17).

In 2012, 19 requests were received under the ICC Expertise Rules: 10 for the proposal of an expert, 9 for the appointment of an expert (see '2013 Statistical Report' published in *ICC International Court of Arbitration Bulletin*, Paris, Vol. 24/Nr. 1 – 2013, p. 17).

In 2011, 35 requests were received under the ICC Expertise Rules: 22 for the proposal of an expert, 8 for the appointment of an expert and 5 for the administration of expertise proceedings. The requests for the proposal of an expert were made by ICC arbitral tribunals in 11 cases. The experts were requested to provide technical expertise in 19 cases, financial expertise in 4 cases, legal expertise in 2 cases and combinations of legal and technical expertise in 4 cases, financial and technical expertise in 1 case and legal and financial expertise in 1 case (see '2011 Statistical Report' published in *ICC International Court of Arbitration Bulletin*, Paris, Vol. 23/Nr. 1 – 2012, p. 17).

In 2010, 29 requests were received under the ICC Expertise Rules: 17 for the proposal of an expert, 7 for the appointment of an expert and in the remaining 5 cases to administer the expertise proceedings. The requests for the proposal of an expert were made by ICC arbitral tribunals in 10 cases. The experts were requested to provide technical expertise in 20 cases, financial expertise in 5 cases, legal expertise in 2 cases and a combinations of technical and legal expertise in the remaining 2 cases (see '2010 Statistical Report' published in *ICC International Court of Arbitration Bulletin*, Paris, Vol. 22/Nr. 1 - 2011, p. 16).

In 2009, 15 requests were received under the ICC Expertise Rules: 11 for the proposal of an expert, 3 for the appointment of an expert and 1 case to administer the expertise proceedings. The areas in which expertise was sought were construction (4 cases), vehicle and railway engineering (4 cases), general engineering (2 cases), technical equipment (2 cases), law (2 cases) and finance (1 case) (see '2009 Statistical Report' published in *ICC International Court of Arbitration Bulletin*, Paris, Vol. 21/Nr. 1 - 2010, p. 16).

1. Proposal of Experts

Parties do not need to include in their contract a clause referring to the ICC International Centre for ADR in order to submit a request for names of qualified experts. Any party, counsel, arbitral tribunal or state court may ask the ICC International Centre for ADR to propose names of experts. The request should contain the following: (i) the name and address of the person filing the request, (ii) a statement indicating that the requesting person seeks the proposal of an expert or of a neutral by the Centre, (iii) a description of the required area of expertise, (iv) a description of any matters that would disqualify a potential expert; and (v) a description of the work to be carried out by the expert and the desired time frame for completing the work (Article 1 of the ICC Rules for the Proposal of Experts and Neutrals). The Centre will process the request only if it is accompanied by a non-refundable payment of US$ 3 000 to cover administrative expenses per expert or neutral to be proposed (Appendix II - Costs, Article 1). However, no payment is required if the proposal of an expert is sought by an arbitral tribunal conducting proceedings under the ICC Rules of Arbitration (Appendix II - Costs, Article 3(1)) or if the request for proposal of a neutral who shall act as mediator is made jointly by all parties in an ongoing arbitration under the ICC Rules of Arbitration (Appendix II - Costs, Article 3(2)).

Any proposal of an expert or neutral of the Centre shall be made by the Centre either through an ICC national committee or group; or otherwise (Article 2(1) of the Rules). The ICC International Centre for ADR is well equipped to respond quickly with a proposal. All proposals of experts and neutrals are made by the President of the Standing Committee of the ICC International Centre for ADR, after consultation with the members of the Committee (Appendix I - Statutes of the Standing Committee, Article 3(3)).

Before a proposal is made, the Centre asks the prospective expert or neutral to sign a statement of acceptance, availability, impartiality and independence and disclose in writing any facts or circumstances that might be of such a nature as to call into question his or her independence in the eyes of the person making the request for a proposal (Article 2(3) of the Rules). The Centre will forward such information to the requesting party, who will be given a time limit within which to submit any comments (Article 3(3) of the Rules).

An expert proposed under the Rules may be a physical person or a legal person, such as a company or a partnership (Article 4(1) of the Rules).

If the Centre is not able to identify an expert or neutral having all the attributes set out by the requesting party, the Centre may ask the requesting party whether it wishes the Centre to propose more than one expert or more than one neutral who between them have the requested attributes, or whether the attributes set out in the request for a proposal may be modified (Article 2(2) of the Rules).

The requesting party is free to decide whether or not to make use of the proposed expert's services. The Centre will not notify any other person of the request for a proposal, unless the requesting party specifically requests it to do so (Article 1(3) of the Rules).

Where, prior to the date of entry into force of the 2015 Rules, the parties have agreed to request the proposal of an expert or of a neutral pursuant to the earlier Rules for Expertise of the ICC, they shall be deemed to have agreed to make their request pursuant to the 2015 ICC Rules for the Proposal of Experts and Neutrals, unless any of the parties objects thereto, in which case the earlier Rules for Expertise of the ICC shall apply (Article 4(2) of the Rules).

Like the Arbitration and the Mediation Rules, the Rules for the Proposal of Experts and Neutrals contain a provision excluding the liability of the expert or neutral, the Centre, ICC and its employees, and the ICC national committees and groups and their employees and representatives, for any act or omission in connection with the proposal of an expert or neutral, except to the extent that such limitation of liability is prohibited by law (Article 4(3)). Article 4 of Appendix I – Statutes of the Standing Committee confirms the principle of the confidential nature of the work of the Standing Committee and of the Centre.

2. Appointment of Experts

Requests for the appointment of an expert or neutral by the ICC International Centre for ADR can be accepted only if the parties have previously agreed to have recourse to the Centre for this purpose or if the Centre is otherwise satisfied that there is a sufficient basis for appointing an expert or neutral (Article 1(1) of the ICC Rules for the Appointment of Experts and Neutrals). The request should therefore contain not only the same information as a request for proposal but also a copy of the parties' agreement for the appointment of an expert or neutral by the Centre and/or any other elements constituting the basis for the request (Article 1(2)). It must also be accompanied by a non-refundable payment of US$ 3 000 to cover administrative expenses, without which the request will not be processed (Article 4(1) of the Rules; Appendix II – Costs, Article 1).

If the parties do not act together by jointly requesting the appointment of an expert, or if they fail to agree on the expert's mission, the Centre will notify the request to the other party or parties and give it or them a time limit within which to submit any comments (Article 1(4) of the Rules). It is possible for parties to jointly propose a particular expert for confirmation by the President of the Standing Committee of the Centre (Article 3(2)). Every expert or neutral must be and remain impartial and independent of the parties involved in the proceedings, if any, unless otherwise agreed in writing by the parties (Article 3(3)). As with proposals, prospective experts and neutrals will first be asked to sign a statement of acceptance, availability, impartiality and independence, and to reveal to the Centre any facts or circumstances that could cause the parties to doubt their independence. The Centre in turn notifies the parties of any such facts or circumstances and gives them a time limit within which to submit comments (Article 3(4)). The Centre checks the prospective expert's or the neutral's nationality, residence, training and experience, and the prospective expert's or neutral's availability and ability to conduct the work to be carried out (Article 3(2). If the Centre is not able to identify an expert or neutral having all the attributes set out by the requesting party, the Centre may ask the parties whether they wish the Centre to appoint more than one expert or neutral who between them have the requested attributes, or whether the attributes agreed upon by the parties may be modified (Article 3(2) of the Rules).

An expert appointed under the Rules may be a physical or a legal person, such as a company or a partnership (Article 5(1) of the Rules).

Any appointment of an expert or neutral by the Centre shall be made by the Centre either through an ICC national committee or group, or otherwise (Article 3(1)). The ICC International Centre for ADR is well equipped to respond quickly with an appointment. All appointments of experts and neutrals are made by the President of the Standing Committee of the ICC International Centre for ADR, after consultation with the members of the Committee (Appendix I – Statutes of the Standing Committee, Article 3(3)). The Centre may replace an expert if a party objects that the expert in question does not have the necessary attributes or is not fulfilling his or her functions or is not independent or impartial. Before making its decision, the Centre will consider the observations of the expert and the other party or parties (Article 3(5)).

Where, prior to the date of entry into force of the 2015 Rules, the parties have agreed to request the appointment of an expert or of a neutral pursuant to the earlier Rules for Expertise of the ICC, they shall be deemed to have agreed to make their request pursuant to the 2015 ICC Rules for the Appointment of Experts and Neutrals, unless any of the parties objects thereto, in which case the earlier Rules for Expertise of the ICC shall apply (Article 5(2) of the Rules).

Like the Arbitration and the Mediation Rules, the Rules for the Appointment of Experts and Neutrals contain a provision excluding the liability of the expert or neutral, the Centre, ICC and its employees, and the ICC national committees and groups and their employees and representatives, for any act or omission in connection with the appointment of an expert or neutral, except to the extent that such limitation of liability is prohibited by law (Article 5(3)). Article 4 of Appendix I – Statutes of the Standing Committee confirms the principle of the confidential nature of the work of the Standing Committee and of the Centre.

3. Administration of Expert Proceedings

The ICC International Centre for ADR is also available to administer expert proceedings, if the parties so wish. In this case, there must be an agreement between the parties to have recourse to the Centre for this purpose. The agreement may have been made in the parties' underlying contract or at a later stage, after a dispute has arisen. There may be times when a neutral opinion from an expert is required before the parties sign their contract. In most cases, however, parties will call upon an expert after a conflict has arisen, regardless of whether or not they have made an agreement to this effect.

The ICC Rules for the Administration of Expert Proceedings contain basic provisions applicable at different stages of the procedure, from the filing of a request for the administration of expert proceedings to the notification of the expert's report. The first step is therefore to file a request, which can only be accepted if there is an agreement between the parties to have recourse to the Centre for the administration of expert proceedings, or the Centre is otherwise satisfied that a sufficient basis for administering expert proceedings exists (Article 1(1) of the Rules for the Administration of Expert Proceedings). For this reason, the request should contain not only the same information as a request for the proposal or for the appointment of an expert, but also a copy of the parties' agreement for the administration of expert proceedings by the Centre and/or any other elements upon which the request is based (Article 1(2)). The request must be accompanied by a payment of US$ 3 000 to cover administrative expenses, which is non-refundable and will be credited to the requesting party's or parties' portion of the deposit subsequently requested (Article 1(3) and Article 12(1) of the Rules; Appendix II – Costs, Article 1).

As soon as the Centre has received the initial payment and the required number of copies of the request, it informs the other party or parties of the request (Article 1(5)). At the outset of the proceedings, it will fix an advance on costs sufficient to cover the expert's fees and expenses and the Centre's administrative costs (Article 12(2) of the Rules; Appendix II – Costs, Article 2). The Centre may stay the proceedings until the advance on costs has been paid (Article 12(2)). The fees of the expert shall be calculated on the basis of the time reasonably spent by the expert in the administered expert proceedings, taking into account the diligence and efficiency of the expert and other relevant circumstances. These fees shall be based on an hourly rate fixed by the Centre when appointing or confirming the expert and after having consulted the expert and the parties. The hourly rate shall be reasonable in amount and shall be determined in light of the complexity of the work to be performed by the expert (Appendix II – Costs, Article 3(1)). The amount of reasonable expenses of the expert shall be fixed by the Centre (Appendix II – Costs, Article 3(2)). The Centre fixes the total cost of the proceedings once they have been completed (Article 12(4) of the Rules).

The first stage in the proceedings will be the appointment of an expert by the Centre (Article 3(2)). Alternatively, the parties may jointly nominate an expert for confirmation by the Centre (Article 3(1)). An expert must remain independent of the parties to the proceedings, unless they agree otherwise (Article 4(1)).

As with proposals and appointments, prospective experts will first be asked to sign a statement of acceptance, availability, impartiality and independence, and to reveal to the Centre any facts or circumstances that could cause the parties to doubt their independence. The Centre in turn notifies the parties of such facts or circumstances and gives them a time limit within which to submit comments (Article 3(3)). In confirming or appointing an expert, the Centre shall consider the prospective expert's nationality, residence, training and experience, and the prospective expert's availability and ability to conduct the expert proceedings in accordance with the Rules (Article 3(4)).

An expert appointed under the Rules may be a physical person or a legal person, such as a company or a partnership (Article 14(1) of the Rules).

The ICC International Centre for ADR is well equipped to respond quickly with an appointment or confirmation of an expert. All confirmations or appointments of experts are made by the President of the Standing Committee of the ICC International Centre for ADR, after consultation with the members of the Committee (Appendix I – Statutes of the Standing Committee, Article 3(2)).

Any appointment or confirmation of an expert or neutral of the Centre shall be made by the Centre either on the basis of proposal by an ICC national committee or group, or otherwise (Article 3(5) of the Rules). If the Centre is not able to identify an expert or neutral having all the attributes set out by the requesting party, the Centre may ask the parties whether they wish the Centre to appoint more than one expert who between them have the requested attributes, or whether the attributes agreed upon by the parties may be modified (Article 3(5) of the Rules).

The Rules provide that experts will be replaced in the event of death, resignation or if they are unable to carry out their functions (Article 4(3)). An expert confirmed or appointed by the Centre shall be replaced upon acceptance by the Centre of a written request of all the parties (Article 4(4)). Also, the Centre may replace an expert if a party objects that the expert in question does not have the necessary qualifications or is not fulfilling his or her functions in accordance with the Rules or within any prescribed time limits. Before making its decision, the Centre will consider the observations of the expert and the other party or parties (Article 4(5)).

As soon as the expert has received the file from the Centre, and after having consulted the parties, the expert shall set out his or her mission in a written document (Article 6(2)). The document must include the following: (i) the names and addresses of the parties, (ii) the name(s) and address(es) of the expert or experts, (iii) a list of issues on which the expert shall make findings in the expert's report, (iv) the procedure to be followed by the expert, (v) the place where the expertise will be conducted, and (vi) the language in which the proceedings will be conducted (Article 6(2)). If the parties disagree on the expert's mission, the expert will have the final say (Article 6(4)). Once the document defining the expert's mission has been drawn up, the expert will prepare a procedural timetable for the conduct of the proceedings (Article 7).

The expert's role is to make findings within any time limits laid down in the document defining his or her mission, and after giving the parties an opportunity to make submissions (Article 8(1) of the Rules). Those findings will not be binding on the parties, unless they have agreed in writing that such findings shall be contractually binding upon them (Article 8(2)). The parties will find below some contract clauses recommended by the ICC, with which they can indicate whether or not they wish the expert's findings to be binding and whether they wish to foresee possible arbitration proceedings after the termination of the administered expert proceedings, in case the expert's findings have not resolved the dispute. Even if a party fails to participate in the proceedings, an expert can still make findings, provided that the party concerned has been given the opportunity to participate (Article 11(1)).

The administered expert proceedings are terminated with a written report of the expert, which the Centre notifies to the parties (Article 10). Before being signed, the expert's report is submitted in draft form to the Centre for approval, unless the parties have waived this requirement and the Centre considers such waiver to be appropriate (Article 9(2)). When scrutinizing the expert's report, the Centre may lay down modifications as to the form of the report and, without affecting the expert's liberty of decision, may also draw the expert's attention to points of substance (Article 9(1)). The rules allow the expert's report to be produced in judicial or arbitral proceedings in which all of the parties were also parties to the administered expert proceedings, unless the parties agree otherwise (Article 8(3)).

Where, prior to the date of entry into force of the 2015 Rules, the parties have agreed to refer their dispute to the administration of expertise proceedings pursuant to the earlier Rules for Expertise of the ICC, they shall be deemed to have agreed to make their request pursuant to the 2015 ICC Rules for the Administration of Expert Proceedings, unless any of the parties objects thereto, in which case the earlier Rules for Expertise of the ICC shall apply (Article 14(2) of the Rules).

Like the Arbitration and the Mediation Rules, the Rules for the Administration of Expert Proceedings contain a provision excluding the liability of the expert or neutral, the Centre, ICC and its employees, and the ICC national committees and groups and their employees and representatives, for any act or omission in connection with the appointment of an expert or neutral, except to the extent that such limitation of liability is prohibited by law (Article 14(3)). Article 4 of Appendix I – Statutes of the Standing Committee confirms the principle of the confidential nature of the work of the Standing Committee and of the Centre.

4. Suggested Clauses for ICC Administered Expert Proceedings

ICC suggests the following clauses for ICC administered expert proceedings (see Appendix 26 below):

a) Option to Submit Disputes to ICC Administered Expert Proceedings:

> 'The parties may at any time, without prejudice to any other proceedings, agree to submit any dispute arising out of or in connection with [clause X of the present contract] to administered expert proceedings in accordance with the Rules for the Administration of Expert Proceedings of the International Chamber of Commerce.'

b) Obligation to Submit Disputes to Non-Binding ICC Administered Expert Proceedings:

> 'In the event of any dispute arising out of or in connection with [clause X of the present contract], the parties agree to submit the matter to administered expert proceedings in accordance with the Rules for the Administration of Expert Proceedings of the International Chamber of Commerce.'

c) Obligation to Submit Disputes to Contractually Binding ICC Administered Expert Proceedings:

> 'In the event of any dispute arising out of or in connection with [clause X of the present contract], the parties agree to submit the matter to administered expert proceedings in accordance with the Rules for the Administration of Expert Proceedings of the International Chamber of Commerce. The parties agree that the findings of the expert shall be contractually binding upon them.'

When clause c) is used, the parties should determine the effect under applicable law of their agreement to be contractually bound by the expert's findings.

A more complex tailor made clause may be needed in certain cases (for example, where a price adjustment in an M&A contract is referred to an expert accountancy firm for determination). Such a tailor made clause may still provide for the expert determination to be conducted pursuant to the ICC Rules for the Administration of Expert Proceedings (ICC Publication No. 869-1 E, Paris, 2015, p. 34).

d) Obligation to Submit Disputes to Non-Binding ICC Administered Expert Proceedings, Followed by ICC Arbitration as Required:

> 'In the event of any dispute arising out of or in connection with [clause X of the present contract], the parties agree to submit the dispute, in the first instance, to administered expert proceedings in accordance with the Rules

> for the Administration of Expert Proceedings of the International Chamber of Commerce. After the International Centre for ADR's notification of the termination of the administered expert proceedings, the dispute, if it has not been resolved, shall be finally settled under the Rules of Arbitration of the International Chamber of Commerce by one or more arbitrators appointed in accordance with the said Rules of Arbitration.'

If the parties wish to exclude any recourse to the Emergency Arbitrator Provisions, the following wording should be added to Clause d):

> 'The Emergency Arbitrator Provisions shall not apply.'

If the parties wish to have recourse to the Emergency Arbitrator Provisions, and want that recourse expressly to be available prior to the termination of the expert proceedings, the following wording should be added to Clause d):

> 'The requirement to refer a dispute to the administered expert proceedings, before referring a dispute to arbitration, shall not prevent the parties from making an application, prior to termination of the administered expert proceedings, for Emergency Measures under the Emergency Arbitrator Provisions in the Rules of Arbitration of the International Chamber of Commerce.'

If the parties wish to have recourse to the Emergency Arbitrator Provisions, but only after termination of the administered expert proceedings, the following wording should be added to Clause d):

> 'The parties shall not have the right to make an application for Emergency Measures under the Emergency Arbitrator Provisions in the Rules of Arbitration of the International Chamber of Commerce prior to the International Centre for ADR's notification of the termination of the administered expert proceedings.'

e) ICC Acting as Appointing Authority in 'Ad hoc' Expert Proceedings:

> 'In the event of any dispute arising out of or in connection with [clause X of the present contract], the parties agree to submit the matter to '*ad hoc*' expert proceedings. The expert shall be appointed by the International Centre for ADR in accordance with the Rules for the Appointment of Experts and Neutrals of the International Chamber of Commerce.'

Parties are also advised to take account of any factors, such as mandatory requirements of applicable law, that may have an impact on the effect of a clause or its enforceability under applicable law.

E. ICC DOCDEX RULES

Since 1997, ICC has made available a special set of rules for the international banking community called DOCDEX, which originally stood for documentary credit dispute resolution expertise. In 2002 and in 2015, the rules were revised (the new DOCDEX Rules in force as from 1 May 2015 are contained in Appendix 27 below) and are now intended to help settle disputes related to the following documentary instruments (Article 2(1) of the 2015 ICC DOCDEX Rules):

- a documentary credit,
- a standby letter of credit,

- a bank-to-bank reimbursement,
- a collection,
- a demand guarantee or counter-guarantee,
- a forfaiting transaction,
- a bank payment obligation (BPO), or
- any other trade finance-related instrument, undertaking or agreement.

When a dispute falling within the scope of Article 2(1) of the Rules arises, a party may refer the dispute to the Rules to obtain an independent, impartial and prompt expert decision on the basis of the terms and conditions of the relevant instrument, undertaking or agreement, any applicable ICC Banking Rules and international standard practice in trade finance (Article 2(2) of the 2015 ICC DOCDEX Rules).

If the dispute arises out of or in connection with an instrument, undertaking or agreement that does not provide for the application of ICC Banking Rules, it shall be administered under the Rules only if each claimant and each respondent so agree. Their agreement shall be recorded on Forms 1 and 2 (Article 2(3) of the 2015 ICC DOCDEX Rules).

ICC Banking Rules means any set of rules or standard practices issued from time to time by the Banking Commission, such as the ICC Uniform Customs and Practice for Documentary Credits (UCP), the ICC Uniform Rules for Bank-to-Bank Reimbursements under Documentary Credits (URR), the ICC Uniform Rules for Collections (URC) and the ICC Uniform Rules for Demand Guarantees (URDG). DOCDEX is a rapid, expert-based procedure, conducted exclusively in writing, whereby three experts appointed by the ICC International Centre for Expertise (now called 'ICC International Centre for ADR', as already indicated above) render a decision to resolve a dispute relating to any of the above-listed instruments. The Rules provide for expedited proceedings, with no opportunity for the oral examination of fact or expert witnesses or for oral submissions at a hearing (Article 2(4) and Article 8(7)).The decision is not intended to conform to the same legal requirements as an arbitral award. Although DOCDEX decisions are not binding on the parties, ICC urges banks to respect them on a voluntary basis. If parties wish to increase the enforceability of the decision, they may specify in advance that it will be legally binding upon them (Article 2(6)).

The DOCDEX Rules were drawn up under the auspices of the ICC Banking Commission and the ICC Commission on Arbitration and ADR and are administered by the ICC International Centre for ADR. ICC DOCDEX panels have decided more than 130 cases since the rules were originally introduced.

A prior agreement of the parties to submit their dispute to a DOCDEX procedure is not necessary. As long as the dispute concerns one of the above-mentioned sets of ICC banking rules, one party can decide to initiate a DOCDEX procedure (see J. Fry, S. Greenberg and F. Mazza, *The Secretariat's Guide to ICC Arbitration*, ICC Publication No. 729 E, Paris, 2012, p. 434).

In 2013, 6 cases were filed (see '2013 Statistical Report' published in *ICC International Court of Arbitration Bulletin*, Paris, Vol. 25/Nr. 1 – 2014, p. 17).

In 2011, as in 2010, 6 cases were filed (see '2011 Statistical Report' published in *ICC International Court of Arbitration Bulletin*, Paris, Vol. 23/Nr. 1 – 2012, p. 17).

In 2009, a total of 16 cases were filed. The average duration of DOCDEX cases filed in 2009 was 56 days and the cost for most cases no more than the standard fee of US$ 5 000 set in the Appendix to the DOCDEX Rules (see '2009 Statistical Report' published in *ICC International Court of Arbitration Bulletin*, Paris, Vol. 21/Nr. 1 – 2010, p. 16-17).

1. Conduct of DOCDEX Proceedings

DOCDEX proceedings may be commenced by a joint claim from the parties or an individual request from a single party using the 'form 1' (Article 3(1) and (2) of the 2015 DOCDEX Rules) (the form is made available for users to download from the ICC DOCDEX webpage at: <www.iccdocdex.org>). The claim must contain the names and addresses of the parties, a summary of the dispute and the claim(s), supported by any relevant documents, the issue(s) for a decision (Article 3 of the Rules). In the Claim Form, the party(ies) have to indicate whether it(they) agreed that the decision shall be contractually binding. The Claim and all accompanying documents shall be supplied to the Centre in electronic form, together with one hard copy for each Respondent (Article 3(1) of the Rules). At the time of submitting a Claim, the Claimant must pay the non-refundable fee specified in the Appendix (Article 3(3)) of US$ 5 000 where the amount in dispute does not exceed US$ 1 000 000 (Article 1 of the Appendix to the 2015 DOCDEX Rules) or of US$ 10 000 where the amount in dispute exceeds US$ 1 000 000 (Article 2 of the Appendix to the 2015 DOCDEX Rules).The respondent may file an answer to the Claim using 'form 2' (Article 4(1) of the Rules) (the Form is made available for users to download from the ICC DOCDEX webpage at: <www.iccdocdex.org>), supported by any relevant documents, only in electronic form (Article 4(2)). The answer must be filed within the time limit set by the Centre, which will normally not exceed 30 days following the Centre communication of the claim. Any answer received by the Centre after that date will be disregarded (Article 4(4) of the Rules). If the claimant has proposed in the Claim that the decision should be contractually binding upon the parties, the respondent must indicate in its answer whether it agrees to this proposal of claimant.

The Centre may request the claimant and the respondent to submit specific supplementary information, including copies of documents, relevant to the DOCDEX decision (Article 5(1) of the 2015 DOCDEX Rules), whereupon such information or documents shall be submitted using 'form 3' (Article 5(1)) (the form is made available for users to download from the ICC DOCDEX webpage at: <www.iccdocdex.org>). The supplementary information shall be submitted to the Centre within 14 days of its request, in electronic form only. The Centre shall forward the supplementary information to each claimant and respondent (Article 5(2)).

When it receives a request to open DOCDEX proceedings, the ICC International Centre for ADR shall, if requested, transmit a copy of the claim to the technical adviser, who shall offer guidance to the Centre whether the claim falls within the scope of the Rules (Article 7(3)). The technical adviser shall also provide guidance on the area(s) of expertise that the claim requires and that the appointed experts should possess (Article 7(4)). The ICC Banking Commission maintains an internal list of experts having experience in, and knowledge of, trade finance transaction (Article 7(1)). Before appointing the three experts (Article 1) and designating one of the three to act as president (Article 7(4)), each expert must declare that he or she is impartial and independent of the parties named in the claim (Article 7(5). If an expert becomes unable to carry out his or her functions or if the Centre considers him or her unable to do so, notice of termination must be given and all documents shall promptly be disposed as agreed with the Centre, which will then immediately appoint a replacement from the list (Article 7(10) of the 2015 DOCDEX Rules). The names of the technical adviser and of the experts are not revealed to the parties (Article 12(3)) and the parties may not ask to be heard by the experts (Article 8(7)).

Whilst all the parties are given the opportunity to participate in the DOCDEX proceedings, the failure of any of them to do so will not prevent the panel from rendering a decision.

2. DOCDEX Decision

The experts are required to draft a decision within 30 days of receiving all information and documents they consider necessary to determine the dispute (Article 8(5)), and provided any additional fee that may have been requested by the Centre has been paid (Article 10(3)). If necessary, the president of the panel of the appointed experts may ask the Centre to request the parties to provide supplementary information and/or copies of documents (Article 8(2)).

Once the experts have drafted their decision, the president of the panel submits it in draft form to the ICC International Centre for ADR. The Centre then consults with the technical adviser. The technical adviser may require modifications as to form of the draft decision and, without affecting the appointed experts' liberty of decision, may also draw their attention to points of substance (Article 9(2)), which will be incorporated if accepted by a majority of the experts.

DOCDEX decisions are drafted in English using 'form 4' (Article 9(1)) (the form is made available for users to download from the ICC DOCDEX webpage at: <www.iccdocdex.org>). DOCDEX decisions may be made unanimously or on a majority basis and shall so indicate (Article 9(3)). The appointed experts shall render the decision exclusively on the basis of the claim, any answer and any supplement, the terms and conditions of the trade finance-related instrument, undertaking or agreement, the ICC Banking Rules that may be applicable and international standard practice in trade finance (Article 9(5)). All DOCDEX decisions are deemed to be made in Paris on the date stated therein (Article 9(4)).

The Centre provides the parties with the decision, provided that any additional fee that may have been requested (under Article 10(2) of the Rules) has been paid. The rules allow ICC to publish DOCDEX decisions, so long as the identities of the parties to the dispute or of any other person or entity named in the claim, answer or any supplement are not revealed (Article 12(1)).

The standard fee, which includes administrative expenses and the appointed experts' fees, is US$ 5 000 where the amount in dispute does not exceed US$ 1 000 000. In case the amount in dispute exceeds US$ 1 000 000, the standard fee for the administrative expenses and the appointed experts' fees is US 10 000 000 (Article 1 of the Appendix to the 2015 DOCDEX Rules). An additional fee of 50% of the standard fee may be fixed by the Centre, at its discretion, taking into account the facts and the documents underlying the dispute (Article 10(2) of the Rules; Article 2 of the Appendix to the 2015 DOCDEX Rules). A DOCDEX decision should not be put on a par with an arbitral award. It is not deemed to be a binding decision that finally decides an issue, unless the parties have specifically stated this to be the case (Article 2(6)). Depending on what the parties have specified in their contract, it may therefore be possible for them subsequently to initiate arbitral or judicial proceedings. However, as already mentioned, they are forbidden to call the DOCDEX experts or the officers of the ICC Banking Commission as witnesses, experts or in any similar function in such proceedings.

F. ICC RULES FOR DISPUTE BOARDS

1. Dispute Board Proceedings

In 2004 ICC adopted a new set of rules relating to Dispute Boards. These Rules were revised in 2015 and new ICC Dispute Board Rules entered into force on 1 October 2015.

Conceived to assist parties in the prevention and resolution of disputes in medium and long-term contracts, dispute boards are often provided for in standard forms of contracts relating to large-scale international infrastructure projects, such as those used by the World Bank and the *Fédération Internationale des Ingénieurs-Conseils* (FIDIC) based in Lausanne, Switzerland. They are typically established at the beginning of a contractual relationship as a permanent body to help ensure that the contract is performed as effectively as possible.

One of the principal innovations of the 2015 Rules is to spell out the three basic functions of dispute boards, so as to emphasize the importance of informal as well as formal approaches to disputes. The 2015 Rules explicitly provide that, upon perceiving a potential disagreement, the dispute board may encourage the parties to overcome it on their own without any further involvement of the dispute board. If the parties are unable to avoid the disagreement on their own, the dispute board can intervene with informal assistance to help the parties resolve the matter by agreement, and by issuing conclusions with respect to disputes upon formal referral, or determine a dispute through a recommendation or a decision issued after a procedure of formal referral (Article 16 of the 2015 Dispute Board Rules). Any party may at any time formally refer a disagreement to the dispute board for a conclusion, at which point the 'disagreement' becomes a 'dispute'. During the formal referral there shall be no informal conversations and no separate meetings between any dispute board member and any party with respect to any of the issues covered by the formal referral (Article 18 of the 2015 Dispute Board Rules). The procedure for formal referral of disputes is set out in Articles 19 (Statement of Case), 20 (Response and Additional Documentation) and 21 (Organization and Conduct of Hearings) of the Rules.

The 2015 Rules continue to give parties a choice between three different types of dispute board, each distinguished by the type of conclusion it issues upon a formal referral.

The Dispute Review Board ('DRB') is probably the most common. It involves the creation of a permanent board with the power to issue recommendations, which are not immediately binding on the parties but become so if no party objects within 30 days (Article 4 of the 2015 Dispute Board Rules).

The Dispute Adjudication Board ('DAB') is a more coercive mechanism. Like the DRB, the DAB exists throughout the life of the contract, but has the power to issue a decision which must be complied with immediately and which will be binding upon the parties until revised by an arbitral tribunal or a court (Article 5 of the 2015 Dispute Board Rules).

Parties can also opt for a Combined Dispute Board ('CDB'), which offers an intermediate solution between the DRB and the DAB. A CDB normally issues recommendations with respect to a dispute referred to it but may issue a decision if a party so requests and no other party objects thereto. If a party requests a decision and another party objects thereto, the CDB will decide whether to issue a recommendation or a decision on the basis of the criteria set forth in Article 6(3) of the Rules (Article 6 of the 2015 Dispute Board Rules).

If a party fails to comply with a recommendation of a DAB or CDB or with a decision of DRB or CDB, the other party or parties may refer the failure to arbitration, if the parties have so agreed, or, if not, to any court or competent jurisdiction (Article 4(4) and Article 5(4) of the 2015 Dispute Board Rules).

The 2015 Rules have strengthened the obligation to comply with recommendations and decisions, when so required, by providing that a party that has failed to comply with a recommendation or a decision shall not raise any issue as to the merits of the recommendation or the decision as a defense to its failure to comply without delay to the recommendation or decision (Article 4(4) and 5(4) of the Dispute Board Rules) and by using explicitly 'final' and 'binding' (Article 4(3), 5(3), 5(4) and 6(3) of the 2015 Dispute Board Rules),

Every prospective dispute board member shall sign a statement of acceptance, availability, impartiality and independence and disclose in writing to the parties, to the other dispute board members, and to the ICC International Centre for ADR (the 'Centre'), if the dispute board member is to be appointed by the Centre, any facts or circumstances which might be of such a nature as to call into question his or her independence in the eyes of the parties, as well as any circumstances that could give rise to reasonable doubts as to the dispute board member's impartiality (Article 8(2) of the 2015 Dispute Board Rules).

Before commencing dispute board activities, each member of a dispute board shall sign with all the parties a dispute board member agreement, which shall set out the terms of their mission and also their compensation, including a monthly management fee and a daily fee (Articles 10, 29 and 30 of the 2015 Dispute Board Rules). If the parties and the dispute board members cannot agree upon the fees of the dispute board members, the Centre, at the request of any party or any dispute board member, shall fix such fees after consulting the parties and the dispute board members. The parties shall be bound by the Centre's determination. The dispute board members shall either accept the determination or decline the appointment (Article 28(4) of the 2015 Dispute Board Rules).

In contrast with proceedings conducted under the Mediation Rules and the Expert Rules, ICC does not administer dispute boards (see J. Fry, S. Greenberg and F. Mazza, *The Secretariat's Guide to ICC Arbitration*, ICC Publication No. 729 E, Paris, 2012, p. 433). The ICC Dispute Board Rules may be applied without recourse to the ICC. However, the ICC proposes a number of administrative services to facilitate their application. These include appointing dispute board members, deciding on challenges against them, determining their fees, and reviewing dispute board decisions. These services are provided exclusively by the ICC International Centre for ADR under the conditions set out in the Rules. ICC's administrative expenses include an amount for each appointment of a dispute board member, an amount for each request for the Centre to fix the fees of the dispute board members, an amount for each decision upon a challenge of a dispute board member and, when parties have agreed to submit decisions of a DAB or CDB to ICC for review, an amount for each such review (Article 34(1) of the 2015 Dispute Board Rules). For a request to appoint a dispute board member a non-refundable amount of US 3 000 is due (Article 1 of Appendix – Schedule of Costs to the 2015 Dispute Board Rules). For a decision upon a challenge of a dispute board member a non-refundable amount of US 3 000 is due but the Centre shall fix the administrative expenses in an amount not exceeding the maximum amount of US$ 10 000 (Article 2 of Appendix – Schedule of Costs to the 2015 Dispute Board Rules). For the review of a decision of a DAB or a CDB a non-refundable amount is due of US 3 000 but the Centre shall fix the administrative expenses in an amount not exceeding the maximum amount of US$ 10 000 (Article 3 of Appendix – Schedule of Costs to the 2015 Dispute Board Rules). For a request for the Centre to fix the fees of the dispute board members a non-refundable amount is due of US 3 000 (Article 4 of Appendix – Schedule of Costs to the 2015 Dispute Board Rules).

In 2013, the Centre was requested to appoint members to dispute boards in five cases relating to construction, engineering and energy products (see '2013 Statistical Report' published in *ICC International Court of Arbitration Bulletin*, Paris, Vol. 25/ Nr. 1 – 2014, p. 16-17). No requests were reported in 2012 (see '2012 Statistical Report' published in *ICC International Court of Arbitration Bulletin*, Paris, Vol. 24/Nr. 1 – 2013, p. 16-17) or filed in 2011 (see '2011 Statistical Report' published in *ICC International Court of Arbitration Bulletin*, Paris, Vol. 23/Nr. 1 – 2012, p. 17).

In 2010, the Centre received one request under its Dispute Board Rules. It was for the appointment of a dispute adjudication board (DAB) member for the performance of a construction contract (see '2010 Statistical Report' published in *ICC International Court of Arbitration Bulletin*, Paris, Vol. 22/Nr. 1 – 2011, p. 17).

In 2009, one request was made to ICC pursuant to the ICC Dispute Board Rules (see '2009 Statistical Report' published in *ICC International Court of Arbitration Bulletin*, Paris, Vol. 21/Nr. 1 – 2010, p. 17).

2. Suggested Clauses for ICC Dispute Board Proceedings

ICC suggests the following clauses for ICC dispute board proceedings (see Appendix 29 below):

a) ICC Dispute Review Board followed by ICC arbitration if required:

> 'The Parties hereby agree to establish a Dispute Review Board ("DRB") in accordance with the Dispute Board Rules of the International Chamber of Commerce (the "Rules"), which are incorporated herein by reference. The DRB shall have [one/three/X] member[s] appointed in this Contract or appointed pursuant to the Rules.
>
> All disputes arising out of or in connection with the present Contract shall be submitted, in the first instance, to the DRB in accordance with the Rules. For any given dispute, the DRB shall issue a Recommendation in accordance with the Rules.
>
> If any Party fails to comply with a Recommendation, when required to do so pursuant to the Rules, the other Party may refer the failure itself, without having to refer it to the DRB first, to arbitration under the Rules of Arbitration of the International Chamber of Commerce by one or more arbitrators appointed in accordance with the said Rules of Arbitration. A Party that has failed to comply with a Recommendation, when required to do so pursuant to the Rules, shall not raise any issue as to the merits of the Recommendation as a defence to its failure to comply without delay with the Recommendation.
>
> If any Party sends a written notice to the other Party and the DRB expressing its dissatisfaction with a Recommendation, as provided in the Rules, or if the DRB does not issue the Recommendation within the time limit provided in the Rules, or if the DRB is disbanded pursuant to the Rules prior to issuing

the Recommendation, the dispute shall be finally settled under the Rules of Arbitration of the International Chamber of Commerce by one or more arbitrators appointed in accordance with the said Rules of Arbitration.'

b) ICC Dispute Adjudication Board followed by ICC arbitration if required:

'The Parties hereby agree to establish a Dispute Adjudication Board ("DAB") in accordance with the Dispute Board Rules of the International Chamber of Commerce (the "Rules"), which are incorporated herein by reference. The DAB shall have [one/three/X] member[s] appointed in this Contract or appointed pursuant to the Rules.

All disputes arising out of or in connection with the present Contract shall be submitted, in the first instance, to the DAB in accordance with the Rules. For any given dispute, the DAB shall issue a Decision in accordance with the Rules.*

If any Party fails to comply with a Decision, when required to do so pursuant to the Rules, the other Party may refer the failure itself, without having to refer it to the DAB first, to arbitration under the Rules of Arbitration of the International Chamber of Commerce by one or more arbitrators appointed in accordance with the said Rules of Arbitration. A Party that has failed to comply with a Decision, when required to do so pursuant to the Rules, shall not raise any issue as to the merits of the Decision as a defence to its failure to comply without delay with the Decision.

If any Party sends a written notice to the other Party and the DAB expressing its dissatisfaction with a Decision, as provided in the Rules, or if the DAB does not issue the Decision within the time limit provided in the Rules, or if the DAB is disbanded pursuant to the Rules prior to issuing the Decision, the dispute shall be finally settled under the Rules of Arbitration of the International Chamber of Commerce by one or more arbitrators appointed in accordance with the said Rules of Arbitration.'

[* The Parties may, if they wish, provide for review by the Centre of a DAB's Decisions by inserting the following text in place of the asterisk above:

> The DAB shall submit each Decision to the ICC for review in accordance with Article 23 of the Rules.*]*

c) ICC Combined Dispute Board followed by ICC arbitration if required:

'The Parties hereby agree to establish a Combined Dispute Board ("CDB") in accordance with the Dispute Board Rules of the International Chamber of Commerce (the "Rules"), which are incorporated herein by reference. The CDB shall have [one/three/X] member[s] appointed in this Contract or appointed pursuant to the Rules.

All disputes arising out of or in connection with the present Contract shall be submitted, in the first instance, to the CDB in accordance with the Rules. For any given dispute, the CDB shall issue a Recommendation, unless the Parties agree that it shall render a Decision or it decides to do so upon the request of a Party and in accordance with the Rules.*

If any Party fails to comply with a Recommendation or a Decision, when required to do so pursuant to the Rules, the other Party may refer the failure itself, without having to refer it to the CDB first, to arbitration under the Rules of Arbitration of the International Chamber of Commerce by one or more arbitrators appointed in accordance with the said Rules of Arbitration. A Party that has failed to comply with a Recommendation or a Decision, when required to do so pursuant to the Rules, shall not raise any issue as to the merits of the Recommendation or the Decision as a defence to its failure to comply without delay with the Recommendation or the Decision.

If any Party sends a written notice to the other Party and the CDB expressing its dissatisfaction with a Recommendation or a Decision, as provided in the Rules, or if the CDB does not issue the Recommendation or the Decision within the time limit provided in the Rules, or if the CDB is disbanded pursuant to the Rules prior to issuing the Recommendation or the Decision, the dispute shall be finally settled under the Rules of Arbitration of the International Chamber of Commerce by one or more arbitrators appointed in accordance with the said Rules of Arbitration.'

[*The Parties may, if they wish, provide for review by the Centre of a CDB's Decisions by inserting the following text in place of the asterisk above:

> The CDB shall submit each Decision to the ICC for review in accordance with Article 23 of the Rules.]

The parties should choose whichever kind of dispute board is most appropriate, given the nature of their contract and their relationship. The ICC does not favour any one type of dispute board over the others.

It may be necessary or desirable for parties to adapt the chosen clause to their particular circumstances. For instance, they may wish to stipulate the number of arbitrators, in the event of arbitration. They may also wish to stipulate the language and place of the arbitration and the law applicable to the merits.

When incorporating one of the clauses in their contract, parties are advised to verify its enforceability under applicable law.

CHAPTER 7

STATISTICAL INFORMATION ON ICC ARBITRATION

Official statistics relating to the activity of the ICC International Court of Arbitration are published each year in the *ICC International Court of Arbitration Bulletin*, to which readers are referred for fuller details.

NA = Figure not available

Table 1. Generalities

	2009	2010	2011	2012	2013
Number of arbitration requests filed	817	793	796	759	767
Number of cases pending at year end	1461	1485	1501	1476	1511
Number of parties involved	2095	2145	2293	2036	2120
Number of nationalities (countries/ independent territories) of parties	128	140	139	137	138
Parties from same country	16%	18%	18.5%	18%	20%
Cases with more than two parties	±33%	±33%	31%	31%	33%
Proportion of cases involving state or semi-state parties	9.5%	10%	10.2%	9.9%	11%
Number of arbitrators confirmed or appointed	1305	1331	1341	1301	1329
Number of nationalities (countries /independ. territories) of arbitrators	73	73	78	76	86
Number of challenges of arbitrators	57	46	39	61	66
– number of challenges accepted by Court	5	6	3	13	4
Number of resignations by arbitrators accepted by Court	31	38	30	NA	NA
Proportion of cases in which place of arbitration chosen by the parties	88.4%	89%	87%	90%	88.5%
Proportion of cases in which place of arbitration fixed by Court	11.6%	11%	13%	10%	11.5%
Number of different countries in which place of arbitration located	53	53	63	59	63
Proportion of contracts specifying rules of law applicable to the merits	88%	86%	84%	88%	90%
Number of arbitral awards rendered	415	479	508	491	471
– final awards	265	305	347	341	327
– partial awards	111	130	120	119	104
– awards by consent	39	44	41	31	40

Table 2. Geographical origins of parties – by region

	2009		2010		2011		2012		2013	
	No.	%	No.	%	No.	%	No.	%	No.	%
North & West Europe	857	40	817	38.1	933	40.7	747	36.7	708	33.4
Central & East Europe	268	13	261	12.2	265	11.5	249	12.2	244	11.5
North America	192	9	212	9.9	188	8.2	159	7.9	204	9.6
Latin America and the Caribbean	241	12	297	13.9	247	10.8	292	14.3	279	13.2
North Africa	51	2	59	2.7	101	4.4	41	2	78	3.7
Sub-Saharan Africa	75	4	74	3.4	78	3.4	86	4.2	96	4.5
Central & West Asia	127	6	170	7.9	178	7.8	163	8	199	9.4
South & East Asia	284	14	255	11.9	303	13.2	299	14.7	312	14.7
Total	**2095**		**2145**		**2293**		**2036**		**2120**	

Table 3. Amounts in dispute (percentage of cases filed involving amounts indicated)

	2009	2010	2011	2012	2013
Under US$ 50 000	1.6%	1%	1.1%	1.1%	1.3%
≥ US$ 50 000 < US$ 100 000	1.7%	1.8%	1.1%	1.7%	1.8%
≥ US$ 100 000 < US$ 200 000	3.7%	4.0%	3.1%	3.0%	3.4%
≥ US$ 200 000 < US$ 500 000	8.6%	8.7%	9.6%	8.0%	7.4%
≥ US$ 500 000 < US$ 1 million	7.8%	9.2%	7.9%	11.1%	8.1%
≥ US$ 1 million < US$ 2 million	9.9%	10.5%	11.1%	11.3%	10.1%
≥ US$ 2 million < US$ 5 million	15.6%	14.2%	15.6%	13.5%	14.3%
≥ US$ 5 million < US$ 10 million	10.2%	11.9%	8.9%	11.3%	9.9%
≥ US$ 10 million < US$ 30 million	14.8%	13.9%	15.3%	14.2%	15.7%
≥ US$ 30 million < US$ 50 million	5.3%	3.1%	4.3%	5.1%	6.1%
≥ US$ 50 million < US$ 80 million	3.3%	2.9%	1.9%	4.5%	4.3%
≥ US$ 80 million < US$ 100 million	1.6%	2.0%	0.5%	1.1%	1.8%
≥ US$ 100 million < US$ 500 million	4.4%	2.9%	4.4%	6.3%	6.0%
≥ US$ 500 million	NA	0.5%	1.0%	1.7%	2.2%
Not quantified	11.5%	13.4%	14.2%	6.1%	7.6%

NA: The 2009 ICC Statistical Report only specified the tranche: ≥ US$ 100 million

Table 4. Geographical origins of parties

Countries/territories from which parties originated	2009			2010			2011			2012			2013		
	Cl.	Res.	Total	Cl.	Res.	Total	Cl.	Res.	Total	Cl.	Res.	Total	Cl.	Res.	Total
Europe															
Albania	0	1	1	2	2	4	0	1	1	2	2	4	2	2	4
Andorra	0	0	0	0	0	0	0	0	0	0	0	0	1	0	1
Austria	24	15	39	18	15	33	29	8	37	17	15	32	20	15	35
Belarus	0	1	1	0	0	0	0	0	0	0	1	1	0	0	0
Belgium	11	18	29	30	16	46	21	16	37	11	14	25	12	12	24
Bosnia & Herzegovina	2	4	6	1	0	1	0	1	1	0	3	3	3	3	6
Bulgaria	6	14	20	6	7	13	7	5	12	1	1	2	1	1	2
Channel Islands	4	4	8	5	4	9	7	6	13	2	3	5	3	1	4
Croatia	3	9	12	0	5	5	1	0	1	3	5	8	1	0	1
Cyprus	9	7	16	11	3	14	14	12	26	13	10	23	14	10	24
Czech Republic	16	8	24	9	9	18	7	7	14	5	7	12	4	5	9
Denmark	5	8	13	13	6	19	12	10	22	12	4	16	6	1	7
Estonia	0	0	0	0	0	0	0	0	0	1	1	2	1	0	1
Finland	8	3	11	10	7	17	10	2	12	4	4	8	8	7	15
France	81	73	154	56	75	131	75	54	129	62	62	124	43	59	102
Germany	81	63	144	89	70	159	60	58	118	68	64	132	58	82	140
Gibraltar	0	2	2	2	3	5	0	0	0	1	2	3	0	0	0
Greece	13	14	27	16	11	27	10	17	27	9	9	18	17	12	29
Hungary	1	5	6	1	0	1	3	8	11	2	4	6	0	3	3
Iceland	0	0	0	0	0	0	0	0	0	2	0	2	0	0	0
Ireland	10	9	19	1	5	6	2	3	5	6	3	9	9	2	11
Isle of Man	4	1	5	2	2	4	1	0	1	0	1	1	1	0	1
Italy	33	43	76	38	36	74	51	66	117	34	37	71	37	37	74
Kosovo	0	0	0	1	0	1	0	1	1	0	0	0	0	1	1
Latvia	0	0	0	1	1	2	1	0	1	0	1	1	0	0	0
Liechtenstein	0	1	1	1	6	7	1	0	1	2	0	2	1	1	2
Lithuania	1	1	2	1	1	2	1	2	3	1	3	4	1	0	1
Luxembourg	19	9	28	11	16	27	7	4	11	10	15	25	10	7	17
Macedonia	0	2	2	1	3	4	0	1	1	0	1	1	1	2	3
Malta	2	1	3	1	2	3	2	2	4	1	0	1	4	0	4
Moldova	0	0	0	0	0	0	1	0	1	0	0	0	0	0	0
Montenegro	0	0	0	1	1	2	0	0	0	0	1	1	0	0	0
Monaco	2	1	3	2	5	7	1	2	3	0	1	1	1	0	1
Netherlands	32	37	69	25	21	46	41	30	71	29	25	54	31	29	60
Norway	3	6	9	7	6	13	8	5	13	3	7	10	5	9	14
Poland	7	15	22	14	9	23	13	11	24	10	12	22	7	16	23
Portugal	7	11	18	2	6	8	6	11	17	9	14	23	7	4	11
Romania	7	19	26	7	19	26	18	16	34	27	23	50	11	18	29
Russian Federation	6	11	17	3	10	13	8	17	25	11	12	23	6	7	13
Serbia	5	5	10	4	0	4	5	3	8	5	6	11	2	5	7
Slovakia	1	2	3	2	1	3	3	5	8	3	2	5	3	4	7
Slovenia	0	0	0	3	4	7	2	5	7	2	0	2	0	0	0
Spain	36	41	77	26	39	65	90	54	144	45	28	73	32	41	73
Sweden	7	5	12	14	6	20	8	17	25	9	13	22	3	4	7
Switzerland	31	32	63	25	26	51	26	39	65	19	40	59	20	29	49
Turkey	22	40	62	31	45	76	19	27	46	18	23	41	27	36	63

Countries/territories from which parties originated	2009			2010			2011			2012			2013		
	Cl.	Res.	Total	Cl.	Res.	Total	Cl.	Res.	Total	Cl.	Res.	Total	Cl.	Res.	Total
Turkish Rep. North Cyprus	0	0	0	0	2	2	0	0	0	0	0	0	0	0	0
Ukraine	2	9	11	2	7	9	10	3	13	7	2	9	4	5	9
United Kingdom	25	49	74	24	43	67	46	42	88	27	22	49	20	36	56
Total (Europe)	**526**	**599**	**1125**	**521**	**557**	**1078**	**627**	**571**	**1198**	**493**	**503**	**996**	**441**	**511**	**952**
Americas															
Antigua & Barbuda	0	0	0	0	2	2	0	0	0	0	0	0	0	0	0
Argentina	7	12	19	10	6	16	9	9	18	6	8	14	10	9	19
Bahamas	2	1	3	2	3	5	2	0	2	1	1	2	0	1	1
Barbados	1	1	2	0	1	1	2	1	3	1	1	2	2	2	4
Belize	1	2	3	0	1	1	1	0	1	0	0	0	0	0	0
Bermuda	4	2	6	6	3	9	5	2	7	2	5	7	3	4	7
Bolivia	0	0	0	0	0	0	2	2	4	0	0	0	1	0	1
Brazil	32	54	86	33	41	74	30	51	81	36	46	82	38	53	91
British Virgin Islands	20	8	28	18	19	37	17	12	29	19	13	32	12	7	19
Canada	13	16	29	12	14	26	15	18	33	6	8	14	14	16	30
Cayman Islands	8	3	11	6	7	13	4	2	6	16	2	18	6	9	15
Chile	3	3	6	4	5	9	6	6	12	9	4	13	5	5	10
Colombia	2	3	5	0	1	1	1	9	10	7	4	11	7	10	17
Costa Rica	0	0	0	0	0	0	0	1	1	0	1	1	2	0	2
Cuba	0	1	1	1	1	2	0	0	0	0	12	12	0	5	5
Curaçao	0	0	0	0	0	0	0	0	0	1	3	4	1	0	1
Dominica	0	1	1	1	1	2	0	0	0	0	0	0	0	0	0
Dominican Republic	1	2	3	1	1	2	0	2	2	2	5	7	1	0	1
Ecuador	0	0	0	0	1	1	0	0	0	2	5	7	0	0	0
El Salvador	0	0	0	4	2	6	2	2	4	2	1	3	0	0	0
Guatemala	0	0	0	2	0	2	2	0	2	0	0	0	0	2	2
Guyana	0	0	0	0	0	0	2	1	3	0	0	0	0	0	0
Haïti	0	0	0	0	0	0	0	1	1	0	0	0	0	1	1
Honduras	0	0	0	1	0	1	0	1	1	1	1	2	0	0	0
Jamaica	2	2	4	5	6	11	1	0	1	1	1	2	0	0	0
Mexico	9	9	18	14	48	62	12	16	28	19	25	44	29	18	47
Netherlands Antilles	1	1	2	1	0	1	2	0	2	0	0	0	0	0	0
Nicaragua	1	0	1	0	0	0	0	0	0	1	0	1	0	0	0
Panama	1	12	13	3	4	7	8	5	13	4	8	12	8	3	11
Peru	0	0	0	0	0	0	1	1	2	6	5	11	3	2	5
Puerto Rico	0	0	0	1	1	2	0	0	0	0	0	0	0	0	0
Saint Kitts & Nevis	1	1	2	1	0	1	0	0	0	0	0	0	1	0	1
Saint Vincent & Grenadines	0	0	0	0	0	0	0	0	0	0	0	0	2	1	3
Suriname	0	0	0	0	1	1	0	0	0	0	0	0	0	0	0
Trinidad & Tobago	3	7	10	4	5	9	4	6	10	0	1	1	1	2	3
Turcs & Caicos Islands	1	1	2	0	0	0	0	0	0	0	0	0	0	0	0
Uruguay	2	5	7	1	3	4	1	0	1	3	0	3	5	4	9
USA	85	78	163	86	100	186	73	82	155	80	65	145	82	92	174
US Virgin Islands	0	1	1	0	0	0	0	0	0	0	0	0	1	1	2
Venezuela	0	3	3	3	8	11	2	1	3	1	0	1	0	1	1
Total (Americas)	**204**	**229**	**433**	**221**	**288**	**509**	**204**	**231**	**435**	**226**	**225**	**451**	**234**	**249**	**483**

Countries/territories from which parties originated	2009			2010			2011			2012			2013		
	Cl.	Res.	Total	Cl.	Res.	Total	Cl.	Res.	Total	Cl.	Res.	Total	Cl.	Res.	Total
Africa															
Algeria	3	4	7	5	8	13	5	10	15	5	12	17	8	35	43
Angola	1	0	1	0	0	0	0	0	0	1	1	2	2	1	3
Benin	0	0	0	0	0	0	0	0	0	0	1	1	0	1	1
Botswana	0	0	0	0	0	0	0	0	0	0	0	0	2	1	3
Burkina Faso	0	1	1	1	1	2	0	1	1	0	1	1	0	2	2
Cameroon	0	1	1	1	0	1	1	3	4	0	0	0	0	1	1
Cape Verde	1	0	1	0	0	0	0	0	0	0	0	0	0	0	0
Chad	0	0	0	0	0	0	0	0	0	0	1	1	1	1	2
Comoros	0	0	0	0	0	0	0	0	0	0	1	1	0	0	0
Congo (Dem. Rep.)	2	3	5	2	5	7	2	3	5	0	0	0	2	2	4
Congo (Rep.)	1	2	3	0	1	1	2	0	2	0	0	0	4	4	8
Côte d'Ivoire	0	2	2	0	1	1	0	1	1	1	0	1	0	1	1
Djibouti	0	0	0	0	0	0	0	0	0	0	0	0	0	1	1
Egypt	8	12	20	7	14	21	16	23	39	3	6	9	4	4	8
Equatorial Guinea	0	1	1	0	0	0	2	1	3	0	0	0	0	1	1
Eritrea	0	3	3	0	4	4	0	0	0	0	0	0	0	0	0
Ethiopia	0	0	0	0	1	1	1	2	3	0	1	1	3	2	5
Gabon	0	0	0	0	1	1	0	3	3	2	3	5	0	0	0
Gambia	0	1	1	0	0	0	0	0	0	1	0	1	0	0	0
Ghana	0	0	0	2	0	2	3	2	5	0	1	1	1	1	2
Guinea	0	0	0	1	1	2	0	2	2	0	1	1	1	3	4
Kenya	2	1	3	0	2	2	1	1	2	2	1	3	2	4	6
Liberia	0	0	0	0	0	0	1	0	1	1	0	1	1	0	1
Libya	0	2	2	1	1	2	0	2	2	0	4	4	3	6	9
Madagascar	0	0	0	0	0	0	1	2	3	2	2	4	4	1	5
Malawi	0	1	1	0	0	0	0	0	0	0	0	0	0	0	0
Mali	1	1	2	0	1	1	1	0	1	0	2	2	1	1	2
Mauritania	0	0	0	1	1	2	0	8	8	0	0	0	1	1	2
Mauritius	5	2	7	4	2	6	3	2	5	4	2	6	6	5	11
Morocco	5	8	13	13	7	20	12	15	27	1	6	7	3	9	12
Mozambique	0	0	0	0	0	0	0	0	0	0	0	0	2	3	5
Namibia	0	2	2	0	0	0	0	0	0	0	0	0	0	0	0
Niger	0	0	0	0	0	0	0	0	0	0	0	0	0	1	1
Nigeria	4	11	15	7	8	15	5	5	10	5	9	14	3	2	5
Rwanda	0	0	0	0	1	1	1	3	4	0	0	0	3	0	3
Senegal	1	0	1	0	2	2	1	2	3	0	0	0	0	1	1
Seychelles	0	1	1	0	0	0	0	0	0	1	2	3	1	0	1
Sierra Leone	0	1	1	1	1	2	0	2	2	0	0	0	0	0	0
South Africa	5	7	12	6	5	11	5	3	8	9	9	18	5	3	8
Sudan	1	1	2	0	1	1	0	0	0	0	2	2	1	2	3
Swaziland	0	0	0	0	0	0	2	1	3	0	0	0	0	0	0
Tanzania	0	0	0	0	0	0	0	1	1	0	14	14	1	2	3
Togo	0	0	0	0	0	0	0	0	0	1	0	1	0	0	0
Tunisia	4	5	9	1	0	1	6	4	10	2	2	4	2	2	4
Uganda	0	0	0	2	1	3	0	1	1	0	0	0	0	2	2
Zambia	1	1	2	0	0	0	1	0	1	1	1	2	1	1	2
Zimbabwe	1	0	1	0	7	7	0	4	4	0	0	0	0	0	0
Total (Africa)	**47**	**79**	**126**	**55**	**78**	**133**	**72**	**107**	**179**	**42**	**85**	**127**	**68**	**106**	**174**

Countries/territories from which parties originated	2009			2010			2011			2012			2013		
	Cl.	Res.	Total	Cl.	Res.	Total	Cl.	Res.	Total	Cl.	Res.	Total	Cl.	Res.	Total
Asia & Pacific															
Afghanistan	0	0	0	0	0	0	1	0	1	0	0	0	3	1	4
Armenia	0	0	0	1	1	2	0	1	1	2	0	2	0	0	0
Australia	8	7	15	5	5	10	7	5	12	4	6	10	7	14	21
Azerbaijan	0	0	0	1	1	2	0	2	2	1	0	1	1	5	6
Bahrain	4	4	8	5	4	9	2	3	5	3	1	4	0	0	0
Bangladesh	2	3	5	1	3	4	0	0	0	0	1	1	0	0	0
Cambodia	0	0	0	0	1	1	0	0	0	0	1	1	0	0	0
China	23	26	49	23	28	51	17	31	48	24	31	55	34	52	86
(Mainland China)	(15	18)	(33)	(9)	(18)	(27)	(8)	(29)	(37)	(10)	(18)	(28)	(18	40)	(58)
(Hong Kong)	(7)	(8)	(15)	(14)	(10)	(24)	(9)	(2)	(11)	(13)	(13)	(26)	(16	12)	(28)
(Macau)	(1)	(0)	(1)	(0)	(0)	(0)	(0)	(0)	(0)	(1)	(0)	(1)	(0)	(0)	(0)
Chinese Taipei	5	3	8	2	4	6	9	4	13	5	5	10	3	10	13
Georgia	2	0	2	1	6	7	0	1	1	0	2	2	1	0	1
India	15	37	52	20	51	71	21	32	53	25	56	81	25	30	55
Indonesia	4	8	12	2	8	10	6	13	19	10	7	17	2	8	10
Iran	5	5	10	9	3	12	5	4	9	3	6	9	8	2	10
Iraq	1	0	1	6	0	6	2	0	2	1	2	3	2	0	2
Israel	7	2	9	9	5	14	11	17	28	6	6	12	9	7	16
Japan	13	13	26	7	14	21	13	11	24	8	9	17	6	15	21
Jordan	10	7	17	1	1	2	3	2	5	2	6	8	5	6	11
Kazakhstan	2	1	3	0	2	2	2	3	5	0	3	3	0	1	1
Korea (P.D.R.)	0	0	0	0	0	0	0	1	1	0	0	0	0	0	0
Kuwait	1	5	6	6	4	10	1	4	5	4	7	11	4	3	7
Laos	0	0	0	0	0	0	1	0	1	1	0	1	0	0	0
Lebanon	5	1	6	7	5	12	13	2	15	8	1	9	12	4	16
Malaysia	9	13	22	2	6	8	9	12	21	5	6	11	8	6	14
Maldives	0	0	0	0	0	0	0	0	0	0	1	1	1	1	2
Marshall Islands	1	0	1	0	0	0	1	1	2	1	0	1	1	0	1
Nepal	0	0	0	0	0	0	0	0	0	0	0	0	1	1	2
New Zealand	1	2	3	1	1	2	0	1	1	0	0	0	2	1	3
Oman	1	2	3	3	2	5	0	0	0	0	0	0	3	2	5
Pakistan	1	2	3	2	1	3	1	5	6	0	3	3	4	10	14
Papua New Guinea	0	0	0	0	0	0	0	0	0	1	0	1	0	0	0
Philippines	2	12	14	0	1	1	5	36	41	5	0	5	2	6	8
Qatar	6	5	11	10	7	17	2	10	12	8	1	9	7	5	12
Samoa	0	0	0	0	0	0	0	0	0	1	0	1	0	0	0
Saudi Arabia	6	3	9	4	1	5	5	15	20	5	9	14	9	24	33
Singapore	15	12	27	11	10	21	4	9	13	13	11	24	11	12	23
South Korea	15	16	31	9	14	23	12	14	26	15	26	41	10	14	24
Sri Lanka	1	4	5	2	4	6	0	1	1	1	3	4	1	2	3
Syria	1	2	3	1	1	2	5	1	6	1	2	3	0	2	2
Tajikistan	0	1	1	0	0	0	0	1	1	0	1	1	0	0	0
Thailand	4	1	5	5	5	10	5	3	8	6	3	9	2	5	7
Turkmenistan	0	0	0	0	4	4	0	0	0	0	0	0	0	0	0
United Arab Emirates	19	18	37	24	29	53	25	31	56	21	38	59	30	39	69
Uzbekistan	0	1	1	0	1	1	2	1	3	0	1	1	0	0	0
Vietnam	2	5	7	2	5	7	0	12	12	0	5	5	2	3	5
Western Samoa	0	0	0	0	0	0	1	0	1	0	0	0	0	0	0
Yemen	0	0	0	0	0	0	0	1	1	0	0	0	0	0	0
Total (Asia)	**191**	**220**	**411**	**182**	**238**	**420**	**191**	**290**	**481**	**190**	**272**	**462**	**217**	**294**	**511**

Table 5. Geographical origins of arbitrators (CA: Co-arbitrators; SA: Sole arbitrators; C: Presidents of arbitral tribunals)

Countries/territories from which arbitrators originated	2009			2010			2011			2012			2013		
	CA	SA/P	Total	CA	SA/P	Total	CA	SA/P	Total	CA	SA/P	Total	CA	SA/P	Total
Albania	0	0	0	0	0	0	0	0	0	1	0	1	0	0	0
Algeria	1	0	1	3	0	3	3	0	3	1	0	1	6	0	6
Argentina	10	6	16	20	7	27	6	7	13	11	6	17	11	7	18
Australia	6	14	20	6	13	19	10	18	28	12	7	19	23	16	39
Austria	18	27	45	17	29	46	15	21	36	24	24	48	15	30	45
Bahrain	1	0	1	1	0	1	1	2	3	2	2	4	3	1	4
Bangladesh	0	0	0	0	1	1	1	0	1	0	0	0	0	0	2
Belarus	0	0	0	0	0	0	1	0	1	1	0	1	0	0	0
Belgium	21	25	46	19	29	48	26	24	50	14	19	33	13	21	34
Brazil	26	6	32	26	14	40	24	13	37	28	16	44	36	15	51
Brunei	0	0	0	0	0	0	0	0	0	1	0	1	0	0	0
Bulgaria	5	0	5	4	0	4	2	2	4	2	4	6	0	2	2
Burkina Faso	0	0	0	0	0	0	0	0	0	0	0	0	2	0	2
Cameroon	0	0	0	0	0	0	0	0	0	1	1	2	2	0	2
Canada	17	19	36	8	37	45	16	24	40	17	23	40	7	26	33
Chile	3	4	7	3	1	4	4	1	5	3	1	4	4	2	6
China	2	3	5	5	3	8	2	1	3	7	0	7	5	0	5
(Mainland China)	(1)	(0)	(1)	(N)	(N)	(N)	(N)	(N)	(N)	(N)	(N)	(N)	(N)	(N)	(N)
(Hong Kong)	(1)	(3)	(4)	(N)	(N)	(N)	(N)	(N)	(N)	(N)	(N)	(N)	(N)	(N)	(N)
Chinese Taipei	2	0	2	2	1	3	0	0	0	3	1	4	0	0	0
Colombia	6	6	12	4	5	9	2	4	6	6	11	17	7	10	17
Congo (Rep.)	0	0	0	0	0	0	0	0	0	0	0	0	2	1	3
Costa Rica	0	0	0	0	2	2	0	0	0	1	0	1	1	1	2
Croatia	4	1	5	2	0	2	2	1	3	4	4	0	1	0	1
Cuba	1	0	1	1	0	1	0	0	0	1	0	1	1	0	1
Cyprus	0	0	0	0	0	0	0	0	0	0	0	0	0	2	2
Czech Republic	11	3	14	8	1	9	1	2	3	5	1	6	4	0	4
Denmark	0	1	1	2	1	3	5	5	10	1	3	4	3	3	6
Dominican Republic	0	0	0	2	1	3	2	0	2	0	0	0	0	2	2
Ecuador	0	0	0	0	0	0	1	0	1	0	0	0	1	0	1
Egypt	2	4	6	9	4	13	4	2	6	4	1	5	3	2	5
El Salvador	0	0	0	0	0	0	4	0	4	0	0	0	0	0	0
Estonia	0	0	0	0	0	0	0	1	1	0	0	0	0	1	1
Ethiopia	0	0	0	0	0	0	0	0	0	1	0	1	0	0	0
Finland	1	2	3	0	4	4	2	2	4	5	3	8	4	0	4
France	64	32	96	76	44	120	53	48	101	65	50	115	71	57	128
Georgia	0	0	0	1	0	1	1	0	1	0	0	0	0	0	0
Germany	57	47	104	43	45	88	65	54	119	38	45	83	36	38	74
Ghana	1	0	1	0	0	0	0	0	0	0	0	0	0	0	0
Greece	14	4	18	24	8	32	9	6	15	9	7	16	8	4	12
Guatemala	0	0	0	0	0	0	1	0	1	0	0	0	0	0	0
Hungary	0	0	0	2	3	5	3	1	4	3	0	3	1	2	3
India	14	4	18	13	4	17	10	3	13	13	3	16	17	1	18
Indonesia	1	0	1	0	0	0	1	0	1	1	0	1	5	0	5
Iran	1	2	3	9	2	11	12	2	14	5	3	8	5	3	8
Iraq	0	1	1	0	0	0	1	2	3	0	0	0	1	0	1
Ireland	7	3	10	6	1	7	4	7	11	1	6	7	1	9	10

Countries/territories from which arbitrators originated	2009			2010			2011			2012			2013		
	CA	SA/P	Total	CA	SA/P	Total	CA	SA/P	Total	CA	SA/P	Total	CA	SA/P	Total
Israel	2	1	3	1	0	1	0	2	2	0	0	0	1	1	2
Italy	16	12	28	27	10	37	23	9	32	31	11	42	18	15	33
Jamaica	0	0	0	0	1	1	0	0	0	3	0	3	0	0	0
Japan	2	0	2	0	0	0	3	1	4	1	1	2	2	1	3
Jordan	5	3	8	0	6	6	2	3	5	2	2	4	4	3	7
Kenya	1	1	2	0	0	0	0	0	0	0	0	0	0	0	0
Kuwait	0	0	0	2	0	2	0	0	0	0	0	0	0	0	0
Kyrgyzstan	0	0	0	0	0	0	0	0	0	0	0	0	1	0	1
Lebanon	4	4	8	11	6	17	10	20	30	15	7	22	15	9	24
Libya	2	0	2	0	0	0	0	0	0	0	0	0	0	0	0
Lithuania	0	1	1	0	0	0	0	1	1	0	1	1	0	3	3
Luxembourg	4	0	4	4	0	4	2	1	3	0	0	0	2	0	2
Malaysia	1	4	5	5	4	9	0	5	5	1	8	9	9	7	16
Malta	1	0	1	0	1	1	0	1	1	0	0	0	0	2	2
Mauritius	3	0	3	1	1	2	1	0	1	0	0	0	2	1	3
Mexico	12	5	17	15	9	24	20	11	31	18	11	29	18	13	31
Montenegro	0	0	0	1	0	1	0	0	0	0	0	0	0	0	0
Morocco	0	0	0	3	0	3	2	0	2	2	0	2	0	0	0
Nepal	0	0	0	0	0	0	0	0	0	0	0	0	1	0	1
Netherlands	2	11	13	10	9	19	5	5	10	3	7	10	2	5	7
New Zealand	0	0	0	1	7	8	2	5	7	2	9	11	7	5	12
Nigeria	5	0	5	4	0	4	4	0	4	0	2	2	7	0	7
Norway	2	0	2	1	2	3	8	3	11	2	3	5	9	5	14
Pakistan	1	0	1	2	0	2	2	0	2	2	0	2	0	0	0
Panama	0	0	0	0	0	0	0	0	0	0	0	0	1	0	1
Paraguay	1	0	1	0	0	0	1	0	1	0	0	0	0	0	0
Peru	0	0	0	0	0	0	0	1	1	5	2	7	0	2	2
Philippines	6	2	8	0	0	0	4	0	4	5	0	5	3	0	3
Poland	14	4	18	8	1	9	10	4	14	4	3	7	9	7	16
Portugal	5	2	7	4	2	6	6	5	11	3	3	6	3	2	5
Romania	4	0	4	6	1	7	10	1	11	9	1	10	5	0	5
Russian Federation	0	1	1	4	0	4	2	1	3	5	0	5	3	0	3
Saudi Arabia	1	0	1	0	0	0	0	0	0	1	0	1	6	0	6
Senegal	0	0	0	1	0	1	0	0	0	1	0	1	1	0	1
Serbia	5	0	5	1	0	1	1	1	2	5	0	5	3	0	3
Singapore	12	21	33	10	13	23	9	18	27	14	19	33	15	32	47
Slovakia	2	1	3	2	0	2	3	0	3	0	0	0	3	0	3
Slovenia	1	3	4	0	0	0	0	1	1	0	0	0	2	0	2
South Africa	0	0	0	8	4	12	12	4	16	2	3	5	5	4	9
South Korea	3	4	7	1	0	1	0	1	1	1	0	1	3	0	3
Spain	15	14	29	11	11	22	27	19	46	25	20	45	14	17	31
Sri Lanka	0	1	1	3	1	4	0	0	0	5	0	5	3	0	3
St. Vincent & Grenad.	0	0	0	0	0	0	0	0	0	0	0	0	1	0	1
Sudan	0	0	0	0	0	0	0	0	0	0	0	0	1	0	1
Sweden	5	3	8	11	11	22	8	11	19	13	8	21	10	13	23
Switzerland	78	124	202	72	108	180	64	105	169	86	74	160	67	74	141
Syria	0	0	0	2	0	2	2	1	3	1	0	1	0	0	0
Tanzania	1	0	1	0	0	0	0	0	0	0	0	0	1	0	1
Thailand	1	2	3	3	0	3	1	2	3	0	1	1	0	1	1

Countries/territories from which arbitrators originated	2009 CA	2009 SA/P	2009 Total	2010 CA	2010 SA/P	2010 Total	2011 CA	2011 SA/P	2011 Total	2012 CA	2012 SA/P	2012 Total	2013 CA	2013 SA/P	2013 Total
Togo	0	0	0	0	0	0	0	0	0	0	0	0	1	0	1
Trinidad & Tobago	1	0	1	0	0	0	0	0	0	0	0	0	0	0	0
Tunisia	6	2	8	1	1	2	1	0	1	1	3	4	4	1	5
Turkey	11	2	13	14	3	17	12	2	14	18	4	22	12	2	14
Uganda	1	0	1	0	0	0	0	0	0	1	0	1	0	0	0
Ukraine	0	0	0	5	0	5	2	1	3	1	0	1	4	2	6
United Arab Emirates	2	0	2	3	0	3	1	3	4	6	2	8	1	0	1
United Kingdom	103	93	196	103	74	177	102	67	169	106	73	179	91	79	170
Uruguay	0	0	0	2	3	5	0	2	2	0	0	0	0	0	0
USA	64	35	99	57	43	100	73	39	112	56	31	87	61	32	93
Venezuela	0	0	0	1	1	2	2	0	2	4	0	4	1	1	2
Vietnam	0	0	0	0	0	0	0	0	0	1	0	1	1	0	1
Zambia	0	0	0	0	0	0	0	0	0	1	0	1	1	0	1
Zimbabwe	0	0	0	0	0	0	1	0	1	0	0	0	0	0	0
Total	720	585	1305	593	738	1331	730	611	1341	751	550	1301	734	595	1329

N: Not specified in the ICC Statistical Report

Table 6. Place of arbitration (P: chosen by the parties; C: fixed by the ICC Court)

Countries/territories where places of arb'n were located	2009 P	2009 C	2009 Total	2010 P	2010 C	2010 Total	2011 P	2011 C	2011 Total	2012 P	2012 C	2012 Total	2013 P	2013 C	2013 Total
Albania	0	0	0	0	0	0	0	0	0	1	0	1	0	0	0
Algeria	0	0	0	0	0	0	2	0	2	0	0	0	0	0	0
Angola	0	0	0	0	0	0	0	0	0	1	0	1	0	0	0
Argentina	3	0	3	6	0	6	2	0	2	4	0	4	3	0	3
Australia	3	0	3	1	1	2	1	0	1	0	0	0	5	2	7
Austria	22	4	26	11	2	13	11	1	12	13	0	13	10	2	12
Bahrain	0	1	1	1	1	2	4	2	6	0	1	1	0	0	0
Barbados	0	0	0	0	0	0	0	0	0	0	0	0	1	0	1
Belgium	11	3	14	7	1	8	9	5	14	5	1	6	9	0	9
Bolivia	0	0	0	0	0	0	0	0	0	0	0	0	1	0	1
Botswana	0	0	0	0	0	0	0	0	0	0	0	0	0	1	1
Brazil	11	0	11	11	0	11	14	3	17	14	1	15	22	0	22
Bulgaria	0	0	0	0	0	0	2	0	2	0	0	0	0	0	0
Canada	4	2	6	7	0	7	5	2	7	6	0	6	3	0	3
Chile	3	0	3	3	0	3	0	0	0	1	0	1	4	0	4
China	8	1	9	11	3	14	5	4	9	10	2	12	14	0	14
(Mainland China)	(0)	(0)	(0)	(N)	(N)	(0)	(N)	(N)	(1)	(N)	(N)	(1)	(0)	(0)	(0)
(Hong Kong)	(8)	(1)	(9)	(N)	(N)	(14)	(N)	(N)	(8)	(N)	(N)	(11)	(N)	(N)	(14)
Chinese Taipei	1	0	1	1	0	1	0	0	0	0	1	1	0	0	0
Colombia	0	0	0	0	0	0	0	0	0	0	0	0	3	0	3
Congo (Rep.)	0	0	0	0	0	0	0	0	0	0	0	0	1	0	1
Costa Rica	0	0	0	0	0	0	0	0	0	1	0	1	0	0	0
Croatia	0	0	0	0	0	0	0	0	0	0	0	0	1	0	1
Cyprus	0	0	0	0	0	0	2	0	2	1	0	1	0	1	1
Czech Republic	0	0	0	3	0	3	1	0	1	1	0	1	0	0	0

Countries/territories where places of arb'n were located	2009			2010			2011			2012			2013		
	P	C	Total	P	C	Total	P	C	Total	P	C	Total	P	C	Total
Denmark	0	0	0	2	3	5	4	3	7	2	1	3	4	0	4
Dominican Republic	0	0	0	0	0	0	0	0	0	0	0	0	1	1	2
Ecuador	0	0	0	0	0	0	0	0	0	1	0	1	0	0	0
Egypt	4	1	5	2	0	2	3	0	3	2	0	2	0	0	0
El Salvador	0	0	0	0	0	0	0	1	1	1	0	1	0	0	0
Estonia	0	0	0	0	0	0	0	0	0	1	0	1	0	0	0
Ethiopia	0	0	0	0	0	0	0	0	0	1	0	1	0	0	0
Finland	1	0	1	3	0	3	6	0	6	3	0	3	0	0	0
France	94	19	113	109	15	124	92	20	112	80	21	101	93	26	119
Germany	37	3	40	24	3	27	39	5	44	18	1	19	20	2	22
Greece	6	0	6	9	1	10	3	0	3	6	0	6	4	0	4
Honduras	0	0	0	0	0	0	0	0	0	0	0	0	1	0	1
Hungary	0	0	0	1	0	1	2	0	2	1	0	1	0	0	0
Iceland	0	0	0	0	0	0	0	0	0	1	0	1	0	0	0
India	6	1	7	6	1	7	6	0	6	11	0	11	3	1	4
Indonesia	0	0	0	0	0	0	0	0	0	0	0	0	2	0	2
Ireland	2	0	2	0	0	0	1	0	1	1	0	1	1	2	3
Israel	1	0	1	0	0	0	1	0	1	0	0	0	0	0	0
Italy	6	0	6	6	0	6	6	0	6	3	0	3	6	0	6
Jamaica	0	0	0	1	0	1	0	0	0	0	0	0	0	0	0
Japan	3	2	5	2	1	3	3	2	5	3	0	3	2	0	2
Jordan	2	0	2	0	0	0	0	0	0	0	0	0	2	0	2
Kenya	0	0	0	1	0	1	1	0	1	0	0	0	0	0	0
Kuwait	0	0	0	2	0	2	0	0	0	0	1	1	0	0	0
Lebanon	0	0	0	0	1	1	1	0	1	1	0	1	1	0	1
Liechtenstein	0	0	0	0	1	1	0	0	0	0	0	0	0	0	0
Lithuania	0	1	1	0	0	0	1	0	1	0	0	0	0	0	0
Luxembourg	5	0	5	0	4	4	0	0	0	0	0	0	1	0	1
Malaysia	4	0	4	1	1	2	4	0	4	1	0	1	3	1	4
Mali	1	0	1	0	0	0	0	0	0	0	0	0	0	0	0
Malta	0	0	0	0	0	0	0	0	0	0	0	0	0	1	1
Mauritius	0	1	1	0	0	0	0	1	1	0	0	0	0	1	1
Mexico	6	0	6	12	1	13	10	0	10	11	1	12	8	1	9
Monaco	1	0	1	0	0	0	1	0	1	0	0	0	0	0	0
Morocco	0	0	0	3	0	3	1	0	1	1	0	1	1	0	1
Mozambique	0	0	0	0	0	0	0	0	0	0	0	0	1	0	1
Nepal	0	0	0	0	0	0	0	0	0	1	0	1	0	0	0
Netherlands	6	3	9	5	5	10	5	0	5	4	1	5	4	0	4
New Zealand	0	0	0	0	0	0	0	0	0	0	0	0	1	0	1
Nigeria	1	0	1	0	0	0	0	0	0	0	0	0	1	0	1
Norway	0	0	0	0	0	0	2	0	2	2	1	3	3	0	3
Oman	0	0	0	1	0	1	0	0	0	0	0	0	0	0	0
Pakistan	0	0	0	0	0	0	1	0	1	0	0	0	0	0	0
Panama	0	0	0	0	0	0	1	0	1	1	0	1	1	1	2
Peru	0	0	0	0	0	0	0	0	0	2	0	2	0	0	0
Philippines	4	0	4	0	0	0	2	2	4	1	0	1	1	0	1

Countries/territories where places of arb'n were located	2009			2010			2011			2012			2013		
	P	C	Total	P	C	Total	P	C	Total	P	C	Total	P	C	Total
Poland	7	0	7	4	0	4	7	0	7	2	0	2	6	0	6
Portugal	1	0	1	1	0	1	2	1	3	2	0	2	3	0	3
Qatar	1	1	2	4	1	5	3	0	3	4	0	4	2	0	2
Romania	5	1	6	8	0	8	7	1	8	8	1	9	5	0	5
Russian Federation	0	0	0	1	0	1	1	0	1	0	0	0	1	0	1
Rwanda	0	0	0	0	0	0	1	0	1	0	0	0	0	0	0
Saudi Arabia	0	0	0	0	0	0	1	0	1	0	0	0	0	0	0
Serbia	0	0	0	0	0	0	0	0	0	2	0	2	2	0	2
Singapore	34	4	38	23	1	24	22	2	24	31	5	36	32	1	33
Slovakia	2	0	2	0	0	0	0	0	0	1	0	1	2	0	2
Slovenia	0	0	0	0	0	0	0	1	1	0	0	0	0	0	0
South Africa	1	1	2	0	0	0	2	0	2	2	0	2	1	0	1
South Korea	2	0	2	2	0	2	1	0	1	2	0	2	2	1	3
Spain	11	2	13	8	1	9	15	1	16	7	0	7	8	2	10
Sri Lanka	3	0	3	3	0	3	0	0	0	3	0	3	1	0	1
Sudan	0	0	0	0	1	1	0	0	0	0	0	0	0	0	0
Swaziland	0	0	0	0	0	0	1	0	1	0	0	0	0	0	0
Sweden	6	0	6	6	1	7	5	3	8	5	1	6	15	0	15
Switzerland	109	10	119	79	7	86	88	9	97	115	7	122	88	6	94
Syria	0	0	0	0	0	0	1	0	1	0	0	0	0	0	0
Tanzania	2	0	2	0	0	0	0	0	0	0	0	0	0	1	1
Thailand	2	0	2	4	0	4	1	1	2	0	1	1	2	0	2
Trinidad & Tobago	0	0	0	1	0	1	1	0	1	0	0	0	0	0	0
Tunisia	1	0	1	0	0	0	0	0	0	0	0	0	0	0	0
Turkey	4	0	4	6	0	6	2	0	2	3	0	3	2	1	3
United Arab Emirates	7	0	7	8	4	12	7	0	7	8	0	8	11	0	11
United Kingdom	67	6	73	66	4	70	59	3	62	68	3	71	63	9	72
Uruguay	4	0	4	1	0	1	0	0	0	1	0	1	0	0	0
USA	31	5	36	42	2	44	43	5	48	33	8	41	35	3	38
Venezuela	0	0	0	0	0	0	0	0	0	1	0	1	0	0	0
Vietnam	0	0	0	0	0	0	3	0	3	0	0	0	0	1	1
Zambia	0	1	1	0	0	0	0	1	1	0	0	0	0	0	0
Total	**557**	**73**	**630**	**524**	**67**	**591**	**528**	**79**	**607**	**514**	**59**	**573**	**524**	**68**	**592**

N: Not specified in the ICC Statistical Report

CHAPTER 8

BIBLIOGRAPHY ON ICC ARBITRATION

A. ICC ARBITRAL AWARDS

ICC Dispute Resolution Bulletin

This journal, published by the ICC International Court of Arbitration since 2015 provides extracts of ICC arbitral awards, procedural orders and practice commentaries. Moreover, the Bulletin's coverage extends beyond arbitration to other ICC dispute resolution procedures.

The ***ICC International Court of Arbitration Bulletin / Bulletin de la Cour internationale d'arbitrage de la CCI***, which was published from 1990 until 2014, served as the Court's principal vehicle for external communications. It provided news on the ICC Court and contained, amongst other things, extracts from ICC arbitral awards redacted so as to remove any indication of the parties' identities, as well as reports and notes essential to ICC arbitration practitioners. It also published articles on aspects of arbitration procedure and developments in arbitration law across the world. It was published twice-yearly, together with an annual supplement.

Journal de droit international (Clunet)

This French journal is published quarterly. The last issue of each year contains extracts from ICC arbitral awards commented by specialists. While the commentaries are generally in French, the extracts are from awards rendered in English as well as in French.

Collection of ICC Arbitral Awards (Arnaldez, Derains, Hascher, Jarvin)

This collection presently comprises six volumes containing extracts from ICC arbitral awards, accompanied by commentaries. Some of the extracts are the same as those published in the *Journal de droit international*.

Volume I: S. Jarvin and Y. Derains, *Collection of ICC Arbitral Awards – Recueil des sentences arbitrales de la CCI 1974–1985* (Kluwer Law & Taxation/ICC Publishing, 1990) xlix-581pp.

Volume II: S. Jarvin, Y. Derains and J.-J. Arnaldez, *Collection of ICC Arbitral Awards – Recueil des sentences arbitrales de la CCI 1986–1990* (Kluwer Law and Taxation/ICC Publishing, 1994) cxi-578pp.

Volume III: J.-J. Arnaldez, Y. Derains and D. Hascher, *Collection of ICC Arbitral Awards – Recueil des sentences arbitrales de la CCI 1991–1995* (Kluwer Law International/ ICC Publishing, 1997) ccvii-672pp.

Volume IV: S. Jarvin, Y. Derains and D. Hascher, *Collection of ICC Arbitral Awards – Recueil des sentences arbitrales de la CCI 1996–2000* (Kluwer Law International/ICC Publishing, 2003) ccxxx-617pp.

Volume V: J.-J. Arnaldez, Y. Derains and D. Hascher, *Collection of ICC Arbitral Awards – Recueil des sentences arbitrales de la CCI 2001–2007* (Kluwer Law International/ ICC Publishing, 2009) cclxi-844pp.

Volume VI: J.-J. Arnaldez, Y. Derains and D. Hascher, *Collection of ICC Arbitral Awards – Recueil des sentences arbitrales de la CCI 2008–2011* (Kluwer Law International/ ICC Publishing, 2013) ccxxxvi-1072pp.

Yearbook Commercial Arbitration

This annual publication in English, produced by the International Council for Commercial Arbitration, contains extracts from ICC arbitral awards plus related decisions by state courts. It also contains information on arbitral awards rendered under the auspices of other arbitration institutions, national reports and the full texts of institutional arbitration rules and arbitration laws.

B. BOOKS ON ICC ARBITRATION

M. Bühler and T. Webster, *Handbook of ICC Arbitration, Commentary, Precedents, Materials* (Second Edition, Thomson/Sweet & Maxwell, London, 2008) lxiii-811pp. An article-by-article commentary, in English, on the 1998 ICC Rules of Arbitration.

M. Bühler and T. Webster, *Handbook of ICC Arbitration, Commentary, Precedents, Materials* (Thomson/Sweet & Maxwell, London, 2005) xxxvii-657pp. An article-by-article commentary, in English, on the 1998 ICC Rules of Arbitration.

W. Craig, W. Park and J. Paulsson, *International Chamber of Commerce Arbitration* (3rd Edition, Oceana/ICC Publishing, 2000) xvi-952pp. An English language classic on ICC arbitration.

W. Craig, W. Park and J. Paulsson, *Annotated Guide to the 1998 ICC Arbitration Rules* (Oceana/ICC Publishing, 1998) 236pp. A succinct commentary on the 1998 ICC Rules of Arbitration.

Y. Derains and E. Schwartz, *A Guide to the New ICC Rules of Arbitration* (Second Edition, Kluwer Law International, 2005) xvi-606pp. An article-by-article commentary, in English, on the 1998 ICC Rules of Arbitration.

Y. Derains and E. Schwartz, *A Guide to the New ICC Rules of Arbitration* (Kluwer Law International, 1998) xv-478pp. An article-by-article commentary, in English, on the 1998 ICC Rules of Arbitration.

J. Fry, S. Greenberg and F. Mazza, *The Secretariat's Guide to ICC Arbitration* (ICC Publication No. 729 E, Paris, 2012) xii-506p. An article-by-article commentary, in English, on the 2012 ICC Rules of Arbitration.

J. Grierson and A. Van Hooft, *Arbitrating under the 2012 ICC Rules, An Introductory User's Guide* (Kluwer Law International, 2012) xvi-360pp. A topic-by-topic commentary, in English, on the 2012 ICC Rules of Arbitration.

D. Hascher, *Collection of Procedural Decisions in ICC Arbitration – Recueil des décisions de procédure dans l'arbitrage CCI 1993–1996* (Kluwer Law International/ICC Publishing, 1997) 311pp. A selection of procedural orders rendered by arbitral tribunals in ICC arbitrations. They are accompanied by commentaries, which are mostly in French; many of the decisions are in English.

J.H. Nedden and A. Herzberg, *ICC-SchO/DIS-SchO Praxiskommentar zu den Schiedsgerichtsordnungen* (Verlag Dr. Otto Schmidt, Cologne, 2014) xxii-1130pp. An article-by-article commentary, in German, on the 2012 ICC Rules of Arbitration and on the 1998 Arbitration Rules of the German Institution of Arbitration.

P.M. Patocchi, E. Geisinger and S. Lüke, *Internationales Privatrecht* (Orell Füssli, Zurich, 2000) 1993pp. This book, in German, has an appendix containing a brief commentary on the ICC Rules of Arbitration with references to Swiss case law.

A. Reiner, *ICC Schiedsgerichtsbarkeit: Ein Handbuch für die Praxis* (Manz, Vienna, 1989) 335pp. A detailed commentary in German on the 1988 ICC Rules of Arbitration and the practice of the ICC International Court of Arbitration.

R. Schütze, *Institutional Arbitration, Article-by-Article Commentary on* (C.H.Beck/Hart/Nomos, Munich, 2013) xii-1499pp. This book has an article-by-article commentary, in English, by A. Reiner and C. Aschauer on the 2012 ICC Rules of Arbitration.

E. Schäfer, H. Verbist and C. Imhoos, *ICC Arbitration in Practice* (Kluwer Law International, The Hague/Stämpfli, Berne, 2005) xxiii-379pp. An article-by-article commentary, in English, on the 1998 ICC Rules of Arbitration.

E. Schäfer, H. Verbist and C. Imhoos, *ICC Arbitration in Practice* (in Arabic version, translated in Arabic by I. Sattout) (Editions Sader, Beirut, 2011) 672pp. An article-by-article commentary, in English, on the 1998 ICC Rules of Arbitration.

E. Schäfer, H. Verbist and C. Imhoos, *L'arbitrage de la Chambre de commerce internationale (CCI) en pratique* (Stämpfli, Berne/Bruylant, Brussels, 2002) xxii-357pp. An article-by-article commentary, in French, on the 1998 ICC Rules of Arbitration.

E. Schäfer, H. Verbist and C. Imhoos, *Die ICC Schiedsgerichtsordnung in der Praxis* (Economica, Bonn, 2000) xx-281pp. An article-by-article commentary, in German, on the 1998 ICC Rules of Arbitration.

T. Webster and M. Bühler, *Handbook of ICC Arbitration, Commentary, Precedents, Materials* (Third Edition, Thomson/Sweet & Maxwell, London, 2014) xxxiii-974pp. An article-by-article commentary, in English, on the 2012 ICC Rules of Arbitration.

C. DOSSIERS OF THE ICC INSTITUTE OF WORLD BUSINESS LAW

Arbitration, Money Laundering, Corruption and Fraud, Edited by K. Karsten and A. Berkeley, Dossier I, ICC Publication No. 651, Paris, 2003, 190pp.

Arbitration and Oral Evidence, Edited by K. Lévy and V.V. Veeder, Dossier II, ICC Publication No. 689, Paris, 2004, 197pp.

Parallel State and Arbitral Procedures in International Arbitration, Edited by B. Cremades and J. Lew, Dossier III, ICC Publication No. 692, Paris, 2005, 320pp.

Evaluation of Damages in International Arbitration, Edited by Y. Derains and R. Kreindler, Dossier IV, ICC Publication No. 668, Paris, 2006, 273pp.

Interest, Auxiliary and Alternative Remedies in International Arbitration, Edited by F. De Ly and L. Lévy, Dossier V, ICC Publication No. 684, Paris, 2008, 257pp.

Written Evidence and Discovery in International Arbitration, Edited by T. Giovannini and A. Mourre, Dossier VI, ICC Publication No. 698, Paris, 2009, 509pp.

Multiparty Arbitration, Edited by B. Hanotiau and E. Schwartz, Dossier VII, ICC Publication No. 701 E, Paris, 2010, 272pp.

Is Arbitration Only as Good as the Arbitrator? Status, Powers and Role of the Arbitrator, Edited by Y. Derains and L. Lévy, Dossier VIII, ICC Publication No. 714 E, Paris, 2011, 168pp.

Players' Interaction in International Arbitration, Edited by B. Hanotiau and A. Mourre, Dossier IX, ICC Publication No. 737 E, Paris, 2012, 184pp.

Third-party Funding in International Arbitration, Edited by B. Cremades and A. Dimolitsa, Dossier X, ICC Publication No. 752 E, Paris, 2013, 176pp.

The Application of Substantive Law by International Arbitrators, Edited by F. Bortolotti and P. Mayer, Dossier XI, ICC Publication No. 753 E, Paris, 2014, 171pp.

Jurisdictional Choices in Times of Trouble, Edited by G. Affaki and H. Grigera Naon, Dossier XII, ICC Publication No. 755 E, Paris, 2015, 239pp.

Addressing Issues of Corruption in Commercial and Investment Arbitration, Edited by D. Baizeau and R. Kreindler, Dossier XIII, ICC Publication No. 768 E, Paris, 2015, 219pp.

D. WEB SITES CONTAINING MATERIALS AND INFORMATION ON INTERNATIONAL ARBITRATION

1. Materials Referred to in this Book

The text of the ICC Rules of Arbitration, various national arbitration laws, the 1958 New York Convention and other instruments are now freely available on the Internet.p.

The ICC International Court of Arbitration has a web site containing information on ICC arbitration, the text of the ICC Rules of Arbitration and other material:

< www.iccarbitration.org >

The UNCITRAL Arbitration Rules, the UNCITRAL Model Law, the text of the New York Convention and a list of signatory states may be found at the following web site:

< www.uncitral.org >

The national arbitration laws mentioned in the course of this book are available at the following web sites:

- Belgium (Book 6 JC 2013):
  < www.cepani.be >
- France (Book 4 NCPC 2011):
  < www.legifrance.gouv.fr/html/frame_lois_reglt.htm >
- Germany (Book 10 ZPO 1997):
  < www.dis-arb.de >
- Switzerland (Chapter 12 PILA 1989):
  < www.admin.ch >

2. Other Internet Resources

There are hundreds of web sites containing information on arbitration, of varying quality. The following are those which the authors consider most useful for the purpose of advanced searches.

The International Trade Centre UNCTAD/WTO has a web site containing detailed information on international business law and international commercial arbitration in particular, at:

< www.jurisint.org/pub >

Useful links to national arbitration laws, international conventions, arbitration institutions and other international arbitration resources may be found at the web sites listed below:

- International Commercial Arbitration Resources in Print and Electronic Format (Chicago University):
  < www.lib.uchicago.edu/ ~ llou/intlarb.html >
- Interarb.com – Geographic index of arbitration databases:
  < interarb.com/vl/pages/Geographic_index >

The legal search engine 'Findlaw' is also to be recommended. The relevant addresses are:

< www.findlaw.com/01topics/11disputeres/index.html >
< www.findlaw.com/01topics/24international/index.html >

Lastly, reference may be made to the Kluwer Arbitration web site, where on-line information is available through subscription:

< www.kluwerarbitration.com >

APPENDIX 1

ICC RULES OF ARBITRATION (1 JANUARY 2012)

RULES OF ARBITRATION OF THE INTERNATIONAL CHAMBER OF COMMERCE

In force as from 1 January 2012

INTRODUCTORY PROVISIONS

Article 1: International Court of Arbitration

1. The International Court of Arbitration (the "Court") of the International Chamber of Commerce (the "ICC") is the independent arbitration body of the ICC. The statutes of the Court are set forth in Appendix I.

2. The Court does not itself resolve disputes. It administers the resolution of disputes by arbitral tribunals, in accordance with the Rules of Arbitration of the ICC (the "Rules"). The Court is the only body authorized to administer arbitrations under the Rules, including the scrutiny and approval of awards rendered in accordance with the Rules. It draws up its own internal rules, which are set forth in Appendix II (the "Internal Rules").

3. The President of the Court (the "President") or, in the President's absence or otherwise at the President's request, one of its Vice-Presidents shall have the power to take urgent decisions on behalf of the Court, provided that any such decision is reported to the Court at its next session.

4. As provided for in the Internal Rules, the Court may delegate to one or more committees composed of its members the power to take certain decisions, provided that any such decision is reported to the Court at its next session.

5. The Court is assisted in its work by the Secretariat of the Court (the "Secretariat") under the direction of its Secretary General (the "Secretary General").

Article 2: Definitions

In the Rules:

(i) "arbitral tribunal" includes one or more arbitrators;

(ii) "claimant" includes one or more claimants, "respondent" includes one or more respondents, and "additional party" includes one or more additional parties;
(iii) "party" or "parties" include claimants, respondents or additional parties;
(iv) "claim" or "claims" include any claim by any party against any other party;
(v) "award" includes, *inter alia*, an interim, partial or final award.

Article 3: Written Notifications or Communications; Time Limits

1. All pleadings and other written communications submitted by any party, as well as all documents annexed thereto, shall be supplied in a number of copies sufficient to provide one copy for each party, plus one for each arbitrator, and one for the Secretariat. A copy of any notification or communication from the arbitral tribunal to the parties shall be sent to the Secretariat.

2. All notifications or communications from the Secretariat and the arbitral tribunal shall be made to the last address of the party or its representative for whom the same are intended, as notified either by the party in question or by the other party. Such notification or communication may be made by delivery against receipt, registered post, courier, email, or any other means of telecommunication that provides a record of the sending thereof.

3. A notification or communication shall be deemed to have been made on the day it was received by the party itself or by its representative, or would have been received if made in accordance with Article 3(2).

4. Periods of time specified in or fixed under the Rules shall start to run on the day following the date a notification or communication is deemed to have been made in accordance with Article 3(3). When the day next following such date is an official holiday, or a non-business day in the country where the notification or communication is deemed to have been made, the period of time shall commence on the first following business day. Official holidays and non-business days are included in the calculation of the period of time. If the last day of the relevant period of time granted is an official holiday or a non-business day in the country where the notification or communication is deemed to have been made, the period of time shall expire at the end of the first following business day.

COMMENCING THE ARBITRATION

Article 4: Request for Arbitration

1. A party wishing to have recourse to arbitration under the Rules shall submit its Request for Arbitration (the "Request") to the Secretariat at any of the offices specified in the Internal Rules. The Secretariat shall notify the claimant and respondent of the receipt of the Request and the date of such receipt.

2. The date on which the Request is received by the Secretariat shall, for all purposes, be deemed to be the date of the commencement of the arbitration.

3. The Request shall contain the following information:

a) the name in full, description, address and other contact details of each of the parties;
b) the name in full, address and other contact details of any person(s) representing the claimant in the arbitration;

c) a description of the nature and circumstances of the dispute giving rise to the claims and of the basis upon which the claims are made;
d) a statement of the relief sought, together with the amounts of any quantified claims and, to the extent possible, an estimate of the monetary value of any other claims;
e) any relevant agreements and, in particular, the arbitration agreement(s);
f) where claims are made under more than one arbitration agreement, an indication of the arbitration agreement under which each claim is made;
g) all relevant particulars and any observations or proposals concerning the number of arbitrators and their choice in accordance with the provisions of Articles 12 and 13, and any nomination of an arbitrator required thereby; and
h) all relevant particulars and any observations or proposals as to the place of the arbitration, the applicable rules of law and the language of the arbitration.

The claimant may submit such other documents or information with the Request as it considers appropriate or as may contribute to the efficient resolution of the dispute.

4. Together with the Request, the claimant shall:
a) submit the number of copies thereof required by Article 3(1); and
b) make payment of the filing fee required by Appendix III ("Arbitration Costs and Fees") in force on the date the Request is submitted.

In the event that the claimant fails to comply with either of these requirements, the Secretariat may fix a time limit within which the claimant must comply, failing which the file shall be closed without prejudice to the claimant's right to submit the same claims at a later date in another Request.

5. The Secretariat shall transmit a copy of the Request and the documents annexed thereto to the respondent for its Answer to the Request once the Secretariat has sufficient copies of the Request and the required filing fee.

Article 5: Answer to the Request; Counterclaims

1. Within 30 days from the receipt of the Request from the Secretariat, the respondent shall submit an Answer (the "Answer") which shall contain the following information:
a) its name in full, description, address and other contact details;
b) the name in full, address and other contact details of any person(s) representing the respondent in the arbitration;
c) its comments as to the nature and circumstances of the dispute giving rise to the claims and the basis upon which the claims are made;
d) its response to the relief sought;
e) any observations or proposals concerning the number of arbitrators and their choice in light of the claimant's proposals and in accordance with the provisions of Articles 12 and 13, and any nomination of an arbitrator required thereby; and
f) any observations or proposals as to the place of the arbitration, the applicable rules of law and the language of the arbitration.

The respondent may submit such other documents or information with the Answer as it considers appropriate or as may contribute to the efficient resolution of the dispute.

2. The Secretariat may grant the respondent an extension of the time for submitting the Answer, provided the application for such an extension contains the respondent's

observations or proposals concerning the number of arbitrators and their choice and, where required by Articles 12 and 13, the nomination of an arbitrator. If the respondent fails to do so, the Court shall proceed in accordance with the Rules.

3. The Answer shall be submitted to the Secretariat in the number of copies specified by Article 3(1).

4. The Secretariat shall communicate the Answer and the documents annexed thereto to all other parties.

5. Any counterclaims made by the respondent shall be submitted with the Answer and shall provide:

a) a description of the nature and circumstances of the dispute giving rise to the counterclaims and of the basis upon which the counterclaims are made;
b) a statement of the relief sought together with the amounts of any quantified counterclaims and, to the extent possible, an estimate of the monetary value of any other counterclaims;
c) any relevant agreements and, in particular, the arbitration agreement(s); and
d) where counterclaims are made under more than one arbitration agreement, an indication of the arbitration agreement under which each counterclaim is made.

The respondent may submit such other documents or information with the counterclaims as it considers appropriate or as may contribute to the efficient resolution of the dispute.

6. The claimant shall submit a reply to any counterclaim within 30 days from the date of receipt of the counterclaims communicated by the Secretariat. Prior to the transmission of the file to the arbitral tribunal, the Secretariat may grant the claimant an extension of time for submitting the reply.

Article 6: Effect of the Arbitration Agreement

1. Where the parties have agreed to submit to arbitration under the Rules, they shall be deemed to have submitted *ipso facto* to the Rules in effect on the date of commencement of the arbitration, unless they have agreed to submit to the Rules in effect on the date of their arbitration agreement.

2. By agreeing to arbitration under the Rules, the parties have accepted that the arbitration shall be administered by the Court.

3. If any party against which a claim has been made does not submit an Answer, or raises one or more pleas concerning the existence, validity or scope of the arbitration agreement or concerning whether all of the claims made in the arbitration may be determined together in a single arbitration, the arbitration shall proceed and any question of jurisdiction or of whether the claims may be determined together in that arbitration shall be decided directly by the arbitral tribunal, unless the Secretary General refers the matter to the Court for its decision pursuant to Article 6(4).

4. In all cases referred to the Court under Article 6(3), the Court shall decide whether and to what extent the arbitration shall proceed. The arbitration shall proceed if and to the extent that the Court is *prima facie* satisfied that an arbitration agreement under the Rules may exist. In particular:

(i) where there are more than two parties to the arbitration, the arbitration shall proceed between those of the parties, including any additional parties joined pursuant to Article 7, with respect to which the Court is *prima facie* satisfied that an arbitration agreement under the Rules that binds them all may exist; and

(ii) where claims pursuant to Article 9 are made under more than one arbitration agreement, the arbitration shall proceed as to those claims with respect to which the Court is *prima facie* satisfied (a) that the arbitration agreements under which those claims are made may be compatible, and (b) that all parties to the arbitration may have agreed that those claims can be determined together in a single arbitration.

The Court's decision pursuant to Article 6(4) is without prejudice to the admissibility or merits of any party's plea or pleas.

5. In all matters decided by the Court under Article 6(4), any decision as to the jurisdiction of the arbitral tribunal, except as to parties or claims with respect to which the Court decides that the arbitration cannot proceed, shall then be taken by the arbitral tribunal itself.

6. Where the parties are notified of the Court's decision pursuant to Article 6(4) that the arbitration cannot proceed in respect of some or all of them, any party retains the right to ask any court having jurisdiction whether or not, and in respect of which of them, there is a binding arbitration agreement.

7. Where the Court has decided pursuant to Article 6(4) that the arbitration cannot proceed in respect of any of the claims, such decision shall not prevent a party from reintroducing the same claim at a later date in other proceedings.

8. If any of the parties refuses or fails to take part in the arbitration or any stage thereof, the arbitration shall proceed notwithstanding such refusal or failure.

9. Unless otherwise agreed, the arbitral tribunal shall not cease to have jurisdiction by reason of any allegation that the contract is non-existent or null and void, provided that the arbitral tribunal upholds the validity of the arbitration agreement. The arbitral tribunal shall continue to have jurisdiction to determine the parties' respective rights and to decide their claims and pleas even though the contract itself may be non-existent or null and void.

MULTIPLE PARTIES, MULTIPLE CONTRACTS AND CONSOLIDATION

Article 7: Joinder of Additional Parties

1. A party wishing to join an additional party to the arbitration shall submit its request for arbitration against the additional party (the "Request for Joinder") to the Secretariat. The date on which the Request for Joinder is received by the Secretariat shall, for all purposes, be deemed to be the date of the commencement of arbitration against the additional party. Any such joinder shall be subject to the provisions of Articles 6(3)–6(7) and 9. No additional party may be joined after the confirmation or appointment of any arbitrator, unless all parties, including the additional party, otherwise agree. The Secretariat may fix a time limit for the submission of a Request for Joinder.

2. The Request for Joinder shall contain the following information:

a) the case reference of the existing arbitration;

b) the name in full, description, address and other contact details of each of the parties, including the additional party; and
c) the information specified in Article 4(3), subparagraphs c), d), e) and f).

The party filing the Request for Joinder may submit therewith such other documents or information as it considers appropriate or as may contribute to the efficient resolution of the dispute.

3. The provisions of Articles 4(4) and 4(5) shall apply, *mutatis mutandis,* to the Request for Joinder.

4. The additional party shall submit an Answer in accordance, *mutatis mutandis*, with the provisions of Articles 5(1)–5(4). The additional party may make claims against any other party in accordance with the provisions of Article 8.

Article 8: Claims Between Multiple Parties

1. In an arbitration with multiple parties, claims may be made by any party against any other party, subject to the provisions of Articles 6(3)–6(7) and 9 and provided that no new claims may be made after the Terms of Reference are signed or approved by the Court without the authorization of the arbitral tribunal pursuant to Article 23(4).

2. Any party making a claim pursuant to Article 8(1) shall provide the information specified in Article 4(3), subparagraphs c), d), e) and f).

3. Before the Secretariat transmits the file to the arbitral tribunal in accordance with Article 16, the following provisions shall apply, *mutatis mutandis*, to any claim made: Article 4(4) subparagraph a); Article 4(5); Article 5(1) except for subparagraphs a), b), e) and f); Article 5(2); Article 5(3) and Article 5(4). Thereafter, the arbitral tribunal shall determine the procedure for making a claim.

Article 9: Multiple Contracts

Subject to the provisions of Articles 6(3)–6(7) and 23(4), claims arising out of or in connection with more than one contract may be made in a single arbitration, irrespective of whether such claims are made under one or more than one arbitration agreement under the Rules.

Article 10: Consolidation of Arbitrations

The Court may, at the request of a party, consolidate two or more arbitrations pending under the Rules into a single arbitration, where:

a) the parties have agreed to consolidation; or
b) all of the claims in the arbitrations are made under the same arbitration agreement; or
c) where the claims in the arbitrations are made under more than one arbitration agreement, the arbitrations are between the same parties, the disputes in the arbitrations arise in connection with the same legal relationship, and the Court finds the arbitration agreements to be compatible.

In deciding whether to consolidate, the Court may take into account any circumstances it considers to be relevant, including whether one or more arbitrators have been confirmed or appointed in more than one of the arbitrations and, if so, whether the same or different persons have been confirmed or appointed.

When arbitrations are consolidated, they shall be consolidated into the arbitration that commenced first, unless otherwise agreed by all parties.

THE ARBITRAL TRIBUNAL

Article 11: General Provisions

1. Every arbitrator must be and remain impartial and independent of the parties involved in the arbitration.

2. Before appointment or confirmation, a prospective arbitrator shall sign a statement of acceptance, availability, impartiality and independence. The prospective arbitrator shall disclose in writing to the Secretariat any facts or circumstances which might be of such a nature as to call into question the arbitrator's independence in the eyes of the parties, as well as any circumstances that could give rise to reasonable doubts as to the arbitrator's impartiality. The Secretariat shall provide such information to the parties in writing and fix a time limit for any comments from them.

3. An arbitrator shall immediately disclose in writing to the Secretariat and to the parties any facts or circumstances of a similar nature to those referred to in Article 11(2) concerning the arbitrator's impartiality or independence which may arise during the arbitration.

4. The decisions of the Court as to the appointment, confirmation, challenge or replacement of an arbitrator shall be final, and the reasons for such decisions shall not be communicated.

5. By accepting to serve, arbitrators undertake to carry out their responsibilities in accordance with the Rules.

6. Insofar as the parties have not provided otherwise, the arbitral tribunal shall be constituted in accordance with the provisions of Articles 12 and 13.

Article 12: Constitution of the Arbitral Tribunal

Number of Arbitrators

1. The disputes shall be decided by a sole arbitrator or by three arbitrators.

2. Where the parties have not agreed upon the number of arbitrators, the Court shall appoint a sole arbitrator, save where it appears to the Court that the dispute is such as to warrant the appointment of three arbitrators. In such case, the claimant shall nominate an arbitrator within a period of 15 days from the receipt of the notification of the decision of the Court, and the respondent shall nominate an arbitrator within a period of 15 days from the receipt of the notification of the nomination made by the claimant. If a party fails to nominate an arbitrator, the appointment shall be made by the Court.

Sole Arbitrator

3. Where the parties have agreed that the dispute shall be resolved by a sole arbitrator, they may, by agreement, nominate the sole arbitrator for confirmation. If the parties fail to nominate a sole arbitrator within 30 days from the date when the claimant's Request for Arbitration has been received by the other party, or within such additional

time as may be allowed by the Secretariat, the sole arbitrator shall be appointed by the Court.

Three Arbitrators

4. Where the parties have agreed that the dispute shall be resolved by three arbitrators, each party shall nominate in the Request and the Answer, respectively, one arbitrator for confirmation. If a party fails to nominate an arbitrator, the appointment shall be made by the Court.

5. Where the dispute is to be referred to three arbitrators, the third arbitrator, who will act as president of the arbitral tribunal, shall be appointed by the Court, unless the parties have agreed upon another procedure for such appointment, in which case the nomination will be subject to confirmation pursuant to Article 13. Should such procedure not result in a nomination within 30 days from the confirmation or appointment of the co-arbitrators or any other time limit agreed by the parties or fixed by the Court, the third arbitrator shall be appointed by the Court.

6. Where there are multiple claimants or multiple respondents, and where the dispute is to be referred to three arbitrators, the multiple claimants, jointly, and the multiple respondents, jointly, shall nominate an arbitrator for confirmation pursuant to Article 13.

7. Where an additional party has been joined, and where the dispute is to be referred to three arbitrators, the additional party may, jointly with the claimant(s) or with the respondent(s), nominate an arbitrator for confirmation pursuant to Article 13.

8. In the absence of a joint nomination pursuant to Articles 12(6) or 12(7) and where all parties are unable to agree to a method for the constitution of the arbitral tribunal, the Court may appoint each member of the arbitral tribunal and shall designate one of them to act as president. In such case, the Court shall be at liberty to choose any person it regards as suitable to act as arbitrator, applying Article 13 when it considers this appropriate.

Article 13: Appointment and Confirmation of the Arbitrators

1. In confirming or appointing arbitrators, the Court shall consider the prospective arbitrator's nationality, residence and other relationships with the countries of which the parties or the other arbitrators are nationals and the prospective arbitrator's availability and ability to conduct the arbitration in accordance with the Rules. The same shall apply where the Secretary General confirms arbitrators pursuant to Article 13(2).

2. The Secretary General may confirm as co-arbitrators, sole arbitrators and presidents of arbitral tribunals persons nominated by the parties or pursuant to their particular agreements, provided that the statement they have submitted contains no qualification regarding impartiality or independence or that a qualified statement regarding impartiality or independence has not given rise to objections. Such confirmation shall be reported to the Court at its next session. If the Secretary General considers that a co-arbitrator, sole arbitrator or president of an arbitral tribunal should not be confirmed, the matter shall be submitted to the Court.

3. Where the Court is to appoint an arbitrator, it shall make the appointment upon proposal of a National Committee or Group of the ICC that it considers to be appropriate. If the Court does not accept the proposal made, or if the National Committee or

Group fails to make the proposal requested within the time limit fixed by the Court, the Court may repeat its request, request a proposal from another National Committee or Group that it considers to be appropriate, or appoint directly any person whom it regards as suitable.

4. The Court may also appoint directly to act as arbitrator any person whom it regards as suitable where:

a) one or more of the parties is a state or claims to be a state entity; or
b) the Court considers that it would be appropriate to appoint an arbitrator from a country or territory where there is no National Committee or Group; or
c) the President certifies to the Court that circumstances exist which, in the President's opinion, make a direct appointment necessary and appropriate.

5. The sole arbitrator or the president of the arbitral tribunal shall be of a nationality other than those of the parties. However, in suitable circumstances and provided that none of the parties objects within the time limit fixed by the Court, the sole arbitrator or the president of the arbitral tribunal may be chosen from a country of which any of the parties is a national.

Article 14: Challenge of Arbitrators

1. A challenge of an arbitrator, whether for an alleged lack of impartiality or independence, or otherwise, shall be made by the submission to the Secretariat of a written statement specifying the facts and circumstances on which the challenge is based.

2. For a challenge to be admissible, it must be submitted by a party either within 30 days from receipt by that party of the notification of the appointment or confirmation of the arbitrator, or within 30 days from the date when the party making the challenge was informed of the facts and circumstances on which the challenge is based if such date is subsequent to the receipt of such notification.

3. The Court shall decide on the admissibility and, at the same time, if necessary, on the merits of a challenge after the Secretariat has afforded an opportunity for the arbitrator concerned, the other party or parties and any other members of the arbitral tribunal to comment in writing within a suitable period of time. Such comments shall be communicated to the parties and to the arbitrators.

Article 15: Replacement of Arbitrators

1. An arbitrator shall be replaced upon death, upon acceptance by the Court of the arbitrator's resignation, upon acceptance by the Court of a challenge, or upon acceptance by the Court of a request of all the parties.

2. An arbitrator shall also be replaced on the Court's own initiative when it decides that the arbitrator is prevented *de jure* or *de facto* from fulfilling the arbitrator's functions, or that the arbitrator is not fulfilling those functions in accordance with the Rules or within the prescribed time limits.

3. When, on the basis of information that has come to its attention, the Court considers applying Article 15(2), it shall decide on the matter after the arbitrator concerned, the parties and any other members of the arbitral tribunal have had an opportunity to comment in writing within a suitable period of time. Such comments shall be communicated to the parties and to the arbitrators.

4. When an arbitrator is to be replaced, the Court has discretion to decide whether or not to follow the original nominating process. Once reconstituted, and after having invited the parties to comment, the arbitral tribunal shall determine if and to what extent prior proceedings shall be repeated before the reconstituted arbitral tribunal.

5. Subsequent to the closing of the proceedings, instead of replacing an arbitrator who has died or been removed by the Court pursuant to Articles 15(1) or 15(2), the Court may decide, when it considers it appropriate, that the remaining arbitrators shall continue the arbitration. In making such determination, the Court shall take into account the views of the remaining arbitrators and of the parties and such other matters that it considers appropriate in the circumstances.

THE ARBITRAL PROCEEDINGS

Article 16: Transmission of the File to the Arbitral Tribunal

The Secretariat shall transmit the file to the arbitral tribunal as soon as it has been constituted, provided the advance on costs requested by the Secretariat at this stage has been paid.

Article 17: Proof of Authority

At any time after the commencement of the arbitration, the arbitral tribunal or the Secretariat may require proof of the authority of any party representatives.

Article 18: Place of the Arbitration

1. The place of the arbitration shall be fixed by the Court, unless agreed upon by the parties.

2. The arbitral tribunal may, after consultation with the parties, conduct hearings and meetings at any location it considers appropriate, unless otherwise agreed by the parties.

3. The arbitral tribunal may deliberate at any location it considers appropriate.

Article 19: Rules Governing the Proceedings

The proceedings before the arbitral tribunal shall be governed by the Rules and, where the Rules are silent, by any rules which the parties or, failing them, the arbitral tribunal may settle on, whether or not reference is thereby made to the rules of procedure of a national law to be applied to the arbitration.

Article 20: Language of the Arbitration

In the absence of an agreement by the parties, the arbitral tribunal shall determine the language or languages of the arbitration, due regard being given to all relevant circumstances, including the language of the contract.

Article 21: Applicable Rules of Law

1. The parties shall be free to agree upon the rules of law to be applied by the arbitral tribunal to the merits of the dispute. In the absence of any such agreement, the arbitral tribunal shall apply the rules of law which it determines to be appropriate.

2. The arbitral tribunal shall take account of the provisions of the contract, if any, between the parties and of any relevant trade usages.

3. The arbitral tribunal shall assume the powers of an *amiable compositeur* or decide *ex aequo et bono* only if the parties have agreed to give it such powers.

Article 22: Conduct of the Arbitration

1. The arbitral tribunal and the parties shall make every effort to conduct the arbitration in an expeditious and cost-effective manner, having regard to the complexity and value of the dispute.

2. In order to ensure effective case management, the arbitral tribunal, after consulting the parties, may adopt such procedural measures as it considers appropriate, provided that they are not contrary to any agreement of the parties.

3. Upon the request of any party, the arbitral tribunal may make orders concerning the confidentiality of the arbitration proceedings or of any other matters in connection with the arbitration and may take measures for protecting trade secrets and confidential information.

4. In all cases, the arbitral tribunal shall act fairly and impartially and ensure that each party has a reasonable opportunity to present its case.

5. The parties undertake to comply with any order made by the arbitral tribunal.

Article 23: Terms of Reference

1. As soon as it has received the file from the Secretariat, the arbitral tribunal shall draw up, on the basis of documents or in the presence of the parties and in the light of their most recent submissions, a document defining its Terms of Reference. This document shall include the following particulars:

a) the names in full, description, address and other contact details of each of the parties and of any person(s) representing a party in the arbitration;
b) the addresses to which notifications and communications arising in the course of the arbitration may be made;
c) a summary of the parties' respective claims and of the relief sought by each party, together with the amounts of any quantified claims and, to the extent possible, an estimate of the monetary value of any other claims;
d) unless the arbitral tribunal considers it inappropriate, a list of issues to be determined;
e) the names in full, address and other contact details of each of the arbitrators;
f) the place of the arbitration; and
g) particulars of the applicable procedural rules and, if such is the case, reference to the power conferred upon the arbitral tribunal to act as *amiable compositeur* or to decide *ex aequo et bono*.

2. The Terms of Reference shall be signed by the parties and the arbitral tribunal. Within two months of the date on which the file has been transmitted to it, the arbitral tribunal shall transmit to the Court the Terms of Reference signed by it and by the parties. The Court may extend this time limit pursuant to a reasoned request from the arbitral tribunal or on its own initiative if it decides it is necessary to do so.

3. If any of the parties refuses to take part in the drawing up of the Terms of Reference or to sign the same, they shall be submitted to the Court for approval. When the Terms of Reference have been signed in accordance with Article 23(2) or approved by the Court, the arbitration shall proceed.

4. After the Terms of Reference have been signed or approved by the Court, no party shall make new claims which fall outside the limits of the Terms of Reference unless it has been authorized to do so by the arbitral tribunal, which shall consider the nature of such new claims, the stage of the arbitration and other relevant circumstances.

Article 24: Case Management Conference and Procedural Timetable

1. When drawing up the Terms of Reference or as soon as possible thereafter, the arbitral tribunal shall convene a case management conference to consult the parties on procedural measures that may be adopted pursuant to Article 22(2). Such measures may include one or more of the case management techniques described in Appendix IV.

2. During or following such conference, the arbitral tribunal shall establish the procedural timetable that it intends to follow for the conduct of the arbitration. The procedural timetable and any modifications thereto shall be communicated to the Court and the parties.

3. To ensure continued effective case management, the arbitral tribunal, after consulting the parties by means of a further case management conference or otherwise, may adopt further procedural measures or modify the procedural timetable.

4. Case management conferences may be conducted through a meeting in person, by video conference, telephone or similar means of communication. In the absence of an agreement of the parties, the arbitral tribunal shall determine the means by which the conference will be conducted. The arbitral tribunal may request the parties to submit case management proposals in advance of a case management conference and may request the attendance at any case management conference of the parties in person or through an internal representative.

Article 25: Establishing the Facts of the Case

1. The arbitral tribunal shall proceed within as short a time as possible to establish the facts of the case by all appropriate means.

2. After studying the written submissions of the parties and all documents relied upon, the arbitral tribunal shall hear the parties together in person if any of them so requests or, failing such a request, it may of its own motion decide to hear them.

3. The arbitral tribunal may decide to hear witnesses, experts appointed by the parties or any other person, in the presence of the parties, or in their absence provided they have been duly summoned.

4. The arbitral tribunal, after having consulted the parties, may appoint one or more experts, define their terms of reference and receive their reports. At the request of a party, the parties shall be given the opportunity to question at a hearing any such expert.

5. At any time during the proceedings, the arbitral tribunal may summon any party to provide additional evidence.

6. The arbitral tribunal may decide the case solely on the documents submitted by the parties unless any of the parties requests a hearing.

Article 26: Hearings

1. When a hearing is to be held, the arbitral tribunal, giving reasonable notice, shall summon the parties to appear before it on the day and at the place fixed by it.

2. If any of the parties, although duly summoned, fails to appear without valid excuse, the arbitral tribunal shall have the power to proceed with the hearing.

3. The arbitral tribunal shall be in full charge of the hearings, at which all the parties shall be entitled to be present. Save with the approval of the arbitral tribunal and the parties, persons not involved in the proceedings shall not be admitted.

4. The parties may appear in person or through duly authorized representatives. In addition, they may be assisted by advisers.

Article 27: Closing of the Proceedings and Date for Submission of Draft Awards

As soon as possible after the last hearing concerning matters to be decided in an award or the filing of the last authorized submissions concerning such matters, whichever is later, the arbitral tribunal shall:

a) declare the proceedings closed with respect to the matters to be decided in the award; and
b) inform the Secretariat and the parties of the date by which it expects to submit its draft award to the Court for approval pursuant to Article 33.

After the proceedings are closed, no further submission or argument may be made, or evidence produced, with respect to the matters to be decided in the award, unless requested or authorized by the arbitral tribunal.

Article 28: Conservatory and Interim Measures

1. Unless the parties have otherwise agreed, as soon as the file has been transmitted to it, the arbitral tribunal may, at the request of a party, order any interim or conservatory measure it deems appropriate. The arbitral tribunal may make the granting of any such measure subject to appropriate security being furnished by the requesting party. Any such measure shall take the form of an order, giving reasons, or of an award, as the arbitral tribunal considers appropriate.

2. Before the file is transmitted to the arbitral tribunal, and in appropriate circumstances even thereafter, the parties may apply to any competent judicial authority for interim or conservatory measures. The application of a party to a judicial authority for such measures or for the implementation of any such measures ordered by an arbitral tribunal shall not be deemed to be an infringement or a waiver of the arbitration agreement and shall not affect the relevant powers reserved to the arbitral tribunal. Any such application and any measures taken by the judicial authority must be notified without delay to the Secretariat. The Secretariat shall inform the arbitral tribunal thereof.

Article 29: Emergency Arbitrator

1. A party that needs urgent interim or conservatory measures that cannot await the constitution of an arbitral tribunal ("Emergency Measures") may make an application for such measures pursuant to the Emergency Arbitrator Rules in Appendix V. Any such application shall be accepted only if it is received by the Secretariat prior to the transmission of the file to the arbitral tribunal pursuant to Article 16 and irrespective of whether the party making the application has already submitted its Request for Arbitration.

2. The emergency arbitrator's decision shall take the form of an order. The parties undertake to comply with any order made by the emergency arbitrator.

3. The emergency arbitrator's order shall not bind the arbitral tribunal with respect to any question, issue or dispute determined in the order. The arbitral tribunal may modify, terminate or annul the order or any modification thereto made by the emergency arbitrator.

4. The arbitral tribunal shall decide upon any party's requests or claims related to the emergency arbitrator proceedings, including the reallocation of the costs of such proceedings and any claims arising out of or in connection with the compliance or non-compliance with the order.

5. Articles 29(1)–29(4) and the Emergency Arbitrator Rules set forth in Appendix V (collectively the "Emergency Arbitrator Provisions") shall apply only to parties that are either signatories of the arbitration agreement under the Rules that is relied upon for the application or successors to such signatories.

6. The Emergency Arbitrator Provisions shall not apply if:

a) the arbitration agreement under the Rules was concluded before the date on which the Rules came into force;

b) the parties have agreed to opt out of the Emergency Arbitrator Provisions; or

c) the parties have agreed to another pre-arbitral procedure that provides for the granting of conservatory, interim or similar measures.

7. The Emergency Arbitrator Provisions are not intended to prevent any party from seeking urgent interim or conservatory measures from a competent judicial authority at any time prior to making an application for such measures, and in appropriate circumstances even thereafter, pursuant to the Rules. Any application for such measures from a competent judicial authority shall not be deemed to be an infringement or a waiver of the arbitration agreement. Any such application and any measures taken by the judicial authority must be notified without delay to the Secretariat.

AWARDS

Article 30: Time Limit for the Final Award

1. The time limit within which the arbitral tribunal must render its final award is six months. Such time limit shall start to run from the date of the last signature by the arbitral tribunal or by the parties of the Terms of Reference or, in the case of application of Article 23(3), the date of the notification to the arbitral tribunal by the Secretariat of the approval of the Terms of Reference by the Court. The Court may fix a different time limit based upon the procedural timetable established pursuant to Article 24(2).

2. The Court may extend the time limit pursuant to a reasoned request from the arbitral tribunal or on its own initiative if it decides it is necessary to do so.

Article 31: Making of the Award

1. When the arbitral tribunal is composed of more than one arbitrator, an award is made by a majority decision. If there is no majority, the award shall be made by the president of the arbitral tribunal alone.

2. The award shall state the reasons upon which it is based.

3. The award shall be deemed to be made at the place of the arbitration and on the date stated therein.

Article 32: Award by Consent

If the parties reach a settlement after the file has been transmitted to the arbitral tribunal in accordance with Article 16, the settlement shall be recorded in the form of an award made by consent of the parties, if so requested by the parties and if the arbitral tribunal agrees to do so.

Article 33: Scrutiny of the Award by the Court

Before signing any award, the arbitral tribunal shall submit it in draft form to the Court. The Court may lay down modifications as to the form of the award and, without affecting the arbitral tribunal's liberty of decision, may also draw its attention to points of substance. No award shall be rendered by the arbitral tribunal until it has been approved by the Court as to its form.

Article 34: Notification, Deposit and Enforceability of the Award

1. Once an award has been made, the Secretariat shall notify to the parties the text signed by the arbitral tribunal, provided always that the costs of the arbitration have been fully paid to the ICC by the parties or by one of them.

2. Additional copies certified true by the Secretary General shall be made available on request and at any time to the parties, but to no one else.

3. By virtue of the notification made in accordance with Article 34(1), the parties waive any other form of notification or deposit on the part of the arbitral tribunal.

4. An original of each award made in accordance with the Rules shall be deposited with the Secretariat.

5. The arbitral tribunal and the Secretariat shall assist the parties in complying with whatever further formalities may be necessary.

6. Every award shall be binding on the parties. By submitting the dispute to arbitration under the Rules, the parties undertake to carry out any award without delay and shall be deemed to have waived their right to any form of recourse insofar as such waiver can validly be made.

Article 35: Correction and Interpretation of the Award; Remission of Awards

1. On its own initiative, the arbitral tribunal may correct a clerical, computational or typographical error, or any errors of similar nature contained in an award, provided

such correction is submitted for approval to the Court within 30 days of the date of such award.

2. Any application of a party for the correction of an error of the kind referred to in Article 35(1), or for the interpretation of an award, must be made to the Secretariat within 30 days of the receipt of the award by such party, in a number of copies as stated in Article 3(1). After transmittal of the application to the arbitral tribunal, the latter shall grant the other party a short time limit, normally not exceeding 30 days, from the receipt of the application by that party, to submit any comments thereon. The arbitral tribunal shall submit its decision on the application in draft form to the Court not later than 30 days following the expiration of the time limit for the receipt of any comments from the other party or within such other period as the Court may decide.

3. A decision to correct or to interpret the award shall take the form of an addendum and shall constitute part of the award. The provisions of Articles 31, 33 and 34 shall apply *mutatis mutandis*.

4. Where a court remits an award to the arbitral tribunal, the provisions of Articles 31, 33, 34 and this Article 35 shall apply *mutatis mutandis* to any addendum or award made pursuant to the terms of such remission. The Court may take any steps as may be necessary to enable the arbitral tribunal to comply with the terms of such remission and may fix an advance to cover any additional fees and expenses of the arbitral tribunal and any additional ICC administrative expenses.

COSTS

Article 36: Advance to Cover the Costs of the Arbitration

1. After receipt of the Request, the Secretary General may request the claimant to pay a provisional advance in an amount intended to cover the costs of the arbitration until the Terms of Reference have been drawn up. Any provisional advance paid will be considered as a partial payment by the claimant of any advance on costs fixed by the Court pursuant to this Article 36.

2. As soon as practicable, the Court shall fix the advance on costs in an amount likely to cover the fees and expenses of the arbitrators and the ICC administrative expenses for the claims which have been referred to it by the parties, unless any claims are made under Article 7 or 8 in which case Article 36(4) shall apply. The advance on costs fixed by the Court pursuant to this Article 36(2) shall be payable in equal shares by the claimant and the respondent.

3. Where counterclaims are submitted by the respondent under Article 5 or otherwise, the Court may fix separate advances on costs for the claims and the counterclaims. When the Court has fixed separate advances on costs, each of the parties shall pay the advance on costs corresponding to its claims.

4. Where claims are made under Article 7 or 8, the Court shall fix one or more advances on costs that shall be payable by the parties as decided by the Court. Where the Court has previously fixed any advance on costs pursuant to this Article 36, any such advance shall be replaced by the advance(s) fixed pursuant to this Article 36(4), and the amount of any advance previously paid by any party will be considered as a partial payment by such party of its share of the advance(s) on costs as fixed by the Court pursuant to this Article 36(4).

5. The amount of any advance on costs fixed by the Court pursuant to this Article 36 may be subject to readjustment at any time during the arbitration. In all cases, any party shall be free to pay any other party's share of any advance on costs should such other party fail to pay its share.

6. When a request for an advance on costs has not been complied with, and after consultation with the arbitral tribunal, the Secretary General may direct the arbitral tribunal to suspend its work and set a time limit, which must be not less than 15 days, on the expiry of which the relevant claims shall be considered as withdrawn. Should the party in question wish to object to this measure, it must make a request within the aforementioned period for the matter to be decided by the Court. Such party shall not be prevented, on the ground of such withdrawal, from reintroducing the same claims at a later date in another proceeding.

7. If one of the parties claims a right to a set-off with regard to any claim, such set-off shall be taken into account in determining the advance to cover the costs of the arbitration in the same way as a separate claim insofar as it may require the arbitral tribunal to consider additional matters.

Article 37: Decision as to the Costs of the Arbitration

1. The costs of the arbitration shall include the fees and expenses of the arbitrators and the ICC administrative expenses fixed by the Court, in accordance with the scale in force at the time of the commencement of the arbitration, as well as the fees and expenses of any experts appointed by the arbitral tribunal and the reasonable legal and other costs incurred by the parties for the arbitration.

2. The Court may fix the fees of the arbitrators at a figure higher or lower than that which would result from the application of the relevant scale should this be deemed necessary due to the exceptional circumstances of the case.

3. At any time during the arbitral proceedings, the arbitral tribunal may make decisions on costs, other than those to be fixed by the Court, and order payment.

4. The final award shall fix the costs of the arbitration and decide which of the parties shall bear them or in what proportion they shall be borne by the parties.

5. In making decisions as to costs, the arbitral tribunal may take into account such circumstances as it considers relevant, including the extent to which each party has conducted the arbitration in an expeditious and cost-effective manner.

6. In the event of the withdrawal of all claims or the termination of the arbitration before the rendering of a final award, the Court shall fix the fees and expenses of the arbitrators and the ICC administrative expenses. If the parties have not agreed upon the allocation of the costs of the arbitration or other relevant issues with respect to costs, such matters shall be decided by the arbitral tribunal. If the arbitral tribunal has not been constituted at the time of such withdrawal or termination, any party may request the Court to proceed with the constitution of the arbitral tribunal in accordance with the Rules so that the arbitral tribunal may make decisions as to costs.

MISCELLANEOUS

Article 38: Modified Time Limits

1. The parties may agree to shorten the various time limits set out in the Rules. Any such agreement entered into subsequent to the constitution of an arbitral tribunal shall become effective only upon the approval of the arbitral tribunal.

2. The Court, on its own initiative, may extend any time limit which has been modified pursuant to Article 38(1) if it decides that it is necessary to do so in order that the arbitral tribunal and the Court may fulfil their responsibilities in accordance with the Rules.

Article 39: Waiver

A party which proceeds with the arbitration without raising its objection to a failure to comply with any provision of the Rules, or of any other rules applicable to the proceedings, any direction given by the arbitral tribunal, or any requirement under the arbitration agreement relating to the constitution of the arbitral tribunal or the conduct of the proceedings, shall be deemed to have waived its right to object.

Article 40: Limitation of Liability

The arbitrators, any person appointed by the arbitral tribunal, the emergency arbitrator, the Court and its members, the ICC and its employees, and the ICC National Committees and Groups and their employees and representatives shall not be liable to any person for any act or omission in connection with the arbitration, except to the extent such limitation of liability is prohibited by applicable law.

Article 41: General Rule

In all matters not expressly provided for in the Rules, the Court and the arbitral tribunal shall act in the spirit of the Rules and shall make every effort to make sure that the award is enforceable at law.

APPENDIX I:
STATUTES OF THE INTERNATIONAL COURT OF ARBITRATION

Article 1: Function

1. The function of the International Court of Arbitration of the International Chamber of Commerce (the "Court") is to ensure the application of the Rules of Arbitration of the International Chamber of Commerce, and it has all the necessary powers for that purpose.

2. As an autonomous body, it carries out these functions in complete independence from the ICC and its organs.

3. Its members are independent from the ICC National Committees and Groups.

Article 2: Composition of the Court

The Court shall consist of a President,[1] Vice-Presidents,[2] and members and alternate members (collectively designated as members). In its work it is assisted by its Secretariat (Secretariat of the Court).

Article 3: Appointment

1. The President is elected by the ICC World Council upon the recommendation of the Executive Board of the ICC.

2. The ICC World Council appoints the Vice-Presidents of the Court from among the members of the Court or otherwise.

3. Its members are appointed by the ICC World Council on the proposal of National Committees or Groups, one member for each National Committee or Group.

4. On the proposal of the President of the Court, the World Council may appoint alternate members.

5. The term of office of all members, including, for the purposes of this paragraph, the President and Vice-Presidents, is three years. If a member is no longer in a position to exercise the member's functions, a successor is appointed by the World Council for the remainder of the term. Upon the recommendation of the Executive Board, the duration of the term of office of any member may be extended beyond three years if the World Council so decides.

Article 4: Plenary Session of the Court

The Plenary Sessions of the Court are presided over by the President or, in the President's absence, by one of the Vice-Presidents designated by the President. The deliberations shall be valid when at least six members are present. Decisions are taken by a majority vote, the President or Vice-President, as the case may be, having a casting vote in the event of a tie.

Article 5: Committees

The Court may set up one or more Committees and establish the functions and organization of such Committees.

Article 6: Confidentiality

The work of the Court is of a confidential nature which must be respected by everyone who participates in that work in whatever capacity. The Court lays down the rules regarding the persons who can attend the meetings of the Court and its Committees and who are entitled to have access to materials related to the work of the Court and its Secretariat.

---

1. Referred to as "Chairman of the International Court of Arbitration" in the Constitution of the International Chamber of Commerce.
2. Referred to as "Vice-Chairmen of the International Court of Arbitration" in the Constitution of the International Chamber of Commerce.

Article 7: Modification of the Rules of Arbitration

Any proposal of the Court for a modification of the Rules is laid before the Commission on Arbitration and ADR before submission to the Executive Board of the ICC for approval, provided, however, that the Court, in order to take account of developments in information technology, may propose to modify or supplement the provisions of Article 3 of the Rules or any related provisions in the Rules without laying any such proposal before the Commission.

APPENDIX II:
INTERNAL RULES OF THE INTERNATIONAL COURT OF ARBITRATION

Article 1: Confidential Character of the Work of the International Court of Arbitration

1. For the purposes of this Appendix, members of the Court include the President and Vice-Presidents of the Court.

2. The sessions of the Court, whether plenary or those of a Committee of the Court, are open only to its members and to the Secretariat.

3. However, in exceptional circumstances, the President of the Court may invite other persons to attend. Such persons must respect the confidential nature of the work of the Court.

4. The documents submitted to the Court, or drawn up by it or the Secretariat in the course of the Court's proceedings, are communicated only to the members of the Court and to the Secretariat and to persons authorized by the President to attend Court sessions.

5. The President or the Secretary General of the Court may authorize researchers undertaking work of an academic nature to acquaint themselves with awards and other documents of general interest, with the exception of memoranda, notes, statements and documents remitted by the parties within the framework of arbitration proceedings.

6. Such authorization shall not be given unless the beneficiary has undertaken to respect the confidential character of the documents made available and to refrain from publishing anything based upon information contained therein without having previously submitted the text for approval to the Secretary General of the Court.

7. The Secretariat will in each case submitted to arbitration under the Rules retain in the archives of the Court all awards, Terms of Reference and decisions of the Court, as well as copies of the pertinent correspondence of the Secretariat.

8. Any documents, communications or correspondence submitted by the parties or the arbitrators may be destroyed unless a party or an arbitrator requests in writing within a period fixed by the Secretariat the return of such documents, communications or correspondence. All related costs and expenses for the return of those documents shall be paid by such party or arbitrator.

Article 2: Participation of Members of the International Court of Arbitration in ICC Arbitration

1. The President and the members of the Secretariat of the Court may not act as arbitrators or as counsel in cases submitted to ICC arbitration.

2. The Court shall not appoint Vice-Presidents or members of the Court as arbitrators. They may, however, be proposed for such duties by one or more of the parties, or pursuant to any other procedure agreed upon by the parties, subject to confirmation.

3. When the President, a Vice-President or a member of the Court or of the Secretariat is involved in any capacity whatsoever in proceedings pending before the Court, such person must inform the Secretary General of the Court upon becoming aware of such involvement.

4. Such person must be absent from the Court session whenever the matter is considered by the Court and shall not participate in the discussions or in the decisions of the Court.

5. Such person will not receive any material documentation or information pertaining to such proceedings.

Article 3: Relations Between the Members of the Court and the ICC National Committees and Groups

1. By virtue of their capacity, the members of the Court are independent of the ICC National Committees and Groups which proposed them for appointment by the ICC World Council.

2. Furthermore, they must regard as confidential, vis-à-vis the said National Committees and Groups, any information concerning individual cases with which they have become acquainted in their capacity as members of the Court, except when they have been requested by the President of the Court, by a Vice-President of the Court authorized by the President of the Court, or by the Court's Secretary General to communicate specific information to their respective National Committees or Groups.

Article 4: Committee of the Court

1. In accordance with the provisions of Article 1(4) of the Rules and Article 5 of its statutes (Appendix I), the Court hereby establishes a Committee of the Court.

2. The members of the Committee consist of a president and at least two other members. The President of the Court acts as the president of the Committee. In the President's absence or otherwise at the President's request, a Vice-President of the Court or, in exceptional circumstances, another member of the Court may act as president of the Committee.

3. The other two members of the Committee are appointed by the Court from among the Vice-Presidents or the other members of the Court. At each Plenary Session the Court appoints the members who are to attend the meetings of the Committee to be held before the next Plenary Session.

4. The Committee meets when convened by its president. Two members constitute a quorum.

5. (a) The Court shall determine the decisions that may be taken by the Committee.

(b) The decisions of the Committee are taken unanimously.
(c) When the Committee cannot reach a decision or deems it preferable to abstain, it transfers the case to the next Plenary Session, making any suggestions it deems appropriate.
(d) The Committee's decisions are brought to the notice of the Court at its next Plenary Session.

Article 5: Court Secretariat

1. In the Secretary General's absence or otherwise at the Secretary General's request, the Deputy Secretary General and/or the General Counsel shall have the authority to refer matters to the Court, confirm arbitrators, certify true copies of awards and request the payment of a provisional advance, respectively provided for in Articles 6(3), 13(2), 34 (2) and 36(1) of the Rules.

2. The Secretariat may, with the approval of the Court, issue notes and other documents for the information of the parties and the arbitrators, or as necessary for the proper conduct of the arbitral proceedings.

3. Offices of the Secretariat may be established outside the headquarters of the ICC. The Secretariat shall keep a list of offices designated by the Secretary General. Requests for Arbitration may be submitted to the Secretariat at any of its offices, and the Secretariat's functions under the Rules may be carried out from any of its offices, as instructed by the Secretary General, Deputy Secretary General or General Counsel.

Article 6: Scrutiny of Arbitral Awards

When the Court scrutinizes draft awards in accordance with Article 33 of the Rules, it considers, to the extent practicable, the requirements of mandatory law at the place of the arbitration.

APPENDIX III:
ARBITRATION COSTS AND FEES

Article 1: Advance on Costs

1. Each request to commence an arbitration pursuant to the Rules must be accompanied by a filing fee of US$ 3,000. Such payment is non-refundable and shall be credited to the claimant's portion of the advance on costs.

2. The provisional advance fixed by the Secretary General according to Article 36(1) of the Rules shall normally not exceed the amount obtained by adding together the ICC administrative expenses, the minimum of the fees (as set out in the scale hereinafter) based upon the amount of the claim and the expected reimbursable expenses of the arbitral tribunal incurred with respect to the drafting of the Terms of Reference. If such amount is not quantified, the provisional advance shall be fixed at the discretion of the Secretary General. Payment by the claimant shall be credited to its share of the advance on costs fixed by the Court.

3. In general, after the Terms of Reference have been signed or approved by the Court and the procedural timetable has been established, the arbitral tribunal shall, in

accordance with Article 36(6) of the Rules, proceed only with respect to those claims or counterclaims in regard to which the whole of the advance on costs has been paid.

4. The advance on costs fixed by the Court according to Articles 36(2) or 36(4) of the Rules comprises the fees of the arbitrator or arbitrators (hereinafter referred to as "arbitrator"), any arbitration-related expenses of the arbitrator and the ICC administrative expenses.

5. Each party shall pay its share of the total advance on costs in cash. However, if a party's share of the advance on costs is greater than US$ 500,000 (the "Threshold Amount"), such party may post a bank guarantee for any amount above the Threshold Amount. The Court may modify the Threshold Amount at any time at its discretion.

6. The Court may authorize the payment of advances on costs, or any party's share thereof, in instalments, subject to such conditions as the Court thinks fit, including the payment of additional ICC administrative expenses.

7. A party that has already paid in full its share of the advance on costs fixed by the Court may, in accordance with Article 36(5) of the Rules, pay the unpaid portion of the advance owed by the defaulting party by posting a bank guarantee.

8. When the Court has fixed separate advances on costs pursuant to Article 36(3) of the Rules, the Secretariat shall invite each party to pay the amount of the advance corresponding to its respective claim(s).

9. When, as a result of the fixing of separate advances on costs, the separate advance fixed for the claim of either party exceeds one half of such global advance as was previously fixed (in respect of the same claims and counterclaims that are the subject of separate advances), a bank guarantee may be posted to cover any such excess amount. In the event that the amount of the separate advance is subsequently increased, at least one half of the increase shall be paid in cash.

10. The Secretariat shall establish the terms governing all bank guarantees which the parties may post pursuant to the above provisions.

11. As provided in Article 36(5) of the Rules, the advance on costs may be subject to readjustment at any time during the arbitration, in particular to take into account fluctuations in the amount in dispute, changes in the amount of the estimated expenses of the arbitrator, or the evolving difficulty or complexity of arbitration proceedings.

12. Before any expertise ordered by the arbitral tribunal can be commenced, the parties, or one of them, shall pay an advance on costs fixed by the arbitral tribunal sufficient to cover the expected fees and expenses of the expert as determined by the arbitral tribunal. The arbitral tribunal shall be responsible for ensuring the payment by the parties of such fees and expenses.

13. The amounts paid as advances on costs do not yield interest for the parties or the arbitrator.

Article 2: Costs and Fees

1. Subject to Article 37(2) of the Rules, the Court shall fix the fees of the arbitrator in accordance with the scale hereinafter set out or, where the amount in dispute is not stated, at its discretion.

2. In setting the arbitrator's fees, the Court shall take into consideration the diligence and efficiency of the arbitrator, the time spent, the rapidity of the proceedings, the complexity of the dispute and the timeliness of the submission of the draft award, so as to arrive at a figure within the limits specified or, in exceptional circumstances (Article 37(2) of the Rules), at a figure higher or lower than those limits.

3. When a case is submitted to more than one arbitrator, the Court, at its discretion, shall have the right to increase the total fees up to a maximum which shall normally not exceed three times the fees of one arbitrator.

4. The arbitrator's fees and expenses shall be fixed exclusively by the Court as required by the Rules. Separate fee arrangements between the parties and the arbitrator are contrary to the Rules.

5. The Court shall fix the ICC administrative expenses of each arbitration in accordance with the scale hereinafter set out or, where the amount in dispute is not stated, at its discretion. In exceptional circumstances, the Court may fix the ICC administrative expenses at a lower or higher figure than that which would result from the application of such scale, provided that such expenses shall normally not exceed the maximum amount of the scale.

6. At any time during the arbitration, the Court may fix as payable a portion of the ICC administrative expenses corresponding to services that have already been performed by the Court and the Secretariat.

7. The Court may require the payment of administrative expenses in addition to those provided in the scale of administrative expenses as a condition for holding an arbitration in abeyance at the request of the parties or of one of them with the acquiescence of the other.

8. If an arbitration terminates before the rendering of a final award, the Court shall fix the fees and expenses of the arbitrators and the ICC administrative expenses at its discretion, taking into account the stage attained by the arbitral proceedings and any other relevant circumstances.

9. Any amount paid by the parties as an advance on costs exceeding the costs of the arbitration fixed by the Court shall be reimbursed to the parties having regard to the amounts paid.

10. In the case of an application under Article 35(2) of the Rules or of a remission pursuant to Article 35(4) of the Rules, the Court may fix an advance to cover additional fees and expenses of the arbitral tribunal and additional ICC administrative expenses and may make the transmission of such application to the arbitral tribunal subject to the prior cash payment in full to the ICC of such advance. The Court shall fix at its discretion the costs of the procedure following an application or a remission, which shall include any possible fees of the arbitrator and ICC administrative expenses, when approving the decision of the arbitral tribunal.

11. The Secretariat may require the payment of administrative expenses in addition to those provided in the scale of administrative expenses for any expenses arising in relation to a request pursuant to Article 34(5) of the Rules.

12. When an arbitration is preceded by proceedings under the ICC Mediation Rules, one half of the ICC administrative expenses paid for such proceedings shall be credited to the ICC administrative expenses of the arbitration.

13. Amounts paid to the arbitrator do not include any possible value added tax (VAT) or other taxes or charges and imposts applicable to the arbitrator's fees. Parties have a duty to pay any such taxes or charges; however, the recovery of any such charges or taxes is a matter solely between the arbitrator and the parties.

14. Any ICC administrative expenses may be subject to value added tax (VAT) or charges of a similar nature at the prevailing rate.

Article 3: ICC as Appointing Authority

Any request received for an authority of the ICC to act as appointing authority will be treated in accordance with the Rules of ICC as Appointing Authority in UNCITRAL or Other *Ad Hoc* Arbitration Proceedings and shall be accompanied by a non-refundable filing fee of US$ 3,000. No request shall be processed unless accompanied by the said filing fee. For additional services, the ICC may at its discretion fix ICC administrative expenses, which shall be commensurate with the services provided and shall normally not exceed the maximum amount of US$ 10,000.

Article 4: Scales of Administrative Expenses and Arbitrator's Fees

1. The Scales of Administrative Expenses and Arbitrator's Fees set forth below shall be effective as of 1 January 2012 in respect of all arbitrations commenced on or after such date, irrespective of the version of the Rules applying to such arbitrations.

2. To calculate the ICC administrative expenses and the arbitrator's fees, the amounts calculated for each successive tranche of the amount in dispute must be added together, except that where the amount in dispute is over US$ 500 million, a flat amount of US$ 113,215 shall constitute the entirety of the ICC administrative expenses.

3. All amounts fixed by the Court or pursuant to any of the appendices to the Rules are payable in US$ except where prohibited by law, in which case the ICC may apply a different scale and fee arrangement in another currency.

A. ADMINISTRATIVE EXPENSES

Amount in dispute (in US Dollars)				Administrative expenses(*)
up to			50,000	$3,000
from	50,001	to	100,000	4.73%
from	100,001	to	200,000	2.53%
from	200,001	to	500,000	2.09%
from	500,001	to	1,000,000	1.51%
from	1,000,001	to	2,000,000	0.95%
from	2,000,001	to	5,000,000	0.46%
from	5,000,001	to	10,000,000	0.25%
from	10,000,001	to	30,000,000	0.10%
from	30,000,001	to	50,000,000	0.09%
from	50,000,001	to	80,000,000	0.01%
from	80,000,001	to	500,000,000	0.0035%
over	500,000,000			$113,215

(*) For illustrative purposes only, the table on the following page indicates the resulting administrative expenses in US$ when the proper calculations have been made.

B. ARBITRATOR'S FEES

Amount in dispute (in US Dollars)				Fees (**) minimum	maximum
up to	50,000			$3,000	18.0200%
from	50,001	to	100,000	2.6500%	13.5680%
from	100,001	to	200,000	1.4310%	7.6850%
from	200,001	to	500,000	1.3670%	6.8370%
from	500,001	to	1,000,000	0.9540%	4.0280%
from	1,000,001	to	2,000,000	0.6890%	3.6040%
from	2,000,001	to	5,000,000	0.3750%	1.3910%
from	5,000,001	to	10,000,000	0.1280%	0.9100%
from	10,000,001	to	30,000,000	0.0640%	0.2410%
from	30,000,001	to	50,000,000	0.0590%	0.2280%
from	50,000,001	to	80,000,000	0.0330%	0.1570%
from	80,000,001	to	100,000,000	0.0210%	0.1150%
from	100,000,001	to	500,000,000	0.0110%	0.0580%
over	500,000,000			0.0100%	0.0400%

(**) For illustrative purposes only, the table on the following page indicates the resulting range of fees in US$ when the proper calculations have been made.

AMOUNT IN DISPUTE (in US Dollars)	A. ADMINISTRATIVE EXPENSES (*) (in US Dollars)	B. ARBITRATOR'S FEES (**) (in US Dollars)	
		Minimum	Maximum
up to 50,000	3,000	3,000	18.02% of amount in dispute
from 50,001 to 100,000	3,000 + 4.73% of amt. over 50,000	3,000 + 2.6500% of amt. over 50,000	9,010 + 13.568% of amt. over 50,000
from 100,001 to 200,000	5,365 + 2.53% of amt. over 100,000	4,325 + 1.4310% of amt. over 100,000	15,794 + 7.6850% of amt. over 100,000
from 200,001 to 500,000	7,895 + 2.09% of amt. over 200,000	5,756 + 1.3670% of amt. over 200,000	23,479 + 6.8370% of amt. over 200,000
from 500,001 to 1,000,000	14,165 + 1.51% of amt. over 500,000	9,857 + 0.9540% of amt. over 500,000	43,990 + 4.0280% of amt. over 500,000
from 1,000,001 to 2,000,000	21,715 + 0.95% of amt. over 1,000,000	14,627 + 0.6890% of amt. over 1,000,000	64,130 + 3.6040% of amt. over 1,000,000
from 2,000,001 to 5,000,000	31,215 + 0.46% of amt. over 2,000,000	21,517 + 0.3750% of amt. over 2,000,000	100,170 + 1.3910% of amt. over 2,000,000
from 5,000,001 to 10,000,000	45,015 + 0.25% of amt. over 5,000,000	32,767 + 0.1280% of amt. over 5,000,000	141,900 + 0.9100% of amt. over 5,000,000
from 10,000,001 to 30,000,000	57,515 + 0.10% of amt. over 10,000,000	39,167 + 0.0640% of amt. over 10,000,000	187,400 + 0.2410% of amt. over 10,000,000
from 30,000,001 to 50,000,000	77,515 + 0.09% of amt. over 30,000,000	51,967 + 0.0590% of amt. over 30,000,000	235,600 + 0.2280% of amt. over 30,000,000
from 50,000,001 to 80,000,000	95,515 + 0.01% of amt. over 50,000,000	63,767 + 0.0330% of amt. over 50,000,000	281,200 + 0.1570% of amt. over 50,000,000
from 80,000,001 to 100,000,000	98,515 + 0.0035% of amt. over 80,000,000	73,667 + 0.0210% of amt. over 80,000,000	328,300 + 0.1150% of amt. over 80,000,000
from 100,000,001 to 500,000,000	99,215 + 0.0035% of amt. over 100,000,000	77,867 + 0.0110% of amt. over 100,000,000	351,300 + 0.0580% of amt. over 100,000,000
over 500,000,000	113,215	121,867 + 0.0100% of amt. over 500,000,000	583,300 + 0.0400% of amt. over 500,000,000

(*)(**) See preceding page

APPENDIX IV: CASE MANAGEMENT TECHNIQUES

The following are examples of case management techniques that can be used by the arbitral tribunal and the parties for controlling time and cost. Appropriate control of time and cost is important in all cases. In cases of low complexity and low value, it is particularly important to ensure that time and costs are proportionate to what is at stake in the dispute.

a) Bifurcating the proceedings or rendering one or more partial awards on key issues, when doing so may genuinely be expected to result in a more efficient resolution of the case.
b) Identifying issues that can be resolved by agreement between the parties or their experts.
c) Identifying issues to be decided solely on the basis of documents rather than through oral evidence or legal argument at a hearing.
d) Production of documentary evidence:
   (i) requiring the parties to produce with their submissions the documents on which they rely;
   (ii) avoiding requests for document production when appropriate in order to control time and cost;
   (iii) in those cases where requests for document production are considered appropriate, limiting such requests to documents or categories of documents that are relevant and material to the outcome of the case;
   (iv) establishing reasonable time limits for the production of documents;
   (v) using a schedule of document production to facilitate the resolution of issues in relation to the production of documents.
e) Limiting the length and scope of written submissions and written and oral witness evidence (both fact witnesses and experts) so as to avoid repetition and maintain a focus on key issues.
f) Using telephone or video conferencing for procedural and other hearings where attendance in person is not essential and use of IT that enables online communication among the parties, the arbitral tribunal and the Secretariat of the Court.
g) Organizing a pre-hearing conference with the arbitral tribunal at which arrangements for a hearing can be discussed and agreed and the arbitral tribunal can indicate to the parties issues on which it would like the parties to focus at the hearing.
h) Settlement of disputes:
   (i) informing the parties that they are free to settle all or part of the dispute either by negotiation or through any form of amicable dispute resolution methods such as, for example, mediation under the ICC Mediation Rules;
   (ii) where agreed between the parties and the arbitral tribunal, the arbitral tribunal may take steps to facilitate settlement of the dispute, provided that every effort is made to ensure that any subsequent award is enforceable at law.

Additional techniques are described in the ICC publication entitled "Controlling Time and Costs in Arbitration".

APPENDIX V:
EMERGENCY ARBITRATOR RULES

Article 1: Application for Emergency Measures

1. A party wishing to have recourse to an emergency arbitrator pursuant to Article 29 of the Rules of Arbitration of the ICC (the "Rules") shall submit its Application for Emergency Measures (the "Application") to the Secretariat at any of the offices specified in the Internal Rules of the Court in Appendix II to the Rules.

2. The Application shall be supplied in a number of copies sufficient to provide one copy for each party, plus one for the emergency arbitrator, and one for the Secretariat.

3. The Application shall contain the following information:

a) the name in full, description, address and other contact details of each of the parties;

b) the name in full, address and other contact details of any person(s) representing the applicant;

c) a description of the circumstances giving rise to the Application and of the underlying dispute referred or to be referred to arbitration;

d) a statement of the Emergency Measures sought;

e) the reasons why the applicant needs urgent interim or conservatory measures that cannot await the constitution of an arbitral tribunal;

f) any relevant agreements and, in particular, the arbitration agreement;

g) any agreement as to the place of the arbitration, the applicable rules of law or the language of the arbitration;

h) proof of payment of the amount referred to in Article 7(1) of this Appendix; and

i) any Request for Arbitration and any other submissions in connection with the underlying dispute, which have been filed with the Secretariat by any of the parties to the emergency arbitrator proceedings prior to the making of the Application.

The Application may contain such other documents or information as the applicant considers appropriate or as may contribute to the efficient examination of the Application.

4. The Application shall be drawn up in the language of the arbitration if agreed upon by the parties or, in the absence of any such agreement, in the language of the arbitration agreement.

5. If and to the extent that the President of the Court (the "President") considers, on the basis of the information contained in the Application, that the Emergency Arbitrator Provisions apply with reference to Article 29(5) and Article 29(6) of the Rules, the Secretariat shall transmit a copy of the Application and the documents annexed thereto to the responding party. If and to the extent that the President considers otherwise, the Secretariat shall inform the parties that the emergency arbitrator proceedings shall not take place with respect to some or all of the parties and shall transmit a copy of the Application to them for information.

6. The President shall terminate the emergency arbitrator proceedings if a Request for Arbitration has not been received by the Secretariat from the applicant within 10

days of the Secretariat's receipt of the Application, unless the emergency arbitrator determines that a longer period of time is necessary.

Article 2: Appointment of the Emergency Arbitrator; Transmission of the File

1. The President shall appoint an emergency arbitrator within as short a time as possible, normally within two days from the Secretariat's receipt of the Application.

2. No emergency arbitrator shall be appointed after the file has been transmitted to the arbitral tribunal pursuant to Article 16 of the Rules. An emergency arbitrator appointed prior thereto shall retain the power to make an order within the time limit permitted by Article 6(4) of this Appendix.

3. Once the emergency arbitrator has been appointed, the Secretariat shall so notify the parties and shall transmit the file to the emergency arbitrator. Thereafter, all written communications from the parties shall be submitted directly to the emergency arbitrator with a copy to the other party and the Secretariat. A copy of any written communications from the emergency arbitrator to the parties shall be submitted to the Secretariat.

4. Every emergency arbitrator shall be and remain impartial and independent of the parties involved in the dispute.

5. Before being appointed, a prospective emergency arbitrator shall sign a statement of acceptance, availability, impartiality and independence. The Secretariat shall provide a copy of such statement to the parties.

6. An emergency arbitrator shall not act as an arbitrator in any arbitration relating to the dispute that gave rise to the Application.

Article 3: Challenge of an Emergency Arbitrator

1. A challenge against the emergency arbitrator must be made within three days from receipt by the party making the challenge of the notification of the appointment or from the date when that party was informed of the facts and circumstances on which the challenge is based if such date is subsequent to the receipt of such notification.

2. The challenge shall be decided by the Court after the Secretariat has afforded an opportunity for the emergency arbitrator and the other party or parties to provide comments in writing within a suitable period of time.

Article 4: Place of the Emergency Arbitrator Proceedings

1. If the parties have agreed upon the place of the arbitration, such place shall be the place of the emergency arbitrator proceedings. In the absence of such agreement, the President shall fix the place of the emergency arbitrator proceedings, without prejudice to the determination of the place of the arbitration pursuant to Article 18(1) of the Rules.

2. Any meetings with the emergency arbitrator may be conducted through a meeting in person at any location the emergency arbitrator considers appropriate or by video conference, telephone or similar means of communication.

Article 5: Proceedings

1. The emergency arbitrator shall establish a procedural timetable for the emergency arbitrator proceedings within as short a time as possible, normally within two days from the transmission of the file to the emergency arbitrator pursuant to Article 2(3) of this Appendix.

2. The emergency arbitrator shall conduct the proceedings in the manner which the emergency arbitrator considers to be appropriate, taking into account the nature and the urgency of the Application. In all cases, the emergency arbitrator shall act fairly and impartially and ensure that each party has a reasonable opportunity to present its case.

Article 6: Order

1. Pursuant to Article 29(2) of the Rules, the emergency arbitrator's decision shall take the form of an order (the "Order").

2. In the Order, the emergency arbitrator shall determine whether the Application is admissible pursuant to Article 29(1) of the Rules and whether the emergency arbitrator has jurisdiction to order Emergency Measures.

3. The Order shall be made in writing and shall state the reasons upon which it is based. It shall be dated and signed by the emergency arbitrator.

4. The Order shall be made no later than 15 days from the date on which the file was transmitted to the emergency arbitrator pursuant to Article 2(3) of this Appendix. The President may extend the time limit pursuant to a reasoned request from the emergency arbitrator or on the President's own initiative if the President decides it is necessary to do so.

5. Within the time limit established pursuant to Article 6(4) of this Appendix, the emergency arbitrator shall send the Order to the parties, with a copy to the Secretariat, by any of the means of communication permitted by Article 3(2) of the Rules that the emergency arbitrator considers will ensure prompt receipt.

6. The Order shall cease to be binding on the parties upon:

a) the President's termination of the emergency arbitrator proceedings pursuant to Article 1(6) of this Appendix;
b) the acceptance by the Court of a challenge against the emergency arbitrator pursuant to Article 3 of this Appendix;
c) the arbitral tribunal's final award, unless the arbitral tribunal expressly decides otherwise; or
d) the withdrawal of all claims or the termination of the arbitration before the rendering of a final award.

7. The emergency arbitrator may make the Order subject to such conditions as the emergency arbitrator thinks fit, including requiring the provision of appropriate security.

8. Upon a reasoned request by a party made prior to the transmission of the file to the arbitral tribunal pursuant to Article 16 of the Rules, the emergency arbitrator may modify, terminate or annul the Order.

Article 7: Costs of the Emergency Arbitrator Proceedings

1. The applicant must pay an amount of US$ 40,000, consisting of US$ 10,000 for ICC administrative expenses and US$ 30,000 for the emergency arbitrator's fees and expenses. Notwithstanding Article 1(5) of this Appendix, the Application shall not be notified until the payment of US$ 40,000 is received by the Secretariat.

2. The President may, at any time during the emergency arbitrator proceedings, decide to increase the emergency arbitrator's fees or the ICC administrative expenses taking into account, *inter alia*, the nature of the case and the nature and amount of work performed by the emergency arbitrator, the Court, the President and the Secretariat. If the party which submitted the Application fails to pay the increased costs within the time limit fixed by the Secretariat, the Application shall be considered as withdrawn.

3. The emergency arbitrator's Order shall fix the costs of the emergency arbitrator proceedings and decide which of the parties shall bear them or in what proportion they shall be borne by the parties.

4. The costs of the emergency arbitrator proceedings include the ICC administrative expenses, the emergency arbitrator's fees and expenses and the reasonable legal and other costs incurred by the parties for the emergency arbitrator proceedings.

5. In the event that the emergency arbitrator proceedings do not take place pursuant to Article 1(5) of this Appendix or are otherwise terminated prior to the making of an Order, the President shall determine the amount to be reimbursed to the applicant, if any. An amount of US$ 5,000 for ICC administrative expenses is non-refundable in all cases.

Article 8: General Rule

1. The President shall have the power to decide, at the President's discretion, all matters relating to the administration of the emergency arbitrator proceedings not expressly provided for in this Appendix.

2. In the President's absence or otherwise at the President's request, any of the Vice-Presidents of the Court shall have the power to take decisions on behalf of the President.

3. In all matters concerning emergency arbitrator proceedings not expressly provided for in this Appendix, the Court, the President and the emergency arbitrator shall act in the spirit of the Rules and this Appendix.

APPENDIX 2

ICC ARBITRATOR STATEMENT OF ACCEPTANCE, AVAILABILITY, IMPARTIALITY AND INDEPENDENCE (2012 RULES)

Case No. __________

Family Name(s): ______________________

Given Name(s): ___________________________

Please tick all relevant boxes.

1. ACCEPTANCE

Acceptance

☐ **I agree** to serve as arbitrator under and in accordance with the 2012 ICC Rules of Arbitration ("**Rules**"). I confirm that I am familiar with the Rules. I accept that my fees and expenses will be fixed exclusively by the ICC Court (Article 2(4) of Appendix III to the Rules).

Non-Acceptance

☐ **I decline** to serve as arbitrator in this case. *(If you tick here, simply date and sign the form without completing any other sections.)*

2. AVAILABILITY

☐ **I confirm**, on the basis of the information presently available to me, that I can devote the time necessary to conduct this arbitration diligently, efficiently and in accordance with the time limits in the Rules, subject to any extensions granted by the Court pursuant to Articles 23(2) and 30 of the Rules. I understand that it is important to complete the arbitration as promptly as reasonably practicable and that the ICC Court will consider the duration and conduct of the proceedings when fixing my fees (Article 2(2) of Appendix III to the Rules). My *current* professional engagements are as below for the information of the ICC Court and the parties.

Principal professional activity

(e.g. lawyer, arbitrator, academic): ___________________________________

Number of *currently pending* cases in which I am involved *(i.e. arbitrations and activities pending now, not previous experience; additional details you wish to make known to the ICC Court and to the parties in relation to these matters can be provided on a separate sheet):*

	As tribunal chair / sole arbitrator	As co-arbitrator	As counsel
Arbitrations			
Court litigation	*Not applicable*	*Not applicable*	

Furthermore, I am aware of commitments which might preclude me from devoting time to this arbitration during the following periods (*please provide details regarding such periods below or on a separate sheet*):

3. INDEPENDENCE and IMPARTIALITY

(Tick one box and provide details below and/or, if necessary, on a separate sheet)

In deciding which box to tick, you should take into account, having regard to Article 11(2) of the Rules, whether there exists any past or present relationship, direct or indirect, between you and any of the parties, their related entities or their lawyers or other representatives, whether financial, professional or of any other kind. *Any doubt must be resolved in favour of disclosure.* Any disclosure should be complete and specific, identifying *inter alia* relevant dates (both start and end dates), financial arrangements, details of companies and individuals, and all other relevant information.

☐ **Nothing to disclose**: I am impartial and independent and intend to remain so. To the best of my knowledge, and having made due enquiry, there are no facts or circumstances, past or present, that I should disclose because they might be of such a nature as to call into question my independence in the eyes of any of the parties and no circumstances that could give rise to reasonable doubts as to my impartiality.

☐ **Acceptance with disclosure**: I am impartial and independent and intend to remain so. However, mindful of my obligation to disclose any facts or circumstances which might be of such a nature as to call into question my independence in the eyes of any of the parties or that could give rise to reasonable doubts as to my impartiality, I draw attention to the matters below and/or on the attached sheet.

Date: ________________ Signature: ________________________________

Disclaimer: The information requested in this form will be considered by the ICC for its Dispute Resolution Services, and will be stored in case management database systems. Pursuant to the French Law on "Informatique et Libertés" of 6 January 1978, particularly Articles 32 and 40, you may access this information and ask for rectification by writing to the Court's Secretariat.

APPENDIX 3

MODEL CURRICULUM VITAE FOR ICC ARBITRATORS

Case No. ________

CURRICULUM VITAE

For the confidential use of the ICC International Court of Arbitration and communication to the parties. To be completed in English.

Personal Information

☐ Mr ☐ Mrs ☐ Miss ☐ Ms

Family Name(s):

Given Name(s):

Date of birth:

Nationality(ies):

Personal Address

Address:

ZIP / City:

Country:

Telephone: Telefax:

E-Mail:

Business Address

Company or firm name where applicable:

Address:

ZIP / City:

Country:

Telephone: Telefax: Mobile:

E-Mail:

Website:

Please indicate which address you wish to be used for any correspondence:

☐ Personal ☐ Business

Please indicate which email you wish to be used for all notifications and communications:

☐ Personal ☐ Business

For the confidential use of the ICC International Court of Arbitration and communication to the parties. To be completed in English.

Academic Degrees / Qualifications *(Use separate sheet if necessary)*

Current Professional Activity(ies) and Position(s) *(Use separate sheet if necessary)*

Professional Experience *(Use separate sheet if necessary)*

Additional Information *(Use separate sheet if necessary)*

Languages

Mark all languages, including your native language, in which you consider yourself able to conduct an arbitration and to draft an award without the assistance of an interpreter or translator:

☐ English	☐ French	☐ German	☐ Italian
☐ Spanish	☐ Portuguese	☐ Russian	☐ Polish
☐ Arabic	☐ Chinese	☐ Japanese	☐ Other __________

Please indicate other languages of which you have good knowledge:

Date: ______________ Signature: ____________________________

Disclaimer: The information requested in this form will be considered by the ICC for its Dispute Resolution Services, and will be stored in case management database systems. Pursuant to the French Law on "Informatique et Libertés" of 6 January 1978, particularly Articles 32 and 40, you may access this information and ask for rectification by writing to the Court's Secretariat.

Case No. ________

For the confidential use of the ICC International Court of Arbitration only. To be completed in English.

Family Name(s):

Given Name(s):

Fields of Legal Expertise *(Use separate sheet if necessary)*

- ☐ Civil law – specify jurisdiction(s):
- ☐ Common law – specify jurisdiction(s):
- ☐ European law
- ☐ International law
- ☐ Islamic law – specify jurisdiction(s):
- ☐ Other laws – please specify:

Specialisation (Mark the appropriate box or boxes)

- ☐ Administrative Law
- ☐ Agency (Representation)
- ☐ Competition
- ☐ Construction, Engineering
- ☐ Corporate Law
- ☐ Criminal Law
- ☐ Distribution, Franchising
- ☐ Employment
- ☐ Energy and Natural Resources
- ☐ Environment
- ☐ Finance and Banking
- ☐ Information and Communication Technologies
- ☐ Insurance
- ☐ Intellectual Property
- ☐ Investment
- ☐ Joint Ventures, Consortia, Cooperation
- ☐ Maritime
- ☐ Pharmaceutical
- ☐ Real Estate
- ☐ Sales, Purchases
- ☐ Taxation
- ☐ Transport
- ☐ Other:

For the confidential use of the ICC International Court of Arbitration only. To be completed in English.

Arbitration Experience *(Use separate sheet if necessary)*

Number of arbitration cases in which you have acted as:

		Chair of tribunal	Sole arbitrator	Co-arbitrator	Party's Counsel	Secretary or other
International Institutional Arbitration	ICC					
	Other					
International Ad Hoc Arbitration						
Domestic Arbitration						

Other Alternative Dispute Resolution Experience *(Use separate sheet if necessary)*

Date: _______________ Signature:____________________________

Disclaimer: The information requested in this form will be considered by the ICC for its Dispute Resolution Services, and will be stored in case management database systems. Pursuant to the French Law on "Informatique et Libertés" of 6 January 1978, particularly Articles 32 and 40, you may access this information and ask for rectification by writing to the Court's Secretariat.

APPENDIX 4

SECRETARIAT'S NOTE TO PARTIES IN PROCEEDINGS UNDER THE 2012 ICC RULES OF ARBITRATION

This Note highlights key aspects of ICC arbitration and provides practical guidance regarding the impact of the ICC Rules of Arbitration in force as of 1 January 2012 ("Rules"). The Note is intended to assist parties in using ICC arbitration to good effect.

ICC International Court of Arbitration ("Court")

1. The Court is an administrative body which ensures that ICC arbitrations are conducted in accordance with the Rules. It does not itself resolve disputes (Article 1(2)).

2. The Court is the only body authorized to administer arbitrations under the Rules, including the scrutiny and approval of all awards rendered in accordance with the Rules (Article 1(2)). An arbitration that is not administered by the Court is not an ICC arbitration.

3. The Court is assisted day-to-day by its Secretariat (Article 1(5)) which, under my direction of the Secretary General, acts as a neutral interface between the parties, their representatives and the Court. Should any questions arise relating to the Rules or ICC procedures, parties may contact the team in charge of arbitration at their convenience.

4. Disputes are resolved by arbitral tribunals, the members of which will either be confirmed, in the case of arbitrators nominated by the parties or the co-arbitrators (Articles 13(1) and 13(2)) or appointed by the Court (Articles 13(3) and 13(4)).

5. The Court's administration of arbitrations includes closely monitoring the progress of the proceedings.

Where Requests for Arbitration can be submitted

6. ICC arbitration is commenced upon the Secretariat's receipt of a Request for Arbitration at any of its offices (Article 4(1) and Article 5(3) of Appendix II). The Secretariat has offices in Paris and Hong Kong, and SICANA serves as an office of the Secretariat in New York for purposes of Articles 4(1) and 5(3) of Appendix II

Pleas on jurisdiction

7. In order to expedite proceedings where any party:
   (i) does not file an answer,

(ii) raises one or more pleas concerning the existence, validity or scope of the arbitration agreement, or
(iii) questions whether all of the claims may be determined together in a single arbitration,

the arbitration will proceed and the arbitral tribunal shall decide such issue, unless the Secretary General refers the matter to the Court for a decision (Articles 6(3) and 6(4)).

8. If the Secretary General refers the case to the Court, it will then decide whether and to what extent the arbitration shall proceed. An arbitration will proceed if and to the extent that the Court is prima facie satisfied that an arbitration agreement under the Rules may exist (Article 6(4)).

Joinder of additional parties, claims between multiple parties, multiple contracts

9. For the first time, the Rules expressly provide for a transparent procedure in relation to (i) requests to join additional parties to an arbitration (Article 7); (ii) claims made in an arbitration involving multiple parties (Article 8); and (iii) claims arising out of more than one contract in a single arbitration (Article 9).

10. Requests for joinder of a party are similar to Requests for Arbitration (Article 7). When a request for joinder is submitted, the additional party becomes a party to the arbitration and may raise pleas pursuant to Article 6(3) of the Rules. It is important to be aware of the timing for such joinder, as no additional party may be joined after the confirmation or appointment of an arbitrator, unless the parties and the additional party agree otherwise. Thus, a party to an arbitration wishing to join an additional party must file its request for joinder before any arbitrator is confirmed or appointed under the Rules.

Consolidation of arbitrations

11. The Court may consolidate two or more pending arbitrations at the request of a party, provided that any of the three situations set out in Article 10 of the Rules exist. Factors that the Court may take into account include whether one or more arbitrators have been confirmed or appointed in more than one of the arbitration and, if so, whether the same or different persons have been confirmed or appointed.

Arbitral tribunal

12. The Court requires all potential arbitrators to complete and sign a Statement of Acceptance, Availability, Impartiality and Independence (Article 11(2)). Recent additions to this Statement concern arbitrators' availability and impartiality.

13. Potential arbitrators must indicate the number of arbitrations in which they currently act, specifying whether they act as president, sole arbitrator, co-arbitrator or as parties' counsel, as well as their availability over the next 12 to 18 months. This is intended to encourage prospective arbitrators to focus on their duty to conduct arbitrations in an expeditious and cost-effective manner (Article 22).

14. Furthermore, arbitrators are obliged to act at all times in an impartial and independent manner (Articles 11 and 22(4)).

Case management techniques

15. A report of the ICC Commission on Arbitration and ADR entitled Controlling Time and Costs in Arbitration and available on the ICC website, provides a compilation of techniques widely acknowledged to be a valuable aid to controlling time and costs in a manner proportionate with the value and/or complexity of an arbitration. The second edition of the report relates to the 2012 Rules and can be used in conjunction with those Rules.

16. Articles 22 and 24 of the Rules and Appendix V thereto include provisions to encourage the effective management of the arbitration. The parties must comply with directions issued by arbitral tribunals.

Advance on Costs

17. A provisional advance is fixed by the Secretary General upon receipt of the Request for Arbitration (Article 36(1)). It is intended to cover the costs of the arbitration until the Terms of Reference have been drawn up.

18. Payment of the provisional advance will be considered as a partial payment by the claimant of the advance on costs subsequently fixed by the Court. Transmission of the file to the arbitral tribunal, once constituted, will be subject to prior payment of the provisional advance (Article 16).

19. The advance on costs is intended to cover the arbitral tribunal's fees and expenses, as well as the ICC administrative expenses (Article 36 and Article 1(4) of Appendix III). The advance on costs may be readjusted by the Court if the development of the arbitration so requires (Article 36(5)).

20. The parties will be invited to pay the advance on costs in accordance with paragraphs 2, 3, 4 and 5 of Article 36 of the Rules. The payment must originate from a party to the case in which the payment has been requested. All bank charges must be borne by the party making the payment.

Costs of arbitration

21. Arbitral tribunals may make decisions as to costs, except for those to be fixed by the Court, and order payment thereof at any time during the proceedings (Article 37(3)).

22. In making decisions as to costs, the arbitral tribunal may take into account such circumstances as it considers relevant, including the extent to which each party has conducted the arbitration in an expeditious and cost effective manner (Article 37(5)).

23. If the parties withdraw their claims or the arbitration terminates before the rendering of a final award, the Court shall fix the fees and expenses of the arbitrators and the ICC administrative expenses. If the parties have not agreed upon the allocation of the costs of the arbitration or other relevant issues with respect to costs, such matters shall be decided by the arbitral tribunal (Article 37(6)). In case the arbitral tribunal is not yet constituted at the time of the withdrawal, any party may request the Court to proceed with the constitution of the arbitral tribunal so that it may make decisions as to costs.

Closing of the proceedings and scrutiny of awards

24. An arbitral tribunal should declare the proceedings closed as soon as possible after the last hearing or the last authorized submission filed in relation to matters to

be decided in an award, whether final or otherwise (Article 27). Upon doing so, the arbitral tribunal must inform the Secretariat and the parties of the date by which it expects to submit the draft award for the Court's scrutiny (Article 33).

25. The scrutiny process carried out by the Court with the assistance of its Secretariat is a unique and thorough procedure designed to ensure that all awards are of the best possible quality and are more likely to be more enforced by state courts. All draft awards undergo a three-step review process, starting with the counsel of the team in charge of the arbitration that has followed the proceedings since the inception of the arbitration, followed by review by myself, the Deputy Secretary General, the General Counsel, or the Managing Counsel, before being submitted for the Court's scrutiny. For certain arbitrations, generally those involving state parties or dissenting opinions, a Court member will draft a report with recommendations on the draft award.

ICC International Centre for ADR

26. Parties are free to settle their dispute amicably at any time during an arbitration. The parties may wish to consider conducting an amicable dispute resolution procedure pursuant to the ICC Mediation Rules, which in addition to mediation, also allow for the use of other amicable settlement procedures. ICC can assist the parties in finding a suitable mediator. Further information is available from the ICC International Centre for ADR at +33 1 49 53 30 53 or adr@iccwbo.org or www.iccadr.org.

ICC International Centre for Expertise

27. If a party requires the assistance of an expert, the ICC International Centre for Expertise ("Centre") can, upon request, propose experts with a wide range of specialisations. The fee for this service is US$ 2,500. Further information is available from the Centre at +33 1 49 53 30 53 or expertise@iccwbo.org or www.iccexpertise.org.

Contact with the Secretariat

28. Finally, the parties and/or their legal representatives are encouraged to communicate with the team in charge of the arbitration. Alternatively, the parties may communicate with the management, namely the Secretary General, the Deputy Secretary General, the General Counsel or the Managing Counsel, should they have any queries or comments at any moment before or during the proceedings.

29. At the end of the arbitration you will be invited to complete an evaluation. Your answers will be confidential and will allow us to evaluate and improve the quality of our services.

APPENDIX 5

SECRETARIAT'S NOTE ON ARTICLE 36(4) OF THE 2012 ICC RULES OF ARBITRATION

1. The International Court of Arbitration of the International Chamber of Commerce ("Court") fixes advances on costs to cover the fees and expenses of the arbitral tribunal and the ICC administrative expenses ("advance on costs").

2. This Note provides information on how the Court will fix advances on costs when:
   (i) one or more additional parties are joined in an arbitration (Article 7); and/or
   (ii) claims are made between multiple parties (Article 8).

3. In such situations, the Court shall fix the advance on costs and the respective portions thereof to be paid by each party (Article 36(4)).

4. In all other situations, the Court shall fix the advance on costs which shall be payable by each side in equal shares (Article 36(2)). The Court may fix separate advances on costs where counterclaims are submitted by Respondents, in which case, each of the parties shall pay the advance on costs corresponding to its claims (Article 36(3)).

Advance on costs

5. The Court may fix one or more advances on costs where claims are made under Articles 7 and 8 of the Rules. However, in most situations including those outlined at (i) and (ii) above, the Court is likely to fix one advance on costs.

6. We invite you to refer to the Cost Calculator on the ICC website www.iccarbitration.org to estimate the advance on costs.

7. Where the Court apportions the advance on costs, it determines the amount that each party must pay towards the advance on costs. When doing so, the Court will ensure that a party shall only contribute towards the claim or claims in which it is involved ("Claims"). The amount payable by each party shall be proportionate to the value of those Claims in relation to the total amount in dispute in the arbitration.

Apportionment of the advance on costs

8. The Court will apportion the advance on costs by:
   (i) calculating advances for each set of Claims ("Partial Advance");
   (ii) adding up the Partial Advances; and

(iii) calculating the percentage that each Partial Advance forms as part of the total amount ("Percentage").

9. Such apportionment generally will not increase the advance on costs fixed by the Court.

Calculation of the amount to be paid by each party

10. The Percentages are applied to the advance on costs to calculate the respective amounts payable by each party in relation to each set of Claims ("Amounts Payable").

11. The Amounts Payable by a party are then added together to form that party's share of the advance on costs.

12. Please inform the Secretariat of any agreement between some or all of the parties in relation to payment of the advance on costs so that each party's share of the advance on costs may be calculated accordingly. Absent any such agreement, if the Court apportions the advance on costs, it will determine the apportionment as follows:

(i) For each set of Claims, the portion shall be payable fifty percent by the parties bringing said Claims and fifty percent by the parties defending said Claims.

(ii) If there are multiple parties either bringing or defending each set of Claims, the co-claimants or co-respondents respectively will bear their fifty percent share equally.

13. Should a party fail to pay one or more of the Amounts Payable that form its share of the advance on costs, the Secretariat will invite the other parties involved in that set of Claims to pay the outstanding Amounts Payable.

APPENDIX 6

SECRETARIAT'S NOTE ON ICC EMERGENCY ARBITRATOR PROCEEDINGS (2012 RULES)

This Note emphasizes some essential elements that the emergency arbitrator should take into account throughout the proceedings under the Emergency Arbitration Provisions in the Rules of Arbitration of the International Chamber of Commerce ("Rules").

Request for Arbitration

1. The President of the International Court of Arbitration of the International Chamber of Commerce ("President") will terminate the emergency arbitrator proceedings if a Request for Arbitration has not been received by the Secretariat within 10 days of the Secretariat's receipt of the Application, unless the emergency arbitrator determines that a longer period of time is necessary (Article 1(6) of Appendix V).

Procedural timetable

2. The Emergency Arbitrator's first task is to establish a procedural timetable as soon as possible, normally within two days from the transmission of the file to the emergency arbitrator (Article 5 of Appendix V).

3. In doing so, the emergency arbitrator must ensure that the responding party is granted time to comment on the Application.

The Order

4. The Order must be made no later than 15 days from the date on which the file was transmitted to the emergency arbitrator (Article 6(4) of Appendix V). The President may extend the time limit pursuant to a reasoned request or on the President's own initiative if he decides it is necessary to do so (Article 6(4) of Appendix V).

5. As emergency arbitrator proceedings do not provide for scrutiny of any Order rendered, the ICC Emergency Arbitrator Order Checklist may serve as guidance to the emergency arbitrator in drafting the Order, particularly regarding decisions on jurisdiction, the place or language of the emergency arbitrator proceedings.

6. When notifying the Order to the parties, the emergency arbitrator must send to the Secretariat two originals of the Order. The Secretariat will retain such originals in its records together with the correspondence and other decisions taken by the President and the Court.

Acting as arbitrator

7. An emergency arbitrator must not act as an arbitrator in any arbitration relating to the dispute that gave rise to the Application (Article 2(6) Appendix V).

APPENDIX 7

EMERGENCY ARBITRATOR'S STATEMENT OF ACCEPTANCE, AVAILABILITY, IMPARTIALITY AND INDEPENDENCE (2012 RULES)

Case No. ____________________

Family Name(s): ____________________ Given Name(s): ____________________

Please tick all relevant boxes.

1. ACCEPTANCE

Acceptance

☐ I agree to serve as emergency arbitrator under and in accordance with the 2012 ICC Rules of Arbitration ("Rules"). I am aware that (i) other candidates may have been contacted by the ICC to serve as emergency arbitrator in this case and (ii) the urgency of the proceedings may require the ICC to appoint another candidate before receiving my response. I confirm that I am familiar with the Rules, in particular Article 29 and Appendix V. I accept that my remuneration will be in accordance with Article 7 of Appendix V.

Non-Acceptance

☐ I decline to serve as emergency arbitrator in this case. (*If you tick here, simply date and sign the form without completing any other sections.*)

2. AVAILABILITY

☐ I confirm, on the basis of the information presently available to me, that I can devote the time necessary to conduct this emergency arbitrator proceeding diligently, efficiently and in accordance with the time limit in Article 6(4) of Appendix V to the Rules, subject to any extensions granted by the President. I understand that it is important to complete these proceedings as promptly as reasonably practicable. Furthermore, I am not aware of any commitments which might preclude me from completing the emergency arbitrator proceeding on time, or from devoting to them the attention that they require.

3. INDEPENDENCE and IMPARTIALITY

(Tick one box and provide details below and/or, if necessary, on a separate sheet.)

In deciding which box to tick, you should take into account, having regard to Article 2(4) of Appendix V to the Rules, whether there exists any past or present relationship, direct or indirect, between you and any of the parties to this emergency arbitrator proceeding, their related entities or their lawyers or other representatives, whether financial, professional or of any other kind. Any doubt must be resolved in favour of disclosure. Any disclosure should be complete and specific, identifying *inter alia* relevant dates (both start and end dates), financial arrangements, details of companies and individuals, and all other relevant information.

☐ Nothing to disclose: I am impartial and independent and intend to remain so. To the best of my knowledge, and having made due enquiry, there are no facts or circumstances, past or present, that I should disclose because they might be of such a nature as to call into question my independence in the eyes of any of the parties to this emergency arbitrator proceeding and no circumstances that could give rise to reasonable doubts as to my impartiality.

☐ Acceptance with disclosure: I am impartial and independent and intend to remain so. However, mindful of my obligation to disclose any facts or circumstances which might be of such a nature as to call into question my independence in the eyes of any of the parties to this emergency arbitrator proceeding or that could give rise to reasonable doubts as to my impartiality, I draw attention to the matters below and/or on the attached sheet.

Date:______________ Signature: ______________________________

Disclaimer: The information requested in this form will be considered by the ICC for its Dispute Resolution Services, and will be stored in case management database systems. Pursuant to the French Law on "Informatique et Libertés" of 6 January 1978, particularly Articles 32 and 40, you may access this information and ask for rectification by writing to the Court's Secretariat.

APPENDIX 8

SECRETARIAT'S ICC EMERGENCY ARBITRATOR ORDER CHECKLIST (2012 RULES)

Case No. ________

Disclaimer: This Checklist is intended to provide emergency arbitrators acting under the ICC Rules of Arbitration with guidance in addition to the Note on ICC Emergency Arbitrator Proceedings. It does not constitute an exhaustive, mandatory or otherwise binding document. It should not be thought to reflect the opinion of the President of the International Court of Arbitration of the International Chamber of Commerce ("Court"), the Court or its Secretariat, but is simply intended to facilitate the emergency arbitrators' mission.

1. General

☐ A. ICC case reference number mentioned in full on front page.

☐ B. Document clearly identified in its title as an Order.

☐ C. Paragraphs numbered.

☐ D. Pages numbered.

☐ E. Table of contents included (unless Order is short and does not need one).

☐ F. Abbreviations defined and used consistently.

☐ G. Preferably translations of quotations in languages other than the language(s) of the Order.

☐ H. Quotation of entire arbitration agreement(s) and record of any agreed amendments to the arbitration agreement(s)

☐ I. Quotation of relevant choice-of-law clause.

2. Identification of the parties, their representatives and the emergency arbitrator

☐ A. Parties' complete addresses and correct names. Clarify the identity of any parties to the emergency arbitrator proceedings.

☐ B. Addresses of parties' representatives.

☐ C. Emergency arbitrator's address.

3. History of the emergency arbitrator proceedings

☐ A. Summary of all procedural steps to date (e.g. Application, appointment of the emergency arbitrator, transmission of the file to the emergency arbitrator, timetable for the emergency arbitrator proceedings).

☐ B. Place of the emergency arbitrator proceedings (decision of the President if applicable).

☐ C. Indication of means used by the emergency arbitrator for notification of the Order (Article 6(5) Appendix V) and clarification that the Order was made by the emergency arbitrator in due time (Article 6(4) Appendix V).

☐ D. Time extension for rendering the Order.

4. Admissibility/jurisdiction

☐ A. Indication of the President's decisions regarding Article 1(5) of the Appendix V.

☐ B. Admissibility pursuant to Article 29(1): Emergency Measures are so urgent that they cannot await the constitution of the arbitral tribunal.

☐ C. Compliance of the Application with Articles 29(5) and 29(6):

☐ i. parties are signatories/successors to such signatories;

☐ ii. arbitration agreement(s) concluded after 1 January 2012;

☐ iii. no agreement to opt out;

☐ iv. no agreement to resort to other pre-arbitral procedure for urgent conservatory or interim measures.

☐ D. Any other issue regarding admissibility/jurisdiction.

5. Cost of the emergency arbitrator proceedings (Articles 7(3) and 7(4), Appendix V)

☐ i. US$ 40 000 or any amount as increased pursuant to Article 7(2), Appendix V.

☐ ii. Parties' legal costs.

☐ iii. Allocation of the costs of the emergency arbitrator proceedings.

6. Dispositive section, place of the emergency arbitrator proceedings, date, signature

☐ A. Order contains a dispositive section mentioning all decisions made (including the decision on admissibility and jurisdiction) and nothing more.

☐ B. Order deals with all Emergency Measures sought by the applicant (which should be stated clearly).

☐ C. State in the dispositive section of the Order that all other requests are rejected.

☐ D. Indication of any conditions for the Order, including appropriate security, if any (Article 6(7), Appendix V).

☐ E. After the dispositive section, add the date on which the Order is made and the signature in the following manner:

Place of the emergency arbitrator proceedings: City (Country)

Date: ______________ Signature: ________________________________

APPENDIX 9

SECRETARIAT'S NOTE TO THE ARBITRAL TRIBUNAL ON THE CONDUCT OF THE ARBITRATION (2012 RULES)

This Note is intended to provide the arbitral tribunal with information concerning the conduct of arbitration under the 2012 ICC Rules of Arbitration ("Rules"). It incorporates notes previously published separately on (i) personal and arbitral tribunal expenses, (ii) VAT, taxes, charges and imposts applicable to arbitrators' fees, and (iii) appointment, duties and remuneration of administrative secretaries. For previous versions of the Rules, contact the Secretariat of the International Court of Arbitration of the International Chamber of Commerce ("Secretariat").

Time limits under the Rules

1. Rapid resolution of arbitrations is a priority of the International Court of Arbitration of the International Chamber of Commerce ("Court"). Arbitrators should devote the time and effort necessary to conduct the arbitration within the requirements of the Rules. The Rules contain strict time limits, in particular:

- Terms of Reference: must be established within two months from the transmission of the file to the arbitral tribunal (Article 23(2)).
- Case management conference: must be convened with the parties when drawing up the Terms of Reference or as soon as possible thereafter (Article 24(1)).
- Procedural timetable: must be established during or immediately following the case management conference and transmitted to the Court and the parties (Article 24(2)).
- Closing of the proceedings: must be done as soon as possible after the last hearing concerning matters to be decided in an award, or the filing of the last authorised submissions concerning such matters (Article 27).
- Date for submission of draft awards: must be indicated to the Secretariat and the parties when the arbitral tribunal closes the proceedings in relation to the award (Article 27).
- Final award: must be rendered within the time limit fixed by the Court based upon the procedural timetable or, if the Court does not fix such time limit, within six months from the date of the last signature or notification of the approval of the Terms of Reference. (Article 30(1)). The Court expects sole arbitrators to

submit draft awards within two months and three-member arbitral tribunals to submit draft awards within three months of the last hearing concerning matters to be decided in such award or the filing of the last authorised submission concerning such matters, whichever is later (Article 27).

Conduct of the arbitration and techniques for controlling time and costs

2. The Rules require the arbitral tribunal and the parties to make every effort to conduct the arbitration in an expeditious and cost-effective manner, having regard to the complexity and value of the dispute (Article 22(1)).

3. In order to ensure effective case management, the arbitral tribunal, after consulting the parties, may adopt such procedural measures as it considers appropriate, provided that they are not contrary to any agreement of the parties (Article 22(2)). The arbitral tribunal should consider the case management techniques referred to in Appendix IV to the Rules and the report of the ICC Commission on Arbitration and ADR entitled *Controlling Time and Costs in Arbitration*, available on the ICC website.

4. Although extensions of the time limits indicated above may be granted by the Court, in setting an arbitrator's fees, the Court considers the diligence and efficiency of the arbitrator, the time spent, the rapidity of the proceedings, the complexity of the dispute and the timeliness of the submission of the draft award when fixing arbitrators' fees (Article 2(2) of Appendix III).

5. The Court can replace an arbitrator when it decides that such arbitrator is not fulfilling his or her functions within the prescribed time limits (Article 15(2)).

ICC International Centre for ADR ("Centre")

6. Parties are free to settle their dispute amicably prior to or at any time during an arbitration. Where appropriate, arbitrators may wish to remind the parties about the Mediation Rules of the International Chamber of Commerce, which, in addition to mediation, also allow for the use of other amicable settlement procedures. The Centre can also assist the parties in finding a suitable mediator.

7. If the assistance of an expert is required, the Centre can, upon request, propose experts from a wide range of specializations. This service is provided free of charge to arbitrators.

8. Further information is available from the Centre at +33 1 49 53 30 53 or adr@iccwbo.org or www.iccadr.org.

Replacement of arbitrators

9. When an arbitrator is replaced, the reconstituted arbitral tribunal shall invite the parties to comment and then determine if and to what extent prior proceedings shall be repeated (Article 15(4)).

10. When fixing the arbitral tribunal's fees, the Court generally deducts the fees of the previous arbitrator from the fees of the replacement arbitrator.

11. Subsequent to the closing of the proceeding, taking into account the views of the remaining arbitrators and the parties, instead of replacing an arbitrator who has died or been removed by the Court pursuant to Article 15(1) or 15(2), the Court may

decide, when it considers it appropriate, that the remaining arbitrator shall continue the arbitration (Article 15(5)).

ICC Award Checklist ("Checklist")

12. The Checklist is intended to provide arbitrators with guidance when drafting awards and is not an exhaustive, mandatory or otherwise binding document. It should not be thought to reflect the opinion of the members of the Court or its Secretariat, but is intended to facilitate the arbitrators' mission. It may not be published or used for any purpose other than the conduct of ICC arbitrations. The Checklist is not exhaustive of issues that may be raised by the Court under Article 33 of the Rules.

Originals of Terms of Reference and Awards

13. An original of the Terms of Reference signed by the parties and the arbitral tribunal must be provided to each party, each member of the arbitral tribunal and the Secretariat. The arbitral tribunal must verify with the parties the number of originals they need. When the Terms of Reference are submitted to the Court for approval (Article 23(3)), the necessary number of originals must be prepared.

14. Similarly, each party, each arbitrator and the Secretariat receive an original of the awards signed by the arbitrators after approval of the drafts by the Court. The arbitral tribunal must thus provide the Secretariat with the required number of originals (unbound) to be notified to the parties.

Advance on costs

15. The advance on costs is intended to cover the arbitral tribunal's fees and arbitration related expenses, as well as the ICC administrative expenses (Article 36 and Article 1(4) of Appendix III).

16. The advance on costs may be readjusted by the Court if the development of the arbitration so requires (Article 36). The arbitral tribunal should inform the Secretariat of any developments in the value and complexity of the arbitration or any other issues it considers relevant.

17. The arbitral tribunal should clarify with the parties whether they will be directly responsible for the costs of any hearing or whether such costs should be included in the arbitration-related expenses. If hearing costs will be included in the arbitration-related expenses, the arbitral tribunal should provide the Secretariat with an estimate of such costs. Thereafter, the Secretariat will examine whether it is appropriate to invite the Court to reconsider the advance on costs.

The arbitral tribunal's fees

18. The arbitral tribunal is encouraged to consult the Cost Calculator on the ICC website (www.iccarbitration.org). Fees are fixed exclusively by the Court. Separate fee arrangements between the parties and arbitrators are not permitted.

19. The Court fixes arbitrators' fees at the end of the arbitration, although advances on fees may be granted upon completion of concrete steps in the arbitration.

20. In setting an arbitrator's fees, the Court considers the diligence and efficiency of the arbitrator, the time spent, the rapidity of the proceedings, the complexity of the dispute

and the timeliness of the submission of draft award, so as to arrive at a figure within the time limits specified or, in exceptional circumstances (Article 37(2)), at a figure higher or lower than those limits (Article 2(2) of Appendix III to the Rules). The Court does not consider the arbitrator's usual hourly rates or remuneration.

21. When there is a three-member arbitral tribunal, arbitrators should consider the time spent and the work done by each arbitrator and inform the Secretariat of their opinion of a fair and appropriate allocation of the fees for each arbitrator. Unless the Secretariat is advised in writing that the arbitral tribunal has agreed to a different allocation, the Court normally fixes the arbitrators' fees so that the president receives 40% of the total fees and each co-arbitrator receives 30%. The Court may decide upon a different allocation based on the circumstances. Unless otherwise agreed, the same allocation will apply to any advances on fees granted by the Court.

22. Under French tax laws, the ICC is required to declare the amount of fees, including advances on fees, paid to any arbitrator during each calendar year, as well as any expenses reimbursed during the same period.

Personal and arbitral tribunal expenses (as of 1 September 2013)

How to submit a request for expenses

23. The Secretariat will reimburse expenses and pay *per diem* allowances only upon receipt of a request in a readily comprehensible form including a cover page listing each payment claimed and the reason for it. Expense reimbursement claims must be supported by original receipts. This is necessary so that the Secretariat can carry out its accounting responsibilities and, from time to time, provide the parties with comprehensive statements of expenses incurred by arbitrators.

When to submit a request for expenses

24. Arbitrators should submit their requests for the reimbursement of expenses and/or the payment of *per diem* allowances, together with any required supporting documentation as specified below, as soon as possible after expenses are incurred. This will help ensure that the advance on costs paid by the parties is adequate to cover the costs of the arbitration.

25. All requests for the reimbursement of expenses and/or the payment of *per diem* allowances relating to any period prior to the submission of the draft final award must be provided at the latest when the draft final award is submitted to the Secretariat. Three-member arbitral tribunals should co-ordinate their submission of requests for reimbursement of expenses and/or payment of *per diem* allowances in order to ensure that they reach the Secretariat no later than the draft final award. Requests for the reimbursement of expenses and/or the payment of *per diem* allowances submitted after the Court has approved the final award will not be taken into account by the Court when fixing the costs of the arbitration and will not be paid save in exceptional circumstances as decided by the Secretary General.

26. In the event of the withdrawal of all claims or the termination of the arbitration before the rendering of a final award, all requests for the reimbursement of expenses and/or the payment of *per diem* allowances must be submitted within the time limit granted by the Secretariat. Requests for the reimbursement of expenses and/or the

payment of *per diem* allowances submitted after the date the Court fixes the costs of arbitration will not be taken into account by the Court and will not be paid.

Travel expenses

27. If required to travel for the purpose of an ICC arbitration, an arbitrator will be reimbursed for the actual travel expenses he or she incurs travelling from and returning to his or her usual place of business as indicated on the *curriculum vitae* filed for the relevant ICC arbitration. Travel expenses will be reimbursed in accordance with paragraphs 28 to 30.

28. A request for reimbursement of travel expenses must be accompanied by the originals of all receipts claimed or other proper substantiation if receipts are unavailable. Travel expenses that are not fully and comprehensively justified will not be reimbursed.

29. The reimbursement of travel expenses is subject to the following strict limits:

(a) Air travel: an airfare equivalent to the applicable standard business class airfare.
(b) Rail travel: the applicable first class train fare.
(c) Transport to and from airport(s) and/or train station(s): the applicable standard taxi fare.
(d) Travel by private car: a flat rate for every kilometre driven, plus all necessary actual parking and toll charges incurred. The flat rate is US$ 0.80 per kilometre.

30. Except for expenses claimed pursuant to paragraph 29(d) above, travel expenses will, where possible, be reimbursed in the same currency in which they were incurred. An arbitrator may alternatively request reimbursement in US dollars provided that the request is accompanied by a statement of the US dollar amount and evidence of the exchange rate (for example, a print out from www.oanda.com). The date for the currency conversion should be the date the expense was incurred.

Per diem allowance

31. In addition to travel expenses, an arbitrator will be paid a flat-rate *per diem* allowance in accordance with paragraphs 32 to 35 for every day of an ICC arbitration that he or she is required to spend outside his or her usual place of business as indicated on the *curriculum vitae* filed for the relevant ICC arbitration. The arbitrator is not required to submit receipts in order to claim the *per diem* allowance, but simply evidence of the travel for purposes of the arbitration.

32. If the arbitrator is not required to use overnight hotel accommodation, the flat-rate *per diem* allowance is US$ 400.

33. If the arbitrator is required to use overnight hotel accommodation, the flat-rate *per diem* allowance is US$ 1,200.

34. The applicable *per diem* allowance is deemed to cover fully all personal living expenses of whatever nature and of whatever actual value (other than travel expenses) incurred by an arbitrator. In particular, the applicable *per diem* allowance is deemed to cover, among other expenses, the total cost of:

- Accommodation (except where paragraph 32 above applies)
- Meals
- Laundry/ironing/dry cleaning and other housekeeping or similar services

- Inner-city transport
- Telephone calls, faxes, emails and other means of communication
- Gratuities

35. For the avoidance of doubt, no *per diem* allowance will be paid in respect of time spent by an arbitrator travelling to or from the relevant destination.

36. Since the *per diem* allowance is deemed to cover all personal living expenses incurred by an arbitrator while outside his or her usual place of business on ICC arbitration business, the Secretariat will not reimburse expenses over and above the applicable *per diem* allowance under any circumstances.

General office expenses and courier charges

37. General office expenses and overheads incurred in the ordinary course of business by an arbitrator or an arbitral tribunal in connection with an ICC arbitration will not be reimbursed. However, an arbitrator or an arbitral tribunal may request to be reimbursed at cost for any courier, photocopying, facsimile or telephone charges incurred for the purposes of an ICC arbitration, provided such request is accompanied by detailed receipts.

Advance payments on expenses

38. An arbitrator may request an advance payment of travel expenses and/or the applicable *per diem* allowance in accordance with paragraphs 27 to 36 above. If an advance is granted, the arbitrator must subsequently submit the relevant supporting documentation to the Secretariat, including all receipts and a statement of working days and nights spent outside of his or her usual place of business on ICC arbitration business.

VAT, taxes, charges and imposts applicable to arbitrators' fees (as of 13 October 2010)

39. Amounts paid to an arbitrator do not include any possible value added taxes (VAT) or other taxes or charges and imposts applicable to the arbitrator's fees (Article 2(13) of Appendix III). Parties have a duty to pay any such taxes or charges; however, the recovery of any such charges or taxes is a matter solely between the arbitrator and the parties.

40. ICC nonetheless offers arbitrators subject to VAT and other taxes, charges and imposts (hereinafter "VAT"), who expressly request in writing, a service allowing them to have the funds corresponding to their estimate of the VAT due on their fees and expenses (hereinafter "fees") administered by ICC.

41. This service is totally separate from, and has no effect on, the procedure for paying advances as set out in the Rules. Should the parties fail to pay the VAT on the arbitrators' fees, this cannot be invoked by the arbitrators before the Court, for instance as a ground for suspending the arbitral proceedings.

42. Any arbitrator subject to VAT may take advantage of this service. ICC acts as the 'depositary' of the funds, receives funds from parties who have been instructed to this effect by an arbitrator, and makes the payments corresponding to the VAT at the arbitrator's request.

43. The initiative of requesting that a VAT account be opened, of calling advances for the payment of VAT on fees ("VAT advance") and paying arbitrators on the basis of the amounts deposited lies solely with the arbitrators.

44. This service is available to arbitrators from any country.

45. The VAT advance is only administered in US dollars and does not yield interest for the parties or the arbitrators.

46. It is the arbitrators' sole responsibility to ensure that the procedure described below complies with the tax law provisions applicable to the exercise of their profession as arbitrators, including the payment of their fees. Arbitrators are encouraged to check the basis on which they should calculate the amount of VAT due.

47. The ICC acts exclusively as depositary and is not in a position to advise the arbitrators on any tax law.

48. *Procedure*

Step 1: Request for VAT account
Any arbitrator wishing to use this service shall inform the Secretariat in writing and request ICC to act as depositary for the sums paid by the parties as an advance on the VAT due on the arbitrators' fees.

Step 2: Estimation of amounts
The arbitrator determines the amount of VAT on his or her fees in light of the rules that apply at the place where he or she is taxable.

Arbitrators may use the Cost Calculator on the ICC website (www.iccarbitration.org) to estimate the amount of the fees that may be payable. They are however reminded that the proportions in which the total amount of the fees is divided between the members of the arbitral tribunal (40% for the President, 30% for each co-arbitrator) are given merely as a guide and may be changed by the Court.

If, in the course of an arbitration, the amount of the advance is increased pursuant to a decision of the Court, this step may be repeated.

Step 3: Disclosure of the estimated amounts of VAT
The arbitrator fixes a time limit in this respect and requests the parties:

- to pay the VAT advance in US dollars
- bear any banking charges associated with the payment
- use the following banking instructions:

Beneficiary (*Account holder*):	International Chamber of Commerce 33–43 avenue du Président Wilson 75116 Paris, France
Bank of Beneficiary:	UBS AG Bahnhofstrasse 45 8098 Zurich Switzerland
IBAN:	CH44 0024 0240 2245 3463 G
Code SWIFT/BIC:	UBSWCHZH80A
Reference of the case:	*****/***/VAT Arbitrators Claimant(s)/Respondent(s)

The payment must originate from a party to the case in which the payment has been requested.

The arbitrator must also inform the Secretariat of the substance of this request.

If the president calls for a VAT advance on behalf of the members of the arbitral tribunal subject to VAT, he or she shall inform the Secretariat of the breakdown of this advance arbitrator-by-arbitrator.

Step 4: Acknowledgement of payments and administration
The Secretariat confirms to the arbitrator and the parties the receipt of the amounts paid by the parties.

In the absence of communication to the arbitrator by the Secretariat of any receipt of payments on the advance on VAT made by the parties, it is up to the arbitrator to renew his or her request to the parties and to fix a time limit in this respect.

ICC administers the VAT advance on behalf of the arbitrator.

Step 5: Payments to the arbitrator
When drawing up his or her invoice, the arbitrator requests ICC to pay the amount corresponding to the VAT on the fees due by the parties. This applies at the time of the final award, but also in the event that the Court decides to pay an advance on fees to arbitrators who reside in countries where, under local tax law, VAT becomes payable to the tax authorities when fees are paid in advance.

Payments are made to the arbitrators by ICC on behalf of the parties and within the limits of the VAT advances already provided.

Step 6: Balance of account
At the end of the arbitration proceedings the Secretariat seeks instructions from the arbitrator for closing the VAT advance. On the basis of the information provided by the arbitrator and in accordance with his or her instructions, the Secretariat closes the VAT account and returns to the parties any amounts remaining from the VAT advance deposited with ICC.

After advising the arbitrator, ICC may close the account if no balance remains. The account will be closed even if the parties have not paid any additional VAT advance requested by the arbitrator.

Appointment, duties and remuneration of administrative secretaries (as of 1 August 2012)

49. The ICC Rules of Arbitration ("Rules") are silent as to the appointment, duties and remuneration of arbitral tribunal administrative secretaries or other assistants ("Administrative Secretaries"). This Note replaces the Secretariat's previous note on the same subject. It sets out the policy and practice of the ICC International Court of Arbitration ("Court") and its Secretariat regarding the engagement of Administrative Secretaries by arbitral tribunals. It applies with respect to any Administrative Secretary appointed on or after 1 August 2012. Any arbitral tribunal proposing to appoint an Administrative Secretary shall provide the parties with a copy of this Note.

Appointment

50. Administrative Secretaries can provide a useful service to the parties and arbitral tribunals in ICC arbitration. While principally engaged to assist three-member arbitral tribunals, an Administrative Secretary may also assist a sole arbitrator. Administrative Secretaries can be appointed at any time during an arbitration.

51. If an arbitral tribunal envisages the appointment of an Administrative Secretary, it shall consider carefully whether in the circumstances of that particular case such an appointment would be appropriate.

52. Administrative Secretaries must satisfy the same independence and impartiality requirements as those which apply to arbitrators under the Rules. ICC staff members are not permitted to serve as Administrative Secretaries.

53. There is no formal process for the appointment of an Administrative Secretary. However, before any steps are made to appoint an Administrative Secretary, the arbitral tribunal shall inform the parties of its proposal to do so. For this purpose, the arbitral tribunal shall submit to the parties the proposed Administrative Secretary's *curriculum vitae*, together with a declaration of independence and impartiality, an undertaking on the part of the Administrative Secretary to act in accordance with the present Note and an undertaking on the part of the arbitral tribunal to ensure that this obligation on the part of the Administrative Secretary shall be met.

54. The arbitral tribunal shall make clear to the parties that they may object to such proposal and an Administrative Secretary shall not be appointed if a party has raised an objection.

Duties

55. Administrative Secretaries act upon the arbitral tribunal's instructions and under its strict supervision. The arbitral tribunal shall, at all times, be responsible for the Administrative Secretary's conduct in relation to the arbitration.

56. An Administrative Secretary may perform organizational and administrative tasks such as:

- transmitting documents and communications on behalf of the arbitral tribunal;
- organizing and maintaining the arbitral tribunal's file and locating documents;
- organizing hearings and meetings;
- attending hearings, meetings and deliberations; taking notes or minutes or keeping timc;
- conducting legal or similar research; and
- proof-reading and checking citations, dates and cross-references in procedural orders and awards as well as correcting typographical, grammatical or calculation errors.

57. Under no circumstances may the arbitral tribunal delegate decision-making functions to an Administrative Secretary. Nor should the arbitral tribunal rely on the Administrative Secretary to perform any essential duties of an arbitrator.

58. The Administrative Secretary may not act, or be required to act, in such a manner as to prevent or discourage direct communications among the arbitrators, between the arbitral tribunal and the parties, or between the arbitral tribunal and the Secretariat.

59. A request by an arbitral tribunal to an Administrative Secretary to prepare written notes or memoranda shall in no circumstances release the arbitral tribunal from its duty personally to review the file and/or to draft any decision of the arbitral tribunal.

60. When in doubt about which tasks may be performed by an Administrative Secretary, the arbitral tribunal or the Administrative Secretary should contact the Secretariat.

Remuneration

61. With the exception of the Administrative Secretary's reasonable personal disbursements as provided under point 64, the engagement of an Administrative Secretary should not pose any additional financial burden on the parties. Accordingly, the arbitral tribunal may not look to the parties for the reimbursement of any costs associated with an Administrative Secretary beyond the scope prescribed in this Note.

62. Any remuneration payable to the Administrative Secretary shall be paid by the arbitral tribunal out of the total funds available for the fees of all arbitrators, such that the fees of the Administrative Secretary will not increase the total costs of the arbitration.

63. In no circumstances should the arbitral tribunal seek from the parties any form of compensation for the Administrative Secretary's activity. Direct arrangements between the arbitral tribunal and the parties on the Administrative Secretary's fees are prohibited. Since the fees of the arbitral tribunal are established on an *ad valorem* basis, any compensation to be paid to the Administrative Secretary is deemed to be included in the arbitral tribunal's fees.

Disbursements

64. The arbitral tribunal may seek reimbursement from the parties of the Administrative Secretary's justified reasonable expenses for hearings and meetings.

APPENDIX 10

SECRETARIAT'S NOTE ON ADMINISTRATIVE ISSUES IN PROCEEDINGS UNDER THE 2012 ICC RULES OF ARBITRATION

Communications

1. Pursuant to Article 3(1) of the ICC Rules of Arbitration ("Rules"), parties and arbitrators must send copies of all written correspondence directly to all other parties, arbitrators and the Secretariat of the International Court of Arbitration of the International Chamber of Commerce ("Secretariat").

2. The Secretariat will generally send correspondence by email. As such, parties, their counsel and prospective arbitrators must provide the Secretariat with their email addresses.

3. Pursuant to the Rules, the Request for Arbitration (Article 4), the Answer and any counterclaims (Article 5), and any Request for Joinder (Article 7, 2012 Rules) must be sent to the Secretariat in hard copy as well as in electronic form. To the extent possible, the Secretariat should be provided with any other written documents in electronic form only, even in cases where the arbitral tribunal also requests hard copies.

Dispatch of materials to the ICC and customs fees

3. Materials sent to the ICC (correspondence, submissions, binders, tapes, CDs, etc.) must be sent exclusively as "Documentation". No other description should be indicated on the transportation slip or waybill. Generally, documentation is not subject to customs tax. Other material may be subject to tax, which varies according to the origin, content and weight of such material. Customs fees, if any, will increase the costs of arbitration.

Representation

4. If the parties foresee being represented by counsel, they must inform the Secretariat of the name and address of such counsel.

ICC International Centre for Expertise

5. If a party requires the assistance of an expert, the ICC International Centre for Expertise ("Centre") can, upon request, propose experts from a wide range of specializations.

The fee for this service is US$ 2 500. Further information is available from the Centre at + 33 1 49 53 30 53 or expertise@iccwbo.org or www.iccexpertise.org.

ICC Hearing Centre

6. The ICC Hearing Centre in Paris (France) is an integral part of ICC Services, a wholly-owned affiliate of the ICC. The ICC Hearing Centre offers flexible packages and a range of specialized facilities and services for hearings and meetings. Further information is available on our website at www.icchearingcentre.org.

7. By reserving a room at the ICC Hearing Centre for an ICC arbitration, parties and arbitrators accept that their contact details be communicated by the Secretariat to the ICC Hearing Centre for the needs of this booking only.

Post-arbitration services

8. Disbursements in connection with services requested after this arbitration is closed may be charged to the requesting party.

APPENDIX 11

SECRETARIAT'S ICC AWARD CHECKLIST (1998 AND 2012 RULES)

Disclaimer: This Checklist is intended to provide arbitrators acting under the ICC Rules of Arbitration with guidance when drafting Awards. It does not constitute an exhaustive, mandatory or otherwise binding document. It should not be thought to reflect the opinion of the members of the International Court of Arbitration of the International Chamber of Commerce or of its Secretariat, but is simply intended to facilitate the arbitrators' mission. Moreover, this Checklist is not exhaustive of issues that may be raised by the ICC Court.

Case No.: ________

1. General

☐ A. ICC case reference number mentioned in full on front page.

☐ B. Award clearly identified in its title as interim, partial, final or award by consent.

☐ C. Paragraphs numbered.

☐ D. Pages numbered.

☐ E. Table of contents included (unless award is short and does not need one).

☐ F. Abbreviations defined and used consistently.

☐ G. Translations of quotations in languages other than the language(s) of the arbitration.

☐ H. Indication of the applicable version of the ICC Rules of Arbitration (e.g. 1998 / 2012).

2. Identification of the parties, their representatives and the arbitrator(s)

☐ A. Parties' complete addresses and correct names. Clarify the identity of any parties to the arbitration that are different from the parties to the contract(s).

☐ B. Addresses of parties' representatives.

☐ C. Arbitrators' addresses.

3. Arbitration and choice-of-law agreements

☐ A. Quotation of entire arbitration agreement(s).

☐ B. Record of any agreed amendments to the arbitration agreement(s).

☐ C. Precise indication of the parties to and/or signatories of the arbitration agreement(s).

☐ D. Quotation of relevant choice-of-law clause.

4. History of the arbitral proceedings

☐ A. Summary of all procedural steps to date (e.g. Request for Arbitration, Answer, Terms of Reference, date of the case management conference (Article 24, 2012 Rules), procedural timetable, parties' submissions, hearing).

☐ B. Indication of the ICC Court's decisions regarding (if applicable):

- ☐ i. Article 6(2) (1998 Rules) / 6(4) (2012 Rules);
- ☐ ii. Place of arbitration;
- ☐ iii. Number of arbitrators.

☐ C. Description of the constitution of the arbitral tribunal (including confirmation or appointment decisions).

☐ D. If applicable, reference to the parties' agreement on an alternative method of nominating or appointing the president of the Arbitral Tribunal.

☐ E. Date of closing of the proceedings under Article 22(1) (1998 Rules) / 27 (2012 Rules) (for every award).

☐ F. Indication of the time limit for rendering the final award, including any extensions granted by the Court under Article 24(2) (1998 Rules) / 30(2) (2012 Rules) and the date on which it was granted.

It is recommended that all extensions granted by the Court and the date(s) on which they were granted be specified, especially when Paris is the place of arbitration.

☐ G. If there has been a prior Award, no need to repeat the procedural history set out in the prior Award, but simply:

- ☐ i. restate the information mentioned in sections 1, 2 and 3 above;
- ☐ ii. refer to the previous Award, the date on which it was notified to the parties by the Secretariat, the issues it decided, and the fact that its procedural background is incorporated by reference into the present Award;
- ☐ iii. describe the procedure subsequent to that set out in the previous Award.

5. Jurisdiction

☐ Wherever jurisdiction has been contested, or there is a non-participating party, or the ICC Court has made an Article 6(2) (1998 Rules) / 6(4) (2012 Rules) decision, the award should ordinarily include the Arbitral Tribunal's decision on jurisdiction or state why it is not necessary.

6. Costs of the Arbitration (Final Awards only)

☐ A. Costs of arbitration fixed by the ICC Court and each party's legal costs dealt with separately in both the body of the Award and in the dispositive section.

☐ B. Reference to Article 37 (1998 Rules) / 37(2012 Rules) and to the discretion to allocate costs of arbitration (Article 37(5), 2012 Rules) fixed by the Court and parties' legal costs, and fix the amount to be borne by each party.

7. Dispositive section, place of arbitration, date, signature

☐ A. Award contains a dispositive section mentioning all orders (including the decision on jurisdiction, if applicable) and nothing more.

☐ B. Award deals with all of the issues and parties' claims (which should be stated clearly and precisely somewhere in the Award and compared to the Terms of Reference), including the parties' most recent requests for relief, and decides nothing more than those issues and claims (state clearly if certain claims are reserved for one or more future Awards).

☐ C. State in the dispositive section of Final Awards that all other requests and claims are rejected (unless the nature of the Award makes this unnecessary).

☐ D. After the dispositive section, add the date on which the Award is made and the signatures in the following manner:

Place of arbitration: City (Country)

Date: __/__/____ ____________*[date must be later than the Court session at which the Award was approved and not earlier than when the last arbitrator signs]*

Signature(s):________________________

APPENDIX 12

SECRETARIAT'S NOTE ON CORRECTION AND INTERPRETATION OF ARBITRAL AWARDS (1998 AND 2012 RULES)

PROCEDURE UNDER ARTICLE 29 (1998 RULES) / 35 (2012 RULES)

Article 29 of the 1998 ICC Rules of Arbitration provides:

1. On its own initiative, the Arbitral Tribunal may correct a clerical, computational or typographical error, or any errors of similar nature contained in an Award, provided such correction is submitted for approval to the Court within 30 days of the date of such Award.

2. Any application of a party for the correction of an error of the kind referred to in Article 29(1), or for the interpretation of an Award, must be made to the Secretariat within 30 days of the receipt of the Award by such party, in a number of copies as stated in Article 3(1). After transmittal of the application to the Arbitral Tribunal, it shall grant the other party a short time limit, normally not exceeding 30 days, from the receipt of the application by that party to submit any comments thereon. If the Arbitral Tribunal decides to correct or interpret the Award, it shall submit its decision in draft form to the Court not later than 30 days following the expiration of the time limit for the receipt of any comments from the other party or within such other period as the Court may decide.

3. The decision to correct or to interpret the Award shall take the form of an addendum and shall constitute part of the Award. The provisions of Articles 25, 27 and 28 shall apply *mutatis mutandis*.

Furthermore, Article 2(7) of Appendix III provides:

In the case of an application under Article 29(2) of the Rules, the Court may fix an advance to cover additional fees and expenses of the Arbitral Tribunal and may subordinate the transmission of such application to the Arbitral Tribunal to the prior cash payment in full to the ICC of such advance. The Court shall fix at its discretion any possible fees of the arbitrator when approving the decision of the Arbitral Tribunal.

Article 35 of the 2012 ICC Rules of Arbitration provides:

1. On its own initiative, the arbitral tribunal may correct a clerical, computational or typographical error, or any errors of similar nature contained in an award, provided such correction is submitted for approval to the Court within 30 days of the date of such award.

2. Any application of a party for the correction of an error of the kind referred to in Article 35(1), or for the interpretation of an award, must be made to the Secretariat within 30 days of the receipt of the award by such party, in a number of copies as stated in Article 3(1). After transmittal of the application to the arbitral tribunal, the latter shall grant the other party a short time limit, normally not exceeding 30 days, from the receipt of the application by that party, to submit any comments thereon. The arbitral tribunal shall submit its decision on the application in draft form to the Court not later than 30 days following the expiration of the time limit for the receipt of any comments from the other party or within such other period as the Court may decide.

3. A decision to correct or to interpret the award shall take the form of an addendum and shall constitute part of the award. The provisions of Articles 31, 33 and 34 shall apply *mutatis mutandis*.

Furthermore Article 2(10) of Appendix III provides:

In the case of an application under Article 35(2) of the Rules [...], the Court may fix an advance to cover additional fees and expenses of the arbitral tribunal and additional ICC administrative expenses and may make the transmission of such application to the arbitral tribunal subject to the prior cash payment in full to the ICC of such advance. The Court shall fix at its discretion the costs of the procedure following an application [...], which shall include any possible fees of the arbitrator and ICC administrative expenses, when approving the decision of the arbitral tribunal.

Article 29(1) (1998 Rules) / 35(1) (2012 Rules)

If the arbitral tribunal decides to correct the award on its own initiative, it should inform the parties and the Secretariat of its intention to do so and grant the parties a short time limit to comment. The arbitral tribunal should submit the draft Addendum to the Court for scrutiny within 30 days of the date of the award.

Article 29(2) (1998 Rules) / 35(2) (2012 Rules)

Upon receipt of an Article 29(2) (1998 Rules) / 35(2) (2012 Rules) application, the Secretariat may submit the matter to the Court for it to consider whether, in view of the circumstances of the case, an advance to cover additional fees and expenses of the arbitral tribunal and additional ICC administrative expenses (Article 2(10), Appendix III, 2012 Rules) is warranted. Should the Court fix an additional advance, such advance must be paid before the Secretariat will transmit the application to the arbitral tribunal. Otherwise, the Secretariat will transmit the application directly to the arbitral tribunal. As such, the arbitral tribunal should not address an application until the Secretariat transmits it to them.

If the Court did not ask for an advance on costs at the time when the application was submitted to the Secretariat, it can, in exceptional circumstances, take a decision on costs at the time of the scrutiny and make the notification of the Addendum or the

Decision contingent upon the payment by one or both parties of the costs fixed by the Court.

Upon receipt of the application from the Secretariat the arbitral tribunal should grant the other parties a short time limit, normally not exceeding 30 days, for comments.

The arbitral tribunal should then submit its draft decision to the Court for scrutiny not later than 30 days following the expiration of the time limit granted for comments. Should the arbitral tribunal require an extension of such time limit, it should inform the Secretariat.

Depending upon the arbitral tribunal's decision, such decision can take one of four forms:

1. *Addendum*: if the arbitral tribunal decides to correct or interpret the award, as this shall constitute part of the award.
2. Decision: if the arbitral tribunal decides that the award does not need to be corrected or interpreted and does not take a decision on costs.
3. *Addendum* and Decision: if there are two or more applications and the arbitral tribunal decides to correct or interpret the award on the basis of one or more, but not all applications.
4. Decision and *Addendum* on Costs: if the arbitral tribunal decides that the award does not need to be corrected or interpreted but takes a decision on costs related to the application.

General considerations

All decisions should contain the reasons upon which they are based (Article 25(2) (1998 Rules) / 31(2) (2012 Rules)). They should also include operative conclusions ("*dispositif*") or a finding that the application is rejected. For further guidance about what should be included in the draft decision, see the ICC Checklist on Correction and Interpretation of Arbitral Awards. The Court will scrutinise the draft decision (Article 27 (1998 Rules) / 33 (2012 Rules)), and upon approval thereof it should be signed by the arbitral tribunal (Article 25(1) and (3) (1998 Rules) / 31(1) and (3) (2012 Rules)) and sent to the Secretariat for notification to the parties (Article 28 (1998 Rules) / 34 (2012 Rules).

In all cases the arbitral tribunal must first ensure that mandatory rules of law at the place of arbitration do not exclude the correction or interpretation of an award by the tribunal.

Where the relevant national law or court practice provide specific circumstances in which an arbitral tribunal may render certain decisions other than corrections or interpretation regarding an award which had been approved and notified, such situations shall be treated in the spirit of this Note.

APPENDIX 13

SECRETARIAT'S CHECKLIST ON CORRECTION AND INTERPRETATION OF AWARDS (1998 AND 2012 RULES)

Disclaimer: This Checklist is intended to provide arbitrators acting under the ICC Rules of Arbitration with guidance in addition to the Note on Correction and Interpretation of Arbitral Awards. It does not constitute an exhaustive, mandatory or otherwise binding document. It should not be thought to reflect the opinion of the members of the International Court of Arbitration of the International Chamber of Commerce or of its Secretariat. It is simply intended to facilitate the arbitrators' mission. Moreover, this Checklist is not exhaustive of issues that may be raised by the ICC Court.

Case No.: ________

1. General

☐ A. ICC case reference number mentioned in full on front page.

☐ B. Document clearly identified in its title as:

☐ i. "Addendum", if the Arbitral Tribunal corrects or interprets the Award; all decisions pursuant to Article 29(1) (1998 Rules) / 35(1) (2012 Rules) should be called "Addendum";

☐ ii. "Decision", if the Arbitral Tribunal dismisses the application;

☐ iii. "Decision and Addendum on costs", if the Arbitral Tribunal dismisses the Application but awards costs;

☐ iv. "Decision and Addendum", when there is more than one Application and the Arbitral Tribunal decides to correct or interpret the Award on the basis of one or more but not all Applications.

☐ C. Paragraphs numbered.

☐ D. Pages numbered.

☐ E. Abbreviations defined and used consistently.

☐ F. Translations of quotations in languages other than the language(s) of the arbitration.

---

2. Identification of the parties, their representatives and the arbitrator(s)

☐ A. Parties' complete addresses and correct names.

☐ B. Addresses of parties' representatives.

☐ C. Arbitrators' addresses.

3. Contents

☐ A. Summary of all procedural steps from the approval of the Award to date (e.g., indication of the date of the Award and when it was received by each party).

☐ B. Cases under Article 29(1) (1998 Rules) / 35(1) (2012 Rules)

☐ i. Indication of the date on which the Arbitral Tribunal invited the parties' comments before correcting or interpreting the award upon its own initiative;

☐ ii. Indication of the date on which the parties submitted comments, and the contents thereof;

☐ iii. Indication of the date the Arbitral Tribunal submitted the draft Addendum to the Court for approval.

☐ C. Cases under Article 29(2) (1998 Rules) / 35(2) (2012 Rules)

☐ i. Indication of the date on which the Application was made and whether it was made within the time limit provided under the Rules;

☐ ii. Indication of the time limit and any extension granted by the Court for submitting a decision;

☐ iii. Description of the contents of each of the requests contained in the Application(s);

☐ iv. Reasons for the Arbitral Tribunal's decision to accept or dismiss each of the requests (including an indication of whether the Application falls outside the scope of the Rules);

☐ v. No reasoning added to the reasoning contained in the Award, when an Application is rejected.

4. Costs – Article 29(2) (1998 Rules) / 35(2) (2012 Rules) only

☐ A. If the Court has fixed an additional advance on costs pursuant to Appendix III of the Rules:

☐ i. Indication of the amount of the advance;

☐ ii. Indication of the manner in which the advance was paid by the parties;

☐ iii. Decision on how the advance will be borne by the parties (even if it is just an indication that the party who paid shall bear it).

☐ B. If one or more parties requested a decision on costs:

☐ i. Costs of the Application and each party's legal costs dealt with separately in the body and in the dispositive section;

☐ ii. Fix the amount to be borne by each party.

5. Dispositive section, place of arbitration, date, signature

☐ A. Contains a dispositive section mentioning all orders and nothing more:

☐ i. Indication of whether the award is corrected (or interpreted) and if so how;

☐ ii. Decisions on costs if any (Article 29(2) (1998 Rules) / 35(2) ()2012 Rules only).

☐ B. After the dispositive section, add the date on which the Addendum or Decision is made and the signatures in the following manner:

Place of arbitration: City (Country)

Date: __/__/____ __________[date must be later than the Court session at which the Addendum or Decision was approved and not earlier than when the last arbitrator signs]

Signature(s):__________________________

APPENDIX 14

EFFECTIVE MANAGEMENT OF ARBITRATION: A GUIDE FOR IN-HOUSE COUNSEL AND OTHER PARTY REPRESENTATIVES (2014)

EFFECTIVE MANAGEMENT OF ARBITRATION: A GUIDE FOR IN-HOUSE COUNSEL AND OTHER PARTY REPRESENTATIVES (2014)

The purpose of this guide is to provide in-house counsel and other party representatives, such as managers and government officials, with a practical toolkit for making decisions on how to conduct an arbitration in a time- and cost-effective manner, having regard to the complexity and value of the dispute. The guide can also assist outside counsel in working with party representatives to that effect.

Reflecting the ICC's continuing efforts to provide arbitration users with means to ensure that arbitral proceedings are conducted effectively, the guide focuses on time and cost issues in the management of arbitration. While strategic considerations are of great importance in any arbitration and will have a significant impact on its management, they tend to be case-specific and are beyond the scope of this guide.

While the guide was conceived with the ICC Rules of Arbitration in mind, most of its contents, as well as the dynamic generated by it, can be used in any arbitration. The guide can be useful for both large and small cases.

INTRODUCTION

Arbitration is a dispute resolution mechanism that provides diverse users worldwide with a neutral forum, a uniform system of enforcement and the procedural flexibility that allows parties to tailor-make a procedure to suit their needs in each case. With a joint commitment to efficient management by parties, outside counsel and arbitral tribunals, it can achieve a time- and cost-effective resolution of a dispute. Without that commitment, the opposite can be true: the very flexibility of arbitration can lead to increased time and cost.

As arbitration has become more complex and the scrutiny of dispute resolution mechanisms has intensified, users have expressed the concern that arbitration is often too long and too expensive. One user has queried why a bridge can be built in one or two years but an arbitration to determine responsibility for delays and defects can take as long as three to four years. In light of the concerns of users, the ICC decided to address time- and cost-efficiency in arbitration head-on.

As a first step, in 2007, the ICC Commission on Arbitration (as it was then known) published its report on controlling time and costs in arbitration. Prior research covering a wide range of ICC cases had showed that on average:

- 82% of the costs of an arbitration were party costs, including lawyers' fees and expenses, expenses related to witness and expert evidence, and other costs incurred by the parties for the arbitration;
- 16% of the costs covered arbitrators' fees and expenses; and
- 2% of the costs covered ICC administrative expenses.

It followed that, to minimize costs, special emphasis needed to be placed on reducing the costs connected with the parties' presentation of their cases. The report developed a series of suggested concrete measures for each phase of the arbitration that can be used to reduce time and cost.

Then, in 2009, the Commission began its revision of the ICC Rules of Arbitration. The revised Rules came into force on 1 January 2012. One of the guiding principles for the revision was to improve the time- and cost-efficiency of arbitration. Among the provisions directed to that end is the requirement of an early case management conference during which the parties and the tribunal can establish an appropriate, time- and cost-effective procedure for the arbitration. The suggestions in the 2007 report, many of which are now included as an appendix to the Rules, may be used for that purpose.

The present guide is a continuation of that effort and is designed to help party representatives implement the new provisions and make appropriate decisions for effective case management. The guide will also assist outside counsel in working with party representatives to ensure well-planned and well-managed proceedings.

As noted above, arbitration rules permit flexibility and do not specify precisely how an arbitration is to be conducted. For example, there is nothing in the ICC Rules of Arbitration about the number of rounds of briefs, document production, the examination of witnesses, oral argument, post-hearing memoranda or bifurcation. The open-ended nature of the Rules enables the parties and the arbitral tribunal to tailor-make an effective procedure that suits the needs and particularities of each case. However, when studying the matter, the Commission came to the conclusion that too often the parties and tribunals do not tailor-make the procedure at an early stage, but rather apply boilerplate solutions or simply decide procedural matters piecemeal as the case progresses. This was found to increase time and cost in many arbitrations. Under the new case management provisions in Articles 22-24 of the Rules, which are specifically designed to address that problem, the process of tailor-making the procedure has now become a formal requirement.

Tailor-making the procedure so that the arbitration will be faster and cheaper is not inherently difficult to accomplish. The parties can agree upon faster and cheaper procedures and, failing their agreement, the arbitral tribunal has the power to determine such procedures after consultation with the parties. This will normally be done at the first case management conference. What is more challenging is determining the appropriate level of process and resources to match the value and complexity of the case. It is faster and cheaper to have one round of briefs rather than three, or to hold a three-day rather than a three-week hearing, but an extended opportunity to be heard will necessarily be given up. It is less expensive and less burdensome to present a witness by videoconference, but perhaps also less persuasive. The goal of each party is to present its case in a manner that is most likely to persuade the arbitral tribunal to find in its favour. The time and cost that a party should be willing to devote to that end will vary according to the importance, complexity and value of the dispute. For each phase of the arbitration, cost/risk/benefit decisions have to be made.

Appropriate time and cost decisions can be made when party representatives have a collaborative relationship with outside counsel and actively participate in the making of those decisions. Each party best knows its own internal processes, the value of the underlying transaction and what is ultimately at stake. It is the party's case, the party's risk and the party's money, so the party itself is in the best position to decide what level of risk to accept and what strategic decisions to make. Outside counsel can assist in reaching such decisions on the basis of an informed evaluation of the pros and cons of the available alternatives. In addition, arbitral tribunals play an important role by bringing their experience to bear in devising cost-effective procedures and encouraging all of the parties to assist in conducting the arbitration in an expeditious and cost-effective manner, as contemplated by Article 22(1) of the Rules.

Case management considerations

As a general matter, party representatives should consider the following when managing an arbitration:

- **Early case assessment**. Much time and cost can be saved by not litigating matters with low chances of success, or that are not worth the cost/time/distraction to its personnel. This should be analysed before an arbitration has begun; however, case assessment should also continue during the arbitration.
- **Maintaining realistic schedules**. Setting up of a realistic schedule for the entire arbitration as early as possible and sticking to that schedule, unless there are serious reasons for not doing so, are essential to controlled and predictable proceedings. Parties will be able more accurately to foresee the date of the award and make appropriate financial plans. The arbitral tribunal also has an important role in establishing and maintaining a realistic schedule.
- **Establishing a tailor-made and cost-effective procedure**. Using this guide, party representatives along with outside counsel can determine optimum procedures from the party's perspective. The question then is how to implement those procedures. First, one party may consult with the other party with a view to reaching agreement on the applicable procedures. Any such agreement must be applied pursuant to Article 19 of the Rules. If the parties cannot agree on one or more of the procedures, each can present its position to the arbitral tribunal prior to or during the case management conference. The arbitral tribunal will decide after hearing the parties.
- **Awareness of settlement procedures**. Settlement procedures such as mediation, neutral evaluation and direct settlement discussions can occur at any time before or during an arbitration. As an arbitration progresses, views on the case and parties' needs may change, affecting the desirability and nature of a potential settlement. New facts may come to light, a partial award may be rendered, management changes may occur, and new perspectives in relations between the parties may emerge. The parties should continually reassess their case and determine whether, at any given point in time, there is an opportunity for a meaningful settlement.

Structure of the guide

This guide is composed of three main parts, each of which is designed to assist in making effective time and cost decisions for an arbitration: first, a discussion of settlement considerations; second, a discussion of the case management conference; and third, a series of eleven topic sheets

Each topic sheet deals independently with a specific step in the arbitration process where cost/risk/benefit decisions need to be made. The topic sheets are not intended to cover every aspect of an arbitration; rather, they are designed to provide a methodology for decision-making. They may also serve as a tool to assist in making appropriate decisions on each topic. The following topics are covered:

- Request for arbitration
- Answer and counterclaims
- Multiparty arbitration
- Early determination of issues
- Rounds of written submissions
- Document production
- Need for fact witnesses
- Fact witness statements
- Expert witnesses
- Hearing on the merits
- Post-hearing briefs

Each topic sheet is designed to serve as an executive summary and follows a standard format consisting of a series of separate sections. The first section presents the topic and identifies the issue(s); the second section sets out the options available to the parties for that topic; the third section discusses the pros and cons of the different options; the fourth section analyses the different choices from a cost/risk/benefit perspective; and the fifth section lists useful questions that will help to focus on the key decisions that need to be made. The list of questions could, for example, serve as a basis for discussion between party representatives and outside counsel regarding the choices that need to be made for that particular phase of the arbitration. Where useful, a final section contains other general points to consider.

The topic sheets are not prescriptive and do not provide any definitive answers but rather contain suggestions that can be used to stimulate discussion and decision-making. It is the hope of the Commission that these topic sheets will help in taking the appropriate cost/risk/benefit decisions that need to be made in order to conduct an expeditious and cost-effective arbitration, having regard to the complexity and value of the dispute.

SETTLEMENT CONSIDERATIONS

A negotiated settlement of the dispute can save a great deal of time and cost, and parties would be well advised to maintain focus on the availability of settlement opportunities before and throughout an arbitration. The case management techniques listed in Appendix IV (h) to the ICC Rules of Arbitration indicate that the arbitral tribunal may inform the parties that they are free to settle all or part of the dispute at any time and, where agreed with the parties, may take steps to facilitate a settlement, subject to enforceability considerations under applicable law.

Whether or not to settle

This is a complex question that will depend on each individual case. It is necessary to weigh the chances of success in an arbitration against a series of factors including the costs, burden and distraction caused by the proceedings and the time required to obtain the result. The choice may be affected by matters of principle or the need to eliminate financial or other uncertainties. Additional considerations include:

- **Preservation of relationships**. Parties to an arbitration may have an ongoing relationship which they wish to preserve. Settlement may support that relationship better than litigating the dispute.
- **Difficulties of enforcement**. If a claimant anticipates difficulties in enforcing an arbitral award against a particular respondent, it should factor that difficulty into its assessment of the strength of its case. When enforcement is uncertain, a settlement for a lower amount may be appropriate.
- **Reasons not to settle**. Various factors may militate against settlement. For example, a claimant may wish to obtain a precedent or guidance from a tribunal for use in future cases or may consider that a given settlement offer does not match the chances of success in an arbitration. A respondent may prefer not to settle in order to discourage other potential claimants from seeking a settlement or because it is concerned that a settlement may be interpreted as an admission of liability.
- **Importance of confidentiality**. A settlement may be preferable to an arbitration that is not confidential. ICC arbitration proceedings will not be confidential unless the parties have so agreed, the tribunal has so ordered or applicable law so requires.

Methods of settlement

If the parties have decided to explore settlement, various methods are available to them. They may seek a settlement on their own, with the assistance of counsel or with the assistance of a mediator pursuant to the ICC Mediation Rules. Recourse to the Mediation Rules may be based on an agreement between the parties or a unilateral request by one party subsequently accepted by the other. While providing for mediation, the ICC Mediation Rules also allow the parties to choose any other settlement method that may be better suited to their dispute. Settlement methods that can be used under the ICC Mediation Rules include:

- **Mediation**. The neutral acts as a facilitator to help the parties arrive at a negotiated settlement of their dispute. The neutral is not requested to provide any opinion on the merits of the dispute.
- **Neutral evaluation**. The neutral provides a non-binding opinion or evaluation on any of a wide variety of matters including issues of fact or law, technical questions or the interpretation of a contract.
- **Mini-trial**. A panel consisting of the neutral and an authorized executive of each party hears presentations by the parties, after which either the panel or the neutral can mediate the dispute or express an opinion on the merits.
- **A combination of methods**, such as mediation with a neutral evaluation on a particular issue.

The report of an expert, selected pursuant to the ICC Rules for the Administration of Expert Proceedings to make findings on a disputed matter, may help to facilitate settlement. However, unlike a neutral evaluation and unless the parties agree otherwise, the expert's report will be admissible in judicial or arbitral proceedings if no settlement is reached.

Case management techniques

The parties and their counsel should keep in mind that even where settlement is not feasible before or at the outset of an arbitration, the arbitration can be managed in such a way as to facilitate settlement throughout the proceedings. Appendix IV to the ICC Rules of Arbitration highlights several case management techniques that can be used to that end:

- **Bifurcation**. In appropriate cases, a partial award on jurisdiction or liability may facilitate settlement. For example, if the arbitral tribunal decides that it has jurisdiction, the parties will know that the arbitration will go forward. This could prompt them to discuss settlement. Similarly, if the tribunal finds a party to be liable, the parties may prefer to settle the issue of damages rather than incur the time and expense of completing the arbitration.
- **Early consideration of controlling issues**. In some cases there are issues of law, fact or a mixture of fact and law, which necessarily affect the determination of the claims in the arbitration, yet can be resolved independently at relatively little expense. Examples include the determination of the applicable law, statute of limitations, the interpretation of a particular contractual provision, the determination of a key fact or technical issue or the measure of damages. The parties may find it easier to arrive at a settlement after such issues have been resolved by the tribunal.
- **Engagement of the arbitral tribunal**. Where the parties agree and the applicable law permits, the arbitral tribunal can actively facilitate settlement either by encouraging the parties to pursue one of the settlement methods described above, or through discussions with the parties.

Creativity and open-mindedness

Arbitrations often take on a life of their own once the parties have developed their positions and incurred costs. Parties and their counsel should keep in mind that a settlement can occur at any time during an arbitration and that the ICC Rules of Arbitration encourage the parties to explore this possibility. When exercising their will and their creativity in seeking a settlement, parties often arrive at solutions that are unavailable through arbitration.

CASE MANAGEMENT CONFERENCE

The case management conference provides the mechanism for determining the manner in which the arbitration will be conducted. If it is not possible to determine the entire procedure at the first case management conference, the remaining issues may be decided at a subsequent conference. The decisions made at the case management conference can be modified during the course of the arbitration by agreement of all of the parties or, failing such agreement, by a decision of the arbitral tribunal.

Article 24(1) of the ICC Rules of Arbitration requires the arbitral tribunal to convene an early case management conference to consult the parties on the conduct of the arbitration. Thereafter, pursuant to Article 22(2) of the Rules, the arbitral tribunal may adopt procedural measures for the conduct of the arbitration, provided that they are not contrary to any agreement of the parties. Article 22(1) requires the arbitral tribunal and the parties to make every effort to conduct the arbitration in an expeditious and cost-effective manner, having regard to the complexity and value of the dispute.

Issues to be decided include: the number of rounds of briefs; the extent of document production, if any; the early determination of issues; fact and expert witnesses; and the conduct of the hearing, if any. The topic sheets contained in this guide are designed to assist the parties, along with their counsel and the arbitral tribunal, in making appropriate choices for the conduct of the arbitration.

In practice, after receiving the case file, the arbitral tribunal may invite the parties to make case management proposals. If it does not do so, the parties can seek to agree between themselves upon the conduct of the proceedings. If they arrive at an agreement, it must be followed, subject to any proposals of the arbitral tribunal that are accepted by all of the parties. If the parties do not reach an agreement, the arbitral tribunal, after listening to the parties, will adopt procedural measures that it deems to be appropriate for the case at hand.

While Article 22(1) of the Rules refers to expeditious and cost-effective proceedings, it also makes clear that speed and low cost are not ends in themselves. The complexity and value of the dispute must be taken into account. A cost-effective and expeditious arbitration will be one in which the time and cost devoted to resolving the dispute is appropriate in light of what is at stake. In each case, it is necessary to make a cost/benefit analysis in order to see whether a particular procedural measure is cost-justified.

The objectives of the parties will play a crucial role in making such choices. Some examples of how parties' goals may translate into case management strategy are set forth below:

- When an important matter of principle is at stake, it may be worth the time and expense needed for a thorough examination of the facts and a full articulation of all legal arguments. A party with this objective may be willing to incur the expense of more extensive document production, multiple rounds of written submissions, a larger number of fact and expert witnesses, and the like.
- When neither an important principle nor great sums are at stake, parties may wish the arbitration to be as inexpensive and rapid as possible. Here, in contrast, parties may seek to limit document production, limit the number of witnesses, shorten hearings or minimize submissions.
- When parties wish to settle the case, for example in order to maintain their relationship or mitigate the risk of loss, they may use the case management conference to seek bifurcation of the proceedings or an early determination of controlling issues, the resolution of which might facilitate settlement. The parties may also agree to undertake settlement procedures either before or during the remaining phases of the arbitration.

TOPIC SHEET 1: REQUEST FOR ARBITRATION

Presentation

An ICC arbitration is commenced by the filing of a Request for Arbitration with the Secretariat of the ICC International Court of Arbitration (Article 4 of the ICC Rules of Arbitration). In all cases, the Request must contain the information required by Article 4(3) of the Rules. That provision is intended to elicit sufficient information to enable the respondent to respond to the claimant's claims, as required by Article 5(1) of the

Rules, and for the International Court of Arbitration to fulfil its functions under the Rules with respect to the constitution of the arbitral tribunal and the setting in motion of the arbitration.

Issue: Should the Request contain only the minimum requirements of the Rules or provide a more elaborate statement of the case?

Options

A. File a short Request that satisfies the Rules without providing any more content or evidence than is strictly required by the Rules.

B. File a comprehensive Request that constitutes a full statement of the case, including exhibits.

The above options represent two ends of a spectrum. However, there is also the option of filing a Request that provides a level of content and evidence anywhere between those two ends.

Pros and cons

A shorter and less comprehensive Request can be prepared more economically and more quickly than a more comprehensive document.

On the other hand, a more comprehensive Request may avoid the need for multiple rounds of subsequent submissions and thereby help to expedite the arbitration. In addition, providing more information may increase the impact of the Request on the respondent. Additional detail may also enable the parties and the arbitral tribunal to focus on the key issues in the case as early as possible and thereby facilitate the drawing up of the Terms of Reference and the conduct of the case management conference.

Cost/benefit analysis

In all circumstances, the claimant should seriously consider conducting an early assessment of the nature, strengths and weaknesses of its case before filing a Request. This will allow it to determine, in the first instance, whether the claims are sufficiently strong to warrant bringing the arbitration or whether it would be better to seek a settlement of the dispute. If it decides to proceed with the arbitration, the early case assessment will help to ensure that the Request does not contain errors and that the claimant's claims are correctly described and set forth in the most effective manner. While this assessment requires some time and expenditure, it typically results in a saving of both over the arbitration as a whole.

If the claimant decides to proceed with the arbitration, it must determine whether to file a shorter or longer Request. The decision on how comprehensive the Request should be will be heavily influenced by the circumstances of the case and strategic considerations. Some time and cost may be saved by drafting a shorter Request although this may be a temporary saving if the claimant is ultimately required to supplement such a Request with additional detailed information. When the Request and the Answer respectively constitute a full statement of the case and a full statement of defence, time and cost can be saved by avoiding one or more further rounds of submissions. However, in complex cases this may not be possible, and the Request and Answer may be ultimately superseded by subsequent written submissions.

If a primary purpose for filing a Request is to elicit settlement discussions, consideration should be given to whether this is best accomplished with a shorter or a longer

Request. A shorter Request may be preferable if the respondent is unlikely to discuss settlement unless an arbitration has been commenced and the substantive aspects of the claim would be best dealt with in the settlement discussions. A longer Request may be preferable if the goal is to show the respondent in writing the strengths of the claimant's case before commencing settlement discussions.

Questions to ask

1. What is the desired result of filing the Request (e.g. triggering settlement discussions or having the dispute resolved by arbitration)?

2. Are there any valid reasons for not conducting an early case assessment?

3. Are there any real cost savings in filing a shorter Request? Would they be outweighed by the benefits of filing a longer Request for any of the reasons described above?

4. Are there any other strategic or legal considerations that may affect the timing of the filing of the Request and consequently whether it should be shorter or longer?

Other points to consider

In certain cases, questions of timing may militate in favour of a shorter Request. For example, a Request may need to be filed quickly to avoid being barred by a statute of limitations. A Request may also have to be filed within ten days of receipt by the Secretariat of an application for emergency measures pursuant to Article 1 of the Emergency Arbitrator Rules (Appendix V to the Rules).

Pursuant to Article 23(4) of the Rules, after the Terms of Reference have been established, no new claims may be made without the authorization of the arbitral tribunal. It is therefore prudent for the claimant to make all of its claims prior to the signing of the Terms of Reference.

Article 5(6) of the Rules provides that the claimant shall submit a reply to any counterclaim raised by the respondent pursuant to Article 5(5) of the Rules. The topic sheet relating to the Answer and counterclaims offers guidance on this matter.

TOPIC SHEET 2: ANSWER AND COUNTERCLAIMS

Presentation

The respondent is required to file an Answer to the Request for Arbitration with the Secretariat (Article 5 of the ICC Rules of Arbitration). In all cases, the Answer must contain the information required by Article 5(1) of the Rules. The Answer may contain a counterclaim pursuant to Article 5(5) of the Rules.

Issue: How detailed or extensive should the Answer and any counterclaim be, above and beyond what is required by the Rules?

Options

A. File a short Answer that satisfies the Rules without providing any more content or evidence than is strictly required by the Rules.

B. File a comprehensive Answer that constitutes a full statement of defence, including evidentiary exhibits.

The above options represent two ends of a spectrum. However, there is also the option of filing an Answer that provides a level of content and evidence anywhere between those two ends.

In deciding on the appropriate length of the Answer, the respondent should consider whether or not to match the length and level of detail chosen by the claimant. Specifically, the respondent may choose between the following options:

a) File an Answer that reflects the approach taken by the claimant (e.g. a shorter or a longer document).
b) File an Answer in a form that is different from the form of the Request filed by the claimant.

C. Assert a counterclaim, irrespective of the length and content of the Answer. The raising of a counterclaim is subject to considerations similar to those described in the topic sheet on the Request for Arbitration.

Pros and cons

The pros and cons of filing a shorter or a longer Answer may vary depending on the form of the Request filed by the claimant. If the claimant has filed a shorter Request and the respondent reciprocates with an equally short Answer, the arbitration should be able to proceed more expeditiously to the Terms of Reference and the case management conference, in part because the respondent is less likely to need an extension of time for filing the Answer pursuant to Article 5(2) of the Rules. On the other hand, if the claimant files a longer and more detailed Request, then the respondent may be required to seek an extension of time in order to respond with a detailed Answer.

A shorter and less comprehensive Answer can be prepared more economically and more quickly than a more comprehensive document.

If the claimant has filed a comprehensive Request and the respondent decides to file a comprehensive Answer, this may avoid the need for multiple rounds of subsequent submissions and thereby expedite the arbitration.

In addition, providing more information may increase the impact of the Answer. Additional detail may also increase the ability of the parties and the arbitral tribunal to focus on the key issues in the case as early as possible and thereby facilitate the drawing up of the Terms of Reference and the conduct of the case management conference.

Cost/benefit analysis

To the extent possible in the time available, the respondent should conduct an early assessment of the nature, strengths and weaknesses of its case before filing an Answer. This will allow it to determine, in the first instance, whether the case should be defended or whether settlement should be pursued. If the respondent decides to defend the arbitration, and possibly assert counterclaims, the early case assessment will help to ensure that the Answer does not contain errors and that the respondent's defence and/or counterclaims are correctly described and set forth in the most effective manner. While this assessment requires some time and expenditure, it typically results in a saving of both over the arbitration as a whole.

An additional consideration for the respondent is the limited amount of time available under the Rules for making an early case assessment and filing its Answer. If the respondent has prior knowledge of the dispute, then it may be able to undertake an early case assessment before receiving the Request for Arbitration. If, on the other hand, the receipt of the Request for Arbitration is the respondent's first real opportunity to assess the claimant's claims, the time available to it under the Rules for this purpose will be limited.

Depending on the circumstances described above, the respondent must decide whether to file a shorter or a longer Answer. The decision on how comprehensive the Answer should be will be heavily influenced by the circumstances of the case, strategic considerations and the limited time available for submitting the Answer under the Rules. Some time and cost may be saved by drafting a shorter Answer although this may be a temporary saving if the respondent is ultimately required to supplement such an Answer with additional detailed information.

If the claimant has filed a full statement of the case in its Request and if in the time available it is possible to file a full statement of defence in the Answer, time and cost can be saved by avoiding one or more rounds of further submissions. However, this may not be possible in complex cases.

Consideration should be given to whether filing a shorter or a longer Answer might facilitate settlement discussions. A shorter Answer may be preferable if the substantive aspects of the settlement would best be dealt with in negotiations and there is a reasonable prospect of a settlement. A longer Answer may be preferable if the goal is to show the claimant in writing the strengths of the respondent's defence and any counterclaims for purposes of settlement discussions.

Questions to ask

1. Are there any real cost savings or any other advantages in filing a shorter Answer? Would they be outweighed by the benefits of filing a longer Answer for any of the reasons described above?

2. Is there sufficient time to conduct an early assessment of the defence and file the Answer within the 30 days specified in the Rules, or is it necessary to request an extension of time for filing the Answer pursuant to Article 5(2)?

3. Are there any serious counterclaims that can and should be raised in the arbitration? Should they comply with only the minimum requirements set out in the Rules or be more detailed and accompanied by evidentiary exhibits?

Other points to consider

Pursuant to Article 23(4) of the Rules, after the Terms of Reference have been established, no new claims may be made, without the authorization of the arbitral tribunal. It is therefore prudent for any counterclaims to be made by the respondent prior to the signing of the Terms of Reference.

If the respondent wishes to join an additional party pursuant to Article 7(1) of the Rules, it must be careful to do so within the time limits specified in that Article.

If there are serious objections to jurisdiction, the respondent may consider keeping the Answer short with respect to the merits.

TOPIC SHEET 3: MULTIPARTY ARBITRATION

Presentation

Under the ICC Rules of Arbitration, an arbitration having more than two parties may occur when all of the parties have so agreed. Multiparty arbitrations may result from various procedural choices:

- A claimant may commence an arbitration pursuant to Article 4 of the Rules against two or more respondents.
- Two or more claimants may commence an arbitration pursuant to Article 4 of the Rules against one or more respondents.
- Before the confirmation or appointment of any arbitrator, any party may join another party to the arbitration pursuant to Article 7 of the Rules.
- Upon any party's request, two or more pending arbitrations may be consolidated into a single arbitration by the Court, subject to the requirements of Article 10 of the Rules.

Issue: When is it beneficial to choose a multiparty arbitration?

Options

A. A single arbitration that includes all relevant parties when they have all so agreed.

B. Two or more separate arbitrations.

Pros and cons

A single multiparty arbitration, when possible, results in more comprehensive proceedings and avoids duplication. It also avoids the risk of conflicting decisions in separate arbitrations.

On the other hand, a single multiparty arbitration may result in more complex proceedings, which could increase the length and cost of the arbitration. For example, a party with a small role in the dispute may not wish to participate in a multiparty arbitration and could refuse to do so in the absence of a binding arbitration agreement. Further, in an arbitration where there is to be a three-member arbitral tribunal, choosing to have more than two parties in the arbitration may deprive the parties of their ability to choose a co-arbitrator, because the ICC International Court of Arbitration may decide to appoint the entire tribunal pursuant to Article 12(8) of the Rules.

Cost/benefit analysis

Consideration should be given to whether a single multiparty arbitration, as opposed to two or more separate arbitrations, would save time and money. While a single arbitration will usually be more cost-efficient, there could be situations in which separate arbitrations may still be the more efficient option for one or more parties.

If a single multiparty arbitration is the more time- and cost-efficient option, the parties should consider whether the time and cost benefits outweigh any of the potential disadvantages, such as the risk of losing the opportunity to choose a co-arbitrator because the International Court of Arbitration may find it necessary to appoint the arbitral tribunal pursuant to Article 12(8) of the Rules.

Another important factor to consider in deciding whether a single multiparty arbitration would be beneficial is the contractual role of each party and the specific interests flowing from that role. Arbitration of your dispute with one party may weaken your position with respect to another party. Where, for example, parties share potential liability with respect to their contractual counterparty, it may be tactically imprudent for them to have their internal disputes heard in the arbitration with the contractual counterparty, since their allegations against each other may support the counterparty's case against them.

TOPIC SHEET 4: EARLY DETERMINATION OF ISSUES

Presentation

Issue: In what circumstances would it be beneficial to break out certain issues for early determination by the arbitral tribunal in a partial award?

Various kinds of issues lend themselves to such treatment:

First, there may be threshold issues that could be dispositive of the entire arbitration. Such issues might include:

- whether the tribunal has jurisdiction over the dispute;
- whether the dispute is barred by an applicable statute of limitations;
- whether there is liability;
- whether the dispute is arbitrable;
- whether the parties have capacity to sue or be sued.

For example, were a tribunal to decide that it lacks jurisdiction over the entire dispute, that would result in a final award dismissing all claims made in the arbitration. If the tribunal decides that it has jurisdiction, that decision would result in a partial award and the arbitration would continue, unless the tribunal's decision leads to a settlement. The same pattern would apply, *mutatis mutandis*, to the other examples given above.

Second, there may be discrete issues which could be usefully broken out and decided in a partial award, even though their resolution would not be dispositive of the entire arbitration. The early resolution of a particular issue may narrow or simplify the issues to be decided in the remainder of the arbitration or may facilitate settlement. Such issues may include:

- a decision on the meaning of a contractual provision;
- a decision on the applicable law;
- a decision on certain key facts in dispute;
- a decision on an issue that may significantly affect a party's exposure to one or more claims, such as determination of the types of recoverable damages.

For example, a decision on applicable law may save the parties from having to incur time and cost pleading their case on the basis of alternative applicable laws. The same analysis applies to the other examples above.

Options

A. Do not break out any issues for early determination.

B. Break out one or more issues for early determination by means of an award.

Pros and cons

The early determination of one or more issues in a partial award may resolve the entire dispute, simplify the remainder of the arbitration or facilitate settlement. However, if the award does not achieve one of those objectives, the early determination procedure may result in added time and cost. In addition, breaking out a discrete issue rather than having it decided along with the other issues may affect the way the tribunal decides one or more of the issues.

Cost/benefit analysis

Breaking out issues that could be dispositive of the entire arbitration

A cost/benefit analysis of this question is complicated by the fact that the decision has to be made in the face of important unknowns. When deciding whether or not to break out an issue, the parties cannot know what the arbitral tribunal's decision will be. For example, in a case involving issues of liability and damages, if the issue of liability is broken out and the tribunal decides that there is no liability, a great deal of time and cost will be saved since there will be no need to exchange briefs and hold hearings on damages. On the other hand, if the tribunal finds that there is liability, unless such finding encourages the parties to settle the case, there will have to be a damages phase, and the breaking out of the issue of liability may then actually add to the overall time and cost of the proceedings.

Given these unknowns, the cost/benefit analysis must turn on an appreciation of probabilities and an estimate of potential cost. In deciding whether to break out an issue, it may be useful to estimate likely outcomes as well as time and cost in answer to certain specific questions:

- What is the likelihood that the tribunal's decision will be dispositive of the entire arbitration?
- If the tribunal's decision will not be dispositive of the entire arbitration, what is the likelihood that the tribunal's early determination of the issue may result in a settlement of the case?
- What is the added time and cost likely to result from early determination of the issue in comparison with the likely overall cost, i.e. how much more time and cost would there be if the arbitration were conducted in two parts rather than one?

The answers to these questions can help in deciding whether or not to break out an issue for early determination. The following factors would tend to favour the breaking out of an issue for early determination:

- the likelihood of a dispositive determination is high;
- the likelihood of a settlement, even if there is no dispositive determination, is high;
- the remaining phases are likely to be long and expensive;
- the additional cost caused by early determination is low.

A decision on whether to break out an issue can be made by weighing these factors in relation to each other.

Breaking out issues in a partial award not dispositive of the entire arbitration

A similar type of cost/benefit analysis would apply here, although the relevant questions are slightly different:

- What is the likelihood that the tribunal's early determination of a particular issue will significantly narrow or simplify the other issues to be decided in the remainder of the arbitration?
- What is the likelihood that early determination of a particular issue may result in a settlement of the case?
- What is the additional time and cost likely to result from early determination of a particular issue?

Once again, weighing the answers to those questions against each other can help in deciding whether it is beneficial to break out a particular issue for early determination.

Questions to ask

1. Does the case contain any threshold or discrete issues that could be determined in a separate award?

2. Would the early determination of those issues by the arbitral tribunal be beneficial, in light of the cost/benefit analysis discussed above?

3. Would early determination (a) potentially resolve the entire dispute, (b) facilitate settlement or (c) simplify the rest of the arbitration?

Other points to consider

Article 37(5) of the Rules permits the arbitral tribunal, when allocating the costs of the arbitration, to take into account the extent to which each party has conducted the arbitration in an expeditious and cost-effective manner. The arbitral tribunal might allocate some amount of costs against a party that loses in the early determination of a potentially dispositive issue if that party is considered to have acted in bad faith or otherwise not to have acted in an expeditious and cost-effective manner.

There may be logistical reasons for breaking out one or more issues for early determination, such as the availability of witnesses, hearing facilities, counsel or arbitrators. In addition, it may allow a complex case to be conducted in a more orderly manner.

There may be compelling reasons for deciding certain issues early in an arbitration, e.g. whether claims made under different arbitration agreements may be heard together in a single arbitration. The breaking out of an issue for decision in a partial award could be agreed upon by the parties or determined by the arbitral tribunal in the absence of an agreement by the parties.

TOPIC SHEET 5: ROUNDS OF WRITTEN SUBMISSIONS

Presentation

An ICC arbitration is commenced by the filing of a Request for Arbitration (Article 4 of the ICC Rules of Arbitration). Thereafter, the respondent files an Answer (Article 5). If the Answer contains a counterclaim, the claimant files a reply (Article 5). The Terms of Reference for the arbitration are then established (Article 23).

Issue: How many subsequent rounds of written submissions are appropriate in a particular arbitration?

Options

A. No further written submissions are necessary, since the Request and the Answer sufficiently state the case.

B. One subsequent round of written submissions.

C. Two or more subsequent rounds of written submissions.

D. Post-hearing briefs (assuming there is a hearing).

Pros and cons

Additional rounds of written submissions enable the parties to articulate their positions more extensively and respond to the developing arguments on each side.

However, additional rounds of briefs may lead to unnecessary repetition, excessive detail or dilatory tactics.

Cost/benefit analysis

Each round of written submissions increases the length and cost of the arbitration. It is therefore essential to determine whether, in a particular case, the benefits of an additional round are worth the extra time and cost.

Additional submissions may be particularly useful in certain cases, e.g. where there are complicated issues of fact or law or issues of strategic importance for a party. In such cases, it is very common to have two rounds of pre-hearing written submissions after the initial submissions.

Questions to ask

1. Does the case justify the extra time and cost caused by additional written submissions?

And, in particular,

2. Are additional rounds of submissions genuinely useful or necessary for a party to make its case to the arbitral tribunal, and if so, why?

3. What is the estimated cost of such additional rounds?

4. Is the benefit worth the cost, and if so, why?

Other points to consider

Consider limiting the number of pages of written submissions.

Consider limiting the scope of such submissions, e.g. to issues raised by the other side in its immediately preceding submission.

Consider having the arbitral tribunal indicate issues on which it wishes the parties to focus in any further round of submissions.

Consider whether any subsequent rounds of submissions should be simultaneous or sequential. For example, it may be efficient for post-hearing briefs to be filed simultaneously.

Consider whether post-hearing briefs are genuinely useful or necessary, or whether one round of pre-hearing briefs and one round of post-hearing briefs are sufficient.

The foregoing suggestions could be put into effect either through an agreement between the parties or in an order from the arbitral tribunal upon a party's request.

TOPIC SHEET 6: DOCUMENT PRODUCTION

Presentation

Document production can involve substantial time and cost. Obviously, every party may unilaterally submit documents to support its case. Document production refers to the extent to which one party may demand that another party produce documents.

The ICC Rules of Arbitration contain no specific provisions governing document production. Article 19 of the Rules allows the parties to agree upon the procedures to be applied and empowers the tribunal to decide in the absence of an agreement of the parties. Article 22(4) requires the arbitral tribunal to ensure that each party has a reasonable opportunity to present its case. Article 25(1) provides that the arbitral tribunal shall establish the facts of the case by all appropriate means and Article 25(5) allows it to summon any party to provide additional evidence.

In short, the Rules leave the question of whether and how much document production will occur to the parties and the arbitrators, provided that the parties are treated fairly and impartially and that each party has a reasonable opportunity to present its case. When document production is to occur, the manner in which the process is executed and the degree of production can have a significant impact on time and cost.

In-house counsel or other party representatives, working with outside counsel, should consider whether and to what extent document production is genuinely useful and cost-beneficial. When document production is to occur, time and cost can be significantly reduced by establishing an efficient document production procedure.

Issue: Is document production desirable and, if so, how much document production should there be?

Options

Options range from no document production at all to full document production.

A. No document production.
- The parties may decide to seek no documents from each other and to rely solely on the documents each of them possesses.
- The parties are always free to submit their own documents.
- The parties are also free to request the arbitral tribunal to order the production of specific documents.

B. Production limited to specific documents or narrow categories of documents, which are relevant and material to deciding an issue in the arbitration.

Consider using:
- the IBA Rules on the Taking of Evidence in International Arbitration ("IBA Rules") as a standard;
- the suggestions in the report of the ICC Commission on Arbitration and ADR entitled "Controlling Time and Costs in Arbitration";
- the report of the ICC Commission on Arbitration and ADR entitled "Managing E-Document Production".

C. Broad document production as used in some common law jurisdictions.
- The parties may agree upon broad requests for documents.
- In rare cases, the parties may agree to common law style "discovery" including depositions and/or interrogatories.

When document production is to occur, the parties may agree upon the ground rules for requesting documents from and producing documents to each other.

If the parties cannot agree on whether to have document production or on the extent of document production or the ground rules for such production, the tribunal will decide.

Pros and cons

Document production can be very expensive and time-consuming and the broader the document production the more expensive and time-consuming it tends to be. It requires time and expenditure from the party that searches for and produces documents as well as from the party that must study and analyse the documents that are produced.

On the other hand, if one of the parties has sole possession of documents needed by the other party, document production may be essential. Moreover, document production can provide the parties and the tribunal with a more complete understanding of the case. Given that parties are unlikely to submit documents spontaneously when they are detrimental to their own case, document production puts them under an obligation to do so.

Cost/benefit analysis

In view of the time and cost required for document production, a cost/benefit analysis is necessary in order to decide whether to seek document production at all and, if so, to determine the desired extent of such production. The parties should explore whether they can effectively meet their burden of proof with the documents that are already in their possession and whether the other side is likely to have documents that are genuinely useful for the first party to make its case.

Each party should then estimate the extra time and cost caused by document production and weigh this against the likelihood that document production will genuinely assist it in making its case. For example, if document production is estimated to cost USD 500,000 and it is considered that there is at best a 10% chance that it will yield valuable results, the question arises as to whether that 10% chance is worth the expense of USD 500,000. This is a decision that can best be made jointly by the party, typically represented by in-house counsel, and outside counsel. Many factors may come into play, such as the amount in dispute, whether there are policy issues, whether there is concern about precedent and whether the benefit of obtaining documents from the other side may be outweighed by the detriment of being required to produce documents oneself.

Questions to ask

1. Are any requests for document production genuinely useful or necessary for a party to make its case or can the party rely effectively on the documents in its possession?
2. What extent of document production is genuinely useful and necessary?
3. When should document production occur?
4. What is the estimated cost of searching for and producing documents, as well as the cost of reviewing and analysing documents that have been produced?
5. Is the benefit of document production worth the cost, and if so, why?

Other points to consider

Consider whether it is appropriate to deal with document production in the arbitration clause, for example by agreeing that there will be no document production (e.g. in contracts where it is relatively certain that document production will not assist in resolving potential disputes); by agreeing to limited document production in accordance with the IBA Rules; or by agreeing to broad document production or "discovery".

Consider whether document production should occur once or more than once. Consider whether it should occur prior to or after written submissions.

Consider whether it is appropriate to limit documents transmitted to the arbitral tribunal to a manageable quantity.

Take into account any costs of translation when estimating the cost of document production.

Consider the ground rules to be adopted for implementing document production, including the use of a Redfern Schedule and the setting of the shortest reasonable time frames for production.

Special considerations may be needed if the parties agree upon or the tribunal orders the production of electronic documents. In such cases, the report of the ICC Commission on Arbitration and ADR entitled "Managing E-Document Production" can be used to assist in choosing the most efficient methods of e-document production.

TOPIC SHEET 7: NEED FOR FACT WITNESSES

Presentation

Article 25(1) of the ICC Rules of Arbitration requires the arbitral tribunal to establish the facts of the case by all appropriate means. This can include the hearing of fact witnesses. Article 25(3) of the Rules specifically allows the arbitral tribunal to decide to hear witnesses. However, Article 25(6) allows the arbitral tribunal to decide the case solely on documents, unless a party requests a hearing. This would permit an arbitration with no hearing and no fact witnesses.

Issue: Is there a genuine need for fact witnesses?

Options

A. No fact witnesses at all.

B. One or more fact witnesses.
- Identify the issues on which fact witness testimony is necessary.
- Identify the appropriate fact witnesses for the issues.

Pros and cons

Fact witnesses can be essential to proving a case. However, they significantly increase the length and cost of an arbitration, since there will typically be one or more written witness statements for each witness and the oral testimony of each witness may be required at a hearing.

Cost/benefit analysis

Fact witnesses may be genuinely necessary in order to prove disputed facts or to present a broader picture of the circumstances surrounding the dispute. In determining whether fact witnesses are needed, the following issues can be considered:
- Are there any disputed facts? It may appear from the pleadings that there are disputed facts, but it may turn out after discussion between the parties that those facts are not really disputed. In addition, a party may agree not to

contest certain disputed facts in order to save time and cost when the dispute over those facts is not sufficiently important.
- If there are disputed facts, are they relevant and material for deciding an issue in the dispute? There is no need to incur the extra time and cost involved in having a fact witness testify on disputed facts that will not affect the determination of an issue in the dispute.
- If there are disputed facts that are relevant and material, can they be proved by documents alone or do they genuinely need to be proved through fact witnesses?
- Is it useful to call fact witnesses to make a general presentation on the circumstances of the dispute?

When a party has decided to use fact witnesses, time and cost can be reduced by avoiding having many witnesses testify as to the same facts and by carefully focusing the scope of the testimony of each witness.

Questions to ask

1. Is there a genuine need for fact witnesses at all?

2. If so, who should they be? What should be the scope of their testimony? How many fact witnesses are genuinely necessary to establish a particular fact or present the circumstances of the case?

Other points to consider

Consider using videoconferencing for oral witness testimony to save time and cost.

Consider what is the most effective way of examining the fact witnesses at a hearing: e.g. direct examination and cross-examination; opening presentation by the witness followed by cross-examination; use of the witness's written statement as a substitute for direct examination and proceeding straightaway with cross-examination; questioning of fact witnesses by the tribunal only or by the tribunal followed by questions from counsel.

Determine whether it is preferable for a given witness to testify in the language of the arbitration or in his or her native language. When a witness is testifying in a language other than the language of the arbitration, appropriate translation will often need to be arranged, which will increase time and cost.

TOPIC SHEET 8: FACT WITNESS STATEMENTS

Presentation

Issues arising when a party has decided to present fact witness evidence: Should witness statements be submitted? What should their scope be? When should they be submitted?

Options

Form

A. No written witness statements.

B. Brief summary of the scope of witness evidence (witness summary).

C. Full witness statements.

Scope of full witness statements

A. Lengthy and comprehensive statement.

B. Short statement limited to key factual issues in dispute.

Number and timing

A. One or more rounds of witness statements.

B. Witness statements submitted with written submissions.

C. Witness statements submitted following the exchange of written submissions.

D. Witness statements submitted simultaneously or sequentially.

Pros and cons

Form

Written witness statements increase the length and cost of the pre-hearing phase, but can reduce the length and cost of the hearing by replacing direct examination and allowing for a more focused cross-examination. The absence of witness statements, or the submission of witness summaries only, will reduce pre-hearing costs but can increase the length and cost of the hearing.

Scope

Comprehensive witness statements can be a valuable part of case presentation, allowing witnesses to tell the story of the dispute and place documentary evidence in its context. However, lengthy witness statements will increase time and cost as well as the scope of cross-examination.

Number and timing

More than one round of witness statements provides witnesses with the opportunity to rebut the evidence of other witnesses, but will increase time and cost prior to the hearing.

Submitting witness statements with the written submissions provides direct proof of the facts at the time they are alleged. It also allows the parties to identify and progressively narrow down the factual issues, which may make for shorter, more targeted submissions later.

Submitting witness statements only after the exchange of written submissions may allow the parties to narrow down the factual issues in dispute before preparing and submitting witness statements, which may consequently be more focused on the disputed issues.

Cost/benefit analysis

While witness statements can provide valuable evidence in support of a party's position, they can add significantly to time and cost. The importance of the evidence to be presented must therefore be weighed against the time and expense required to present it. For example, if alternative sources of evidence are available (e.g. contemporaneous documentary evidence), there may be no cost justification for providing a witness statement on those facts. Similarly, if a witness is submitting a statement on a given fact, the submission of another witness statement evidencing the same fact may not be cost-justified, particularly if the fact is of little importance.

Full witness statements require more work and are therefore more expensive to prepare than witness summaries. However, they may subsequently save time and cost during a hearing by obviating the need for lengthy direct examination of the witness at the hearing.

The case management techniques set out in Appendix IV to the Rules include limiting the length and scope of written witness evidence so as to avoid repetition and focus on key issues. In line with Appendix IV, parties may wish to consider how to structure their fact witness evidence as efficiently as possible.

Questions to ask

1. In light of the other sources of evidence available, is the preparation of a given witness statement justified in terms of time and cost?

2. Is a witness statement required to prove a disputed question of fact or provide necessary background information? Is more than one witness statement necessary to accomplish this? Is there a good reason not to limit the witness statement to the key factual issues in dispute?

3. Should the witness evidence be presented in the form of full witness statements or witness summaries?

4. Is it necessary to have more than one round of witness statements?

5. Should the witness statements be filed concurrently with, or only after, the parties' written submissions?

TOPIC SHEET 9: EXPERT WITNESSES (pre-hearing issues)

Presentation

Article 25(3) of the ICC Rules of Arbitration contemplates the possibility of experts appointed by the parties, while Article 25(4) provides that, after consulting the parties, the arbitral tribunal may appoint one or more experts, define their terms of reference, and receive their reports.

Issues: Is there a genuine need to appoint experts? Should they be appointed by the parties, the tribunal, or both? How should they be selected? How should the written expert reports be produced?

Options

Whether and how to appoint experts

A. No experts at all.

B. Party-appointed expert(s) only.

C. Tribunal-appointed expert(s) only.

D. Both party-appointed and tribunal-appointed experts.

How to select party-appointed experts

A. Selection of an expert by the parties or their counsel.

B. Selection of an expert proposed by the ICC International Centre for ADR at a party's request.

How to select tribunal-appointed experts

A. Selection by the tribunal alone after obtaining the parties' comments on the expert to be appointed, including with respect to the expert's independence and impartiality. This option includes the tribunal's selection of an expert proposed by the ICC International Centre for ADR at the tribunal's request.

B. Selection by the tribunal of an expert agreed by the parties or from a list of experts jointly submitted by the parties.

Production of written reports

A. Separate reports by each party-appointed expert.
- These reports can be produced with the parties' briefs or after the parties have produced their fact witness statements.
- These reports can be produced either simultaneously or sequentially.

B. Instead of, or subsequent to, the production of separate reports, the party-appointed experts meet to determine points of agreement and disagreement and produce reports laying out their respective positions on the points of disagreement.

C. Preparation by the tribunal of terms of reference for tribunal-appointed experts after submitting a draft to the parties for comment. Thereafter, the expert produces a written report based upon the terms of reference.

Pros and cons

Certain technical issues may need to be presented through expert opinions. In some cases, expert opinions can be decisive for a case. However, expert witnesses significantly increase the length and cost of an arbitration.

If there are to be experts, the pros and cons of party-appointed experts and/or tribunal-appointed experts must be considered. In particular cases, a tribunal-appointed expert may be the most persuasive expert for arbitrators from certain legal cultures, but reliance on a tribunal-appointed expert deprives the parties of some degree of control. Whether a tribunal-appointed expert should be requested is an important matter of strategy to be considered on a case-by-case basis.

Recourse to a tribunal-appointed expert alone, with no party-appointed experts, will no doubt be the least expensive option. However, there may be cases where a tribunal-appointed expert's views cannot be adequately questioned or tested by the parties without the assistance of party-appointed experts. Recourse to both will increase time and cost.

Cost/benefit analysis

Whether and how to appoint experts

Whether or not to appoint experts can be a complex question requiring consideration of a number of factors, including the nature of the issues, the legal and cultural background of the tribunal, the availability of experts, case strategy and the impact on time and cost. A key consideration will be whether the cost and time associated with expert witnesses is justified by a genuine need in the case at hand.

How to select party-appointed experts

A. Selection of an expert by the parties or their counsel

In order to present evidence on issues requiring expertise, the parties or their counsel may select an outside expert to produce an expert report. Alternatively, evidence on such issues can be presented by the parties' in-house technical experts. The in-house experts may be very knowledgeable in their field and have hands-on knowledge of the specific technical matters at issue. Yet, there is a risk that the tribunal could perceive them as being partial. Outside experts are more expensive and more time-consuming but, depending on their qualifications and professional demeanour, could be viewed as more impartial.

B. Selection of an expert proposed by the ICC International Centre for ADR at a party's request.

The ICC International Centre for ADR offers parties and tribunals a service of finding experts from a wide range of sectors and countries. This may speed up the process of identifying experts and minimize the cost. In addition, the fact that a party-appointed expert has been identified by the ICC International Centre for ADR can reflect well upon the expert's qualifications, independence and impartiality.

How to select tribunal-appointed experts

A. Selection by the tribunal alone after obtaining the parties' comments on the expert to be appointed, including with respect to the expert's independence and impartiality. This option includes the selection by the tribunal of an expert proposed by the ICC International Centre for ADR at the tribunal's request.

The selection of an expert by the arbitral tribunal alone may be more expeditious and may avoid disputes between the parties over the suitability of their respective proposals. Moreover, the appointment of one expert will reduce time and cost. However, this method excludes the parties from the selection process and creates a risk that the chosen expert may fall short of the parties' expectations. From the parties' perspective, a further disadvantage is that the content of the expert's opinion may remain unknown to them until produced before the arbitral tribunal.

B. Selection by the tribunal of an expert agreed by the parties or from a list of experts jointly submitted by the parties.

This is a more time-consuming process than the appointment of an expert by the tribunal alone, but has the advantage of restricting selection to an expert acceptable to the parties and the tribunal. Moreover, the appointment of a single expert will reduce time and cost. However, a potential disadvantage from the parties' perspective will again be that the content of the expert's opinion remains unknown to the parties until produced before the arbitral tribunal.

Production of written reports

A. Separate reports by each party-appointed expert.

- These reports can be produced with the parties' briefs or after the parties have produced their fact witness statements.

  The submission of expert evidence with a party's briefs has the advantage of enabling a more comprehensive understanding of that party's case. It may help to focus the content of any subsequent briefs on the actual rather than the assumed areas in which expert evidence may be submitted. The disadvantage is that the expert evidence may not take account of any evidence introduced by the other party in subsequent witness statements, expert reports or subsequent briefs and may either be incomplete or create a need for supplemental expert evidence.

- These reports can be produced either simultaneously or sequentially.
  In cases where the points of disagreement are sufficiently clear, simultaneous filings will generally be faster than sequential filings because there will be fewer rounds. However, when the points of disagreement are not sufficiently clear, simultaneous filings may result in expert reports that do not correspond or respond to each other, which could actually increase time and cost.

The ultimate choice will also depend upon tactical or strategic considerations that go beyond issues of time and cost.

B. Instead of, or subsequent to, the production of separate reports, the party-appointed experts meet to determine points of agreement and disagreement and produce reports laying out their respective positions on the points of disagreement.

The production of written expert reports can be time-consuming and expensive. Reducing the scope of those reports will reduce time and cost. If the party-appointed experts are given the opportunity to meet and clearly identify the points over which they disagree, their reports can be shortened and focus on the points of disagreement.

C. Preparation by the tribunal of terms of reference for tribunal-appointed experts after submitting a draft to the parties for comment. Thereafter, the expert produces a written report based on the terms of reference.

It is important to ensure that the tribunal-appointed expert focuses and provides an opinion on the specific issues in dispute within the relevant area of expertise. The terms of reference are designed to serve this purpose. By being allowed to comment on and provide input into the terms of reference, the parties will have a degree of control over the process.

Questions to ask

1. Is there a genuine need to appoint experts or can the case be effectively made without expert evidence?

2. Should there be party-appointed experts, tribunal-appointed experts or both?

3. What is the appropriate method for selecting party-appointed experts or tribunal-appointed experts, as the case may be?

4. If there are to be party-appointed experts, how many experts are genuinely necessary?

5. When and in what form should expert reports be produced?

6. Should reports be submitted simultaneously or sequentially?

7. Should party-appointed experts be required to meet in order to determine points of agreement and disagreement?

8. If such a meeting is held, should counsel be present at the meeting?

Other points to consider

Consider avoiding more than one party-appointed expert per topic on each side.

Consider whether it is genuinely necessary to have an expert witness on issues of law. A great deal of time and cost can be saved if legal issues are argued by outside counsel in their briefs and at the hearing.

TOPIC SHEET 10: HEARING ON THE MERITS (including witness issues)

Presentation

Pursuant to Article 25(2) of the ICC Rules of Arbitration, a hearing must be held if requested by any party. In addition, pursuant to Articles 25(2) and 25(3), the arbitral tribunal may hear the parties, witnesses, experts or any other person, if it so decides of its own motion.

Hearings are expensive to hold and the longer they are, the more costly they become.

Issues: Is it genuinely necessary to hold a hearing at all? If so, is there a need for more than one hearing? What is the appropriate length for the hearing and how should it be organized?

Options

A. Hold no hearing and have the case decided solely on the documents submitted by the parties.

B. Hold one or more hearings, as appropriate.

When a hearing is to be held, a certain number of choices need to be made, including:

- appropriate location;
- dates;
- attendees;
- appropriate duration;
- allocation of time between the parties;
- whether there are to be opening and/or closing statements and their duration;
- whether there should be direct examination, cross-examination and/or witness conferencing for fact and expert witnesses;
- whether the hearing should be transcribed and if so, whether daily transcripts and/or live transcripts (i.e. real-time transcripts available electronically to participants during the hearing) should be made;
- when interpreting is needed, whether it should be consecutive or simultaneous;
- whether to use videoconferencing for all or part of the hearing.

Pros and cons

Oral hearings are often considered as a key opportunity for the parties to present their case and for the arbitrators to understand it and assess the evidence.

On the other hand, oral hearings are typically one of the most expensive and time-consuming phases of the arbitral process. Costs are generated by a number of factors, including the extensive preparation that is usually necessary and the number of people attending the hearing. In addition, the arbitration is often delayed by the difficulty of finding a mutually convenient time in the calendars of all relevant participants.

Cost and time can nevertheless be reduced by making appropriate choices with respect to the organization of the hearing.

Cost/benefit analysis

In deciding whether to request or agree upon a hearing, the parties should take various factors into consideration. Hearings tend to be most useful when there are disputed issues of fact to be addressed by fact and expert witnesses. Parties may consider proceeding without a hearing, for example, when:

- the case turns exclusively on questions of contract interpretation that do not require witness testimony;
- the case turns exclusively on a question of law;
- no respondent is participating;
- the value of the dispute is low;
- there is a need for a quick decision.

It should be determined whether the potential benefits of a hearing justify the associated time and cost. The choices made with respect to the organization of the hearing may reduce time and cost and may affect the decision on whether or not to hold a hearing at all.

Appropriate location

Pursuant to Article 18(2) of the Rules, hearings may be conducted at any location and not necessarily at the place of the arbitration. The cost of the hearing can be reduced if a location likely to be advantageous in terms of cost is chosen.

Dates

To avoid delay, the dates for the hearing should be set at the earliest reasonable opportunity and recorded in everyone's calendars. Ideally, the hearing dates should be fixed during the first case management conference.

Attendees

Attendees should be limited to those genuinely necessary for the conduct of the hearing.

Time and cost can be reduced if an informed and knowledgeable party representative with decision-making authority participates in the preparation of and attends the hearing. Such a person will be in a position to make cost/benefit decisions in consultation with outside counsel. For companies, the party representative is often an in-house counsel. For states or state entities, an individual with decision-making authority can be appointed.

Appropriate duration

Under the Rules, there is no prescribed length for hearings. In practice, parties often request hearings that are longer than necessary. However, the longer the hearing, the greater the cost. The length of the hearing should be carefully chosen so as to allow no more time than is necessary for adequately presenting the case.

Use and duration of opening/closing statements

An opening statement is an opportunity to make a summary and synthesis of the case and can help focus the arbitral tribunal's attention on the key issues. The longer the statement, the greater the cost. When the case has already been fully developed in briefs with supporting documents and witness statements, it may not be necessary to repeat these matters in an opening statement.

A closing statement is an opportunity to make a summary and a synthesis of what happened at the hearing. However, if the parties are not given sufficient time to prepare a closing statement, it may be of little use. Furthermore, it may not be necessary to have both a closing statement and a post-hearing brief, as they are likely to repeat each other and unnecessarily increase time and cost.

Direct examination, cross-examination, witness conferencing

In some legal systems, the questioning of witnesses is largely conducted by the arbitral tribunal, with counsel for each side being invited to ask follow-up questions. Under this approach there is no direct examination or cross-examination.

In other legal systems, and increasingly in international arbitration, the questioning of witnesses is largely conducted by counsel through direct examination and cross-examination, with the arbitral tribunal having the right to interject questions or ask questions at the end of the witness's testimony.

The first approach will often result in a shorter and less expensive hearing. The second approach will often allow a more comprehensive examination of the witnesses. Since the first approach leaves the arbitral tribunal largely in control, there is little scope for the parties to make cost/benefit decisions. While the overall duration and cost of the second approach will often be greater, a number of choices can be made to reduce the time and cost, as follows:

Direct examination

Direct examination is the questioning of a witness by the party presenting that witness. In international arbitration, witnesses often submit written witness statements setting forth their evidence. When such statements have been submitted, direct examination may be dispensed with entirely or kept short (e.g. 10 or 15 minutes). This will reduce the length and cost of the hearing.

Cross-examination

Cross-examination is the questioning of a witness presented by the opposing party. If each side is given an overall allocation of time at the hearing, a party is free to determine how much time to use for each witness so long as the total time is not exceeded. Alternatively, time and cost can be reduced by setting time limits on the cross-examination of witnesses.

Consideration should also be given to the appropriate scope of cross-examination. Limiting its scope to matters covered in a witness's statement or in direct examination, if any, may reduce the length and cost of the hearing.

If it is not necessary to cross-examine certain witnesses who have provided statements for the other side, time and cost can be saved by not doing so. However, in that case, it may be necessary to obtain agreement from the other side or an order from the tribunal stipulating that the decision not to cross-examine a witness does not constitute an admission of the truth of that witness's written statement.

Witness conferencing

Witness conferencing can function as an alternative or an addition to cross-examination. In witness conferencing, two or more witnesses dealing with the same area of evidence are questioned together either by the arbitral tribunal first and then by counsel, or vice versa. The witnesses are also given the opportunity to debate with each other.

Witness conferencing (in particular of expert witnesses) can save time and cost insofar as it helps to focus on, clarify and resolve areas of evidential disagreement.

If the witness conferencing is directed by the arbitral tribunal, the arbitrators will need to prepare carefully beforehand in order to be able to fulfil their inquisitorial role effectively. It may deprive the parties of some control over the presentation of the case.

If the witness conferencing is directed by counsel, they retain greater control over the process and debate can still occur between the witnesses. In addition, the tribunal will have the opportunity to ask its own questions. However, some of the benefits of witness conferencing may be lost as the process is likely to be longer, more expensive and less focused.

Nature of transcripts, if needed

Transcripts are expensive, especially daily transcripts and live transcripts (i.e. real-time transcripts available electronically to participants during the hearing). A cost/benefit decision should be made on what is genuinely necessary. A transcript enables the parties and the tribunal to have a complete and accurate record of the evidence adduced at the hearing. It can be very helpful to the parties when preparing post-hearing briefs, if any, and to the tribunal when preparing the award. In very low value or simple cases, it may be possible to save the expense of a transcript at no great loss. In complex cases with many witnesses, the additional cost of daily transcripts and live transcripts may well be justified. They will facilitate effective cross-examination and be useful when preparing further witness questioning.

Consecutive or simultaneous interpreting, if needed

A choice must be made between simultaneous and consecutive interpreting.

Consecutive interpreting requires fewer interpreters and equipment, but is more than twice as long as simultaneous interpreting, which makes it more costly due notably to the extra time lawyers and experts will have to spend at the hearing. While it may be easier to control the accuracy of consecutive interpreting, that benefit must be weighed against the considerable time and cost it may add to the hearing.

Use of videoconferencing for all or part of the hearing

While it is generally preferable to hold hearings in the physical presence of the arbitrators, the parties and the witnesses, the significant time commitment and travel expenditure this may require from certain witnesses can be avoided by using videoconferencing.

Questions to ask

1. Is an oral hearing necessary for the fair determination of the issues in dispute so as to justify the extra time and cost it involves?

2. Is it necessary to test a written witness statement by cross-examining the witnesses at a hearing?

3. Is there a more convenient location for the hearing than the place of arbitration?

4. What is the earliest time at which dates for the hearing can be set?

5. Who genuinely needs to attend the hearing?

6. Should fact witnesses and/or expert witnesses be allowed to attend the hearing while other witnesses are giving testimony?

7. Taking into account the nature of the issues in dispute, the value of the dispute and the number of witnesses, what is the total number of days genuinely necessary for the hearing? Is the proposed length of the hearing justified in terms of cost?

8. How should the total time of the hearing be allocated between the parties?

9. Should there be an opening statement and if so, how long should it be? Is it genuinely necessary to have both a closing statement and a post-hearing brief? If there is to be a closing statement, how long should it be and how much time should be allocated for its preparation?

10. Does every witness need to be cross-examined?

11. Which areas of evidence require examination and what is the most efficient method of examination (cross-examination or witness conferencing)?

12. Should the hearing be transcribed and if so, should there be daily transcripts and/or live transcripts?

13. If interpreting is needed, should it be consecutive or simultaneous?

14. Should videoconferencing be used for all or part of the hearing?

TOPIC SHEET 11: POST-HEARING BRIEFS

Presentation

Parties in an arbitration have the opportunity to present their legal arguments and the relevant facts in pre-hearing submissions and during the hearing itself. The issue here is whether it is necessary or useful for the parties to submit post-hearing briefs.

Post-hearing briefs may be used to draw the arbitral tribunal's attention to relevant facts that have emerged at the hearing and place them in the context of the parties' claims and defences. They may be drafted in a manner that assists the arbitral tribunal with drafting the arbitral award. In some cases, the arbitral tribunal may identify key issues to be addressed by the parties in their post-hearing briefs.

If closing statements are made at the end of a hearing, post-hearing briefs may be unnecessary. Conversely, if there are post-hearing briefs, closing statements may be unnecessary.

Issue: Should there be post-hearing briefs and/or closing statements?

Options

A. Proceed directly from the hearing to an award with no closing statements or post-hearing briefs.

B. Provide for closing statements immediately after the hearing or at some agreed time thereafter, but no post-hearing briefs.

C. Provide for post-hearing briefs but no closing statements.

D. Provide for both closing statements and post-hearing briefs.

E. Post-hearing briefs, if any, can be submitted simultaneously or sequentially, and there can be more than one round of post-hearing briefs.

Pros and cons

The submission of post-hearing briefs can serve a number of useful purposes, as mentioned above. In a long and complex hearing, it may be useful for each party to sum up what they consider to have been demonstrated at the hearing. Post-hearing briefs can include valuable references to the hearing transcript and present a short final synthesis of the evidence and facts of the case, which can be of great value to the arbitral tribunal when drafting the award.

On the other hand, post-hearing briefs add to the cost of the arbitration and may delay the rendering of the award. In addition, they may be of little use if they merely repeat facts and arguments already well understood by the arbitral tribunal.

Cost/benefit analysis

The additional time and expense required for post-hearing briefs need to be balanced against the likelihood that they will genuinely serve one of the purposes indicated above. For example, post-hearing briefs will be especially useful where there are numerous witnesses, complicated or disputed facts, or extensive cross-examination. In all cases, the time and cost associated with post-hearing briefs should be weighed against their likely impact on the arbitral tribunal's decision.

The time and expense required for post-hearing briefs can often be reduced if measures are agreed to keep them relatively short and concise, e.g. limiting the number of pages.

Questions to ask

1. Does the case justify the extra time and expense required for post-hearing briefs, closing statements, or both?

And, in particular,

2. Are post-hearing briefs genuinely useful or necessary for a party to make its case to the arbitral tribunal, and if so, why?

3. What is the estimated cost of preparing the post-hearing briefs?

4. Is the benefit worth the cost, and if so, why?

Other points to consider

Consider limiting the scope, length and timing of any post-hearing briefs.

Consider having post-hearing briefs filed simultaneously to save time.

In some cases, it may be genuinely necessary to allow each party a short period of time in which to reply briefly to the other party's post-hearing brief.

In some cases, simultaneous post-hearing briefs may have the undesirable consequence of creating a need for further rounds of submissions. Care should therefore be taken to define properly the parameters of post-hearing briefs.

Post-hearing briefs may include submissions on costs, which are normally not discussed at the hearing. This can also save time.

APPENDIX 15

COMMISSION REPORT/SECOND EDITION – TECHNIQUES FOR CONTROLLING TIME AND COSTS IN ARBITRATION (2012)

REPORT OF THE ICC COMMISSION ON ARBITRATION AND ADR TASK FORCE ON REDUCING TIME AND COSTS IN ARBITRATION

PREFACE TO THE SECOND EDITION

Arbitration is a valuable tool for the resolution of disputes. However, if it is to serve the needs of its users, it must be time and cost effective. The first edition of this Report, published in August 2007, provided a range of techniques that could be used to increase the time and cost efficiency of arbitration. The final paragraph of the preface to that edition expressed the hope that the Report would be of use in the crafting of efficient arbitration procedures. That hope has become a reality. Since its publication, the Report has been positively received by the users of arbitration, as well as by arbitrators and counsel, and the techniques set out in the Report have been widely applied in institutional and *ad hoc* arbitrations all over the world. The need to focus on the time and cost efficiency of arbitration has become generally recognized, and the ideas in the Report have inspired much discussion as well as a large number of other publications.

In 2009, the ICC Commission on Arbitration (as it was then known) began its revision of the 1998 ICC Rules of Arbitration. A drafting subcommittee (the "DSC") was established to propose modifications to the Rules, taking into account suggestions received from national committees, the ICC International Court of Arbitration and its Secretariat, and the arbitration community at large. The DSC included two in-house counsel who consulted with the user community worldwide. The users proposed that the approach to time and cost efficiency taken in the Report should be incorporated into the Rules. This was accomplished in Articles 22-24 and Appendix IV of the 2012 ICC Rules of Arbitration. Article 22(1) places an explicit obligation on both the arbitral tribunal and the parties to make every effort to conduct the arbitration in an expeditious and cost-effective manner, having regard to the complexity and value of the dispute. Article 22(2) empowers the arbitral tribunal, in the absence of an agreement of the parties, to adopt appropriate procedural measures to ensure effective case management.

Article 24(1) requires the arbitral tribunal to convene a case management conference to consult the parties on appropriate procedural measures to be adopted pursuant to Article 22(2). It is expressly stated that those measures may include one or more of the techniques described in Appendix IV. Those techniques are taken directly from the Report.

In sum, the tailor-making of the arbitral procedure referred to in the preface to the first edition of the Report has become a formal requirement in the 2012 Rules, accomplished through the case management conference. Ideally, party representatives will be present so that they can participate in the choice of appropriate procedures for the case. To make an arbitration faster and cheaper, it may be necessary to forego certain steps, such as additional rounds of briefs, excessive document production, longer hearings, more experts, and the like. The goal at the case management conference is to arrive at procedures that are genuinely useful and necessary for the effective presentation of the case. Any additional procedures are likely to result in time and cost inefficiencies.

What, then, is the nature and function of this second edition of the Report? First, the Report has been updated to reflect the various modifications made in the 2012 Rules. Second, and more importantly, this edition of the Report should be seen as an adjunct to the 2012 Rules. It can be used to enhance the tailor-making process required by the Rules. In this edition the techniques set out in Appendix IV to the Rules are further discussed and explained. Additional techniques beyond those in Appendix IV are also presented. The hope that may be expressed for this edition of the Report is that it will help ensure the success of the tailor-making process under the 2012 Rules and thereby contribute to the increased effectiveness and attractiveness of international arbitration.

Peter M. Wolrich
Chairman, ICC Commission on Arbitration and ADR

PREFACE TO THE FIRST EDITION

One of the salient characteristics of arbitration as a dispute resolution mechanism is that the rules of arbitration themselves present a framework for arbitral proceedings but rarely set out detailed procedures for the conduct of the arbitration. For example, rules of arbitration do not generally specify whether there should be one, two or more exchanges of briefs. They do not contain any detailed provisions concerning document production. They do not specify how hearings should be conducted and how witnesses, if any, should be heard.

This important characteristic entails that the specific procedures can be tailor-made as appropriate for each dispute and adapted to the legal cultures of the parties and the arbitrators. In order to establish the appropriate procedures for a given arbitration, it is useful and efficient for the parties and the tribunal to make conscious decisions as early as possible on the procedures best suited to the dispute at hand. In making those decisions, it is possible to shape the arbitral proceedings so that the duration and cost of the arbitration are commensurate with what is at stake in the case and appropriate in light of the claims and issues presented.

With the above in mind, the Task Force on Reducing Time and Costs in Arbitration, set up by the ICC Commission on Arbitration and excellently co-chaired by Yves Derains and Christopher Newmark, has prepared the following document setting out a large number of techniques which can be used for organizing the arbitral proceedings and controlling their duration and cost. This document can provide valuable assistance to the parties and the tribunal in developing appropriate procedures for their arbitration. It is intended to encourage them to create a new dynamic at the outset of an arbitration, whereby the parties can review the suggested techniques and agree upon appropriate procedures and, if they fail to agree, the tribunal can decide upon such procedures. For example, an arbitral tribunal can send this document to the parties at the start of the proceedings, indicating that early in the proceedings they might seek to agree upon appropriate procedures in consultation with the tribunal. In that process, all may agree upon the use of certain techniques. If one party wishes to use a particular technique and the other party does not, the tribunal, after obtaining the views of each party on the matter, can decide whether or not to adopt that procedure. The use of this approach, coupled with the proactive involvement of the tribunal in the management of the proceedings, can result in meaningful savings of time and cost in the arbitration.

The techniques suggested in the document are not intended to be exhaustive. On the contrary, they are open-ended, and the parties and the tribunal are encouraged to think of this document as a basis from which to develop the procedures to be used. Indeed, it is the intention of the ICC Commission on Arbitration to revise and republish this document in the future, taking into account further suggestions which will emerge from the use of the document. As a corollary, it should be clear that parties and arbitrators are in no way obligated to follow any of the techniques. Moreover, the document is a product of the ICC Commission on Arbitration and not of the ICC International Court of Arbitration and thus it is not part of or interpretative of the ICC Rules of Arbitration or in any way binding upon the Court. Rather, it is a practical tool designed to stimulate the conscious choice of arbitral procedures with a view to organizing an arbitration which is efficient and appropriately tailor-made. Finally, while this document was conceived with the ICC Rules of Arbitration in mind, the vast majority of the techniques as well as the dynamics generated by the document can be used in all arbitrations.

It is the sincere hope of the Task Force that this document will be used and be of use in the crafting of efficient arbitration procedures in which time and cost will be proportionate to the needs of the dispute.

Peter M. Wolrich
Chairman, ICC Commission on Arbitration

INTRODUCTION

Costs incurred by the parties constitute the largest part of the total cost of international arbitration proceedings. It follows that if the overall cost of the arbitral proceedings is to be reduced, special emphasis needs to be placed on steps aimed at lowering the costs connected with the parties' presentation of their cases. Such costs are often caused by unnecessarily long and complicated proceedings with unfocused requests for disclosure of documents and unnecessary witness and expert evidence. Costs can also be unnecessarily increased when counsel from different legal backgrounds use procedures familiar to them in a manner that leads to needless duplication.

The increasing and, on occasion, unnecessary complication of the proceedings seems to be the main explanation for the long duration and high cost of many international arbitrations. The longer the proceedings, the more expensive they will be. The 2012 ICC Rules of Arbitration (the "Rules") have expressly addressed these concerns.

These Techniques for Controlling Time and Costs in Arbitration (the "Techniques") are designed to assist arbitral tribunals, parties and their counsel in devising tailor-made procedures for individual arbitrations pursuant to Articles 22-24 of the Rules.

In particular, the Techniques may be of benefit to the parties and the tribunal when preparing the case management conference and seeking agreement on procedures suitable for their case. If the parties cannot reach agreement, the Techniques may also assist the arbitral tribunal in adopting procedures that it considers appropriate, taking into account its obligation to conduct the arbitration in an expeditious and cost-effective manner. The Techniques are freely accessible online on the ICC's website (www.iccwbo.org) and in the ICC Dispute Resolution Library (www.iccdrl.com). They are in no way prescriptive. Rather, they provide suggestions that may assist in arriving at procedures that are efficient and will reduce both cost and time. Certain procedures will be appropriate for one arbitration, but inappropriate for another. There may be other procedures not mentioned here that are well suited to a particular case. In all instances, it is for the parties and the arbitral tribunal to select the procedures that are best suited for the case. The table of contents to this document can serve as a checklist of points to consider.

While the main focus of the Techniques is to provide guidance on the procedure during the arbitration, the first two sections give suggestions on the drafting of arbitration agreements and the initiation of arbitral proceedings.

ARBITRATION AGREEMENT

1 Keeping clauses simple

Simple, clearly drafted arbitration clauses will avoid uncertainty and disputes over their meaning and effect. They will minimize the risk of time and costs being spent on disputes regarding, for example, the jurisdiction of the arbitral tribunal or the process of appointing arbitrators. In all cases, ensure that the arbitration clause conforms with any relevant applicable laws.

2 Use of the ICC model clause

Use of the standard ICC arbitration clause is recommended. It provides as follows:

> All disputes arising out of or in connection with the present contract shall be finally settled under the Rules of Arbitration of the International Chamber of Commerce by one or more arbitrators appointed in accordance with said Rules.

Modifications to the standard clause can result in unintended and undesirable consequences and therefore should be made only with great care and for specific purposes. In addition to the standard clause, the parties may wish to specify in separate sentences the place of the arbitration, the language of the arbitration and the rules of law governing the contract. Be cautious about adding to this clause further provisions relating to the procedure for the arbitration.

The Rules permit any party in need of urgent or conservatory measures that cannot await the constitution of an arbitral tribunal to make an application to the ICC International Court of Arbitration (the "Court") for the appointment of an emergency arbitrator to decide upon the request for such measures. The parties should consider whether the Emergency Arbitrator Provisions as set out in Article 29 and Appendix V of the Rules are desirable in their particular situation. If the parties do not want the Emergency Arbitrator Provisions to apply, they must agree to opt out of those provisions and may do so by using the following model clause:

All disputes arising out of or in connection with the present contract shall be finally settled under the Rules of Arbitration of the International Chamber of Commerce by one or more arbitrators appointed in accordance with the said Rules. The Emergency Arbitrator Provisions shall not apply.

3 *Selection and appointment of arbitrators*

High-value and complex contracts can give rise to small disputes for which a three-member tribunal may be too expensive. Although parties may desire the certainty of appointing either a one- or a three-member tribunal in their arbitration agreement, consideration should be given to staying with the standard ICC arbitration clause and providing for one or more arbitrators. This will enable the ICC to appoint, or the parties to agree on, a sole arbitrator where the specific nature of any subsequent dispute does not warrant a three-member tribunal (Rules, Article 12(2)).

If the parties wish the ICC to select and appoint all members of the arbitral tribunal (see paragraph 11 below), then the following wording can be used: "All arbitrators shall be selected and appointed by the ICC International Court of Arbitration."

Adding special requirements regarding the expertise and qualifications of arbitrators to be appointed will reduce the pool of available arbitrators and may increase the time taken to select a tribunal.

4 *Fast-track procedures*

Consideration may be given to setting out fast-track procedures in the arbitration clause. Indeed, Article 38(1) of the Rules enables the parties to shorten time limits provided for in the Rules, while Article 38(2) enables the Court to extend those shortened time limits when necessary. Fast-track procedures are designed to enable an arbitration to proceed quickly, given the specific nature of the contract and the disputes that are likely to arise. However, experience shows that in practice it is difficult at the time of drafting the clause to predict with a reasonable degree of certainty the nature of disputes and the procedures that will be suitable for those disputes. Also, disagreements can arise later over the interpretation or application of fast-track clauses. Careful thought should therefore be given before such provisions are included in an arbitration agreement. Once a dispute has arisen, the parties could at that time agree upon a fast-track procedure, if appropriate.

5 *Time limits for rendering the final award*

One commonly used provision that can give rise to significant difficulties is the requirement that a final award be produced within a certain number of weeks or months from the commencement of the arbitration. Such specific time limits can create jurisdictional and enforcement problems if it turns out that the time limit specified is unrealistic or not clearly defined.

6 *More detailed arbitration agreement after the dispute has arisen*

If the parties agree to submit a dispute to ICC arbitration after the dispute has arisen, they can consider specifying in some detail the procedure for the arbitration, taking into account the nature of the dispute in question. This procedure may include some of the suggestions set out below to control time and costs.

INITIATION OF PROCEEDINGS

Selection of counsel

7 Counsel with experience

Consider appointing counsel with the skills necessary for handling the arbitration at hand and who are sensitive to the need for appropriate time and cost efficiency. Such counsel are more likely to be able to work with the arbitral tribunal and the other party's counsel to devise an efficient procedure for the case.

8 Counsel with time

Ensure that the counsel you have selected has sufficient time to devote to the case.

Selection of arbitrators

9 Use of a sole arbitrator

After a dispute has arisen, consider agreeing upon having a sole arbitrator, when appropriate. Generally speaking, a one-member tribunal will be able to act more quickly than a three-member tribunal, since discussions between tribunal members are not needed and diary clashes for hearings will be minimized. A one-member tribunal will obviously also be cheaper.

10 Arbitrators with time

Whether selecting a sole arbitrator or a three-member tribunal, it is advisable to make sufficient enquiries to ensure that the individuals selected have sufficient time to devote to the case in question. If there is a particular need for speed, this must be made clear to the ICC so that it can be taken into consideration when making any appointments.

11 Selection and appointment by the ICC

Consider allowing the ICC to select and appoint the arbitral tribunal, whether it be a sole arbitrator or a three-person tribunal. This will generally be the quickest way to constitute the arbitral tribunal if there is no agreement between the parties on the identity of all arbitrators. It will also reduce the risk of challenges, facilitate the constitution of a tribunal having a variety of specialist skills and create a different dynamic within the arbitral tribunal. If the parties wish to have input into the selection of the tribunal by the ICC, they can request that the ICC provide a list of possible arbitrators to be selected in accordance with a procedure to be agreed upon by the parties in consultation with the ICC.

12 Avoiding objections

Any objection to the appointment of an arbitrator will delay the constitution of the arbitral tribunal. When selecting an arbitrator, give careful thought to whether or not the appointment of that arbitrator might give rise to an objection.

13 Selecting arbitrators with strong case management skills

A tribunal that is proactive and skilled in case management will be able to play its role in managing the arbitration so as to make it as cost and time effective as possible, given the issues in dispute and the number and nature of the parties. Careful consideration should therefore be given to selecting tribunal members, especially the sole arbitrator or chair.

Request for Arbitration and Answer

14 Complying with the Rules

The claimant should ensure that the Request for Arbitration includes all of the elements required by Article 4(3), subparagraphs (a)-(h), of the Rules. Failure to do so may make it necessary for the Secretariat to revert to the Claimant before the Request can be forwarded to the Respondent in accordance with Article 4(5). This causes delay. Similarly, when filing its Answer, the Respondent should include all elements required by Article 5(1), subparagraphs (a)-(f), of the Rules.

15 Setting out a detailed statement of case

The Rules do not require a Request for Arbitration or an Answer to set out a full statement of case for either the claim or the defence (or, where applicable, a counterclaim). Whether or not a full statement is made in the Request can have an impact on the efficient management of the arbitration. Where the Request does contain detailed particulars of the claim, and a similar approach is taken by the respondent in the Answer, the parties and the arbitral tribunal will be in a position to make informed decisions at a very early stage in the proceedings regarding the procedural measures and case management techniques that are appropriate for the case. This will help to optimize the first case management conference held pursuant to Article 24(1).

16 Submitting additional information

The Rules expressly allow the parties to submit with a Request or an Answer any further documents or information that may contribute to the efficient resolution of the dispute (see Articles 4(3) and 5(1)). Those provisions allow for the submission of a full statement of case but also allow the parties simply to submit additional useful information. Consideration should be given to exercising this option, whether or not a full statement of case is provided.

Language of the arbitration

17 Determination of the language by the arbitral tribunal

If the parties have not agreed on the language of the arbitration, the arbitral tribunal, when determining the language, should consider doing so by means of a procedural order pursuant to Article 20 of the Rules, prior to drawing up the Terms of Reference and after ascertaining the positions of the parties.

18 Proceedings involving two or more languages

Having two or more languages of the arbitration will normally increase time and cost. Consideration should be given to whether the use of two or more languages truly justifies the additional time and cost. On the other hand, where there is a single language of the arbitration, the use of an additional language should be considered if it would reduce time and cost. For example, where appropriate, the parties can agree that documents, legal materials and witness testimony in a particular language need not be translated into the language of the arbitration.

If the parties have agreed, or the arbitral tribunal has decided, that the arbitration will be conducted in two or more languages, the parties and the arbitral tribunal should consider agreeing upon practical means to avoid duplication. In cases where the members of the arbitral tribunal are fluent in all applicable languages, it may not be necessary for documents to be translated. Consideration should also be given to avoiding having the Terms of Reference, procedural orders and awards in more than one language. If this cannot be avoided, the parties would be well advised to agree upon the language that will prevail.

ESTABLISHING THE FRAMEWORK OF THE ARBITRAL PROCEEDINGS

The Rules call for the framework of the arbitral proceedings to be established in three steps: the Terms of Reference; the case management conference; and the procedural timetable. The paragraphs that follow provide suggestions on how to use each of these steps to optimize time and cost efficiency.

Terms of reference

19 Summaries of claims and relief sought

The arbitral tribunal should consider whether it is appropriate for it to draft the summary of claims and/or the relief sought itself, or whether it would assist if each party were to provide a draft summary for inclusion in the Terms of Reference in accordance with Article 23(1), subparagraph (c), of the Rules. In the latter case, the arbitral tribunal should consider requesting the parties to limit their summaries to an appropriate fixed number of pages. Further guidance on preparing Terms of Reference can be found in the article of Serge Lazareff, "Terms of Reference", ICC International Court of Arbitration Bulletin, Vol. 17/No. 1 (2006).[1]

20 Empowering the president of the arbitral tribunal on procedural issues

Where there is a three-member tribunal, it may not be necessary for all procedural issues to be decided upon by all three arbitrators. The parties should consider empowering the president of the arbitral tribunal to decide on certain procedural issues alone. In all events, consider authorizing the president to sign procedural orders alone.

21 Administrative secretary to the arbitral tribunal

Consider whether or not an administrative secretary to the arbitral tribunal would assist in reducing time and cost. If it is decided to use such a secretary, the parties and the arbitral tribunal should take into account the Note of the Secretariat of the Court on the Appointment, Duties and Remuneration of Administrative Secretaries. It is distributed to arbitrators in all cases and is reproduced in the ICC International Court of Arbitration Bulletin, Vol. 23/No. 1 (2012)).

22 Need for a physical meeting

Consider whether it is appropriate to agree upon and sign the Terms of Reference without a physical meeting (e.g. by way of a telephone or video conference). In making that decision, the advantages of having a physical meeting at the start of the

1. The Bulletin is available from the ICC Store (www.storeiccwbo.org) and online in the ICC Dispute Resolution Library (www.iccdrl.com).

proceedings should be weighed against the time and cost involved. The holding of the case management conference should also be taken into account when deciding whether or not to hold a physical meeting (see paragraph 31 below).

23 Counterparts

If there is no physical meeting for signing the Terms of Reference, the arbitral tribunal should consider having the Terms of Reference signed in counterparts.

24 Compliance with Article 23(3)

If a party refuses to take part in drawing up the Terms of Reference or refuses to sign them, the arbitral tribunal should make certain that the Terms of Reference to be submitted to the Court for approval pursuant to Article 23(3) of the Rules do not contain any provisions that require the parties' agreement or a decision by the arbitral tribunal.

Case management conferences

25 Timing

Article 24(1) requires the arbitral tribunal to convene a case management conference when drawing up the Terms of Reference or as soon as possible thereafter. Consider whether it is most convenient and efficient to hold the case management conference immediately after the signing of the Terms of Reference and at the same meeting.

26 Preparation

For the case management conference to be most effective, the tribunal should consider asking the parties well in advance of the conference to submit joint or separate case management proposals. This will encourage them actively to consider and exchange views on the procedures and case management techniques that may be appropriate for the case. Any joint or separate proposals from the parties, any agreements between the parties, and any suggestions from the tribunal should be discussed at the case management conference. It should be noted that, in accordance with Article 22(2) of the Rules, the arbitral tribunal may not adopt procedural measures that are contrary to an agreement of the parties.

27 Use of the Techniques

Appendix IV of the Rules sets out examples of available case management techniques. These and additional examples are also contained in this Report. They can be used by the arbitral tribunal and the parties at the case management conference to assist in arriving at the most appropriate procedures for the case (see the section entitled "Subsequent procedure for the arbitration" below).

28 Providing information in advance of the conference

The more information the arbitral tribunal has about the issues in the case prior to the conference, the better placed it will be to assist the parties in devising a procedure that will deal with the dispute as efficiently as possible. For example, a tribunal that has made itself familiar with the details of the case from the outset can be proactive and give appropriate, tailor-made suggestions on the issues to be addressed in documentary and witness evidence, the areas in which it will be assisted by expert evidence, and the extent to which disclosure of documents by the parties is needed to address the issues in dispute.

29 Scope

Whenever possible, the procedure for the entire arbitration should be determined at the first case management conference and reflected in the procedural timetable to be established pursuant to Article 24(2) of the Rules. However, it may not always be possible to do so, for example in very complex cases or in cases where insufficient detail has been provided prior to the first case management conference. In such situations, the procedural timetable would lay out the procedure as far as can be done (e.g. through a first round of briefs) and a second case management conference would be held promptly to determine the remainder of the procedure for the arbitration.

30 Client attendance

Article 24(4) of the Rules expressly allows the arbitral tribunal to request the attendance at the case management conference of the parties in person or through an internal representative. The tribunal should consider *requiring* such attendance. When clients are present at the case management conference, they can play an active role in the decision-making process. They should be empowered to make case management decisions. Such decisions call for a cost-benefit analysis. For example, is an additional round of briefs worth the time and expense? Is a degree of discovery-style document production likely to produce benefits justifying the time and cost?

31 Need for a physical meeting

As with the drawing up of the Terms of Reference (see paragraph 22 above) and as permitted by Article 24(4), consider whether it is appropriate to hold the case management conference by way of telephone, video conference or similar means of communication that do not involve a physical meeting. If the case management conference is to be held at the same time as the Terms of Reference are signed, consider whether that would justify a physical meeting for both purposes.

32 Use of discretion in apportionment of costs

Pursuant to Article 37(5) of the Rules, the extent to which each party has conducted the arbitration in an expeditious and cost-effective manner may be taken into account by the arbitral tribunal in determining who shall bear what portion of the costs of the arbitration. The arbitral tribunal should consider informing the parties at the case management conference that in exercising its discretion to allocate costs pursuant to the Rules, it will take into consideration any unreasonable failure to comply with procedures agreed upon or ordered in the arbitration or any other unreasonable conduct (see paragraph 82 below).

33 Further case management conferences

Consider holding further case management conferences during the course of the arbitration, as appropriate. Such conferences may be held prior to significant phases in the procedure (e.g. the exchange of witness statements) so as to ensure that the procedure provided for that phase remains appropriate. Short telephone conferences may also be held at regular intervals (e.g. once a month) to enable the arbitral tribunal to check on progress and discuss with the parties any unforeseen procedural issues that have arisen or may shortly arise.

Procedural timetable

34 Compliance with the procedural timetable

Consistent with their obligation under Article 22(1) of the Rules to make every effort to conduct the arbitration in an expeditious and cost-effective manner, the arbitrators and the parties should make all reasonable efforts to comply with the procedural timetable. Extensions and revisions of the timetable should be made only when justified. Any revisions should be promptly communicated to the Court and the parties in accordance with Article 24(2) of the Rules.

35 Need for a hearing

Consider whether or not it is necessary for there to be a hearing in order for the arbitral tribunal to decide the case. If it is possible for the arbitral tribunal to decide the case on documents alone, this will significantly reduce costs and time.

36 Fixing the hearing date

If a hearing is necessary, then early in the proceedings (ideally at the first case management conference) consider fixing the date for this hearing. This will reduce the likelihood that the arbitral proceedings become drawn out and will enable the procedure leading up to the hearing to be adapted to the time available.

37 Pre-hearing conference

Consider organizing a conference with the arbitral tribunal, which may be by telephone, to discuss the arrangements for any hearing. At such a pre-hearing conference, held a suitable time before the hearing itself, the parties and the arbitral tribunal can discuss matters such as time allocation, use of transcripts, translation issues, order of witnesses and other practical arrangements that will facilitate the smooth conduct of the hearing. The arbitral tribunal may consider using the occasion of the pre-hearing conference to indicate to the parties the issues on which it would like them to focus at the forthcoming hearing.

38 Short and realistic time periods

When deciding upon the length of the final hearing and the amount of time required for all procedural steps leading up to that hearing, choose the shortest times that are realistic. Unrealistically short periods of time are likely to result in longer rather than shorter proceedings, should they need to be rescheduled.

39 Bifurcation and partial awards

The arbitral tribunal should consider, or the parties could agree on, bifurcating the proceedings or rendering a partial award when doing so may genuinely be expected to result in a more efficient resolution of the case.

40 Briefing everyone involved in the case

As soon as the proceedings start, parties should give thought to the input that will be needed for each step in the anticipated timetable. Once the timetable is set, the parties should consider precisely what is required of them to comply with the timetable. It will be useful for all relevant personnel to be briefed accordingly (e.g. management within the client organization, witnesses, internal and external lawyers, experts). This will greatly assist in enabling everyone to reserve the time needed to provide input at the relevant point in the procedure and will assist in enabling each party to adhere to deadlines set in the timetable.

Settlement

41 Arbitral tribunal's role in promoting settlement

The arbitral tribunal should consider informing the parties that they are free to settle all or part of the dispute at any time during the ongoing arbitration, either through direct negotiations or through any form of ADR proceedings. For example, mediation proceedings can be conducted under the ICC Mediation Rules, further information on which can be found in the ICC International Court of Arbitration Bulletin, Vol. 24/No. 2 (2013).

42 Settlement initiatives taken with the parties' agreement

The parties may request the arbitral tribunal to suspend the arbitration proceedings for a specific period of time while settlement discussions take place. The parties may also agree that the arbitral tribunal should take other steps to facilitate settlement of their dispute, provided that such steps are not inconsistent with the tribunal's duty under Article 41 of the Rules to make every effort to make sure that its award is enforceable at law.

SUBSEQUENT PROCEDURE FOR THE ARBITRATION

The paragraphs that follow give guidance on the points to be discussed by the parties and the arbitral tribunal at the case management conference. They provide suggestions that may assist in reducing the cost and duration of the proceedings.

Written submissions

Written submissions come in different forms and are given different names. They include the Request for Arbitration and the Answer, statements of case and defence, memorials and other written arguments, and opening and closing written submissions. These comments apply to written submissions generally.

43 Setting out the case in full early in the proceedings

If the parties set out their cases in full early in the proceedings, the parties and the arbitral tribunal will be better able to understand the key issues at an early stage. Doing so will help ensure that the procedure defined at the case management conference is efficient and that time and money are not wasted on matters that turn out to be of no direct relevance to the issues to be determined.

44 Avoiding repetition

Avoid unnecessary repetition of arguments. Once a party has set out its position in full, it should not be necessary to repeat the arguments at later stages (e.g. in pre-hearing memorials, oral submissions or post-hearing memorials), and the arbitral tribunal may direct that there be no such repetition.

45 Sequential or simultaneous delivery

Consider whether it is more effective for written submissions to be sequential or simultaneous. Whilst simultaneous submissions enable both parties to inform each other of their cases at the same time (and this may make things quicker), it can also result in inefficiency if the parties raise different issues in their submissions and extensive submissions are required in response.

46 Specifying form and content

Consider specifying the form and content of written submissions. For example, clarify whether the first round of written submissions should or should not be accompanied by witness statements and/or expert reports.

47 Limiting the length of submissions

Consider agreeing on limiting the length of specific submissions. This can help focus attention on the key issues to be addressed and is likely to save time and cost.

48 Limiting the number of submissions

Consider limiting the number of rounds of submissions. This may help to avoid repetition and encourage the parties to present all key issues in their first submissions.

Documentary evidence

49 Organization of documents

From the outset of the case the parties should consider using a coherent system for numbering or otherwise identifying documents produced in the case. This process can start with the Request for Arbitration and the Answer, and a system for the remainder of the arbitration can be established with the arbitral tribunal at the time of the first case management conference.

50 Producing documents on which the parties rely

The parties will normally each produce the documents upon which they intend to rely. Each party should consider avoiding requests for production of documents from another party unless such production is relevant and material to the outcome of the case. When the parties have agreed upon non-controversial facts, no documentary evidence should be needed to prove those facts.

51 Establishing procedure for requests for production

Consider whether requests for production of documents are genuinely necessary. If they are, the parties and the arbitral tribunal should consider establishing a clear and efficient procedure for the submission and exchange of documents. In that regard, they could consider referring to Article 3 of the IBA Rules on the Taking of Evidence in International Arbitration for guidance. In addition, the parties and the arbitral tribunal should consider establishing an appropriate time frame for the production of documents. In most situations, this is likely to be after the parties have set out their cases in full for the first time. If issues concerning the production of electronic documents arise, consider referring to the ICC Commission Report *Managing E-Document Production*[2] for information and guidance on how to manage such production in an efficient and cost-effective manner.

52 Managing requests for production efficiently

Time and costs associated with requests for production of documents, if any, can further be reduced by agreeing upon one or more of the following:

- Limiting the number of requests;
- Limiting requests to the production of documents (whether in paper or electronic form) that are relevant and material to the outcome of the case;
- Establishing reasonable time limits for the production of documents;
- Using the Schedule of Document Production devised by Alan Redfern (often referred to as the Redfern Schedule) in the form of a chart containing the following four columns:
    - First Column: identification of the document(s) or categories of documents that have been requested;
    - Second Column: short description of the reasons for each request;
    - Third Column: summary of the objections by the other party to the production of the document(s) or categories of documents requested; and
    - Fourth Column: left blank for the decision of the arbitral tribunal on each request.

53 Avoiding duplication

It is common for each of the parties to produce copies of the same documents, appended to their statements of case, witness statements or other written submissions. Avoiding duplication where possible will reduce costs.

54 Selection of documents to be provided to the arbitral tribunal

It is wasteful to provide the arbitrators with documents that are not material to their determination of the case. In particular, it will usually not be appropriate to send to the arbitral tribunal all documents produced pursuant to production requests. This not only generates unnecessary costs, but also makes it harder for the arbitral tribunal to prepare efficiently.

55 Keeping hard copies to a minimum

Consider minimizing the volume of paper documents that need to be produced. Exchanging documents in electronic form can reduce costs (see the ICC Commission Report *Managing E-Document Production* and the 2004 Special Supplement of the ICC International Court of Arbitration Bulletin, *Using Technology to Resolve Business Disputes*).

2. Available online at < www.iccwbo.org/about-icc/policy-commissions/arbitration/commission-rules,-reports-and-guidelines/ > and at < www.iccdrl.com >.

56 Translations

Try to agree how translations of any documents are to be dealt with. Reducing the need for certified translations will help to lower costs. Certified translations may be required only where translation issues emerge from unofficial translations.

57 Authenticity of documents

Consider providing that documents produced by the parties are deemed to be authentic unless and until such authenticity is challenged by another party.

Correspondence

58 Correspondence between counsel

Avoid unnecessary correspondence between counsel. The arbitral tribunal may consider informing the parties that the persistent use of such correspondence may be viewed as unreasonable conduct and be taken into consideration by the arbitral tribunal when exercising its discretion in allocating costs pursuant to the Rules (see paragraph 82 below).

59 Sending correspondence to the arbitral tribunal

Avoid sending correspondence between counsel to the arbitral tribunal unless a decision of the arbitral tribunal is required. Any such correspondence that is addressed to the arbitral tribunal should be copied to the Secretariat in accordance with Article 3(1) of the Rules.

Witness statements

60 Limiting the number of witnesses

Every witness adds to the costs, both when a witness statement is prepared and considered and when the witness attends to give oral evidence. Costs can be saved by limiting the number of witnesses to those whose evidence is required on key issues. The arbitral tribunal may assist in identifying those issues on which witness evidence is required and focusing the evidence from witnesses on those issues. This whole process will be facilitated if the parties can reach agreement on non-controversial facts that do not need to be addressed by witness evidence.

61 Minimizing the number of rounds of witness statements

If there are to be witness statements, consider the timing for the exchange of such statements so as to minimize the number of rounds of statements that are required. For example, consider whether it is preferable for witness statements to be exchanged after all documents on which the parties wish to rely have been produced, so that the witnesses can comment on those documents in a single statement.

Expert evidence

62 Presumption that expert evidence not required

It is helpful to start with a presumption that expert evidence will not be required. Depart from this presumption only if expert evidence is needed in order to inform the arbitral tribunal on key issues in dispute.

63 ICC expert services

If either the parties or the arbitral tribunal require assistance in identifying an expert witness, recourse can be had to the ICC International Centre for ADR pursuant to the ICC Rules for the Proposal of Experts and Neutrals or the ICC Rules for the Appointment of Experts and Neutrals. Where an ICC arbitral tribunal seeks a proposal from the Centre for a tribunal-appointed expert, the services of the Centre are available at no cost. Further information regarding the operation of the ICC's rules and services relating to experts can be found on the ICC website at www.iccwbo.org/products-and-services/arbitration-and-adr/expertise/.

64 Clarity regarding the subject matter and scope of reports

It is essential for there to be clarity at an early stage (by agreement, if possible) over the subject matter and scope of any expert evidence to be produced. This will help to ensure that the experts appointed by the parties have similar expertise and address the same issues.

65 Number of experts

Other than in exceptional circumstances, it should not be necessary for there to be more than one expert per party for any particular area of expertise.

66 Number of reports

Consider agreeing on a limit to the number of rounds of expert reports and consider whether simultaneous or sequential exchange will be more efficient.

67 Meetings of experts

Experts will often be able to narrow the issues in dispute if they can meet and discuss their views after they have exchanged reports. Consideration should therefore be given to providing that experts shall take steps to agree on issues in advance of any hearing at which their evidence is to be presented. Time and cost can be saved if the experts draw up a list recording the issues on which they have agreed and those on which they disagree.

68 Use of single expert

Consider whether a single expert appointed either by the arbitral tribunal or jointly by the parties might be more efficient than experts appointed by each party. A single, tribunal-appointed expert may be more efficient in some circumstances. An expert appointed by the arbitral tribunal or jointly by the parties should be given a clear brief and the expert's report should be required by a specified date consistent with the timetable for the arbitration.

Hearings

69 Minimizing the length and number of hearings

Hearings are expensive and time-consuming. If the length and number of hearings requiring the physical attendance of the arbitral tribunal and the parties are minimized, this will significantly reduce the time and cost of the proceedings.

70 Choosing the best location for hearings

Pursuant to Article 18(2) of the Rules, hearings do not need to be held at the place of the arbitration. The arbitral tribunal and the parties can select the most efficient place to hold hearings. In some cases, it may be more cost-effective to hold hearings at a location that, for example, is convenient to the majority of the witnesses due to give evidence at that hearing.

71 Telephone and video conferencing

For procedural hearings in particular, consider the use of telephone and video conferencing, where appropriate. Also, consider whether certain witnesses can give evidence by video link, so as to avoid the need to travel to an evidentiary hearing.

72 Providing submissions in good time

The arbitral tribunal should be provided with all necessary submissions (e.g. pre-hearing briefs, if any) sufficiently in advance of any hearing to be able to read them, prepare and become fully informed of the issues to be addressed.

73 Cut-off date for evidence

In advance of any evidentiary hearing, consider setting a cut-off date after which no new documentary evidence will be admitted unless a compelling reason is shown.

74 Identifying core documents

Consider providing the arbitral tribunal, in advance of any hearing, with a list of the documents it needs to read in preparation for the hearing. Where appropriate, this can be done by preparing and delivering to the arbitral tribunal a bundle of core documents on which the parties rely.

75 Agenda and timetable

Consider agreeing on an agenda and timetable for all hearings, with an equitable division of time between each of the parties. Consider the use of a chess clock to monitor the fair allocation of time.

76 Avoiding repetition

Consideration should be given to whether it is necessary to repeat pre-hearing written submissions in opening oral statements. This is sometimes done because of concern that the arbitral tribunal will not have read or digested the written submissions. If the arbitral tribunal has been provided with the documents it needs to read in advance of the hearing and has prepared properly, no such repetition will be necessary.

77 Need for witnesses to appear

Prior to any hearing, consider whether all witnesses need to give oral evidence. This is a matter on which the parties' counsel can confer and seek to reach agreement.

78 Use of written statements as direct evidence

Cost and time can be saved by limiting or avoiding direct examination of witnesses. When appropriate, witness statements can substitute for direct examination at a hearing.

79 Witness conferencing

Witness conferencing is a technique in which two or more fact or expert witnesses presented by one or more of the parties are questioned together on particular topics by the arbitral tribunal and possibly by counsel. Consider whether this technique is appropriate for the arbitration at hand.

80 Limiting cross-examination

If there is to be cross-examination of witnesses, the arbitral tribunal, after hearing the parties, should consider limiting the time available to each party for such cross-examination.

81 Closing submissions

Consider whether post-hearing submissions can be avoided in order to save time and cost. However, if post-hearing submissions are required, consider providing for either oral or written closing submissions. The use of both will result in additional time and cost. In order to give focus, the arbitral tribunal should consider providing counsel with a list of questions or issues to be addressed by the parties in the closing submissions. Any written closing submissions should be provided by an agreed date as soon as reasonable following the hearing.

Costs

82 Using allocation of costs to encourage efficient conduct of the proceedings

The allocation of costs can be a useful tool to encourage efficient behaviour and discourage unreasonable behaviour. Pursuant to Article 37(5) of the Rules, the arbitral tribunal has discretion to award costs in such a manner as it considers appropriate. It is expressly stated that in making its decisions on costs, the tribunal may take into consideration the extent to which each party has conducted the arbitration in an expeditious and cost-effective manner. The tribunal should consider informing the parties at the outset of the arbitration (e.g. at the case management conference) that it intends to take into account the manner in which each party has conducted the proceedings and to sanction any unreasonable behaviour by a party when deciding on costs. Unreasonable behaviour could include: excessive document requests, excessive legal argument, excessive cross-examination, dilatory tactics, exaggerated claims, failure to comply with procedural orders, unjustified applications for interim relief, and unjustified failure to comply with the procedural calendar.

Deliberations and awards

83 Anticipating the time required

Before closing the proceedings, the arbitral tribunal should ensure that time has been reserved in each of the arbitrators' diaries for deliberation promptly thereafter. The arbitral tribunal should promptly comply with Article 27 of the Rules and indicate to the Secretariat and the parties the date by which it expects to submit its draft award to the Court.

84 Prompt completion of the award

The arbitral tribunal must use its best efforts to submit the draft award as quickly as possible and should follow the guidance on drafting awards in the ICC Award Checklist sent to all arbitrators when the case file is transmitted to them. Further guidance can be found in the article "Drafting Awards in ICC Arbitrations" by Humphrey LLoyd, Marco Darmon, Jean-Pierre Ancel, Lord Dervaird, Christoph Liebscher and Herman Verbist, published in the ICC International Court of Arbitration Bulletin, Vol. 16/No. 2 (2005).

SPECIAL CONSIDERATIONS

Multiparty and multicontract arbitrations

85 Conditions imposed by Articles 7-9 of the Rules

Subject to certain conditions set forth in the Rules, Article 7 expressly permits the joinder of additional parties; Article 8 expressly permits claims between multiple parties; and Article 9 expressly permits claims arising out of more than one contract to be brought in a single arbitration, even if the claims are made under more than one arbitration agreement. Clearly, time and cost will be wasted if a party seeks to apply those provisions when the conditions set forth in the Rules are not met. For example, a Request for Joinder pursuant to Article 7 will be successful only if the joined party is bound by the arbitration agreement under which the claims in the arbitration are made; in addition, no additional party may be joined after the confirmation or appointment of any arbitrator, unless otherwise agreed. While Article 9 allows claims to be made in a single arbitration under more than one arbitration agreement, those claims will only be sustained only if the different arbitration agreements are compatible. The conditions imposed by Articles 7, 8 and 9 should be carefully studied so as to avoid wasting time and money by making claims that will be rejected or by claiming against parties over whom the tribunal will have no jurisdiction.

86 Adapting procedures to multiparty and multicontract cases

The presence of one or more additional parties, the existence of one or more claims between claimants or between respondents, and the existence of claims under more than one contract are likely to complicate the proceedings. Care should be taken at the case management conference to devise tailor-made procedures, appropriate to the specifics of the case at hand, for dealing with the presence of additional parties, cross-claims, and multicontract claims.

Consolidation

87 Consider consolidating related cases

Article 10 of the Rules provides for the consolidation of two or more separate arbitrations brought under the Rules when all of the parties to those arbitrations consent to the consolidation. Consider whether giving such consent would result in a more efficient resolution of the disputes.

Emergency arbitrator proceedings

88 Issues to consider before initiating emergency arbitrator proceedings

Subject to the conditions set forth in the Rules, the Emergency Arbitrator Provisions allow a party to seek urgent interim or conservatory measures from an emergency arbitrator acting under the Rules. The emergency arbitrator offers an alternative forum to state courts for seeking such relief. In deciding whether to file an Application for Emergency Measures, a party should consider a number of issues: first, whether it is genuinely useful and necessary to spend time and money on seeking to obtain interim or conservatory measures; second, whether an application for Emergency Measures under the Rules is preferable to seeking interim measures in a state court. Furthermore, the party should make sure that the conditions for bringing emergency arbitrator proceedings under the Rules are met. For example, the party making the application must be able to demonstrate that it needs urgent interim or conservatory measures that cannot await the constitution of the arbitral tribunal. Also, emergency arbitrator proceedings may only be brought against a signatory of the arbitration agreement or the signatory's successor. An attempt to bring emergency arbitrator proceedings that do not meet all of the conditions will result in needless expenditure and loss of time. Further information on ICC emergency arbitrator proceedings can be found in Jason Fry, Simon Greenberg, Francesca Mazza, The Secretariat's Guide to ICC Arbitration (ICC Publication 729)[3] and in Andrea Carlevaris and José Ricardo Feris, 'Running in the ICC Emergency Arbitrator Rules: The First Ten Cases', published in the ICC International Court of Arbitration Bulletin, Vol. 25/No. 1 (2014).[4]

3. Available from <www.storeiccwbo.org> and online at <www.iccdrl.com>.
4. The article is available as an e-chapter from <www.storeiccwbo.org>.

APPENDIX 16

COMMISSION REPORT – ARBITRATION INVOLVING STATES AND STATE ENTITIES UNDER THE ICC RULES OF ARBITRATION (2012)

REPORT OF THE ICC COMMISSION ON ARBITRATION AND ADR TASK FORCE ON ARBITRATION INVOLVING STATES OR STATE ENTITIES (2012)

Introduction

1. This report has been produced under the auspices of the ICC Commission on Arbitration. Its purpose is to explain how ICC arbitration works in relation to disputes involving states and state entities. It will be of interest to states, state entities and their legal advisers, but also to other organizations and entities that have relations with states and seek information on the options available to them when resolving disputes involving states or state entities.

2. The report is the work of the Commission Task Force on Arbitration Involving States and State Entities. The Task Force was created in recognition of the fact that ICC arbitration, although a powerful dispute resolution tool, was underused in disputes involving states and state entities and that some explanation was required on the advantages it offers and on how the ICC Rules of Arbitration (the "ICC Rules") operate in this context. That explanation is better given in a report than by way of a separate set of rules for state and state entity arbitration.

3. The recent revision of the ICC Rules has made a separate set of rules applicable to cases involving states or state entities unnecessary. The 2012 ICC Rules contain new provisions that reflect the work of the Task Force and are intended to facilitate and further the participation of state parties in ICC arbitration.

4. Users of international arbitration may be unaware of the recommendations, rules and practices that have been developed in the ICC arbitration system to take into account the participation of a state or state entity. This report seeks to raise awareness of those recommendations, rules and practices within the international arbitration community.

---

5. The aforementioned recommendations, rules and practices relate to two aspects of ICC arbitration involving states and state entities: the arbitration agreement and procedure. This report is intended to provide guidance on these matters.

6. The report begins with some background facts on ICC arbitrations involving states and state entities. It then offers recommendations on drafting arbitration agreements. Lastly, it looks at matters of procedure that specifically address arbitrations involving states and state entities.

Background

7. ICC arbitration is often used by states and state entities. Approximately 10 per cent of ICC arbitrations involve a state or a state entity.

8. ICC arbitration is chosen for disputes involving states or state entities in all parts of the world, although there is a concentration of cases from Sub-Saharan Africa, Central and West Asia, and Central and Eastern Europe. Between them, cases from these regions account for about 80 per cent of ICC arbitrations involving states or state entities.

9. ICC arbitrations involving states and state entities cover a wide variety of cases involving both large and small amounts in dispute.

10. Those arbitrations cover both commercial and investment disputes. Claims arising out of commercial contracts constitute the largest category of cases involving states or state entities. The most frequent kinds of contracts are those relating to construction, maintenance and the operation of facilities or systems.

11. Some ICC cases involving states and state entities arise from the breach of a bilateral investment treaty ("BIT"). Such cases represent a minority of the ICC's caseload. At the present time, approximately 18 per cent of BITs allow for the possibility of using the ICC Rules.

The Arbitration Agreement

12. In order to provide for ICC arbitration, a clause or provision should be incorporated into the relevant contract, BIT, investment treaty or domestic investment law.

13. As arbitration agreements for commercial arbitration involving states and state entities are formed differently from those in investment arbitration, the recommendations regarding each will be set out separately.

Commercial arbitration

14. It is recommended that states/state entities and their private contractual counterparties insert the following standard ICC arbitration clause in their contracts:

> All disputes arising out of or in connection with the present contract shall be finally settled under the Rules of Arbitration of the International Chamber of Commerce by one or more arbitrators appointed in accordance with the said Rules.

15. States/state entities and their private contractual counterparties may wish to modify the standard ICC arbitration clause in the preceding paragraph to take into account the following variables arising in arbitrations involving states and state entities:

- Under the ICC Rules, in cases where the size of the arbitral tribunal is not specified, the ICC International Court of Arbitration (the "Court") will decide whether there should be one or three arbitrators. Statistics show that the majority of ICC cases involving states and state entities were submitted to three-member tribunals.[1] States wishing to be sure that their dispute is decided by a three-member panel should modify the standard ICC arbitration clause as follows:

> All disputes arising out of or in connection with the present contract shall be finally settled under the Rules of Arbitration of the International Chamber of Commerce by **three** arbitrators appointed in accordance with the said Rules.

- Under the ICC Rules, in cases submitted to three-member tribunals, each party nominates an arbitrator for confirmation by the Court. The Court appoints the president of a three-member tribunal unless the parties agree on another procedure for such appointment, in which case the nomination will be subject to the confirmation of the Court. States and state entities wishing to have the president of a three-member tribunal nominated by the party-nominated arbitrators or by the parties themselves should accordingly add the following to the standard ICC arbitration clause:

  > The third arbitrator, who shall act as president of the arbitral tribunal, shall be jointly nominated by [the other two arbitrators/the parties] within [30] days of the [confirmation/appointment] of the second arbitrator. If the president of the arbitral tribunal is not nominated within this time period, the Court shall appoint such arbitrator.

- States and state entities may wish to extend the thirty-day time limit for nominating an arbitrator laid down in Article 5(1) of the ICC Rules. To allow for extra time, the standard ICC arbitration clause should be modified as follows:

  > All disputes arising out of or in connection with the present contract shall be finally settled under the Rules of Arbitration of the International Chamber of Commerce by one or more arbitrators appointed in accordance with the said Rules. **The time limit set forth in Article 5(1) of the Rules shall be [60] days**.

- States and state entities may wish to avoid the application of emergency arbitrator proceedings to their cases. This is allowed under Article 29(6) of the ICC Rules, which provides that "[t]he Emergency Arbitrator Provisions shall not apply if: ... b) the parties have agreed to opt out of the Emergency Arbitrator Provisions ..." To opt out, parties to ICC arbitrations involving states and state entities should use the following standard ICC arbitration clause:

  > All disputes arising out of or in connection with the present contract shall be finally settled under the Rules of Arbitration of the International Chamber of Commerce by one or more arbitrators appointed in accordance with the said Rules. The Emergency Arbitrator Provisions shall not apply.

  NB: As will be explained below in paragraphs 51 and 52, emergency arbitrator proceedings cannot apply in ICC investment treaty arbitrations.

- Unless otherwise provided under the applicable law, ICC arbitration is not confidential per se. To protect confidentiality, states/state entities and their

1. 85 per cent of ICC cases involving states and 86 per cent of ICC cases involving state entities were referred to three-member tribunals, as compared to only 57.5 per cent of ICC cases in general.

private contractual counterparties may therefore wish to modify the standard ICC arbitration clause as follows:

> All disputes arising out of or in connection with the present contract shall be finally settled under the Rules of Arbitration of the International Chamber of Commerce by one or more arbitrators appointed in accordance with the said Rules. **The parties agree to keep confidential the existence of the arbitration, the arbitral proceedings, the submissions made by the parties and the decisions made by the arbitral tribunal, including its awards, except as required by applicable law and to the extent not already in the public domain.**

- Conversely, states/state entities and their private contractual counterparties can agree on greater transparency, for example by providing for the award, proceedings or submissions of the parties to be made public. It should be noted that the agreed degree of confidentiality or transparency can be changed in the course of the arbitration proceedings.

16. States and their private contractual counterparties may wish to include in their ICC arbitration clause a provision on the state's immunity from enforcement, especially in view of the interpretations that have been given by national courts to Article 28(6) of the 1998 ICC Rules (Article 34(6) of the 2012 ICC Rules).

17. States contemplating other deviations from the ICC Rules should first verify these modifications with the Secretariat of the Court so as to ensure that they are compatible with the ICC's offer to administer the process.

18. It is also recommended that states/state entities and their private contractual counterparties explore the possibility of including an obligation to submit the dispute to amicable dispute resolution prior to arbitration. To that end, the following clause could be included in contracts signed by states or state entities:

> In the event of any dispute arising out of or in connection with the present contract, the parties agree to submit the matter to settlement proceedings under the ICC Mediation Rules. If the dispute has not been settled pursuant to the said Rules within 45 days following the filing of a Request for Mediation or within such other period as the parties may agree in writing, such dispute shall be finally settled under the Rules of Arbitration of the International Chamber of Commerce by one or more arbitrators appointed in accordance with the said Rules of Arbitration.

Investment arbitration

19. Contracting states may wish to include in new BITs, multilateral investment treaties, investment chapters in Free Trade Agreements ("FTA"), or domestic investment laws a provision giving investors the possibility of resorting to ICC arbitration. In this case, it is sufficient to identify the dispute and provide that it shall be submitted "to arbitration under the Rules of Arbitration of the International Chamber of Commerce".

20. Contracting states may also wish to offer the possibility of using other ICC dispute resolution services. If a state wishes ICC mediation to be used, the parties should identify the dispute and provide that it shall be submitted "to settlement proceedings under the ICC Mediation Rules. If the dispute has not been settled pursuant to the said Rules within 45 days following the filing of a Request for Mediation or within such other period as the parties may agree in writing, such dispute shall be finally settled

under the Rules of Arbitration of the International Chamber of Commerce by one or more arbitrators appointed in accordance with the said Rules of Arbitration."

21. States seeking transparency in investment arbitration may wish the Court to communicate the reasons for its decisions on objections to the confirmation of arbitrators, non-confirmations of arbitrators, and challenges and replacements of arbitrators. Contracting States may therefore wish to include the following in their BIT, multilateral investment treaty, investment chapter in their FTA, or domestic investment law:

> The Parties agree that the ICC International Court of Arbitration shall communicate the reasons for its decisions on the disputed confirmation, non-confirmation, challenge and replacement of arbitrators, in derogation of Article 11(4) of the ICC Rules of Arbitration.

The derogation does not extend to appointment decisions: the reasons for appointments should normally be apparent from an appointee's CV.

22. States can also agree on modifications to the ICC Rules similar to those described above in respect of commercial arbitration, in which case equivalent wording should be applied, *mutatis mutandis*, to the provisions referring to ICC arbitration in BITs, multilateral investment treaties, investment chapters in FTAs, and domestic investment laws.

23. States contemplating other deviations from the ICC Rules should first verify these modifications with the Secretariat so as to ensure that they are compatible with the ICC's offer to administer the process.

Procedure

24. ICC arbitration procedure is made up of the provisions set forth in the ICC Rules and the practices developed by the Court and its Secretariat.

Provisions added to the ICC Rules in 2012 to take into account the particularities of ICC arbitration involving states and state entities

25. The 2012 ICC Rules contain the following provisions addressing the participation of states/state entities in ICC arbitration:

Articles 1(1) and 1(2): disputes referable to ICC arbitration

26. Article 1(1) of the 1998 ICC Rules provided:

> The International Court of Arbitration (the "Court") of the International Chamber of Commerce (the "ICC") is the arbitration body attached to the ICC. ... The function of the Court is to provide for the settlement by arbitration of **business disputes** ... [Emphasis added.]

27. Articles 1(1) and 1(2) of the 2012 ICC Rules read as follows:

> Article 1(1)
>
> The International Court of Arbitration (the "Court") of the International Chamber of Commerce (the "ICC") is the independent arbitration body of the ICC. The statutes of the Court are set forth in Appendix I.
>
> Article 1(2)

> The Court does not itself resolve disputes. It administers the resolution of disputes by arbitral tribunals, in accordance with the Rules of Arbitration of the ICC (the "Rules"). The Court is the only body authorized to administer arbitrations under the Rules, including the scrutiny and approval of awards rendered in accordance with the Rules. It draws up its own internal rules, which are set forth in Appendix II (the "Internal Rules").

28. Given that Article 1 now refers to "disputes" rather than to "business disputes", the 2012 ICC Rules make it clear that investment treaty disputes are covered.

Articles 6(3)-6(5): prima facie analysis of the arbitration agreement

29. Article 6(2) of the 1998 ICC Rules provided:

> If the Respondent does not file an Answer, as provided by Article 5, or if any party raises one or more pleas concerning the existence, validity or scope of the arbitration agreement, the Court may decide, without prejudice to the admissibility or merits of the plea or pleas, that the arbitration shall proceed if it is *prima facie* satisfied that an arbitration agreement under the Rules may exist. In such a case, any decision as to the jurisdiction of the Arbitral Tribunal shall be taken by the Arbitral Tribunal itself. If the Court is not so satisfied, the parties shall be notified that the arbitration cannot proceed. In such a case, any party retains the right to ask any court having jurisdiction whether or not there is a binding arbitration agreement.

30. Articles 6(3) and 6(4) of the 2012 ICC Rules provide that the Secretary General shall now screen pleas concerning the existence, validity or scope of the arbitration agreement, and decide whether the matter at issue should be referred to the Court.

31. Articles 6(3) and 6(4) accordingly provide as follows:

> Article 6(3)
>
> If any party against which a claim has been made does not submit an Answer, or raises one or more pleas concerning the existence, validity or scope of the arbitration agreement or concerning whether all of the claims made in the arbitration may be determined together in a single arbitration, the arbitration shall proceed and any question of jurisdiction or of whether the claims may be determined together in that arbitration shall be decided directly by the arbitral tribunal, unless the Secretary General refers the matter to the Court for its decision pursuant to Article 6(4).
>
> Article 6(4)
>
> In all cases referred to the Court under Article 6(3), the Court shall decide whether and to what extent the arbitration shall proceed. The arbitration shall proceed if and to the extent that the Court is *prima facie* satisfied that an arbitration agreement under the Rules may exist. In particular:
>
> (i) where there are more than two parties to the arbitration, the arbitration shall proceed between those of the parties, including any additional parties joined pursuant to Article 7, with respect to which the Court is *prima facie* satisfied that an arbitration agreement under the Rules that binds them all may exist; and

(ii) where claims pursuant to Article 9 are made under more than one arbitration agreement, the arbitration shall proceed as to those claims with respect to which the Court is *prima facie* satisfied (a) that the arbitration agreements under which those claims are made may be compatible, and (b) that all parties to the arbitration may have agreed that those claims can be determined together in a single arbitration.

The Court's decision pursuant to Article 6(4) is without prejudice to the admissibility or merits of any party's plea or pleas.

32. ICC statistics showed that Article 6(2) of the 1998 ICC Rules was applied slightly more frequently in ICC arbitrations involving states or state entities than in other ICC arbitrations and that, accordingly, the possibility of raising pleas concerning the existence, validity or scope of the arbitration agreement was an important factor for states and state entities.

33. Under the 2012 ICC Rules, the arbitral tribunal will continue to decide on preliminary jurisdictional objections, irrespective of whether the Secretary General decides to refer the question concerning the existence, validity or scope of the arbitration agreement to the Court.

34. The change made in the 2012 Rules was intended, in particular, to ensure that when a non-signatory party objects to the extension of an arbitration agreement to it and when claims are brought together under one or more instruments, the matter would be sent to the Court by the Secretary General.

35. It is of course always open to the Court to send the matter thereafter to the arbitral tribunal for a decision, as it frequently does.

Article 13(4): appointment of sole arbitrators, presidents of arbitral tribunals, and co-arbitrators failing a nomination

36. Pursuant to Article 9(3) of the 1998 ICC Rules, unless otherwise agreed by the parties, sole arbitrators and presidents of arbitral tribunals were appointed by the Court upon the proposal of one of the ICC National Committees. Likewise, pursuant to Article 9(6), co-arbitrators were appointed by the Court upon the proposal of an ICC National Committee failing a nomination by the parties.

37. Article 13(4) of the 2012 ICC Rules provides as follows:

The Court may also appoint directly to act as arbitrator any person whom it regards as suitable where:

a) one or more of the parties is a state or claims to be a state entity; or,
b) the Court considers that it would be appropriate to appoint an arbitrator from a country or territory where there is no National Committee or Group; or,
c) the President certifies to the Court that circumstances exist which, in the President's opinion, make a direct appointment necessary and appropriate.

38. One of the concerns expressed by states was the role played by ICC National Committees in the appointment of a sole arbitrator or the president of an arbitral tribunal. There was a perception that ICC National Committees lacked neutrality owing to the

fact that they are often composed of leading companies and business associations in their respective countries.

39. Article 13(4) of the 2012 ICC Rules addresses this concern by giving the Court discretion to appoint a sole arbitrator or the president of an arbitral tribunal directly, rather than upon the proposal of an ICC National Committee, in cases where one or more of the parties is a state or state entity.

40. Further concerns were expressed over how the Court would determine whether one of the parties was a "state entity" and how "state entity" should be defined for the purposes of Article 13(4) of the 2012 ICC Rules. This issue was dealt with by providing that the Court *may* make a direct appointment in a case where a party "claims to be a state entity." It was emphasized that, in any event, the Court always has the discretion to decide whether or not to make a direct appointment.

Articles 11 and 14: addition of "impartiality"

41. ICC arbitration provides for an independent and impartial method of dispute resolution. This is now made clear in the 2012 ICC Rules, which expressly require arbitrators to be impartial as well as independent.

42. The term "impartiality" was not explicitly referred to in the 1998 ICC Rules. Only Article 15(2) of the 1998 ICC Rules referred to impartiality in connection with the rules governing the arbitral proceedings:

> In all cases, the Arbitral Tribunal shall act fairly and **impartially** and ensure that each party has a reasonable opportunity to present its case. [Emphasis added.]

43. The term "impartiality" is now included in Articles 11 (concerning the appointment of arbitrators) and 14 (concerning the challenge of arbitrators) of the 2012 ICC Rules.

Article 21(2): non-application of contracts and trade usages

44. Article 17(2) of the 1998 ICC Rules provided:

> In all cases the Arbitral Tribunal shall take account of the provisions of the contract and the relevant trade usages.

45. Article 21(2) of the 2012 ICC Rules provides as follows:

> The arbitral tribunal shall take account of the provisions of the contract, if any, between the parties and of any relevant trade usages.

46. A concern was raised that Article 17(2) of the 1998 ICC Rules directed the arbitral tribunal in all cases to take account of the provisions of the contract and that many investment disputes involving states arise under BITs where there is no relevant contract.

47. This concern has been addressed by Article 21(2) of the 2012 ICC Rules which proposes that the arbitral tribunal shall take into account the provisions of the contract, *if any*.

48. A further concern was raised that, in investment arbitration, no trade usages should normally apply.

49. This second concern was also addressed by Article 21(2) of the 2012 ICC Rules which proposes that the arbitral tribunal shall take account of *any* relevant trade usages.

50. Article 21(1) of the 2012 ICC Rules, which refers to "rules of law", is broad enough to encompass the issue of the applicable law in investment treaty cases.

Article 29(5): non-application of the Emergency Arbitrator Provisions

51. One of the purposes of Article 29(5) of the 2012 ICC Rules was to exclude investment arbitration from the scope of emergency arbitrator proceedings. Article 29(5) provides:

> Articles 29(1)–29(4) and the Emergency Arbitrator Rules set forth in Appendix V (collectively the "Emergency Arbitrator Provisions") shall apply only to parties that are either signatories of the arbitration agreement under the Rules that is relied upon for the application or successors to such signatories.

52. When drafting this provision, the ICC considered that the investor and the host state are not signatories of the arbitration agreement formed by the state's offer contained in the BIT and the investor's acceptance contained in its notice of claim or request for arbitration.

Bifurcation of proceedings

53. Although the 2012 ICC Rules do not contain any provisions on the bifurcation of the arbitral proceedings when a state/state entity objects to the jurisdiction of the arbitral tribunal or the admissibility of one or more claims, Appendix IV to the ICC Rules lists the following as one of the case management techniques that can be used by arbitral tribunals and parties:

> Bifurcating the proceedings or rendering one or more partial awards on key issues, when doing so may genuinely be expected to result in a more efficient resolution of the case.

54. The reference to "key issues" was intended to cover, amongst other situations, serious jurisdictional objections raised by a state or state entity.

Practices of the Court in ICC arbitrations involving states and state entities

55. Practices relevant to ICC arbitration involving states or state entities concern the role of the Court and ICC National Committees, the *prima facie* assessment of the arbitration agreement, the constitution of the arbitral tribunal, the fixing of the place of the arbitration and the scrutiny of draft awards.

Role of the Court and ICC National Committees

56. States and state entities have raised concerns about the role of the Court and ICC National Committees in ICC arbitration.

57. It must be pointed out that the members of the Court are usually private practitioners of international arbitration with no personal interest in the outcome of the disputes brought before the Court.

58. It must further be pointed out that, during the scrutiny of a draft award by the Court, the Court's long-standing practice is to exclude from the session any Court member who may be interested in the case, including, for example, the Court member proposed by the ICC National Committee in any state involved in the case.

59. It must lastly be pointed out that, as provided for in Article 13(4) of the 2012 ICC Rules, in cases involving states or state entities the Court no longer needs to appoint a sole arbitrator or the president of an arbitral tribunal upon a proposal from an ICC National Committee.

Application of Articles 6(3) and 6(4) to situations in which one of the parties seeks the extension of the arbitration agreement to a non-signatory state or state entity

60. Evidence suggests that the Court was always more restrictive in applying Article 6(2) of the 1998 ICC Rules where one of the parties sought the extension of the arbitration agreement to a non-signatory state or state entity.

61. Articles 6(3) and 6(4) of the 2012 ICC Rules were drafted in the expectation that the Court would maintain the rigour it applies to requests for the extension of an arbitration agreement to a non-signatory party, whether public or private, and that the Secretary General would be more likely to exercise his/her discretion and refer this matter to the Court.

Constitution of the arbitral tribunal (Articles 11-15)

Number of arbitrators

62. It is the Court's practice to submit disputes involving states and state entities to a three-member arbitral tribunal.

63. According to ICC statistics, states and state entities often prefer a three-member arbitral tribunal.

64. An exception to this may occur when the state or state entity specifically requests that the dispute be submitted to a sole arbitrator.

Appointment of a co-arbitrator on behalf of a state or state entity that has failed to make a nomination

65. It has been the Court's practice, when appointing a co-arbitrator on behalf of a state or state entity that has failed to make a nomination, to appoint an arbitrator either from that state or from a state with which that state has cultural affinities.

66. However, the Task Force on Arbitration Involving States and State Entities has recommended, and the ICC has accepted, that the Court's discretion when appointing a co-arbitrator on behalf of a state or state entity that has failed to make a nomination should not be limited to appointing a co-arbitrator from the same or a culturally related state.

67. The Court will take into consideration all facts and circumstances when appointing a co-arbitrator on behalf of a state or state entity that has failed to make a nomination.

Fixing of the place of the arbitration (Article 18)

68. Article 18(1) of the 2012 ICC Rules, like Article 14(1) of the 1998 ICC Rules, provides:

> The place of the arbitration shall be fixed by the Court, unless agreed upon by the parties.

69. It is the Court's practice to fix the place of the arbitration in cases involving states or state entities in a neutral location situated in a country that has ratified the New York Convention.

Scrutiny of draft awards (Article 33)

70. When an ICC arbitral tribunal submits its draft award to the ICC for approval, the Counsel in charge of the case at the Secretariat of the Court will review the draft award and may offer comments or observations. Once the draft award has been revised in light of any comments the Counsel may have made, it is submitted to the Court together with the Terms of Reference. A Court member is appointed as *rapporteur* to submit a report to the Court, which then deliberates and decides whether or not to approve the award.

71. The Court may (i) approve the draft award, (ii) approve the draft award but invite the arbitral tribunal to make changes to it when finalizing it for notification to the parties, or (iii) invite the arbitral tribunal to make changes to the draft award and to submit a revised version to a future session.

72. Pursuant to Article 33 of the ICC Rules, the award must be approved as to form. Requirements of form include, for example, whether reasons have been provided, whether the arbitral tribunal has dealt with all of the issues submitted to it, and whether formal requirements at the place of the arbitration have been met. However, Article 33 also permits the Court to make comments on the substance "without affecting the arbitral tribunal's liberty of decision". Examples include problems of computation, contradictory findings of fact or law, decisions made *ultra petita*, and failure to apply or make reference to the applicable law.

73. The Court's practice is to scrutinize draft awards rendered in ICC arbitrations involving states or state entities at its plenary sessions.

74. The scrutiny of draft awards is an important and attractive feature of ICC arbitration as it generally improves their quality and enhances the enforceability of the award. The advantages of scrutiny are strengthened for states and state entities by the fact that it is conducted at a plenary session of the Court.

75. Scrutiny is a fundamental feature of ICC arbitration and it increases confidence in the ICC arbitral process. It distinguishes ICC arbitration from proceedings conducted under other major international arbitration rules such as those of UNCITRAL or ICSID, which do not contain any equivalent provisions.

APPENDIX 17

COMMISSION REPORT – TECHNIQUES FOR MANAGING ELECTRONIC DOCUMENT PRODUCTION WHEN IT IS PERMITTED OR REQUIRED IN INTERNATIONAL ARBITRATION (2012)

REPORT OF THE ICC COMMISSION ON ARBITRATION AND ADR

Task Force on the Production of Electronic Documents in International Arbitration (2012)

There is no automatic duty to disclose documents, or right to request or obtain document production, in international arbitration, and the advent of electronic documents should not lead to any expansion of the traditional and prevailing approach to document production. Thus, requests for the production of electronic documents, like requests for the production of paper documents – to the extent they are deemed necessary and appropriate in any given arbitration – should remain limited, tailored to the specific circumstances of the case and subject to the general document production principles of specificity, relevance, materiality and proportionality. Without endorsing any particular practice or scope of document production, this Report and the accompanying Appendices identify several techniques that arbitrators and parties may wish to consider using in order to manage, in a fair and efficient manner, any issues that may arise when production of electronic documents is permitted or required and, importantly, to ensure that international arbitration does not fall prey to the inefficiencies of electronic document production that have plagued litigation in certain national court jurisdictions like the United States.

1. Introduction

1.1. Mindful of the need constantly to monitor the effectiveness of international arbitration in delivering fair and efficient dispute resolution, the ICC Commission on Arbitration (as it was then known) constituted a Task Force on the Production of Electronic Documents in International Arbitration. The Task Force was co-chaired by Loretta Malintoppi and Robert Smit and was comprised of international arbitration users, practitioners, academics and technical experts from around the world. The Task

Force analysed the issues raised by the production of electronic documents in international arbitration and prepared this report with the aim of providing information of practical utility to parties and arbitrators who may be confronted with those issues.

1.2. A characteristic of international business disputes is the importance of documentary evidence. With the advent of the electronic age, communications and other information that used to be recorded in paper documents are now often created and stored in electronic form ("electronic documents"). Accordingly, much of the documentary evidence now produced in business disputes consists of electronic documents. The move from paper to electronic documentation has been accompanied by an exponential increase in the volume of material that is recorded in a permanent fashion.

1.3. Documentary evidence may be introduced into dispute resolution proceedings in broadly two ways. First, a party will typically submit documentary evidence in support of its own case. Secondly, depending on the procedural framework under which the dispute is being resolved, a party may also be able to obtain the production of such evidence in the possession or control of its opponent. The scope and efficiency of any document production process can affect the efficiency of the entire proceedings.

1.4. The extent to which a party to court litigation may obtain documents in the possession or control of its opponent differs considerably between jurisdictions. In some jurisdictions in which there is a general right to disclosure or discovery of documentary evidence in the hands of an opponent, the advent of electronic documents, and the increase in the volume of material, has given rise to challenges to the efficiency of the litigation process. This has been well documented in the United States, where document discovery is particularly wide-ranging. Other common law jurisdictions which provide for the disclosure of documents as a standard feature of litigation have also had to consider how to adapt those processes to the advent of electronic documents, and have sought to avoid the problems experienced in the United States. Conversely, most civil law jurisdictions do not consider extensive production of documents by the opponent to be a necessary or even appropriate tool to further procedural fairness. Indeed, for cultural, historic and constitutional reasons, there is a deeply-seated resistance in many such jurisdictions to requiring a party to legal proceedings to assist the other side in gathering information that might be used against the producing party in court.

1.5. As noted above, in international arbitration, each party is responsible for submitting the documentary evidence on which it intends to rely to support its case and there is no automatic right to the production of documentary evidence in the possession or control of another party. Moreover, when a party is ordered to produce documents, the prevailing practice is that the scope of such production should be limited to specifically identified documents or to narrow and specific categories of relevant and material documents. Accordingly, the move from paper to electronic documentation in international arbitration has not generally occasioned the same difficulties as have been experienced in court litigation in those jurisdictions in which broad document discovery or disclosure is a standard feature.

2. Executive summary

2.1. Under the ICC Rules of Arbitration (the 'ICC Rules') arbitral tribunals have the power to decide whether or not to order the production of documentary evidence, including electronic documents, and to manage any such process in a fair and efficient way. In addition, the framework for the production of documents set out in the IBA Rules on the Taking of Evidence in International Arbitration (the 'IBA Rules of Evidence') is a valuable resource to help parties and arbitrators deal with the issue of document production, and expressly encompasses the production of electronic documents. As reflected in the IBA Rules of Evidence, the same principles of specificity, relevance, materiality and proportionality apply to the production of both paper and electronic documents.

2.2. It does not seem necessary to prescribe specific 'rules' or 'guidelines' applicable specifically to the production of electronic documents. Furthermore, it may be undesirable to do so to the extent that such rules or guidelines may compromise the parties' and arbitrators' flexibility to address issues in light of the particular circumstances of each case. In particular, the production of electronic documents, if any, should not jeopardize the efficient and cost-effective use of arbitration and thus its attractiveness as a method of dispute resolution.

2.3. Typical practice in international arbitration, and a widely-shared concern of users, is that requests for the production of documents by an opponent, when available at all, should be limited to specifically identified documents or to narrow and specific categories of relevant and material documents. Moreover, an arbitral tribunal should also consider the proportionality of ordering any requested production: it should weigh the relevance and materiality of a document or category of documents against the likely burden of searching for, retrieving, reviewing and producing it.

2.4. In deciding whether to allow, and in managing, the production of electronic documents, parties and arbitrators should take account of particular features of such documents that give rise to additional or different practical considerations from those that arise in connection with paper documents. In so doing, it is essential not to discourage businesses from having recourse to arbitration by proposing approaches that are likely to increase the expense of the proceedings and the disruption to their business activities.

2.5. This Report describes the key features of electronic documents and how they may be managed, which is facilitated by a co-operative approach by the parties, by a focus on avoiding steps that will occasion unnecessary cost or delay, and by active case management by the arbitral tribunal. However, the advent of electronic documents should not lead to any expansion of the traditional and prevailing approach to document production, if any, in arbitration. Requests for the production of electronic documents, like requests for the production of paper documents, to the extent that they are necessary at all, should be limited and tailored to the specific circumstances of the case. The key to maintaining the efficiency of international arbitration, and avoiding the problems occasioned in some jurisdictions by the advent of electronic documents, is for parties and arbitral tribunals to continue to adhere to these general principles of specificity, relevance, materiality and proportionality.

2.6. Two Appendices accompany this Report. Appendix I provides a Primer – for the benefit of parties and arbitrators less knowledgeable about information technology – which contains a description of some of the differences between paper documents and electronic documents and explains how the latter are created, stored, searched, transmitted and deleted. This basic information about electronic documents is intended to assist parties and arbitrators in dealing with some of the practical considerations that may arise when addressing questions relating to electronic documents and to help them manage any production of such documents in a fair and efficient manner. Appendix II contains a Glossary of relevant terms relating to electronic documents.

3. Existing international arbitration rules

(A) ICC Rules

3.1. As noted in the preface to the ICC Commission on Arbitration and ADR's Report on 'Techniques for Controlling Time and Costs in Arbitration' ('Controlling Time and Costs'), a salient characteristic of arbitration is that 'rules of arbitration themselves present a framework for arbitration proceedings but rarely set out detailed procedures for the conduct of the arbitration'. This facilitates the flexibility of arbitration as a method of dispute resolution, and allows the parties and (where they cannot agree) the tribunal to decide the specific procedures for a particular dispute.

3.2. This general characteristic of arbitration applies equally to the production of documents (whether paper or electronic). The ICC Rules contain no specific provision governing the production of documents, and ICC tribunals enjoy wide discretion in managing the proceedings under the Rules. The most pertinent provisions are Articles 19, 22 and 25 of the 2012 ICC Rules in force as of 1 January 2012.

(a) Under Article 19, arbitral proceedings are governed by the ICC Rules and, where the Rules are silent, by any rules which the parties or, failing party agreement, the Arbitral Tribunal shall deem appropriate. Article 19 also explicitly states that parties and arbitrators need not apply the rules of procedure of any national law, subject to the need to take account of any applicable mandatory arbitral procedures prescribed by the national arbitration law in force at the place of arbitration.

(b) Article 22(4) of the Rules requires that the Arbitral Tribunal 'shall act fairly and impartially and ensure that each party has a reasonable opportunity to present its case'.

(c) Article 25(1) further provides that the Arbitral Tribunal 'shall proceed within as short a time as possible to establish the facts of the case by all appropriate means'.

(d) Article 25(5) provides that '[a]t any time during the proceedings, the Arbitral Tribunal may summon any party to provide additional evidence'.

3.3. Accordingly, under the ICC Rules, issues such as whether and how much production of either paper or electronic documents will occur – i.e. whether document production is an appropriate means to establish the facts of the case – are left up to the parties and the arbitrators, provided that the parties are treated fairly and impartially and that each party has a reasonable opportunity to present its case.

3.4. Importantly, and unlike the practice before courts in some jurisdictions, under the ICC Rules there is no general duty on a party to disclose paper or electronic documents to its opponent; nor is there any automatic right for a party to request such documents from an opponent. Furthermore, and again unlike the case in litigation before some courts, a party is not placed under a duty to preserve paper or electronic documents, or other evidence, for the purposes of the arbitration. These features of the ICC Rules reflect the general practice in international arbitration.

(B) IBA Rules of Evidence

3.5. The IBA Rules of Evidence, originally adopted in 1999 and revised by a resolution of the IBA Council of 29 May 2010, are intended to provide a resource to parties and to arbitrators for the efficient, economical and fair taking of evidence in international arbitration, particularly when the parties come from different legal backgrounds and cultures. They provide a detailed framework for addressing the production of documents in arbitration, including the production of electronic documents. While the IBA Rules of Evidence are not themselves binding, parties and/or arbitral tribunals may agree to adopt them, or use them as guidelines, in their entirety or in part, for the conduct of arbitral proceedings.

3.6. The IBA Rules of Evidence have always applied to both paper and electronic documents: 'document', as defined in the 1999 version of these rules, meant 'a writing of any kind' and expressly included writing recorded by 'electronic means'. The 2010 version of the IBA Rules of Evidence contains a new definition of a document which also encompasses electronic documents: 'a writing, communication, picture, drawing, program or data of any kind, whether recorded or maintained on paper or by electronic, audio, visual or any other means'. Accordingly, the principles governing the production of paper documents under the IBA Rules of Evidence apply equally to the production of electronic documents in order to ensure an efficient and economical document production process.

3.7. The IBA Rules of Evidence provide for:

(a) The production by each party, within the time ordered by the arbitral tribunal, of all documents on which it intends to rely to support its case (Article 3(1)); and

(b) A party's right to request, and the arbitral tribunal's authority to order, the production of either a specifically identified document, or 'a narrow and specific requested category of Documents that are reasonably believed to exist', provided that they are not in the possession, custody and control of the requesting party, the 'Documents requested are relevant to the case and material to its outcome', and production is not objectionable under Article 9(2) (Articles 3(3) and 3(7)). Article 9(2) instructs the Arbitral Tribunal to 'exclude from evidence or production any Document' on relevance, materiality, burden, privilege, fairness and other listed grounds, such as compelling grounds of commercial confidentiality.

3.8. The IBA Rules of Evidence leave it to parties and arbitrators to determine what documents are 'relevant and material' in an individual case, and, assuming that document production takes place at all, when it takes place – i.e. before, concurrent with or after the parties submit written memorials.

3.9. The IBA Rules of Evidence also leave it to the parties and arbitrators in individual cases to determine what constitutes a 'narrow and specific' category of documents for the purpose of those document requests that are not limited to specific documents. With respect to electronic documents, Article 3(3) of the IBA Rules of Evidence adds only that: 'in the case of Documents maintained in electronic form, the requesting Party may, or the Arbitral Tribunal may order that it shall be required to, identify specific files, search terms, individuals or other means of searching for such Documents in an efficient and economical manner' This provision was inserted as part of the 2010 revision of the rules.

3.10. Article 9(5) of the IBA Rules of Evidence provides that an arbitral tribunal may infer that a document would have been adverse to the interests of a party that, without satisfactory explanation, fails to produce it after being ordered to so. However, no provision is made for a duty to preserve documents (including electronic documents) or other evidence. Amongst the grounds for refusing production of a document, Article 9(2)(d) lists the 'loss or destruction of the Document that has been shown with reasonable likelihood to have occurred'.

(C) General principles

3.11. As noted above, the IBA Rules of Evidence apply to both paper and electronic documents, and subject requests for the production of documents in both categories to the same principles. This reflects prevailing practice in international arbitration. There is and there should be no difference in principle between the production of paper documents and the production of electronic documents in arbitration. The mere fact that relevant and material information is or may be stored electronically rather than on paper (or may be stored in both formats) is not, in itself, a reason to grant or deny production of that information. The move from predominantly paper-based to predominantly electronic storage of information within businesses therefore requires no general reconsideration of the principles of document production in international arbitration. Application, however, of the principle of proportionality – i.e. that the burdens of production be proportionate to, and not outweigh, the likely benefits of production – may dictate different conclusions in particular cases with respect to the production of paper documents and electronic documents in light of practical challenges and opportunities presented by the way electronic documents are created, stored, searched, retrieved and produced. Arbitrators have sufficient powers under the ICC Rules and/or IBA Rules of Evidence to address those practical considerations and manage the production of either kind of document in a fair and efficient manner.

3.12. In determining the scope and means of document production (whether it concerns paper or electronic documents), parties and arbitrators should be guided by the basic principles of specificity, relevance, materiality and proportionality. First, only adequately identified, relevant and material documents (whether electronic or paper documents) should be subject to production. If the arbitrators are satisfied that the document or category of documents sought is sufficiently identified, relevant and material and all other applicable criteria for the production of documents are met (in particular, pursuant to the IBA Rules of Evidence or generally accepted 'best practices'), they should then consider whether the requested production would be likely to impose an unreasonable burden on the producing party.

3.13. This process requires arbitrators to consider the balance between the likely benefits of production to parties and arbitrators and the potential costs, delay and other burdens that the production exercise may entail. It requires consideration of the specific circumstances of the case at hand. Parties and arbitral tribunals therefore require a degree of flexibility in this respect. The ICC Rules (as supplemented from time to time in the practice of arbitral tribunals by the IBA Rules of Evidence or generally accepted best practices) recognize as much and provide for an appropriate degree of flexibility. This might be lost if detailed new rules or guidelines were introduced.

4. Characteristics of electronic documents

4.1. In applying the general principles discussed above, parties and arbitral tribunals need to take account of a number of features of electronic documents which can give rise to practical considerations different from or additional to those that arise in relation to paper documents. This section sets out the key features of electronic documents and the practical considerations.

(A) Increased volume of material

4.2. Computers have made it possible for individuals and businesses to generate, accumulate and disseminate vastly greater quantities of information in electronic form than was the case when the principal means of written communication and record-keeping was in a physical, paper format. The simplicity and ubiquity of email invites voluminous, written records of information that previously would not have been recorded or communicated in written form.

4.3. The following practical considerations arise:

(a) Emails, and electronic documents generally, may provide additional contemporaneous written evidence which may assist a tribunal in identifying the facts of a dispute and reduce the extent to which it must rely on the recollection of witnesses.

(b) However, if a party is placed under an obligation to produce documents framed in broad terms, the retrieval, review and production of electronic documents in accordance with that obligation may give rise to considerable expense and delay. This has, indeed, been the experience in litigation in the United States, where parties are placed under particularly wide-ranging document discovery obligations.

(c) The volume of electronic documents may also mean that searching for a particular document held electronically in response to a document request – to the extent such document requests are allowed – is a more extensive process than it might have been when documents were predominantly paper-based.

(d) While parties of course review their own documents to some extent to prepare for or during the course of an arbitration, given the vast scope of and numerous sources for potential electronic documents, they often do not review the entire universe of documents that may have some relevance to the arbitration. Thus, such internal review typically does not suffice in case of extensive disclosure requests by the opposing party. As a consequence, the often costly and disruptive consequences of broad document requests cannot necessarily be avoided merely because a party has already undertaken some internal review of its own documents.

(B) Dispersal

4.4. Electronic documents relating to a transaction or event may be dispersed more widely than the relevant paper documents. Whereas paper documents relating to a transaction or event may typically be stored in a limited number of physical locations (e.g. a number of files, boxes, drawers, a warehouse), electronic documents may reside simultaneously in several different locations (mainframe computers, network servers, personal desktop or laptop computers, BlackBerries or other hand-held devices, electronic back-up or disaster recovery systems).

4.5. The following practical considerations arise:

(a) The dispersal of electronic documents may lead to the retention of evidence that is relevant and material to a dispute when physical paper documents are no longer available.

(b) However, there may be a greater number of potential places to search for electronic documents in response to a document request than is the case for paper documents. This may increase the burden of any search ordered by an arbitral tribunal. It also requires the requesting party to show that the documents requested are not in its own possession or under its own control or at least not reasonably accessible.

(c) Electronic documents are often more accessible in some locations than in others. Electronic documents that are in everyday use will typically be readily accessible, although potentially voluminous. Electronic documents held for back-up or disaster recovery purposes will often be relatively inaccessible, and retrieving data from such a source may require the restoration of a large volume of material which may then have to be processed and searched. Each party's system is different; for example, the accessibility of archived electronic documents may vary depending on how well organised a party's archive is. The time and cost of retrieving electronic documents may vary considerably depending on how accessible they are.

(d) There may be significant duplication of electronic documents across a party's computer system. Several electronic copies of the same document may exist in various repositories within a party's system or network.

(C) Durability and fragility

4.6. Electronic documents are both more durable and more fragile than paper documents.

(a) Even after they are 'deleted' and even if no copies exist, emails and other electronic documents may nevertheless continue to exist and remain potentially recoverable. (A 'deleted' electronic document is often simply moved to another location in a computer system, the space which it occupied is designated as available for storage of new data, and the document may only be lost as and when the system overwrites it with new data.) Such 'deleted' material may not, however, be easily accessible and may be incomplete (i.e. an electronic document may only be recoverable in part). Recovery of such electronic documents may only be possible with the assistance of forensic specialists and attendant costs.

(b) Unlike paper documents, electronic documents are easily edited, modified or over-written, sometimes automatically without any human intervention (e.g. as with 'auto-delete' functions). Everyday use of a system (e.g. accessing, copying or printing an electronic document) may result in changes to electronic documents (particularly metadata, as to which, see below). As a result, electronic documents are more vulnerable to being changed inadvertently or for improper purposes. Preserving an electronic document in the precise state it is in on a given date will typically require active steps, such as taking copies or forensically 'imaging' it. Forensically preserving any large volume of electronic documents will typically involve significant costs and cause disruption to a party's ongoing business.

(D) Use of hardware and software

4.7. Computer hardware and software is used to create, read and render an electronic document in a form that is viewable and printable.

(a) Most of the electronic documents created by a business are likely to be created and stored using well-known commercially available and reasonably standard hardware and software, to which other parties, counsel and arbitrators also have access.

(b) However, many electronic documents may not be readily accessible by others. They may be created and/or stored on specialised or even bespoke or obsolete hardware or software. Another party to a dispute, counsel and/or arbitrators may not have access to the hardware or software needed to view or print such electronic documents. A similar situation may arise with respect to documents created with standard commercial software that is not or not yet in use by that party or person (such as a different email system or a new version of a standard software product). It may be possible to convert such documents into another, more accessible format. For example, many of the major software providers enable new software releases to be 'backward compatible' (i.e. able to access documents produced on earlier versions of the software) to a point. However, the time and costs involved to undertake such a conversion can vary depending on the nature of the electronic documents in question.

(E) Metadata

4.8. 'Metadata' is, literally, data about (electronically stored) data. Documents or files created on a computer will typically contain embedded information that is not readily apparent on the screen view of a file or in a printed version of the document or file. This secondary 'metadata' is information about the electronic document or file that describes its characteristics, origins, or usage. There are three basic categories of metadata:

(i) 'Substantive' (or 'application') metadata is created by the software used to create the document, and reflects (among other things) editing changes or comments made to the document over time. Substantive metadata is embedded in the document it describes – and therefore remains with, and arguably part of, the document when it is copied, moved or produced – and may be useful in showing the genesis of a document and the history of proposed and/or accepted revisions to the document.

(ii) 'Systems' metadata reflects automatically generated information about the creation or revision of a document, such as the document's author or the date and time of its creation, modification or delivery. Systems metadata is not necessarily embedded in the document but can be generated by the computer system on which the document was created, and can be relevant if a document's authenticity is at issue or there are issues as to who received a document (including blind copy recipients that do not appear on the face of a document) or when it was received.

(iii) "'Embedded' metadata is inputted into a document by its creator or users but cannot be seen in the document's display, and commonly includes the formulas used to create spreadsheets, hidden columns, references, fields or linked files. Embedded metadata can be critical to understanding complex spreadsheets (such as those often used, for example, in construction projects) which on their face do not explain the mathematical formulas underlying or relating to the various rows or columns of information that are displayed on a computer screen or printed version of the spreadsheet.

4.9. 'Visible' metadata should be distinguished from 'hidden' metadata. Visible metadata is commonly displayed on screen and/or in print-outs and hidden metadata is not. In the case of an email, strictly speaking, all its constituent fields are metadata. Examples of visible metadata include the to/from/cc/date/title fields. Examples of hidden metadata would include the route the email took over the internet and the IP address from which it was sent. Most of the metadata mentioned in sub-paragraphs (i) to (iii) above is hidden metadata.

4.10. The following practical considerations arise:

(a) Visible metadata (e.g. the visible fields of an email mentioned above) and embedded metadata (e.g. the formulas used in a spreadsheet) will often be necessary to understand the data in an electronic document.

(b) Where there is a suspicion of fraud, forgery or deliberate tampering with evidence, hidden metadata may be valuable evidence. However, in most cases hidden metadata will not be relevant or material to the issues in dispute.

(c) Metadata is particularly vulnerable to inadvertent modification. Metadata may also be lost if an electronic document is converted from one format to another. It may be possible to preserve metadata forensically, but at a cost.

(d) If an electronic document is produced in 'native' format (i.e. the format in which it was originally created), or something close to native format (e.g. a format created by review software which approximates the native format but allows it to be searched and handled more easily), the substantive and embedded metadata will normally be included in it. Typically, a document produced in such a format will be searchable by the receiving party to the same extent as it was by the producing party (provided the receiving party has similar software available to it). It may be possible to remove substantive or embedded metadata from an electronic 'document', either by using software which strips out (some of) the metadata, or by converting the document into another format. Doing so is likely to incur a cost for the producing party, and (depending on the alternative format into which the document is converted) may reduce the searchability of the document in the hands of the receiving party, thus increasing the costs of review for the receiving party.

(e) In connection with US-style e-discovery, the review of hidden metadata involves significant attendant costs. Although millions of pages of documents are frequently produced in a US commercial lawsuit, the number of documents containing hidden metadata material to the case is typically very small. To avoid the costs of review, parties in US litigation frequently agree not to produce most of their documents in their native format, but instead to produce them in a format that allows the documents to be searched but which does not include hidden metadata, and which therefore avoids the review of a significant volume of irrelevant hidden metadata by lawyers. Other jurisdictions that require disclosure of documents in litigation have taken a different approach to this. For example, in England and Wales, the presumption is that documents should be produced in native or near-native format, but that the hidden metadata (other than the date of creation of the document) is likely to be irrelevant and therefore need not be preserved or reviewed.

(F) Electronic search and review tools and techniques

4.11. Computer technology offers a number of tools that may assist the process of searching for, organizing and producing electronic documents. Electronic tools may allow for the automatic searching and ordering of volumes of material for documents which satisfy certain parameters, based for example on key words, date ranges, file types, custodian or location on a computer system. Electronic tools may also allow the automatic de-duplication of documents.

4.12. The following practical considerations arise:

(a) A party may have access to some electronic tools as part of its computer system which it uses as part of its everyday business, and which it and counsel may use in identifying evidence in support of its case or to respond to a document request. However, the sophistication of such tools may vary widely. Specialist tools are available, but at a cost. Some counsel in international arbitration may have access to such specialist tools. In other cases, external experts would need to be engaged at additional cost. The most sophisticated specialist tools may be expected to be needed only to respond to broad document requests, of the kind that is generally inappropriate in international arbitration.

(b) All electronic search tools have their limitations. For example, date restrictions may be easier to implement in relation to emails than for other types of electronic documents. The effectiveness of key word searching depends upon the ability to identify search terms that are likely to feature in relevant material and unlikely to feature in irrelevant material. Where electronic documents are stored in multiple languages, care should be taken to identify appropriate key words in each language.

(c) Electronic tools may assist in identifying electronic documents that are potentially responsive to a document request. However, they can rarely, if ever, replace a manual review by counsel of at least some documents. The related costs have to be considered when such a document production request is submitted.

(d) The technique of data sampling entails the retrieval, review and production of only a portion of the repositories potentially containing relevant and material documents in order to assess whether the benefits of further review and production justify the costs and burdens of such review and production.

5. Techniques for managing any production of electronic documents

5.1. If international arbitration is to remain an attractive method of dispute resolution, it must avoid the problems to which electronic documents have given rise in court litigation in some jurisdictions. The production of electronic documents does not usually give use to particular difficulties in international arbitration, due (among other reasons) to the disciplined scope of document production in most international arbitrations and the arbitrators' management of the arbitral process. If and to the extent electronic document production issues arise, however, this section discusses techniques and approaches that parties and tribunals may adopt to address those issues in a fair and efficient manner. Nothing in this Report, however, should be interpreted as an endorsement of any particular technique, approach or practice, which remain the exclusive province of parties and arbitrators to decide in light of the particular circumstances of each case.

5.2. Parties are generally free to produce whatever evidence they wish to rely upon. Although some issues concerning the production of electronic documents (such as the format in which a document is produced) apply equally to documents on which a party relies and to requests for documents, most of the issues considered in this section relate only to the latter.

(A) Electronic document production in context

5.3. The production of electronic documents is simply an aspect of document production. Since most documents today are created electronically, and many are stored electronically, almost every time a tribunal may be called upon to consider the production of documentary evidence, it will be considering the production of electronic documents.

5.4. Document production is but one of many procedural matters to be addressed by arbitrators as part of their task of managing the arbitral proceedings. As a general rule, parties and arbitrators should heed the two fundamental principles set forth in the introduction to Controlling Time and Costs, namely (i) that they should, wherever possible, make a conscious and deliberate choice early in the proceedings about the specific procedures suitable for the case, and (ii) that the arbitral tribunal should work proactively with the parties to manage the procedure from the start.

In addition, further guidance may be found in Appendix IV to the 2012 ICC Rules, which include case management techniques available to arbitral tribunals and parties to manage document production, paper and electronic alike.

5.5. In light of these principles, parties and arbitral tribunals may consider taking the following steps:

(a) Parties or tribunals may consider expressly adopting the IBA Rules of Evidence, either in whole or in part and either directly or by way of general guidance, to govern the production of documents, including electronic documents, in the arbitration. Logical junctures at which to consider this include at the time the arbitration agreement is drafted, at the time of adoption of the Terms of Reference, and/or in an early procedural order.

(b) Tribunals should encourage the parties to consider document production issues (including the production of electronic documents) as early as possible in the proceedings. Controlling Time and Costs and the ICC Rules recommend that an early case-management conference be convened, either at the time the Terms of Reference are finalized or (if later) once the parties have set out their cases in sufficient detail. The production of documents (including electronic documents) may be included on the agenda for such a conference.

(c) The parties and tribunal should consider whether any questions relating to document production can be resolved at the case-management conference. For example, it may be possible to devise a system for the organization of documents, agree on the format in which electronic documents are to be produced (either by a party in support of its own case or in response to document requests, if there are to be any), and/or agree on the time at which each party is to produce the documents on which it relies. Depending upon the extent to which the issues in dispute are sufficiently clear, it may also be possible at the case-management conference to consider issues of principle relating to document requests, such as whether there are to be any document requests at all and, if so, what procedure is to be followed (see Controlling Time and Costs and Appendix IV to the ICC Rules).

(d) Tribunals should be wary of imposing on parties detailed technical requirements relating to the production of electronic documents, and should only do so after obtaining a clear understanding of the time and costs involved in complying with those requirements. Tribunals should encourage parties to reach agreement regarding such requirements wherever possible, but should be willing to engage with the technical detail in order to resolve disputes. Parties should ensure that they have a clear understanding of the implications of technical requirements (and obtain advice if necessary) before agreeing to them. Parties and tribunals should demonstrate flexibility and be willing to reconsider technical requirements if necessary as an arbitration progresses.

(B) Scope of production

5.6. The advent of electronic documents should not lead to any expansion of the traditional and prevailing approach to document production in arbitration. Under the IBA Rules of Evidence, for example, requests for the production of electronic documents, like requests for the production of paper documents, should remain limited to specific documents or narrow categories of documents relevant and material to the issues in dispute in the arbitration. The primary solution to the question of how to avoid the problems caused by the advent of electronic documents in some jurisdictions lies in parties and tribunals adhering to the existing prevailing practice in international arbitration as to the appropriate scope of document production. Parties and arbitrators should bear in mind the following general considerations:

(a) There is no automatic right in international arbitration to obtain documents from an opponent. Parties and tribunals should consider whether document requests are necessary or desirable in the context of the case at hand.

(b) Where document requests are allowed, parties and arbitrators should ensure that they are narrowly drawn in the manner envisaged in the IBA Rules of Evidence, that only documents relevant and material to the outcome of the case are requested and ordered to be produced, and that the benefits and burdens of production are properly assessed before production is ordered. 'Fishing expeditions' should be avoided.

(c) Most of the burden, in terms of time and cost, of responding to a document request is often associated with searching for the responsive document or documents (including retrieving electronic documents from a party's computer system and reviewing them for responsiveness and privilege). Parties and tribunals should therefore consider not only the volume of documents that a responding party is being asked to produce, but also, and more importantly, the process it may be expected to undertake to locate and identify those documents if they are not readily available.

(d) Tribunals should avoid broad, US-style discovery, which is inappropriate in international arbitration, unless the parties have specifically agreed that they wish to adopt such an approach.

(e) Finally, parties may view and address electronic documents – their production, dissemination and storage – in very different ways, depending on various factors, including their legal culture, the frequency with which they take part in litigation or arbitration, regulatory requirements to which they are subject, and their size, resources and relative IT sophistication. For example, a party which regularly conducts litigation under rules which impose broad obligations to produce documents may have standard procedures in place designed to facilitate this, whereas a party that does not have such experience is unlikely to have such resources. In some cases, this may mean that a document production requirement which, on its face, applies equally to all parties to an arbitration is in practice more difficult for one party to comply with than for another party. At the same time, however, differences between the parties' relative sophistication in such matters should not be used to justify unfairly disproportionate obligations. Arbitrators should consider whether such factors affect the reasonableness of the proposed scope of production in a particular case and ensure that document production requirements are fair to all parties.

5.7. In implementing these general considerations, parties and tribunals should consider the following practical steps and issues to maintain the fairness and efficiency of the proceedings:

(i) Timing, number and focus of requests

5.8. The scope of document (including electronic document) production may be restricted by limiting the number of document requests a party may make and by permitting requests only in respect of documents relevant and material to particular issues in dispute. Delaying the submission of document requests until after the parties have submitted their memorials and the documents on which they wish to rely may facilitate more focused document requests. Requests can be confined to specific factual issues that are raised in the memorials and on which there are gaps in the documentary evidence already submitted. In general, in view of the requirements of relevance, materiality and proportionality, a tribunal will usually be in a better position to make an informed decision on requests for document production after at least a first round of submissions on the merits.

(ii) Specificity of requests

5.9. Generally speaking, the broader the scope of document requests allowed, the greater will be the cost and burden of production. Document requests should therefore identify, with the greatest specificity practicable, the specific document or specific and narrow category of documents sought. As envisaged in Article 3(3) of the IBA Rules of Evidence, the specificity of a request relating to electronic documents may be enhanced by identifying and/or limiting the scope of what is sought or ordered by reference to various characteristics of the electronic documents requested.

(a) The starting point should be to limit a document request by reference to what is sought (e.g. an email, a report, minutes of a meeting). Requests for specifically identified documents, whether paper or electronic, will ordinarily entail the least burden on the producing party.

(b) Where a specific and narrow category of documents is requested, limits may also be imposed by reference to a limited number of specific custodians who are expected to be in possession of the electronic documents in question, the sources of electronic documents to be reviewed, date restrictions and, if appropriate, the use of specific search terms to assist in locating relevant and material documents.

(c) As the party responding to a document request will typically be more familiar with its internal IT infrastructure and would therefore be in a better position to decide where and how to search for responsive electronic documents, it may be appropriate for the responding party to identify first the parameters of any search for responsive documents it intends to conduct, and then provide an opportunity for the requesting party to comment on the proposed parameters.

(iii) Accessibility of sources

5.10. The relevance and materiality of the electronic documents requested should be carefully weighed against the burden on the requested party of searching for, retrieving, reviewing and producing them. An important factor in this balance is the relative accessibility of the potential sources of the electronic documents requested. Electronic documents are most easily accessed from a party's office, personal computers, network servers and other computers on databases that are in active use during the ordinary course of a party's business operations. They are less readily accessible from removable storage media such as CDs, DVDs or USB drives, Blackberries or Palm Pilots, home office computers or off-site internet storage, which are not sources accessed in the ordinary course of a party's business or may simply be duplicative of other more readily accessible sources. Electronic documents are least accessible when they have been deleted and/or are located only on off-site or back-up storage data (such as back-up tapes) not used in a party's ordinary course of business.

(a) A tribunal should avoid ordering a party to search a less accessible source if a copy of a relevant and material electronic document is likely to be available from a more easily accessible source. A party should consider structuring any search for documents (whether for documents on which it wishes to rely, or in response to a document request) by searching the most accessible sources first, and only searching less accessible sources if it does not find the documents sought and the burden of extending the search is proportionate to the likely evidential value of the documents if they are found.

(b) In most cases, it should be sufficient to limit searches to sources of electronic documents used by a party in its ordinary business operations. If a document is likely only to be available from a less accessible source, a tribunal should consider carefully whether its likely relevance and materiality justify the inconvenience, cost and potential delay involved in retrieving it. Tribunals should ordinarily not order the production of electronic documents in back-up, deleted or archived files that are not readily accessible, unless the requesting party establishes a degree of relevance and materiality that outweighs the burden and costs involved.

(c) Article 3(12)(c) of the IBA Rules of Evidence provides that a party is not obligated to produce multiple copies of documents that are essentially identical unless the tribunal decides otherwise. This presumption against requiring production of multiple copies contributes to the efficiency of the process. A tribunal should generally avoid ordering a party to search for duplicate copies of a document in more than one location, even if they are all easily accessible. An exception to this might occur where identifying the location of copies of a document is itself of evidentiary value (for example, because it identifies which individuals had access to the document and this is of material importance in the arbitration).

(iv) Metadata

5.11. As explained above, whereas visible metadata will typically be required to understand an electronic document that is being produced, hidden metadata will usually be irrelevant to the dispute and it will therefore be unnecessary to produce them. Even where metadata is potentially relevant, the burdens of production may outweigh its potential evidentiary value. Tribunals should consider applying a presumption against requiring the production of hidden metadata associated with a document that is to be produced, unless the requesting party establishes a degree of relevance and materiality that outweighs the burden and costs involved.

5.12. Some of the relevant factors in addressing requests for production of hidden metadata, in addition to the general factors relevant to any document request, include: (a) the importance of the particular type of metadata requested to facilitating the parties' review, production and understanding of the documents to which the metadata relates; (b) the accessibility of the metadata sought; (c) the timing of the request for metadata; and (d) the ease and efficiency with which the metadata can be produced and used.

(v) Use of electronic tools and search methods

5.13. Parties should be encouraged to use technology where this can reduce the burden associated with document production, but parties and tribunals should be aware and take account of the limitations of and costs involved in using the available electronic tools. Computer technology enables parties to search large volumes of electronic documents for specific relevant words, names, subjects or phrases, which may pertain to the particular dispute concerned. This can be both more efficient and more accurate than human document review of paper documents. Although not all electronic documents are searchable in their native form, they may be convertible into a searchable format. However, the processes available to render electronic documents word-searchable may be expensive, and parties and tribunals will need to consider and weigh the extent to which such techniques are appropriate in the context of the circumstances of each individual case.

5.14. In addition to the use of simple key word searches – which risks either identifying too large a universe of responsive documents or missing relevant and material documents that do not include the key word – parties may consider using the ever-expanding array of more sophisticated search technologies (e.g. 'Boolean"' searches, 'fuzzy' searches, algebraic searches, probabilistic searches) designed to enhance the accuracy of electronic document searches. A manual review of at least some of the electronic documents identified by a key word or other automated search will invariably be required, but the volume of electronic documents that needs to be reviewed by the parties' lawyers should be much less than otherwise. This may, therefore, lead to a significant cost saving.

5.15. Key word searches can be used in different ways to enhance the efficiency of electronic document production. The requesting or responding party may choose, or be required to identify, with its request for production or response, search terms to be used to locate responsive relevant and material electronic documents. Absent objection, use of those search terms may be deemed to satisfy the responding party's obligation to search for and produce responsive electronic documents in good faith. It will often be desirable for the parties to agree on (or the tribunal to order) the relevant key words to be used before searches are undertaken, in order to avoid a search having to be repeated if there is a dispute about the adequacy of the search terms used. When electronic documents are stored in different languages, care should be taken to identify appropriate key words in each language.

5.16. Where relevant and material responsive information may potentially be located in several, or in voluminous, electronic document repositories, parties and arbitrators may wish to consider the technique of data sampling. Data sampling entails the retrieval, review and production of only a portion of the electronic document repositories potentially containing relevant and material information in order to assess whether the benefits of further review and production justify the cost and burden of such review and production. As with electronic document search terms, in appropriate circumstances, a responding party may be deemed to have satisfied its good faith obligation to produce responsive electronic documents by conducting such data sampling.

5.17. The use of the foregoing electronic search tools should be limited to those particular cases involving a large volume of electronic documents, or different sources of electronic documents, in which the parties and arbitrators conclude that the benefits of such electronic searches outweigh their costs and burdens. In no event should the mere availability of those electronic search tools to search potentially large volumes of electronic documents justify inappropriately broad electronic document requests.

(C) IT expertise

5.18. An understanding of a party's IT system will be important to the efficient management of any document production exercise. In most cases, a party's in-house IT staff is likely to be able to provide the necessary expertise to that party, in conjunction with counsel. In particularly complex or high-value disputes, a party may also seek advice from external experts.

5.19. In all but the most exceptional cases, parties, with the assistance of their advisers, should provide (and should be able to provide) the tribunal with sufficient information on their IT systems for the tribunal to manage the process. In the exceptional case, ICC tribunals have the authority to appoint their own IT expert under Article 25(4) of the ICC Rules. In deciding whether and how to appoint such an IT expert, tribunals should consider the guidelines for tribunal-appointed experts set forth in the report of the ICC Commission on Arbitration Task Force on Guidelines for ICC Expertise Proceedings entitled 'Issues for Arbitrators to Consider Regarding Experts', published in the *ICC International Court of Arbitration Bulletin* Vol. 21 No. 1 (2010) 31. A tribunal-appointed IT expert, however, should be reserved for the rare case in light of the additional expense, delay and intrusion into the party's IT systems that a tribunal-appointed IT expert may entail.

(D) Cost shifting

5.20. Normally, the production of both paper and e-documents, if ordered at all by a tribunal, should be contained and should not give rise to large volumes of documents produced and exchanged. In the rare and very exceptional cases where the volume of electronic documents to be searched and produced is large and/or review and production from less accessible sources of electronic documents is warranted, parties and arbitrators may wish to consider requests for electronic documents only on the condition that some or all of the costs of searching for, retrieving and/or producing those electronic documents is shifted from the responding party to the requesting party. The requesting party, for example, may be required either to (a) pay to the responding party the costs of extraordinary electronic document search and retrieval techniques, or of production in a particular electronic format, as such costs are incurred during or following the electronic document production process; (b) advance those costs to the responding party during the production process, subject to reallocation in the arbitration award in light of the results of the production process and/or the final outcome of the case; or (c) pay those costs once the arbitration award is rendered pursuant to the allocation of arbitration costs set forth in the award.

5.21. However, arbitrators should be mindful of a number of factors which may militate against cost shifting: (i) cost shifting does not reduce the overall cost of the arbitration; (ii) it may become a substitute for disciplined limitations on the scope of document production generally permitted in international arbitration; (iii) it does not give rise to the perceived ability of a party to 'purchase' greater access to electronic document production than would otherwise be available; and (iv) it may become a tool for abuse between parties of unequal financial means.

5.22. More generally, arbitrators should be mindful that, like electronic discovery generally in the United States, the standards and practices of US courts with respect to the shifting of costs for the search and production of electronic documents are not generally relevant or appropriate in international arbitration due to the stark differences between US litigation and international arbitration practices with respect to document production and costs. In US litigation, the scope of document discovery is broad and parties ordinarily bear their own costs. In international arbitration, by contrast, the scope of document production is tailored and limited, and arbitrators (as under Article 37(4) of the ICC Rules) are empowered to allocate the costs of the arbitration (including the parties' reasonable attorney fees and other costs) between the parties and in the proportions the arbitrators deem appropriate. In allocating the arbitration costs of the parties, arbitrators may take account of the reasonableness with which a party has conducted the case as well as the outcome of the arbitration.

5.23. Cost shifting should therefore ordinarily be reserved for extraordinary circumstances and imposed only after a weighing of the relevant factors such as, for instance, the volume and accessibility of electronic documents to be reviewed, which party bears the burden of proof and persuasion in the case, the relative financial resources of the parties, and the amounts at stake in the arbitration.

(E) Form of production

5.24. The form in which electronic documents are produced by a party in support of its case or in response to a document request may impact their utility to the other party and the arbitrators receiving the documents. Parties and arbitrators should therefore address at an early stage of the proceedings the form in which electronic documents should be produced. As noted above, this may be done at the case-management conference.

5.25. Electronic documents generally should be produced in the most expeditious, cost-effective and efficient form appropriate in the circumstances.

(a) Parties and arbitral tribunals should note that requiring electronic documents to be converted into a particular format for production may increase costs (possibly significantly so), unless that format is carefully chosen. A producing party may incur conversion costs, only for the requesting party to incur further costs converting the documents into another format. For example, a producing party may incur costs upon converting electronic documents to paper form and filing such paper documents, only for the other party to then incur the additional and unnecessary cost of scanning the documents produced in paper form back into an electronic form with keyword-searchable or other electronic functionalities.

(b) Article 3(12)(b) of the IBA Rules of Evidence provide that, absent specific agreement by the parties or directions by the tribunal, documents in electronic form should be submitted or produced by the party that maintains them 'in the form most convenient or economical to it that is reasonably usable by the recipients'. This is helpful guidance. In order to avoid unnecessary discussions and potential disruption of the arbitration timetable, in case of doubt about accessibility, the producing party should discuss the format with the receiving party before production and endeavour to reach agreement about such format. In some cases, it may be sensible to convert the electronic documents to a searchable format which all parties and the tribunal are able to access. Conversion may result in the loss of metadata but, unless the lost metadata is likely to be relevant (e.g. visible metadata necessary to understand the document or, exceptionally, hidden metadata if there are doubts as to the authenticity of the document) this is likely to be acceptable, and may save time and costs if the parties otherwise would have reviewed that metadata. However, since the parties in any case should be discouraged from spending time and costs on reviewing irrelevant material, an alternative is for the parties to produce the documents in native format but not to review the hidden metadata, thus also avoiding conversion costs.

(c) Parties may also consider using a web-based repository to which both sides have access as a means of producing electronic documents.

5.26. If the receiving party objects to the producing party's proposed form of production, and the parties are unable to resolve the objection by agreement, arbitrators may consider requiring the receiving party to show that the need for an electronic document in the form it prefers outweighs the burden and cost of providing production in that form.

(F) Privilege

5.27. As noted above, documents, including electronic documents, may be withheld from production in international arbitration on grounds of privilege.

5.28. Production of a document to which privilege attaches may amount, in certain jurisdictions, to an inadvertent waiver of that privilege. In cases in which a large volume of electronic documents must be searched and produced (perhaps using automated techniques) inadvertent waiver of privilege is a real concern for parties. The following techniques may be used in an effort to avoid this:

(a) *Privilege search term.* One technique is to apply appropriate search terms to the electronic documents identified in response to a document request, including for the surnames of known lawyers whose names may appear on emails or other documents associated with the gathered material, and for other key words that may appear on documents like 'privileged' or 'confidential'. Documents containing these search terms may then be segregated from the larger set of responsive information and manually reviewed for any applicable privilege. Like all key-word searching, however, this has limitations: for example, many organizations have adopted the practice of incorporating 'privileged' and 'confidential' notations on all email communications, reducing the efficacy of such search terms.

(b) *'Claw-back' agreements.* Another technique is the use of 'claw-back' agreements. A claw-back agreement provides ground rules in advance of production for each producing party to be able to retrieve inadvertently produced privileged documents without risk of waiver. A party may not feel the need to review all documents for privilege before it produces them if such a 'claw back' agreement is made. However, the potential drawbacks of claw-back agreements include: (i) they may encourage swamping one's opponent with irrelevant documents, which is entirely inappropriate in international arbitration; (ii) they may not avoid the risk of waiver of privilege with respect to third parties in all jurisdictions; and (iii) they may not effectively protect the inadvertently produced privileged information since the receiving party will have seen the privileged material and may be able to take advantage of that information without actually using the document.

5.29. Use of these techniques should be reserved for extraordinary cases in light of the limited and tailored scope of document production generally available in international arbitration. Moreover, the availability of these techniques should not be used to justify an unduly broad scope of document production.

(G) Preservation of and failure to produce electronic documents

5.30. As explained above, electronic documents (in particular, metadata) may easily be altered or destroyed inadvertently, for example by the operation of routine day-to-day computer network functions (including any 'auto-delete' functions). Freezing, disabling or deactivating such functions may cause serious inconvenience to a party. In US litigation, procedures are often put in place to preserve and retrieve electronic documents forensically because the mere act of accessing or copying an electronic document will cause changes to be made to its metadata. This is an important factor which greatly contributes to the cost of discovery in US litigation.

5.31. As noted above, international arbitration operates under a very different regime. Tribunals should avoid importing from other systems notions with regard to the preservation of evidence that may give rise to unnecessary inconvenience or expense. While a party's intentional efforts to thwart disclosure of relevant and material evidence by destroying or altering an electronic document may warrant appropriate sanctions (such as an adverse inference contemplated by Article 9(5) of the IBA Rules of Evidence), inadvertent destruction or alteration of an electronic document as a result of routine operation of that party's computer network does not ordinarily reflect any culpable conduct or warrant any such sanctions. Moreover, whilst a party may wish, for its own benefit, to take steps to preserve relevant evidence, it is under no automatic duty to do so. Nor should a tribunal consider imposing such a duty absent a specific reason to do so, such as credible allegations of fraud, forgery or deliberate tampering with evidence.

5.32. If a party wishes to preserve evidence in its possession and control, it should focus its efforts on the most likely sources of relevant and material evidence and avoid taking steps that are likely to give rise to unnecessary inconvenience and expense.

(a) For example, attempting to freeze day-to-day functions across an entire computer network is likely to give rise to severe disruption and costs. Likewise, unless the circumstances of the particular case indicate that hidden metadata may be relevant and material to the dispute, a party should not be expected or required by the tribunal to incur the cost of obtaining a forensic snapshot of all or even a subset of its electronic documents.

(b) On the other hand, a party may consider taking a copy of a limited number of electronic documents from reasonably accessible sources and focused by reference to appropriate parameters (such as key custodians and/or particular electronic folders in which relevant transaction documents are held), and to put that copy to one side or entrust it to counsel for safekeeping. The electronic documents so preserved may provide a resource upon which the party may draw for evidence in support of its own case. It may also provide a convenient starting point for a search for documents in response to a document request.

5.33. Finally, in light of the fragility of electronic documents, if there is a dispute regarding their destruction or alteration, parties and arbitrators should consider placing the burden on the requesting party to show that the responding party has acted wrongfully, rather than on the responding party to show that its actions or inactions were reasonable and in good faith.

6. Conclusion

6.1. While each party is of course free to submit any documents in support of its claim or defence, absent a specific agreement between the parties to a case, or an order of the tribunal, there is no obligation to produce documents, including electronic documents, in international arbitration. In deciding whether to order electronic document production, tribunals should be guided by the principles of specificity, relevance, materiality and proportionality.

6.2. Keeping in mind this important framework, it is hoped that this Report will offer concrete assistance to tribunals and parties on how to address and manage as efficiently as possible any electronic document issues that arise, and control any costs and delays that may result when electronic document production is permitted or required in international arbitration.

APPENDIX I
A PRIMER ON ELECTRONIC DOCUMENTS

DIAGRAM OF A TYPICAL OFFICE COMPUTER NETWORK 1.

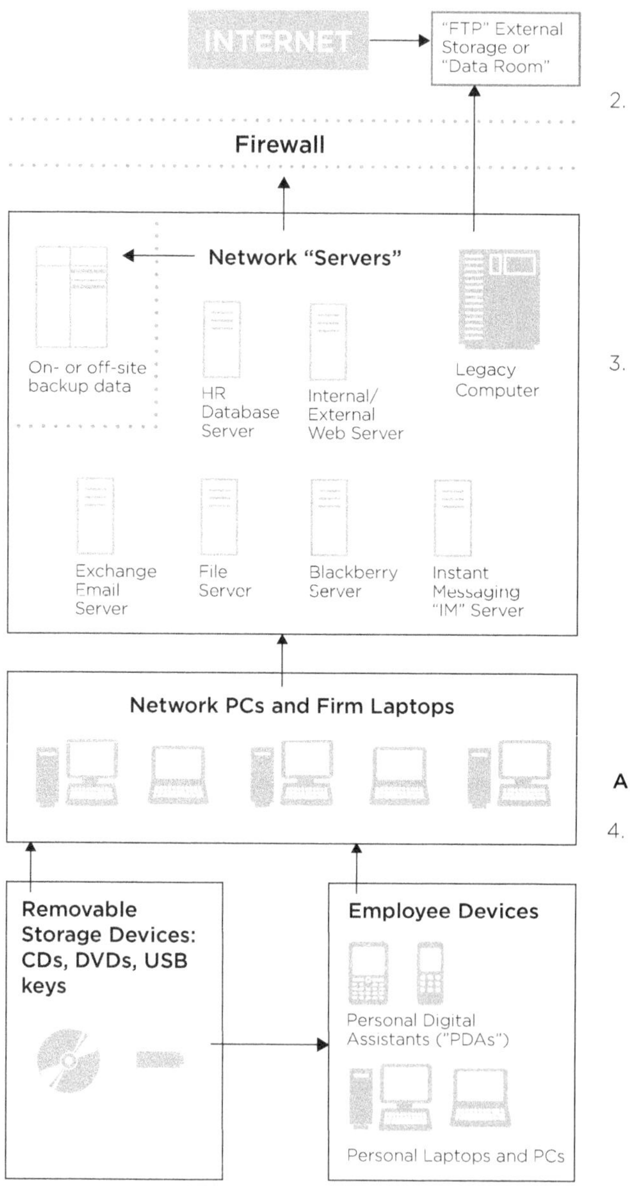

1. This Appendix provides an overview of how electronic documents are created, managed and stored, and identifies some of the questions, challenges and opportunities that arise in the production of electronic documents as a result of its unique characteristics.

2. To address electronic document production issues that may arise, it is useful to have a basic understanding of how a typical office computer network works and where electronic documents responsive to a document request may potentially be located and retrieved. Electronic documents may potentially be located either in relatively accessible 'active' sources or in less accessible 'inactive' back-up, fragmented or deleted sources.

3. 'Active' electronic documents – which ordinarily should be the sole source of production of any electronic documents in international arbitration – are generally stored in a readily usable format and are relatively easy to access. 'Inactive' electronic documents are generally harder and more expensive to access and produce. The diagram below illustrates a simplified office computer network and the hardware components that may be used to create, manage and store electronic documents, and the sections that follow describe the 'active' and 'inactive' sources of electronic documents, as well as the data about electronic documents known as 'metadata'

A. 'Active' electronic documents

4. Personal computers: At a basic level, when a human being (a 'user' or document 'custodian') sits down at his or her 'workstation' or desk and writes an email, drafts a word-processing document, populates an electronic spreadsheet (i.e. creates, stores or manipulates electronic documents), he/she does so on a 'personal computer' (or 'PC') – either a 'desktop' or 'laptop' computer. The PC will typically have a 'local' hard drive where electronic documents created on that PC may be electronically located, stored and accessible only through that specific computer. The kinds of electronic documents that may exist on the local hard drive of a personal computer include virtually any variety of document or file a person can create using today's vast array of computer software 'applications'. In a business context, these will most commonly include word-processing files, emails, spreadsheets, slide presentations – the familiar array of files that most office PCs are equipped to create.

5. Electronic documents created on any given user's PC may also be located wherever else those electronic documents may have been sent by the user, or otherwise automatically stored. For example, when a user sends an email, it will typically be recorded in the sender's 'sent' box; it will also appear in the 'in' box of one or many recipients. The email's recipients in turn may have forwarded the same email to other recipients. On a network, a copy of the email may reside on the PC hard drives of the sender and/or one or more recipients. As described below, it may also be recorded on a shared server, as well as a 'personal digital assistant' ('PDA') device such as a Blackberry, which replicates each user's email remotely. The user's PC becomes an input and viewing device for electronic documents located on a server elsewhere.

6. Shared servers: To maximize computer efficiency and to promote office interconnectedness, each user/custodian's PC located at his or her desk will typically be part of a 'network' of many such workstation PCs. A network of individual PCs will usually be constructed around a number of shared 'server' computers, which constitute a second potential source of 'active' electronic documents. A 'server' computer is a separate computer from the PC computer located on each user's desk, located and operated

centrally, that contains software to perform specific functions for all of the PCs (or 'clients') in the network that are interconnected by the server. One example would be a shared email server. Office computer networks will typically have one or more servers that do nothing but 'serve' the network's email needs for all of the users in the network. Thus, instead of each user having their own emails created, sent, received and stored on their individual PC at their desk, all of the emails created, sent, received and stored by all users in the network will reside on one or more shared server computers that do nothing but process emails. The result is that a particular user's email, which they access from their PC, may not actually be located on their individual PC, but instead may be located entirely or in large part on a shared server computer, physically located somewhere else, to which their PC is connected, and which centrally provides email for all network users whose PCs are connected to that email server.

7. The shared functions within an office computer network that may be performed by servers rather than by each individual user's PC can be just about anything. Servers may be dedicated to providing network user access to the Internet, providing internal kinds of messaging applications separate from email, managing the printing of all documents in the office, managing and storing electronic documents created by Blackberry or other handheld devices, or maintaining other kinds of network electronic documents, like all word-processing files or all accounting or staff personnel files in a centrally accessible location. Having dedicated 'servers' perform different aspects of a company's business on behalf of all PCs in a network enables centralization and administrative control over a company's electronic documents, whereby a company's 'Information Technology' ('IT') officer or department can monitor use, or assign or withhold different user access rights, for instance by limiting the number of users/custodians who may access the server containing the company's staff personnel files or other sensitive need-to-know data.

8. When shared servers are used to create an office network, electronic documents generated by an individual network user at his or her PC may actually be stored in a shared server computer located somewhere else, which that individual user's PC accesses for the particular kind of electronic documents involved – email, word-processing, accounting data, and so on – rather than located on the hard drive of the individual user's desktop or laptop PC. Consequently, a file created by one user in the network may be equally accessible to all or several other users in the network, who can equally access, copy, modify, delete, overwrite or send a particular document or file that was created by another user on the shared server.

9. 'Legacy computers': Sometimes a company's network of computers may include 'legacy computers', i.e. outdated computer hardware containing antiquated software or data that is still necessary to perform certain aspects of the company's business. For example, a company may have an antiquated or custom-designed accounting system, which resides on a specific computer that can still support the accounting application the company has been using for many years. The speed at which new hardware and software is introduced on the market to replace, supplement or update a company's existing computer systems may often result in piecemeal changes and updates to an existing computer network, requiring phased integration of old and new hardware and software over an extended period of time. Electronic documents created and stored on legacy computers may only be located on one or more specific legacy computers in the network and may not be accessible or readable on any of the company's other computers since other forms of hardware do not support the data concerned. Such

legacy electronic documents may be difficult to retrieve and produce in an accessible format if the outdated hardware or software used to create those documents is required to read and use them. Many of the major software providers enable new software releases to be 'backward-compatible' (i.e. able to access electronic documents produced on earlier versions of the software) to a point. However, this is not always the case, for example if a company is operating a bespoke system.

10. PDAs: In addition to serving individual PC and laptop workstations connected within the office network, specific servers may also serve other kinds of client computers, such as personal digital assistants – an ever-expanding array of portable handheld devices, including BlackBerries, smart phones and Palm Pilots – as well as remote PCs or laptops maintained by company employees at home or otherwise outside the office. All of these remote or wireless devices are capable of creating, managing and storing electronic documents in their own right, and remotely accessing, altering, deleting and exchanging electronic documents located on the office network servers via an Internet connection. PDAs will typically contain hard drives of their own where electronic documents may also be stored, in addition to accessing remotely electronic documents that are located on the office network. However, in many cases, any document received, created or sent by a PDA will be automatically synchronized back to a central server.

11. Third-party PCs, servers, and data rooms: Electronic documents may also be found on third-party servers or PCs, completely external to a company's network. For example, data and files may be sent to and then stored on a third-party's PC or network through a 'file transfer protocol' ('FTP') client, which allows easy transfer of large amounts of data and files through the Internet. Electronic documents might also be found on an external server in a virtual 'data room'. Data rooms usually are password-protected, but are often accessible to multiple parties through the Internet. Data rooms may be maintained by the company or a third-party vendor that provides off-site data storage and management, and can contain data and files of both the company and third parties.

12. Removable media: Finally, 'active' electronic documents can also be stored on removable media, such as CDs, DVDs, disks, tapes, and USB portable drives. These compact storage devices for electronic information can be used on any computer. They effectively provide a removable and portable hard drive, capable of storing any of the same kinds of electronic documents that a PC can generate, and may be located virtually anywhere – in the office, at home, in a car, in a briefcase, a pocket, with a third party, etc.

B. 'Inactive' electronic documents

13. In addition to the foregoing components of a typical 'active' computer network, business computer networks typically will also include 'archived' or 'inactive' electronic documents. Such inactive electronic documents can be located on the same clients and servers that are part of a company's active network, or on dedicated back-up servers or removable disks or tapes, which are maintained separately from the active network so as to protect and preserve electronic documents that can be vital to a business's survival in the event that a catastrophe compromises the company's active computer system and the electronic documents it contains. Depending on a company's business practices, archived electronic documents may be stored within an organized structure. In contrast, back-up servers or tapes will typically maintain a 'snapshot' of

all or specific portions of a company's active electronic documents, taken on a periodic basis to preserve the company's data in the event of catastrophic system failure, loss or damage such as may be caused by a fire, earthquake, virus contamination, or other core threats to a company's business. Back-up servers or tapes should not, therefore, be expected to provide a comprehensive set of all of a business's electronic documents. Furthermore, back-up electronic documents are typically not maintained in a format that is readily accessible or searchable, as they are intended only for disaster-recovery purposes. Typically, back-up tapes are not well structured. Therefore, it is usually necessary to restore the entire tape or collection of tapes (at considerable expense) in order to investigate only a small part that may be relevant to a particular dispute.

14. 'Deleted' electronic documents: "Deleted" electronic documents are another form of inactive electronic documents. 'Deleted' is a misnomer insofar as 'deletion' of a document or file on a computer may serve only to move it from one location (e.g. an email inbox) to another (e.g. an email 'trash' or 'recycle' folder) where it remains and can readily be retrieved for some period of time. When an electronic document is then deleted from a trash or recycle file, that typically means only that the digital storage space required to maintain that particular electronic document has been designated as available for the storage of different information as and when the computer automatically determines that the same space is needed to store new or different information. But the deleted item continues to reside on the computer until it is overwritten with new and different information. This can result in 'fragmented' files, as computers will move and divide data designated as deleted in order to efficiently make room for new data. However, computer forensic techniques exist even to retrieve deleted electronic document long after it has been designated as such.

15. It is also worth noting that even when an electronic document is deleted from one location on one computer, PDA or storage device, an identical copy may continue to exist somewhere else on a company's computer system. For example, if the sender of an email deletes the email from his or her sent box at work, the email may continue to exist in a multitude of other email folders of other network users.

C. Metadata

16. "Metadata" is, literally, data about (electronically stored) data. Documents or files created on a computer will typically contain embedded information that is not readily apparent on the screen view of a file or in a printed version of the document or file. This secondary metadata is information about the electronic document or file that describes its characteristics, origins, or usage. There are three basic categories of metadata:

(i) 'Substantive' (or 'application') metadata is created by the software used to create the document, and reflects (among other things) editing changes or comments made to the document over time. Substantive metadata is embedded in the document it describes – and therefore remains with the document when it is copied, moved or produced – and may be useful in showing the genesis of a document and the history of proposed and/or accepted revisions to the document.

(ii) 'Systems' metadata reflects automatically generated information about the creation or revision of a document, such as the document's author or the date and time of its creation, modification or delivery. Systems metadata is not necessarily embedded in the document but can be generated by the computer system on which the document was created, and can be relevant if a document's authenticity is at issue or there are issues as to who received a document (including blind copy recipients that do not appear on the face of a document) or when it was received.

(iii) 'Embedded' metadata is inputted into a document by its creator or users but cannot be seen in the document's display, and commonly includes the formulas used to create spreadsheets, hidden columns, references, fields or linked files. Embedded metadata can be critical to understanding complex spreadsheets (such as those often used, for example, in construction projects) which on their face do not explain the mathematical formulas underlying or relating to the various rows or columns of information that are displayed on a computer screen or a printed version of the spreadsheet.

17. It should be noted that 'visible' metadata should be distinguished from 'hidden' metadata. Visible metadata is commonly displayed on screen and/or in print-outs and hidden metadata is not. In the case of an email, strictly speaking, all its constituent fields are metadata. Examples of visible metadata include the to/from/cc/date/title fields. Examples of hidden metadata would include the route the email took over the Internet and the IP address from which it was sent. Most of the metadata mentioned in sub-paragraphs (i) to (iii) above is hidden metadata.

18. Metadata is most commonly produced either in (a) a pdf or tagged image format (TIFF) with an accompanying 'load file' which permits the recipient to search the document for the relevant metadata, or (b) in the 'native' format in which the document being produced was created and which provides the recipient with all of the information available to the original user.

APPENDIX II
A GLOSSARY OF ELECTRONIC DOCUMENT TERMS

Note: Words in *Italics* refer to entries in this Glossary.

Archived Electronic Sources: means *Electronic Sources* that are stored for a shorter or longer term for the purpose of preservation. Storage for the purpose of archiving (preservation) means that a copy of the *Electronic Source* is made and stored on a *Data Carrier* to preserve it in the actual state without subsequent alterations of its substance. Normally, *Electronic Sources* are archived on dedicated *Data Carriers* which are logically and/or physically kept separate from electronic information that is in use. *Archived Electronic Sources* are a 'snapshot' of the archived data in existence at the time the archive was created. *Archived Electronic Sources* may be a complete 'snapshot' of this data or incremental. Incremental means that, if compared to the last *Back-up,* only new or changed data is archived.

Authenticity, of electronic document: Archiving or backing up electronic data is mostly done by using dedicated *Computer Programs* that allow tracking the date and time of any modification to data included in the archive. Some of these programs comply with national legal requirements for preserving the data integrity, i.e. *Authenticity.*

Authenticity of an *Electronic Document* is a non-technical attribute ascribed to it in a communication context, here a dispute. An *Electronic Document* is considered as being authentic if (i) the author or creator who figures as such in the context of the information displayed in the document or identified by somebody as being the author/creator really is or is determined by the arbitrators to be the 'real' author/creator; (ii) that this author/creator did produce exactly this *Electronic Document* at the moment ascribed to it by him or a third party; and (iii) that the *Electronic Document* was not subsequently altered by anybody.

Back-up: means a copy of electronic data for the purposes of preservation. See also *Archived Electronic Sources.*

Client: refers to dedicated *Software* that is locally installed on a *Computer* linked to a *Network* within which a *Server* is accessed by the *Client,* to which it provides a service. For example an *Email Client* interacts with an *Email Server,* such as MS Outlook with MS Exchange or a Lotus Domino *Server* with a Lotus Notes *Client.* Therefore, *Network* System architecture using *Servers* and *Clients* is referred to as *Server-Client*-Architecture.

For the purpose of *eDocument* disclosure it is useful to know, that a *Client* may, but need not always locally and permanently store copies of *ESD,* and that certain *Server-Client*-Systems may store *ESD* permanently only in a *Directory* of the *File System* pertaining to a *Server* (this may be increasingly the case where web-based services are employed in the relevant sphere of control, especially if cloud computing is used). This may be relevant for identifying *Custodians.*

Cloud Computing: is a catch-all term essentially referring to *Network* based computing systems within which software applications are being provided to local *Computers* by remote *Servers* as a service on demand. Furthermore, *Cloud Computing* is generally characterized by exclusive permanent storage of *ESI* in *Directories* of the *File Systems* pertaining to *Servers* in the so called cloud. A further common feature of *Cloud Computing* is virtualization of *Servers.* Virtualization means that the *Server* software is dissociated from the *Server*-computer (also called *Server*) hardware and may move from one computer location to another.

The same applies to *Directories* of the *File Systems* pertaining to the *Server-Software*. Application service software is often provided by third parties on the basis of complex service providing or outsourcing agreements. This may be relevant for identifying *Custodians* and/or the identification of the physical location of hardware means for *ESI* storage.

Typically, the *User* may access *Cloud Computing* services from any computer in the network using a *User*-ID and password, if such computer is equipped with a web-front-end and software pertaining thereto (e.g. a web-browser such as Mozilla Firefox, Safari, MS Explorer, Java-Runtime). The front-end software may also be referred to as *Client*, which is rather general-purpose and not dedicated (specialized) software. However, *Cloud Computing* may also require dedicated software for certain services.

An example of *Cloud Computing* most people may know are the so called 'web-mailers' for managing personal *email* accounts.

Computer Forensics: refers to a branch of forensics dealing with (i) security threats to computing systems and intrusions, but also (ii) data recovery and verification of data integrity, which are relevant to *eDisclosure*. *Computer Forensics* is a service provided by experts and comprises *inter alia*:
- Extraction of relevant data from computer systems and data carriers.
- Recovery of deleted data.
- Data analysis for establishing the 'history' of data and *Authenticity*.

Computer Hardware: refers to physically existing devices that generate, process, store and display any kind of data, such as *inter alia*: computers, displays, printers, network devices, disk drives and tape drives.

Computer Programs: refers to a recorded machine readable and executable code that is used to operate data processing devices and/or process data. *Computer Programs* usually consist of many *Files* that may also have different formats. *Computer Programs* are normally dedicated for a specific purpose, such as word-processing, spreadsheet calculation, visual presentations, data conversion, data back-up, voice- or video communication.

Computer Programs must be compatible with their environment, i.e. other programs such as the operating system (e.g. Windows, Linux, MacOS, Unix) and possibly other dedicated programs, since they use functions of these programs during operation, by exchanging data through software interfaces.

Computer Programs are normally protected by intellectual property rights, e.g. usually copyright and sometimes patents. Therefore, they may only be used in accordance with the terms and conditions of the licence of the holder of the rights.

Copy: is the reproduction of the original data. In relation to electronically recorded data, the problem is to distinguish copy from original. For example, if you send an *email*, a copy of which is stored in the (virtual) out-box of the sender's *Email Client*, the question may arise whether the copy of the message in the (virtual) in-box of the recipient's *email Client* or the copy in the out-box of the sender's *email Client* is the original. When processing data, computer programs may create several virtually identical *Files* in the background that are stored in different places. Therefore, unlike a sheet of paper with text and signatures, it may be a futile to try to distinguish the original *eDocument* from a copy. The question then is whether the copy is authentic (see: *Authenticity*). In our example one could compare the copy in the out-box with the one in the in-box.

Custodian, of electronic data: refers to a natural or legal person that has had or has control over electronic data, such as a specific word-processor file. Such control comprises physical access to a medium on which the electronic data is stored and the rights of access to the electronic data. Physical access means access to a computer or terminal that is technically enabled to access the storage medium on which the data is stored. This access may take place over a *Network*. Technically, access rights are controlled by computer software that is configured by the system operator (SysOp) according to the applicable policies. Access rights range from 'read' to 'read/write', 'delete', 'create' to 'change name'. Access rights are also defined by company policy or legal regulations to which natural persons who are *Custodians* may be subjected. Legal and natural persons who are *Custodians* may be subjected to contractual restrictions and/or legal rules that govern their rights of access to or authority over disclosed electronic data.

Data Mining: originally relates to the extraction of knowledge (information) from databases in a meaningful (intelligible) format for analysis for a specific purpose. Also useful is the context of the production of relevant *ESD*, since parties are required to produce not only *ESD* they know to exist but also which they happen to find by chance. Rather, they must extract and provide the existing *ESD* that falls under an agreed or ordered definition. The dispersion of *ESD* on *Data Carriers*, the variety of possible *File Formats*, and the sheer quantity of *ESD* that must be searched during the process, prevents this process from being carried out manually. Therefore, the use of *Search Tools* is required to extract potentially disclosable *ESD* at a first stage, which is followed by an analysis carried out by somebody at a second stage. This is followed by the extraction and organization of the *ESD* meeting the definition(s). Such *ESD* is mostly organized using Software that relies on relational databases. Finally, 'mined' *ESD* meeting the definition is disclosed in specified formats, unless *ESD* is privileged.

Data Carrier: means any tangible object on which electronic data is stored. (See: *Electronic Means of Storing or Recording Information*)

Data Deletion: refers to data, usually a *File* or *Directory* with regard to which somebody has completed the command 'delete'. Deletion will cause the relevant *Computer Program*, usually the operating system, to treat the data as non-existent, i.e. the *File* or *Directory* is no longer displayed (the logical pointers to the data in the *File System* and data disk sectors are removed). However, this does not mean that the relevant data has disappeared from the *Data Carrier* on which it was stored, unless the sections where bits and bytes of which it is composed are overwritten. Often, all or some deleted data can be recovered even after deletion. This requires dedicated recovery software and, possibly, special technical expertise (see *Computer Forensics*).

Data Erasure: refers to more than *Data Deletion*, since erased data is overwritten and thereby completely destroyed on the storage medium on which the erasure is carried out.

Data Recovery: refers to the complete or partial reconstruction of deleted or erased data using dedicated recovery tools, i.e. programs that analyze and reassemble residual deleted or erased data on a *Data Carrier* (see *Computer Forensics*).

Data Room: This term refers to a dedicated *File Repository* on a *Server* that uses advanced web technology.

Deleted eDocument: refers to a copy of an *eDocument* with regard to which somebody has performed the command 'delete'. Deletion will cause the relevant *Computer Program*, usually the operating system, to treat the *eDocument* as non-existent, i.e. the copy of the *eDocument* is no longer displayed. However, this does not mean that the relevant data has disappeared from the *Data Carrier* on which it was stored, unless the sections where bits and bytes of which it is composed are overwritten (see *Data Deletion, Computer Forensics*).

Disaster Recovery System: refers to a system consisting of hard- and *Software* with procedures that allow the technological infrastructure, including data, to be recovered or resumed should that infrastructure be hit by a disaster. For this purpose, such system will include periodical *Back-up* of critical *ESI* contained in the primary system.

Directory: refers to a hierarchical system (the *File System*) for organizing and retrieving electronic data used by *Computer Programs*, including the operating system, which is or may also be made visible as a 'folder' or 'drawer' (icons) via the graphical *User* interface, i.e. the display. With the exception of the so-called 'desk top', *Directories* are always logically placed and visualized below one or more physical or logical *Data Carriers*. A *Directory* may contain *Files* or sub-*Directories*. Sub-*Directories* are *Directories* located in another *Directory*, i.e. at a lower point in the logical hierarchy. Each *Directory* has an identifier, i.e. name. *Directories* on the same level in the hierarchy may not have identical names.

eDisclosure: is a non-standardized term used herein. It refers to the process by which a party to an arbitration or any third entity extracts data in electronic format from the *Data Carriers* in its custody and provides one or more other parties to the arbitration with such data in a certain format under the control of the arbitral tribunal and/or in accordance with the terms these parties have agreed. *eDisclosure* also comprises disclosure of copies of physically existing material (e.g. documents, photographs) that have been reduced into digital format.

Electronic Document (eDocument): may, but need not necessarily be, a 'photographic' copy of a physical document that was digitized (scanned). Herein *eDocument* is understood as falling within the definition of 'Document' in the IBA Rules on the Taking of Evidence in International Arbitration [2010]. The term *eDocument* is a subcategory of *ESI*, which is the broader term.

Black's Law Dictionary defines the term 'Document' as meaning something tangible on which words, symbols or marks are recorded. In short, a document is something tangible on which information that is intelligible by humans is recorded. An *Electronic Document* is a document that is not tangible but may be displayed or printed with the aid of a computer and its peripherals.

In most instances *Electronic Documents* are recorded as *Files*. However, it is also possible that a document is assembled automatically from several *Files* or some information contained in a file by a *Computer Program* for the purpose of displaying or printing the *Electronic Document*.

Electronic Documents may also contain or consist of video or audio recordings.

Electronic Mail (email): is a means of communicating via computer *Networks* including the *World Wide Web* by using POP or SMTP protocols. *Email* is the primary source of material for *eDisclosure*, since it is intensively used for intra-company communications. *Emails* can be sent and received by any person or logical entity that has an *email* account, i.e. an *email* address and a system with the software required for sending and receiving messages pertaining to this address. To access or send *emails*, *Users* either use a locally installed dedicated program that is called *email Client*, or they access a *Server* with the required *Software* via their web browser over a *Network*.

Email is mainly a means for text-based communication. However, *Files* can and often are 'attached' to *emails*.

A sent *email* is normally locally stored by the *Client* or the *Server* behind the web-front-end and then forwarded by *email* computer *Server* systems in blocks (data segments) via *Network*(s) to the *email* Server of the domain to which the recipient's *email* address belongs. This *Server* stores the *email* and forwards it to the *email Client* that is configured for receiving *emails* sent to the *email* account to which the recipient's *email* address belongs, if this *Client* (automatically) sends a signal to the Server indicating that it 'wants' to or can receive messages.

Each copy of an *email* that was created during the process can be deleted by a person with the required access rights, or automatically (normally after a certain period of time) where the system is configured to allow automatic deletion. However, the existence of large numbers of copies, as happens when there are multiple recipients, increases the probability that one or more copies remain available somewhere.

Proving actual receipt of an *email* by an intended recipient, in the event the recipient denies receipt, may be difficult for technical reasons. However, the content of other available information (documents) may indirectly prove receipt. *Computer Forensics* may also be used to clarify the issue.

Issues relating to *Authenticity* or subsequent alterations of messages (technically easy) may be resolved by comparing copies of *emails*. Otherwise, *Computer Forensics* may also be used to clarify the issue.

Electronic Means of Storing or Recording Information: refers to dedicated computer hardware for storing data, such as hard disks, memory cards, diskettes, back-up tape machines, USB-sticks, CD/DVD/Blu-ray drives and the discs they use, as well as the software for carrying out read/write operations. Storing implies a certain duration; the random access memory (RAM) used by computers to store transient bits and bytes during processing is not included.

Electronic Sources: mean information of any kind stored in machine-readable electronic format that may be relevant for the outcome of the dispute in relation to disclosure.

ESD: is an acronym for *eDocument* (see *ESI, Electronic Sources, File*).

ESI: is an acronym for electronically stored information or information stored in digital format (see *eDocument*, *Electronic Sources, File*).

ESI, active: refers to *ESI* that is accessible to *Custodians* within a computer or a *Network* without any need to access *Back-up ESI*.

ESI, inactive: refers to *ESI* that is not accessible to *Custodians* within a computer or a *Network* and requires access to *Back-up ESI*.

Extranet: see *Intranet*.

File: refers to a finite sequence of bytes representing information that are flagged as pertaining to this file when used in relation to computing. *Files* are normally stored for a certain duration on a storage medium. *Files* are part of the *File System*. Each *File* has an identifier (e.g. *File Name*) that must be unique within the *Directory* where it is located. The name is followed by a suffix describing the *File Type*.

Unless a *File* is 'flagged' to restrict certain operations such as deletion, the operating system is enabled to carry out read/write, renaming and deletion or erase actions. Apart from *Files* incorporating executable program codes, the arrangement of the information in a *File* is defined for the *File* to be used by a program such as a word-processor or media player. The type of program to which the *File* pertains may in such case be seen from the suffix. Without the correct program, the information may not be extracted correctly from the *File* and information cannot be correctly written into the *File* without expert knowledge and special tools.

Although a *File* is treated within a computer system as single logical entity, this does not mean that it is stored as one single sequence on the storage medium. Depending on the way storage is organized on such a medium, a *File* may be stored in blocks of bytes at different logical locations on the storage medium. Logical flags and indices used by the operation software manage these blocks (see: *File Fragment*).

File, accessible: is not a technical term and refers to a *File* that is accessible to a *Custodian*. Unless there are legal impediments, *active Files* are accessible. *Deleted Files* are normally no longer accessible to programs, including search tools, or may only be accessible with unreasonable effort using dedicated recovery tools, since they have disappeared from the *File System*. *Erased Files* are inaccessible unless dedicated tools used by *Computer Forensics* can recover all or some fragments from a *Data Carrier*. The required effort may be unreasonable, especially if the purpose of the search is not defined. Finally, a *File* may be inaccessible to a certain person or entity because that person or entity no longer has physical access to or the legal right of access to the computer/system to which the *Data Carrier* on which the *File* is stored is related.

File, active: is not a technical term and refers to a *File* that is not archived and may be accessed by a *User* with the required rights during normal operations.

File, deleted / erased: see *Data Deletion*, *Data Erasure*.

File Format: refers to *File* type represented by the suffix. The suffix indicates to *Users* the programs and what kind of programs should be enabled to properly extract, use/manipulate, visualize or make audible the information in the *File*, since the structure and arrangement of the bytes in the *File* have been defined by the programmer to be used by that specific program or kind of programs. Certain *File* types have been subject to considerable standardization efforts but others are proprietary. If a *User* knows the file extension he or she can search the corresponding program(s) on the *Internet* (see e.g. at <www.file-extension.com/>, <www.filext.com/>, <www.file-extensions.org/>).

File Fragment: refers to a block of data pertaining to a *File*. When *Data Recovery* is carried out, file fragments are retrieved, identified and reassembled to the extent that this is technically possible (see *Computer Forensics*),

File Name: refers to a unique and arbitrary identifier for a *File* within a *Directory* of a *File System*. Depending on the operating system a *File Name* must comply with certain requirements. Certain applications, such as word-processors, allow *Users* to determine the prefix of the *File Name*. It is good practice to use a meaningful and systematic approach to naming *Files*. Automatically created *Files* are assigned prefixes consisting of strings in accordance with a programmed naming system. Today, the prefix is followed by a dot and a suffix (file extension/type) that is normally assigned automatically. This suffix indicates the *File Format*.

Active Files can easily be searched in a *File System* on the basis of their (truncated) *File Name* using available search tools.

File Repository: refers to a logical place, normally accessible via a *Network*, where *Files* are stored for retrieval. In most instances, the *User* accesses the *File Repository* through the interface of dedicated document management software (DMS) that is either locally installed (in part) or via the web browser and allows *Files* to be uploaded, downloaded, visualized and processed, depending on *User* rights, which can often be defined down to the level of a particular *File*. The DMS normally comprises relational data *Software* allowing additional information to be associated with any *File* and versions and *User* access to be tracked. In most cases the *Files* in the *File Repository* are presented to the *User* in a hierarchical structure of folders that resembles the structure of the *File System*, even if the actual visual representation may be more sophisticated. The DMS usually allows complex search operations and can include functions such as optical character recognition (OCR).

File Repositories may be particularly useful for disclosure of *eDocuments* and/or electronic filing.

File System: refers to a defined system by which electronic data in *File Format* is organized for access, processing and storage. On a PC the *File System* may be visualized by icons that are mostly arranged in a hierarchical structure comprising *Directories*, sub-directories and *Files*, which reside in physical *Data Carriers*.

However, there are also virtual *File Systems* that overlay more specific *File Systems*, each of which may have a different specification according to the interface provided by the virtual *File System*. Global *File Systems* are cluster-*File Systems* that comprise *Directories* and *Files* on a multitude of physical *Data Carriers* within a storage data area *Network*. *Network File Systems* support *File* sharing over a *Network*, mostly by using a *Server*.

Format, of disclosure of eDocument: refers to the *File Format* in which *eDocuments* are disclosed to the other side. The *File Format* for disclosure may, but need not necessarily be the same format which is used for submissions to the arbitral tribunal. Sometimes it is suggested that *eDocuments* be disclosed in their original format, so that all *Metadata* included in the 'original' *eDocument* is preserved. However, unless the recipients of disclosed *eDocuments* already have a licence to the Software to which the original format pertains, such party may have difficulty accessing the information in the *File* with reasonable effort.

Format, of submission for eDocument: refers to the *File Format* in which *eDocuments* are filed with the arbitral tribunal. *eDocuments* are often submitted to the arbitral tribunal as a print-out or, if provided in digital format, as a PDF copy, since it is reasonable to submit *eDocuments* in a format that any addressee (other parties, arbitrators) can open and read without needing to subscribe to special software, which may not otherwise be easily available on acceptable conditions. However, this approach may sometimes not be useful due to the particular nature of the *eDocument* or because the original version of the *eDocument* includes relevant Metadata that would not be preserved if the *eDocument* is produced in a different easily accessible *Format*.

Handheld Devices (Blackberry): refers to small data-processing units that are small enough to fit into a person's hand and are from time to time, or most of the time, connected to a *Network* (mobile telephone networks, WLAN, Bluetooth, USB, etc.) for communication purposes. *Handheld Devices* are extensively used for text messaging, *email* or instant messaging (SMS). In- and outgoing messages are stored on the mobile device for a variable duration, depending on the *Data Carrier* that may be built into the device, or may be exchangeable (see: *Archived Electronic Source, Custodian*).

Internet: refers to the global *Network* of computers consisting of a decentralized structure of *Networks*, comprising hard- and *Software* within which connected computers can exchange data, using the standard *Internet* protocol suite (TCP/IP). The *Internet* comprises various services/application types, such as the *World Wide Web, email, File* transfer (e.g. using FTP).

Intranet: refers to a *Network* that is used to communicate and share information in electronic format among a defined group of *Users* related to an organization, normally a company or a group of companies. However, persons or entities that do not belong to the organization but interact with it, such as suppliers and customers, may have certain rights to access information within the *Intranet*. An *Intranet* usually interfaces with the *Internet*. Sometimes a distinction is made between an *Intranet*, whose *Users* are attached to the organization and an extranet which includes the aforementioned external *Users*.

In any event, virtualization removes the need to distinguish between *Inter- Intra-*, and extranets, since what matters is the access to the *Networks* defined by the *User* ID, password, and rights of access to a secure environment (data encryption) that has been defined as a *Network*.

Laptop: refers to a kind of portable *Personal Computer*.

Legacy Hard- and Software: refers to older hard- and *Software* that has become obsolete due to technical progress and is not fully compatible with the system now used by the organization in question. Such outdated hard- or *Software* may be kept available within organizations for the purpose of accessing *Back-ups* or other *ESI*.

Local Means of Storage: local refers to system devices or computers that are located at the workplace of the *Custodian*, e.g. a *Laptop* or *Personal Computer*. Means of storage refers to *Electronic Means of Storing or Recording Information*.

Mainframe Computer: refers traditionally to high-performance central computers run by big organizations that were accessed via terminals. Today, *Mainframe Computers* operate in *Networks* using *Internet* protocols and may host *Network Servers*.

Metadata: refers to data that is related to other data, such as *Files*, and describes attributes thereof. Certain *Metadata* provides book-keeping information within *File Systems*, such as file creation, modification, storage dates, *File Format*, access permission settings, and can often be easily visualized. Other *Metadata* depends on the *File Format* and/or the application *Software* environment. *File Repositories*, case management *Software* and other applications use database *Software* for creating, managing and storing arbitrarily defined categories of *Metadata*.

Network: (also referred to as 'Computer *Network*') may refer to the cables and devices by which computers and peripherals are connected and can exchange data. *Networks* can be classified as Local Area *Network* (LAN), Wide Area *Network* (*WAN*), Virtual Private *Network* (VPN), etc. However, the relevant hardware and *Network Software* constitute only the *Network* infrastructure, since the devices relate to a specific *Network* only because they were arbitrarily made to do so. For this purpose each device has a unique identifier and defined access rights within the *Network* to which the *User*'s rights correspond. A device that is not 'flagged' as being part of the *Network* does not belong to it.

Network Server: refers to a *Server* that is linked to a specific *Network*.

Original, of Electronic Document: see *Authenticity, Copy, File*.

PDA: is the abbreviation for personal digital assistant and means a mobile hand held device. Technologically, PDA's merge into mobile communication devices such as smart phones like Blackberry's, iPhones and the like.

Personal Computer (PC): refers to 'stand-alone' computers, such as desktop computers, *Laptops*, etc. These computers are characterized by consisting of hard- and *Software* that allows them to be used independently of a *Network* connection. Prior to the advent of *PCs*, *Mainframe Computers*, to which *Users* connected via terminals without local storage capacity, were used. Today, *PCs* are nearly all permanently or temporarily connected to *Networks*, and the software they use is not always or not completely installed locally. More importantly, data processed on a *PC* may not be stored, or not permanently stored, on a local *Data Carrier*, but also be held on *Network* storage devices.

Search Tool: refers to *Software* for *Data Mining*. The technical sophistication of such tools for predictably reliable results is crucial, since the tool must allow complex (multi-criteria) search operations and be capable of using these on a maximum of *File Formats* or at least those formats in which the *ESD* that are searched will in all likelihood exist. It is important to know that while many *File Formats* contain information that is directly machine readable (i.e. using search words), bit map *File Formats* (digital photocopies) may not be searchable unless converted using optical character recognition (OCR).

However, the best *Search Tool* will provide only results of a quality that is determined by the quality of the search instructions. Thus, search methodology is crucial, and transparency in this regard is commendable.

Server: sometimes refers to a dedicated computer that is connected to a *Network* on which *Server* applications are running. However, the term essentially refers to *Computer Programs* providing services to other *Computer Programs*, usually in a *Network* by using *Network* protocols. *Server* programs may run on *Mainframe Computers*.

In the context of *eDisclosure* it is important to know that much data exchanged inside or outside an organization is managed by a *Server*. The storage media where such data is held may be directly connected to the computer on which the *Server* runs. However, the trend is to have *Servers* run in virtual operating system environments, i.e. in an environment where devices are logical and to a certain extent disconnected from the actual hardware, allowing processed and/or stored data to move around or to be stored in several physical locations. The metaphor for this delocalized existence is '*Cloud*'

Shared Server: is a *Server*, normally a *Network Server*, hosting *ESI* for defined groups of *Users* having defined rights with regard to the hosted data.

Software: see *Computer Programs*.

User: is a logical entity possessing the access rights for using a computer or *Software* or accessing a *Network*. A *User* may have the right to carry out any operation (e.g. system administrator) or be assigned restricted rights (e.g. normal *User*) with regard to operations and/or access to *ESI* for which usage restrictions have been implemented. For managing *User*-rights, systems use *User*-names (*User*-ID) and access codes (e.g. passwords or biometrical data). A physical person possessing such access information will be treated by the system as the logical *User* with whom this set of data is associated and is also called *User*. Depending on the assigned rights, a person who is a *User* may be a *Custodian*.

Version history: refers to the different stages of 'existence' of data, especially *Files*, such as creation or modification dates. Certain basic historic information is nearly always stored as *Metadata*. Depending on the *Format*, or the *Software* used, historic information may be more complete. *File Repositories* and other dedicated *Software* systems (e.g. case-management systems) may store data including the complete version history of a *File* and, possibly, any different versions of such File.

WAN: is an acronym meaning Wide Area *Network* (see *Network*, *World Wide Web*).

World Wide Web: refers to the global *Network* of hypertext pages served through *Servers* via the *Internet* according to agreed standards and includes small *Software* programs and services that enable a vast array of operations via the *Internet*.

APPENDIX 18

COMMISSION REPORT – ISSUES FOR ARBITRATORS TO CONSIDER REGARDING EXPERTISE (2010)

REPORT OF THE ICC COMMISSION ON ARBITRATION AND ADR (2010)*

* This report is being updated in the light of the 2012 ICC Rules of Arbitration, mainly in regard to references to new provisions

I. Introduction

This text[1] is intended to help guide arbitrators on issues that they should consider regarding tribunal-appointed and party-appointed experts in arbitrations under the ICC Rules of Arbitration ('Rules of Arbitration'). The text may also be useful in arbitrations to which the Rules of Arbitration do not apply. Specifically, the text explores how to use experts effectively and efficiently, with an eye toward avoiding certain approaches that may cause problems during or even after the arbitration.

In ICC arbitrations, experts may be used to prove or establish facts that are relevant to the merits of the parties' dispute. Experts also may be used to help arbitrators understand relevant issues of law that will govern the tribunal's decision on the merits (e.g., where the arbitrators are unfamiliar with the laws applicable to the dispute).

The Rules of Arbitration include two distinct mechanisms for the appointment and use of experts. Under Article 20(3), the tribunal may hear testimony from experts whom one or more parties appoint to offer testimony relevant to the parties' dispute. Under Article 20(4), after consulting with the parties, the arbitral tribunal may retain one or more experts directly, define their terms of reference, receive their reports, and permit the parties to question them at the hearing. Whether the expert is party-appointed or tribunal-appointed, the Rules of Arbitration give the tribunal considerable flexibility regarding how experts may be used in the arbitration, and likely more flexibility than would be available in national courts.

---

1. This document was produced under the auspices of the ICC Commission on Arbitration and is a report of the Task Force on Guidelines for ICC Expertise Proceedings co-chaired by Erik Schäfer and David B. Wilson. It follows two earlier reports: 'Guide to ICC Expertise' published in the *ICC International Court of Arbitration Bulletin* Vol. 16 No. 1 (2005) 19, and 'Issues for Experts Acting Under the ICC Rules for Expertise or the ICC Rules of Arbitration' published in the *ICC International Court of Arbitration Bulletin* Vol. 20 No. 1 (2009) 23.

II. Party-appointed experts

A. What is a party-appointed expert's role and status?

Although parties also may retain expert consultants who will not be called to testify, the only party-appointed experts who are likely to concern the arbitral tribunal are those retained to testify before the tribunal as witnesses. Experts may be appointed by one or more parties.

It is up to the party to decide whether to attempt to prove its case through evidence from a party-appointed expert. The party or parties who retain the expert are responsible for defining the expert's tasks and for arranging remuneration and other practical issues with the expert.

Regardless of which party or parties appoint them, party-appointed experts are witnesses-nothing more and nothing less. As with any other witness, the arbitral tribunal may reasonably expect and require that a party-appointed expert tell the truth when he or she testifies. The expert's duty to testify truthfully overrides any other duty that an expert might believe that he or she owes to a party. See also Section II(F) below.

Whatever the expert's qualifications, the expert is not the decision-maker in the arbitration. The arbitral tribunal remains solely responsible for determining the facts of the case and applying the law to the facts to resolve the parties' dispute. The tribunal cannot delegate its role to an expert.

Thus, the arbitral tribunal is and remains responsible for giving whatever weight it deems appropriate to an expert witness's testimony, just as the tribunal would for any other witness in the arbitration. When weighing an expert's testimony, the arbitral tribunal should consider factors such as:

- the factual and legal issues presented in the arbitration;
- the expert's qualifications and experience;
- the care and attention that the expert used when formulating his or her opinions;
- whether the expert is biased towards a party or conclusion;
- whether the expert's opinions were derived based on a methodology recognized by other experts in the field;
- whether the expert reached unreasonable or irrelevant findings;
- whether the expert's answers to questions from opposing counsel or the tribunal reduce the value of the expert's opinions;
- the expert's overall credibility while testifying; and
- other factors that the arbitral tribunal deems relevant.

B. What directions, if any, should the arbitral tribunal issue concerning experts before a party appoints an expert?

Subject to the arbitral tribunal's oversight and direction (see Section II(C) below), the parties may agree on the timing and method of presenting expert evidence. If the parties do not agree, the arbitral tribunal usually will discuss these issues with the parties and issue appropriate directions. Usually, this is done early in the arbitration during the procedural conference at which the time schedule for the proceedings is established, although the tribunal may decide to issue directions later in the proceedings if the tribunal believes that it does not yet have sufficient information about the need for expert testimony.

Moreover, if the circumstances warrant and subject to any prior agreements between the parties, the arbitral tribunal, after consulting the parties and in accordance with Article 15(1) of the Rules of Arbitration, may establish an explicit rule requiring any expert to certify that the findings set forth in the expert's report are true and that the opinions expressed are correct to the best of the expert's knowledge. This duty may or may not exist in the national legal systems with which the expert is familiar. The tribunal can provide further clarifying directions, as necessary. By providing early notice of this requirement, the tribunal can help to avoid surprises later in the proceedings.

C. Must the arbitral tribunal agree to hear testimony from an expert witness if one or more parties wish to offer expert evidence?

No. Under Article 20(3) of the Rules of Arbitration the arbitral tribunal retains discretion to decide whether to hear expert evidence from party-appointed experts. Nonetheless, under Article 15(2) of Rules of Arbitration, the arbitral tribunal is responsible for ensuring that each party has a 'reasonable opportunity to present its case'. Thus, the arbitral tribunal may be reluctant to refuse a party's request to offer expert testimony, out of concern that it might deprive the party of its rights and expose the arbitral award to the risk of being set aside. As a practical matter, expert evidence concerning specific, disputed matters that are relevant to the arbitral tribunal's decision normally should be heard.

The tension between Article 15(2) and Article 20(3) often can be resolved through guidance from the arbitral tribunal, as discussed in subsection (D) below.

D. When should the arbitral tribunal encourage or discourage the parties from relying on expert evidence?

When formulating the Terms of Reference and otherwise in administering the arbitration, it is entirely appropriate for the arbitral tribunal to provide guidance to the parties on whether expert evidence is likely to help the tribunal to resolve disputed issues in the arbitration. If the tribunal indicates that expert evidence is unlikely to be helpful, most parties will not attempt to offer it. Likewise, the tribunal may indicate the need to narrow the scope of the expert's evidence to specific relevant issues.

When deciding what guidance to provide, the arbitral tribunal may wish to consider the following questions:

(i) Does the resolution of the parties' dispute require technical or other specialized knowledge?

In many cases, the answer to this question will be no. In this case, expert evidence will be unnecessary. For example, although a dispute over defects in the construction of a power plant is likely to require technical or other specialized knowledge, a dispute involving a routine claim for breach of a commercial contract will not, except perhaps with regard to damages.

(ii) Does the tribunal already possess the necessary technical or specialized knowledge?

Even where technical or other specialized knowledge is required to resolve the parties' dispute, expert evidence may be unnecessary if the tribunal itself has the needed expertise. Thus, for example, if the dispute involves an issue of Swedish law and the tribunal includes Swedish attorneys, it may not be helpful for the tribunal to hear testimony from attorneys or law professors on Swedish law. Likewise, if the dispute involves a dispute over construction defects, it may not always be helpful to hear expert evidence if the arbitrator is an engineer with expertise in the area relevant to the parties' dispute and thus understands the relevant technical issues without the need for further explanation from a party-appointed expert.

If the dispute involves specialized knowledge other than the applicable law (which falls squarely within the tribunal's duties) and only one member of a three-arbitrator tribunal possesses the required expert knowledge, the situation becomes more complex because of the need to avoid a de facto in camera expertise proceeding. In other words, unless the parties expressly agree, it is neither expected nor recommended that one arbitrator will perform an independent expert investigation or evaluation on which the other arbitrators would rely in making their decision. Many problems exist with this approach, not the least of which is that it reduces the parties' ability to comment on, ask questions about and, if appropriate, challenge what the expert has done.

In some arbitrations, all parties have intended that the tribunal should include arbitrators with certain expert skills, so as to avoid the need to educate the arbitral tribunal on specific issues through a retained expert. In these circumstances, the arbitral tribunal should ensure that:

- adequate procedural protections can be implemented to avoid what would amount to an in camera expertise proceeding;
- the scope of expert fact-finding activities can be delegated and carried out by the arbitrator(s) concerned in a more cost and time-efficient manner than could a tribunal-appointed or party-appointed expert; and
- the relationship among the arbitrators is such that they are comfortable entrusting one of their number with the task.

(iii) Are the parties' employees or officers able to testify competently concerning the disputed issues?

Evidence from retained experts is not necessary in every arbitration. Officers or employees of the parties may be experts in the relevant industries and thus able to testify competently on technical matters in a manner that helps the arbitral tribunal understand and resolve disputed factual issues.

(iv) What impact will expert evidence have on the costs of the arbitration?

Retained expert witnesses do not work for free, nor are they inexpensive. Expert witness fees can materially increase the overall costs of the arbitration, even without taking into account the corollary impact on attorneys' fees and hearing time. The potential benefit of a party-appointed expert should thus be evaluated in the light of these increased costs.

(v) How else can the arbitral tribunal help the parties to save time and costs when retaining experts?

To reduce time and costs, the arbitral tribunal may wish to encourage the parties jointly to retain a single expert on a particular subject, rather than one expert on each side.

The arbitral tribunal should candidly discuss all of these issues with the parties and try to obtain a consensus on whether these costs are likely to be worthwhile given the particular issues in dispute.

E. How should the arbitral tribunal communicate with party-appointed experts?

In general, the tribunal does not communicate directly with a party-appointed expert, except when the expert is testifying at a hearing. If the tribunal has a question regarding a procedural matter, it should raise this question through counsel to the party who engaged the expert.

F. What duties does the expert owe to the arbitral tribunal?

The tribunal should insist that the expert testify truthfully in response to all questions from the arbitral tribunal and the parties' respective counsel.

The expert must comply with the tribunal's directions regarding expert testimony, including for example, whether expert testimony will be allowed, the form of the expert's work product, when the work product is due, whether the witness will be accepted as an expert, how long the expert will be permitted to testify, directions to answer particular questions; and so forth.

In some countries, an expert witness also may have certain obligations to the tribunal under the regulations of a professional body or licensing authority to which the expert is subject or otherwise under national law.

In some national court systems,[2] party-appointed experts who are designated as testimonial witnesses are deemed to have an affirmative duty to assist the court that overrides the expert's duty to the appointing party. Apparently, this duty is construed to be broader than the expert's duty to testify truthfully.

Neither the Rules of Arbitration nor arbitration laws, such as those based on the UNCITRAL Model Law on International Commercial Arbitration, presently include an explicit rule to this effect.

Although the parties may agree on such a procedural rule (e.g., in the agreement to arbitrate or in the Terms of Reference signed by all parties), it is far from clear whether arbitrators may or should establish or apply a rule of this kind.

Some arbitrators and arbitration practitioners argue that the arbitral tribunal should issue directions establishing an affirmative 'duty to assist the tribunal' upon party-appointed experts in ICC arbitration. The proponents of this approach argue that establishing such a duty will encourage experts to be independent and thus more likely to help the tribunal determine the true facts and issue a just award. Although the proponents acknowledge that such a duty is not specified in the Rules of Arbitration, they argue that unless the parties agree otherwise, the tribunal has the power to establish the duty through an order under Articles 15(1) and 20(1) of the Rules. The proponents of this approach argue that enabling the arbitral tribunal to issue instructions directly to the expert is a practical solution to a possible 'battle of experts', which might otherwise cause the tribunal to appoint its own expert as permitted under Article 20(4) of the Rules of Arbitration.

---

2. These include the United Kingdom, Hong Kong, Australia and New Zealand, but not the USA.

Other arbitrators and arbitration practitioners argue that imposing an affirmative duty to assist the tribunal upon party-appointed experts ignores the distinction in the Rules of Arbitration between party-appointed experts and tribunal-appointed experts. Although Article 20(4) gives the arbitral tribunal the right to define the terms of reference for tribunal-appointed experts, Article 20(3) does not mention a similar right with respect to a party-appointed expert. When appointing an expert under Article 20(4), the tribunal, in consultation with the parties, defines the expert's mission. By contrast, a party-appointed expert's mission is negotiated between the expert and the party or parties who appoint the expert, taking into account factors such as:

- the expert's expertise and how the expert can help the party prove its case;
- the expert's fees for performing the needed analysis; and
- the time required to perform that analysis.

The distinction between party-appointed experts and tribunal appointed experts is important when one tries to understand precisely what the 'duty to assist' the tribunal would entail. Because the Rules of Arbitration do not mention such a duty, the arbitral tribunal must define the duty's scope directly or by reference to some body of law. As a practical matter, this means that the duty's scope would vary from case to case and from tribunal to tribunal. Under either scenario, if the duty to assist is broader than the duty to testify truthfully, serious problems exist in connection with defining any objective standard for the duty's limits. For example, would the duty require the expert to perform analyses that interest the tribunal, but which (a) the appointing party cannot afford or considers irrelevant; (b) would delay the arbitration's timely completion; or (c) would go beyond the expert's defined mission? Further, if the arbitral tribunal believes that the expert has testified truthfully but has not sufficiently 'assisted' the tribunal, is the appointing party subject to some sort of consequence (e.g., adverse inferences)?

In summary, opponents of the 'duty to assist' approach argue that if the arbitral tribunal is concerned that a party-appointed expert would not be sufficiently independent or 'helpful', the tribunal should consider appointing an expert itself. If the tribunal believes that a party-appointed expert is slanting his or her findings or testimony for the benefit of the appointing party, the tribunal may properly decide to give the expert's testimony little or no weight. See Section II(A) above. The tribunal will need to weigh testimony and judge the credibility of expert witnesses regardless of whether the tribunal establishes a duty to assist.

G. What directions, if any, should the arbitral tribunal issue regarding the expert's report or other work product?

The tribunal has discretion to decide whether to require the expert to provide a report or other work product in advance of the hearing and the form that the report or other work product should take. Tribunals frequently order reports in one of two forms:

- a detailed narrative report of the expert's analysis and conclusions, or
- a witness statement setting out the expert's analysis and conclusions in the form of an affidavit or declaration.[3]

3. See Appendix II below and 'Issues for Experts Acting Under the ICC Rules for Expertise or the ICC Rules of Arbitration' (2009) 20:1 ICC Arb. Bull. 23 at 34.

In almost all arbitrations, directions from the tribunal requiring the expert to submit his or her work product in advance of the hearing will be helpful to the tribunal and the parties. This approach is also likely to shorten the time needed for the hearing.

The arbitral tribunal should require the expert's work product to be communicated to all parties in accordance with a set or agreed time schedule. Normally, it will help to expedite the hearing and focus the issues if the tribunal also gives the parties the opportunity to comment on or rebut the opposing party's expert's report before the hearing and to supplement the expert's report to clarify issues that the opposing side raises. See Sections (H) and (I) below.

1. What can the arbitral tribunal do if a proposed expert lacks the qualifications to testify competently, if the expert's methodology is unsatisfactory, or if the expert's report is otherwise deficient?

The tribunal has discretion to decide how to address and resolve these sorts of issues.

When doubts arise regarding the witness's qualifications to testify as an expert or the methodology that the witness used to reach his or her conclusions, the question is usually whether the tribunal should refuse to permit the expert to testify at all or whether the tribunal should address these concerns when weighing the witness's testimony. Thus, where the tribunal believes that the witness is not really an expert or where the witness's methodology is fatally flawed, the tribunal might permit the witness to testify, but choose to give the witness's testimony little or no weight.

On the other hand, if the expert's qualifications are not in dispute, but the expert fails to comply with the tribunal's directions regarding the submission of a satisfactory pre-hearing report or witness statement, the question is whether the expert's failure to comply prejudices the opposing party's ability to prepare for and present its case at the hearing. Under these circumstances, the tribunal might issue remedial directions, such as barring the expert from testifying (at least until the deficiency is corrected) or limiting the expert's testimony to the material specifically addressed in the report or witness statement.

2. How does the arbitral tribunal resolve a party's objections to another party's party-appointed expert or an expert jointly retained by both parties?

The arbitral tribunal should resolve objections after hearing from the parties, and taking into account each party's right to have a reasonable opportunity to present its case. Objections can take several forms, including for example:

(a) Objections alleging a conflict of interest

A party may object based on the allegation that the expert has a conflict of interest that would preclude the expert from testifying.

(i) Prior service to or relationship with the party who retained the expert

Where the basis of the alleged conflict is the expert's prior service to or relationship with the party that calls the expert, the tribunal usually will find that the conflict does not preclude the expert from testifying, but may affect the weight that the arbitral tribunal gives to the expert's testimony.

(ii) Prior service to or relationship with the objecting party

Where the objecting party alleges that the expert's prior service to or relationship with the objecting party should preclude the expert from testifying, the issue usually is whether the expert previously obtained trade secrets or other confidential information from the objecting party, and is precluded by contract or applicable law from using or disclosing that information. This fact pattern can be difficult to resolve, and requires the arbitral tribunal to evaluate factors, including:

- the dates, nature and duration of the prior relationship between the objecting party and the expert;
- whether the expert obtained trade secrets or other confidential information from the objecting party;
- contractual or legal prohibitions on the disclosure of that information;
- the nature of the expert's engagement in the arbitration;
- the likelihood that the expert will use or disclose the protected information when serving the opposing party; and
- whether the objecting party has waived the conflict.

(iii) Prior service to or relationship with one or more members of the arbitral tribunal

Here, a party objects to the opposing party's expert because the expert has a personal or professional relationship with one or more members of the tribunal that is alleged to compromise the tribunal's ability to hear and weigh the expert's testimony objectively and impartially. Examples of relationships that might result in objections include:

- an existing or previous business relationship with one or more of the arbitrators (e.g., expert and arbitrator both partners in the same firm), and
- an existing or prior consulting or other relationship with one or more of the arbitrators (e.g., the arbitrator is currently using the expert in a case in which the arbitrator is counsel; the expert is acting as arbitrator in a case in which the arbitrator is counsel; the expert retained the arbitrator in some capacity, etc.).

In these circumstances, the arbitral tribunal must decide whether allowing the expert to testify would create the appearance of impropriety; and the hardship that would result to the party who retained the expert if the expert is not permitted to testify. Arbitrators should deal with these situations with due regard to the specific case and the parties' legitimate expectations. If any doubt exists as to whether a party might object, the relationship with the expert should be disclosed to the parties as soon as practicable.

(b) Objections to the expert's qualifications

Based on the expert's professional biography or statements made by the expert orally or in writing a party may object to the opposing party's expert's qualifications. See Section G(1).

(c) Objections to the expert's methodology

A party may argue that expert's methodology is not a proper basis for the expert's opinion. See Section G(1).

(d) Objections based on contacts between the expert and counsel for the party who retained him or her

A party may sometimes challenge the opposing party's expert's credibility based on contacts between the expert and the party who appointed him or her. These contacts occur in almost every case because counsel usually needs to be educated by the expert concerning the subject matter of the expert's expertise, in order for counsel to present his or her client's case competently. In common law systems, this approach is completely appropriate and acceptable. Otherwise the retaining party would also need to retain an additional expert (a so-called 'shadow expert') to assist counsel, thus resulting in additional costs.

Thus, the question may arise as to whether and to what extent information exchanged between counsel and the expert must be disclosed. Opinions are divided in this regard. In many civil law systems, only court-appointed experts are regarded as acceptable and any ex parte contacts between a party and an expert is inappropriate. Common law systems allow such contacts, but usually require communications between counsel and expert to be disclosed when the expert is endorsed as a testimonial witness. Communications with experts who are not expected to testify (i.e., consulting experts) remain privileged and non-discloseable. In systems where privilege may be waived, this sometimes results in extensive requests for discovery and extensive questioning of the expert during testimony concerning the expert's communications with the appointing counsel.

The Rules of Arbitration, most lex arbitri, and arbitration practice do not provide guidance in this regard. Thus, the issue of privilege should be resolved by agreement of the parties or if the parties do not agree, by the arbitral tribunal under Article 15(1) of the Rules of Arbitration, whenever practicable, after hearing from the parties.

The following approach is recommended:

- The issue should be addressed and resolved as early as practicable and before testimonial expert witnesses are named in the arbitral proceedings.
- Experts who give evidence should be required to disclose the facts upon which they rely in forming their opinions, including the source from which these facts have been obtained (e.g., test results, project documentation and any other source).
- Where the information provided to the expert involves trade secrets or other non-public business information, the arbitral tribunal may enter an appropriate protective order that would preclude the opposing party from using or disclosing the information outside of the arbitration. If the party asserting a trade secret or other confidential information refuses to disclose the information provided to the expert, the arbitral tribunal may choose to preclude the expert from testifying or to limit the weight given to the expert's testimony.

H. What techniques may the arbitral tribunal employ to reduce conflicts in the opinions of party-appointed experts?

When each side calls its own expert and the experts disagree on one or more material issues, the arbitral tribunal may find it difficult to determine which (if either) expert should be believed and how to weigh the experts' testimony. This is because the arbitrators usually do not have the same technical expertise as the experts.

For example, the experts may differ in the structure of their respective work product, their basic underlying data, or their methodology. Conflicting expert opinions are particularly challenging for the tribunal to resolve where the tribunal cannot find flaws in the experts' methodologies or findings that would enable the tribunal to conclude that one expert's conclusions are more likely to be correct than the other's.

To avoid the difficulty that 'dueling experts' sometimes create, some arbitral tribunals appoint their own experts instead of or in addition to party-appointed experts or use witness conferencing. See Section II(K) below.

I. May the arbitral tribunal direct party-appointed experts to work together to bridge disagreements and, if so, how?

Another approach is to require the experts to meet in private to attempt to narrow specific areas of disagreement, which the arbitral tribunal should identify to them. Where the differences cannot be bridged, the arbitral tribunal may require the experts to explain to the tribunal and the parties, in writing, the reasons for the differences and whether the experts' differing approaches both can withstand peer review.

If practicable, this approach works best after the tribunal has received written expert opinions and any comments the parties may have provided, thereby helping the tribunal to focus the hearing on the relevant issues concerning which the experts disagree.

J. What directions, if any, should the arbitral tribunal issue on questioning experts at the hearing?

The Rules of Arbitration give the arbitral tribunal broad discretion regarding how to conduct the hearing. If the case warrants, the arbitral tribunal will discuss appropriate directions with the parties at a pre-hearing conference. See Section II(B) above. In most cases, after the experts have submitted their written reports, the arbitral tribunal will summon the experts to attend a hearing, either because a party requests a hearing or because the arbitral tribunal finds that a hearing would be helpful.

The order and duration of the questioning is up to the arbitrators, unless the parties have agreed otherwise. For example, the arbitral tribunal may direct that counsel for the party who retained the expert should go first, followed by the opposing party's counsel, and then the tribunal. Or the arbitral tribunal may permit the opposing party's counsel to go first, followed by the counsel for the party who retained the expert, and then the tribunal. The tribunal may also decide to ask its questions first, intervene with questions at any time, or ask its questions once the parties have asked their questions.

If the tribunal believes it appropriate, the tribunal may direct or authorize an expert to put questions to other experts or witnesses in relation to the subject matter of the expert's assignment.

K. What is witness conferencing and how can this technique be used?

If there are several party-appointed experts, the tribunal alternatively may direct that a so-called 'witness conference' be conducted during which the expert, the other experts and any knowledgeable fact witnesses will be heard together. The arbitral tribunal directs the experts and witnesses present in the hearing room to address issues that it considers relevant. Each expert may thus be confronted with what other experts state or asked to engage in a discussion with them. This method is increasingly used to resolve the differences between conflicting expert opinions, but requires the tribunal's active participation and supervision in order to maintain order at the hearing.

L. How should the tribunal use a party-appointed expert's findings when making its decision?

The tribunal has discretion to decide how much, if any, weight to give to the expert's testimony. See Section II(A) above.

M. May the arbitral tribunal award costs and expenses of party-appointed experts?

Under Article 31(1) of the Rules of Arbitration, costs of the arbitration can include amounts paid to party-appointed experts. Under Article 33(3), the arbitral tribunal has discretion to decide what costs to award and which party or parties shall bear them and in what proportion. As a practical matter, this means that the tribunal can award all, part or none of the experts' fees to the party that advanced those fees.

In international arbitration, the most common approach is to award costs. Some arbitrators award costs in proportion to the outcome of the principal claims. This approach, however, would not preclude capping the recoverability of certain costs, if they are unreasonable. Another approach is for the tribunal to consider costs by categories and to determine the extent to which the party needed to incur these costs in order to establish its case.[4]

III. Tribunal-appointed experts

A. Under what circumstances should the arbitral tribunal retain an expert?

The arbitral tribunal has a duty to establish the facts of the case and to apply the law to the facts. It may not delegate these duties to an expert.

Article 20(4) of the Rules of Arbitration gives the arbitral tribunal broad authority to retain one or more experts directly, after consulting the parties.[5] The arbitral tribunal can appoint an expert, even if none of the parties ask the tribunal to do so. If, however, all parties object to the tribunal's appointment of an expert, the tribunal should not make the appointment, as at least one party must be willing to pay an advance on the expert's costs. See Rules of Arbitration, Appendix III, Article 1(11).

In general, the arbitral tribunal may appoint an expert for two reasons:

- to provide evidence regarding disputed facts that require technical expertise or other specialized knowledge to understand or explain (evidentiary function);
- to advise the arbitral tribunal regarding and to illustrate and explain issues that are difficult to understand (although not necessarily disputed) and to prepare the tribunal to hear evidence from the parties, including any party-appointed experts (advisory function).

In determining whether to appoint an expert, the tribunal should consider the following factors:

---

4. ICC Commission on Arbitration Report, *Techniques for Controlling Time and Costs in Arbitration*, ICC Publication No. 843 (2007), p. 40, para. 85.
5. Article 6.1 of the IBA Rules on the Taking of Evidence in International Commercial Arbitration (1 June 1999) also provides that the parties should be consulted before the tribunal appoints an expert.

(i) Have one or more parties asked or suggested that the tribunal appoint an expert to assist in establishing relevant disputed facts?

If so, is there a reason why the tribunal should not honor this request, such as irrelevance of the subject matter of the expert's proposed testimony to the outcome of the dispute?

(ii) Does the arbitral tribunal itself have the expertise to determine the issue?

See Section II(D)(ii) above regarding the need to avoid a de facto in camera expertise proceedings. If the arbitral tribunal does not intend to appoint an expert, but prefers to rely on its own specific knowledge of factual matters to be addressed in the award, this should be discussed with the parties. Before rendering its award, the tribunal should also give the parties an opportunity to comment on any findings that are based on its personal knowledge.

(iii) Does a party object to a tribunal-appointed expert? If so, does the objection have merit?

A party might object to a tribunal-appointed expert for various reasons, including, for example (i) unfamiliarity with the process, (ii) sensitivity to the cost of retaining experts in general or a specific candidate whom the tribunal proposes, (iii) dissatisfaction with the qualifications of a specific candidate whom the tribunal proposes, and (iv) a preference for party-appointed experts, rather than a tribunal-appointed expert. Although the tribunal may appoint an expert over a party's objections, it is helpful if the tribunal can build consensus among the parties that an expert should be appointed and that a specific candidate or candidates are suitable to all parties.

(iv) Would the expected benefits of appointing an expert reduce the efficiency of the proceedings and increase time and costs in such a way that the adverse effects might outweigh the benefits?

Not every arbitration needs an expert. See Section II(D) above. If the parties already have obtained and submitted expert evidence, it would be unusual (and expensive) for the arbitral tribunal to appoint one or more experts of its own to evaluate the party-appointed experts' work. But if the technical issues involved are sufficiently complex (and the value at stake is sufficiently high), this approach is an option.[6]

1. At what stage of the arbitral proceedings should the arbitral tribunal appoint an expert?

The tribunal should appoint an expert as soon as possible after the tribunal has precisely identified the issues calling for expertise. In many cases, identifying the specific issues will require that the parties have submitted at least one, if not two, rounds of detailed pleadings. To further clarify the issues, the tribunal may need to issue directions requiring the parties to provide further particulars concerning certain facts and issues.

---

6. See N. Blackaby, C. Partasides with A. Redfern & M. Hunter, *Redfern and Hunter on International Arbitration*, Oxford University Press (2009) at paras 5-22 and 6-158.

2. What process should the arbitral tribunal use to appoint an expert?

Once it has determined that an expert is required, the arbitral tribunal searches for prospective experts with the necessary skills.

The tribunal may use its own contacts to identify a suitable expert, and may also seek assistance from a specialized institution, such as the ICC International Centre for Expertise.[7] A proposal by the latter may enhance the expert's credibility.

The arbitral tribunal usually will find it helpful to seek the parties' input on whether the proposed expert is suitable. Thus, the tribunal can:

- invite the parties to agree jointly on an expert; or
- propose the candidate it considers best suited and give the parties an opportunity to comment, in case they have legitimate objections;
- present the parties with a list of suitable experts, from which they may delete those to whom they object (eventually, limiting the number of candidates who may be deleted); or
- present the parties with a list of suitable experts, whom the parties can rank in order of preference, with the candidate scoring the most points selected.

(a) Initial contacts

The tribunal's initial contacts with a potential expert should focus on whether the candidate:

- possesses the required skills,
- is willing and available to serve without delaying the schedule for the arbitration,
- is independent and neutral,
- is willing to accept appropriate compensation for completing the required tasks,
- is willing to agree to appropriate confidentiality, and
- does not have a conflict of interest that should preclude the expert from serving.

(b) Defining the expert's mission

After obtaining a formal assurance of independence and neutrality from the chosen expert, the arbitral tribunal should require the expert to accept a written retainer agreement (including the expert's terms of reference) that covers the following:

- the specific tasks that the expert is requested to accomplish;
- the procedural directions that the expert is expected to follow; and
- the terms of the expert's financial remuneration and reimbursement of the expert's expenses.

See Appendix 1 below. Experts sometimes propose their own format for the retainer agreement and other commercial terms. Depending on the circumstances, these may need to be reviewed and, discarded or amended, as appropriate.

7. Under Article 2(1) of the ICC Rules for Expertise, the ICC International Centre for Expertise will propose an expert, if an arbitral tribunal so requests. Such a proposal is free of charge in ICC arbitrations. See ICC Rules for Expertise, Appendix II, Article 1; see also ICC Commission on Arbitration Report, *Techniques for Controlling Time and Costs in Arbitration*, ICC Publication No. 843 (2007) at 35ff.

When the expert has executed the retainer agreement, the tribunal formally appoints the expert. This is usually accomplished through a procedural order to which the retainer agreement is attached and which also requires the parties to submit a deposit securing the expert's remuneration.

Although Article 20(4) of the Rules of Arbitration requires the arbitral tribunal to 'consult' with the parties before appointing an expert, the Rules of Arbitration do not address the parties' role in any detail. Normally, in addition to seeking the parties' comments on whether the tribunal should appoint an expert, the tribunal also will find it helpful, at a minimum, to obtain their comments on the facts to be proved or explained by the expert, how to select the expert, and the terms of the expert's compensation.

3. How can the arbitral tribunal select the 'right' expert?

Normally, the expert appointed is an individual person, but the tribunal also may appoint legal entities and 'expert teams' as experts.[8] If so, all persons involved (other than purely clerical staff carrying out secretarial or menial tasks) should be disclosed to the parties and be available for questioning at a hearing.

In all circumstances, the arbitral tribunal should select an expert with care and give attention to the following criteria:

(a) Personal acceptability and trustworthiness

The arbitrator(s) and, to the extent possible, the parties should trust the expert's objectiveness and impartiality. For the expert, this requirement amounts to the same standard of objectiveness and impartiality as is expected of arbitrators, including for example:

- the absence of any appearance of bias caused by the expert's cultural background;
- the absence of any appearance of bias caused by any personal interest in the outcome of the dispute;
- the absence of a subject-matter bias – i.e., the expert should not have reached a conclusion before starting to work on the assignment;
- the absence of a conflict of interest that should preclude the expert from serving.

(b) Communication skills

The expert often will not work in his or her usual work environment, communication culture or preferred working language. In international arbitration, this means that the expert should possess the linguistic skills required to carry out the assignment. It also means that the expert should be capable of presenting his or her findings to the arbitral tribunal and the parties in a structured manner and a way that they can understand as laypersons in the specific field of expertise.

(c) Availability and reliability

It is important that the expert can adhere to an acceptable time schedule for carrying out the agreed mission. When accepting the assignment, the expert should therefore

8. See H. Charrin, 'The ICC International Center for Expertise Realities and Prospects' (1995) 6:2 ICC ICArb. Bull. 33 at 35.

be able to forecast whether he or she is available, and should remain available to the extent required for carrying out the mission.

(d) Professional qualifications and expert skills

The expert's skill and expertise are the main reasons why the expert is retained, and the arbitral tribunal should give this factor the most weight when selecting an expert. Because the required skills will vary from case to case, the tribunal should define the type of expertise that is required as thoroughly and precisely as possible, taking into account the relevant disputed issues.

If the arbitral tribunal seeks assistance from the ICC International Centre for Expertise or another specialized institution, it should inform the institution about the relevant criteria when requesting a proposal.

4. What terms should the expert's retainer agreement contain?

The expert will perform services on a contractual basis. The legal framework, including the issue of who is contracting with the expert, depends on the specific legal setting and thus will vary from case to case. Normally, this does not cause problems, so long as the expert's remuneration is secured by an advance payment for fees and expenses.

(a) Parties to the contract

Several different approaches exist for identifying who should be the parties to the retainer agreement:

The most common approach is for the arbitral tribunal to contract with an expert in the name and on behalf of all parties to the dispute. The arbitral tribunal's authority to do so comes from Article 20(1) of the Rules of Arbitration, which empowers the tribunal 'to establish the facts of the case by all appropriate means'.

Alternatively, the arbitral tribunal may make the appointment in its own name, relying on its explicit authority to appoint experts. If so, liability for the expert's remuneration should be shifted to the parties by means of an advance on costs paid by the parties (see Rule of Arbitration, Appendix III, Article 1(11)) or by incorporating an appropriate provision in the Terms of Reference.

The parties' arbitration agreement, as well as applicable mandatory law (e.g., lex arbitri) also may impact the terms of the agreement with the expert.

(b) Terms concerning the expert's mission[9] and the tribunal's procedural requirements

The Rules of Arbitration do not specify formal requirements, such as the need to have the terms signed by the parties or the expert. In practice, the arbitral tribunal often includes the terms of the expert's mission in the procedural order formally appointing the expert.

Even then, however, the arbitral tribunal should make appropriate agreements with the expert because the expert is not a party to the arbitration, and the procedural order will not bind the expert unless the expert agrees to it.

Although the Rules of Arbitration do not expressly require the parties to be involved in drafting the expert's retainer agreement, it is good practice for the arbitral tribunal

9. See Appendix II and section III(d)(2) of the prior report 'Issues for Experts Acting Under the ICC Rules for Expertise on the ICC Rules of Arbitration' (2009) 20:1 ICC ICArb. Bull. 23 at 33.

to draft the expert's retainer agreement and then submit its draft to the parties for comments. These comments should be directed at the scope of the expert's mission, with the goal of securing as much agreement as possible.

In appropriate circumstances, it may be useful to involve the expert in the drafting of his or her mission, as the parties and the tribunal might not have fully have grasped the extent of the relevant problem. On the other hand, the expert may not yet have been appointed and the expert's remuneration may not yet be secured by a deposit for fees and expenses. Nor is the expert likely to be in possession of all information needed to provide meaningful suggestions.

Moreover, because the wording of the issues to be addressed by the expert may give rise to debates between the parties, it may be preferable not to involve the expert too much at this stage. Instead, the tribunal should include an umbrella provision in the expert's mission along the following lines:

If the expert, while carrying out the mission, becomes aware that any issue to be addressed in the expert report is not appropriately phrased, or if the expert becomes aware of a relevant issue not mentioned in these terms of reference, then the expert shall advise the arbitral tribunal thereof immediately. The arbitral tribunal shall have the right to modify and/or amend these terms of reference as it deems fit after having heard the parties.

The expert's terms of reference can be attached as an exhibit to the retainer agreement or referenced in the retainer agreement and defined in a separate document. Normally, the arbitral tribunal will want to cover the following: (i) identification of the arbitration; (ii) expert's name and address (if a legal entity is appointed as expert, the responsible individual should be named); (iii) identification of the information (e.g., documents, specimens, etc.) to be communicated to the expert; (iv) general description of the tasks that the expert is expected to perform; (v) description of the expert's right to remuneration and reimbursement of expenses (including fees for the expert's employees, allowances for appropriate travel and accommodation, etc.) and any advance payments; (vi) duty to maintain confidentiality; (vii) obligation to be truthful and impartial; (viii) duty to disclose the expert's contacts with the parties[10] or potential sources of conflicts of interest before and during the arbitration; (ix) basic rules for communications among the expert, the parties and the tribunal so as to protect the transparency of the expert's performance; (x) basic rules for monitoring costs and readjusting the advance on the expert's costs; (xi) provisional timetable; (xii) scope of the expert's liability and grounds for termination; (xiii) affirmation of the parties' right to comment on the expert's report and to question the expert at the hearing; and (xiv) the arbitral tribunal's power to adjust the expert's terms of reference as necessary.[11]

(c) Defining the expert's mission

The arbitral tribunal should clearly describe the scope and substance of the questions to be answered by the expert, and clearly distinguish between the disputed and the undisputed facts of the matter.

---

10. Unlike party-appointed expert witnesses, tribunal-appointed experts normally should not have any private contact with any of the parties. Contacts with a party outside the arbitral tribunal's control are inappropriate. Consequently, all contacts with a party or counsel are subject to full disclosure.

11. A checklist for experts' terms of reference is attached as Appendix I.

(d) Procedures regarding remuneration

For obvious practical reasons, the arbitral tribunal should not permit the expert to begin work without obtaining agreement on the expert's remuneration and reimbursement of the expert's expenses and the parties' payment of an advance on costs and expenses. This is explicitly addressed in Articles 31(1) and (3) of the Rules of Arbitration and Appendix III, Article 1(11).

The arbitral tribunal should fix the advance on the expert's costs and expenses at an amount that will in all likelihood cover the total anticipated amount of the expert's costs and expenses. Thus, the tribunal should ask the expert to report as soon as the expert believes that the advance is likely to be insufficient.

The Rules of Arbitration do not specify how the parties are to bear the advance on costs, and the tribunal has discretion in this regard. If one party refuses to pay its share, the arbitral tribunal may request the other party to pay that share, if appropriate under the circumstances. If a party does not pay the advance on costs, the expert's work thus will not proceed, and the arbitral tribunal may take adverse inferences against the party who refused to pay. In regard to the final allocation of expert costs, see Section III(B)(3) below.

Likewise, the Rules of Arbitration do not address the question as to who shall administer the advance payment of the expert's costs. Although it is possible to request that the advance payment be made to the expert, who will then render account to the arbitral tribunal and the parties, this approach is not recommended. A better practice is for the arbitral tribunal to require that payment be made into a special account that it administers (normally through the chairman, in the case of a panel) or to order payment into an ICC account administered by the Secretariat of the ICC International Court of Arbitration under the arbitral tribunal's direction. The expert will submit requests for advance payments or invoices to the arbitral tribunal, which will review them and arrange for payments to the expert.

5. What should be the arbitral tribunal's role in directing the expert's work?

The arbitral tribunal will order the expert to commence carrying out the expert's mission.

For practical reasons, the expert will have a high degree of independence when carrying out the mission. But because the arbitral tribunal is responsible for establishing the truth, ensuring efficient proceedings, and rendering an enforceable award, the tribunal retains supervisory responsibility over the expert's conduct and performance.

The arbitral tribunal should adopt appropriate measures to ensure that the expert receives from the parties the support needed to carry out the mission. If necessary or if the expert requests, the arbitral tribunal should require the parties to support the expert, for example, by responding to the expert's questions, by granting access to sites and physical evidence and by accompanying the expert during site visits and attending meetings if the expert requests.

In most cases, this sort of assistance from the tribunal will be needed only if one party does not voluntarily cooperate with the expert.

The arbitral tribunal should also adopt appropriate measures to ensure that the expert observes the parties' right to be heard and respects the terms of reference defining the scope of the expert's mission. Thus, for example, the arbitral tribunal should include the following measures to ensure transparency in the flow of information:

- Generally, the expert should not communicate with a party without the other party being included (i.e., no private meetings, no letters unless copied to all, no telephone conferences unless all parties may listen).
- If the expert absolutely must communicate with one party, the arbitral tribunal should make sure (to the extent possible) that the other party is informed of this communication and its purpose and contents as soon as possible.
- Both parties must have a chance to be present if the expert questions one party or visits a site. The other party must be informed if the expert requests documents from one party. Documents obtained from one party must be made available to the other party. If the expert works on a site owned by a party, the arbitral tribunal should ensure that the other party is duly informed and also obtains access to the site.
- According to the second sentence of Article 20(4) of the Rules of Arbitration, the arbitral tribunal, upon its own initiative or a party's request, must give the parties the opportunity to question any tribunal-appointed expert at a hearing.

Where the information to be provided to the expert involves trade secrets or other non-public business information, the arbitral tribunal should provide appropriate directions that address the parties' legitimate interests in protecting confidential business information. See Section II(G)2.d above.

When fulfilling its responsibilities, the arbitral tribunal may need to communicate with the expert, and the expert may need to communicate with the arbitral tribunal whenever a difficulty arises. These communications are often informal and may be essential to the efficient completion of the expert's mission. The parties may be concerned about such communications taking place without the parties being fully informed. Opinions are divided as to whether private communications between the arbitral tribunal and the expert should be allowed and, if so, to what extent. Thus, the arbitral tribunal should exercise great caution in this regard.[12]

B. What guidance should the arbitral tribunal provide regarding the expert's report?

It is common practice in international arbitration for a tribunal-appointed expert to provide the arbitral tribunal and the parties with one or more written reports.

The Rules of Arbitration do not contain any requirements regarding the form or content of the expert's report. Thus, unless the applicable law or the expert's terms of reference provide otherwise, issues relating to the form of the report are up to the expert.

That said, the arbitral tribunal may wish to include, in the expert's terms of reference or separately, guidance on how the report is to be presented and structured and on the issues to be covered. The report should meet at least the following basic requirements:

---

12. If the IBA Rules on the Taking of Evidence in International Commercial Arbitration apply, the arbitral tribunal should comply with Article 6(5), which states: 'The Parties may examine any document that the Tribunal-Appointed Expert has examined and any correspondence between the Arbitral Tribunal and the Tribunal-Appointed Expert.'

- The report should answer the questions contained in the expert's mission in a comprehensive manner.
- The report should allow the arbitral tribunal to form its own opinion on the issues that were submitted to the expert.
- The report should be self-contained in the sense that the arbitral tribunal and the parties may understand how and why the expert arrived at each specific conclusion.

It also is entirely appropriate for the tribunal to provide guidance to the expert on communications with parties during preparatory work, as well as concerning site visits, reporting duties, time scheduling and other issues that have nothing to do with the expert's findings.

1. What should the arbitral tribunal do with the expert's report?

Once the expert submits his written report to the arbitral tribunal (in a sufficient number of copies), the tribunal should communicate it to the parties with further procedural directions. Normally, the parties will be given the opportunity to comment in writing before the oral hearing, at which they will have the right to examine the expert.

The tribunal may instruct the expert first to submit a draft report, so as to ascertain that the report has the required quality and form. Experience shows that this method of quality control is useful.

If the parties agree or the arbitral tribunal directs, the expert may be invited to present a summary of the draft report at a meeting, at which the parties will be invited to comment on the preliminary findings. The expert can then take into account these comments when finalizing the report. This approach has the advantage of allowing corrections and amendments to be made, but may occasionally result in protracted discussions and unjustified attacks on the expert's credibility.

2. What directions, if any, should the arbitral tribunal issue on the questioning of experts during the hearing?

(a) Procedural aspects

From a common law perspective, the expert's written report is to be regarded as direct testimony, and the expert's oral evidence is limited to responses to questions from the arbitral tribunal and the parties and their representatives. From a civil law perspective, the report is also considered as evidence, although with special probative value as it is evidence from a knowledgeable neutral third party acting under the arbitral tribunal's control. Regardless of the expert's conclusions, the authority to establish the facts rests with the arbitral tribunal, which retains the right not to follow the expert's findings.

The Rules of Arbitration (and, in most cases, the applicable law) do not require a specific form of questioning. Unless the parties have agreed that the questioning shall be conducted in a particular manner, or the Terms of Reference so require, the arbitral tribunal will usually discuss and determine at a preparatory conference how experts are to be questioned.

The method chosen will depend on each individual case. The emerging trend is for the parties to drive the expert's examination, as one would expect under the common law approach. Another approach is for the arbitral tribunal to take an active role in the questioning, leaving the parties with the right to submit additional relevant questions.

(b) Disagreements that may occur at the hearing

The following matters relating to experts may be a cause of disagreement during the hearing:

(i) Whether and which additional questions should be put to the expert

After consulting the parties, the arbitral tribunal has discretion regarding whether the expert must supplement the expert report (either because it did not answer all questions that the arbitral tribunal defined or because further questions have arisen). If the parties agree that no additional questions should be put to the expert, this is not an issue. The arbitral tribunal also must decide whether an expert must answer questions to which the other party objects.

(ii) Whether another expert should be appointed

In rare cases, the arbitral tribunal, the parties, or both may have the impression that the expert has not done a good job or is incompetent. In this case, the tribunal must decide, after hearing from the parties, whether another expert should be appointed. The tribunal may appoint a second expert only if at least one party agrees and is willing to make the advance payment.

(iii) The expert's conclusions

The arbitral tribunal must assess the expert's conclusions and decide the case after hearing from the parties. This does not apply, however, in the rare cases where the parties stipulate regarding certain facts or conclusions after receiving and jointly disagreeing with the expert's report.

3. What directions or decisions may the arbitral tribunal issue regarding the costs and expenses of tribunal-appointed experts?

The same principles applicable to party-appointed experts govern the allocation of the fees and expenses of a tribunal-appointed expert. See Section II(M). The only difference is that in most cases these expenses are paid out of a deposit to which one or all parties have contributed as directed by the arbitral tribunal. The parties' respective contributions to the deposit should be in the final award allocating costs.

4. May the arbitral tribunal use an expert as advisor in private meetings and, if so, how?

Parties and counsel may be instinctively opposed to an expert acting as advisor to the arbitrators in private meetings.

In certain complex and technically difficult cases, however, an expert capable of explaining certain technical terms or other experts' reports may be useful in helping the arbitrators to understand the facts correctly and assure the quality of the reasoning underlying the award.

If the arbitral tribunal wishes to use an expert as an internal advisor, it is good practice for the tribunal to raise the issue beforehand with the parties and to obtain their explicit agreement in advance.

When the tribunal wishes to use an expert as an advisor, the tribunal, the expert and the parties should all understand the following:

- the expert shall only function as an advisor, and shall not be responsible for finding any new facts or evaluating facts;
- the expert's task will be limited to explaining information on technical issues submitted by the parties (including any party-appointed experts); and
- the expert will not become a decision-maker and will not exceed the role described above.

The above should be recorded in writing. Unless such an agreement is reached, arbitral tribunals usually will abstain from adopting this approach.

APPENDIX I – CHECKLIST FOR EXPERTS' TERMS OF REFERENCE

An expert's terms of reference normally will cover the following topics:

- Identification of the arbitration proceedings
- Name and address of the expert (in case of a legal entity appointed as expert, the responsible individual also should be named)
- Identification of information (documents, specimens, etc.) to be communicated to the expert
- Definition of the expert's tasks
- Definition of the expert's rights:
  - Remuneration and reimbursement of expenses (including fees for the expert's employees and charges for travel and accommodation, if appropriate)
  - Advance payments
- The expert's secondary obligations:
  - Duty to maintain confidentiality
  - Obligation to be truthful and impartial
  - Duty to disclose the expert's contacts with the parties and potential conflicts of interests prior to and during arbitral proceedings
- General rules for the conduct of the expertise:
  - Basic rules for communications between the expert, the parties and the tribunal to ensure the expertise proceedings are fully transparent
  - Basic rules for monitoring costs and readjusting the advance on expert's costs
  - Provisional timetable
  - Power of the arbitral tribunal to adjust the expert's terms of reference if so required by the expert's findings (normally exercised after consulting the parties)
- Items that might be included:
  - Scope of the expert's liability
  - Grounds for dismissal
  - Affirmation of the parties' right to comment on the expert's report and to question the expert at an oral hearing upon request

APPENDIX II – CHECKLIST FOR EXPERT REPORTS

A. Structure

An expert report that follows a structure similar to the following will usually be helpful to the arbitral tribunal:

(i) A summary identifying the party or parties, the expert (including professional biography) and the arbitration procedure.

(ii) A summary of the expert's mission

(iii) A summary of the methodology and the standards that the expert used; and, if applicable, the professional or ethical rules by which the expert abides.

(iv) A summary of the information on which the expert relies, including comprehensive references to literature and other sources used. Sometimes, it is appropriate to include this in an attachment.

(v) The expert's factual findings and reasoned opinion and conclusion regarding the issues that were submitted for the expert to evaluate. In many cases, it will be appropriate to set forth separately the parties' respective positions, the experts' factual findings and the conclusions separately, on an issue-by-issue basis. Alternatively, it is possible to summarize the parties' respective positions and the factual findings in one section and the reasoned conclusions in another section. If known to the expert, he or she may also specifically refer to reports by other experts on relevant issues. Regardless of the structure the expert, the report should be easily and fully understandable to any non-experts who are expected to read it. In other words, if only other experts are likely to understand the report, its value to the arbitral tribunal is reduced.

(vi) A statement that the report and its findings set forth in the report are true and that the opinions expressed are correct to the expert's best knowledge.

(vii) Date and signature

B. Methodology and standards

The expert should use the methodology and standards that are generally accepted in the expert's field of expertise. If the expert deviates from these for justified reasons, the expert should clearly state why and how. The basic rule is that the expert's report should withstand the test of peer review. The expert should assume that the report will be subjected to some sort of peer review because this is highly probable.

APPENDIX 19

ISSUES FOR EXPERTS ACTING UNDER THE ICC RULES FOR EXPERTISE OR THE ICC RULES OF ARBITRATION (2009)

REPORT OF THE ICC COMMISSION ON ARBITRATION AND ADR (2009)*

* This report is being updated in the light of the 2012 ICC Rules of Arbitration, mainly in regard to references to new provisions

I. Introduction

This text[1] is intended to provide general guidance regarding issues that should be considered by individuals who have been retained to serve as an expert in proceedings under the ICC Rules for Expertise or the ICC Rules of Arbitration or who are contemplating such an engagement. It also provides information that may be useful for other expert services to which these rules do not apply.

Experts provide a valuable service in helping to avoid or resolve disputes, and can serve several different roles under the Rules for Expertise and the Rules of Arbitration:

– Expertise

- Consulting expert services. At the request of a party, an expert can analyze facts and assist in finding solutions to specific problems before or during a dispute.
- Independent impartial expert services and non-binding evaluation. Either in connection with a pending arbitration or as the parties otherwise agree, the parties can engage an expert to establish the 'true' facts, to evaluate these facts, or to provide a non-binding, impartial evaluation of a disputed issue within the expert's expertise.

---

1. This document was produced under the auspices of the ICC Commission on Arbitration and is a report of the Task Force on Guidelines for ICC Expertise Proceedings co-chaired by Erik Schäfer and David B. Wilson. It follows an earlier report entitled 'Guide to ICC Expertise' published in the ICC International Court of Arbitration Bulletin Vol. 16 No. 1 (Spring 2005) 19.

- Independent binding adjudication[2] / determination by an impartial expert. Either in connection with a pending arbitration or as the parties otherwise agree, the parties can engage an expert to provide a binding determination regarding the solution of a disputed issue within the expert's expertise. The extent to which the expert determination is contractually binding or otherwise will depend on the applicable law.[3]

– Arbitration

- Expert witness. In arbitrations, where the expert's expertise helps the arbitral tribunal to understand the issues and resolve the dispute, one or more parties or the arbitral tribunal may engage an expert to evaluate certain facts relevant to disputed issues and to provide an expert opinion regarding the results of that evaluation.
- Expert consultant. In arbitrations, one or more parties may engage an expert to assist counsel in efficiently presenting the case.
- Expert as arbitrator. An expert also can be appointed to serve as an arbitrator in an arbitration. In this situation, the expert is not a witness, but a decision maker, who ensures that the arbitration is conducted consistently with the Rules, decides disputed factual issues, and applies the law to the facts to resolve the parties' dispute. Experts who are acting as arbitrators should conduct themselves in the same manner as arbitrators who are not experts, and further discussion of arbitrator behavior is beyond the scope of this text.

II. What are the differences between serving as an expert under institutional rules and being engaged directly by one party or all parties?

A. What determines my rights and duties?

1. Direct appointment by one party or all parties

The agreement under which you promise to provide your services defines your rights and duties. Typically, this will be an agreement between you and the party or parties who engage you to provide services.

Your agreement will be governed by the law to which you and the parties agree or, in the absence of an agreement regarding the applicable law, determined by the competent authority, which can be either an arbitral tribunal or a national court. The applicable law may be relevant to define your duties-for example, through such concepts as implied duties (obligations that you may have, even if they are not expressly stated in your engagement) and the consequences of any failure in the performance of these duties, such as late or defective performance, and excuses for such failures. Ultimately, the choice of law depends on the circumstances of your case, and is not addressed here. But in your agreement with the parties, you should take care to agree

2. 'Adjudication' is a term coined in the United Kingdom for a swift and informal agreed process by which the expert determines rights and obligations of the parties involved. Other national laws provide for procedures with a similar result, but the terms used and certain legal requirements may vary. 'Adjudication' must not be confused with 'arbitration'.
3. Many (if not most) countries allow parties to authorize an expert to determine their contractual rights and duties. On rare occasions, such determinations may be easier to enforce than a contract. Some countries require the expert to observe certain minimum 'procedural standards'. As addressed below, this will vary, depending on the applicable law.

explicitly on all relevant rights and duties with the appropriate level of detail and on the applicable law. In general, the terms to which the parties agree are binding and enforceable.

2. Appointment under institutional rules

If the parties have agreed to proceed under the ICC Rules for Expertise or the ICC Rules of Arbitration, you will be expected to provide your services in a manner consistent with these rules, and the rules are part of your engagement. For example, as provided in the agreed set of rules, the institution or the arbitral tribunal will make certain determinations (e.g., the scope of your assignment, the form of your expert report, when your report is due, your compensation). Thus, before you accept an appointment, you should ask whether the parties have agreed to a particular set of rules and read those rules carefully. You cannot unilaterally change the rules to which the parties have agreed, and if the rules or the time-line under which you are expected to provide your services are unacceptable, you should not accept the engagement unless all parties agree to suitable modifications.

B. To which ethical standards am I subject?

1. Professional standards

If you are a member of a professional society or subject to licensure requirements or other professional or legal standards, the rules that normally apply to your professional activities probably also apply to you when you serve as an expert. Thus, if your agreement with the parties would require services or behavior that conflict with the mandatory rules to which your profession is subject, you should consider declining or terminating your engagement. In case of doubt, you should consider obtaining advice from the professional body to which you belong, but be careful not to violate any obligation to maintain confidentiality.

Of course, you should also conduct yourself in a manner that is consistent with the trust that the parties placed in you when they retained you. You should act honestly and in a manner that will withstand peer review. If you are retained as 'neutral' expert, you shall also act impartially without any bias for a party or a position.

2. Standards under institutional rules

Institutional rules to which the parties agree may include ethical standards; e.g., with regard to the expert's independence and impartiality. When you accept your engagement, you agree to comply with these standards. See section II(A)(2) above.

(a) Independence. Article 3(3) of the ICC Rules for Expertise requires that experts who are being proposed by the Centre need to disclose any circumstances that could compromise their independence in the eyes of the party or parties requesting the proposal. Under Article 7(3) and 7(4) of the Rules for Expertise, any expert appointed by the Centre must provide a written declaration confirming independence and disclosing relevant facts, and the expert must be and remain independent of the parties. Under Article 11(1) of the Rules for Expertise, in administered proceedings, regardless of whether the expert was appointed or agreed by the parties, the expert must remain independent throughout these proceedings, although the parties may expressly waive this requirement.

Normally, a common sense approach will allow you easily to decide whether to decline an engagement for lack of independence.

'Independent' means that you may not reasonably be perceived as having any financial or personal interest whatsoever in the outcome of your assignment. Whether you are independent depends on an evaluation of your relationships and business and financial interests. Thus, only general guidance can be provided in this regard. You are responsible for determining whether these relationships and interests can be seen as compromising your independence. Although directed at arbitrators and not binding upon ICC, the IBA Guidelines on Conflicts of Interest in International Arbitration[4] might provide you with guidance in evaluating difficult questions.

(b) When acting under the ICC Rules for Expertise, you should assume that the standards applicable to your impartiality and independence are the same as those applied to arbitrators under the ICC Rules of Arbitration. For example, factors that could compromise your independence or require disclosure include:
   (i) A close personal relationship with one of the parties (e.g., being married to the CEO of a party or a company belonging to the same organization or group as a party, or current or former status as an employee or consultant of that party). Depending on their character and duration, even certain past relationships of this kind may continue to be relevant.
   (ii) A material financial interest (e.g., owning a stake in one of the parties, or past or present contractual relationships with a party or a member of the group of companies to which a party belongs).
   (iii) Prior and non-trivial services to a party or prior services related to the disputed subject matter.
   (iv) A similarly close relationship with a third party that has an interest in the outcome of the dispute may also need to be taken into account.

(c) Disclosure is essential in case of doubt. Nonetheless, a vast 'grey area' exists, where reasonable people might disagree as to whether the expert has a conflict that would compromise the expert's independence or impartiality. Thus, if you have questions about whether a particular interest or relationship creates a conflict, you should disclose it. See ICC Rules for Expertise, Article 3(3). Once these relationships and interests are fully disclosed, the issue is resolved if the concerned parties do not object or explicitly waive the requirement.

Moreover, by providing full disclosure, you reinforce the perception of your honesty and credibility. By contrast, undisclosed relevant facts that come to light later on may substantially affect your credibility, reputation and the authoritative character of your work product, even if the parties would not have objected upon early disclosure. More important, failure to disclose may violate your duties to the parties under applicable law.

(d) Impartiality. 'Impartiality' is synonymous with 'neutrality', and the essence of both terms is broadly the same. If the parties have entrusted you with the mission of being an impartial expert evaluator or adjudicator, you also are responsible for the process and should strive to meet the justified expectations

4. The IBA Guidelines on Conflicts of Interest in International Arbitration, which are for arbitrators but also provide helpful guidance for experts, can be accessed at: <www.ibanet.org/images/downloads/ Arbitration_guidelines_2007.pdf>.

of all parties regarding how a party standing in their shoes would expect to be treated. You should be impartial and disinterested in the outcome of the proceeding or the conclusions to be drawn from your work product (i.e., your 'deliverable'). You should proceed in a fair and just manner, and treat the parties equally. You also should proceed in a transparent manner. This means that you should spell out what you expect of the parties, and ensure that the parties are privy to any flow of information, unless exceptional circumstances require otherwise. See sections III(C) and IV(D) below. Moreover, the expert who is perceived to be impartial and disinterested will tend to be more persuasive.

Thus, the question is whether you would be able to reserve judgment and reach a conclusion based on the same professional standards and criteria that your peer experts would apply to the same facts or whether external factors (e.g., a dislike for a party or its counsel) might cause you to reach a different conclusion than your peers would under the same circumstances.

Finally, you may not be impartial if you already have formed such a strong opinion regarding a certain matter that you are unlikely to be able to take an objective look at the situation based on the facts of the specific case. If, however, a substantial number or most of your peers would share your professional opinion, your previous opinion need not automatically mean that you are not impartial. If you have questions about how a previous opinion might impact your impartiality, you should consider disclosing the issue to the party or parties who are requesting your services.

C. How do the different types of assignment affect my role?

1. Considerations for expert witnesses in arbitration and expert evaluators or adjudicators in expertise proceedings

Unless the parties agree or the tribunal directs otherwise, any statement of fact that you make in writing or orally during an arbitration hearing or in the report that you issue in connection with an arbitration or expertise proceedings must be true to the best of your knowledge, and any opinion that you give must be correct to the best of your professional ability. You may assume certain facts or proceed on the basis of hypothetical facts if the parties or the arbitral tribunal instruct you to do so and you make this explicit. But unless the parties expressly agree, you may not tacitly assume or invent facts or omit relevant facts that are known to you. A witness who knowingly provides untrue evidence may be subject to civil and criminal liability under applicable law. Likewise, you should not provide opinions or evaluations that you or any equally qualified peer expert would know are not sustainable in the light of the recognized state of the art in your field.

2. Considerations for experts who are only proposed by the Centre to one party or to parties with convergent interests

If the work is assigned to you by only one party or by parties who have identical interests and you are not appointed under the ICC Rules for Expertise, the above principles may not fully apply.

(a) If you are retained to provide a work product for one or more parties for their internal use only, your duties are governed by your agreement with the parties and by the professional standards to which you are subject. See section

II(B)(1) above. If you are a proposed expert under the ICC Rules for Expertise, Article 3(3) requires you to provide an initial statement of independence and disclosures.

(b) If you are retained to provide services related to a nascent dispute or as expert evidence in litigation or arbitration, you should distinguish between the following situations: either you act exclusively as expert consultant assisting counsel or you are retained as expert witness. In some instances, you may first be retained as a consultant and later designated as an expert witness.
   (i) If you will be acting exclusively as an expert consultant, the principles set forth in section II(C)(2)(a) apply. Laws or procedural rules governing the behavior of advisors may also apply.
   (ii) If you will be acting as expert witness, the standards and rules set forth in section IV apply. Additionally, you will have to provide the party or parties requesting the proposal with an initial statement of independence and disclosures. See section II(B)(2) above.

(c) If possible, you should try to clarify your role before you accept the engagement or as soon as possible thereafter. If there is any possibility that you will be asked to serve as an expert witness, you may want to behave differently from how you would if you are only to be a consultant. The counsel with whom you are working should be able to guide you regarding specific legal and ethical requirements. If the party provides guidance or instructions that you believe to be illegal or inconsistent with your professional duties, consider declining the engagement or terminating it early.

D. How does my role affect my initial contacts with a party?

1. Questions to ask

Your services may be required for different roles, each of which require specific behavior and may be subject to different legal and ethical standards. Thus, before you begin discussions about the substance of the assignment, you should obtain basic information, including:

(a) Who is contacting you and in what capacity?
(b) Who are the other parties/stakeholders?
(c) For what purpose are your expert services required?
(d) What is the expertise that the parties require?
(e) Are there any agreements or applicable rules that define terms and conditions of an eventual assignment?
(f) What is the time frame for completing the assignment?
(g) How will you be paid?

If you cover these points, you should be able to determine whether you have the needed expertise, have a conflict of interest, need to disclose certain facts, are available, and are willing to accept the assignment.

2. What to avoid

(a) Avoid acting in a way that would be inappropriate once you accept the assignment.
(b) Avoid providing opinions, judgments or partisan statements that might be relevant in the expertise proceedings or arbitration.

(c) Avoid accepting the assignment before you have determined that there is no conflict of interest and no other impediment to your acting as expert.

If one party contacts you regarding a proposed impartial engagement as expert (e.g., expert evaluator, adjudicator or arbitrator), you should avoid any further contacts with fewer than all parties beyond the initial exchange of basic information. For example, it is generally inappropriate to accept and study documents or other information, especially if the other party is unaware. If a meeting or preliminary study of documents and other information is appropriate, you should get all parties involved and afford them the opportunity to participate in any preliminary meetings or conference calls.

III. Experts operating under the ICC Rules for Expertise

A. What can be my role under the ICC Rules for Expertise?

1. Proposed or appointed expert, without administration

Upon request by one or more parties, the ICC International Centre for Expertise (Centre) will propose or appoint an expert. An arbitral tribunal may request a proposal.

(a) If an expert is proposed by the Centre, the party or parties who have requested the proposal will have to decide whether to appoint the expert and negotiate the terms of his engagement. The ICC Rules for Expertise normally will not apply to the expert's engagement. Rather, the scope and nature of the expert's activities are governed by the terms and conditions of the agreement made between the expert and the party or parties. See section II(A) above.

(b) The Centre appoints the expert on the parties' behalf and based on the parties' agreement. In most instances, however, the parties' agreement will need to be supplemented by an agreement with the expert to define the scope and nature of the expert's activities and remuneration. See section II(A) above. After the expert is appointed, the Centre has no further involvement, and the Rules of Expertise will apply only to the extent the parties have agreed. Thus, unless specifically agreed, the ICC Rules for Expertise will not apply to the expert's engagement. Rather, the scope and nature of the expert's activities are governed by the terms and conditions of the agreement made between the expert and the party or parties. See sections II (A) and II(B)(2) above.

2. Administered expertise proceedings

In administered expertise proceedings, the ICC Rules for Expertise govern the expert's activities, including issues related to remuneration. The Centre also retains certain responsibility to ensure that the proceedings comply with the Rules and has certain powers to assure quality. This avoids the need to negotiate many details of the expert's activities.

When the parties have agreed to administered expertise proceedings, the parties can select an expert directly or agree upon an expert proposed by the Centre, or, if they cannot agree, the Centre will appoint the expert on the parties' behalf and based on their agreement. The Rules for Expertise continue to govern the expert's activities as described above under section II(A)(2).

3. Nature of the expert's work product

Your role also depends on the type of work product that is requested from you:

(a) Non-binding expert findings. If you are retained by one party as consultant or expert witness or appointed as an expert by an arbitral tribunal, your expert findings will be authoritative but will not directly or conclusively establish rights and duties of any concerned party.

(b) Binding expert findings. If the parties agree, your findings will conclusively affect or create the parties' rights and duties. This does not mean that you act as an arbitrator who renders an arbitral award. Rather, it means that the parties have agreed that you will determine certain of their rights and duties in a given situation for a specific purpose and that your determination becomes part of the parties' agreement. For example, the parties may agree that you will establish certain facts or technical issues concerning which the parties may not further argue. See ICC Rules for Expertise, Article 12(3). Because your authority flows from the parties' agreement, you should at all times bear in mind what the parties have agreed and act accordingly. If the parties' agreement appears to be unclear or incomplete, you should seek clarification from the parties.

The law applicable to your agreement with the parties, as well as the professional standards to which you are subject, may contain rules that affect your power to make binding findings or impose certain formal or other requirements related to your service as an expert. If you have questions or doubts, you should also seek clarification from the parties. Although it is unrealistic to try to address all possible scenarios, if you have a question, it is better to seek clarification early in the engagement, before a problem arises concerning how you should proceed.

B. What factors should I consider before accepting an appointment?

Before accepting an appointment, you should strive to obtain all of the information that you need to make an informed decision concerning whether to accept. If you accept an engagement and then it turns out that you lack the required expertise or cannot otherwise perform (e.g., because of a conflict of interest), you will hurt the parties and your professional reputation, and potentially could be dragged into legal proceedings. If the parties do not provide all of the information you need to evaluate a potential engagement, do not be afraid to ask.

1. Do I have the experience to serve?

First, you should obtain the information that you need to understand the nature and scope of the issues for which your subject matter expertise is requested, so that you can decide whether your expertise is the same as the type of expertise required. In making this determination, you should keep in mind that your first contact may not be with a person skilled in your field of expertise, and thus the description of the problem may be inaccurate. Further, if your first contact is with only one of several parties with whom you are expected to work, the party's description of the problem may not fully match the description that the other side would provide.

Second, you should also ask questions regarding the purpose of the expertise proceedings. This will allow you to evaluate whether you have the necessary 'procedural' skills. For example, if the parties seek a binding expert opinion or adjudication, you will need dispute resolution skills that enable you successfully to manage proceedings where the parties are in a contentious dispute. In such cases, your communication and persuasion skills are important, given that you normally lack the power to compel the parties to comply with your requests.

Finally, you should ask whether there are language requirements that could diminish your ability to carry out the assignment efficiently. For example, if all relevant project documents are in Chinese, or if the parties speak only French, and you are fluent in English only, it may be difficult or impossible for you to serve as an expert.

Once you have this information, you should personally and honestly assess whether you are the expert the parties are looking for. If you conclude that substantial effort and time would be needed to familiarize yourself with the issues at hand, if you detect a serious communication issue, or if you believe that you will have to subcontract another expert, you should either decline the engagement or raise the issue with the party or parties before accepting.

2. Am I impartial and independent of the parties?

Independence and impartiality can be tricky issues, especially where you are one of very few experts in your field. Independence and impartiality may have different meanings depending on the applicable law and the type of proceedings. See sections II(A)-(B) above.

3. What obligation do I have to disclose potential conflicts of interest to the parties?

Potential conflicts should be disclosed. See section II(B) above.

4. Do I have the time to serve?

Always ask about the parties' time schedule and when the parties need to receive your work product. In nearly all cases, time is of the essence to the parties. The parties may have decided to use your services as an alternative to arbitral or court proceedings because they want and need a swift result. Sometimes the parties' agreement may fix a rigid time schedule within which your work product is required.

You should also ask for the information needed to determine what needs to be done (site visits, experiments, etc.), so that you can realistically estimate the time you will need to accomplish your mission, taking into account the inevitable 'surprises' along the way.

If your forecast and the parties' time schedule do not match and it is unlikely that you or anybody else will be able to meet the parties' requirements, you should raise the issue with the parties, in case they may be willing to modify their agreement.

If your other professional or personal commitments make it impossible for you to adhere to the proposed time schedule, you should raise this issue with the parties before accepting and ask whether they are willing to retain your services with an adjusted time schedule. If they are not, you should decline the engagement.

5. How will I be compensated and how will my expenses be paid?

(a) Non-administered expertise proceedings. You are entitled to be paid for your services, but you will need to reach agreement with the parties regarding who will compensate you, in what amount, and how. Unless you want to risk being surprised later, you should not accept a mandate as expert without making satisfactory arrangements regarding payment.

Your fee can be based on your normal hourly or daily rates. Or you could agree to a lump sum fee. You should agree on how out-of-pocket expenses are going to be repaid, as well as other payment terms, such as due dates, invoicing procedures, currency of payment, etc. Your fees should not depend in any way on the outcome of the expertise proceedings, as this would seriously compromise your impartiality.

Because it may be particularly cumbersome to enforce claims for fees in an international environment, you should consider requiring a deposit or advance payment to cover the fees and expenses for the services that you will render, along with permission from the parties to pay your fees out of the deposit. You should also consider requiring the deposit to be 'refreshed' if and when it is exhausted.

(b) Administered expertise proceedings. In administered ICC expertise proceedings, these issues are governed by Articles 9(5)(c) and 14 and Appendix II, Article 3 of the ICC Rules for Expertise. Under these rules, you will be paid for the time that you reasonably spend at a daily rate that the Centre fixes after consultation with you and the parties and taking into account the complexity and other relevant circumstances of the case. The Centre will also fix your reasonable expenses.

Your fees and expenses will be paid out of a deposit fixed at the beginning and adjusted as required. Thus, you should provide the Centre with reliable information concerning the time you anticipate to complete your mission, the complexity of the case, and your usual daily fee. You should also estimate your out-of-pocket expenses.

You should address these financial issues with the Centre as soon as you have the basic information about the engagement. If your expectations about fees are unlikely to be met, you should consider declining the engagement.

If unforeseen circumstances will cause you to perform more work than you originally anticipated, you should provide the Centre with the updated information as soon as possible.

C. How may I communicate with the parties?

1. Expertise under agreement with one party

If only one party has retained you to provide services, you and the party may communicate as either of you deems fit. If the party retaining your services plans to use your work product as expert evidence in court or arbitration proceedings, your communications with the party may be subject to certain legal rules and requirements that can vary depending on the circumstances. Thus, you should ask the party that retained you about any requirements concerning communication, especially anything that might limit the usefulness of your work product. Keep in mind that your communications with the party may be subject to full disclosure in the court or arbitration proceedings.

2. Expertise under agreement with all parties

If all parties retain your expert services to resolve a dispute between them, you should avoid communications with only one party unless all other parties are privy to those communications. The parties expect to be treated fairly and transparently. If they suspect that something might be taking place behind their backs, your credibility and thus the persuasiveness of your work product will be reduced. Moreover, if you engage in ex parte communications with a party, the other parties may have a basis to challenge your independence or impartiality.

Before working on the assignment, you should define in writing the communication protocol that you and the parties will follow. An open discussion with the parties about these issues is useful because it allows you to obtain a feeling for whether the parties' approach is cooperative or more adversarial.

(a) Written materials. Try to get agreement that the parties will jointly provide you with all materials, objects and other information that you will need in electronic or tangible format. Alternatively, you should require that each party simultaneously provide the other parties with a true and complete copy of anything that a party sends to you. You should keep a list itemizing what you have received and provide the parties with a copy of the list before you prepare and submit your work product.

    The parties have a responsibility to comply with the communication procedures that you and they agree, but if you suspect that the other side has not received certain information, you should raise your concern with the parties.

(b) Meetings. Unless all parties agree, you should not meet with only one party unless all other parties are present or have a reasonable opportunity to be present. The same applies to site visits. Thus, any meeting or site visit should be scheduled with the parties and announced far enough in advance so that the date can be adjusted if a party or parties are unavailable.

    It may be useful to provide the parties with a written summary of any meeting or site visit within a reasonably short period thereafter, including the date, place, participants and results of the meeting or site visit. If the parties have agreed on facts that were previously disputed, it is important to record this agreement in writing.

(c) Telephone communications. In general, you should participate in a telephone conference with a party only if the other parties are privy. Experience shows, however, that a party may call you or you may need to call a party about a non-substantive issue (e.g., payment). In this instance, try to avoid discussing issues of substance. Generally, you should create a note that summarizes the conversation, and make it available to all parties.

D. How do I define my mission as an expert?

The quality of the questions often determines the quality of the answers. Your active participation in defining your mission may increase the efficiency of the proceedings, as well as the quality of your work product. Although the nature of your mission is ultimately up to the parties, your expertise may help you to guide the parties to define your mission in a way that will help to promote efficiency, reduce costs and result in a work product that is more likely to assist the parties to resolve their dispute. Thus, you should avoid skipping the sometimes cumbersome exercise of working with the parties until you are satisfied that the mission enables you to perform your duties in a manner consistent with the state of the art in your field of expertise.

If shortcomings in the agreed mission become apparent only later, carefully raise the issue with the parties and seek agreement on the desirable modifications as early as possible.

1. Expertise under agreement with one party

The party will define your mission. If you become aware of any deficiencies or possible improvements, you may raise the point with the party.

2. Expertise under agreement with all parties

Here, the challenge is to work with the parties so that they are able to agree on your mission. Parties in a dispute may tend to phrase the questions posed to you differently and in a way that each believes is likely to lead to the desired answer. Thus, even if the parties broadly agree on your mission, they still may disagree on many specific points. Accordingly, the wording of your mission should be discussed and, to the extent possible, agreed during a meeting or a telephone conference.

In administered proceedings under the ICC Rules for Expertise, Article 12(1) requires you to define your mission in writing after consulting all parties. You also may modify your mission after consulting all parties. Although you cannot deviate completely from what the parties have asked you to do when they commenced the expertise proceedings, you have the flexibility needed to overcome an impasse caused by disagreement over details of your mission, if your efforts to reach agreement fail.

Basically, you have three options to resolve disagreement regarding your mission:

(a) Define your mission broadly, with words to which all parties are willing to agree.

(b) Define your mission by including each party's questions where they disagree and a question requiring you to decide, if necessary, which question is appropriate.

(c) Define your mission by rephrasing the questions over which the parties disagree.

You should use your judgment to decide which of these approaches is preferable in the specific circumstances. You also should make a reasonable effort to keep the mission from being flawed with imprecise or irrelevant questions.

E. What sort of work product is expected from me?

As a general rule, your work product should satisfy any formal requirements established in your mission and cover all points defined therein. Unless the parties agree, you should not exceed your initially defined mission or deviate from it.

Normally you will be expected to present a report, setting out your analysis and findings, as described in further detail below. Sometimes, you may be required to report on findings of fact, such as the observations you made during a test run, at an inspection, or in perusing accounting records. Occasionally, other services may be required of an expert, such as ongoing advice on certain issues or the drafting of texts.

If a party wishes your report to deal with an issue where the parties have diverging interests, you should make sure that your report addresses only what the parties agreed, and avoid exceeding your mission based upon a unilateral and contested request. You should resolve any dispute over whether to include this type of divergent request early in your engagement, rather than surprise one party with your work product by addressing an issue that fewer than all parties agreed that you should address.

1. Non-administered expertise proceedings

In non-administered expertise proceedings under the ICC Rules for Expertise, the party or parties retaining your services will define the form of your work product. This should be clearly stated in your written agreement with the parties. As the expert, you may need to elicit from the party or parties what they have in mind and then take the lead by proposing the form of your work product and level of detail required.

2. Administered expertise proceedings

In administered expertise proceedings, Article 12(6) of the ICC Rules for Expertise requires a written report to be reviewed by the Centre, which has the right to require formal adjustments. This helps to ensure good quality and may be helpful to you because you can draw on the Centre's experience.

The ICC Rules for Expertise do not include specific requirements regarding the content or quality of the report, as this depends on the nature of the expertise and how the report will be used. Thus, it may be useful to discuss with the parties specific requirements as to form and substance and record those in your expert's mission. See section III(D) above. The parties can provide you with any applicable legal requirements regarding form.

3. General guidelines for a persuasive work product

(a) Methodology and standards. You should use the methodology and standards that are generally accepted in your field of expertise. If you deviate from these for justified reasons, you should clearly state why and how you did so. The basic rule is that your report should stand the test of peer review, and you should assume that your report will be subjected to some sort of peer review because it possibly will be.

(b) Structure. In most instances, the report follows a structure similar to the following:

   (i) A summary identifying the party or parties and yourself.

   (ii) A summary of your mission.

   (iii) A summary of the methodology and the standards you have used and, if applicable, the professional or ethical rules by which you abide.

   (iv) A summary of the information on which you rely, including comprehensive references to literature and other sources that you used. Sometimes, it is appropriate to include this in an attachment.

   (v) Your factual findings and your reasoned opinion and conclusion regarding the issues that were submitted to you. In many cases, it will be appropriate to set forth separately the parties' respective positions, your factual findings, and the conclusions on an issue-by-issue basis. But it is also possible to summarize the parties' respective positions and factual findings in one section and the reasoned conclusions in another section. If known to you, you may also specifically refer to reports of other experts on the relevant issues in this context. Regardless of which structure you choose, your report should be easily and fully understandable to the non-experts who are expected to read it. In other words, if only experts are able to understand your report, the report's value to the parties will be reduced.

(c) If only one party assigned the work to you, the same principles apply. If the party requires your report for a nascent dispute or as expert evidence in litigation or arbitration (rather than only for the party's internal use), you should proceed as an independent impartial expert and provide your work product accordingly. You may seek instructions from the party regarding any specific legal requirements. If the party provides guidance or instructions that you believe to be problematic, illegal or inconsistent with your professional duties, consider terminating your engagement.

IV. Expert witnesses operating under the ICC Rules of Arbitration

A. What role can I have in arbitration proceedings?

As described above in the introduction, you may be asked to serve in one of several distinct roles in an arbitration: (1) party-appointed expert witness, (2) tribunal-appointed expert witness, or (3) non-testifying expert consultant.

The role of expert consultants is discussed in section II(C)(2)(b) above. As described there, experts are sometimes initially retained as consultants and later designated as testifying expert witnesses. Considerations for party-appointed and tribunal-appointed expert witnesses are discussed below.

B. What factors should I consider before accepting an appointment as an expert witness in arbitration?

Under the ICC Rules of Arbitration, an expert witness can be retained by one or more parties or by the arbitral tribunal. Under Article 20(3), party-appointed experts are engaged to offer testimony on behalf of one or more parties. Under Article 20(4), after consulting with the parties, the arbitral tribunal may retain one or more experts directly, define their terms of reference, receive their reports, and permit the parties to question them at the hearing.

Regardless of who retains you, before accepting an engagement as an expert in an arbitration, you should strive to obtain all of the information that you need to make an informed decision concerning whether to accept, including the following:

1. Do I have the experience to serve?

As described in section III(B)(1) above, you should evaluate whether you have the substantive expertise, procedural skills and language ability necessary to fulfill your engagement.

2. Am I impartial and independent of the parties?

The concepts of 'independence' and 'impartiality' are discussed above in section III(B)(2). The ICC Rules of Arbitration do not expressly require expert witnesses to be independent or impartial. Nonetheless, you may be subject to independence and impartiality requirements under applicable law or professional standards to which you are subject. See section II (B)(1) above. In addition, if your appointment as an expert witness comes through a proposal from the Centre, you must satisfy the requirements for independence and impartiality under the ICC Rules for Expertise. See section II(B)(2) above. In this context, if the arbitral tribunal requested that the Centre propose an expert, Article 3(3) of the ICC Rules for Expertise requires you to be independent of the parties also and not only the arbitral tribunal. If you are appointed by the Centre, Article 7(3) of the Rules for Expertise will apply. See section II(A)(2) above.

As a practical matter, if you are a tribunal-appointed expert, your terms of reference, the rules to which the parties have agreed,[5] or the applicable arbitration law will likely require you to be and remain impartial and independent of the parties.

If you are a party-appointed expert, the party or parties who engage you will likely require you to disclose potential conflicts of interest or other information related to your independence or impartiality. If all parties retain you to serve as a party-appointed expert, the parties will likely require you to be and remain independent of and impartial towards all parties.

If fewer than all parties retain you, these parties will likely want to make sure, at a minimum, that you do not have a conflict of interest with any opposing party. Moreover, regardless of legal requirements and professional standards, if your relationships or interests would cause the arbitral tribunal to view you as biased towards a particular party or outcome, your testimony is unlikely to be persuasive to the arbitral tribunal. Thus, even where fewer than all parties retain you, you may be required to be and remain independent of all parties and to demonstrate a lack of predetermined bias towards a particular outcome.

If you have any questions or concerns about whether you are sufficiently independent or impartial, you should raise these concerns with the persons who propose to engage you before you accept the engagement. If you accepted the engagement before your concern arose, you should work to address the concern as quickly as possible with the persons who engaged you. If you have any doubt about whether you should disclose a particular relationship or interest, you should disclose it.

3. *Do I have the time to serve?*

ICC arbitrations have a procedural timetable that will vary depending on the circumstances of each case. Therefore, it is essential that you can complete your assignment within the period of time allotted by the procedural timetable. Thus, before accepting an engagement, you need to ask sufficient questions of the party that is engaging you to understand (a) when you will be expected to complete your work product, (b) how long it likely will take you to complete your work product, and (c) the dates of any hearings at which you would be expected to testify. If you cannot meet any of these deadlines, you should not accept the engagement.

4. *How will I be compensated and how will my expenses be paid?*

Whether you are a party-appointed or tribunal-appointed expert, your fees and expenses are the subject of negotiation and agreement between you and the persons who engage you. Your fee can be based on your normal hourly or daily rates, or you could agree to a lump-sum fee. You should agree on how out-of-pocket expenses are going to be repaid, as well as other payment terms, such as due dates, invoicing procedures, currency of payment, etc. You should reduce your agreement regarding payment of fees and expenses to writing before your engagement begins. You should also assume

5. E.g., Article 6.2 of the IBA Rules on the Taking of Evidence in International Commercial Arbitration (1999) details various requirements concerning the expert's independence and impartiality. See supra note 4.

that your agreement regarding payment of fees and expenses will be disclosed to the opposite side.

Regarding deposits or advances on fees and expenses, see section III(B)(5)(a) above. If you are appointed by the arbitral tribunal, and the tribunal manages a deposit, most of the considerations in section III(B)(5)(b) above will apply.

C. What duties do I owe to the parties to the arbitration and to the arbitral tribunal?

1. Overview

Your duties as an expert in arbitration proceedings arise from several sources. First, your duties are determined by the terms and conditions of your engagement. Second, your role is governed by the applicable procedural rules and the applicable arbitration law. Third, the arbitral tribunal may issue instructions that pertain to you. Regardless of the differences in agreements, procedures and law that may exist from case to case, your role in the arbitration will always be to assist in establishing the truth. Moreover, an expert witness who is perceived to be independent and disinterested in a particular outcome will tend to be more persuasive.

(a) If you are a tribunal-appointed expert and operate under terms of reference that the tribunal has established, you will normally be considered as a 'fact finding aide' to the tribunal. This role should be distinguished from that of a 'witness of fact'.

(b) If you are an expert appointed by all parties, you will operate under the terms and conditions of your engagement, which will usually require a neutral approach as described in sections II(C)(1), III(C)(2), III(D)(2) above. Unless the parties have agreed that you should act as a tribunal-appointed expert, the considerations in (c) below apply.

(c) If you are a party-appointed expert, you may sometimes perceive tension between your relationship with the party that retained you and your role in the proceedings. Ultimately, you should bear in mind that a party-appointed expert is an expert witness. Under applicable law, you must testify truthfully and cannot make up things that did not happen. Likewise, you must not try to create a false impression by omitting known, relevant information.

2. Duties to all parties

You should testify truthfully in any report or witness statement that you provide, as well as at the hearing. At the hearing, you should answer questions from the opposing party courteously and without evasion. If you fail to testify truthfully, you may be subject to penalties under applicable law for providing false testimony

3. Duties to the arbitral tribunal

The arbitral tribunal is responsible for determining how the arbitration will proceed, subject to the applicable rules and any agreements of the parties. Among other things, this means that regardless of whether you are a party-appointed or tribunal-appointed expert, the tribunal will determine whether expert testimony will be allowed, the form of your work product, when your work product is due, whether you will be accepted as an expert, how long you will be permitted to testify, the limits of cross-examination, and so forth. You will need to comply with the requirements set by the tribunal.

In addition, if you are a tribunal-appointed expert, the tribunal is acting as your principal. You will need to comply with your terms of reference agreed between the tribunal and you. Regarding your terms of reference, see section III(D) above. If you have suggestions, questions or concerns about how your terms of reference should be defined, you should raise them with the arbitral tribunal, which will determine the proper course of action, usually after consulting the parties.

You must testify truthfully in response to any questions from the arbitral tribunal.

4. Duties to the party or parties who appointed me

You should discharge the terms of your engagement, including the preparation of your work product, on time and in a manner consistent with the professional standards to which you are subject and applicable rules of law. Regarding your terms of reference, see section III(D) above. You should strive to create a work product that would withstand scrutiny from your peers in your field of expertise.

D. How may I communicate with the parties and the arbitral tribunal?

You should distinguish between two issues: (i) whether and how you may communicate with the parties or the arbitral tribunal and (ii) whether the substance of your communications with the party or tribunal who retained you is appropriate under the circumstances.

1. Party-appointed expert

(a) Communications with the parties who retained you. If you are retained by one or more parties but fewer than all parties, you may communicate with the parties who retained you as you deem appropriate, unless the arbitral tribunal's order or applicable rules restrict those communications. You should be aware, however, that in some cases all parties or, in case of disagreement, upon request by one party, the arbitral tribunal may decide to require you to disclose to the other parties any written communications between you and the parties who retained you or their counsel and that the other parties may be permitted to question you at the hearing about any communications between you and the parties who retained you or their counsel. See section III(C)(1) above. Whether and to what extent such disclosure can be required depends on the tribunal's directions or other rules applicable to the specific case. Given that these directions may not be known to you from the beginning, your communications should be guided by the 'working hypothesis' that they are not privileged and that their disclosure might be required later.

If you are retained by all parties, you should be careful to ensure that you do not communicate with one party in the absence of the other parties. See section III(C)(2) above.

(b) Communications with the opposing party. In general, as a party-appointed expert, you should not communicate with the opposing party or its counsel unless counsel to the party that engaged you is present or if specifically instructed to do so by the party that appointed you or by the arbitral tribunal.

(c) Communications with other expert witnesses. In general, as a party-appointed expert, you should not communicate with other expert witnesses unless counsel to the parties are present or if specifically instructed to do so by agreement with the parties or the arbitral tribunal.

(d) Communications with the arbitral tribunal. In general, as a party-appointed expert, you should not need to communicate with the arbitral tribunal, except when testifying at the hearing. If you have a question regarding a procedural matter, you should raise this question through the counsel to the party that engaged you.

(e) Substance of the communications. As a party-appointed expert, the substance of your communications with that party is usually not governed by specific rules. Nonetheless, your communications should be consistent with the professional standards to which you are subject, applicable rules of law, and your role in helping to find the truth in the arbitration. Put another way, no party or its counsel should ask you to do something that is illegal, unethical or dishonest. If this sort of conflict arises, you should raise the issue with the party that appointed you, and if you are unable to resolve the issue, you should decline or terminate your engagement.

2. *Tribunal-appointed expert*

(a) Communications with the tribunal. If you are retained by the arbitral tribunal, the tribunal should define in your terms of reference or otherwise any communication protocols that the tribunal would like you to follow. Thus, for example, the tribunal ordinarily should provide directions to you regarding (i) whether you should communicate only with all members of the tribunal simultaneously (e.g., in writing or through a conference call); and (ii) whether and when the parties' counsel should be present when you communicate with the tribunal and whether and when counsel should receive copies of your written communications to the tribunal. If you have any questions or concerns about what the tribunal requires, you should seek clarification from the tribunal.

(b) Communications with the parties. The arbitral tribunal will control your communications with the parties and provide you with guidance regarding how and to what extent you may communicate with the parties or their counsel outside the tribunal's presence. In general, where the tribunal directs you to interview a party, to visit a party's facility, or otherwise to communicate with a party, you should make sure that the other parties or their counsel have the opportunity to attend and observe. Unless for some reason the tribunal directs otherwise, written communications to one party should be copied to all other parties. Again, if you have any questions or concerns, you should ask the tribunal to clarify.

(c) Substance of the communications. As a tribunal-appointed expert, the substance of your communications with any party is governed by the requirements of independence and impartiality. Ideally, all parties and the arbitral tribunal should be privy to any such communication. Communications with only one party should take place only when absolutely necessary, and should be limited to minor logistical or similar issues (e.g., instructions on how to get to the plant or other site), as opposed to contentious or substantive issues. The arbitral tribunal may issue directions or guidelines in this regard. See section III(C)(2) above.

E. What powers do I have to obtain information (including access to a site) from the parties and the arbitral tribunal?

1. Party-appointed expert

If you are a party-appointed expert, you may ask the parties that engaged you to provide the documents or other things (including access to a site) within those parties' possession, custody or control that you need to complete your work product. If the required documents or things are within the opposing party's possession, custody or control, you should ask counsel with whom you are working to request the needed documents or things on your behalf. If the opposing party is unwilling to cooperate, counsel can ask the arbitral tribunal to direct the opposing party to provide you with the required information and documents. Nothing guarantees, however, that the arbitral tribunal will issue the requested directions. Thus, you may need to complete your work product without the opposite side's full cooperation and without obtaining all information that you might want from the opposite side.

2. Tribunal-appointed expert

You should tell the arbitral tribunal what sort of information and documents you need. If the information and documents are within a party's possession, custody or control, the arbitral tribunal can direct the party to provide you with the required information and documents.

F. What sort of report or other work product will I be expected to produce?

For general guidance regarding written expert reports, see section III(E)(3) above.

Party-appointed experts and tribunal-appointed experts almost will always be expected to prepare some sort of written work product, which usually will take one of two forms: (a) a narrative report of your analysis and conclusions or (b) a witness statement setting out your analysis and conclusions in the form of an affidavit or declaration. The persons who engaged you can provide guidance regarding the type of work product, its format, and the level of detail required.

Tribunal-appointed experts will operate according to a procedural order or 'terms of reference' that generally require the submission of a written report. See section III(E)(3) above.

Your report or other work product should be prepared using the same methods that equally or better skilled experts in your field of expertise would use in the same or similar circumstances. If you fail to apply recognized methodologies or if peers in your field of expertise would be unable to repeat your analysis or are likely to disagree, your work product may be subject to criticism that will significantly reduce or even eliminate its usefulness to the parties and the arbitral tribunal.

G. What can I expect after submitting my work product but before a hearing?

Regardless of whether you are a party-appointed expert or a tribunal-appointed expert, your work product will be communicated to all parties, who will normally be afforded an opportunity to comment on or rebut your report before the hearing. If you are a party-appointed expert, the party that appointed you may instruct you to review and analyze any reports from the opposite side's experts and to supplement your own work product, as appropriate.

If the opposing parties have each appointed an expert witness, the various experts often disagree on crucial issues. Where, for example, the experts differ in the structure of their work product, their basic underlying data or their methodology, the experts' disagreement may create a substantial hurdle for the arbitral tribunal to overcome, given that the arbitrators usually do not have the same technical expertise as the experts. To avoid the difficulty that 'dueling experts' sometimes create, some arbitral tribunals may resort to appointing their own expert in place of, or in addition to, party-appointed experts.

Another approach is to require you and the other expert(s) to meet in private to attempt to narrow the areas of disagreement. Where the differences cannot be bridged, the arbitral tribunal may require the experts to explain in writing to the tribunal and the parties the reasons for the differences and whether the experts' differing approaches can both withstand peer review.

If you were appointed by the arbitral tribunal and there are no party-appointed experts, the tribunal may instruct you to supplement or clarify your report in light of the parties' comments or questions.

H. What can I expect at the hearing?

The ICC Rules of Arbitration give the arbitral tribunal broad discretion regarding how to conduct the hearing, but the tribunal will work to provide each party with a full and fair opportunity to present its case. In most cases, after the experts have submitted their written reports, the arbitral tribunal will summon the experts to attend a hearing, either because a party requests a hearing or because the arbitral tribunal finds that a hearing would be helpful.

Hearings are usually held in a large conference room at an 'impartial venue' where seating arrangements tend to mimic (to a greater or lesser extent) those in a court of law. If you will need technical equipment to present your expert opinion or to answer questions, you should make sure that the required arrangements are made and document your request for the equipment.

You may be asked to testify from the conference table or from a separate 'witness chair'. Before you start testifying, the arbitral tribunal will likely ask you to affirm that your testimony is true and correct. In appropriate circumstances, you may also be required to testify under oath.

Then, some combination of the parties' counsel and the tribunal will ask you questions about your background as an expert, your assignment in this case, what you did, your analysis and your conclusions. You may also be asked, for example, about the details of your report, articles and books that you have written, documents produced as evidence in the case, and other matters relevant to the disputed issues in the case. The arbitral tribunal will instruct counsel to stop if the tribunal finds that a particular question or line of questioning is irrelevant or otherwise improper. If you find a question to be improper, you may say so, and the arbitral tribunal will ultimately decide whether you should answer the question.

The order of questioning is up to the arbitral tribunal. If you are party-appointed expert, for example, the arbitral tribunal may direct that counsel for the party that retained you will go first, followed by the opposing party's counsel, and then the tribunal. Alternatively, the arbitral tribunal may permit the opposing party's counsel to go first, followed by the counsel for the party that retained you, and then the tribunal.

If you are a tribunal-appointed expert, the arbitral tribunal will permit each party's counsel to question you, after which the tribunal may also have questions. Alternatively, the tribunal may switch this order.

Regardless of your role and who asks the questions, you must answer all questions truthfully.

Some arbitral tribunals may direct or authorize you to put questions to other experts or witnesses in relation to the subject matter of your assignment. Actual practice in this regard varies depending on the arbitrators and the dispute.

Finally, if there are several party-appointed experts, the tribunal may direct that a so-called 'witness conference' be conducted in which you will be heard together with the other experts and knowledgeable fact witnesses, if any. During a witness conference, several experts or witnesses will be present in the hearing room and the arbitral tribunal will direct them to address certain issues which it deems relevant. You may be confronted with what other experts state or directed to engage in a discussion with them. This method is increasingly used to resolve differences between conflicting expert opinions.

APPENDIX 20

RULES OF ICC AS APPOINTING AUTHORITY IN UNCITRAL OR OTHER AD HOC ARBITRATION PROCEEDINGS (1 JANUARY 2004)

RULES OF ICC AS APPOINTING AUTHORITY IN UNCITRAL OR OTHER *AD HOC* ARBITRATION PROCEEDINGS

In force as from 1 January 2004

Article 1: ICC as Appointing Authority in UNCITRAL or Other Ad Hoc *Arbitration Proceedings*

1. If so empowered by an arbitration clause, a subsequent agreement of the parties, a designation by the Secretary-General of the Permanent Court of Arbitration in The Hague, or otherwise, the International Chamber of Commerce ('ICC') shall act as appointing authority in accordance with the parties' agreement and/or the UNCITRAL Arbitration Rules.

2. The present Rules shall also apply where an authority within ICC[1] is requested to act as appointing authority in accordance with the parties' agreement or is designated by the Secretary-General of the Permanent Court of Arbitration in The Hague. References to ICC in these Rules include such other authorities.

3. Where ICC is empowered or requested to act as appointing authority under Articles 1(1) or 1(2), the function shall be carried out by the ICC International Court of Arbitration (the 'Court'). To fulfil this role, the Court shall create a special committee (the 'Special Committee') consisting of the President[2] of the Court and two other members of the Court. The President may designate a Vice-President of the Court to replace him at a meeting of the Special Committee. Unless otherwise provided, the Special Committee shall carry out the functions of the Court under these Rules. The Special Committee's decisions shall be taken unanimously. In the event that a unanimous decision cannot be reached, the matter shall be referred to the Court sitting as a special

1. Such as the Chairman or Secretary General of ICC or the President or Secretary General of the ICC International Court of Arbitration.
2. *Editor's note*: Originally "Chairman". Replaced by "President" in keeping with the change of terminology in the ICC Rules of Arbitration in force as from 1 January 2012.

plenary session (the 'Special Plenary Session'). When making decisions upon challenges pursuant to these Rules, the Court shall do so at a Special Plenary Session.

Article 2: Request for ICC to Act as Appointing Authority

1. In cases referred to in Article 1 of these Rules, a party wishing ICC to act as appointing authority shall submit a request (the 'Request') to the Secretariat of the Court (the 'Secretariat'), which shall notify the other party or parties of the receipt of the Request and the date of such receipt.

2. The Request shall contain all the information that the requesting party deems appropriate to allow the Court to make the requested appointment.

3. The Request and all documents annexed thereto shall be supplied in a sufficient number of copies to provide one for each party and one for the Secretariat. When submitting its Request, the requesting party shall make the payment required by Article 6 of these Rules. Should the requesting party fail to comply with either of these requirements, the Secretariat may set a time limit for compliance. Failing compliance within the time limit, the file shall be closed without prejudice to the right of the requesting party to resubmit its Request at a later date.

Article 3: The Court Acting as Appointing Authority under the UNCITRAL Arbitration Rules

1. When acting as the appointing authority for the purpose of appointing a sole or presiding (third) arbitrator pursuant to Articles 6(2) and 7(3) of the UNCITRAL Arbitration Rules, the Court shall follow the list-procedure set forth in Article 6(3) of the UNCITRAL Arbitration Rules, unless all parties agree that the list-procedure should not be used or the Court determines in its discretion that the use of the list-procedure is not appropriate for the case.

2. When following the list-procedure, the Court shall prepare a list of at least three candidates which shall be communicated to the parties by the Secretariat. Within 15 days of receiving this list, each party may return the list to the Secretariat after deleting the name or names to which it objects and numbering the remaining names on the list in the order of its preference. After expiration of the aforementioned 15-day time limit, the Court shall appoint the sole or presiding arbitrator from among the names approved on the list returned to the Secretariat and in accordance with the order of preference indicated by the parties. If for any reason the appointment cannot be made according to this procedure, the Court may exercise its discretion in appointing the sole or presiding arbitrator.

3. In accordance with Article 6(4) of the UNCITRAL Arbitration Rules, when making the appointment, the Court shall have regard to such considerations as are likely to secure the appointment of an independent and impartial arbitrator and shall take into account as well the advisability of appointing an arbitrator of a nationality other than that of the parties.

4. When appointing an arbitrator on behalf of a party in default under Article 7 of the UNCITRAL Arbitration Rules, the Court may exercise its discretion in making the appointment.

5. When making decisions upon challenges submitted by any party under Article 12 of the UNCITRAL Arbitration Rules, the Court will do so at a Special Plenary Session

after the Secretariat has afforded an opportunity for the arbitrator concerned, the other party or parties and any other members of the arbitral tribunal to comment in writing within a suitable period of time. Such comments shall be communicated to the parties and to the arbitrators, before being submitted to the Court.

6. When appointing a substitute arbitrator under Articles 12(2) and 13 of the UNCITRAL Arbitration Rules, the Court shall follow the procedure set forth in the preceding paragraphs.

7. At the request of any party and pursuant to Article 39(4) of the UNCITRAL Arbitration Rules, the Court may, on a consultative basis, provide a statement concerning the fees of the arbitrators, taking into account the ICC Scale of Arbitrator's Fees for cases conducted under the ICC Rules of Arbitration.

8. At the request of any party and pursuant to Article 41(3) of the UNCITRAL Arbitration Rules, the Court may, on a consultative basis, give the arbitral tribunal any comments it deems appropriate concerning the amount of any deposit or supplementary deposit to be made under Article 41 of the UNCITRAL Arbitration Rules.

Article 4: The Court Acting as Appointing Authority in Ad Hoc, *Non-UNCITRAL Arbitration Proceedings*

1. Where the parties have agreed or where an applicable text provides that ICC shall act as appointing authority in *ad hoc*, non-UNCITRAL (hereafter, non-UNCITRAL) arbitral proceedings, the Court, exercising its discretion within the limits fixed by the parties in their agreement(s), or the limits contained in the applicable text, shall appoint an arbitrator independent of the parties involved in the arbitration.

2. The parties to non-UNCITRAL arbitral proceedings may agree that the Court, as appointing authority, shall have the power to decide upon a challenge made by any of the parties against any member of the arbitral tribunal. A challenge shall be made by submitting to the Secretariat a written statement specifying the facts and circumstances on which the challenge is based.

3. The Court shall decide on the challenge at a Special Plenary Session after the Secretariat has afforded an opportunity for the arbitrator concerned, the other party or parties and any other members of the arbitral tribunal to comment in writing within a suitable period of time. Such comments shall be communicated to the parties and to the arbitrators, before being submitted to the Court.

Article 5: General Provisions

1. When requested to act under these Rules, the Court shall proceed if it is satisfied that an agreement authorizing it to act as appointing authority may exist.

2. If so empowered by an arbitration clause, a subsequent agreement of the parties, or otherwise, the Court shall consider providing services, besides those specifically indicated in these Rules, in accordance with the parties' agreement.

3. Before appointment in cases provided for under Articles 3 and 4 of these Rules, a prospective arbitrator shall sign a declaration of acceptance and a statement of independence and disclose in writing to the Secretariat any facts or circumstances which might be of such a nature as to call into question the arbitrator's independence in the eyes of the parties.

4. The reasons for the decisions taken by the Court under these Rules shall not be communicated.

5. Neither the Court and its members, nor the International Chamber of Commerce and its employees shall be liable to any person for any act or omission in connection with the activities performed under these Rules.

Article 6: ICC Costs for Services Rendered as Appointing Authority

1. Each Request submitted to the Secretariat must be accompanied by payment to ICC of a non-refundable sum, the amount of which shall be determined according to the Appendix to these Rules.

2. For services provided pursuant to Article 5(2) of these Rules, the Court may fix administrative expenses commensurate with these services, which shall be paid by the requesting party or parties.

APPENDIX
ICC COSTS FOR SERVICES RENDERED AS APPOINTING AUTHORITY

Article 1

The non-refundable amount referred to in Article 6(1) of these Rules is US$ 3,000. The non-refundable amount is payable by the party or parties submitting the Request. No Request shall be processed unless accompanied by the requisite payment.

Article 2

The administrative expenses of ICC for the services rendered pursuant to Article 5(2) of these Rules shall be fixed at ICC's discretion depending on the tasks carried out by ICC. Such administrative expenses shall be commensurate with said services and shall not exceed the maximum sum of US$ 10,000.

International Chamber of Commerce
International Court of Arbitration
33-43 avenue du Président Wilson
75116 Paris
France
Tel. +33 1 49 53 29 05
Fax +33 1 49 53 29 33
E-mail arb@iccwbo.org
www.iccarbitration.org

APPENDIX 21

ICC RULES FOR A PRE-ARBITRAL REFEREE PROCEDURE (1 JANUARY 1990)

RULES FOR A PRE-ARBITRAL REFEREE PROCEDURE OF THE INTERNATIONAL CHAMBER OF COMMERCE

In force as from 1 January 1990

Introduction

During the course of many contracts, especially those made for long-term transactions, problems can arise which require an urgent response. It is frequently not possible to obtain in the time required a final decision from an arbitral tribunal or from a court.

Accordingly, the International Chamber of Commerce (ICC) has set out the following Rules for a Pre-Arbitral Referee Procedure in order to enable parties that have so agreed to have rapid recourse to a person (called a "Referee") empowered to make an order designed to meet the urgent problem in issue, including the power to order the preservation or recording of evidence. The order should therefore provide a temporary resolution of the dispute and may lay the foundations for its final settlement either by agreement or otherwise.

Use of the Pre-Arbitral Referee Procedure does not usurp the jurisdiction of any entity (whether arbitral tribunal or national court) that is ultimately responsible for deciding the merits of any underlying dispute.

Article 1: Definitions

1.1. These Rules concern a procedure called the "Pre-Arbitral Referee Procedure", which provides for the immediate appointment of a person (the "Referee") who has the power to make certain Orders prior to the arbitral tribunal or national court competent to deal with the case (the "Competent Authority") being seized of it.

1.2. The Secretariat of the ICC International Court of Arbitration (the "Secretariat") shall act as the Secretariat of the Pre-Arbitral Referee Procedure.

1.3

a) In these Rules any reference to a party includes a party's employees or agents.

---

b) Any reference to the "President"[1] means the President of the ICC International Court of Arbitration and includes, in his absence, a Vice-President.

Article 2: Powers of the Referee

2.1. The powers of the Referee are:

a) to order any conservatory measures or any measures of restoration that are urgently necessary to prevent either immediate damage or irreparable loss and so to safeguard any of the rights or property of one of the parties;
b) to order a party to make to any other party or to another person any payment which ought to be made;
c) to order a party to take any step which ought to be taken according to the contract between the parties, including the signing or delivery of any document or the procuring by a party of the signature or delivery of a document;
d) to order any measures necessary to preserve or establish evidence.

2.1.1. These powers may be altered by express written agreement between the parties.

2.2. The Referee shall not have power to make any Order other than that requested by any party in accordance with Article 3.

2.3. Unless the parties otherwise agree in writing, a Referee appointed in accordance with these Rules shall not act as arbitrator in any subsequent proceedings between those parties or in any other proceedings in which there is any issue or question that is the same as or connected with any raised in the proceedings before the Referee.

2.4. If the Competent Authority becomes seized of the case after the appointment of the Referee, the Referee shall nevertheless retain the power to make an Order within the time provided by Article 6.2, unless the parties otherwise agree or the Competent Authority orders otherwise.

2.4.1. Except as provided in Article 2.4 above, once the Competent Authority becomes seized of the case it alone may order, under the rules applicable to it, any further provisional or conservatory measures that it considers necessary. For such purpose the Competent Authority, if its rules so permit, shall be deemed to have been authorized by the parties to exercise the powers conferred on the Referee by Article 2.1.

Article 3: Request for Referee and Answer

3.1. An agreement to use the Pre-Arbitral Referee Procedure must be in writing.

3.2. A party requiring the appointment of a Referee must send two copies of its Request and of any annexed documents to the Secretariat. Such party must at the same time notify the other party or parties of the Request by the quickest method of delivery available, including telefax.

3.2.1. Each such Request must be accompanied by the amount required to open the file, as set out in Article B.1 of the Appendix to these Rules.

3.2.2. The Request must be drawn up in whatever language may have been agreed upon in writing by the parties or, in the absence of any such agreement, in the same language as the agreement to use the Pre-Arbitral Referee Procedure. If this language is

1. *Editor's note*: Originally "Chairman". Replaced by "President" in keeping with the change of terminology in the ICC Rules of Arbitration in force as from 1 January 2012.

not English, French or German, a translation of the Request into one of these languages must accompany the Request. The annexed documents may be submitted in their original language without translation except where it is necessary in order to understand the Request. The Request shall be in writing and shall contain in particular:

a) the names and addresses of the parties to the agreement together with a brief description of the legal relationships between the parties;
b) a copy of the agreement on which the Request is based;
c) the Order or Orders requested and an explanation of the grounds relied on so as to show that the Request falls within Article 2.1;
d) as the case may be, the name of the Referee chosen by agreement of the parties;
e) any information concerning the choice of the Referee required to be appointed, including, as appropriate, technical or professional qualifications, nationality and language requirements;
f) confirmation that the request has been sent to every other party, stating the means by which this has been done and enclosing proof of transmission, such as postal registration form, receipt from a private courier, or telefax receipt.

3.3. The requesting party shall, if required by the Secretariat, establish when a copy of the Request was received by each party to whom it was sent or when it should be treated as having been received by said party.

3.4. The other party or parties must submit to the Secretariat in writing an Answer to the Request within eight days from receipt of the copy of the Request sent in accordance with Article 3.2 above, and must send at the same time a copy to the requesting party and to any other party, using the quickest method of delivery available, including telefax. The Answer must state any Order requested by that party or parties.

Article 4: Appointment of the Referee and transmission of the file

4.1. The Referee may be chosen by the parties by agreement before or after a Request is made pursuant to Article 3, in which case the name and address of the Referee shall be sent immediately to the Secretariat. Upon receipt of the Answer or, at the latest, upon the expiry of the time limit set out in Article 3.4, and having verified the *prima facie* existence of the agreement of the parties, the President shall promptly appoint the Referee agreed upon.

4.2. If a Referee is to be appointed under Article 3.2.2(e), the President shall, upon the expiry of the time limit set out in Article 3.4, appoint the Referee in the shortest time possible, taking account of his technical or professional qualifications, nationality, residence, other relationships with the countries in which the parties are established or with which they are otherwise connected, and any submissions of any party concerning the choice of a Referee.

4.3. Once the Referee has been appointed, the Secretariat shall so notify the parties and shall transmit the file to him. Thereafter, all documentation from the parties must be sent directly to the Referee with a copy to the Secretariat. All documentation from the Referee to the parties must be copied to the Secretariat.

4.4. Any party may challenge a Referee appointed under Article 4.2. In such case the President, after giving the other party and the Referee an opportunity to comment, shall take within the shortest time possible a final decision as to the validity of the challenge. His decision shall be within his sole discretion and shall not itself be subject to challenge or appeal by any party.

4.5. Another person shall be appointed (a) where a Referee dies or is prevented or unable to carry out his functions, or (b) it is decided under Article 4.4. that a challenge is valid or (c) if the President decides, after giving the Referee an opportunity to comment, that he is not fulfilling his functions in accordance with the Rules or within any applicable time limit. Such an appointment shall be made in accordance with Article 4.2 (but subject to Article 4.4). In such case the new Referee shall proceed afresh.

4.6. The reasons for any decision about an appointment, challenge or replacement of any Referee shall not be disclosed.

Article 5: The proceedings

5.1. If any party has not presented an Answer by the time the file is transmitted to the Referee, the requesting party may be required by the Referee to establish to his satisfaction that a copy of the Request was received or should be treated as having been received by that party before he proceeds further. If the Referee is not so satisfied he shall notify the relevant party of its right to submit an Answer and shall set a time limit within which the Answer shall be submitted. Any such action by the Referee shall not affect the validity of his appointment.

5.2. Any decision as to the Referee's jurisdiction shall be taken by the Referee.

5.3. Within the limits of the powers conferred on him by Article 2.1 and subject to any agreement of the parties, the Referee shall conduct the proceedings in the manner which he considers appropriate for the purpose for which he was appointed including:

- considering the written documents submitted by the parties,
- informing the parties of any further investigation or inquiry that he may consider necessary,
- making such further investigation or inquiry, which may include his visiting any place where the contract is being carried out, or the premises of the parties, or any other relevant place; obtaining the report of an expert; and hearing any person he chooses in connection with the dispute, either in the presence of the parties or, if they have been duly convened, in their absence. The results of these investigations and inquiries shall be communicated to the parties for comment.

5.4. In agreeing to these Rules the parties undertake to provide the Referee with every facility to implement his terms of reference and, in particular, to make available to him all documents which he may consider necessary and also to grant free access to any place for the purpose of any investigation or inquiry. The information given to the Referee shall remain confidential between the parties and the Referee.

5.5. The Referee may convene the parties to appear before him within the shortest time limit possible on a date and at a place fixed by him.

5.6. If one of the parties fails to make a submission or to comment or appear as required by the Referee, and the Referee is satisfied that the party concerned has received or should have received the relevant communication, he may nonetheless continue with the proceedings and may make his Order.

Article 6: The Order

6.1. The decisions taken by the Referee shall be sent by him to the Secretariat in the form of an Order giving reasons.

6.2. The Referee shall make and send the Order within 30 days from the date on which the file was transmitted to him. This time limit may be extended by the President upon a reasoned request from the Referee or on his own initiative if he thinks it is necessary to do so.

6.3. The Referee's Order does not pre-judge the substance of the case, nor shall it bind any Competent Authority, which may hear any question, issue or dispute in respect of which the Order has been made. The Order of the Referee shall however remain in force unless and until the Referee or the Competent Authority has decided otherwise.

6.4. The Referee may make the carrying out of his Order subject to such conditions as he thinks fit including (a) that a party shall commence proceedings before the Competent Authority on the substance of the case within a specified period, (b) that a party for whose benefit an Order is made shall provide adequate security.

6.5. The Secretariat shall notify the parties of the Order of the Referee provided it has received the full amount of the advance on costs fixed by the Secretariat. Only Orders so notified are binding upon the parties.

6.6. The parties agree to carry out the Referee's Order without delay and waive their right to all means of appeal or recourse or opposition to a request to a court or to any other authority to implement the Order, insofar as such waiver can validly be made.

6.7. Unless otherwise agreed between the parties and subject to any mandatory order, any submissions, communications or documents (other than the Order) established or made solely for the purposes of the Pre-Arbitral Referee Procedure shall be confidential and shall not be given to the Competent Authority.

6.8. The Referee shall not be obliged to explain or give further additional reasons for any Order after it has been notified by the Secretariat under Article 6.5. Neither the ICC nor any of its employees or persons acting as President or Vice-President, nor any person acting as Referee shall be liable to any person for any loss or damage arising out of any act or omission in connection with the Rules, except that the Referee may be liable for the consequences of conscious and deliberate wrongdoing.

6.8.1. The Competent Authority may determine whether any party that refuses or fails to carry out an Order of the Referee is liable to any other party for loss or damage caused by such refusal or failure.

6.8.2. The Competent Authority may determine whether a party that requested the Referee to issue an Order, the carrying out of which caused damage to another party, is liable to such other party.

Article 7: Costs

7.1. The costs of the Pre-Arbitral Referee Procedure comprise: (a) an administrative charge as set out in the Appendix to these Rules, (b) the fees and expenses of the Referee to be determined as set out in the Appendix and (c) the costs of any expert. The Referee's Order shall state who shall bear the costs of the Pre-Arbitral Referee Procedure and in what proportion. A party that made an advance or other payment in respect of costs for which it was not liable under the Referee's Order shall be entitled to recover the amount paid from the party that ought to have made the payment.

7.2. The costs of and payment for any procedure under these Rules are as set out in the Appendix hereto.

APPENDIX: COSTS AND PAYMENT FOR A PRE-ARBITRAL REFEREE PROCEDURE

A. Costs

1. An administrative charge of US$ 2,500 is payable by the requesting party in respect of each Request made to the ICC to appoint a Referee or to administer a Pre-Arbitral Referee Procedure.

The charge covers all services rendered by the ICC that may be required by the Rules, but not any services required by alterations to or extensions of the Pre-Arbitral Referee Procedure. The administrative charge is not refundable and becomes the property of the ICC.

2. The amount of the fees and expenses of the Referee shall be fixed by the Secretary General of the ICC International Court of Arbitration. The amount shall be reasonable, taking into consideration the time spent, the complexity of the matter and any other relevant circumstances.

3. The costs of the procedure shall also include any fees and expenses of any expert.

B. Payment

1. The amount required to open the file (Article 3.2.1 of the Rules) is US$ 5,000, of which US$ 2,500 constitutes the administrative charge as set out above and US$ 2,500 constitutes an advance on the fees and expenses of the Referee and any expert. No Request for the appointment of a Referee or for the administration of an ICC Pre-Arbitral Referee Procedure will be entertained unless accompanied by this amount.

2. As soon as possible after the file has been sent to the Referee and after such consultation as is possible with the Referee and the parties, the Secretariat shall fix an advance on costs to cover the estimated costs of the Pre-Arbitral Referee Procedure (Article 7.1 of the Rules). Such advance on costs is subject to readjustment by the Secretariat.

The requesting party shall pay the whole of this advance on costs, except insofar as the Secretariat may request the other party or parties to contribute to the advance on costs in the light of any request for an Order by the Referee which any other party may have made.

3. No Order of the Referee shall be notified by the Secretariat or be valid unless the advance on costs has been received (Article 6.5 of the Rules). Where two or more parties have been asked to contribute to the advance on costs and have not paid their contribution, only the Order requested by the party or parties that have fully paid the advance or contribution shall be notified and be valid.

International Chamber of Commerce
International Court of Arbitration
33-43 avenue du Président Wilson, 75116 Paris, France
Tel +33 1 49 53 29 05
Fax +33 1 49 53 29 33
Email arb@iccwbo.org
www.iccarbitration.org

APPENDIX 22

PRE-ARBITRAL REFEREE'S STATEMENT OF ACCEPTANCE, AVAILABILITY AND INDEPENDENCE

ICC RULES FOR A PRE-ARBITRAL REFEREE PROCEDURE

Case No.: __________

Family Name(s): ____________________ Given Name(s): ________________________

Please tick all relevant boxes.

1. ACCEPTANCE

Acceptance

☐ I agree to serve as referee under and in accordance with the ICC Rules for a Pre-arbitral Referee Procedure ("Rules"). I confirm that I am familiar with the requirements of the Rules, and am able and available to serve as a referee in accordance with all of the requirements of those Rules. I accept that my fees and expenses will be fixed exclusively in accordance with the Rules.

Non-acceptance

☐ I decline to serve as referee in this case. *(If you tick here, simply date and sign the form without completing any other sections.)*

2. AVAILABILITY

☐ I confirm, on the basis of the information presently available to me, that I can devote the time necessary to conduct this procedure diligently, efficiently and in accordance with the time limit in the Rules, subject to any extension granted by the Chairman pursuant to Article 6(2) of the Rules. I understand that it is important to complete the procedure as promptly as reasonably practicable and that the Chairman will consider the duration and conduct of the proceedings when fixing my fees (Article A.2 of the Appendix to the Rules). My <u>current</u> professional engagements are as below for the information of the Secretariat and the parties.

Principal professional activity *(e.g. lawyer, arbitrator, academic):*

____

Number of currently pending cases in which I am involved *(i.e. dispute resolution procedures and activities pending now, not previous experience; additional details you wish to make known to the Secretariat and to the parties in relation to these matters can be provided on a separate sheet):*

	As referee	As counsel
Out of Court dispute resolution procedures		
Court litigation	*Not applicable*	

Furthermore, I am aware of commitments which might preclude me from devoting time to this arbitration during the following periods *(please provide details regarding such periods below or on a separate sheet):*

3. INDEPENDENCE *(Tick one box and provide detailed information, if necessary.)*

In deciding which box to tick, you should take into account whether there exists any past or present relationship, direct or indirect, between you and any of the parties, their related entities or their lawyers or other representatives, whether financial, professional or of any other kind. Any doubt must be resolved in favour of disclosure. Any disclosure should be complete and specific, identifying inter alia relevant dates (both start and end dates), financial arrangements, details of companies and individuals, and all other relevant information.

☐ Nothing to disclose: I am independent and intend to remain so. To the best of my knowledge, and having made due enquiry, there are no facts or circumstances, past or present, that I should disclose because they might be of such a nature as to call into question my independence in the eyes of any of the parties.

☐ Acceptance with disclosure: I am independent and intend to remain so. However, mindful of my obligation to disclose any facts or circumstances which might be of such a nature as to call into question my independence in the eyes of any of the parties, I draw attention to the matters on the attached sheet.

Date: ______________ Signature: ______________________________________

Disclaimer: The information requested in this form will be considered by the ICC for its Dispute Resolution Services, and will be stored in case management database systems. Pursuant to the French Law on "Informatique et Libertés" of 6 January 1978, particularly Articles 32 and 40, you may access this information and ask for rectification by writing to the Court's Secretariat.

APPENDIX 23

ICC MEDIATION RULES (1 JANUARY 2014)

ICC MEDIATION RULES

In force as from 1 January 2014

Article 1. Introductory Provisions

1. The Mediation Rules (the 'Rules') of the International Chamber of Commerce (the 'ICC') are administered by the ICC International Centre for ADR (the 'Centre'), which is a separate administrative body within the ICC.

2. The Rules provide for the appointment of a neutral third party (the 'Mediator') to assist the parties in settling their dispute.

3. Mediation shall be used under the Rules unless, prior to the confirmation or appointment of the Mediator or with the agreement of the Mediator, the parties agree upon a different settlement procedure or a combination of settlement procedures. The term 'mediation' as used in the Rules shall be deemed to cover such settlement procedure or procedures and the term 'Mediator' shall be deemed to cover the neutral who conducts such settlement procedure or procedures. Whatever settlement procedure is used, the term 'Proceedings' as used in the Rules refers to the process beginning with its commencement and ending with its termination pursuant to the Rules.

4. All of the parties may agree to modify any of the provisions of the Rules, provided, however, that the Centre may decide not to administer the Proceedings if, in its discretion, it considers that any such modification is not in the spirit of the Rules. At any time after the confirmation or appointment of the Mediator, any agreement to modify the provisions of the Rules shall also be subject to the approval of the Mediator.

5. The Centre is the only body authorized to administer Proceedings under the Rules.

Article 2. Commencement Where there is an Agreement to Refer to the Rules

1. Where there is an agreement between the parties to refer their dispute to the Rules, any party or parties wishing to commence mediation pursuant to the Rules shall file a written Request for Mediation (the 'Request') with the Centre. The Request shall include:

a) the names, addresses, telephone numbers, email addresses and any other contact details of the parties to the dispute and of any person(s) representing the parties in the Proceedings;
b) a description of the dispute including, if possible, an assessment of its value;
c) any agreement to use a settlement procedure other than mediation, or, in the absence thereof, any proposal for such other settlement procedure that the party filing the Request may wish to make;
d) any agreement as to time limits for conducting the mediation, or, in the absence thereof, any proposal with respect thereto;
e) any agreement as to the language(s) of the mediation, or, in the absence thereof, any proposal as to such language(s);
f) any agreement as to the location of any physical meetings, or, in the absence thereof, any proposal as to such location;
g) any joint nomination by all of the parties of a Mediator or any agreement of all of the parties as to the attributes of a Mediator to be appointed by the Centre where no joint nomination has been made, or, in the absence of any such agreement, any proposal as to the attributes of a Mediator;
h) a copy of any written agreement under which the Request is made.

2. Together with the Request, the party or parties filing the Request shall pay the filing fee required by the Appendix hereto in force on the date the Request is filed.

3. The party or parties filing the Request shall simultaneously send a copy of the Request to all other parties, unless the Request has been filed jointly by all parties.

4. The Centre shall acknowledge receipt of the Request and of the filing fee in writing to the parties.

5. Where there is an agreement to refer to the Rules, the date on which the Request is received by the Centre shall, for all purposes, be deemed to be the date of the commencement of the Proceedings.

6. Where the parties have agreed that a time limit for settling the dispute pursuant to the Rules shall start running from the filing of a Request, such filing, for the exclusive purpose of determining the starting point of the time limit, shall be deemed to have been made on the date the Centre acknowledges receipt of the Request or of the filing fee, whichever is later.

Article 3. Commencement Where there is No Prior Agreement to Refer to the Rules

1. In the absence of an agreement of the parties to refer their dispute to the Rules, any party that wishes to propose referring the dispute to the Rules to another party may do so by sending a written Request to the Centre containing the information specified in Article 2(1), subparagraphs a)-g). Upon receipt of such Request, the Centre will inform all other parties of the proposal and may assist the parties in considering the proposal.

2. Together with the Request, the party or parties filing the Request shall pay the filing fee required by the Appendix hereto in force on the date the Request is filed.

3. Where the parties reach an agreement to refer their dispute to the Rules, the Proceedings shall commence on the date on which the Centre sends written confirmation to the parties that such an agreement has been reached.

4. Where the parties do not reach an agreement to refer their dispute to the Rules within 15 days from the date of the receipt of the Request by the Centre or within such additional time as may be reasonably determined by the Centre, the Proceedings shall not commence.

Article 4. Place and Language(s) of the Mediation

1. In the absence of an agreement of the parties, the Centre may determine the location of any physical meeting of the Mediator and the parties or may invite the Mediator to do so after the Mediator has been confirmed or appointed.

2. In the absence of an agreement of the parties, the Centre may determine the language(s) in which the mediation shall be conducted or may invite the Mediator to do so after the Mediator has been confirmed or appointed.

Article 5. Selection of the Mediator

1. The parties may jointly nominate a Mediator for confirmation by the Centre.

2. In the absence of a joint nomination of a Mediator by the parties, the Centre shall, after consulting the parties, either appoint a Mediator or propose a list of Mediators to the parties. All of the parties may jointly nominate a Mediator from the said list for confirmation by the Centre, failing which the Centre shall appoint a Mediator.

3. Before appointment or confirmation, a prospective Mediator shall sign a statement of acceptance, availability, impartiality and independence. The prospective Mediator shall disclose in writing to the Centre any facts or circumstances which might be of such a nature as to call into question the Mediator's independence in the eyes of the parties, as well as any circumstances that could give rise to reasonable doubts as to the Mediator's impartiality. The Centre shall provide such information to the parties in writing and shall fix a time limit for any comments from them.

4. When confirming or appointing a Mediator, the Centre shall consider the prospective Mediator's attributes, including but not limited to nationality, language skills, training, qualifications and experience, and the prospective Mediator's availability and ability to conduct the mediation in accordance with the Rules.

5. Where the Centre appoints a Mediator, it shall do so either on the basis of a proposal by an ICC National Committee or Group, or otherwise. The Centre shall make all reasonable efforts to appoint a Mediator having the attributes, if any, which have been agreed upon by all of the parties. If any party objects to the Mediator appointed by the Centre and notifies the Centre and all other parties in writing, stating the reasons for such objection, within 15 days of receipt of notification of the appointment, the Centre shall appoint another Mediator.

6. Upon agreement of all of the parties, the parties may nominate more than one Mediator or request the Centre to appoint more than one Mediator, in accordance with the provisions of the Rules. In appropriate circumstances, the Centre may propose to the parties that there be more than one Mediator.

Article 6. Fees and Costs

1. The party or parties filing a Request shall include with the Request the non-refundable filing fee required by Article 2(2) or Article 3(2) of the Rules, as set out

in the Appendix hereto. No Request shall be processed unless accompanied by the filing fee.

2. Following the receipt of a Request pursuant to Article 3, the Centre may request that the party filing the Request pay a deposit to cover the administrative expenses of the Centre.

3. Following the commencement of the Proceedings, the Centre shall request the parties to pay one or more deposits to cover the administrative expenses of the Centre and the fees and expenses of the Mediator, as set out in the Appendix hereto.

4. The Centre may stay or terminate the Proceedings under the Rules if any requested deposit is not paid.

5. Upon termination of the Proceedings, the Centre shall fix the total costs of the Proceedings and shall, as the case may be, reimburse the parties for any excess payment or bill the parties for any balance required pursuant to the Rules.

6. With respect to Proceedings that have commenced under the Rules, all deposits requested and costs fixed shall be borne in equal shares by the parties, unless they agree otherwise in writing. However, any party shall be free to pay the unpaid balance of such deposits and costs should another party fail to pay its share.

7. A party's other expenditure shall remain the responsibility of that party, unless otherwise agreed by the parties.

Article 7. Conduct of the Mediation

1. The Mediator and the parties shall promptly discuss the manner in which the mediation shall be conducted.

2. After such discussion, the Mediator shall promptly provide the parties with a written note informing them of the manner in which the mediation shall be conducted. Each party, by agreeing to refer a dispute to the Rules, agrees to participate in the Proceedings at least until receipt of such note from the Mediator or earlier termination of the Proceedings pursuant to Article 8(1) of the Rules.

3. In establishing and conducting the mediation, the Mediator shall be guided by the wishes of the parties and shall treat them with fairness and impartiality.

4. Each party shall act in good faith throughout the mediation.

Article 8. Termination of the Proceedings

1. Proceedings which have been commenced pursuant to the Rules shall terminate upon written confirmation of termination by the Centre to the parties after the occurrence of the earliest of:

a) the signing by the parties of a settlement agreement;
b) the notification in writing made to the Mediator by any party, at any time after it has received the Mediator's note referred to in Article 7(2), that such party has decided no longer to pursue the mediation;
c) the notification in writing by the Mediator to the parties that the mediation has been completed;
d) the notification in writing by the Mediator to the parties that, in the Mediator's opinion, the mediation will not resolve the dispute between the parties;

e) the notification in writing by the Centre to the parties that any time limit set for the Proceedings, including any extension thereof, has expired;
f) the notification in writing by the Centre to the parties, not less than seven days after the due date for any payment by one or more parties pursuant to the Rules, that such payment has not been made; or
g) the notification in writing by the Centre to the parties that, in the judgment of the Centre, there has been a failure to nominate a Mediator or that it has not been reasonably possible to appoint a Mediator.

2. The Mediator shall promptly notify the Centre of the signing of a settlement agreement by the parties or of any notification given to or by the Mediator pursuant to Article 8(1), subparagraphs b)-d), and shall provide the Centre with a copy of any such notification.

Article 9. Confidentiality

1. In the absence of any agreement of the parties to the contrary and unless prohibited by applicable law:
   a) the Proceedings, but not the fact that they are taking place, have taken place or will take place, are private and confidential;
   b) any settlement agreement between the parties shall be kept confidential, except that a party shall have the right to disclose it to the extent that such disclosure is required by applicable law or necessary for purposes of its implementation or enforcement.

2. Unless required to do so by applicable law and in the absence of any agreement of the parties to the contrary, a party shall not in any manner produce as evidence in any judicial, arbitral or similar proceedings:
   a) any documents, statements or communications which are submitted by another party or by the Mediator in or for the Proceedings, unless they can be obtained independently by the party seeking to produce them in the judicial, arbitral or similar proceedings;
   b) any views expressed or suggestions made by any party within the Proceedings with regard to the dispute or the possible settlement of the dispute;
   c) any admissions made by another party within the Proceedings;
   d) any views or proposals put forward by the Mediator within the Proceedings; or
   e) the fact that any party indicated within the Proceedings that it was ready to accept a proposal for a settlement.

Article 10. General Provisions

1. Where, prior to the date of the entry into force of the Rules, the parties have agreed to refer their dispute to the ICC ADR Rules, they shall be deemed to have referred their dispute to the ICC Mediation Rules, unless any of the parties objects thereto, in which case the ICC ADR Rules shall apply.

2. Unless all of the parties have agreed otherwise in writing or unless prohibited by applicable law, the parties may commence or continue any judicial, arbitral or similar proceedings in respect of the dispute, notwithstanding the Proceedings under the Rules.

3. Unless all of the parties agree otherwise in writing, a Mediator shall not act nor shall have acted in any judicial, arbitral or similar proceedings relating to the dispute

which is or was the subject of the Proceedings under the Rules, whether as a judge, an arbitrator, an expert or a representative or advisor of a party.

4. Unless required by applicable law or unless all of the parties and the Mediator agree otherwise in writing, the Mediator shall not give testimony in any judicial, arbitral or similar proceedings concerning any aspect of the Proceedings under the Rules.

5. The Mediator, the Centre, the ICC and its employees, the ICC National Committees and Groups and their employees and representatives shall not be liable to any person for any act or omission in connection with the Proceedings, except to the extent such limitation of liability is prohibited by applicable law.

6. In all matters not expressly provided for in the Rules, the Centre and the Mediator shall act in the spirit of the Rules.

APPENDIX – FEES AND COSTS

Article 1. Filing Fee

Each Request pursuant to the Rules must be accompanied by a filing fee of US$ 2,000. The filing fee is non-refundable and shall be credited towards the deposit of the party or parties having filed the Request.

Article 2. Administrative Expenses

1. The administrative expenses of the ICC for the proceedings shall be fixed at the Centre's discretion depending on the tasks carried out by the Centre and shall normally not exceed the following:

- US$ 5,000 for amounts in dispute up to and including US$ 200,000;
- US$ 10,000 for amounts in dispute between US$200,001 and US$ 2,000,000;
- US$ 15,000 for amounts in dispute between US$ 2,000,001 and US$ 10,000,000;
- US$ 20,000 for amounts in dispute between US$ 10,000,001 and US$ 50,000,000;
- US$ 25,000 for amounts in dispute between US$ 50,000,001 and US$ 100,000,000;
- US$ 30,000 for amounts in dispute over US$ 100,000,000.

2. Where the amount in dispute is not stated, the administrative expenses may be fixed by the Centre at its discretion, taking into account all the circumstances of the case, including indications regarding the value of the dispute, but they shall normally not exceed US$ 20,000.

3. In exceptional circumstances, the Centre may fix the administrative expenses at a higher figure than that which would result from the application of the above scale, provided that the Centre shall inform the parties of such possibility beforehand and shall normally not exceed the maximum amount for administrative expenses foreseen in the scale.

4. The Centre may require the payment of administrative expenses in addition to those provided in the scale described in Article 2(1) of this Appendix as a condition for holding the proceedings in abeyance at the request of the parties or of one of them with

the acquiescence of the other. Such abeyance fee shall normally not exceed US$ 1,000 per party per year.

Article 3. Mediator's Fees and Expenses

1. Unless otherwise agreed by the parties and the Mediator, the fees of the Mediator shall be calculated on the basis of the time reasonably spent by the Mediator in the proceedings. These fees shall be based on an hourly rate fixed by the Centre when appointing or confirming the Mediator and after having consulted the Mediator and the parties. The hourly rate shall be reasonable in amount and shall be determined in light of the complexity of the dispute and any other relevant circumstances.

2. If agreed by the parties and the Mediator, the Centre may fix the Mediator's fees on the basis of a single fixed fee for the whole proceedings, rather than an hourly rate. The single fixed fee shall be reasonable in amount and shall be determined in light of the complexity of the dispute, the amount of work that the parties and the Mediator anticipate will be required of the Mediator, and any other relevant circumstances. The Centre, at its discretion, may increase or decrease the amount of the single fixed fee based upon a reasoned request of a party or the Mediator. Prior to increasing or decreasing the single fixed fee, the Centre shall invite observations from all parties and the Mediator.

3. The amount of reasonable expenses of the Mediator shall be fixed by the Centre.

4. The Mediator's fees and expenses shall be fixed exclusively by the Centre as required by the Rules. Separate fee arrangements between the parties and the Mediator are not permitted by the Rules.

Article 4. Prior ICC Arbitration

When a mediation is preceded by the submission of a request for arbitration pursuant to the ICC Rules of Arbitration concerning the same parties and the same or parts of the same dispute, the filing fee paid for such arbitration proceedings shall be credited to the administrative expenses of the mediation, if the total administrative expenses paid with respect to the arbitration exceed US$ 7,500.

Article 5. Currency, VAT and Scope

1. All amounts fixed by the Centre or pursuant to any Appendix to the Rules are payable in US$ except where prohibited by law, in which case the ICC may apply a different scale and fee arrangement in another currency.

2. Amounts paid to the Mediator do not include any possible value added tax (VAT) or other taxes or charges and imposts applicable to the Mediator's fees. Parties have a duty to pay any such taxes or charges; however, the recovery of any such taxes or charges is a matter solely between the Mediator and the parties.

3. Any ICC administrative expenses may be subject to value added tax (VAT) or charges of a similar nature at the prevailing rate.

4. The above provisions on the costs of proceedings shall be effective as of 1 January 2014 in respect of all proceedings commenced on or after such date under the present Rules or the ICC ADR Rules.

Article 6. ICC as Appointing Authority

Any request received for an authority of the ICC to appoint a Mediator will be treated in accordance with the ICC Rules for Appointment of Experts or Neutrals and shall be accompanied by a non-refundable filing fee of US$ 2,000 per Mediator. No request shall be processed unless accompanied by the said filing fee. For additional services, the ICC may at its discretion fix ICC administrative expenses, which shall be commensurate with the services provided and shall normally not exceed the maximum amount of US$ 10,000.

APPENDIX 24

ICC MEDIATION CLAUSES (2014)

MEDIATION RULES – ICC MEDIATION CLAUSES

Parties wishing to use proceedings under the ICC Mediation Rules should consider choosing one of the clauses below, which cover different situations and needs. Parties are free to adapt the chosen clause to their particular circumstances. For instance, they may wish to specify the use of a settlement procedure other than mediation. Further, they may wish to stipulate the language and place of any mediation and/or arbitration proceedings.

The notes below each clause are intended to help parties select the clause that best meets their specific requirements.

At all times, care must be taken to avoid any risk of ambiguity in the drafting of the clause. Unclear wording causes uncertainty and delay and can hinder or even compromise the dispute resolution process.

When incorporating any of these clauses in their contracts, parties are advised to take account of any factors that may affect their enforceability under applicable law.

Clause A: Option to Use the ICC Mediation Rules

The parties may at any time, without prejudice to any other proceedings, seek to settle any dispute arising out of or in connection with the present contract in accordance with the ICC Mediation Rules.

Notes: By including this clause, the parties acknowledge that proceedings under the ICC Mediation Rules are available to them at any time. This clause does not commit the parties to do anything, but the presence of the clause is designed to remind them of the possibility of using mediation or some other settlement procedure at any time. In addition, it can provide a basis for one party to propose mediation to the other party. One or more parties may also ask the ICC International Centre for ADR for its assistance in this process.

Clause B: Obligation to Consider the ICC Mediation Rules

In the event of any dispute arising out of or in connection with the present contract, the parties agree in the first instance to discuss and consider referring the dispute to the ICC Mediation Rules.

Notes: This clause goes a step further than Clause A and requires the parties, when a dispute arises, to discuss and consider together referring the dispute to proceedings under the ICC Mediation Rules. One or more parties may ask the ICC International Centre for ADR for its assistance in this process.

This clause may be appropriate where the parties do not wish to commit to referring a dispute to proceedings under the Rules at the outset but prefer to retain flexibility as to whether to use mediation to try and settle a dispute.

Clause C: Obligation to Refer Dispute to the ICC Mediation Rules While Permitting Parallel Arbitration Proceedings if Required

(x) In the event of any dispute arising out of or in connection with the present contract, the parties shall first refer the dispute to proceedings under the ICC Mediation Rules. The commencement of proceedings under the ICC Mediation Rules shall not prevent any party from commencing arbitration in accordance with sub-clause y below.

(y) All disputes arising out of or in connection with the present contract shall be finally settled under the Rules of Arbitration of the International Chamber of Commerce by one or more arbitrators appointed in accordance with the said Rules.

Notes: This clause creates an obligation to refer a dispute to proceedings under the ICC Mediation Rules. It is designed to ensure that when a dispute arises, the parties will attempt to settle the dispute using proceedings under the Rules.

The clause also makes it clear that the parties do not need to conclude the proceedings under the ICC Mediation Rules, or wait for an agreed period of time, before commencing arbitration proceedings. This is also the default position under Article 10(2) of the Rules.

The clause provides for ICC arbitration as the forum for final determination of the dispute. If desired, the clause can be adapted to provide instead for a different form of arbitration, or for judicial or other similar proceedings.

Clause D: Obligation to Refer Dispute to the ICC Mediation Rules, Followed by Arbitration if Required

In the event of any dispute arising out of or in connection with the present contract, the parties shall first refer the dispute to proceedings under the ICC Mediation Rules. If the dispute has not been settled pursuant to the said Rules within [45] days following the filing of a Request for Mediation or within such other period as the parties may agree in writing, such dispute shall thereafter be finally settled under the Rules of Arbitration of the International Chamber of Commerce by one or more arbitrators appointed in accordance with the said Rules of Arbitration.

Notes: Like Clause C, this clause creates an obligation to refer a dispute to proceedings under the ICC Mediation Rules.

Unlike Clause C, this clause provides that arbitration proceedings may not be commenced until an agreed period has elapsed following the filing of a Request for Mediation. The lapse of time suggested in the model clause is 45 days, but parties should select a period that they consider to be appropriate for the contract in question.

Clause D changes the default position under Article 10(2) of the ICC Mediation Rules allowing judicial, arbitral or similar proceedings to be commenced in parallel with proceedings under the ICC Mediation Rules.

Like Clause C, Clause D provides for ICC arbitration as the forum for final determination of the dispute. If desired, the clause can be adapted to provide instead for a different form of arbitration, or for judicial or other similar proceedings.

Specific Issues Concerning the Emergency Arbitrator Provisions

The parties should determine whether they wish to have recourse to the Emergency Arbitrator Provisions under Clauses C and D.

Clauses C and D

If the parties wish to exclude any recourse to the Emergency Arbitrator Provisions, the following wording should be added to Clause C or D as applicable:

> *The Emergency Arbitrator Provisions shall not apply.*

Clause D

1. If the parties wish to have recourse to the Emergency Arbitrator Provisions, and want that recourse expressly to be available prior to expiry of the 45-day or other agreed period following filing of the Request for Mediation, the following wording should be added to Clause D:

> *The requirement to wait [45] days, or any other agreed period, following the filing of a Request for Mediation, before referring a dispute to arbitration shall not prevent the parties from making an application, prior to expiry of those [45] days or other agreed period, for Emergency Measures under the Emergency Arbitrator Provisions in the Rules of Arbitration of the International Chamber of Commerce.*

2. If the parties wish to have recourse to the Emergency Arbitrator Provisions, but only after expiry of the 45-day or other agreed period following filing of the Request for Mediation, the following wording should be added to Clause D:

> *The parties shall not have the right to make an application for Emergency Measures under the Emergency Arbitrator Provisions in the Rules of Arbitration of the International Chamber of Commerce prior to expiry of the [45] days or other agreed period following the filing of a Request for Mediation.*

APPENDIX 25

ICC EXPERT RULES (1 FEBRUARY 2015)

ICC RULES FOR THE PROPOSAL OF EXPERTS AND NEUTRALS

In force as from 1 February 2015

Preamble

The ICC Rules for the Proposal of Experts and Neutrals (the "Rules") are administered by the ICC International Centre for ADR (the "Centre"), which is a separate administrative body within the International Chamber of Commerce (the "ICC"). In administering the Rules, the Centre is assisted by a Standing Committee, the statutes of which are set forth in Appendix I.

Upon the request of any physical or legal person(s) or any court or tribunal (the "Person"), the Centre can provide the name of one or more experts in a particular field of activity or the name of one or more neutrals. An expert proposed under the Rules may be a physical person or a legal person, such as a company or a partnership.

Under the Rules, the Centre's role is limited to proposing the name of one or more experts or neutrals. The Person requesting a proposal may then contact directly the proposed expert(s) or neutral(s) and, as the case may be, agree with such expert(s) or neutral(s) on the scope of the appropriate mission and fees. There is no obligation to make use of the services of an expert or a neutral proposed by the Centre.

The proposal of an expert may be useful in many different contexts. A person may require an expert in connection with its ongoing business activities or in connection with contractual relations. A party to an arbitration or other contentious process may wish to obtain the name of a potential expert witness. A court or arbitral tribunal that has decided to appoint an expert may wish to obtain the proposal of an expert.

The proposal of a neutral may be useful to parties who wish to use the services of a neutral as a mediator or a dispute board member, or to assist them with the resolution of a dispute in a similar procedure that is not administered by the ICC.

Article 1. Recourse to the Centre

1. Any Person may ask the Centre to propose one or more experts or neutrals by submitting a request for the proposal of an expert or a neutral (the "Request for Proposal") to the Centre.

---

2. The Request for Proposal shall include:
   a) the name, address, telephone number, email address and any other contact details of each Person filing the Request for Proposal;
   b) if applicable, the name and contact details of any person or entity relevant for checking potential conflicts of interest of the expert or neutral;
   c) when the Request for Proposal is for an expert:
      (i) a description of the field of activity of the expert to be proposed;
      (ii) any desired attributes of the expert, including but not limited to education, qualifications, language skills and professional experience;
      (iii) any undesired attributes of the expert and a description of any matters that would disqualify a potential expert;
      (iv) a detailed description of the work to be carried out by the expert, including whether an expert report or site visits will be required;
      (v) the desired time frame for completing such work;
      (vi) the language(s) in which the expert is to carry out such work; and
      (vii) the proposed location of any physical meetings with the expert;
   d) when the Request for Proposal is for a neutral:
      (i) a description of the dispute resolution or other procedure for which the neutral's assistance is sought;
      (ii) a description of the dispute, if any;
      (iii) any desired attributes of the neutral, including but not limited to education, qualifications, language skills and professional experience;
      (iv) any undesired attributes of the neutral and a description of any matters which would disqualify a potential neutral;
      (v) the desired time frame for conducting and completing the procedure;
      (vi) the agreed location of any physical meetings with the neutral, or any proposal regarding such location; and
      (vii) the agreed language(s) of the procedure, or any proposal regarding such language.

3. Unless requested to do so by the Person seeking the proposal of an expert or a neutral, the Centre will not inform any other person of the filing of a Request for Proposal except as needed in order to find the prospective expert or neutral.

Article 2. The Proposal

1. Any proposal of an expert or a neutral by the Centre shall be made by the Centre either through an ICC National Committee or Group, or otherwise. The Centre's role under the Rules ends upon the notification of the proposal.

2. The Centre shall make all reasonable efforts to propose an expert or a neutral having the attributes set out by the requesting party pursuant to Article 1(2). If, despite such efforts, the Centre is not able to identify an expert or neutral having all of the attributes set out by the requesting party, the Centre may ask the requesting party whether it wishes the Centre to propose more than one expert or a neutral (who between them have the requested attributes), or whether the attributes set out in the Request for Proposal may be modified.

3. Before a proposal is made, a prospective expert or neutral shall sign a statement of acceptance, availability, impartiality and independence. The prospective expert or neutral shall disclose in writing to the Centre any facts or circumstances which might

be of such a nature as to call into question the expert's or neutral's independence in the eyes of the Person filing the Request for Proposal, as well as any circumstances that could give rise to reasonable doubts as to the expert's or neutral's impartiality. The Centre shall provide such information in writing to such Person and shall fix a time limit for any comments from such Person.

4. Any information or documents given to the prospective expert or neutral by the Centre or any party in connection with the proposal shall be used by the prospective expert or neutral only for the purposes of the proposal and shall be treated by the prospective expert or neutral as confidential.

Article 3. Costs for the Proposal

1. Each Request for Proposal must be accompanied by the non-refundable filing fee specified in Article 1 of Appendix II. No Request for Proposal shall be processed unless accompanied by the filing fee.

2. When the Centre is requested to propose more than one expert or more than one neutral, the non-refundable filing fee accompanying the Request for Proposal and to be paid by the requesting Person is the amount referred to in the preceding paragraph multiplied by the number of experts or neutrals requested.

3. After taking into consideration the specificities of the case, the Centre may fix an additional fee, as specified in Article 2 of Appendix II, to be paid by the party or parties having filed the Request for Proposal.

4. The Centre may cease acting if any requested additional fee has not been paid.

Article 4. General Provisions

1. An expert proposed under the Rules may be a physical person or a legal person, such as a company or a partnership. The term "expert" as used in the Rules applies *mutatis mutandis* to both physical and legal persons.

2. Where, prior to the date of the entry into force of the Rules, the parties have agreed to request the proposal of an expert or a neutral pursuant to the Rules for Expertise of the ICC, they shall be deemed to have agreed to make their request pursuant to the ICC Rules for the Proposal of Experts and Neutrals, unless any of the parties objects thereto, in which case the Rules for Expertise of the ICC shall apply.

3. The expert or neutral, the Centre, the ICC and its employees, and the ICC National Committees and Groups and their employees and representatives shall not be liable to any person for any act or omission in connection with the proposal of an expert or a neutral, except to the extent such limitation of liability is prohibited by applicable law.

4. In all matters not expressly provided for in the Rules, the Centre shall act in the spirit of the Rules.

ICC RULES FOR THE PROPOSAL OF EXPERTS AND NEUTRALS APPENDIX I – STATUTES OF THE STANDING COMMITTEE

Article 1. Composition of the Standing Committee

The Standing Committee is composed of a maximum of fifteen members (a president, three vice-presidents and up to eleven other members) appointed by the ICC for a three-year renewable term.

Article 2. Meetings

A meeting of the Standing Committee shall be convened by its president whenever necessary.

Article 3. Function and Duties of the Standing Committee

1. The Standing Committee shall advise the Centre concerning all aspects of the services carried out by the Centre pursuant to the Rules, in order to help ensure the quality of those services. It shall assist the Centre in reviewing the attributes of the experts or neutrals to be proposed under the Rules.

2. The Centre shall inform the members of the Standing Committee about all Requests for Proposal and ask the members for their advice.

3. The president shall make the final decision on the proposal of the expert or neutral.

4. In the absence of the president, or otherwise at the president's request, one of the three vice-presidents shall be authorized by the Centre to fulfil the tasks of the president, including taking decisions pursuant to these statutes.

Article 4. Confidentiality

The work of the Standing Committee and the Centre is of a confidential nature, which must be respected by everyone who participates in that work in whatever capacity.

ICC RULES FOR THE PROPOSAL OF EXPERTS AND NEUTRALS APPENDIX II – COSTS

Article 1. Filing Fee

Save as provided in Article 3 below, each Request for Proposal pursuant to the Rules must be accompanied by a filing fee of US$ 3,000 per expert or neutral to be proposed. The filing fee is non-refundable. No Request for Proposal shall be processed unless accompanied by the requisite payment.

Article 2. Additional Fee for Proposal

1. Depending on the specificities of the case, the Centre may request the payment of an additional fee from the party or parties by which the Request for Proposal has been filed.

2. When fixing the additional fee, the Centre shall take into account all circumstances of the case, including the requested attributes of the expert or neutral, the specific

nature of the case, including the amount of time needed by the Centre to identify suitable candidates, the time frame in which the Centre shall proceed with the proposal and any other relevant circumstances.

3. The additional fee shall not exceed US$ 3,000 per expert or neutral to be proposed.

Article 3. Proposal of an Expert or a Neutral in an ICC Arbitration

1. If the Request for Proposal of an expert is made by an arbitral tribunal acting pursuant to the ICC Rules of Arbitration, the services of the Centre shall be provided free of charge.

2. If the Request for Proposal of a neutral who shall act as mediator is made jointly by all the parties in ongoing proceedings pursuant to the ICC Rules of Arbitration, the services of the Centre shall be provided free of charge.

Article 4. Currency, VAT and Scope

1. All amounts fixed by the Centre or pursuant to any Appendix to the Rules are payable in US dollars except where prohibited by law, in which case the ICC may apply a different scale and fee arrangement in another currency.

2. Any ICC administrative expenses, including the filing fee and the additional fee, may be subject to value added tax (VAT) or charges of a similar nature at the prevailing rate.

3. The above provisions on the costs of proposals of experts and neutrals shall be effective as of 1 February 2015 in respect of any Request for Proposal filed on or after such date under the present Rules and in respect of any request for the proposal of an expert filed on or after such date under the Rules for Expertise of the ICC.

ICC RULES FOR THE APPOINTMENT OF EXPERTS AND NEUTRALS IN FORCE AS FROM 1 FEBRUARY 2015

Preamble

The ICC Rules for the Appointment of Experts and Neutrals (the "Rules") are administered by the ICC International Centre for ADR (the "Centre"), which is a separate administrative body within the International Chamber of Commerce (the "ICC"). In administering the Rules, the Centre is assisted by a Standing Committee, the statutes of which are set forth in Appendix I.

The Centre will appoint an expert or a neutral pursuant to the Rules in situations where the parties have agreed to use the Centre as the appointing authority or where the Centre is otherwise satisfied that there is a sufficient basis for appointing an expert or a neutral. In such cases the appointment by the Centre shall be binding on the parties. An expert appointed under the Rules may be a physical person or a legal person, such as a company or a partnership. The Centre's role is limited to the process of appointing the expert or neutral in question and the Centre does not administer any proceedings under the Rules.

There are various situations in which the parties may agree to have an expert appointed by the Centre. Experts from a broad range of specializations may be appointed. Such specializations include accounting, finance, engineering, information technology, construction, energy and law. The parties may agree to appoint an expert to give a contractually binding expert determination or to give non-binding advice. This can be in either a contentious or non-contentious context.

There are also various situations in which the parties may agree to have a neutral appointed by the Centre. An appointed neutral may serve as a mediator or dispute board member or may assist them with the resolution of a dispute in any similar procedure that is not administered by the ICC.

Article 1. Recourse to the Centre

1. Any request for the appointment of an expert or a neutral (the "Request for Appointment") shall be submitted to the Centre. Any Request for Appointment shall be processed by the Centre only when it is based upon an agreement between the parties for the appointment of an expert or a neutral by the Centre or when the Centre is otherwise satisfied that there is a sufficient basis for appointing an expert or a neutral.

2. The Request for Appointment shall include:

- a) the names, addresses, telephone numbers, email addresses and any other contact details of:
  - (i) each person filing the Request for Appointment and any other person involved in the relevant proceedings, including any other parties to the agreement for the appointment of an expert or a neutral; and
  - (ii) any person representing each person filing the Request for Appointment;
- b) if applicable, the name and contact details of any person or entity relevant for checking potential conflicts of interest of the expert or neutral;
- c) when the Request for Appointment is for an expert:
  - (i) a description of the field of activity of the expert to be appointed;
  - (ii) any desired attributes of the expert, including but not limited to education, qualifications, language skills and professional experience;
  - (iii) any undesired attributes of the expert and a description of any matters that would disqualify a potential expert;
  - (iv) a detailed description of the work to be carried out by the expert, including whether an expert report or site visits will be required;
  - (v) the desired time frame for completing such work;
  - (vi) any agreement as to the language(s) to be used by the expert or, in the absence thereof, any proposal as to such language(s);
  - (vii) any agreement as to the location of any physical meetings or, in the absence thereof, any proposal as to such location; and
  - (viii) a copy of any agreement for the appointment of an expert by the Centre and/or of any other elements which form the basis of the Request for Appointment;
- d) when the Request for Appointment is for a neutral:
  - (i) a description of the dispute resolution or other procedure for which a neutral's assistance is sought;
  - (ii) a description of the dispute, if any;
  - (iii) any desired attributes of the neutral, including but not limited to education, qualifications, language skills and professional experience;
  - (iv) any undesired attributes of the neutral and a description of any matters which would disqualify a potential neutral;
  - (v) the desired time frame for conducting and completing the procedure;

(vi) any agreement as to the language(s) to be used by the neutral or, in the absence thereof, any proposal as to such language(s);
(vii) any agreement as to the location of any physical meetings or, in the absence thereof, any proposal as to such location; and
(viii) a copy of any agreement for the appointment of a neutral by the Centre and/or of any other elements which form the basis of the Request for Appointment.

3. The Centre shall inform the other party or parties in writing of the Request for Appointment once the Centre has sufficient copies of the Request for Appointment and has received the filing fee required under Article 4.

4. When the Request for Appointment is not made jointly by all of the parties, and/or when the parties do not agree on the attributes of the expert or the neutral, and/or when the parties do not agree on the expert's work or the neutral's role, the Centre shall send a copy of the Request for Appointment to the other party or parties, who may make observations within a time limit fixed by the Centre. Observations received shall be communicated by the Centre to the other party or parties for comments within a time limit fixed by the Centre.

5. The Centre shall proceed with the Request for Appointment as it sees fit and will inform the parties of how it will proceed.

Article 2. Written Notifications or Communications

1. All written communications submitted to the Centre by any party, as well as all documents annexed thereto, shall be supplied in a number of copies sufficient to provide one copy for the Centre and one copy for each party.

2. All notifications or communications from the Centre shall be made to the last address of the party or its representative for whom the same are intended, as notified either by the party in question or by the other party. Such notification or communication may be made by delivery against receipt, registered post, courier, email or any other means of telecommunication that provides a record of the sending thereof.

3. A notification or communication shall be deemed to have been made on the day it was received by the party itself or by its representative, or would have been received if made in accordance with the preceding paragraph.

Article 3. The Appointment

1. Any appointment of an expert or a neutral by the Centre shall be made by the Centre either through an ICC National Committee or Group, or otherwise. The Centre's role under the Rules ends upon the notification of the appointment, except as provided in Article 3(5) below.

2. In confirming or appointing an expert or a neutral, the Centre shall consider the prospective expert's or neutral's nationality, residence, training and experience, and the prospective expert's or neutral's availability and ability to conduct the work to be carried out. The Centre shall make all reasonable efforts to appoint an expert or a neutral having the attributes, if any, which have been agreed upon by all of the parties. If, despite such efforts, the Centre is not able to identify an expert or a neutral having all of the attributes agreed upon by all of the parties, the Centre may ask the parties whether they wish the Centre to appoint more than one expert or neutral (who

between them have the requested attributes), or whether the attributes agreed upon by the parties may be modified.

3. Every expert or neutral must be and remain impartial and independent of the parties involved in the proceedings, if any, unless otherwise agreed in writing by such parties.

4. Before an appointment, a prospective expert or neutral shall sign a statement of acceptance, availability, impartiality and independence. The prospective expert or neutral shall disclose in writing to the Centre any facts or circumstances which might be of such a nature as to call into question the expert's or neutral's independence in the eyes of the parties, as well as any circumstances that could give rise to reasonable doubts as to the expert's or neutral's impartiality. The Centre shall provide such information to the parties in writing and shall fix a time limit for any comments from them.

5. If any party files a written objection with the Centre asserting that the expert or neutral does not have the necessary attributes, is not fulfilling the expert's or neutral's functions or is not independent or impartial, the Centre may replace the expert or neutral after having considered the observations of the expert or neutral and the other party or parties.

6. Any information or documents given to the expert or the neutral by the Centre or any party in connection with the appointment shall be used by the expert or the neutral only for the purposes of the appointment and shall be treated by the expert or the neutral as confidential.

Article 4. Costs for the Appointment

1. Each Request for Appointment must be accompanied by the non-refundable filing fee specified in Article 1 of Appendix II. No Request for Appointment shall be processed unless accompanied by the filing fee.

2. When the Centre is requested to appoint more than one expert or more than one neutral, the non-refundable filing fee accompanying the Request for Appointment and to be paid by the requesting Person is the amount referred to in the preceding paragraph multiplied by the number of experts or neutrals requested.

3. After taking into consideration the specificities of the case, the Centre may fix an additional fee, as specified in Article 2 of Appendix II, to be paid by the party or parties having filed the Request for Appointment.

4. Each written objection pursuant to Article 3(5) of the Rules must be accompanied by the non-refundable amount specified in Article 1 of Appendix II. No objection shall be processed unless accompanied by the requisite payment.

5. The Centre may cease acting if any requested additional fee or amount has not been paid.

6. When the Centre is requested to appoint an expert who has already been proposed by the Centre under the ICC Rules for the Proposal of Experts and Neutrals in connection with the same matter, the Centre shall charge a maximum of one half of the non-refundable filing fee specified in Article 1 of Appendix II in addition to the amount already paid pursuant to the ICC Rules for the Proposal of Experts and Neutrals.

Article 5. General Provisions

1. An expert appointed under the Rules may be a physical person or a legal person, such as a company or a partnership. The term "expert" as used in the Rules applies *mutatis mutandis* to both physical and legal persons.

2. Where, prior to the date of the entry into force of the Rules, the parties have agreed to the appointment of an expert or a neutral pursuant to the Rules for Expertise of the ICC, they shall be deemed to have agreed to such appointment pursuant to the ICC Rules for the Appointment of Experts and Neutrals, unless any of the parties objects thereto, in which case the Rules for Expertise of the ICC shall apply.

3. The expert or neutral, the Centre, the ICC and its employees, and the ICC National Committees and Groups and their employees and representatives shall not be liable to any person for any act or omission in connection with the appointment of an expert or a neutral, except to the extent such limitation of liability is prohibited by applicable law.

4. In all matters not expressly provided for in the Rules, the Centre shall act in the spirit of the Rules.

ICC RULES FOR THE APPOINTMENT OF EXPERTS AND NEUTRALS APPENDIX I – STATUTES OF THE STANDING COMMITTEE

Article 1. Composition of the Standing Committee

The Standing Committee is composed of a maximum of fifteen members (a president, three vice-presidents and up to eleven other members) appointed by the ICC for a three-year renewable term.

Article 2. Meetings

A meeting of the Standing Committee shall be convened by its president whenever necessary.

Article 3. Function and Duties of the Standing Committee

1. The Standing Committee shall advise the Centre concerning all aspects of the services carried out by the Centre pursuant to the Rules, in order to help ensure the quality of those services. It shall assist the Centre in reviewing the attributes of the experts or neutrals to be appointed under the Rules.

2. The Centre shall inform the members of the Standing Committee about all Requests for Appointment and ask the members for their advice.

3. The president shall make the final decision on the appointment of the expert or neutral.

4. The president will decide whether an objection is justified and shall decide on the manner in which a replacement will be made.

5. In the absence of the president, or otherwise at the president's request, one of the three vice-presidents shall be authorized by the Centre to fulfil the tasks of the president, including taking decisions pursuant to these statutes.

Article 4. Confidentiality

The work of the Standing Committee and the Centre is of a confidential nature, which must be respected by everyone who participates in that work in whatever capacity.

ICC RULES FOR THE APPOINTMENT OF EXPERTS AND NEUTRALS APPENDIX II – COSTS

Article 1. Filing Fee

Save as provided in Article 3 below, each Request for Appointment pursuant to the Rules must be accompanied by a filing fee of US$ 3,000 per expert or neutral to be appointed. The filing fee is non-refundable. No Request for Appointment shall be processed unless accompanied by the requisite payment.

Article 2. Additional Fee for Appointment

1. Depending on the specificities of the case, the Centre may request the payment of an additional fee from the party or parties having filed the Request for Appointment.

2. When fixing the additional fee, the Centre shall take into account all circumstances of the case, including the requested attributes of the expert or neutral to be appointed, the specific nature of the case, including the amount of time needed by the Centre to identify suitable candidates, the time frame in which the Centre shall proceed with the appointment and any other relevant circumstances.

3. The additional fee shall not exceed US$ 3,000 per expert or neutral to be appointed.

Article 3. Appointment of a Neutral to act as Mediator

If the appointment of a neutral who shall act as a mediator is made at the joint request of all of the parties in ongoing proceedings pursuant to the ICC Rules of Arbitration, the appointment of the neutral shall be free of charge.

Article 4. Additional Costs for Objection and Replacement

Each written objection to the appointment of an expert or a neutral by the Centre pursuant to Article 3(5) of the Rules shall be accompanied by a non-refundable amount of US$ 3,000. The amount is to be paid by the party or parties filing the objection. No objection shall be processed unless accompanied by the requisite payment.

Article 5. Administrative Expenses

For additional services, the Centre may at its discretion fix ICC administrative expenses, which shall be commensurate with the services provided and shall normally not exceed a maximum amount of US$ 10,000.

Article 6. Currency, VAT and Scope

1. All amounts fixed by the Centre or pursuant to any Appendices to the Rules are payable in US dollars except where prohibited by law, in which case the ICC may apply a different scale and fee arrangement in another currency.

2. Any ICC administrative expenses, including the filing fee and the additional fee, may be subject to value added tax (VAT) or charges of a similar nature at the prevailing rate.

3. The above provisions on the costs of appointments of experts and neutrals shall be effective as of 1 February 2015 in respect of any Request for Appointment filed on or after such date under the present Rules and in respect of any request for the appointment of an expert filed on or after such date under the Rules for Expertise of the ICC.

ICC RULES FOR THE ADMINISTRATION OF EXPERT PROCEEDINGS IN FORCE AS FROM 1 FEBRUARY 2015

Preamble

The ICC Rules for the Administration of Expert Proceedings (the "Rules") are administered by the ICC International Centre for ADR (the "Centre"), which is a separate administrative body within the International Chamber of Commerce (the "ICC"). In administering the Rules, the Centre is assisted by a Standing Committee, the statutes of which are set forth in Appendix I.

When disputes or differences arise, parties may wish to have recourse to an expert who can provide findings on specified issues through expert proceedings administered by the ICC. Such issues may concern specialist areas such as accounting, finance, engineering, information technology, construction, energy and law. The expert may be a physical person or a legal person, such as a company or a partnership.

In the absence of an agreement of the parties to the contrary, the expert's findings shall be non-binding and can be used by the parties as a basis for negotiations with a view to reaching a settlement of their dispute or differences. However, the parties may agree, subject to applicable law, that the expert's findings shall constitute a contractually binding expert determination. In all cases, an expert appointed under the Rules is not an arbitrator, and the expert's findings are not enforceable like an arbitral award. Unless otherwise agreed by the parties, the expert's report shall be admissible in any judicial or arbitral proceedings between the same parties.

The Centre will administer expert proceedings pursuant to the Rules when all of the parties have agreed to refer a dispute to the Rules or where the Centre is otherwise satisfied that there is a sufficient basis for administering expert proceedings under the Rules. In administering the proceedings, the Centre appoints the expert in the absence of a joint nomination by the parties, coordinates between the parties and the expert, initiates the appropriate steps to encourage the expeditious completion of the expert proceedings, supervises the financial aspects of the proceedings and scrutinizes the expert's report.

Article 1. Recourse to the Centre

1. Any request for the administration of expert proceedings (the "Request") shall be submitted to the Centre. Any Request shall be processed by the Centre only when it is based upon an agreement for the administration of expert proceedings by the Centre or when the Centre is otherwise satisfied that there is a sufficient basis for administering expert proceedings.

2. The Request shall include:
   a) the names, addresses, telephone numbers, email addresses and any other contact details of the parties to the dispute and any person(s) representing the parties in the proceedings;
   b) if applicable, the name and contact details of any person or entity relevant for checking potential conflicts of interest of the expert;
   c) a description of the dispute including, if possible, an assessment of its value;
   d) a description of the field of activity of the expert to be appointed;
   e) any desired attributes of the expert, including but not limited to education, qualifications, language skills and professional experience;
   f) any undesired attributes of the expert and a description of any matters that would disqualify a potential expert;
   g) a detailed description of the work to be carried out by the expert, including whether site visits will be required;
   h) the desired time frame for completing such work;
   i) any agreement as to the location of any physical meetings between the expert and the parties or, in the absence thereof, any proposal as to such location;
   j) any agreement as to the language(s) of the proceedings or, in the absence thereof, any proposal as to such language(s);
   k) any agreement that the findings of the expert shall be contractually binding on the parties or, in the absence thereof, any proposal to that effect; and
   l) a copy of any agreement for the administration of expert proceedings by the Centre and/or of any other elements which form the basis of the Request.

3. Together with the Request, the party or parties filing the Request shall pay the non-refundable amount specified in Article 1 of Appendix II.

4. The Centre shall acknowledge receipt of the Request and of the filing fee in writing to the party or parties that filed the Request.

5. The Centre shall notify the other party or parties in writing of the Request once the Centre has sufficient copies of the Request and has received the filing fee required under Article 12.

6. The date on which the Request is received by the Centre shall, for all purposes, be deemed to be the date of the commencement of the expert proceedings.

Article 2. Written Notifications or Communications

1. All written communications submitted to the Centre by any party to the expert proceedings, as well as all documents annexed thereto, shall be supplied in a number of copies sufficient to provide one copy for the Centre, one copy for each party and one copy for each expert.

2. All notifications or communications from the Centre and the expert shall be made to the last address of the party or its representative for whom the same are intended, as notified either by the party in question or by the other party. Such notification or communication may be made by delivery against receipt, registered post, courier, email or any other means of telecommunication that provides a record of the sending thereof.

3. A notification or communication shall be deemed to have been made on the day it was received by the party itself or by its representative, or would have been received if made in accordance with the preceding paragraph.

Article 3. Selection of the Expert

1. The parties may jointly nominate an expert for confirmation by the Centre.

2. In the absence of a joint nomination of an expert by the parties, the Centre shall appoint an expert.

3. Before appointment or confirmation, a prospective expert shall sign a statement of acceptance, availability, impartiality and independence. The prospective expert shall disclose in writing to the Centre any facts or circumstances which might be of such a nature as to call into question the expert's independence in the eyes of the parties, as well as any circumstances that could give rise to reasonable doubts as to the expert's impartiality. The Centre shall provide such information to the parties in writing and shall fix a time limit for any comments from them.

4. In confirming or appointing an expert, the Centre shall consider the prospective expert's nationality, residence, training and experience, and the prospective expert's availability and ability to conduct the expert proceedings in accordance with the Rules.

5. Where the Centre appoints an expert, it shall do so either on the basis of a proposal by an ICC National Committee or Group, or otherwise. The Centre shall make all reasonable efforts to appoint an expert having the attributes, if any, that have been agreed upon by all of the parties. If, despite such efforts, the Centre is not able to identify an expert having all of the attributes agreed upon by all parties, the Centre may ask the parties whether they wish the Centre to appoint more than one expert (who between them have the requested attributes), or whether the attributes agreed upon by the parties may be modified.

6. Upon agreement of all of the parties, the parties may nominate more than one expert or request the Centre to appoint more than one expert, in accordance with the provisions of the Rules. In appropriate circumstances, the Centre may propose to the parties that there be more than one expert.

7. The Centre may terminate the administered expert proceedings by notifying the parties that, in the judgment of the Centre, there has been a failure to nominate an expert or that it has not been reasonably possible to appoint an expert.

Article 4. Continued Impartiality and Independence of the Expert – Replacement of the Expert

1. Every expert must be and remain impartial and independent of the parties involved in the expert proceedings, unless otherwise agreed in writing by such parties.

2. An expert shall immediately disclose in writing to the Centre and to the parties any facts or circumstances of a similar nature to those referred to in Article 3(3) concerning the expert's impartiality or independence which may arise during the expert proceedings.

3. An expert confirmed or appointed by the Centre, who has died or resigned or is unable to carry out the expert's functions, shall be replaced.

4. An expert confirmed or appointed by the Centre shall be replaced upon acceptance by the Centre of a written request of all of the parties.

5. If any party files a written objection with the Centre asserting that the expert does not have the necessary attributes, is not fulfilling the expert's functions in accordance

with the Rules or in a timely fashion, or is not independent or impartial, the Centre may replace the expert after having considered the observations of the expert and the other party or parties.

6. When an expert is to be replaced, the Centre has discretion to decide whether or not to follow the original appointing process.

Article 5. Location and Language(s) of the Expert Proceedings

1. In the absence of an agreement of the parties, the expert, after consulting the parties, shall determine the location of any physical meeting of the expert and the parties.

2. In the absence of an agreement of the parties, the expert, after consulting the parties, shall determine the language(s) in which the expert proceedings shall be conducted.

Article 6. The Expert's Mission

1. The expert and the parties shall make every effort to conduct the expert proceedings in an expeditious and cost-effective manner, having regard to the complexity and value of the findings to be made in the expert's report.

2. As soon as the expert has received the file from the Centre, the expert, after having consulted the parties, shall set out the expert's mission in a written document. That document shall be consistent with the Rules and any agreement of all of the parties. It shall be communicated to the parties and to the Centre and shall include:

a) the names in full, descriptions, addresses and other contact details of the expert, of each of the parties and of any person(s) representing a party in the administered expert proceedings;
b) addresses to which notifications and communications arising in the course of the administered expert proceedings may be made;
c) a list of the issues on which the expert shall make findings in the expert's report;
d) the procedure to be followed by the expert; and
e) the location of any physical meeting of the expert and the parties and the language(s) in which the administered expert proceedings will be conducted.

3. Modifications to the expert's mission may be made by the expert, in writing, only after consultation with the parties. Any such written modifications shall be communicated to the parties and to the Centre.

4. In the event of a disagreement between the parties as to the scope of the expert's mandate, the expert may continue with the administered expert proceedings to the extent the expert considers that the issues set out in the expert's mission fall within the scope of the expert's mandate. Unless otherwise agreed by all of the parties, the expert shall give reasons for such considerations. The continuation of the administered expert proceedings shall be without prejudice to any determination by an arbitral tribunal or a competent judicial authority as to the scope of the expert's mandate.

Article 7. Procedural Timetable

Upon preparing the document setting out the expert's mission or as soon as possible thereafter, the expert, after having consulted the parties, shall prepare a procedural timetable for the conduct of the administered expert proceedings. The procedural timetable shall be communicated to the parties and to the Centre. Any subsequent modifications to the provisional timetable shall be promptly communicated to the parties and to the Centre.

Article 8. The Expert's Report

1. The expert's main task is to make findings in a written expert's report within the limits set by the expert's mission after giving each party a reasonable opportunity to present its case. Unless otherwise agreed by all of the parties, the expert's report shall give reasons for the findings made.

2. The findings of the expert shall not be binding on the parties, unless all of the parties expressly agree in writing that such findings shall be contractually binding upon them.

3. Unless otherwise agreed by all of the parties, the expert's report shall be admissible in any judicial or arbitral proceedings in which all of the parties thereto were parties to the administered expert proceedings in which such report was prepared.

Article 9. Scrutiny of the Expert's Report by the Centre

1. The expert's report shall be submitted in draft form to the Centre before it is signed. The Centre may lay down modifications as to the form of the report and, without affecting the expert's liberty of decision, may also draw the expert's attention to points of substance. No report shall be communicated to the parties by the expert. No report shall be signed by the expert prior to the Centre's approval of such report.

2. The Centre may waive the requirements laid down in Article 9(1) if expressly requested to do so in writing by all the parties and if the Centre considers that such a waiver is appropriate under the circumstances of the case.

Article 10. Notification of the Expert's Report and Termination of the Administered Expert Proceedings

The expert's report, once signed by the expert, shall be sent to the Centre in as many copies as there are parties plus one for the Centre. Thereafter, the Centre shall notify the expert's report to the party or parties and declare in writing that the administered expert proceedings have been terminated.

Article 11. Duties and Responsibilities of the Parties and the Expert

1. The non-participation of a party in the administered expert proceedings does not deprive the expert of the power to make findings and render the expert's report, provided that such party has been given the opportunity to participate.

2. In agreeing to the application of the Rules, the parties shall provide the expert with all necessary means to implement the expert's mission and, in particular, make available all documents the expert may consider necessary and also grant the expert free access to any place where the expert may be required to go for the proper completion of the expert's mission. The expert shall give each party the opportunity to comment on any information or documents provided by any other party.

3. Any information or documents given to the expert by the Centre or any party in connection with the administered expert proceedings shall be used by the expert only for the purposes of such proceedings and shall be treated by the expert as confidential.

Article 12. Fees and Costs

1. Each Request must be accompanied by the non-refundable filing fee specified in Article 1 of Appendix II. This amount will be credited to the requesting party's or parties' portion of the deposit pursuant to Article 12(2). No Request shall be processed unless accompanied by the filing fee.

2. Following the receipt of a Request, the Centre shall request the parties to pay one or more deposits in an amount likely to cover the administrative costs of the Centre and the fees and expenses of the expert for the administered expert proceedings, as set out in Articles 2 and 3 of Appendix II. The Centre may stay such proceedings until payment of such deposit has been received by the Centre, or the Centre may set a time limit on the expiry of which the administered expert proceedings may be considered withdrawn.

3. Each written objection pursuant to Article 4(5) of the Rules must be accompanied by the non-refundable amount specified in Article 1 of Appendix II. No objection shall be processed unless accompanied by the requisite payment.

4. Upon the termination of administered expert proceedings, the Centre shall fix the total costs of the proceedings and shall, as the case may be, reimburse the party or parties for any excess payment or bill the party or parties for any balance required pursuant to the Rules. The balance, if any, shall be payable before the notification of the final expert's report to the party or parties.

5. All above deposits and costs shall be borne in equal shares by the parties, unless they agree otherwise in writing. However, any party shall be free to pay the unpaid balance of such deposits and costs should the other party or parties fail to pay its or their share.

6. A party's other expenditure shall remain the responsibility of that party, unless otherwise agreed by the parties.

Article 13. Waiver

A party that proceeds with the administered expert proceedings without raising an objection to a failure to comply with any provision of the Rules, any direction given by the Centre or by the expert, any requirement of the expert's mission, or any requirement relating to the appointment of an expert or to the conduct of the administered expert proceedings, shall be deemed to have waived its right to object.

Article 14. General Provisions

1. An expert appointed under the Rules may be a physical person or a legal person, such as a company or a partnership. The term "expert" as used in the Rules applies *mutatis mutandis* to both physical and legal persons.

2. Where, prior to the date of the entry into force of the Rules, the parties have agreed to refer their dispute to the administration of expertise proceedings pursuant to the Rules for Expertise of the ICC, they shall be deemed to have referred to the ICC Rules for the Administration of Expert Proceedings, unless any of the parties objects thereto, in which case the Rules for Expertise of the ICC shall apply.

3. The expert, the Centre, the ICC and its employees, and the ICC National Committees and Groups and their employees and representatives shall not be liable to any person

for any act or omission in connection with the administration of expert proceedings, except to the extent such limitation of liability is prohibited by applicable law.

4. In all matters not expressly provided for in the Rules, the Centre and the expert shall act in the spirit of the Rules.

ICC RULES FOR THE ADMINISTRATION OF EXPERT PROCEEDINGS APPENDIX I – STATUTES OF THE STANDING COMMITTEE

Article 1. Composition of the Standing Committee

The Standing Committee is composed of a maximum of fifteen members (a president, three vice-presidents and up to eleven members) appointed by the ICC for a three-year renewable term.

Article 2. Meetings

A meeting of the Standing Committee shall be convened by its president whenever necessary.

Article 3. Function and Duties of the Standing Committee

1. The Standing Committee shall advise the Centre concerning all aspects of the proceedings, in order to help ensure the quality of the services carried out by the Centre. It shall assist the Centre in reviewing the attributes of the experts to be confirmed or appointed and in scrutinizing the expert's report pursuant to the Rules.

2. The president shall make the final decision on the confirmation or appointment of experts.

3. The Standing Committee shall be informed of the death or resignation of any expert, of any objection by a party or parties or the Centre concerning an expert, or of any other matter requiring the replacement of an expert. It shall provide recommendations to the president as to whether there is any reason not to comply with a request of all of the parties pursuant to Article 4(4) of the Rules and as to whether the objection of a party pursuant to Article 4(5) of the Rules is justified.

4. The president will make the final decision on whether the objection is justified and on the manner in which a replacement will be made.

5. Upon the termination of administered expert proceedings, the president shall fix the expert's fees and expenses in accordance with the Rules.

6. In the absence of the president, or otherwise at the president's request, one of the three vice-presidents shall be authorized by the Centre to fulfil the tasks of the president, including taking decisions pursuant to these statutes.

Article 4. Confidentiality

The work of the Standing Committee and the Centre is of a confidential nature, which must be respected by everyone who participates in that work in whatever capacity.

APPENDIX II – COSTS

Article 1. Filing Fee

Each Request pursuant to the Rules must be accompanied by a filing fee of US$ 3,000. The filing fee is non-refundable and shall be credited towards the deposit of the party or parties having filed the Request. No Request shall be processed unless accompanied by the requisite payment.

Article 2. Administrative Expenses

1. The administrative expenses of the ICC for the administration of expert proceedings shall be fixed at the Centre's discretion depending on the tasks carried out by the Centre. The administrative expenses are added to the filing fee; they shall normally not be less than US$ 2,500 and they shall not exceed the following:

- US$ 10,000, for amounts in dispute up to and including US$ 200,000;
- US$ 15,000, for amounts in dispute between US$ 200,001 and US$ 2,000,000;
- US$ 20,000, for amounts in dispute between US$ 2,000,001 and US$ 10,000,000;
- US$ 30,000, for amounts in dispute between US$ 10,000,001 and US$ 50,000,000;
- US$ 40,000, for amounts in dispute between US$ 50,000,001 and US$ 100,000,000;
- US$ 50,000, for amounts in dispute over US$ 100,000,000.

2. Where the amount in dispute is not stated, the administrative expenses may be fixed by the Centre at its discretion, taking into account all the circumstances of the case, including indications regarding the value of the dispute, but they shall not exceed US$ 50,000.

3. In exceptional circumstances, the Centre may fix the administrative expenses at a higher figure than that which would result from the application of the above scale, provided that such expenses shall normally not exceed the maximum amount of the scale.

4. The Centre may require the payment of administrative expenses in addition to those provided in the scale described in Article 2(1) of this Appendix as a condition for holding the proceedings in abeyance at the request of the parties or of one of them with the acquiescence of the other. Such abeyance fee shall normally not exceed US$ 2,000 per party per year.

Article 3. Expert's Fees and Expenses

1. The fees of the expert shall be calculated on the basis of the time reasonably spent by the expert in the administered expert proceedings, taking into account the diligence and efficiency of the expert and any other relevant circumstances. These fees shall be based on an hourly rate fixed by the Centre when appointing or confirming the expert and after having consulted the expert and the parties. The hourly rate shall be reasonable in amount and shall be determined in light of the complexity of the work to be performed by the expert.

2. The amount of reasonable expenses of the expert shall be fixed by the Centre.

3. The expert's fees and expenses shall be fixed exclusively by the Centre as required by the Rules. Separate fee arrangements between the parties and the expert are not permitted by the Rules.

Article 4. Additional Costs for Objection and Replacement

Each written objection to the appointment of an expert by the Centre pursuant to Article 4(5) of the Rules shall be accompanied by a non-refundable amount of US$ 3,000. The amount is to be paid by the party or parties filing the objection. No objection shall be processed unless accompanied by the requisite payment.

Article 5. Early Termination

If administered expert proceedings terminate before the notification of the expert's report, the Centre shall fix the costs of the administered expert proceedings, including the fees and expenses of the expert and the ICC administrative expenses, at its discretion, taking into account the stage attained in the administered expert proceedings and any other relevant circumstances.

Article 6. Currency, VAT and Scope

1. All amounts fixed by the Centre or pursuant to any Appendix to the Rules are payable in US dollars except where prohibited by law, in which case the ICC may apply a different scale and fee arrangement in another currency.

2. Amounts paid to the expert do not include any possible value added tax (VAT) or other taxes or charges and imposts applicable to the expert's fees. Parties have a duty to pay any such taxes or charges; however, the recovery of any such taxes or charges is a matter solely between the expert and the parties.

3. Any ICC administrative expenses may be subject to value added tax (VAT) or charges of a similar nature at the prevailing rate.

4. The above provisions on the costs of the administration of expert proceedings shall be effective as of 1 February 2015 in respect of all proceedings commenced on or after such date under the present Rules and in respect of the administration of any expertise proceedings commenced on or after such date under the Rules for Expertise of the ICC.

APPENDIX 26

ICC EXPERT CLAUSES (2015)

EXPERT RULES – ICC EXPERT CLAUSES (2015)

SUGGESTED CLAUSE PROVIDING FOR THE ICC AS APPOINTING AUTHORITY FOR EXPERT PROCEEDINGS

Set out below is a suggested clause for use by parties who wish to have the ICC appoint an expert for *ad hoc* expert proceedings that are not administered by the ICC.

> *In the event of any dispute arising out of or in connection with [clause X of the present contract], the parties agree to submit the dispute to ad hoc expert proceedings. The expert shall be appointed by the ICC International Centre for ADR in accordance with the Rules for the Appointment of Experts and Neutrals of the International Chamber of Commerce.*

Notes: The above clause may be used where the parties have provided in their contract for *ad hoc* expert proceedings (i.e. expert proceedings that are not administered by the ICC) but wish to have the ICC International Centre for ADR appoint the expert. In order to use the above clause, the parties will need to replace the phrase "[clause X of the present contract]" with a reference to the relevant contractual provision(s), so as to identify clearly the type of dispute(s) to be referred to the expert proceedings.

Parties are also advised to take account of any factors, such as the requirements of mandatory law, that may have an impact on the effect of a clause or its enforceability under applicable law.

Notes on Drafting a Clause Providing for the ICC as Appointing Authority for Neutrals

Parties may wish to have the ICC appoint a neutral for *ad hoc* mediation, neutral evaluation, dispute boards or other similar dispute resolution proceedings. Given the broad range of situations in which parties may wish to have a neutral appointed, it is not possible to offer a suggested clause that easily fits every situation. These notes are therefore provided to assist parties in drafting their tailor-made clause.

The clause should:

- clearly describe the type of dispute which is to be the subject of the proceedings (e.g. any dispute arising out of or in connection with the present contract or disputes arising under specific provisions of the contract);

- clearly describe the type of proceedings that the neutral and the parties are to use (e.g. mediation, neutral evaluation or dispute board); and
- state that the neutral shall be appointed by the ICC International Centre for ADR in accordance with the Rules for the Appointment of Experts and Neutrals of the International Chamber of Commerce.

At all times, care must be taken to avoid any risk of ambiguity in the drafting of the clause. Unclear wording causes uncertainty and delay and can hinder or even compromise the dispute resolution process.

SUGGESTED CLAUSES REFERRING TO THE ICC RULES FOR THE ADMINISTRATION OF EXPERT PROCEEDINGS

Set out below are suggested clauses covering different situations. Parties should use whichever clause corresponds to their needs. It may be necessary or desirable for them to adapt the chosen clause to their particular circumstances.

At all times, care must be taken to avoid any risk of ambiguity in the drafting of the clause. Unclear wording causes uncertainty and delay and can hinder or even compromise the dispute resolution process. When incorporating any of the clauses below in their contracts, parties are advised to take account of any factors, such as the requirements of mandatory law, that may have an impact on their effect or enforceability under applicable law.

Clause A: Optional Administered Expert Proceedings

> *The parties may at any time, without prejudice to any other proceedings, agree to submit any dispute arising out of or in connection with [clause X of the present contract] to administered expert proceedings in accordance with the Rules for the Administration of Expert Proceedings of the International Chamber of Commerce.*

Notes: By including this clause, the parties acknowledge that proceedings under the ICC Rules for the Administration of Expert Proceedings are available to them at any time. This clause does not commit the parties to do anything, but the presence of the clause is designed to remind them of the possibility of using administered expert proceedings. In addition, it can provide a basis for one party to propose expert proceedings to the other party.

In order to use Clause A, the parties will need to replace the phrase "[clause X of the present contract]" in the suggested clause with a reference to the relevant contractual provision(s), so as to identify clearly the type of dispute(s) that may be referred to expert proceedings.

Clause B: Obligation to Submit Dispute to Non-Binding Administered Expert Proceedings

> *In the event of any dispute arising out of or in connection with [clause X of the present contract], the parties agree to submit the dispute to administered expert proceedings in accordance with the Rules for the Administration of Expert Proceedings of the International Chamber of Commerce.*

Notes: Under the ICC Rules for the Administration of Expert Proceedings, the expert's findings are not binding upon the parties unless the parties expressly agree to be bound by them. Clause B, by referring generally to the Rules, creates an obligation to refer a dispute to non-binding expert proceedings under the ICC Rules for the Administration of Expert Proceedings. It is designed to ensure that when a dispute of a specified type arises, the parties will attempt to resolve the dispute by submitting it to expert proceedings under the Rules.

Clause B may be appropriate, for example, where the parties intend to use the expert's non-binding findings as a basis for reaching an agreed settlement of the dispute that is the subject of the proceedings.

In order to use Clause B, the parties will need to replace the phrase "[clause X of the present contract]" in the suggested clause with a reference to the relevant contractual provision(s), so as to identify clearly the type of dispute(s) to be referred to the expert proceedings.

Clause C: Obligation to Submit Dispute to Contractually Binding Administered Expert Proceedings

> *In the event of any dispute arising out of or in connection with [clause X of the present contract], the parties agree to submit the dispute to administered expert proceedings in accordance with the Rules for the Administration of Expert Proceedings of the International Chamber of Commerce. The parties agree that the findings of the expert shall be contractually binding upon them.*

Notes: Clause C provides a simple form of clause for binding expert proceedings, sometimes referred to as expert determination proceedings. Clause C creates an obligation to refer a dispute to binding expert proceedings under the ICC Rules for the Administration of Expert Proceedings. It is designed to ensure that when a dispute of a specified type arises, the parties will resolve the dispute by submitting it to expert proceedings under the Rules.

Clause C is appropriate where the parties want to be contractually bound by the expert's findings.

In order to use Clause C, the parties will need to replace the phrase "[clause X of the present contract]" in the suggested clause with a reference to the relevant contractual provision(s), so as to identify clearly the type of dispute(s) to be referred to the expert proceedings.

When Clause C is used, the parties should determine the effect under applicable law of their agreement to be contractually bound by the expert's findings.

A more complex tailor-made clause may be needed in certain cases (for example, where a price adjustment in an M&A contract is referred to an expert accountancy firm for determination). Such a tailor-made clause may still provide for the expert determination to be conducted pursuant to the ICC Rules for the Administration of Expert Proceedings.

Clause D: Obligation to Submit Dispute to Non-Binding Administered Expert Proceedings, Followed by Arbitration if Required

> *In the event of any dispute arising out of or in connection with [clause X of the present contract], the parties agree to submit the dispute, in the first instance, to administered expert proceedings in accordance with the Rules for the Administration of Expert Proceedings of the International Chamber of Commerce. After the International Centre for ADR's notification of the termination of the administered expert proceedings, the dispute, if it has not been resolved, shall be finally settled under the Rules of Arbitration of the International Chamber*

of Commerce by one or more arbitrators appointed in accordance with the said Rules of Arbitration.

Notes: Clause D is appropriate where the parties intend to use the expert's non-binding findings as a basis for reaching an agreed settlement of the dispute that is the subject of the administered expert proceedings. If no settlement is reached, then the dispute is referred to ICC arbitration.

In order to use Clause D, the parties will need to replace the phrase "[clause X of the present contract]" in the suggested clause with a reference to the relevant contractual provision(s), so as to identify clearly the type of dispute(s) to be referred to the expert proceedings and subsequently to ICC arbitration proceedings.

If desired, Clause D can be modified to provide instead for judicial or other similar proceedings following the administered expert proceedings.

Specific Issues Concerning the Emergency Arbitrator Provisions

The parties should determine whether they wish to have recourse to the Emergency Arbitrator Provisions in the ICC Arbitration Rules under Clause D.

If the parties wish to exclude any recourse to the Emergency Arbitrator Provisions, the following wording should be added to Clause D:

The Emergency Arbitrator Provisions shall not apply.

If the parties wish to have recourse to the Emergency Arbitrator Provisions, and want that recourse expressly to be available prior to the termination of the expert proceedings, the following wording should be added to Clause D:

The requirement to refer a dispute to administered expert proceedings, before referring a dispute to arbitration, shall not prevent the parties from making an application, prior to termination of the administered expert proceedings, for Emergency Measures under the Emergency Arbitrator Provisions in the Rules of Arbitration of the International Chamber of Commerce.

If the parties wish to have recourse to the Emergency Arbitrator Provisions, but only after termination of the administered expert proceedings, the following wording should be added to Clause D:

The parties shall not have the right to make an application for Emergency Measures under the Emergency Arbitrator Provisions in the Rules of Arbitration of the International Chamber of Commerce prior to the International Centre for ADR's notification of the termination of the administered expert proceedings.

APPENDIX 27

ICC DOCDEX RULES (1 MAY 2015)

ICC RULES FOR DOCUMENTARY INSTRUMENTS DISPUTE RESOLUTION EXPERTISE (ICC DOCDEX RULES)

In force as from 1 May 2015

Preamble

The DOCDEX Rules (the "Rules") of the International Chamber of Commerce (the "ICC") are for use in proceedings called Documentary Instruments Dispute Resolution Expertise ("DOCDEX"), which are administered by the ICC International Centre for ADR (the "Centre"), a separate administrative body within the ICC.

Article 1. Definitions

In the Rules:

"Appendix" means the Appendix entitled "Fees and Costs" set out hereinafter and at www.iccdocdex.org, where it may from time to time be updated.

"Appointed Experts" means a panel of three experts and "Appointed Expert" any member of that panel appointed by the Centre, having regard to the guidance provided by the Technical Adviser pursuant to Article 7(4), to render a Decision as defined below.

"Banking Commission" means the ICC Banking Commission.

"Claimant"/"Claimants" means a party or parties that submit(s) a Claim to the Centre in the manner described in Article 3 for a Decision as defined below.

"Decision" means the final decision rendered by the Appointed Experts pursuant to Article 9.

"Form" means one of the four forms set out hereinafter, available to download at www.iccdocdex.org.

"ICC Banking Rules" means any set of rules or standard practices issued from time to time by the Banking Commission, such as the ICC Uniform Customs and Practice for Documentary Credits (UCP), the ICC Uniform Rules for Bank-to-Bank Reimbursements under Documentary Credits (URR), the ICC Uniform Rules for Collections (URC) and the ICC Uniform Rules for Demand Guarantees (URDG).

"Respondent"/"Respondents" means a party or parties named as such in the Claim.

"Technical Adviser" means one of the Banking Commission's technical Advisers or alternate technical Advisers appointed by the Chair of the Banking Commission to provide guidance as indicated in Articles 2(1), 7(3) and 7(4) and comments on any draft Decision of the Appointed Experts as indicated in Article 9(2).

Article 2. Scope

1. The Rules are available for any dispute which the Centre, in consultation with the Technical Adviser and subject to Articles 2(2) and 2(3) of the Rules, may agree to administer and which relates to:

- a documentary credit,
- a standby letter of credit,
- a bank-to-bank reimbursement,
- a collection,
- a demand guarantee or counter-guarantee,
- a forfaiting transaction,
- a bank payment obligation (BPO), or
- any other trade finance-related instrument, undertaking or agreement.

2. When a dispute falling within the scope of Article 2(1) of the Rules arises, a party may refer the dispute to the Rules to obtain an independent, impartial and prompt expert decision on the basis of the terms and conditions of the relevant instrument, undertaking or agreement, any applicable ICC Banking Rules and international standard practice in trade finance.

3. If the dispute arises out of or is in connection with an instrument, undertaking or agreement that does not provide for the application of ICC Banking Rules, it shall be administered under the Rules only if each Claimant and each Respondent so agree. Their agreement shall be recorded on Forms 1 and 2.

4. The Rules provide for expedited proceedings, with no opportunity for the oral examination of fact or expert witnesses or for oral submissions at a hearing. Accordingly, the Rules are not appropriate where such examination or submissions are required to resolve any factual or legal issues raised by the Claim.

5. Proceedings under the Rules are not arbitral proceedings and a Decision is not an arbitral award.

6. A Decision shall not be binding on any Claimant or Respondent unless each Claimant and Respondent agrees that the Decision shall be contractually binding upon them. Any such agreement shall be recorded on Forms 1 and 2.

Article 3. Claim

1. A Claimant shall apply for a Decision by submitting a claim to the Centre using Form 1 (the "Claim"). The Claim shall be accompanied by all documents that the Claimant considers necessary to support its Claim. The Claim and all accompanying documents shall be supplied to the Centre in electronic form, together with one hard copy for each Respondent.

2. A Claimant may submit a Claim individually or jointly with one or more other Claimants.

3. At the time of submitting a Claim, the Claimant shall pay the fee specified in the Appendix.

4. Subject to Article 3(6) of the Rules, the Centre shall acknowledge receipt of the Claim and the fee to the Claimant.

5. Subject to Article 3(6) of the Rules, once the Centre has received the electronic and hard copies of the Claim and the fee, it shall send a hard copy of the Claim and any accompanying documents to each Respondent identified in the Claim for its Answer, as provided in Article 11(1) of the Rules.

6. If the Centre finds a Claim or part of a Claim to be outside the scope of the Rules, or considers in its discretion that the administration of a Claim or part of a Claim would not be in the spirit of the Rules, the Centre may reject all or part of that Claim at any time, before or after acknowledging receipt, and in such event shall so inform the Claimant and any Respondent to which the Centre has sent a copy of the Claim. The Centre shall also refund all or part of any fee received pursuant to Article 3(3) of the Rules, as appropriate.

7. In considering whether or not to reject a Claim or part of a Claim prior to the appointment of the Appointed Experts, the Centre may seek guidance from the Technical Adviser pursuant to Articles 2(1) and 7(3) of the Rules. Following the appointment of the Appointed Experts, the Centre shall reject a Claim or part of a Claim if informed by a majority of the Appointed Experts pursuant to Article 8(3) that they consider it to be outside the scope of the Rules.

Article 4. Answer

1. A Respondent may submit an answer to a Claim (the "Answer") using Form 2. The Answer, if any, shall be accompanied by any additional documents that the Respondent considers necessary to support its Answer.

2. The Answer and all accompanying documents shall be supplied to the Centre only in electronic form in accordance with Article 11(2) of the Rules. The Centre shall forward the Answer and any accompanying documents to the Claimant and any other Respondent.

3. A Respondent may submit its Answer individually or jointly with one or more other Respondents.

4. An Answer must be received by the Centre within the period it specifies when sending the Claim to each Respondent, which shall not exceed 30 days, save exceptional circumstances. Any Answer received by the Centre after the expiry of the specified period shall be disregarded.

5. If a Respondent does not submit an Answer, the proceedings shall nonetheless continue.

Article 5. Supplementary Information and Additional Documents

1. The Centre may request a Claimant or Respondent to submit supplementary information or copies of documents that the Centre considers relevant to the rendering of a Decision, whereupon such information or documents shall be submitted using Form 3 (the "Supplement").

2. A Supplement shall be submitted to the Centre within 14 days of its request, in electronic form only. The Centre shall forward the Supplement to each Claimant and Respondent.

3. A Supplement shall be submitted to the Centre only in response to a request from the Centre. Any unsolicited submission made to the Centre by any Claimant or Respondent shall be disregarded. The Centre may, at its discretion, accede to a request from a Claimant or Respondent for permission to make a new or additional submission, whereupon such submission shall be supplied in the form of a Supplement within the period indicated by the Centre.

4. No submission by any person other than a Claimant or Respondent shall be admitted in the proceedings and any such submission received by the Centre shall be disregarded.

Article 6. Filing and Finality of Submissions

1. In addition to the requirements set out in Articles 3(1), 4(1) and 5(1) of the Rules with regard to the form of a Claim, Answer and Supplement, the Centre may require any document to be submitted in hard copy or for the electronic copy to be submitted in a particular electronic form.

2. All fields in the relevant Form shall be completed concisely, in English, and shall contain all necessary information clearly presented.

3. If a document accompanying a Claim, Answer or Supplement contains data not drafted in English, it shall be accompanied by an English translation, unless the Centre agrees otherwise in writing.

4. A Claim, Answer and Supplement shall be considered final as received and may not be amended.

Article 7. Appointment of Experts

1. The Banking Commission maintains a list of experts (the "List") having experience in, and knowledge of, trade finance transactions. The Chair of the Banking Commission is the repository of the List and can add or remove experts from the List at any time, as need be.

2. The Centre shall transmit a copy of the Claim to the Technical Adviser after verifying the Technical Adviser's independence with respect to the parties referred to in the Claim.

3. The Technical Adviser shall, if requested, offer guidance to the Centre on whether the Claim falls within the scope of the Rules.

4. The Technical Adviser shall also provide guidance on the area(s) of expertise that the Claim requires and that the Appointed Experts should possess. Having regard to this guidance, the Centre shall make the appointments and designate one of the Appointed Experts to act as president (the "President").

5. Each Appointed Expert must be and remain impartial and independent of the parties involved in the dispute.

6. An Appointed Expert shall not act or have acted, nor shall any Claimant or Respondent seek to have an Appointed Expert act, in any judicial, arbitral or similar

proceedings relating to the dispute that is or was the subject of proceedings under the Rules, whether as a judge, an arbitrator, an expert or fact witness, or a representative or Adviser.

7. Before any appointment, prospective Appointed Experts shall sign a statement of acceptance, availability, impartiality and independence and shall disclose in writing to the Centre any facts or circumstances which might be of such a nature as to call into question their independence in the eyes of any Claimant or Respondent, as well as any circumstances that could give rise to reasonable doubts as to their impartiality. The Centre shall take any such disclosure into account before making the appointment.

8. An Appointed Expert shall immediately disclose in writing to the Centre any facts or circumstances of a similar nature to those referred to in Article 7(7) of the Rules concerning the Appointed Expert's impartiality or independence which may arise during the proceedings.

9. By accepting to serve, an Appointed Expert undertakes to carry out the Appointed Expert's responsibilities in accordance with the Rules.

10. An Appointed Expert who becomes unable to carry out the functions entrusted by the Centre shall so inform the Centre without delay. When the Centre deems that an Appointed Expert is unable to carry out the Appointed Expert's role under the Rules, it shall immediately give notice of termination to such Appointed Expert. The Centre shall inform the other Appointed Experts of such termination and make another appointment from the List.

11. Upon receipt of a notice of termination, an Appointed Expert shall promptly dispose of any documents received from the Centre in an appropriate manner as agreed with the Centre.

Article 8. The Proceedings

1. Unless the Centre has rejected the Claim pursuant to Article 3(6) of the Rules, the Centre shall transmit the Claim, any Answer and any Supplement(s) to the Appointed Experts.

2. When considered necessary by the Appointed Experts, the President may ask the Centre to request any Claimant or Respondent to submit a Supplement in accordance with Article 5 of the Rules.

3. If the Appointed Experts consider that the Claim is outside the scope of the Rules, they shall so inform the Centre, which shall reject the Claim pursuant to Article 3(6) of the Rules.

4. Notwithstanding any disagreement between the Claimant and Respondent as to whether the Claim falls within the scope of the Rules, the Appointed Experts shall continue with the proceedings and render a Decision to the extent that they consider the Claim to fall within the scope of the Rules.

5. Following deliberations among the Appointed Experts, the President shall prepare and submit to the Centre a draft of the Decision for scrutiny pursuant to Article 9(2) of the Rules. The draft Decision shall be submitted within 30 days of receipt by the Appointed Experts of all information and documents they consider necessary for determining the issues in dispute.

6. In exceptional circumstances, and upon a reasoned request submitted by the President, the Centre may extend the time limit for the Appointed Experts to render their draft Decision.

7. There shall be no oral hearing before the Appointed Experts.

Article 9. The Decision

1. The Decision shall be drafted in English using Form 4.

2. Upon receipt of the draft Decision from the President, the Centre shall transmit it forthwith to the Technical Adviser for scrutiny. The Technical Adviser may lay down modifications as to the form of the draft Decision and, without affecting the Appointed Experts' liberty of decision, may also draw their attention to points of substance. No Decision shall be rendered by the Appointed Experts until it has been approved by the Technical Adviser as to its form.

3. The Decision may be made unanimously or on a majority basis and shall so indicate.

4. The Decision shall be deemed to have been made on the date stated therein.

5. The Appointed Experts shall render the Decision exclusively on the basis of the Claim, any Answer and any Supplement, the terms and conditions of the trade finance-related instrument, undertaking or agreement, the ICC Banking Rules that may be applicable and international standard practice in trade finance.

6. Once a Decision has been made, the Centre shall make it available to each Claimant and to any Respondent that has submitted an Answer pursuant to Article 4 of the Rules.

Article 10. Costs

1. The costs of the DOCDEX proceedings shall be the standard fee set out in the Appendix. The standard fee shall be non-refundable, unless the Centre rejects all or part of the Claim pursuant to Article 3(6) of the Rules.

2. An additional fee may be fixed by the Centre, at its discretion, taking into account the facts and documents underlying the dispute and subject to the maximum specified in Article 2 of the Appendix.

3. The Centre shall fix a time limit for the payment of the additional fee. The Centre may instruct the Appointed Experts to suspend their work until the additional fee has been paid.

Article 11. Notifications or Communications; Time Limits

1. A hard copy of the Claim shall be sent by the Centre to each Respondent pursuant to Article 3(5) of the Rules. It shall be sent by delivery against receipt, registered post or courier to the address of the Respondent provided by the Claimant in the Claim.

2. Subject to Article 11(1) of the Rules, all notifications or communications to and from the Centre shall be made by email or by any other means of telecommunications, excluding fax, that provides a record of the sending thereof. Such notifications or communications shall be made to the last email or other electronic address of the Claimant or Respondent, or its representative for whom the same are intended, as notified for this purpose by the party in question. If the Respondent fails to notify the

Centre of an email or other electronic address, then the Centre may use the address for the Respondent that is provided by the Claimant.

3. A notification or communication shall be deemed to have been made on the day it was received by the Claimant or Respondent itself or by its representative, or would have been received if made in accordance with Article 11(2) of the Rules.

4. Periods of time specified in or fixed under the Rules shall start to run on the day following the date a notification or communication is deemed to have been made in accordance with Article 11(3) of the Rules. When the day following such date is an official holiday or a non-business day in the country where the notification or communication is deemed to have been made, the period of time shall commence on the first following business day. Official holidays and non-business days are included in the calculation of the period of time. If the last day of the relevant period of time granted is an official holiday or a non-business day in the country where the notification or communication is deemed to have been made, the period of time shall expire at the end of the first following business day.

Article 12. General

1. The Centre may authorize the publication of any Decision, provided that the identities of each Claimant, Respondent and any other person or entity named in the Claim, Answer or any Supplement are not disclosed.

2. Any information or documents given by the Centre to the Technical Adviser or the Appointed Experts in connection with proceedings under the Rules shall be used by the Technical Adviser and the Appointed Experts only for the purpose of such proceedings and shall be treated by them, as well as by the Centre, as confidential.

3. The Centre, the Technical Adviser and the Appointed Experts shall not reveal the identities of the Appointed Experts and the Technical Adviser to any Claimant, Respondent or other person.

4. In all matters not expressly provided for in the Rules, the Technical Adviser, the Appointed Experts and the Centre shall act in the spirit of the Rules.

5. The Technical Adviser, the Appointed Experts, the Centre, the ICC and its employees, and the ICC National Committees and Groups and their employees and representatives shall not be liable to any person for any act or omission in connection with any proceedings or Decision under the Rules, except to the extent such limitation of liability is prohibited by applicable law.

6. The version of the Rules that is applicable at the time of submission of a Claim shall apply to the proceedings, unless otherwise agreed by each Claimant and Respondent.

APPENDIX

Fees and Costs

Article 1. Standard Fee

Where the amount in dispute does not exceed US$ 1,000,000, the standard fee is US$ 5,000, which includes the Centre's administrative expenses and the Appointed

Experts' fees. For all amounts in dispute exceeding US$ 1,000,000, the standard fee is US$ 10,000.

Article 2. Additional Fee

As indicated in Article 10(2) of the Rules, the Centre may charge an additional fee of up to 50% of the standard fee.

Article 3. Payment

1. Payment shall be made by bank transfer to the account of the International Chamber of Commerce shown below, carrying the reference "DOCDEX case".

UBS AG
Bahnhofstrasse 45
8098 Zurich
Switzerland
Swift code: UBSWCHZH80A
IBAN: CH06 0024 0240 2245 3461 R

2. At the time of payment, an advice in writing should be sent to:

ICC International Centre for ADR
33-43 avenue du Président Wilson
75116 Paris, France
docdex@iccwbo.org

stating the following data:

DOCDEX case number (if known to the Claimant)

date of Claim

name of Claimant

date and amount of payment

postal address

Article 4. Currency, VAT and Scope

1. All amounts fixed by the Centre or pursuant to the Rules and the Appendix are payable in US dollars except were prohibited by law, in which case the ICC may apply a different scale and fee arrangement in another currency.

2. Any standard or additional fee may be subject to value added tax (VAT) or charges of a similar nature at the prevailing rate.

3. The above provisions on the costs of proceedings shall be effective as of 1 May 2015 in respect of all proceedings commenced on or after such date under the present or any previous version of the ICC DOCDEX Rules.

Article 5. Disclaimer

This Appendix is subject to change without notice. Please refer to www.iccdocdex.org for the current version.

APPENDIX 28

ICC DISPUTE BOARD RULES (1 OCTOBER 2015)

DISPUTE BOARD RULES OF THE INTERNATIONAL CHAMBER OF COMMERCE

In force as from 1 October 2015

INTRODUCTORY PROVISIONS

Article 1: Scope of the Rules

1. Dispute Boards established in accordance with the Dispute Board Rules of the International Chamber of Commerce (the "Rules") aid the Parties in avoiding or resolving their Disagreements and Disputes. They may assist the Parties (i) in avoiding Disagreements under Article 16, (ii) in resolving Disagreements through informal assistance under Article 17, or (iii) in resolving Disputes by issuing Conclusions under Article 18.

2. Dispute Boards are not arbitral tribunals and their Conclusions are not enforceable like arbitral awards. Rather, the Parties contractually agree to be bound by the Conclusions under certain specific conditions set forth herein. In application of the Rules, the International Chamber of Commerce (the "ICC"), through its International Centre for ADR (the "Centre"), which is a separate administrative body within the ICC, can provide administrative services to the Parties. These services include appointing Dispute Board members ("DB Members"), deciding upon challenges against DB Members, determining the fees of DB Members, and reviewing Decisions.

Article 2: Definitions

In the Rules:

(i) "Contract" means the agreement of the Parties that contains or is subject to provisions for establishing a Dispute Board under the Rules.

(ii) "Conclusion" means either a Recommendation or a Decision, issued in writing by the Dispute Board, as described in the Rules.

(iii) "Disagreement" means any difference between the Parties arising out of or in connection with the Contract that has not yet become a Dispute, including Disagreements that are subject to avoidance under Article 16 of the Rules or informal assistance under Article 17 of the Rules.

(iv) "Dispute" means any Disagreement that is formally referred to a Dispute Board for a Conclusion under the terms of the Contract and pursuant to Article 18 of the Rules.

(v) "Dispute Board" ("DB") means a Dispute Review Board ("DRB"), a Dispute Adjudication Board ("DAB") or a Combined Dispute Board ("CDB"), composed of one, three or more DB Members.

(vi) "Party" means a party to the Contract and includes one or more parties, as appropriate.

Article 3: Agreement to Submit to the Rules

1. Unless otherwise agreed, the Parties shall establish the DB at the time of entering into the Contract. The Parties shall specify whether the DB shall be a DRB, a DAB or a CDB.

2. The Parties shall cooperate with each other and with the DB in the application of the Rules.

TYPES OF DISPUTE BOARDS

Article 4: Dispute Review Boards (DRBs)

1. DRBs may assist the Parties in avoiding Disagreements, in resolving them through informal assistance, and by issuing Conclusions with respect to Disputes upon formal referral. In formal referrals, DRBs render Recommendations with respect to Disputes.

2. Upon receipt of a Recommendation, the Parties may comply with it voluntarily but are not required to do so.

3. The Parties agree that if no Party has given a written notice to the other Party and the DRB expressing its dissatisfaction with a Recommendation within 30 days of receiving it, the Recommendation shall become final and binding on the Parties. The Parties shall comply without delay with a Recommendation that has become final and binding and agree not to contest that Recommendation, unless such agreement is prohibited by applicable law.

4. If any Party fails to comply with a Recommendation when required to do so pursuant to this Article 4, the other Party may refer the failure itself, without having to refer it to the DRB first, either to arbitration, if the Parties have so agreed, or, if not, to any court of competent jurisdiction. A Party that has failed to comply with a Recommendation, when required to do so, shall not raise any issue as to the merits of the Recommendation as a defence to its failure to comply without delay with the Recommendation.

5. Any Party that is dissatisfied with a Recommendation shall, within 30 days of receiving it, give written notice expressing its dissatisfaction to the other Party and the DRB. Such notice may specify the reasons for the Party's dissatisfaction, in the absence of which the DRB may request the Party to provide the DRB and the other Party with brief reasons for its dissatisfaction.

6. If any Party gives such a written notice expressing its dissatisfaction with a Recommendation, or if the DRB does not render its Recommendation within the time limit prescribed in Article 22, or if the DRB is disbanded pursuant to the Rules before a Recommendation regarding a Dispute has been rendered, the Dispute in question shall be finally settled by arbitration, if the parties have so agreed, or, if not, by any court of competent jurisdiction.

Article 5: Dispute Adjudication Boards (DABs)

1. DABs may assist the Parties in avoiding Disagreements, in resolving them through informal assistance, and by issuing Conclusions with respect to Disputes upon formal referral. In formal referrals, DABs render Decisions with respect to Disputes.

2. A Decision is binding on the Parties upon its receipt. The Parties shall comply with it without delay, notwithstanding any expression of dissatisfaction pursuant to this Article 5.

3. The Parties agree that if no Party has given written notice to the other Party and the DAB expressing its dissatisfaction with the Decision within 30 days of receiving it, the Decision shall remain binding and shall become final. The Parties agree not to contest a Decision that has become final, unless such agreement is prohibited by applicable law.

4. If any Party fails to comply with a Decision rendered pursuant to this Article 5, whether it be binding or both final and binding, the other Party may refer the failure itself, without having to refer it to the DAB first, either to arbitration, if the Parties have so agreed, or, if not, to any court of competent jurisdiction. A Party that has failed to comply with a Decision shall not raise any issue as to the merits of the Decision as a defence to its failure to comply without delay with the Decision.

5. Any Party that is dissatisfied with a Decision shall, within 30 days of receiving it, give written notice expressing its dissatisfaction to the other Party and the DAB. Such notice may specify the reasons for the Party's dissatisfaction, in the absence of which the DAB may request the Party to provide the DAB and the other Party with brief reasons for its dissatisfaction.

6. If any Party gives such written notice expressing its dissatisfaction with a Decision, or if the DAB does not render its Decision within the time limit prescribed in Article 22, or if the DAB is disbanded pursuant to the Rules before a Decision regarding a Dispute has been rendered, the Dispute in question shall be finally settled by arbitration, if the Parties have so agreed, or, if not, by any court of competent jurisdiction. Until the Dispute is finally settled by arbitration or otherwise, or unless the arbitral tribunal or the court decides otherwise, the Parties remain bound to comply with any Decision rendered within the prescribed time limit.

Article 6: Combined Dispute Boards (CDBs)

1. CDBs may assist the Parties in avoiding Disagreements, in resolving them through informal assistance, and by issuing Conclusions with respect to Disputes upon formal referral. In formal referrals, CDBs render Recommendations with respect to Disputes pursuant to Article 4, but may render Decisions pursuant to Article 5, as provided in paragraphs 2 and 3 of this Article 6.

2. If any Party requests a Decision with respect to a given Dispute and no other Party objects thereto, the CDB shall render a Decision.

3. If any Party requests a Decision and another Party objects thereto, the CDB shall make a final decision as to whether it will render a Recommendation or a Decision. In so deciding, the CDB shall consider, without being limited to, the following factors:

- whether, due to the urgency of the situation or other relevant considerations, a Decision would facilitate the performance of the Contract or prevent substantial loss or harm to any Party;

- whether a Decision would prevent disruption of the Contract; and
- whether a Decision is necessary to preserve evidence.

4. Any request for a Decision by the Party referring a Dispute to the CDB shall be made in the Statement of Case pursuant to Article 19. Any such request by another Party should be made in writing no later than in its Response pursuant to Article 20.

ESTABLISHMENT OF THE DISPUTE BOARD

Article 7: Appointment of the DB Members

1. The DB shall be established in accordance with the provisions of the Contract or, where the Contract is silent, in accordance with the Rules.

2. Where the Parties have agreed to establish a DB in accordance with the Rules but have not agreed on the number of DB Members, the DB shall be composed of three members.

3. Where the Parties have agreed that the DB shall have a sole DB Member, they shall jointly appoint the sole DB Member. If the Parties fail to appoint the sole DB Member within 30 days after signing the Contract or within 30 days after the commencement of any performance under the Contract, whichever occurs earlier, or within any other time period agreed upon by the Parties, the sole DB Member shall be appointed by the Centre upon the request of any Party.

4. When the DB is composed of three DB Members, the Parties shall jointly appoint the first two DB Members. If the Parties fail to appoint one or both DB Members within 30 days after signing the Contract or within 30 days after the commencement of any performance under the Contract, whichever occurs earlier, or within any other time period agreed upon by the Parties, both DB Members shall be appointed by the Centre upon the request of any Party.

5. The third DB Member shall be proposed to the Parties by the first two DB Members within 30 days following the appointment of the second DB Member. If the Parties do not appoint the proposed third DB Member within 15 days of receiving the proposal, or if the first two DB Members fail to propose the third DB Member, the third DB Member shall be appointed by the Centre upon the request of any Party. The third DB Member shall act as president of the DB unless all DB Members agree upon another president with the consent of the Parties.

6. When a DB Member has to be replaced due to death, resignation, termination or removal, the new DB Member shall be appointed in the same manner, *mutatis mutandis*, as the DB Member being replaced, unless otherwise agreed by the Parties. All actions taken by the DB prior to the replacement of a DB Member shall remain valid. When the DB is composed of three or more DB Members and when one of the DB Members is to be replaced, the other members shall continue to be DB Members. Prior to the replacement of the DB Member, the remaining DB Members shall not hold hearings or issue Conclusions without the agreement of all of the Parties.

7. The appointment of any DB Member shall be made by the Centre upon the request of any Party if the Centre is satisfied that doing so is justified in order to ensure the proper application of the Rules.

8. When appointing a DB Member, the Centre shall consider the prospective DB Member's attributes, including but not limited to nationality, residence, language skills,

training, qualifications and experience, availability and ability to conduct the work to be carried out, as well as any observations, comments or requests made by the Parties. The Centre shall make all reasonable efforts to appoint a DB Member having the attributes, if any, that have been agreed upon by all of the Parties.

Article 8: Independence

1. Every DB Member must be and remain impartial and independent of the Parties.

2. Every prospective DB Member shall sign a statement of acceptance, availability, impartiality and independence and disclose in writing to the Parties, the other DB Members, and to the Centre if such DB Member is to be appointed by the Centre, any facts or circumstances which might be of such a nature as to call into question the DB Member's independence in the eyes of the Parties, as well as any circumstances that could give rise to reasonable doubts as to the DB Member's impartiality.

3. A DB Member shall immediately disclose in writing to the Parties and the other DB Members any facts or circumstances of a similar nature to those referred to in Article 8(2) concerning the DB Member's impartiality or independence which may arise in the course of such DB Member's tenure.

4. Should any Party wish to challenge a DB Member on the basis of an alleged lack of impartiality, independence or otherwise, it may, within 15 days of learning of the facts upon which the challenge is based, submit to the Centre a request for a decision upon the challenge including a written statement of such facts. The Centre will finally decide the challenge after having given the challenged DB Member, any other DB Members and the other Party an opportunity to comment on the challenge.

5. If a DB Member is successfully challenged, that DB Member shall be removed forthwith and the DB Member Agreement, if any, between that DB Member and the Parties shall be terminated.

Article 9: Work of the DB and Confidentiality

1. By accepting to serve, DB Members undertake to carry out their responsibilities in accordance with the Rules.

2. Unless otherwise agreed by the Parties or otherwise required by applicable law, any information obtained by a DB Member during the course of the DB's activities shall be used by the DB Member only for the purposes of the DB's activities and shall be treated by the DB Member as confidential.

3. Unless otherwise agreed in writing by all of the Parties, a DB Member shall not act nor shall have acted in any judicial, arbitral or similar proceedings relating to the Contract, whether as a judge, an arbitrator, an expert or a representative or adviser of a Party.

Article 10: DB Member Agreement

1. Before commencing DB activities, every DB Member shall sign with all of the Parties a DB Member Agreement. If there are three or more DB Members, each DB Member Agreement shall have substantive terms that are identical to the other DB Member Agreements, unless otherwise agreed by the Parties and the DB Member concerned.

2. The Parties may at any time, without cause and with immediate effect, jointly terminate the DB Member Agreement of any DB Member but shall pay the monthly

management fee to such DB Member for a minimum of three months following the termination, unless otherwise agreed by the Parties and the DB Member concerned.

3. Every DB Member may terminate the DB Member Agreement at any time by giving a minimum of three months' written notice to the Parties, unless otherwise agreed by the Parties and the DB Member concerned.

OBLIGATION TO COOPERATE

Article 11: Providing of Information

1. The Parties shall fully cooperate with the DB and communicate information to it in a timely manner. In particular, the Parties and the DB shall cooperate to ensure that, as soon as possible after the DB has been constituted, the DB becomes fully informed about the Contract and its performance by the Parties.

2. The Parties shall ensure that the DB is kept informed of the performance of the Contract and of any Disagreements arising in the course thereof by such means as progress reports, meetings and, if relevant to the Contract, site visits.

3. The DB shall, after consultation with the Parties, inform them in writing of the nature, format and frequency of any progress reports that the Parties shall send to the DB.

4. If requested by the DB, the Parties shall provide the DB, during meetings and site visits, with adequate working space, accommodation, means of communication, typing facilities and all necessary office and information technology equipment allowing the DB to fulfil its functions.

Article 12: Meetings and Site Visits

1. At the beginning of its activities the DB, in consultation with the Parties, shall establish a schedule of meetings and, if relevant to the Contract, site visits. The frequency of scheduled meetings and site visits shall be sufficient to keep the DB informed of the performance of the Contract and of any Disagreements. Unless otherwise agreed by the Parties and the DB, when site visits are relevant to the Contract there shall be a minimum of three such visits per year. The Parties and the DB shall attend all such meetings and site visits, during which the DB Members may engage in informal conversations with one or more representatives of the Parties. In the event that a Party fails to attend, the DB may nevertheless decide to proceed. In the event that a DB Member fails to attend, the DB may proceed if the Parties so agree or the DB so decides.

2. Site visits occur at the site or sites where the Contract is being performed. Meetings can be held at any location or by telephone or videoconference, as agreed by the Parties and the DB. If they do not agree on where or how to hold a meeting, such matters shall be decided by the DB after consultation with the Parties.

3. During scheduled meetings and site visits the DB shall review the performance of the Contract with the Parties and may assist the Parties in avoiding Disagreements pursuant to Article 16 or may provide informal assistance with respect to any Disagreements pursuant to Article 17.

4. Any Party may request an urgent meeting or site visit in addition to the scheduled meetings and site visits. The DB Members shall accommodate such a request at the earliest possible time and shall use their best efforts to make themselves available for urgent physical meetings or site visits within 30 days of the request.

5. After every meeting and site visit, the DB shall prepare a written summary of the meeting or site visit, including a list of those present.

Article 13: Written Notifications or Communications; Time Limits

1. All written notifications or communications from a Party to the DB or from the DB to the Parties, together with any enclosures and attachments, shall be communicated simultaneously to all Parties and DB Members at the address on file for each of them.

2. Written notifications or communications shall be sent in the manner agreed between the Parties and the DB or in any manner that provides the sender with a record of the sending thereof.

3. All written notifications or communications from a Party to the Centre shall be communicated simultaneously to all Parties at the address on file for each Party.

4. A notification or communication shall be deemed to have been made on the date that it was received by the intended recipient or by its representative or would have been received if made in accordance with this Article 13.

5. Periods of time specified in or fixed under the Rules shall start to run on the day following the date a notification or communication is deemed to have been made in accordance with the preceding paragraph. When the day next following such date is an official holiday or non-business day in the country in which the notification or communication is deemed to have been made, the period of time shall commence on the first following business day. Official holidays and non-business days are included in the calculation of the period of time. If the last day of the relevant period of time granted is an official holiday or a non-business day in the country where the notification or communication is deemed to have been made, the period of time shall expire at the end of the first following business day.

OPERATION OF THE DISPUTE BOARD

Article 14: Beginning and End of the DB's Activities

1. The DB shall begin its activities after every DB Member and the Parties have signed the DB Member Agreement(s).

2. Unless otherwise agreed by the Parties, the DB shall end its activities upon receiving notice from the Parties of their joint decision to disband the DB.

3. A DB Member may resign from the DB at any time by giving three months' written notice to the Parties, unless otherwise agreed in the DB Member Agreement(s).

4. Any dispute that may arise after the DB has been disbanded shall be finally settled by arbitration, if the Parties have so agreed, or, if not, by any court of competent jurisdiction.

Article 15: Powers of the DB

1. The proceedings before the DB shall be governed by the Rules and, where the Rules are silent, by any rules which the Parties or, failing them, the DB may settle on. In particular, in the absence of an agreement of the Parties with respect thereto, the DB shall have the power, *inter alia*, to:

- determine the language or languages of the proceedings before the DB, due regard being given to all relevant circumstances, including the language of the Contract;
- require the Parties to produce any documents that the DB deems necessary in order to fulfil its function;
- call meetings, site visits and hearings;
- decide on all procedural matters arising during any meeting, site visit or hearing;
- question the Parties, their representatives and any witnesses they may call, in the sequence it chooses;
- appoint one or more experts, with the agreement of the parties;
- issue a Conclusion even if a Party fails to comply with a request of the DB;
- decide upon any provisional relief such as interim or conservatory measures; and
- take any measures necessary for it to fulfil its function as a DB.

2. Decisions of the DB regarding the rules governing the proceedings shall be taken by the sole DB Member or, when there are three or more DB Members, by a majority vote. If there is no majority, the decision shall be made by the president of the DB alone.

3. The DB may take measures for protecting trade secrets and confidential information.

4. If there are more than two Parties to the Contract, the application of the Rules may be adapted, as appropriate, to the multiparty situation by agreement of all of the Parties or, failing such agreement, by the DB.

THE THREE SERVICES PROVIDED BY THE DISPUTE BOARD

Article 16: Avoidance of Disagreements

If at any time, in particular during meetings or site visits, the DB considers that there may be a potential Disagreement between the parties, the DB may raise this with the Parties with a view to encouraging them to avoid the Disagreement on their own without any further involvement of the DB. In so doing, the DB may assist the Parties in defining the potential Disagreement. The DB may suggest a specific process that the Parties could follow to avoid the Disagreement, while making it clear to the Parties that it stands ready to provide informal assistance or to issue a Conclusion in the event that the Parties are unable to avoid the Disagreement on their own.

Article 17: Informal Assistance with Disagreements

1. On its own initiative or upon the request of any Party and in either case with the agreement of all of the Parties, the DB may informally assist the Parties in resolving any Disagreements that have arisen during the performance of the Contract. Such informal assistance may occur during any meeting or site visit. A Party proposing informal assistance from the DB shall endeavour to inform the DB and the other Party thereof well in advance of the meeting or site visit during which such informal assistance would occur.

2. The informal assistance of the DB may take the form of a conversation among the DB and the Parties; one or more separate meetings between the DB and any Party with the prior agreement of all of the Parties; informal views given by the DB to the Parties; a written note from the DB to the Parties; or any other form of assistance that may help the Parties resolve the Disagreement.

3. If called upon to issue a Conclusion in connection with a Disagreement on which it has provided informal assistance, the DB shall not be bound by any views, whether expressed orally or in writing, that it may have given in the course of its informal assistance, nor shall it take into account any information that has not been available to all Parties.

Article 18: Formal Referral for a Conclusion

Any Party may at any time formally refer a Disagreement to the DB for a Conclusion, at which point the Disagreement becomes a Dispute. During the formal referral there shall be no informal conversations and no separate meetings between any DB Member and any Party with respect to any of the issues covered by the formal referral. The procedures set forth below shall apply to formal referrals.

PROCEDURE FOR FORMAL REFERRAL OF DISPUTES

Article 19: Statement of Case

1. Any Party shall refer a Dispute to the DB by submitting a concise written statement of its case (the "Statement of Case") to the other Party and the DB. The Statement of Case shall include:

- a clear and concise description of the nature and circumstances of the Dispute;
- a list of the issues submitted to the DB for a Conclusion and a statement of the referring Party's position thereon, including any relevant facts and law;
- relevant support for the referring Party's position such as documents, drawings, schedules and correspondence;
- a statement of the relief sought, together with the amounts of any quantified claims and, to the extent possible, an estimate of the monetary value of any other claims;
- any request for interim or conservatory measures; and
- in the case of a CDB, if the referring Party wishes the CDB to render a Decision, its request for a Decision and the reasons why it believes that the CDB should render a Decision rather than a Recommendation.

2. The date on which the Statement of Case is received by the sole DB Member or the president of the DB, as the case may be, shall, for all purposes, be deemed to be the date of the commencement of the referral (the "Date of Commencement").

3. The Parties remain free to settle the Dispute at any time, with or without the assistance of the DB.

Article 20: Response and Additional Documentation

1. Unless the Parties agree otherwise or the DB orders otherwise, within 30 days of receiving the Statement of Case the responding Party shall respond in writing (the "Response"). The Response shall include:

- a clear and concise statement of the responding Party's position with respect to the Dispute;
- relevant support for its position such as documents, drawings, schedules and correspondence;
- a statement of the issues on which the responding Party requests the DB's Conclusion, including any request for interim or conservatory measures;

- in the case of a CDB, a response to any request for a Decision made by the referring Party or, if the referring Party has not made such a request, any request for a Decision by the responding Party, including the reasons why it believes that the CDB should issue the type of Conclusion it desires.

2. The DB may at any time request a Party to submit additional written statements or documentation to assist the DB in preparing its Conclusion. Each such request shall be communicated in writing by the DB to the Parties.

Article 21: Organization and Conduct of Hearings

1. A hearing regarding a Dispute shall be held unless the Parties and the DB agree otherwise.

2. Unless the DB orders otherwise, hearings shall be held within 15 days of the date on which the sole DB Member or the president of the DB, as the case may be, receives the Response.

3. Hearings shall be held in the presence of all DB Members unless the DB decides, in the circumstances and after consultation with the Parties, that it is appropriate to hold the hearing in the absence of a DB Member. Prior to the replacement of a DB Member, a hearing may be held with the remaining DB Members only with the agreement of all of the Parties pursuant to Article 7(6).

4. If any of the Parties refuses or fails to take part in the DB procedure or any stage thereof, the DB may proceed notwithstanding such refusal or failure.

5. The DB shall be in full charge of the hearings.

6. The DB shall act fairly and impartially and ensure that each Party has a reasonable opportunity to present its case.

7. The Parties shall appear in person or through duly authorized representatives who are in charge of the performance of the Contract. In addition, they may be assisted by advisers.

8. Unless the DB decides otherwise, the hearing shall proceed as follows:
   - presentation of the case, first by the referring Party and then by the responding Party;
   - identification by the DB of any matters that need further clarification;
   - clarification by the Parties concerning the matters identified by the DB;
   - responses by each Party to clarifications made by the other Party, to the extent that new issues have been raised in such clarifications.

9. The DB may request the Parties to provide written summaries of their presentations.

10. The DB may deliberate at any location it considers appropriate before issuing its Conclusion.

CONCLUSIONS OF THE DISPUTE BOARD

Article 22: Time Limit for Issuing a Conclusion

1. The DB shall issue its Conclusion promptly and, in any event, within 90 days of the Date of Commencement as defined in Article 19(2). However, the DB may extend the time limit with the agreement of the Parties. In the absence of such agreement, the DB may, after consulting the Parties, extend the time limit by the shortest time it considers

necessary, provided, however, that the total duration of any such extensions shall not exceed 20 days. In deciding whether to extend the time limit, the DB and the Parties shall take into account the nature and complexity of the Dispute and other relevant circumstances.

2. Where the Parties have agreed to submit Decisions to the ICC for review, the time limit for rendering a Decision shall be extended by the time required for the Centre to review the Decision. The Centre shall complete its review within 30 days of its receipt of the Decision or of the payment of the filing fee referred to in Article 3 of the Appendix, whichever occurs later. However, if additional time is required for such review, the Centre shall notify the DB and the Parties thereof in writing before the expiration of the 30 days, specifying the new date by which the Centre's review shall be completed.

Article 23: Review of Decisions by the Centre

Where the Parties have provided for review by the Centre of the Decisions of a DAB or a CDB, the DB shall submit the Decision in draft form to the Centre before it is signed. Each Decision shall be accompanied by the filing fee referred to in Article 3 of the Appendix. The Centre may lay down modifications only as to the form of the Decision. No Decision shall be signed by the DB Members or communicated to the Parties until it has been approved by the Centre.

Article 24: Contents of a Conclusion

Conclusions shall indicate the date on which they are issued and shall state the findings of the DB as well as the reasons upon which they are based. Conclusions may also include, without limitation and not necessarily in the following order:

- a summary of the Dispute, the respective positions of the Parties and the Conclusion requested;
- a summary of the relevant provisions of the Contract;
- a chronology of relevant events;
- a summary of the procedure followed by the DB; and
- a list of the submissions and documents produced by the Parties in the course of the procedure.

Article 25: Issuing the Conclusion

When the DB is composed of three or more DB Members, the DB shall make every effort to achieve unanimity. If this cannot be achieved, a Conclusion is rendered by a majority of the DB Members. If there is no majority, the Conclusion shall be rendered by the president of the DB alone. Any DB Member who disagrees with the Conclusion shall give the reasons for such disagreement in a separate written document that shall not form part of the Conclusion but shall be communicated to the Parties. The failure of a DB Member to give such reasons shall not prevent the Conclusion from being issued or taking effect.

Article 26: Correction and Interpretation of Conclusions

1. On its own initiative, the DB may correct a clerical, computational or typographical error, or any errors of a similar nature contained in a Conclusion, provided such correction is submitted to the Parties within 30 days of the date of such Conclusion.

2. Any Party may apply to the DB for the correction of an error of the kind referred to in Article 26(1), or for the interpretation of a Conclusion. Such application shall be made to the DB within 30 days of the receipt of the Conclusion by such Party. After receipt of the application by the sole DB Member or the president of the DB, as the case may be, the DB shall grant the other Party a short time limit from the receipt of the application by that Party, to submit any comments thereon. Any correction or interpretation made by the DB shall be issued within 30 days following the expiration of the time limit for the receipt of any comments from the other Party. However, the Parties may agree to extend the time limit for issuing any correction or interpretation.

3. Should the DB issue a correction or interpretation of the Conclusion, all time limits associated with the Conclusion shall start to run afresh upon receipt by the Parties of the correction or interpretation of the Conclusion.

Article 27: Admissibility of Conclusions in Subsequent Proceedings

Unless otherwise agreed by the Parties, any Conclusion, and any separate written document issued pursuant to Article 25, shall be admissible in any judicial or arbitral proceedings in which all of the parties thereto were Parties to the DB proceedings in which the Conclusion was issued.

COMPENSATION OF THE DISPUTE BOARD MEMBERS AND THE ICC

Article 28: General Considerations

1. All fees and expenses of the DB Members shall be shared equally by the Parties, unless otherwise agreed by the Parties.

2. Unless otherwise agreed by the Parties, when there are three or more DB Members, they shall all be treated equally and shall receive the same monthly management fee and the same daily fee for work performed as a DB Member.

3. Unless otherwise provided in the DB Member Agreement(s), the fees shall be fixed for the first 24 months following the signature of the DB Member Agreement(s) and thereafter shall be adjusted on each anniversary of the DB Member Agreement(s) in accordance with the terms thereof.

4. If the Parties and the DB Members cannot agree upon the fees of the DB Members, the Centre, at the request of any Party or any DB Member, shall fix such fees after consulting the Parties and the DB Members. The Parties shall be bound by the Centre's determination. The DB Members shall either accept the determination or decline the appointment.

Article 29: Monthly Management Fee

1. Unless otherwise provided in the DB Member Agreement(s), each DB Member shall receive a monthly management fee, as set out in the DB Member Agreement(s), to cover the following:

- becoming and remaining conversant with the Contract and the progress of its performance;
- activities in managing and coordinating the operation of the DB;
- studying progress reports in order, *inter alia*, to evaluate the progress of performance and identify potential Disagreements;
- reviewing all correspondence between the Parties copied to the DB;

- being available to attend all DB meetings with the Parties, internal DB meetings, and site visits; and
- fixed office overhead expenses.

2. Unless otherwise agreed in the DB Member Agreement(s), the monthly management fee shall be equal to three times the daily fee set out in the DB Member Agreement(s) and shall be payable from the date of signature of the DB Member Agreement(s) until termination of the DB Member Agreement(s), except as provided in Article 10(2).

Article 30: Daily Fee

Unless otherwise agreed in the DB Member Agreement (s), each DB Member shall receive a daily fee, as set out in the DB Member Agreement(s), to cover time spent on the following activities:

- meetings and site visits;
- travel;
- internal meetings of the DB;
- study of documents submitted by the Parties in connection with procedures before the DB;
- work in connection with avoidance of Disagreements;
- work in connection with informal assistance with Disagreements; and
- work in connection with a formal referral for a Conclusion, including hearings.

Article 31: Travel Costs and Other Expenses

1. Unless otherwise provided in the DB Member Agreement(s), air travel expenses shall be reimbursed at unrestricted business class rates between a DB Member's home and the destination. Expenses incurred for hotels and meals when travelling shall be reimbursed at cost.

2. Unless otherwise provided in the DB Member Agreement(s), expenses incurred in DB work for ground transport, long distance telephone calls, courier services, photocopying, postage, visas, etc., shall be reimbursed at cost.

Article 32: Taxes and Charges

1. No taxes and charges, except for value added tax (VAT), levied in connection with the services rendered by a DB Member by the country of the residence or nationality of the DB Member shall be reimbursed by the Parties.

2. All taxes and charges levied in connection with such services by any country other than the DB Member's country of residence or nationality, as well as VAT wherever levied, shall be reimbursed by the Parties.

Article 33: Payment Arrangements

1. Unless otherwise agreed, invoices shall be submitted by each DB Member to each Party for payment as follows:

- monthly management fees shall be invoiced and paid on a quarterly basis in advance for the next three-month period.
- daily fees and travel expenses shall be invoiced and paid after each meeting, site visit, hearing or Conclusion.

2. Invoices of DB Members shall be paid within 30 days of receipt.

3. The failure of any Party to pay its share of fees and expenses within 30 days of receiving a DB Member's invoice shall entitle the DB Member, in addition to any other rights, to suspend work 15 days after providing a notice of suspension to the Parties and any other DB Members, such suspension remaining in effect until receipt of full payment of all outstanding amounts plus simple interest at one-year LIBOR plus two per cent, or the twelve-month prime interest rate in the currency agreed between the Parties and the DB Members.

4. In the event that a Party fails to pay its share of the fees and expenses of a DB Member when due, any other Party, without waiving its rights, may pay the outstanding amount. The Party making such payment, in addition to any other rights, shall be entitled to reimbursement from the non-paying Party of all such sums paid, plus, unless prohibited by applicable law, simple interest at one-year LIBOR plus two per cent, or the twelve-month prime interest rate in the currency agreed between the Parties and the DB Members.

5. Upon signing the DB Member Agreement, the Parties shall provide the DB Member with the form of the invoice to be sent by DB Members, including the invoicing address, number of copies of invoices required, and VAT number, if applicable.

Article 34: Administrative Expenses of the Centre

1. The Centre's administrative expenses include an amount for each appointment of a DB Member, an amount for each request for the Centre to fix the fees of the DB Members, an amount for each decision upon a challenge of a DB Member and, when the Parties have agreed to submit Decisions of a DAB or a CDB to the Centre for review, an amount for each such review.

2. For each request for appointment of a DB Member, the Centre shall receive the non-refundable amount specified in Article 1 of the Appendix. This amount shall represent the total cost for the appointment of one DB Member by the Centre. The Centre shall not proceed with the appointment unless the requisite payment has been received. The cost of each appointment by the Centre shall be shared equally by the Parties.

3. For each decision upon a challenge of a DB Member, the Centre shall fix administrative expenses in an amount not exceeding the maximum sum specified in Article 2 of the Appendix. This amount shall represent the total cost for the Centre's decision upon one challenge of a DB Member. The Centre shall not proceed with the rendering of its decision, and the making of the challenge shall have no effect, unless the said amount has been received by the Centre. The cost of each decision by the Centre shall be borne by the Party making the challenge.

4. Where the Parties have provided for the review by the Centre of a DAB's or a CDB's Decisions, the Centre shall fix administrative expenses for the review of each Decision in an amount not exceeding the maximum sum specified in Article 3 of the Appendix. This amount shall represent the total cost for the review of one Decision by the Centre. The Centre shall not approve a Decision unless the said amount has been received by the Centre. The cost of reviewing each Decision shall be shared equally by the Parties.

5. For each request for the Centre to fix the fees of the DB Members, the Centre shall receive the non-refundable amount specified in Article 4 of the Appendix. This amount shall represent the total cost for determination of the DB members' fees by the Centre. The Centre shall not proceed with fixing the fees of the DB Members unless the

requisite payment has been received. The cost of the Centre's services in fixing the DB Members' fees shall be shared equally by the Parties.

6. If a Party fails to pay its share of the administrative expenses of the Centre, the other Party shall be free to pay the entire amount of such administrative expenses.

Article 35: General Provisions

1. Where the parties have agreed upon the application of the Rules after the date of the entry into force of the 2015 ICC Dispute Board Rules, they shall be deemed to have agreed upon the application of that version of the Rules, unless they have agreed otherwise.

2. The DB Members, the Centre, the ICC and its employees, the ICC National Committees and Groups and their employees and representatives shall not be liable to any person for any act or omission in connection with the DB proceedings, except to the extent such limitation of liability is prohibited by applicable law.

3. In all matters not expressly provided for in the Rules, the DB and the Centre shall act in the spirit of the Rules and the DB shall make every effort to make sure that Conclusions are issued in accordance with the Rules.

APPENDIX – SCHEDULE OF COSTS

Article 1

Each request for appointment of a DB Member must be accompanied by a filing fee of US$ 3,000 per DB Member to be appointed. The filing fee is non-refundable. No request for appointment of a DB Member shall be processed unless accompanied by the requisite payment.

Article 2

Each request for a decision upon a challenge of a DB Member must be accompanied by a filing fee of US$ 3,000. No request for a decision upon a challenge of a DB member shall be processed unless accompanied by the requisite payment. The filing fee is non refundable and shall be credited to the administrative expenses for a decision upon a challenge. The Centre shall fix said administrative expenses in an amount not exceeding the maximum sum of US$ 10,000.

Article 3

Each decision of a DAB or a CDB submitted to the Centre for review must be accompanied by a filing fee of US$ 3,000. No Decision shall be reviewed unless accompanied by the requisite payment. The filing fee is non-refundable and shall be credited to the administrative expenses for the review of each Decision. The Centre shall fix said administrative expenses in an amount not exceeding the maximum sum of US$ 10,000.

Article 4

Each request for the Centre to fix the fees of the DB Members must be accompanied by a filing fee of US$ 3,000. The filing fee is non-refundable. No request for the Centre to fix the fees of the DB Members shall be processed unless accompanied by the requisite payment.

APPENDIX 29

ICC DISPUTE BOARD CLAUSES (2015)

DISPUTE BOARD RULES – ICC DISPUTE BOARD CLAUSES (2015)

Below are standard clauses for use by parties who wish to set up and operate a dispute board under the Rules contained in this booklet.

ICC Dispute Review Board followed by ICC arbitration if required

The Parties hereby agree to establish a Dispute Review Board ("DRB") in accordance with the Dispute Board Rules of the International Chamber of Commerce (the "Rules"), which are incorporated herein by reference. The DRB shall have [one/three/X] member[s] appointed in this Contract or appointed pursuant to the Rules.

All disputes arising out of or in connection with the present Contract shall be submitted, in the first instance, to the DRB in accordance with the Rules. For any given dispute, the DRB shall issue a Recommendation in accordance with the Rules.

If any Party fails to comply with a Recommendation, when required to do so pursuant to the Rules, the other Party may refer the failure itself, without having to refer it to the DRB first, to arbitration under the Rules of Arbitration of the International Chamber of Commerce by one or more arbitrators appointed in accordance with the said Rules of Arbitration. A Party that has failed to comply with a Recommendation, when required to do so pursuant to the Rules, shall not raise any issue as to the merits of the Recommendation as a defence to its failure to comply without delay with the Recommendation.

If any Party sends a written notice to the other Party and the DRB expressing its dissatisfaction with a Recommendation, as provided in the Rules, or if the DRB does not issue the Recommendation within the time limit provided in the Rules, or if the DRB is disbanded pursuant to the Rules prior to issuing the Recommendation, the dispute shall be finally settled under the Rules of Arbitration of the International Chamber of Commerce by one or more arbitrators appointed in accordance with the said Rules of Arbitration.

ICC Dispute Adjudication Board followed by ICC arbitration if required

The Parties hereby agree to establish a Dispute Adjudication Board ("DAB") in accordance with the Dispute Board Rules of the International Chamber of Commerce (the

"Rules"), which are incorporated herein by reference. The DAB shall have [one/three/X] member[s] appointed in this Contract or appointed pursuant to the Rules.

All disputes arising out of or in connection with the present Contract shall be submitted, in the first instance, to the DAB in accordance with the Rules. For any given dispute, the DAB shall issue a Decision in accordance with the Rules. *

If any Party fails to comply with a Decision, when required to do so pursuant to the Rules, the other Party may refer the failure itself, without having to refer it to the DAB first, to arbitration under the Rules of Arbitration of the International Chamber of Commerce by one or more arbitrators appointed in accordance with the said Rules of Arbitration. A Party that has failed to comply with a Decision, when required to do so pursuant to the Rules, shall not raise any issue as to the merits of the Decision as a defence to its failure to comply without delay with the Decision.

If any Party sends a written notice to the other Party and the DAB expressing its dissatisfaction with a Decision, as provided in the Rules, or if the DAB does not issue the Decision within the time limit provided in the Rules, or if the DAB is disbanded pursuant to the Rules prior to issuing the Decision, the dispute shall be finally settled under the Rules of Arbitration of the International Chamber of Commerce by one or more arbitrators appointed in accordance with the said Rules of Arbitration.

[* The Parties may, if they wish, provide for review by the Centre of a DAB's Decisions by inserting the following text in place of the asterisk above: The DAB shall submit each Decision to the ICC for review in accordance with Article 23 of the Rules.]

ICC Combined Dispute Board followed by ICC arbitration if required

The Parties hereby agree to establish a Combined Dispute Board ("CDB") in accordance with the Dispute Board Rules of the International Chamber of Commerce (the "Rules"), which are incorporated herein by reference. The CDB shall have [one/three/X] member[s] appointed in this Contract or appointed pursuant to the Rules.

All disputes arising out of or in connection with the present Contract shall be submitted, in the first instance, to the CDB in accordance with the Rules. For any given dispute, the CDB shall issue a Recommendation, unless the Parties agree that it shall render a Decision or it decides to do so upon the request of a Party and in accordance with the Rules. *

If any Party fails to comply with a Recommendation or a Decision, when required to do so pursuant to the Rules, the other Party may refer the failure itself, without having to refer it to the CDB first, to arbitration under the Rules of Arbitration of the International Chamber of Commerce by one or more arbitrators appointed in accordance with the said Rules of Arbitration. A Party that has failed to comply with a Recommendation or a Decision, when required to do so pursuant to the Rules, shall not raise any issue as to the merits of the Recommendation or the Decision as a defence to its failure to comply without delay with the Recommendation or the Decision.

If any Party sends a written notice to the other Party and the CDB expressing its dissatisfaction with a Recommendation or a Decision, as provided in the Rules, or if the CDB does not issue the Recommendation or the Decision within the time limit provided in the Rules, or if the CDB is disbanded pursuant to the Rules prior to issuing the Recommendation or the Decision, the dispute shall be finally settled under the Rules of Arbitration of the International Chamber of Commerce by one or more arbitrators appointed in accordance with the said Rules of Arbitration.

[*The Parties may, if they wish, provide for review by the Centre of a CDB's Decisions by inserting the following text in place of the asterisk above: The CDB shall submit each Decision to the ICC for review in accordance with Article 23 of the Rules.]

How to use these clauses

Each of the above clauses provides for a different type of dispute board, followed by arbitration as the ultimate recourse if a dispute is not resolved through the dispute board.

The parties should choose whichever kind of dispute board is most appropriate, given the nature of their contract and their relationship. The ICC does not favour any one type of dispute board over the others.

It may be necessary or desirable for parties to adapt the chosen clause to their particular circumstances. For instance, they may wish to stipulate the number of arbitrators, in the event of arbitration. They may also wish to stipulate the language and place of the arbitration and the law applicable to the merits.

At all times, care must be taken to avoid any risk of ambiguity in the drafting of the clause. Unclear wording causes uncertainty and delay and can hinder or even compromise the dispute resolution process.

When incorporating one of the clauses in their contract, parties are advised to verify its enforceability under applicable law.

Translations of the above clauses can be found at <www.iccdisputeboards.org>.

INDEX AND TABLE OF FIGURES

A. ALPHABETICAL INDEX

A

Acceptance
- arbitrator 63, 65, 66
- emergency arbitrator 160, 161, 163, 167, 324, 325f.
- statement of 63, 65f., 160, 167, 272, 301, 546, 575 (*See also* Statement of acceptance, availability, impartiality and independence)

Acknowledgement of receipt 25, 149

Additional party
- filing of claim 38, 45
- filing of request for, 54, 55
- joinder 23, 44, 53ff. (*See also* Joinder – of additional parties)

Administrative secretary 151, 217. *See also* Assistant to arbitral tribunal

ADR proceedings. *See* Mediation proceedings

Advance on costs of arbitration 33, 36f., 98, 195ff.
- calculation 199f.
- consolidation 63
- cross-claims 59
- definitive 19, 199f.
- duty to pay 202
- emergency arbitrator 171
- expert 145, 264
- failure to pay advance on costs 205ff.
- global 44, 197, 202f.
- increase 133, 201f.
- joinder of additional party 56, 204
- new claims 133
- payment 202f., 205ff., 243 (*See also* Bank guarantee)
- provisional advance on costs 19, 37, 98f., 195f., 198f., 201, 205, 243
- readjustment (reconsideration) 98, 201f.
- reimbursement 219, 221
- separate advances 195ff., 202f.
- set-off 211
- special 143
- to cover arbitrator's fees and expenses 6

Advance on costs for expert proceedings 264

Advance on costs of pre-arbitral referee procedure 248

Advance on fees and expenses of experts 21, 146, 212

Advance to cover additional fees and costs for correction/interpretation of award 193, 214, 218, 361

Advance to cover costs related to hearings 151

Affidavits 142

American Arbitration Association 112

'Amiable compositeur' 116, 119f.

'Amiable composition' 119f.

Amicable dispute resolution 37, 136, 234

Amicable negotiations 25, 259

Amicable settlement 218, 234, 248, 259

Amount in dispute 33, 41, 59, 63, 74, 85, 98, 128, 133, 137, 147, 197ff., 213ff., 218ff., 237
- decrease 37
- increase 37, 45
- unquantified 198

Answer to request for arbitration 38ff.
- time limit 43f., 230f.

Apostille 189

Appointing authority 226, 246, 515ff.
Appointment. *See* Arbitrator
Approval
- of addendum 194, 242, 310
- of draft award 154, 156, 182ff., 216, 237
- of modified time limit 226
- of Terms of Reference 131, 210
Arbitrability
- of dispute 117, 118, 233
- of subject matter of dispute 40, 103, 190
- restrictions on 103
Arbitral award
- addendum 191ff., 310, 361f.
- by consent 180ff., 218f.
- contradicting that of first tribunal 134
- correction and interpretation 191ff., 219, 242, 310, 361ff.
- domestic 109, 179
- draft award 11, 18, 21, 97, 107, 150, 153, 154, 156, 173, 176, 178, 179, 181, 182ff., 193, 216, 230, 237, 242
  - submission to ICC Court 237
- enforceable 9, 85, 106, 156, 157, 175, 180, 245 (*See also* Enforceability; Enforcement)
- enforceable at law 182, 229f.
- final 9, 10, 23, 88, 143, 145, 154, 156, 173, 175, 181, 182, 185, 191, 201, 218
- foreign 2, 109, 179
- interim (partial) 9, 23, 145, 175, 182, 185
- international arbitration awards 5
- nationality 179
- original 14, 185, 187, 188
- partial (interim) 9, 23, 145, 175, 185
- place where rendered 179
- reasoned 119
- recognition 2ff., 48, 103, 106, 119, 124, 181, 190, 228, 233, 237
- remission 195, 243
- rendering of award 97, 107, 108, 242
- setting aside 4, 7, 9, 25, 88, 103, 109, 119, 124, 190, 228, 229, 233
- void 190
- withholding of award 188
Arbitral tribunal 97ff.
- acting unfairly or partially 108, 228
- a-national character 2
- assistant (*See* Administrative secretary)
- composition, make-up 10, 41, 144, 146
- comprising one or three members 41, 235
- comprising three members (*See* three-member)
- comprising two members 235f.
- constitution, setting up 6f., 10, 32, 37, 41ff., 67, 72, 79, 73ff., 107, 232, 236
- incorrectly constituted 88
- international 44, 117, 146
- liberty of decision 182, 184
- majority of its members 9, 132, 175, 194
- permanent 6
- president of 75, 78, 79, 84, 86, 302, 427
- reconstituted 92, 96
- seat 101, 104, 114f., 118
- suspension of its work 19, 196, 205, 243
- three-member 6, 34ff., 41f., 72ff., 75f., 76, 97, 98, 111, 132, 198, 237, 240f., 348 (*See also* Arbitrator – three)
- truncated 97
Arbitration
- *ad hoc* 6, 10, 27
- conduct of 7f., 174, 241 (*See also* Proceedings – conduct of)
- domestic 2, 64
- fast track 226f., 485
- institutional 10, 232
- international 2, 5, 7, 8, 30, 48, 103, 109, 112, 118, 119, 131, 136, 137, 140, 142, 146, 152, 175, 229, 259
- multilingual 112
- multiparty 50, 52, 53, 57, 59, 75, 121, 138, 166, 204, 235
Arbitration agreement 2, 3, 6, 34f., 42, 52, 56, 60, 74, 117, 132, 172f., 174, 190, 215, 226, 227, 231ff. *See also* Arbitration clause
- absence 113
- applicable law 233
- compatible 46, 50, 56, 60ff.
- contents 7, 10

- effect 45ff.
- existence 5, 48
- made before 1 January 1998 47
- made before 1 January 2012 47, 156
- more than one 33, 46, 50f., 54, 60ff.
- not empowered to sign 48
- nullity 190
- objection to 48
- scope 48
- separability 52
- signed after 1 January 2012 163
- validity 48, 52, 55, 57, 60, 132, 233f.
- void 1, 48, 233

Arbitration clause 16, 21, 43, 102, 134, 231ff.
- standard ICC arbitration clause 48, 231ff., 245

Arbitrator
- abilities 78
- additional 235
- appointment 3, 16f., 19, 25, 72ff., 78ff., 91, 232, 241
  - direct appointment 76, 86f.
- background (*See* origins)
- challenge 3, 4, 7, 8, 16, 25, 64, 67, 70, 71, 88ff., 108, 109, 123, 152, 160, 168, 171, 216, 226, 228, 241
- criterion for selecting sole arbitrator or president of arbitral tribunal 35
- death 92f.
- failure to fulfil duties 90
- independence 64ff., 79
- international 8, 115
- nomination 27, 34f., 42, 43, 58, 66, 72, 77f., 111, 236, 240f.
  - by third party 6, 236
  - joint nomination of arbitrator 34, 73, 76
  - joint nomination of sole arbitrator 74
- number of 6, 34, 36, 38, 41, 42, 72, 74, 231, 232, 236, 240
- no agreement on number 74
- objection to 67, 76
- origins 7, 103
- place of residence 2, 78f., 222
- prospective 67ff., 76, 79
- record of expenses 21
- relations with a party or its counsel 90
- remaining 97
- removal from office
  - by parties 93f.
  - by state court 228
- replacement 3, 4, 7, 10, 70f., 92ff., 241
- resignation 92f., 216
- sole 6, 34, 35, 41f., 73ff., 76, 85, 103, 117, 184, 198, 200, 236, 237, 240
- third (president of arbitral tribunal) 6, 72, 75f., 98, 236, 240
- three 6, 34, 37, 41f., 72ff., 73, 76, 98, 111, 132, 198, 200, 215, 235, 236, 237 (*See also* Co-arbitrator; Number – of arbitrators; Arbitral tribunal)
- two 73, 97, 98, 216, 235 (*See also* Co-arbitrator; Number – of arbitrators; Arbitral tribunal)

Assistant to arbitral tribunal 151, 217. *See also* Administrative secretary

Attachment (seizure) 157

Availability
- statement of 63ff., 309 (*See also* Statement of acceptance, availability, impartiality and independence)

Authority
- proof of 100, 101, 153, 165, 304

Autonomy
- of arbitration agreement 52
- party autonomy 72, 93f., 105, 122, 133, 144, 146, 226, 227, 236

Award. *See* Arbitral award

B

Bank guarantee 202, 211f.

Battle of forms 48

Belgium 2, 4, 5, 64, 101, 156, 181

Burden of proof 145f.

B. von Hoffmann v. Finanzamt Trier 222

C

Calculation
- of advance 196ff., 212
- of time limits 26, 239, 296
- of administrative expenses 222ff.
- of arbitrators' fees 222f.

Capacity to contract 117

Case management

- conference 7, 14, 41, 72, 106, 131, 135ff., 150, 174, 241, 306, 345, 370, 374f., 402, 409ff., 419, 444, 450
- procedural measures 106, 120, 122, 131, 135, 137, 241, 305, 306, 346, 374, 375, 401f., 407, 409
- procedural timetable 121, 135ff., 174, 241f., 306, 345, 358, 408, 410
- techniques 15, 122, 135ff., 149, 215, 306, 322, 335, 346, 372, 374, 390, 407, 409, 429, 444

Chair
- of arbitral tribunal (*See* Arbitral tribunal – president, Arbitrator – third)

Challenge of arbitrators 3, 7, 25, 88ff., 97, 108, 152, 168, 226, 241
- administrative procedure 88

Charges 214, 222, 258. *See also* Taxes

Choice
- between arbitral tribunal and judicial authority 157
- choice-of-law rules 9
- of arbitrators 27, 34, 38, 41f., 65, 79, 85, 96, 114, 237, 239 (*See also* Nomination)
  - independent arbitrator 65
- of domicile 128
- of expert 144
- of ICC Rules of Arbitration 47
- of language 112f (*See also* Language)
- of law 113f.
  - clause 114
  - negative 114f.
- of means of communication 25
- of national committee or group 85
- of party representative 152 (*See also* Party representation)
- of previous version of the Rules 47
- of place of the arbitration 101
- of a rapporteur 18
- of rules of law 113
- of third arbitrator 75, 98, 236
- of three-member arbitral tribunal 74, 237

Civil law 44, 107f., 127, 140, 146, 229, 259

Claim(s) 57, 32f., 37, 47, 48, 98, 118, 119, 127, 128, 130, 134, 150, 175, 203, 233
- considered as withdrawn 210f.
- excessive 198
- for set-off 44, 181, 203, 211 (*See also* Set-off)
- frivolous 198
- in currency other than US dollars 200
- multiple parties 52, 56ff., 204, 300, 334, 337, 338, 419
- new 129, 133ff., 175
  - authorization of new claims 37, 133f.
- of claimant 39, 98, 211
- of respondent 39, 40, 98
- original claim 134
- principal 200, 202, 212
- reintroduction 52
- quantified 33, 58, 128, 200
- unquantified 41, 54, 128, 200
- unwarranted 157
- withdrawal 180

Closing
- of deliberations 97
- of proceedings 91, 133, 134, 148, 153f., 191, 242

Co-arbitrator 73
- appointment 6, 42, 70, 241
- confirmation (*See* Confirmation)
- fees 215
- joint nomination 76
- nationality 85
- nomination 6, 37, 42, 75, 85, 240f.
- power to choose president of arbitral tribunal 75, 236

Committee (of the Court) 16f., 21, 94, 185, 199

Common law 9, 107f., 143, 146, 179, 259

Communication(s) 7, 24ff., 39, 146f., 179, 239, 243. *See also* Notification

Competence competence. *See* Jurisdiction

Complexity
- of the case 14, 74
- of the proceedings 152, 174, 201, 215, 252, 317

Compromise 180. *See also* Settlement

Conciliation 2f., 245

Conduct
- case management 120, 305
- compliance with order 160
- confidentiality 120, 305
- controlling time and costs 99, 120ff., 346

- cost effectiveness 72, 120ff., 138, 213, 220, 305, 311, 334, 335, 346, 369, 371, 372, 410, 411, 552
- fairness and impartiality 254, 530
- procedural measures 120, 305, 346, 374
- proceedings 7ff., 120f. (*See also* Proceedings)

Confidential information 124
Confidentiality 13, 18, 25, 124, 146f., 151, 179, 189, 255f. *See also* Secrecy
Confirmation
- of arbitrators 16f., 19, 73, 78ff., 88, 91, 236, 240
  - co-arbitrator 75
  - sole arbitrator 42, 240
- of place of the arbitration 101

Conflicts of interest 18, 67, 70, 76, 125, 153
Conservatory and interim measures 5, 124, 155ff., 175
Consolidation
- conditions 61ff.
- of arbitrations 17, 52f., 60ff. (*See also* Multiple parties)

Contract 3, 10, 33, 48, 133ff., 118, 127, 134, 140, 229
- applicable law 237
- arbitration agreement 231ff.
- centre of gravity 116
- freedom to 118
- international 117, 237
- interpretation 112, 226
- language 33, 42, 110
- validity 116
- void 118, 233

Correction of errors. *See* Errors
Costs 7, 19, 41, 212ff. (*See also* Advance on costs of arbitration; expenses)
- additional 151, 193, 195, 219, 362
- administrative expenses 17, 33, 36, 51, 62, 71, 91, 96, 121, 128, 162, 181, 187, 188, 191, 193, 195, 217, 256
- controlling 15, 99, 102, 120f., 128, 135ff., 215
- decision on costs 145, 184, 192, 201, 212ff., 218, 220
- definition 214ff.
- emergency arbitrator proceedings 158, 162, 170, 171
- for making written record of hearing 143, 151
- incurred by ICC Court and Secretariat 202, 217
- incurred by parties for arbitration 41, 121, 215, 218
- interpretation costs 143
- mediation 256f.
- of administrative secretary 151
- of arbitration 181, 187, 197, 212ff.
- of experts 143, 145f., 212, 217, 264
- of witnesses 143
- pre-arbitral referee 248
- procedural costs 33, 152, 154 (*See also* Costs – decision on costs)
- translating costs 112, 113
- withdrawal of claims 221

Counsel. *See also* Lawyer
- in-house 153
- of Secretariat 18ff., 184
- to parties 9, 18, 30, 85, 117, 141f., 153

Counterclaim 38ff., 44, 74, 98, 128, 133, 138, 181, 195ff.
- reply to counterclaim 20, 39, 45, 240

Court. 1ff., 2, 3ff., 32, 49, 73, 88, 101f., 109, 115, 118f., 124, 143, 146, 157f., 190, 228f., 233, 246f. *See also* Judicial authority; ICC International Court of Arbitration
- jurisdiction 2, 3ff., 105, 117f., 143, 155f., 232
- review 9, 88, 229

Curriculum vitae 17, 67, 100, 151, 253, 329ff.

D

Date. *See also* Hearing; Procedural timetable; Time limits
- commencement of proceedings (*litispendence*) 31, 53f.
- expected date of award 154
- of award 179
- of delivery 26
- of notification 26

Declaration of acceptance 68. *See also* Statement of independence
Deliberations 68f., 154, 187
- place 104f.

Delivery 25, 26, 149, 247. *See also* Means of communication
Dépeçage 117
Deposit. *See also* Advance on costs
- award 189
- as security 157
- for expert proceedings 264
- for mediation proceedings 256
Deputy Secretary General 19, 184
Dilatory tactics 132, 134, 202
DIS 112
Discovery 8,
- pre-trial discovery 8
Dispute Boards 245, 271f.
- Dispute Adjudication Board 250, 271
- Dispute Review Board 3, 250, 271
Dissenting opinion 178f., 182, 185
DOCDEX proceedings 269f.
Due process 107, 141f., 145, 150, 152, 254
Dutco 75f.
Duty. *See also* Obligation
- duties of arbitrator 7, 70f., 90, 98, 106, 108, 120, 123f., 136
  - to be impartial and independent 64f.
  - to disclose 67, 90
- of parties to collaborate 10
  - financial duties of parties (*See* Advance on costs of arbitration)
- to carry out the award 190
- to disclose documents 140, 146
- to maintain confidentiality (*See* Confidentiality)

E

Emergency arbitrator proceedings
- application for emergency measures 158ff., 344, 420
- commencement 164ff.
- costs 162, 170ff., 308, 326, 344
- emergency arbitrator
  - appointment 160, 167, 344
  - challenge 160, 168, 324
- judicial authority 158f.
- language 165f., 339
- order 161, 169f., 325, 339
- place 160f., 165ff., 168f., 324, 339, 344
- termination 160ff., 167, 170ff., 323ff., 339
Emergency arbitrator provisions
- application 158f., 163, 165ff., 172f., 323, 429
- limitation of liability 173
Emergency measures
- application 158ff., 164ff., 267, 308, 323ff., 377, 420
Enforceability. *See also* Enforcement
- award 1ff., 9, 141, 156, 179, 182, 186, 229f.
- conservatory and interim measures 157
Enforcement
- of awards 2, 109, 179, 189f.
  - compulsory 4, 189
  - foreign awards 4f.
  - refusal 6, 190, 229
- of decisions of foreign courts 4
- of procedural orders 157
- order 127, 189
Equity 2, 9, 119
Error (correction of)
- clerical 191, 242, 309
- computational 151, 182, 191, 193, 194, 242, 309
- in award 193f., 219
- typographical 151, 182, 191, 193, 194, 242, 309f.
Evidence 8, 9, 30, 32, 40, 44, 112, 134, 138, 140ff., 152, 211, 237
- additional evidence 139, 146, 211
- assessment of evidence 9, 139, 146, 148
- IBA Rules 8, 106, 130, 147, 385, 413, 435, 437f., 444ff., 451, 452, 463
- new evidence 154
- of expert 30, 121, 140, 215
- of witness 8, 30, 121, 149, 215
- physical evidence 104
- preservation of evidence 156, 189, 247, 249, 452, 453, 520, 574
- rules of 177
- summons to provide evidence 146, 385, 436
- taking of 8, 106, 121, 130, 142, 147, 154, 200, 385, 413, 435, 437, 463
'Ex aequo et bono' 9, 113, 119
Exequatur proceedings 119. *See also* Enforcement

Expenses. *See also* Costs
- administrative expenses 128, 187, 198ff., 202, 217, 256, 261, 262, 264
  - advance payment of 36, 196ff.
  - of arbitral tribunal 198, 199, 215f.
  - reimbursement 348
- of arbitrators 6, 187, 202, 216
- of experts 21, 144, 213, 217f.
- of parties (*See* Costs – parties' costs)
- procedural 112 (*See also* Costs)
- reimbursement 6, 9, 21, 41, 155, 200, 216, 483

Expert 8, 11, 30, 131, 140, 141ff.
- admissibility of expert opinions 142
- appointment 144, 262, 264
- appointed by arbitral tribunal 140, 142, 144f.
- appointed by parties 141ff., 143f.
- costs 212f., 214ff. (*See also* Costs; Expenses)
- independent expert 156
- legal expert opinions 112
- mission 143f., 265
- proposal 261
- report 145, 156, 265
- testimony 142

Expert witnesses 143

Expert proceedings
- administration 260, 262ff.

Expert Rules. *See* ICC Expert Rules

F

Failure. *See also* Duty
- to appear 143, 149f. (*See also* Judgments – default)
- to apply ICC Rules of Arbitration 227, 243
- to comply with procedural orders 122, 147, 227, 243
- to nominate arbitrator 78ff.
- to respect mandatory law 119 (*See also* Enforceability; Exequatur proceedings)
- to pay advance 205 (*See also* Duty)

Fédération Internationale des Ingénieurs-Conseils (FIDIC) 271

Fees. *See also* Costs; Expenses
- additional 193, 361
- of arbitrators 6, 10, 16, 21, 187, 198, 203, 210, 212, 214f., 223ff.
- of experts 21, 213, 215, 217f.
- of lawyers 221

Form
- electronic 147, 433ff.
- evaluation 188f.
- of award 5, 119, 133, 145, 156f., 175, 179, 180f.
- of interim decision of arbitral tribunal 156f.
- of notification 187, 189
- of order 5, 161, 169, 183
- of summons 149
- scrutiny of form by ICC Court 182ff. (*See also* Award)

France 2, 13f., 30, 64, 88, 250

'Functus officio' 191

G

General Counsel 19ff., 188, 189, 316, 336. *See also* ICC International Court of Arbitration

General principles of law 114, 116f. *See also* Law
- general principles of private international law 116
- general principles of procedure 123, 141, 229

Geneva Convention 190

Germany 3ff., 64, 115, 156, 157, 181, 195, 292

Group, of ICC. *See also* ICC group
- proposal of arbitrators 76, 78, 302

H

Hague Convention 189. *See also* Apostille

Hague Convention on the Law Applicable to International Sales of Goods 116

Hearing 9, 108, 141ff., 148f. *See also* Meeting
- adjournment 149
- cancellation or postponement 107
- conduct 149, 150f.
- date 148f.
- exclusion of parties 141
- failure to appear 149f.
- language of hearing (*See* Language – of hearing)
- new 96f., 150
- of witnesses 112, 139, 141ff., 152

- place 104, 148
- record 143, 150f.
- rental of premises 21
- re-opening of hearing 154
- repetition 97, 150
- right to take part in 141, 150
- summons 139, 141f., 148f., 306f.
- translation 109
- use of administrative secretary 151
- waiver of right to 148

Hybrid procedures 3

I

IBA. *See* International Bar Association
ICC ADR Rules. *See* ICC Mediation Rules
ICC Banking Commission 14, 269
ICC Banking Rules 268, 270
ICC Commission on Arbitration and ADR 15, 87, 99, 121, 122, 215, 268, 355, 385, 401ff., 434ff., 471ff., 493ff.
ICC Dispute Board Rules 571ff.
ICC DOCDEX Rules 267ff., 563ff.
ICC Expert Rules 145, 259ff., 539ff.
ICC Executive Board 15, 313f.
ICC group. *See* Group
ICC International Centre for Expertise 13, 14, 145, 245, 260, 268, 336, 356, 483, 485, 499. *See also* ICC International Centre for ADR
- President of Standing Committee 262, 263, 542

ICC International Court of Arbitration 10f., 13ff.
- decision 17, 34ff., 42, 44f., 48ff., 55, 60ff., 70f., 74, 77, 85, 88, 91f., 94, 96f., 133, 173, 182ff., 187f., 202, 216, 218f.
- Deputy Secretary General (*See* Deputy Secretary General)
- General Counsel (*See* General Counsel)
- Internal Rules 15, 18, 19, 314ff.
- members 15, 94, 124
- plenary session 16, 91, 94, 185
- powers 10, 88, 233 (*See also* Advance on costs of arbitration; Appointment; Award; Challenge; Costs; Replacement; Joinder)
- practice 47, 76, 102
- President (*See* President of ICC Court)
- reasons 17, 48, 51, 61, 64, 70f., 91, 94, 96
- Secretary General (*See* Secretary General)
- Statutes 13, 15, 18, 312ff.
- structure 15
- urgent decision 17
- Vice-Presidents 15ff., 162, 172

ICC Mediation Rules 100, 136, 214, 217, 234, 248ff., 373, 424, 527f., 535f.
ICC national committee. *See* National committee(s)
ICC Pre-Arbitral Referee Procedure 156, 245f., 246ff., 519ff.
ICC Rules for a Pre-Arbitral Referee Procedure 246, 519ff.
ICC Rules for Expertise. *See* ICC Expert Rules
ICC Rules of Optional Conciliation. *See* ICC Mediation Rules
ICC Uniform Customs and Practice for Documentary Credits (UCP) 268, 563
ICC Uniform Rules for Bank-to-Bank Reimbursement under Documentary Credits (URR) 268, 563
ICC Uniform Rules for Collections (URC) 268, 563
ICC Uniform Rules for Demand Guarantees (URDG) 268, 563
Immunity
- arbitrator 229 (*See also* Liability)
- judicial 229
- state 118, 424

Impartiality
- arbitrator 63ff., 70, 79, 90, 301
- emergency arbitrator 160, 167, 324, 342
- statement of 19, 65ff., 75, 79, 85, 151 (*See also* Statement of acceptance, availability, impartiality and independence)

Imposts 99, 214, 222, 258, 319, 345, 350, 533, 537. *See also* Charges; Taxes
Independence
- arbitrator 63ff., 85, 90, 236, 240, 301, 517
- emergency arbitrator 160, 167, 324, 342

- statement of 70, 79, 83f., 90, 151, 240, 498, 517 (*See also* Statement of acceptance, availability, impartiality and independence)

Information
- confidential 120, 134ff., 125, 478, 479, 578
- disclosure 66
- expenses of arbitrator 100
- fixing advance on costs 37, 45
- fixing arbitrator's fees 215, 224, 346
- to be disclosed 479
- to be included in application for emergency measures 164
- to be included in request for arbitration 32

Inspection of sites 125, 142

Interim measures. *See* Conservatory and interim measures

International Bar Association
- Guidelines on Conflicts of Interest in International Arbitration 66, 67, 496
- Guidelines on Party Representation in International Arbitration 8, 153
- Rules on Taking of Evidence in International Commercial Arbitration 8, 106, 130, 147, 385, 413, 435, 437ff.

International conventions 114, 116, 157, 222, 237, 245, 293

Interest (claim for) 33, 128, 200

Investment
- arbitration 15, 87, 113, 125, 292, 422, 424f., 428, 429
- treaty 87, 113, 125, 163, 422, 423, 424, 426, 429

Issues to be determined 126f., 260. *See also* Terms of Reference

J

Joinder
- of additional parties 53ff., 76f., 299f., 334, 419 (*See also* Multiple parties)
- of arbitrations 23, 39, 52, 56, 204 (*See also* Consolidation)

Judgments 124. *See also* Courts
- default 148, 150
- foreign 4

Judicial authority 155ff., 172, 189, 230. *See also* Courts

Jurisdiction 2, 3ff., 118, 123
- Competence competence 49, 61, 233
- decision on 52, 56, 58, 130, 160, 166
- Kompetenz-Kompetenz 49, 233
- objection to 32, 40, 48, 49, 183
- of arbitral tribunal 34, 47ff., 127, 132, 175, 192, 233
  - conservatory and interim measures 155f.
- of courts 2, 4f., 118, 129, 133, 183, 232
- of ICC (lack of) 6f., 40, 43, 48, 94
- 'prima facie' decision on 51, 55, 58, 60, 71

K

Kompetenz-Kompetenz. *See* Jurisdiction

L

Language
- courts 1
- foreign language 140
- of applicable rules of law 112f.
- of arbitration 34f., 42, 85, 103f., 107, 109ff., 127, 140, 237
- of contract 109f., 232
- of documents submitted 17, 140
- of hearing 112, 150 (*See also* Language – of arbitration)
- of initial pleadings 21, 39, 111f.
- of proceedings (*See* Language – of arbitration)
- of request for arbitration. (*See* Language – of initial pleadings)
- of answer to request for arbitration. (*See* Language – of initial pleadings)
- official/working language of ICC Court 18, 111

Law. *See also* Rules of law
- agreed 2, 113
- antitrust 118
- applicable
  - at place of the arbitration 110 (*See also* Law – applicable to procedure)
  - at place of enforcement of award 183, 190

- to a party's personal status 118
- to contract 237
- to merits/substance 34f., 42, 85, 113ff., 177, 183
- to procedure 1ff., 10, 88, 103ff., 175 (*See also* '*Lex arbitri*')
- Belgian 1, 3, 6, 155, 231f.
- cantonal 3, 5f., 231, 239
- competition (*See* Antitrust)
- determination of 9, 114ff.
- foreign 152, 228
- French 6, 113
- German 6, 113, 118, 179, 190, 195, 211, 231
- mandatory 8, 88, 94, 103, 115, 117ff., 125, 142, 152f., 155f., 179, 181, 189, 193, 230, 316, 485, 559
- national 2, 10, 48, 103, 105, 113ff.
- of country from which parties originate 117
- procedural 1ff., 8, 10, 67, 105, 115, 131, 141, 146, 155, 190, 232 (*See also* Arbitration law)
  - US procedural law 8
- substantive 9, 42, 85, 115
- Swiss 2, 6, 113, 118, 179, 211

Lawyers 32, 40, 64ff., 70, 79, 101, 124, 153, 215. *See also* Counsel
- duty of discretion as arbitrator 124
- parties' lawyers 66, 103, 110, 112f., 131, 138, 149, 164
  - claimant's lawyer 31, 32
  - fees 215, 218, 221, 258
  - representation by 127f., 152f., 165
  - respondent's lawyer 40
  - secrecy of communications with client 146

'*Lex arbitri*' 7ff., 88, 108, 125, 142f., 152, 175, 191, 194

'*Lex mercatoria*' 114f., 116f.

Liability 48
- exclusion of 229
- limitation of 228

Limitation
- of liability 173, 228f., 256, 262f., 266, 312
- period 36 (*See also* Statutes of limitation; Time bar)

Linguistic skills, requirements
- arbitrators 79, 110, 237
- ICC Court, Secretariat 18, 20
- parties 110
- parties' lawyers 110, 112

List of issues to be determined 126, 128ff. *See also* Issues to be determined

M

Mandatory provisions/rules. *See also* Law – mandatory
- concerning conservatory and interim measures 156
- of lex arbitri 8, 125, 142, 152, 194
- of place of the arbitration 104, 115, 152, 156, 179, 182, 189, 193, 230
- of procedure 88, 103, 105, 115, 141

Means of communication 25, 103, 135, 137, 161, 170, 179

Mediation 2f., 136, 138, 153, 234, 248ff. *See also* ICC Mediation Rules
- commencement 252f.
- conduct 254
- termination 255

Mediator 234, 249ff. *See also* Neutral

Meetings 7, 17, 90, 101, 104, 129, 131, 133, 135, 137, 149, 151, 161, 169, 177, 217, 250, 254, 258. *See also* Hearing

Merits 3, 5, 9, 46, 88f., 113ff., 138, 247. *See also* Substance

Mini-trial 153, 373

Modification
- of amount in dispute 200ff.
- of award as to form 182
- of time limits 226f.

Multiple contracts
- claims 52f., 59f.
- constitution of arbitral tribunal 54, 60f.
- 'prima facie' control 60

Multiple parties
- advance on costs 56
- claims between 56f.
- consolidation of arbitration 60ff.
- constitution of arbitral tribunal 62f.
- joinder 53ff.
- limits 57
- multiple contracts 59f.
- 'prima facie' control 56, 58

N

National committee(s) 13f., 30, 70, 84f., 173, 228
- proposal of arbitrators 70, 78ff.,241

Nationality
- of arbitrator (sole, co-arbitrator, president of arbitral tribunal) 87
- of award 179
- of parties 76

Nature
- of award 190
- of case 85, 162, 171
- of dispute 4, 27, 32, 38, 40, 54, 58, 405
- of ICC Court decisions 17, 51, 61, 71, 94
- of new claims 127, 133, 135
- of Terms of Reference 101, 125

Neutral
- expert 143f.
- fees and expenses 256
- mediator (mediation proceedings) 234, 250, 253ff.

Neutral evaluation 251
Neutrality 21, 87, 427
New York Convention 4, 7, 25, 103, 109, 119, 124, 127, 141, 175, 179ff., 189f., 233, 237, 245
Nomination. *See* Arbitrator
Notification 24ff. *See also* Communication(s)
- address for notification 126ff., 138
- by e-mail 25, 149
- by fax 149
- by registered letter 149
- communication 305, 569
- date of notification 173, 193, 210
- of addendum to award 191
- of answer to request for arbitration 45
- of application for emergency measures 166
- of appointment or confirmation of arbitrator 88, 91, 241
- of approval of Terms of Reference 173, 242
- of arbitration procedure 7, 193
- of award 174, 185, 187f., 193, 220, 242
- of counterclaim 45
- of expert report 263f.
- of hearing 149
- of ICC Court decision 77, 88, 133, 240
- of nomination of arbitrator 34, 77, 301
- of President's decision 168
- of reply to counterclaim 45
- of request for arbitration 20, 36f., 240
- of request for joinder 54
- to the parties' lawyers 149

Number
- of arbitrators 6, 27, 34, 36, 38, 41f., 45, 58, 72ff., 77, 84, 87, 198, 231, 232, 235, 236, 239
- of copies of application for emergency measures 159, 164
- of copies of answer to request for arbitration 29, 38f., 45, 99
- of copies of request for arbitration 24, 27f., 36, 99, 239
- of copies of request for joinder 55
- of copies of pleadings and communications 24
- of copies of request for correction or interpretation 191
- of originals of the arbitral award 185

O

Oath 142, 512
Obligation. *See also* Duty
- confidentiality obligation 124, 146
- to act impartially 71, 108, 123
- to carry out the award 190
- to comply with orders made by the arbitral tribunal 126
- to decide on the costs of arbitration 220
- to disclose circumstances relating to arbitrator's independence 90
- to establish Terms of Reference 16, 127
- to ensure that the arbitral award is enforceable at law 106
- to hear a party 152
- to organize a case management conference 120
- to pay advance on costs 201, 202, 205, 210

- to pay VAT 222
- to submit a draft award for scrutiny to the ICC Court 182

On-site visit 121, 139
Oral proceedings 9

P

Parties
- multiple 52ff., 73, 204, 233
- origins 85, 103, 115, 117, 121, 137, 144, 152, 278ff.
- representatives 7, 17f., 24, 32, 40, 69, 100f., 121f., 128, 138, 140ff., 148ff., 164, 176, 183, 215, 355
  - legal background 7
- will of parties 101

Party representation 8, 101, 152. *See also* Choice – of party representative
Pending case 44, 68, 277, 328
Pending proceedings 18, 33
Per diem 217, 348ff.
Place. *See also* Seat
- of the arbitration 2, 4f., 8, 10, 24, 27, 33ff., 42ff., 50, 56, 60ff., 79, 85, 101ff., 115, 126, 129, 150, 152, 155f., 159f., 165f., 168, 175, 177, 179f., 182f., 190, 193, 200, 230, 232, 237, 277ff.
- neutral 2, 35, 103, 118
- of deliberations 104f.
- of enforcement of award 7
- of hearings 104, 129
- of performance 116, 232
- of conservatory/interim measure 156
- of residence 2, 104, 116, 222
  - of arbitrator 2, 79, 222
- of seller 116

Pleadings 21, 24f., 30, 39f., 43, 110, 111f., 126, 138, 140, 144, 149f., 154
Powers
- of '*amiable composition*' 113, 116, 119, 126 (*See also 'Amiable compositeur'*)
- of arbitral tribunal 8, 52, 100, 137, 139, 143, 148, 155, 175, 191, 217, 229, 233
- of arbitration institution 10, 88
- of attorney 101, 233 (*See also* Proof of authority)
- of co-arbitrators to choose third arbitrator 75, 98, 236
- of Dispute Board 271
- of emergency arbitrator 163, 167
- of expert 260
- of ICC Court 10, 13f., 47, 50, 62, 79, 88, 106, 174, 186, 204, 228, 229
- of pre-arbitral referee 162, 246ff.
- of President of the Court 163, 166, 172, 185
- of representation 117
- of Secretariat 19, 43, 49, 54, 67, 79, 85, 100, 228
- of state courts 103

Pre-Arbitral Referee Procedure. *See* ICC Pre-Arbitral Referee Procedure
President of ICC Court 15, 18, 166f., 185, 247
'Prima facie' 17, 33, 46, 49ff., 55ff., 58, 60, 61, 71, 90, 166, 247
Procedural agreements 107
Procedural defect 5, 228, 229
Procedural order 7, 106, 110, 119, 122f., 129f., 132f., 138, 140, 145, 150f., 156f., 175, 183, 220
Procedural rules 10, 103, 105f., 108, 126f., 129, 133, 152, 156, 190, 228, 258
Procedural timetable 72, 121, 127, 135f., 138f., 140, 161, 169, 173f., 201, 241
Proceedings
- closing. *See* Closing – of proceedings
- conduct of 7ff., 20, 35, 64, 91, 130, 149ff., 228, 237, 243, 254f., 265, 269, 375, 411, 418, 437 (*See also* Arbitration – conduct of)
- continuation of 48, 96f.
- defect (*See* Procedural defect)
- emergency arbitrator 20, 121, 158ff., 323ff., 339f., 419f. (*See also* Emergency arbitrator)
- enforcement/exequatur proceedings 119, 189f.
- expert proceedings 131, 145, 235, 259ff.
- for recognition or enforcement of award 7, 237
- oral proceedings 9
- pending 31, 33 (*See also* Pending case)
- repetition of prior proceedings 93, 96
- replacement proceedings 17, 71, 96

- setting aside proceedings 25, 88, 124, 190, 195, 229
Proof
- burden of 145f., 386, 450
- of authority 32, 40, 100f., 165
Provisional advance on costs 19, 98, 195f., 198f., 206, 243, 310
Provisional timetable. *See* Procedural timetable
Public policy 5, 105, 118f., 190
- international public policy 9, 118f.

R
Reasons
- application for emergency measures 159, 165
- arbitral award 175ff., 182ff., 221
- extension of time limit 379
- ICC Court decision 17, 51, 61, 64, 70, 71, 96
- order of emergency arbitrator 170
- prayer for relief 40f.
Recognition of arbitral award 2ff., 9, 48, 103, 106, 119, 124, 179f., 189f., 233, 237, 245. *See also* Enforcement
Referee 156, 162f. *See also* Pre-Arbitral Referee Procedure
Refusal
- alteration of core features of ICC arbitration 15
- conservatory and interim measure 157
- enforcement of arbitral award 4, 7, 119, 179, 190, 229, 233
- hearing 169
- mediation 253
- plea of party 108, 123
- state court jurisdiction 48
- resignation of arbitrator 93
- to administer arbitration 107
- to appear 142
- to appoint arbitrator 66
- to authorize new claims 134
- to comply with procedural order 147, 157
- to comply with terms of arbitral award 147, 157
- to confirm arbitrator 79
- to hear expert 141
- to hear witness 141
- to nominate arbitrator 3, 42
- to pay advance on costs 44, 46, 202
- to set arbitration in motion 41, 49, 235
- to sign Terms of Reference 132, 173, 210, 241, 242
- to take part in proceedings 6, 33, 46, 97, 126, 149, 227
Registered letter/post 24, 149
Registration fee 253, 256
Reply to counterclaim. *See* Counterclaim
Request for arbitration 26ff.
- answer to (*See* Answer to request for arbitration)
- cursory examination by Secretariat 20f.
- filing 7, 20, 27
- information to be included 32ff.
- joinder/consolidation 204
- language 35, 110, 111
- notification 36
- number of copies 36
- payment of advance on administrative expenses 36
- time limit 36, 239
- withdrawal 9f.
Request for mediation 234, 252f., 424
Rome Convention 116
Rome I Regulation 118
Rule of reason 118
Rules
- applicable to making of award 177
- choice-of-law rules 9
- currency exchange rules 210
- governing proceedings 105ff.
- mandatory rules 8, 88, 94, 103, 117f., 125, 153, 179, 193f.
- of conflict of laws 115, 116 (*See also* Choice-of-law rules)
- of procedure. (*See* Procedural rules)
- procedural rules 10, 103, 105f., 108, 126f., 129, 133, 152, 190, 228, 258
Rules of ICC as Appointing Authority 259, 267, 319, 515ff.
Rules of law. *See also* Law
- applicable 27, 34f., 42, 44, 58, 88, 105ff., 112ff., 125, 130, 159, 165, 177, 211, 233ff.
- national 152
- substantive 42, 85, 115

S

Scales of administrative expenses and arbitrators' fees 33, 128, 196, 198ff., 213ff., 222ff.
Scrutiny of awards 11, 16, 18, 37, 99, 107, 120, 154, 170, 176ff., 182ff., 191ff.
Seat. *See* Place of the arbitration
Secrecy 124. *See also* Confidentiality
- of communications 146f.
Secretary General 18ff., 28, 31, 33, 42, 46, 49, 55f., 60, 67, 72, 75, 78ff., 98, 130, 184, 187, 189, 195, 196, 198, 210, 239
Seizure of goods 156
Separability. *See* Autonomy
Set-off *See also* Claim(s)
- for set-off 39, 44, 181, 196, 202f., 205, 211
Settlement 2, 9f., 138, 180f., 218f., 221, 234, 248ff., 322. *See also* Compromise
- settlement agreement 180, 255
Siemens v. *Dutco* 75
Staff meeting 21
State court. *See* Courts
State entities 74, 78, 86f., 113, 163, 303, 395, 421ff.
State immunity 118, 424
Statement of acceptance, availability, impartiality and independence 19, 65ff., 75, 79ff., 90, 151, 160, 165, 167, 240
States 4, 16, 87, 113, 163, 421ff.
Statutes of limitation 31, 184. *See also* Limitation period; Time bar
Substance 117, 119, 121, 127, 130, 132, 163, 166, 178, 182ff., 247
Suggested ICC clauses
- arbitration 232, 587
- dispute boards 273
- expert proceedings 265, 559
- mediation 251, 535
- pre-arbitral referee 246
Sum in dispute. *See* Amount in dispute
Summon
- expert 480
- to arbitration 32
- to hearing 139, 141, 142, 148, 149, 306, 307
- to provide evidence 146, 385, 436
- witness 5
Sweden 190
Switzerland 2, 4, 5, 64, 88, 115, 118, 156, 181, 190, 192, 195, 271

T

Taxes 99f., 188, 215, 221f., 258, 350f. *See also* Charges; Imposts
Technology
- information (*See* Information technology)
Terms of Reference 126ff., 305ff.
- content 127ff.
- drafting 14, 19, 30, 33, 35, 39, 44, 98, 106, 110, 121, 126
- failure to sign 131f.
- function 127
- initial draft 41
- limited to the question of jurisdiction 132
- limits 33, 60, 126
- new 96
- origin 127
- original 131
- relating to the substance of the dispute 132
- rider 129, 135
- signature 57, 99, 101, 129, 131f., 180
- submission to the ICC Court 98, 132
- timetable (*See* Procedural timetable)
- time limit (*See* Time limit)
Testimony 125, 140, 141, 143, 256, 387, 396
Time bar 45, 52, 85, 99, 116. *See also* Limitation period; Statutes of limitation
Time limits 24f., 26, 139ff.
- answer to request for arbitration 43f., 58, 77, 199, 239
- appointment of arbitrator 77, 85, 241
- challenge of arbitrator 91, 241
- comments on qualified statement of independence 67, 70, 240
- correction/interpretation of award 191ff., 242
- drawing up of Terms of Reference 99, 131, 202, 241
- expiry of time limit for payment 210
- extension agreed by the parties 107, 174

- extension by ICC Court 126, 132, 138, 151, 154, 173f., 210, 218, 226, 241
- extension by President of ICC Court 161, 170
- extension by Secretariat 19, 42ff., 77, 202, 240
- ICC Court's decision not to extend 175
- make order on application for emergency measures 167, 169, 170
- modification 174, 226f., 243
- monitoring 11
- nomination of arbitrator 77ff., 103f.
- payment of advance on costs 196, 205, 210, 264
- payment of provisional advance on costs 198, 201, 243
- presentation of arguments 8
- raising an objection 228
- reasonable opportunity to present case 107
- rendering of award 107, 154, 173f., 183, 210, 242
- replacement of arbitrator 94, 241
- reply to counterclaim 45, 240
- request for arbitration 36, 170, 239
- request for joinder 53ff.
- shortening 226f., 243
- signing of Terms of Reference 131f., 241

Trade secrets
- protection of 120, 124f., 141, 146f.

Transcript 143, 150, 218

Translations 18, 109, 111, 112ff., 140, 185, 218, 246

Transmission of file to arbitral tribunal 97f., 167
- delay 36, 202

Treaties
- international 32, 40, 48
- investment 87, 113, 125, 163, 422ff.
- bilateral, multilateral 4, 103, 237

Treaty on the Functioning of the European Union 118

Tunisia 14, 190

U

Ultra petita 184, 431

Umpire 235

UNIDROIT Principles of International Commercial Contracts 114, 117

United Kingdom 250

United Nations Convention on Contracts for the International Sale of Goods 114, 117

V

Validity
- of arbitration agreement 46, 52, 55, 57, 60, 132, 233
- of award 141
- of contract 116

Value added tax (VAT) 214f., 221f., 258f.

Verbatim transcript 143, 151

Video conferencing 17, 104, 135, 142, 149, 161, 169, 177, 370

Voie directe 116

von Hoffmann. *See B. von Hoffmann v. Finanzamt Trier*

W

Waiver
- of arbitration agreement 155, 159
- of deposit 189
- of objection 227ff., 243
- of recourse 187, 190ff.

Witnesses 5, 30, 96, 102ff., 124, 141ff., 152, 176, 259, 372ff., 383, 387ff. *See also* Expert
- affidavit 142
- costs 215, 218, 370, 389, 399
- hearing of 112, 121, 131, 138ff., 141f., 148, 200, 268
- oath 142
- opinion, statement 30, 121, 142, 372, 387

World Bank 271

World Intellectual Property Organization (WIPO) 226

B. TABLE OF FIGURES

Figure 1. Communications between the parties, the Secretariat of the ICC Court and the arbitral tribunal 28

Figure 2. Formation of a three-member arbitral tribunal 80

Figure 3. Appointment of an arbitrator on behalf of a party 82

Figure 4. Arbitration agreement providing for a sole arbitrator 83

Figure 5. Unspecified number of arbitrators 84

Figure 6. Challenge of arbitrators 89

Figure 7. Replacement of arbitrators 95

Figure 8. Advance on costs (i) 206

Figure 9. Advance on costs (ii) 207

Figure 10. Advance on costs (iii) 208

Figure 11. Advance on costs during the arbitration 209